Analyzing and Managing Risky Investments

By:
John M. Campbell, Jr.
John M. Campbell, Sr.
Robert A. Campbell

Analyzing and Managing

Risky Investments

First Edition

1st Printing, April 2001

Printed and Bound in the U.S.A.

ISBN #: 0-9709607-0-0

DISCLAIMER

The author, John M. Campbell, takes no position as to whether any method, apparatus or product mentioned herein is or will be covered by a patent or other intellectual property. Furthermore, the information contained herein does not grant the right, by implication or otherwise, to manufacture, sell, offer for sale or use any method, apparatus or product covered by a patent or other intellectual property right; nor does it insure anyone against liability for infringement of same.

Neither John M. Campbell nor any co-author or other party involved with the writing, preparation, publishing or distribution of these materials shall be responsible or liable in any way for any loss, damage or claim with respect to the use of the information, apparatus, equipment, methods or processes disclosed or described herein. There is no warranty or representation, express or implied, with respect to the accuracy, completeness, or usefulness of the information contained herein. **All express or implied warranties, including any warranty of fitness for any particular purpose, are expressly disclaimed.**

Published by: JOHN M. CAMPBELL
2806 Bruce
Norman, Oklahoma U.S.A. 73072
Phone: (405) 329-7149
Fax: (405) 329-7149
E-mail: RiskyBiker@CS.com

LIST OF CHAPTERS

TABLE OF CONTENTS

LIST OF FIGURES

LIST OF TABLES

LIST OF SCREENS

PREFACE

The edition of Analyzing and Managing Risky Investments reflects the ongoing improvements in assessing and managing risk when making investment decisions. Previous editions emphasized deterministic techniques for identifying, evaluating, and ranking investment projects. Much of the foundation for modern investment valuation, which formally recognizes risk, rather than burying it in imprecise approximations, began over 50 years ago. The rapid increase in computer power, combined with declining cost and easy to use software allows investors to improve their traditional decision making processes.

Professionals today must respond to a more fluid, less certain business environment than their predecessors. These dynamics, along with increasing globalization, require a broader set of skills. One still must be as good an engineer, geologist, geophysicist, accountant, lawyer, and so one as ever. Now, communication skills, continuous improvement, adding value, team building, networking, and other buzzwords have crept into our daily activity. These activities are nothing new. Good/successful professionals always practiced these activities. Only the emphasis has changed.

This book focuses on changes in the business environment and work place which impact investment decision making. Changes in investment objectives, project selection, ranking, the decision making process, the global economy, etc. greatly compound the always difficult task of investing limited capital resources, wisely and effectively. Investing wisely, however, is harder now than ever before. Many seek a formula or procedure which guarantees success, without having to face painful choices and risks. If we, or anyone else, could eliminate risk, it is doubtful they would publish the solution in a book. Why would anyone want to create competitors? We believe that companies and individuals can achieve their objectives in a multitude of ways. The path to these ends varies according to size of organization, attitudes toward risk, characteristics of individuals involved, and so on. This book includes tools and processes to help establish those goals, and to evaluate alternative paths to achieve those objectives. We cannot, nor should not, recommend objectives. But, we can help evaluate the likelihood and consequences of pursuing different options.

Fundamental to evaluating investments is understanding variability or risk. This book runs counter to most academic training. Most disciplines train students to reduce the unknown to one or more equations, where numbers are plugged in and an answer results. The first lesson learned by most professionals is that "in the real world we can't control all the variables. We don't even know how many (variables) there are, much less their identities or how to control them." Balancing time constraints with the demands for good investment decisions, with limited information and inexact equations, constitutes the basic philosophy of this book.

The book tries to bridge the gap between the traditional or classical valuation process and the modern approach which addresses risk formally, rather than informally. As such, it may try to achieve too much. The first five chapters duplicate previous texts by the authors, addressing the technology of business and the basics of investment valuation. The intended audience is the young professional needing to learn about NCF, NPV, IRR, financial analysis, ROCE, etc., and experienced professionals needing a refresher on the material. The chapters emphasize how and why computations are made, along with a detailed discussion about applying the concepts. The main departure from previous texts is new material about the limitations of the process, which is intended to lay the foundation for why successful investors are moving to the modern investment valuation process.

Traditional decision criteria involve several major assumptions, including

- A large number of investment opportunities,
- Low cost to identify and acquire investment opportunities,
- Each investment is a minimal component of the budget, and
- Failure of one project wouldn't impact corporate solvency.

If these assumptions were ever true, they aren't now. These invalid assumptions were compounded by the sequential decision making process, where each discipline worked alone, with little or no consultation with other disciplines. Designing production facilities when the number of wells and flow rates were determined elsewhere, or running project economics when all input values are treated as independent, certainly ignores the impact one input has on another. Flow rate determines size of facilities for example. Ignoring interdependencies restricts our ability to reduce risk, increase profits, or both.

The second five chapters began with a review of tools for measuring variability, and then extends the classical process to formally recognize that variability (Chapters 6, 7, and 8). Chapter 9 compares and contrasts the classical and modern valuations of traditional investment opportunities. Chapter 10 combines risk assessment methods and optimization, which is the only true way to maximize shareholder value. The intended audience is the person desiring to learn the basic concepts, or the sceptic wanting information about the benefits of changing to the modern approach. Each chapter could be and has been expanded to be a complete book in itself.

Will these new methods guarantee success? No!!!! As complexity, cost, risk, and profitability of investments increase, combining risk assessment and optimization helps immensely. The second benefit accrues from a better understanding of the incentive systems being implemented today. Self interest is the basis of the capitalistic system. What is new is the set of criteria used to measure success. Unfortunately, these objectives often contradict each other. The objective to increase production and value (measured by project performance like PV, IRR, NPV/INV, or financial measures like return on equity or return on capital employed), while reducing operating and capital expenditures is the ultimate contradiction. Ability to understand and make these trade offs, however, will be the hallmark of the successful investors.

We hope everyone enjoys the book, whether it is learning the basic tools or expanding on years of practice. We apologize for the errors that exist in the book in advance. Frankly, no matter how hard we try, errors always go unnoticed until the book is in print. Those of you who have never had a mistake in a report are free to be critical. For the rest of you, please let us know what is unclear or what we could do to improve the product. Enjoy.

ACKNOWLEDGMENT

This book, like its predecessors, continues to respond to the ever changing business environment. Authors never develop ideas in a vacuum, but respond to the needs and interests of their students and colleagues. This version of the book reflects our interpretation of the insights and knowledge shared with us by others. While we are responsible of for the mistakes, the book reflects fellowship of humanity, which continues to amaze us. It is always dangerous to name individuals, because deserving people are always omitted. To our students, we have learned more from you than we can ever communicate. Some that we can remember include Dr. Stewart Brown, Charlie Busler, Richard Rowe, Tim Baumgart, Truett Enloe, Chris Cox, John Howell, Ellen Cooper Smith, Glenn McMaster, Ipo Retsema, Laureens Gaarenstroom, Bill Diggons, Reidar Bratvold, and many, many others.

Two people deserve special acknowledgment. One is Dr. Steve Begg, who we first met when teaching a risk class for BP. This new edition would not have been written without his encouragement and interest in the subject. We had actually planned to never finish the book, lacking the necessary motivation and interest or preferring other outdoor activities, until Steve rekindled the flame with his enthusiasm. We can never fully acknowledge his contribution, except to say that we truly enjoy his professional perspective and consider him a true friend.

For every motivator, someone has to live with the author, with all the emotional vicissitudes associated with the roller coaster of writing a book. Linda Campbell experienced all this, and helped immensely to get through the tough parts. She emulated Florence Nightengale in healing the sick and often injured mind of the author. Without her support, the book would never have been finished.

Special thanks goes to two other people. One is Jennifer Campbell, the granddaughter of Dr. Campbell Sr., who prepared the cover for the book. Thanks Jennifer. Second, Danny Stowe prepared the final copy and the layout for the book. His dedication and improvements are much appreciated.

THE CAMPBELLS

John Jr., John Sr., and Robert

Norman, Oklahoma, USA
April 2001

Other books by the author's

- Petroleum Property Analysis
- Successful Communication: Strategies and Practices

Call (405) 360-2784.

CHAPTER 1

THE TECHNOLOGY OF BUSINESS

The Greek philosopher, Heraclitus, said, "there is nothing permanent but change." Most people's lives never follow the path they envisioned in their youth, and these changes continue even as we age. Accepting and understanding the dynamics of change is a critical component along the path to achieving professional excellence; otherwise, one merely responds with limited understanding, lessening the chance of achieving those dreams and ambitions. Understanding the subtle difference between change and growth is crucial for anyone involved in professional affairs. Growth change for the better, while all change is not growth; nor all movement an improvement. Change and growth are crucial elements in understanding the dynamic business environment, especially as technology accelerates the transition time.

Change, often dramatic and always challenging, characterizes the major upheavals in the business environment recently, including organizational structure, incentives, location, employment security, etc. The rapid rise and then fall of the Internet start-up companies, mergers and acquisitions totaling hundreds of billions of dollars, and the telecommunication revolution challenge traditional models of business organization and operation. These changes shift the focus from older, established industries, to the newer, often-faddish businesses. Who wants to work for old, stodgy companies, like Microsoft, when exciting job opportunities, with huge stock options, await in the Dot.Com or telecommunication industries? This attitude toward embracing change surprises, if not amazes, many. Rapid technological change alters peoples perceptions toward changing, usually either causing them to embrace it, or fight it.

Whatever the attitude toward change, it can be emotionally painful or enriching, and disruptive to productivity, especially in the near term. Change seeks to promote growth over the longer term by harnessing the knowledge accumulating in the relevant disciplines, but most experienced personnel realize change faces the same risks as all investment decision – failure occurs as often as success.

Organizations combine knowledge from many disciplines to provide goods and services desired by customers. This chapter introduces the basic framework for understanding the contribution and interaction among the involved disciplines and the information each contributes to the successful operation of an organization. Whatever popular opinion may be, the disciplines hired in a business context exist for a reason, not for creating jobs. This book is motivated by two distinct events: one is the dramatic change in the organizational structure of business, and the second concerns the ongoing change in the way investment decisions are made.

With regards to the first issue, many technically educated professionals have never been exposed to or made aware of their role in an organization. People study science to learn the tools and techniques that lead to a well paying, satisfying job. This glaring omission disturbs new graduates, and perplexes experienced professionals, often to the point of being emotionally traumatic. The shortfall in business understanding partially explains the trend toward selecting upper management from non-technical disciplines.

The reduced focus on technical disciplines in management provides the motivation for educational change. Many universities and national engineering organizations are revising their curriculums to correct the shortfall in the knowledge gap. The MBA was created to provide business acumen for engineers and scientists, but the fast pace of today's society prevents many from being able to take the time to earn that MBA. Expanding the new curricula to include formal business principles is crucial to insuring that change becomes growth.

This chapter outlines the overall issues facing organizations and how disciplines interact. The underlying life cycle, and, hence the natural changes in business is shown in Table 1.1. Understanding any business requires knowing how it evolves. An analogy would be a doctor applying the same rules to an infant and a senior citizen without allowing for physical differences.

TABLE 1.1

Organizational and Discipline Life Cycle

Dominant Issue	Stage 1 *Birth*	Stage 2 *Growth*	Stage 3 *Maturity*	Stage 4 *Decline*	Stage 5 *Death*
Popular strategies	Concentration in a niche	Horizontal and vertical integration	Concentric and conglomerate diversification	Profit strategy followed by retrenchment	Liquidation or bankruptcy
Likely structure	Entrepreneur dominated	Functional management	Profit or investment centers	Structural surgery	Dismemberment of structure
Lead discipline	Explorationist	Geoscience to engineering	Engineering and commercial	Commercial	Legal

That organizations change over time shouldn't surprise anyone. For example, the petroleum industry was created by conditions beyond it's control. The shift away from whale oil for lighting during U. S. Civil War gave birth to the industry, and, later, the industrial revolution formed the foundation for the growth stage. At it's zenith in the late 1970's and early 1980's, the industry made historical profits. Since the early 1980's, most corporations have shifted the focus away from North America and the North Sea, and radically restructured to be leaner and more responsive. The old British Petroleum has reformed itself as Beyond Petroleum as part of their move into newer, more dynamic businesses.

The life-cycle characterization hides as much interesting information, as it conveys. Geographically, the petroleum industry in North America and the North Sea are most often characterized as being in Stage 3 or 4, while, other areas, like Russia, China, South America, and Vietnam, might fall in Stage 2 or 3, depending on one's view. The more serious question is the status of petroleum worldwide. Demand for crude oil has been stagnant in Europe and North America, with the emerging economies of Asia providing the best hope for increasing demand. Worries about future demand heighten when combined with petroleum's contribution to global warming and other environmental issues.

Analysis at the general levels, like petroleum, becomes even more interesting when the components of petroleum, gas versus oil, are considered. While crude oil demand may decline, the perception that environmentally gas demand will climb astronomically dominates many organizational views of future changes.

Disciplines play different roles during these stages as well. When demand first emerges, providing a steady, reliable supply takes precedence; hence the reliance on exploration. Engineers become more important as the infrastructure for delivering product at each location takes priority. After the infrastructure is established, commercial issues and the disciplines that provide commercial skills predominate. Each discipline is involved at each stage; just the relative importance changes.

Most disciplines, and especially technical ones, spend years learning the nuances of their respective skill sets, sometimes without ever appreciating the complex dynamics of the environment the skills must operate in. In the book The Collapse of Chaos, the authors provide an excellent discussion of how complexity emanates from simple instructions (*chaos*), like the Mandlebrot set in fractal geometry, and the converse, *antichaos,* where complex causes yield simple effects[1.1]. "The history of science is the tale of a lengthy battle to dig out the secret simplicities of a complicated world". Reducing complex events to simple laws (the reductionist approach) began with the Renaissance, continues today, and has provided the foundation for most of the progress in human knowledge. For all of the benefits of the reductionist strategy, it fails certain tests. Reductionism becomes less successful as complexity increases, especially when the number of variable interactions increases. The authors argue that this is the reason the laws in disciplines, like ecology, epidemiology and economics, are more imprecise than the natural sciences. This is important because the business world is filled with complex interactions that must be understood for the successful formulation and implementation of objectives. Rebellion against the reductionist model has led one scientist to say, "science has narrowed itself so thoroughly that it doesn't look at very interesting issues anymore."[1.2]

No single book can explain the complex interaction of knowledge that comprises the core of the changes that dominate the business landscape today. But, we can understand what we don't know and how that lack of knowledge forces change. This book focuses on the primary objective of most organizations: adding value through sound investment decisions. The organization may be privately or publicly owned, or even a government. Nevertheless, the organization exists to improve the well being of its stakeholders. The next section outlines simple schematics of how business harnesses knowledge to achieve their objectives. The following section then reformulates the problem to define and discuss the business environment. The chapter concludes with an outline of the book and how the various chapters fill the gap in the knowledge base.

THE KNOWLEDGE SYSTEM: AN OVERVIEW

Knowledge depends on understanding the complex interaction among physical, political and economic systems, most of which are beyond anyone's control, if measurable at all. Pursuit of knowledge is motivated by many forces, ranging from greed and self interest to improving the well being of others. A simplified format for understanding the evolution of knowledge and the interaction among the disciplines is specified in Figure 1.1.

Debates and jokes over the relative importance and merits of disciplines have raged for centuries. It is easy to get caught up in this ultimately, self-defeating process, if taken seriously. Managing successful businesses requires harmony and cooperation among the involved disciplines. Most business failures arise when one or more disciplines fall short in the application of their skill sets. The old adage about the weak link is very real. Arguing about the relative contribution of each discipline is still fun after work, but clouds the major issues if done inappropriately. We just finished two books: one arguing that engineers were just technicians with limited creativity, and the other arguing that engineering knowledge is the foundation of the modern world.

Figure 1.1 could be drawn in a variety of ways. But the basic principle is that the philosophy or reductionism has dominated the evolution of knowledge and the disciplines created to study and apply that knowledge. The three early disciplines – science, mathematics, and language – developed to help understand and improve the general environment. Each of these continues to search for better understanding of basic knowledge. The figure draws the arrows in one direction, but recognize that the motivation for change in the basic disciplines emanates from problems arising in life sciences, natural sciences, engineering, etc. Add arrows in the drawing to recognize the reverse impacts, if you like.

Business knowledge is built on the foundation of the preceding disciplines. Most organizations incorporate knowledge acquired from these disciplines, plus adding some of their own to meet specific needs. The main business disciplines – accounting, management, marketing, etc. – evolved to address the complex iterations arising from the foundation disciplines. Like all disciplines, the business areas have sought to reduce the complexity to simpler ideas, which when followed religiously, may yield the desired outcome. Reductionism has many merits, but, too often, professionals forget about the complexity that

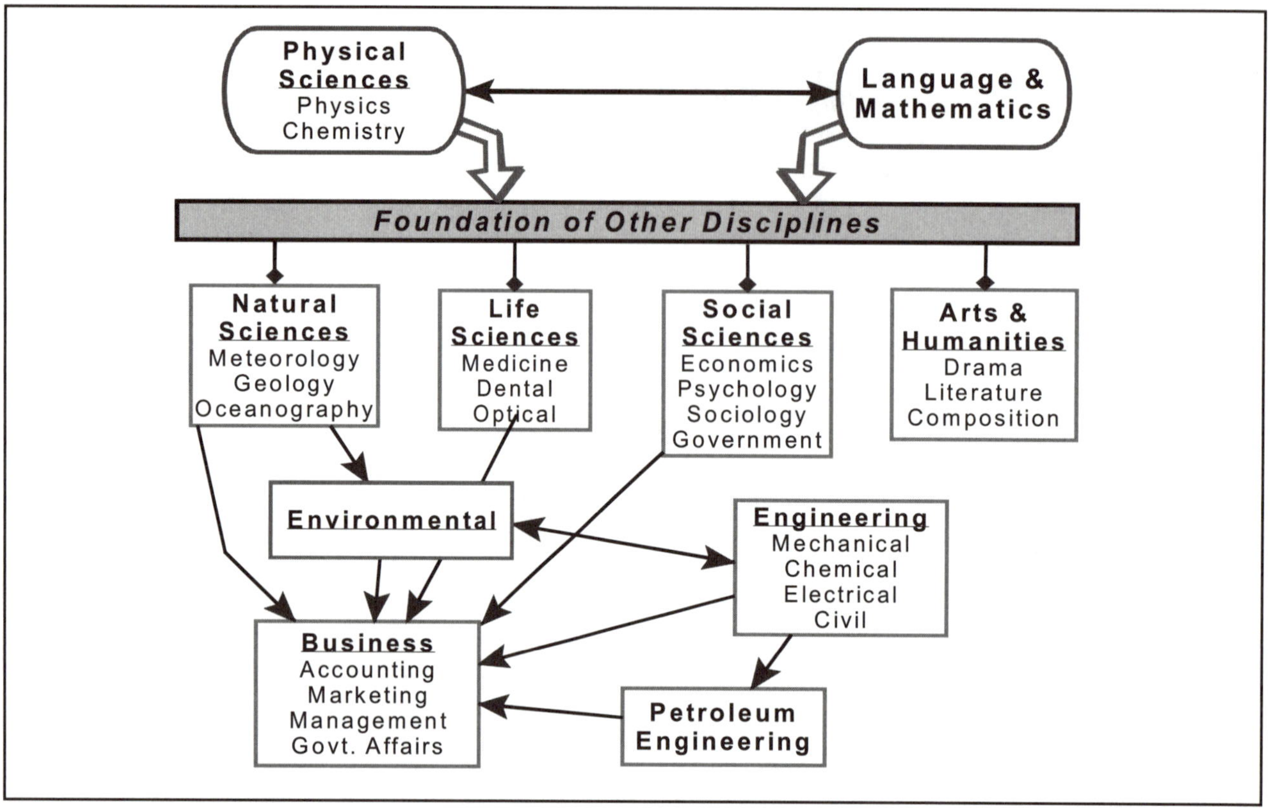

Figure 1.1 One view of the structure of human knowledge

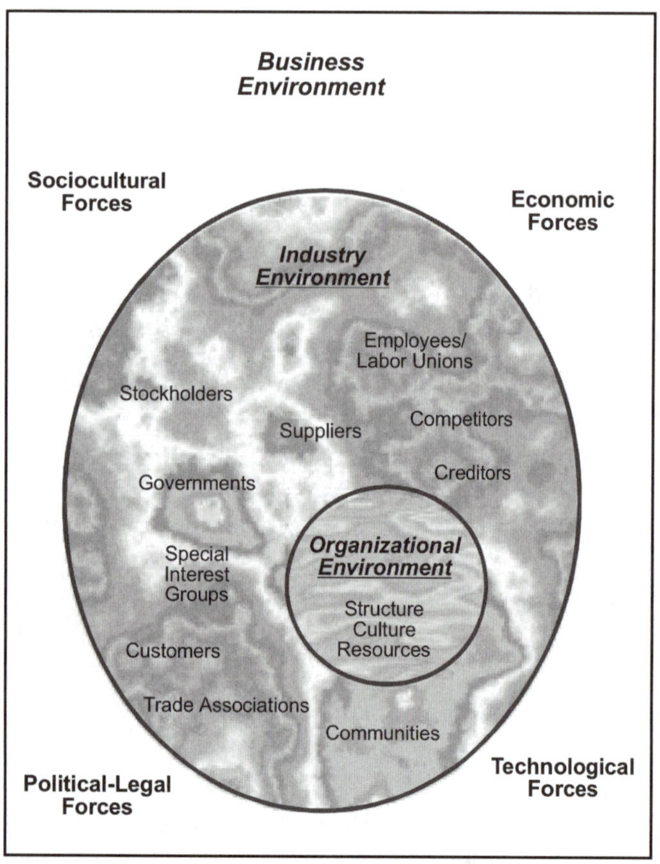

Figure 1.2 A view of the business environment

gave life to those simple rules. Failure to understand the underlying complexity expressed in simple ideas usually frustrates organizational change, no matter how well intended.

Figure 1.2 shifts dramatically from knowledge to the business perspective and the knowledge base necessary to cope with the business environment. Organizations have adopted the latest fads in management, total quality management, reengineering, etc. in the hope of becoming more competitive. The term business environment can be taken as the natural environment that we live in, as the top and bottom headings in the figure suggest. The smallest circle in the interior reflects issues directly under control by the organization – structure, culture and resources used. Forces influencing these items include the elements identified in the industry environment, like competitors, stockholders, employees, governments, suppliers, etc. Most organizations focus on trying to understand and predict these elements.

Moving out from the center shows the major forces influencing the individual organizations and industry. These include sociological, technological, economic, and, lastly, political and legal constraints. Tying the technical forces label back to the relevant disciplines provides the linkage between the structure of the human knowledge base, and business activity. Science, engineering, math, etc. provide foundation knowledge in order for the organization to complete its *mission and vision* (two other popular terms). Most organizations combine elements of all disciplines to achieve desired or mandated goals and objectives.

Figure 1.2 identifies the basic components, but ignores the relationship between the elements. Economics views this situation from the perspective of what it calls markets. Figure 1.3 defines the basic idea of a market. The business organization acquires land, labor, capital, and other resources at a cost to produce a product that households hopefully want. Households provide labor and savings to earn income to purchase the products produced by business. This circularity around the outside describes the flow of money and resources among the elements in the economy outline in traditional economic texts.[1.3] This flow is like a typical heat or material balance equation; it assumes that international and national balances of money flows are equal.

Figure 1.3 emphasizes the business perspective, rather than a traditional economic view. Governments participate in the flow of money and markets by taxing everyone. Governments also impose laws and regulations governing the flow money and services. The Securities and Exchange Commission (SEC) controls reporting requirements, for example. Other agencies formulate policies on environmental rules and regulations, safety standards, etc. Services provided in return include security, health and welfare programs, retirement security, etc. Debate always rages over the merits of these programs, but that is natural and should be expected and encouraged.

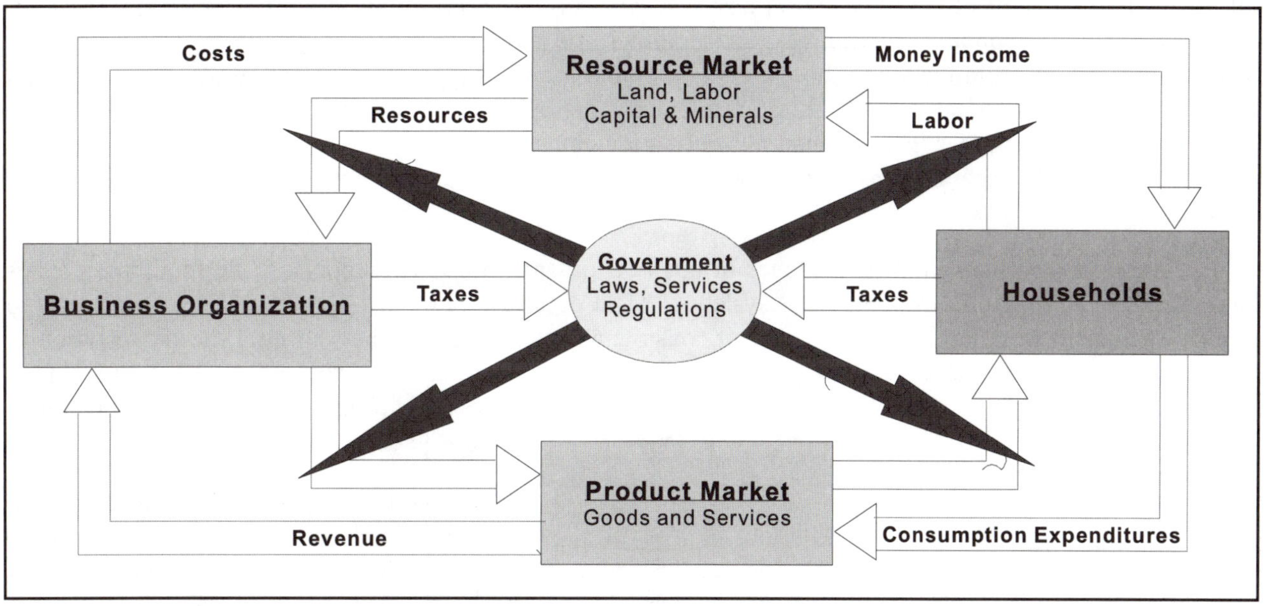

Figure 1.3 Relationships between markets in business environment

Each component shown in Figure 1.3 faces different, often conflicting goals. Governments reflect political as well as economic or monetary objectives, which greatly increase the complexity of their task. Business exists to collect the talent and resources needed to produce goods and services desired by the market. We'll let you define what the objectives of your household. Businesses traditionally define their objective to be:

- make a profit
- stability in earnings and dividends
- maintain *liquidity*, and
- remain *solvent*.

Making a profit makes sense to everyone. *Stability* captures the needs of many investors for fairly predictable dividends and profits. To observe this phenomenon, notice how often a firms stock price changes dramatically as the actual profits deviate from expectations. Liquidity refers to the ability to pay our bills, while solvency reflects the ability to repay debts. Both liquidity and solvency are the same in our personal lives: we have to pay our bills and meet our debt obligations.

This simplified framework captures the essential elements of the knowledge base that underlies the business system. Actual practice involves considerable more complexity, as it should from the application of the reductionist approach. The next section provides an overview of organizational structures, and then moves on to the changes that have been made already and likely to occur in the future.

ORGANIZATIONAL STRUCTURE

The number of ways to structure interrelationships within an organization is almost unlimited. Two of the simplest, oldest, common and most effective are the vertical and horizontal formats. In spite of their simplicity, they have dominated the world for centuries. Figure 1.4 contrasts the two forms of organization. Military and religious organizations follow the vertical structure, and, therefore, is probably the oldest, longest lasting format. It follows the typical pyramid scheme, because each level has multiple persons reporting to the upper level. The pyramid doesn't evolve here since only one group is shown for each level. The graph omits several levels of military organization.

The horizontal organization typifies the traditional legal and accounting format. Whereas the vertical organization assumes the leader knows best and gives orders to be followed without question, the horizontal organization embodies flexibility. Each partner and associate responds freely to local conditions without interference from the top, although general guidelines are supposed to be followed. The horizontal approach is under fire today with the multitude of lawsuits being leveled at auditors and lawyers. Notice that it reflects a current management mantra: only a few layers from the bottom to the top. A current and growing objective of organizations is to reduce layers of management. The horizontal organization already does this.

Figure 1.4 reflects the two extremes of business organizations, as democracy and totalitarian states form the boundary conditions of political systems. Most organizations form hybrids of these two states to achieve management objectives. Management consultants offer advice on how to alter the organization to redirect the focus. Many changes are illusory, but impact everyone.

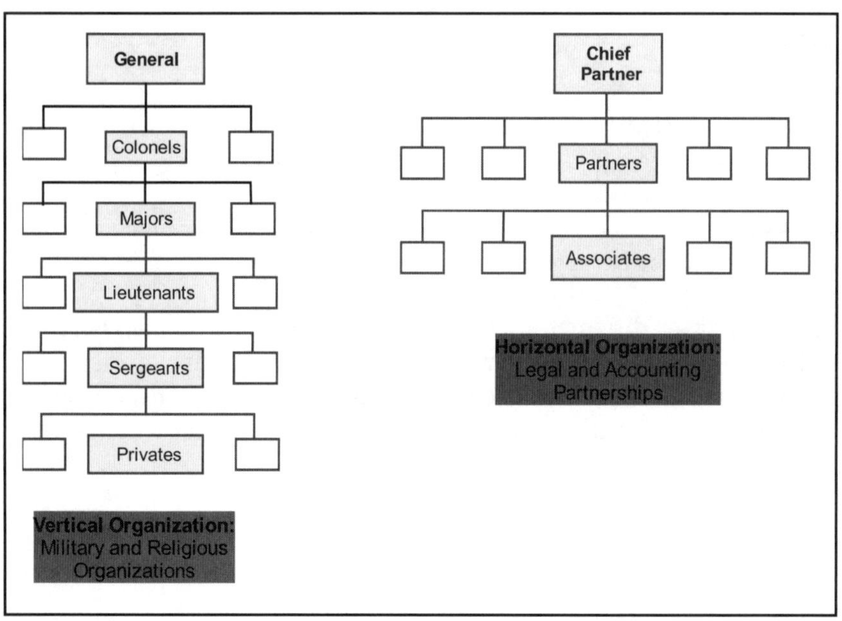

Figure 1.4 Vertical and horizontal structured organizations

Figure 1.5 highlights a hybrid, but common structure. Here, the general office is labeled headquarters for lack of a better term. The headquarters houses the upper management and their support staff. Below them are the divisions of the typical integrated company. These include chemicals, production, refining, and retail. These groups could be further divided geographically. Each area includes contributions from various disciplines: engineering, geoscience, commercial,

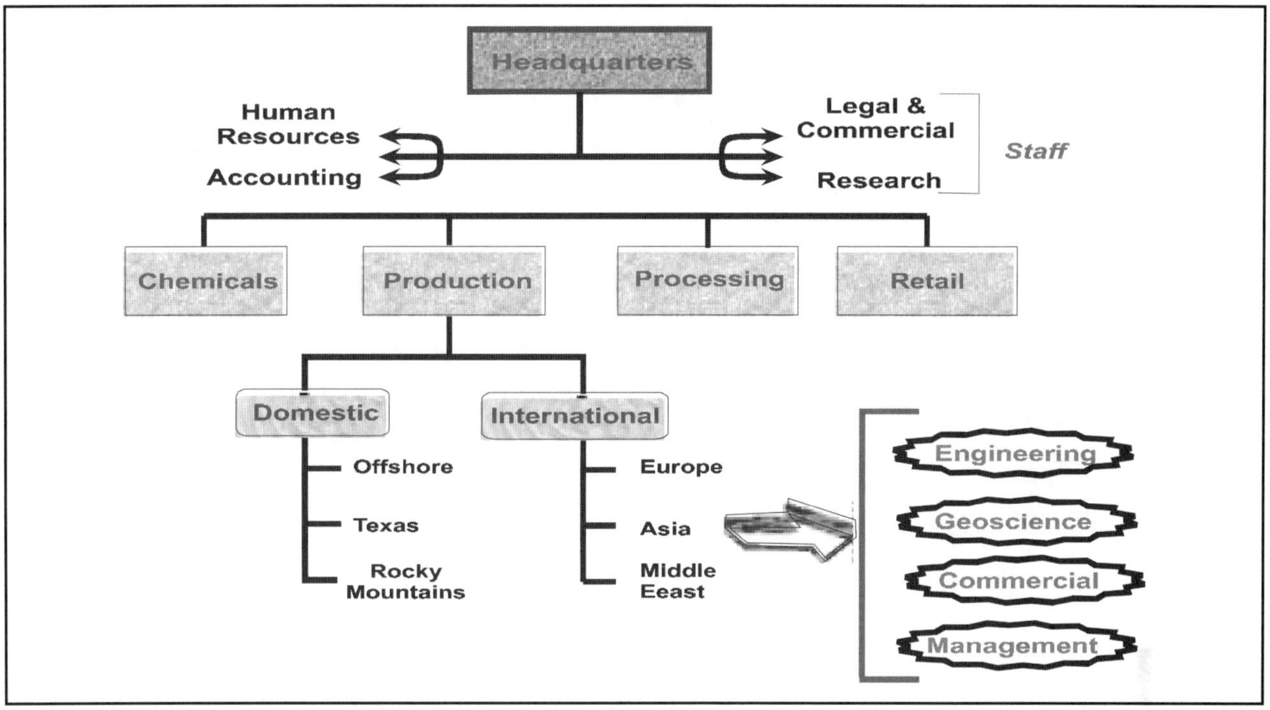

Figure 1.5 Typical business organization

and management. These disciplines are included at every level, although the mix differs depending on the tasks of each unit. Retail includes more marketing and advertising, while production gives greater attention to engineering and geoscience skills. A popular perspective views the system in three stages: the enterprise (the organization as a whole), the asset (geographical business unit), and the project.

Here again the skills relate to the knowledge base outlined earlier. Each discipline provides inputs about the business and industrial environment to the decision making process. The traditional role of headquarters has been to provide the focus and overall strategies for the organization. The divisions are then responsible for implementing the respective strategies.

Headquarters staff provides inputs to the division decision-making process to achieve consistency. Classic examples include information on product prices, country exchange rates, tax obligations, etc. The need for consistency cannot be understated. Examples abound of one division assuming selling prices for the product that is inconsistent with that divisions assumed purchasing price, especially when international boundaries are crossed. Maintaining effective communication has been forced on the lower divisions by using standardized prices and other forecasts.

Staff at the lower levels often chafe, if not outright, bitch about the reporting requirements within their organization, usually during the annual planning process. The assumption is that the headquarters demands data of little use to anyone and takes away from productive work. With less staff, excessive reporting requirements certainly do limit time available for immediate work assignments. It is also fair to say that some of the reports are unproductive, though the data requests are intended to generate useful information. It is also fair to say some of the budgeting and planning process generates more information than is ever used effectively.

The issue is of kind, not of substance. Planning and budgeting are pertinent tasks in organizations of all ages. As many organization failures are attributable to poor planning and budgeting than perhaps any other cause. Several organizations were bankrupted, and billions of dollars invested poorly, because of poor planning. The classic example is AT&T spending over $600 billion to integrate several disparate product lines, and then dismantling the entire endeavor in less than two years: because their strategic plan changed.

This is a continuation of the reductionist thought process. Most disciplines viewed from afar appear quite easy. Only performing the tasks allows one to appreciate the complexity associated with the respective disciplines. The question of whether too much time and energy is committed to individual tasks within these disciplines is another matter, however.

Figure 1.6 outlines a simplified format for the activities performed by headquarters staff. The flow of information in the operating companies provides the basis for a complex set of activities. Although every company differs, five main functions dominate staff activity: legal, public and government affairs, investor relations, controller or treasurer's issues, and planning and economics. Ignored here are the staffs providing technical commentary to management. The technical component flows from the respective operating companies, so there is no need to repeat it here.

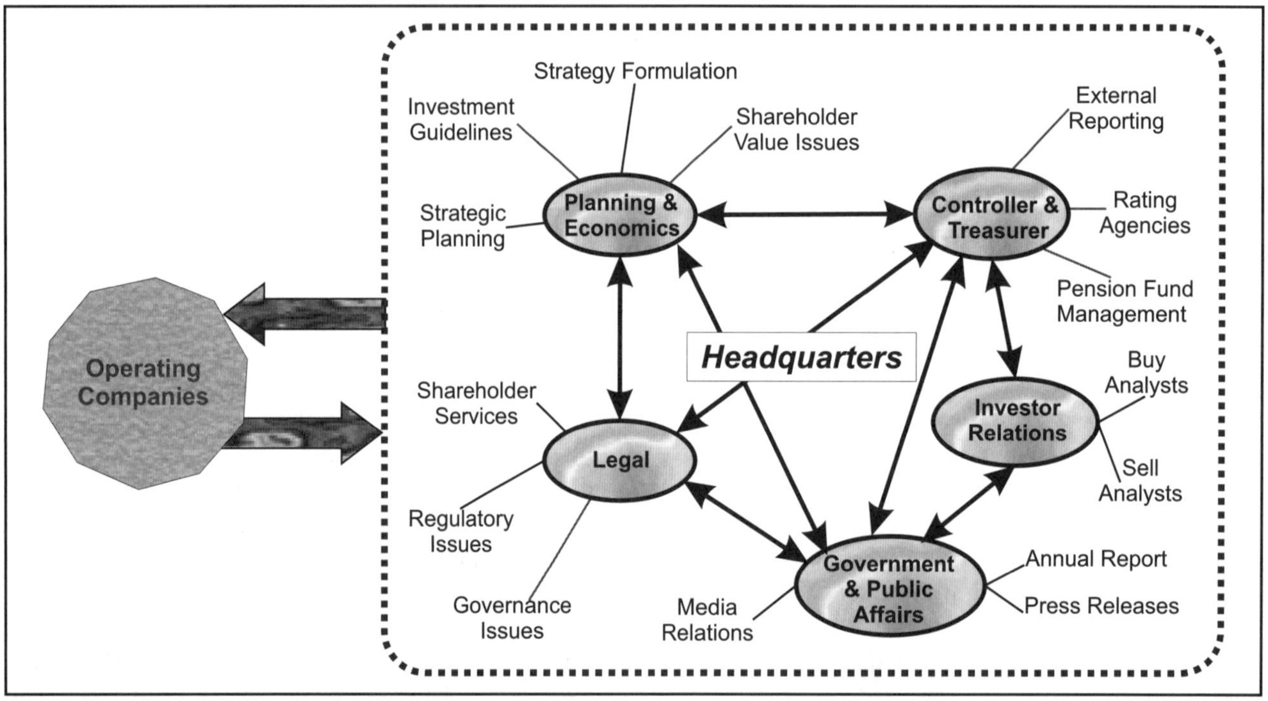

Figure 1.6 Tasks performed by headquarters staff

Public and government affairs interact with outside parties, primarily communicating the organization's position. Investor relations deal with potential and current owners of company stocks and bonds. Almost every company holds annual meetings to communicate their position to these analysts. Some actually sponsor these meetings monthly, if not more frequently. Legal is obvious. None of the tasks performed by these three groups is addressed in this book.

The controllers and treasurers group is usually a mixture of accountants and financial staff. The one issue of concern to this book is the external reporting task. Every public company is required to issue annual reports by the Securities and Exchange Commission (SEC) in the U. S. Other countries use similar bodies to control external reporting. External reporting covers any information provided to groups outside of the organization. This includes analysts, investor's, governments, etc. The external report of interest here is the annual report, which is covered in Chapter 4. The annual report dominates many decisions, because it provides consistency regardless of the company or industry. Once one learns the language and principles of auditing, reading annual reports helps understand and evaluate the issuer's performance, even across countries, with some modifications.

The external reporting format followed in annual reports also impacts the new trend toward formalized incentive systems. SEC guidelines in the U. S. requires organization's to quantify the incentive systems for bonuses and other reward schemes; otherwise, the incentives cannot be deducted from income taxes. Most organizations use the external reports, usually return on capital employed (*ROCE*), return on equity (*ROE*), return on assets (*ROA*), etc., to measure performance. These standards apply to management and employees alike. So, understanding the external reporting format impacts employees directly via incentive systems, and indirectly thru the influence on outside forces. Chapter 4 discusses these principles

Control also monitors tax obligations. Every investment, whether successful or a failure, has tax implications. Taxes, regardless of the form levied (sales versus income taxes), reduce the cash flow of the organization. Without understanding tax obligations, the danger of over spending, either this year or in the future, increases. Careful tax monitoring reduces the odds of having to borrow money to pay this years taxes. This is bad enough for households, but often disastrous for companies.

The role of the commercial and planning department governs most of the topics of this book. The areas of interest are: strategy formulation, investment guidelines, and external environment analysis. Every organization follows a strategy, some consciously, other unconsciously. This chapter reviews basic strategic planning a bit later. Investment guidelines are covered in Chapter 3, Estimating the Flow of Money, and Chapter 5, Measures of Value. Investment guidelines include tax assumptions (Chapter 3), discount rates and valuation methods (Chapter 5), and risk assessment and management (Chapter 5-10).

Most of the book is oriented around the operating companies implementing the strategies and guidelines. Very often, the complexity of our knowledge structure is reduced to simple rules and guidelines, which the operating companies are expected to apply without thinking. Failing to grasp the limitations of the simplicities passed down from above makes sound investing practically impossible in our view. Operating companies are free to modify general guidelines to fit their specific environments in the most successful organizations.

STRATEGIC PLANNING & CHANGE MANAGEMENT

The term *strategic planning* has been used and abused over the years, evolving from the concept of long-range planning that originated in the 1960's. The strategic planning process seeks to identify sources of change in the business environment, and plan methods of for positioning the organization to take advantage of those changes when they occur. Ideally, the process minimizes the cost and risk of change management as well. Once the bailiwick of economists, all disciplines now contribute to the process, though some question whether economists should be included.[1.4]

While *strategic planning* can be nothing more than justification for requesting numbers from operating groups, extensive number crunching by headquarters' staff, and inordinate committee meetings, strategic planning can also be the salvation for struggling organizations and the means for future prosperity. Strategic planning adds value when it motivates organizations to carefully peruse the business environment for signs of changing business conditions. Then, and only then, can the organization develop plans for taking advantage of future conditions, or, as is often the case, minimizing risks.

The basic process of strategic planning is outlined in Figure 1.7. The environmental scanning (the first box) implies someone constantly appraises the external environment, looking at technological, political-legal, environmental, sociological and economic forces as outlined in Figure 1.2. Most organizations assign environmental scanning to headquarters staff, which then establishes the strategy formulation, strategy implementation, and performance metrics. The arrows flowing from headquarters to the operating companies in Figure 1.6 indicate the top down planning process.

Figure 1.7 outlines an iterative process, with all levels of the organization actively involved. The bottom line in the graph, labeled feedback, allows the operating companies to respond to every single

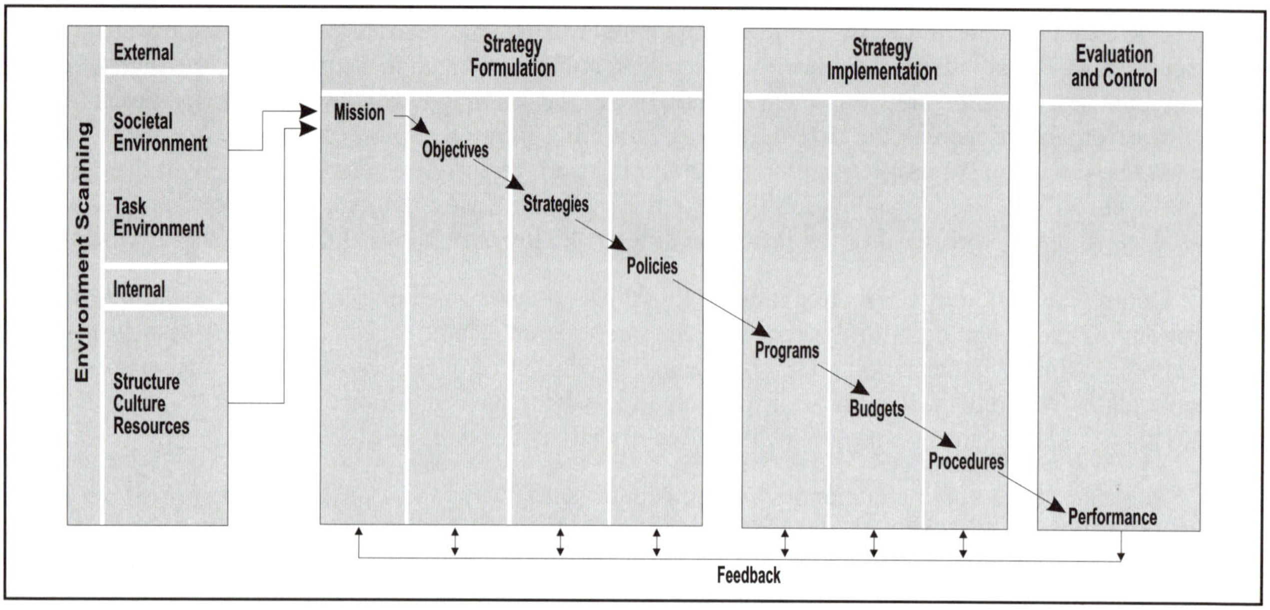

Figure 1.7 Example outline of the strategic planning process

component of the strategic planning process, not just bits and pieces. Most management evidence suggests that this is the critical stage in the process. Part of the driving force behind the movement to business units (profit centers) is the recognition that headquarters staff misses or overlooks many important changes, because they are too far removed from the daily activity of the profit making operations (the operating companies). Testing these perceptions against the knowledge gained by working specific areas validates the process. Strategies and performance measures failing practical experience require further knowledge.

Not all failures reflect poor knowledge or strategy formulation, but result from limited perspectives at the operating level. An equally valid concern arises from the operating centers focusing too much on the current, at the expense of addressing the future. Too often, the operating center is profitable, and acts as if that profitability will exist forever, without any product improvement.

The top down strategic planning process dominates today, primarily because it is easier and quicker to implement. Modern change management theory suggests that a better approach would be for every business unit to initiate the process of strategy formulation, implementation, evaluation and control, the three boxes defined above. When headquarters defines mission, objectives, strategies, and policies (strategy formulation), often with little or no input from the business unit, the business unit then submits programs, budgets, procedures, and performance measures (this is benchmarking) for headquarter approval. Anyone who has ever been told to make a profit, given an incentive system, but forced to use archaic, inefficient accounting, computer or other systems imposed from above should appreciate this point.

The best strategic planning process works by having every business entity, however defined, initiate the very first box of strategy formulation. Headquarters should provide nothing, not even guidelines about the business environment; letting each business entity formulate their own process, subject to the approval of headquarters. Headquarters undermines the entire strategic planning process when it asks the operating companies to respond, rather than participate. The top-down, instead of the top-down with feedback, approach eliminates responsibility for the final decision, and, for establishing the performance metrics.

The critical step in the process comes when the performance measures are set, based on the strategic plan. Too often, those metrics fail, in one or more important ways, to reflect the key aspects of the strategy, encouraging the operating units to invest money contrary to the strategic plan. A simple example will suffice. Most multinationals sought to become the low cost producers, so the performance measure encouraged everyone to reduce operating cost, and this was pushed down to the lowest levels in the hierarchy. At the lowest level, one engineer's primary operating cost was painting the equipment exposed to corrosives (saltwater). By ignoring the painting, at a savings of $50,00 per year, they met their operating cost objective. Unfortunately, the equipment rusted out and had to be replaced at a cost of over $2 million (but the engineer had retired).

Encouraging the operating companies to develop an independent view of the business environment stimulates deeper and more creative thought than just responding rotely to a mandated format. Strategy formulation, implementation, and measurement works much better if the operating companies have actively participated in the entire system, not just followed and responded as requested. Active participation is key. For example, asking participants to indicate how they would respond to each performance metric conveys fascinating feedback.

After each profit center has developed a strategic plan, headquarters staff consolidates the information. Inconsistencies, conflicts in views, and other variations will emerge, but the process of understanding and resolving conflicting views promotes the dialogue that is the essential part of strategic planning. Seeing the big picture (the business environment) is important, as early parts of this chapter emphasized. But, the big picture must also be consistent with the details of the operating environment. Like the knowledge structure discussion, for strategic planning to work correctly, the reductionist view of profit centers must be constantly checked with the complexities of the business environment, and vice versa. That model exists in the most successful organizations, but could be implemented in many more.

Identifying where the organization wants to be only satisfies part of the question. The next issue concerns the steps needed to get to that point. This is the subject of *change management.* The effort to improve and correct deficiencies motivates organizations to pursue, what often appears to be, strange quests. The entire field of management consulting seeks to provide such insights, often with poor or limited success, but sometimes with sterling results. As many bad jokes exist about management consulting, usually equating them with modern day witch doctors as any other profession (three samples: consultants borrow your watch to tell you what time it is then walk off with it; they are people out of work; they know 100 ways to make love but know no one of the opposite sex). Like the discussion so far, management consultancy encompasses a range of thoughts and ideas.[1.5] Management consultants gave us *just in time inventory systems, total quality control, downsizing, re-engineering, profit centers, multidisciplinary discipline teams,* etc. The jokes aside, our favorite citation comments on the approach of managing change by saying:

> *"The average management fad, like the average love-affair, goes through a fairly predictable cycle from infatuation to disillusionment. First, a management guru comes with an idea, coins a buzzword, and sweet-talks the press. Next, one or two big companies threatened with bankruptcy or desperate to seem with it, give the idea a go. Stories are published about sensational results, the corporate world clamors for the advice; the guru forms a multi-million dollar consultancy. Finally some business school professor provides an authoritative report arguing that the fad is a fraud; the press discovers a raft of sensational failures; and the guru, muttering that he was misunderstood, comes up with another idea."*[1.6]

The litany of problems with new, alternative management systems is self evident to people who have lived through the changes. Every organization must change or evolve to swings in the business environment. Failure to respond means loss of market share or lowered profitability, and, ultimately, surgical removal when change does come. Strategic planning, if done wisely, seeks to anticipate these changes and adapt in an orderly, logical process, rather than implementing surgical removal of the offending parts of the organization.

INCENTIVE SYSTEMS AND ORGANIZATIONAL CULTURE

The ongoing changes in management philosophy recognize the importance of the incentive system to successfully modifying organization behavior. This works at every layer in the organization. Whatever the strategic plan, whatever the organizational structure, putting the organizational philosophy into practice is crucial. With all of the systems that have been tried, like *management by objectives, re-engineering, total quality management, team building, etc.,* certain prevailing deficiencies have emerged in all structures. These include:

- ⇒ failure to set clear, controllable objectives,
- ⇒ inconsistency between reward systems and pattern of organization,
- ⇒ understanding the training and political ramifications of change,
- ⇒ failing to understand the variability in professionals motivation, and
- ⇒ poorly designed incentive systems

Other characteristics could certainly be added to this list. Some item may actually overlap with other deficiencies because of the complexity of the system. Management by objectives (MBO) was supposed to set clear objectives, which it felt it did by establishing benchmarks for performance. The argument for setting clear objectives is that MBO would foster hard work and promote the best efforts by all. The lessons of MBO suggest that it may actually increase tension, lessen cooperation, and reduce teamwork. For benchmarking to work, it has to reflect the real needs of the organization and the desires of the professionals. Setting objectives is necessary, but precisely specified bad objectives are worse than imprecise, but sound, objectives.

Efforts to build teamwork illustrate other deficiencies. In complex processes, one estimate of the time required to achieve teamwork is 6 to 10 years.[1.7] Incentive systems and objectives seldom recognize such time lags to reward effective team builders. More importantly, teams are often viewed as nothing more than a means of replacing a middle management power structure with peer pressure. Trying to live up to peer pressure is just as hard as responding to pressure from middle managers. Forcing everyone to become a team player distracts everyone from the task of achieving organizational objectives. There is little or no room on most teams for the maverick professional; yet, most books by successful entrepreneurs emphasize the idea "tap the energy of the anarchist and they will be the one to push your company ahead; irritation is the source of energy and creativity."[1.8]

If creativity is a necessary condition to reach the fountain of success, one author claims that two necessary ingredients for creativity are: a childlike ability to see the world as it is, not as it appears (the Emperors Clothes), and the confidence to speak their mind, "secure in the knowledge that it is the world that is confused, not they (a cynic)."[1.9] Anyone who has worked with colleagues with either trait probably used other, much harsher phrases to describe such colleagues.

Creating effective incentive systems must recognize the differences among personnel: in goals, objectives, abilities, personalities, etc, all changing over time. Any system forcing everyone to behave in the same manner, at the same time, will probably underachieve its objectives. For the aggressive, management oriented employees; the path to success lies in looking and behaving like the immediate managers. Others are perfectly happy doing good technical work with little or no managerial aspirations. The day usually arrives when they realize that no technical ladder really exists, so leaving their love for science, they move into management.

At the core of many professionals psyche today is fear. The successive waves of downsizing, delayering, contracting out has destroyed the concept of a job for life. Fearful employees are seldom productive employees, no matter how well the system is organized and planned. This fear reflects the change in technology and is probably unfounded, but still very real. Technical change destroys old, traditional jobs, as it has done for centuries. Most readers are in very different professions than your immediate parents, grandparents, and so on. The demand for your job probably originated in technical change. Just as likely, the job your grandchildren undertake will bear little resemblance to your job. Change is with us and everyone should plan for change, not fear it.

Talking about the psychology and impetus for change relative to the incentive systems leads to the realization that most incentive systems have changed little for decades. Most professionals still work for piece rates, no different from mill workers in the last century. The objectives set by most organizations, be they output objectives, profit objectives, etc., tie pay as a function to some activity. Money makes a difference to all of us, but people vary according to the amount of money desired and the time spent willing to pursue the acquisition of money. One author, Dr. Campbell Sr., gave an SPE lecture in the 1950's entitled. "Horatio Alger, May He Forever Be Dead." The premise is that not everyone wants to be management or become wealthy, and the incentive system must accommodate these objectives, void of any criticism.

Most everyone's pay comes in differing degrees of three components: base salary, a bonus tied to short term profit targets and longer term incentives tied to company share price (stock options and/or retirement schemes). Management, especially senior management, benefits primarily from stock options, although all the staff benefits if their pension is partly in the form of company stock. Professionals have historically received a base pay and just recently been tied to short-term bonus incentives.

The fundamental philosophy behind incentives is that everyone works better and more productively with higher incentives. This assumption is being challenged. Professionals often lament that current management is shortsighted and risk avoiders; others go further and accuse management of being corporate bureaucrats. There may be some truth to this in some organizations. The risk aversion arises from an incentive system, which has not changed to fit the current environment. Changes in the incentive system are in the offing, but most proposed changes are reactions to perception of current problems, with little understanding of the underlying problem.

Management incentives used to be based on contractual negotiation, often extending the previous management contract with little relationship to actual performance. That's how managers get millions in bonuses even when the company loses money. The current trend is toward benchmarking the incentive systems around the performance of competitors, usually an industry average. This system is enhanced by the recent law passed in the U. S. disallowing the tax deductibility of incentive systems unless a formal performance objective was specified. Common measures include *return on equity (ROE*) or *return on capital employed (ROCE)*, as explained in Chapter 4.

All incentive systems fail when focusing on short-run, accounting valuation measures. Managers will always be conservative when their wealth is based on the value of their firm's share price. Most people diversify their savings to reduce risk; yet, most incentive systems tie future savings value to a single asset, the company stock. Encouraging more aggressive behavior would be easy to implement. Just pay the managers a salary equivalent to an entry professional with a stock option, where the exercise price is 3 to 5 times the current price. Since the manager makes less than most employees, a real incentive to take risks exists. Is this likely to produce good results for the shareholders and the employees, and what is the downside to such a system? The answer to this question is crucial.

In truth no one really knows whether genuine performance incentives are effective, because they have been tried so rarely. Secondly, the level of salaries is now so high that money is unlikely to be the best motivator for senior management.

The same problem holds true for staff incentives. Most major companies have adopted a tiered approach where certain thresholds have to be exceeded before a bonus is paid. The problem is that most plans include features, like company ROCE must exceed the average return of the industry. For those in a business unit or asset team, a successful year can be totally undone by failures elsewhere; hence, no bonus is paid. With no direct control over the bonus system, what little incentive that exists in the first place is totally destroyed. The classic failure of incentive systems arises in the programs designed to encourage productivity improvements. We recently watched an award ceremony where a team of ten professionals developed and implemented an idea that reduced costs around $40 million dollars that one year. The team was acknowledged with a plaque, public accolades, and a check for $3000, to be split amongst the ten people. Needless to say, they had some very pointed comments about their future motivation.

MANAGING CHANGE

Probably no single system can cope with the complexities of the ever-changing business environment, at all times and all places. But, certain philosophies must be integrated into the planning system. Many, including us, believe the approach espoused by Deming's focus on emphasizing quality offers a starting point. Deming felt that most monetary incentive systems "destroy teamwork, setting worker against worker and manager against manager. Deming's view of the world is illustrated by Figure 1.8.[(1.10)]

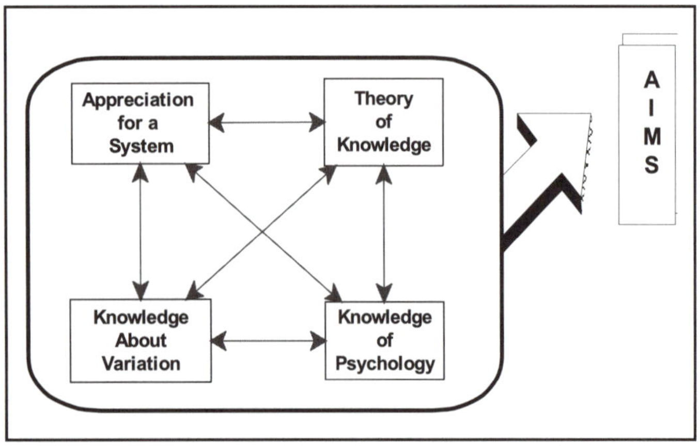

Figure 1.8 A system of profound knowledge

Professor Deming was the father of the quality movement that was adopted in Japan after WWII. Deming's thoughts dominated business development in Japan beginning in the 1960's. Deming eschewed the dogmatic rigid management approach that characterizes current activity. He believed that any organizational structure would work if the leadership and employees understood the system they operated in; conversely, every system, which ignores the complexities of the operating world, will fail.

The Appreciation for a System and Theory of Knowledge components were outlined in Figures 1.1 to 1.7. The knowledge of psychology is especially relevant in technical organizations facing change. Motivating, encouraging, organizing, etc. are rare skills, but are crucial element in determining success or failure, and the relative successes of organizations. The last component, Knowledge About Variation, reflects Deming's training in statistics. He recognized that abandoning deterministic thought processes and analytical procedures was crucial for adopting methods for handling the inevitable change in the business environment. Modern decision methods, including real options, testify to the merits of this approach.

Many now recognize that the critical element in handling change is leadership. Good leaders are able to specify the aims of the organization, and then integrate the components of knowledge to achieve those aims. They are usually quite good at the details of specific disciplines, but also understand the system. Quite honestly the major shortfall at all organizational levels is the paucity of leadership, be it business, government, education, etc. "You cannot encourage good leadership with money. In fact, you can discourage it. The kinds of people who make good leaders are not obsessed with money."[(1.11)] These and other ideas have been expressed more fully in several articles.[(1.12, 1.13)]

ABOUT THE BOOK

The search from the structure of knowledge through the organization of business lays the foundation for the information discussed in this book. *Analyzing and Managing Risky Investments (AMRI)* integrates the ideas and concepts into a formal process for achieving the aims of the organization, however defined. Specification of the aims is beyond the realm of the book, though a fascinating topic in its own right. Once the aims and organizational structure are established, investing limited capital effectively, to achieve those aims, dominates organizational behavior. To invest effectively, the lessons of the chapters that follow must be heeded. We present details of the current knowledge base, and explore the often contradictory measures of investment performance and success. To sort out the relative merits of each metric requires understanding the system and the variability contained therein, especially the contributions of the respective disciplines and their knowledge or lack of knowledge. The book follows the reductionist approach in dealing with the details of specific disciplines, but hope to remind you of the overall system as we move along.

The objectives are several fold. Perhaps the simplest is to make better investment decisions, or, at the very least, development of an understanding of the risks and returns in investments. A broader goal is to develop some breadth in your knowledge base. The typical reader of this book should acquire considerable knowledge in the respective topic areas. We hopefully can increase your appreciation for the knowledge brought to bear on investment issues by other disciplines. Figure 1.9 highlights the knowledge areas expected to be improved after reading the book, in a very rough perspective. This figure assumes one is an engineer. Other disciplines would obviously be affected differently.

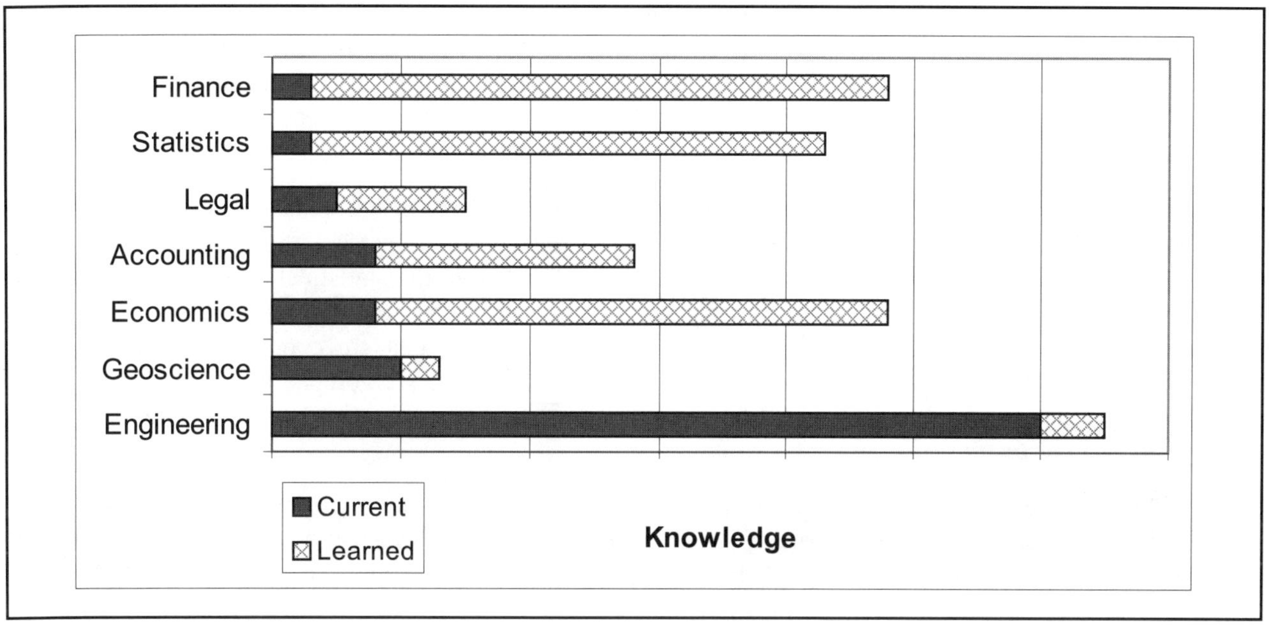

Figure 1.9 Knowledge acquired from book

The book contains ten chapters including this one. Each chapter addresses particular topics relative to the analysis and management of investments. Chapter 2 reviews the basic process of analyzing investments from a general perspective in the classical investment process. The basic steps for formulating and evaluating investment opportunities are covered, along with the basic components that go into successful investments, leaving the specific details for later chapters. The Chapter includes information about the relative importance of the investment components and information on historical investment performance, with a summary of where mistakes have been made (called post-appraisal, look-backs, follow-ups, etc.).

The technical inputs with forecasted values are combined in Chapter 3 to determine the tax burden for most of the financial and economic investment calculations. First, the data are converted into monetary units, including estimates of the tax burdens associated with the project. Tax examples for various countries – U. S., U. K., Norway and Indonesia – are included to illustrate the impact of tax regimes on economic value estimates.

Chapter 4 represents the management setting and how organizations report their performance to interested parties external to the firm. This is often called financial accounting or auditing, and is a specialized area in accounting. The external reports, called annual reports, are covered in detail regarding assumptions, methods, interpretations, and most importantly, misuses of the information. The reader should be able to read an annual report at the end of the chapter.

Chapter 5 builds on the monetary estimates to produce traditional measures of value, like *Net Present Value* (NPV), ratios like *NPV to investment* (NPV/Inv), etc. The chapter includes one of the few serious appraisals of the deficiencies of these methods, with proposed alternatives to rectify some of the deficiencies. *Options theory* and *Modern Investment Valuation* (MIV), and its criticisms of classical DCF are introduced. One of the major causes of poor investment performance is the thoughtless application of biased measures of value.

Chapter 6 discusses basic statistical procedures applied to risk assessment. The optimal approach for getting the best estimate of variability is to prepare the variability estimates initially. The tools, with examples, for estimating variability are analyzed in some detail since this is the basic for the notion of risk.

Chapter 7 addresses the basic issues in building time-series models in general, with application to three of the main components of investment decision-making: product prices, inflation, and exchange rates. These are elements of the business environment from earlier figures that flow into specific investment appraisal. The basic approach for forecasting prices, some simple examples, and the accuracy of price forecasts are addressed. Similar topics are covered for exchange rates for those dealing in an international environment.

In Chapter 8 the measures of value, both traditional and modern, are expanded to include formal risk assessment. This includes detailed appraisal of the chances of a project losing money, the magnitude of the loss and methods for managing the risk. The chapter builds on the statistical applications presented in Chapter 4, and the money derivation (Chapter 6), and Chapter 7. These methods are then applied to common investment decisions in Chapter 9. Real investment decisions are compared to illustrate the proper methods of analysis and then common deterministic outcomes are compared to risked outcomes. Chapter 9 highlights the need to move from the reductionist process to an integrated modeling approach for making proper investment decisions.

Chapter 10 evaluates detailed optimization methods for choosing among projects, including budgeting, planning, and selection of best project option. Traditional brute force methods are contrasted with better risk management practices. Chapter 11 summarizes the pain and suffering of reading the book

Figure 1.10 gives an overview of the book.

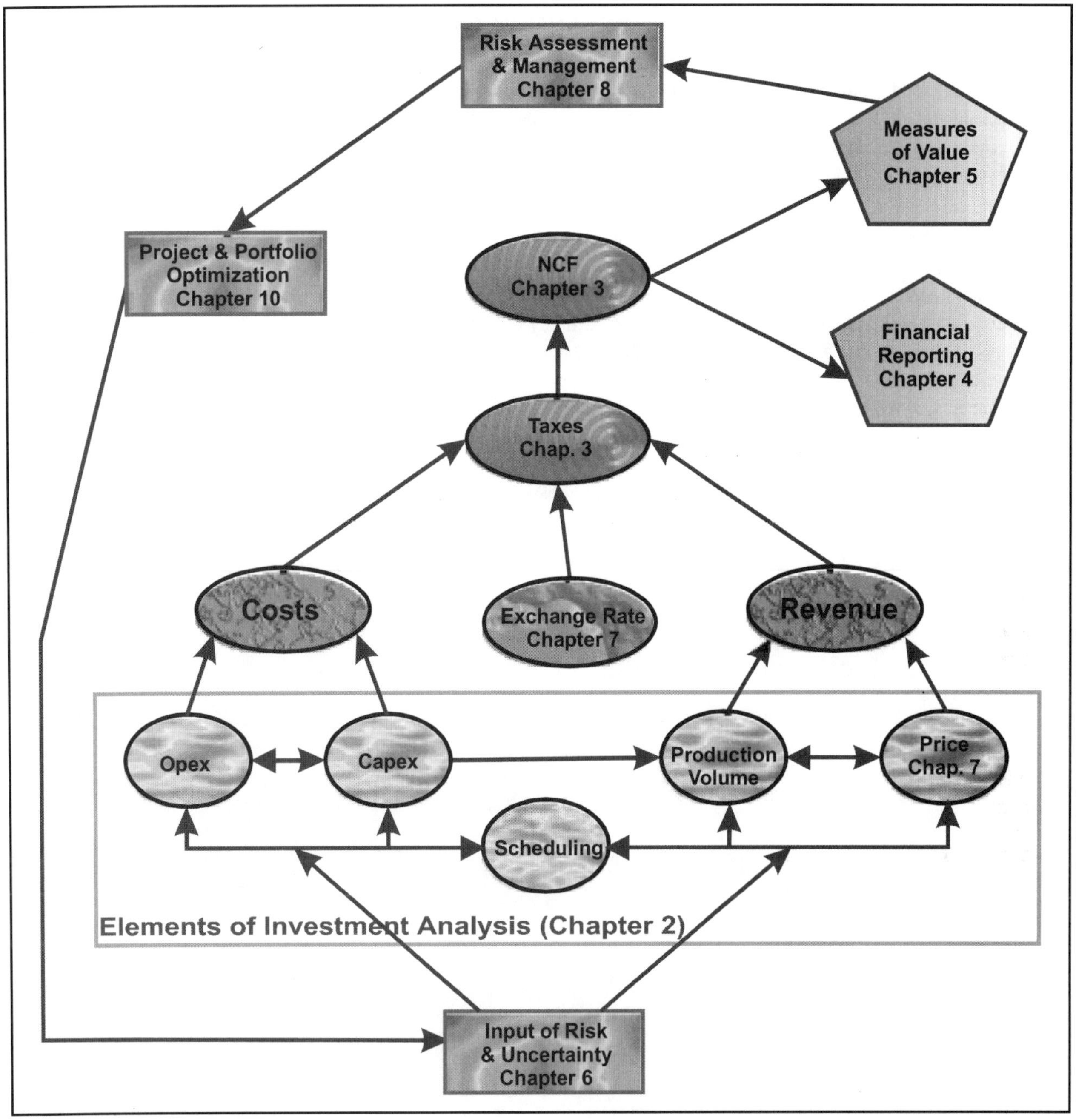

Figure 1.10 Influence diagram of book

REFERENCES

1.1 Cohen, J. and I. Stewart, *The Collapse of Chaos: Discovering Simplicity in a Complex World.* Viking Press (1994).

1.2 Knapp, Ed., "Multidisciplinary Office Spurs Debate." *Science* (3 Feb., 1995), p. 615.

1.3 McConnell, C. and Stanley Brue, *Economics.* McGraw-Hill Publishing Co. (1990).

1.4 Hudson, W., *Business Without Economists.* American Management Association (1987).

1.5 "Management Consultancy" *The Economist* (13 Feb. 1988), pp. 1-18.

1.6 "Re-engineering reviewed," *The Economist* (2 July 1994), p. 66.

1.7 "The trouble with teams," The Economist (14 Jan., 1995), p. 61.

1.8 Anita Roddick, *Body and Soul*, Crown Publishers (1991).

1.9 Zukav, Gary, *The Dancing Wu Li Masters.* Bantam Books (1980).

1.10 Deming, W. E., *The New Economics for Industry, Government, Education.* MIT, Center for Advanced Engineering Study (1993).

1.11 Kotter, K., *The Economist* (1 Feb. 1992), p. 19.

1.12 Gibbons, J. and K. Murphy, "Relative Performance Evaluation of Chief Executive Officers." *Industrial and Labor Relations Review*, Vol. 43, No. 3, pp. 30-51.

1.13 Jensen, M. and K. Murphy, "CEO Incentives – It's Not How Much You Pay, But How". *Harvard Business Review* (May-June, 1990).

CHAPTER 2

ANALYZING INVESTMENT OPPORTUNITIES

Assessing and managing investments involves the complex interaction of the knowledge outlined in Chapter 1. The difficulty in mastering the details of every discipline necessitates simplifying the process, or creating complex structures to integrate that knowledge. Even as later chapters describe the details of the process, the basic process *involves the orderly, dispassionate, and planned analysis of all available information to best estimate value and risk.* Though quite general, this definition identifies a general philosophy for analyzing investments in a professional manner. The key element here is professional manner, as opposed to an approach based on whim, fancy, or wishful thinking. Professional analysis often intermingles with wishful thinking in actual practice, unhappily.

Professional analysis differs significantly from the informal process applied by everyone, everyday. Each time one makes a purchase, some form of evaluation is made, at least subconsciously. When buying a car, for example, one usually raises the hood to look at the motor for leaks or other defects, kick a tire or two, slam a door, and take a test drive. If the car survives this exhaustive test, and the color, brand, upholstery, and price meet the requirements, we buy it. Deals occur when the price asked by the seller seems fair to the buyer. Fair means the value of the item is to the buyer is greater than the asking price. Another buyer might collect the same set of ***facts*** and reach a negative decision.

Applying the same reasoning to investment appraisals leads to several important conclusions.

1. The measure of success of an evaluation is whether it accomplishes it's intended purpose, not how technical it is.
2. The relative importance and interpretation of available data varies with the person performing the evaluation.
3. Value varies according to the involved parties estimates of risk, time, taxes and strategies.

Item 1 formally recognizes the need to understand all facets of the problem, particularly those considered important by the recipient, and not just a rote application of scientific methods. Probably the most common source of investment failures is the undue, over reliance on the calculation procedure with little, if any, regard, for the limitations of the initial data and methodologies. Sound judgment is absolutely necessary at every stage in the evaluation.

Dr. Campbell Sr. has always argued that *"engineers make the calculations they know how to make and like to make."* While this is true, the same observation applies to every other discipline as well. One may be practicing professional principles following this process, but it is doubtful that the needs of your clients and employers are being met. Just doing what you like or know how to do fails the test of being a professional, unless the objectives of the client/employer are kept in mind.

The valuation process is about determining value, and "*value can only be established by an arms-length transaction between two or more independent parties*." The word independent signifies that the parties enter into the transaction without coercion and are independent entities. Without coercion means the transaction can be stopped if either party decides to. Eminent domain, taxes on estates, liquidation, etc. illustrate coercive situations. Likewise, transfer prices between two groups in the same organization can violate the independence requirement. Value reflects the interaction of competitive forces, driven by self-interest, not an artifact designed to reduce taxes or favor one part of the company at the expense of another.

Understanding this, realize that professionals only estimate value and do not determine it. Value may be determined only by a transaction. The professional must, of necessity, understand the objectives of the analysis, and the parties involved have conflicting objectives.

This book is concerned with the economic, engineering, geological, legal and other technical forces interacting in investment appraisals. None of these elements is known with certainty. This chapter outlines the basic components of investment appraisals, and areas where mistakes take place in the process. Then a formalized process for analyzing investment opportunities that hopefully, when followed carefully, minimizes the chance of a mistake is presented. Please realize that no process yields perfect answers, all the time.

ELEMENTS OF AN INVESTMENT APPRAISAL

Before discussing historical investment failures, a brief understanding of the process is in order. Valuing investment opportunities requires accurately estimating the costs and benefits of a project. Some have compared the process to balancing a checkbook – measuring the money flows into and out of the checking account each period. Real world investing is actually more complex, but essentially the same process. The process estimates money (revenue) received, then deducts all costs (investment cost, operating cost, and taxes).

Equation 2.1 outlines the basic format for measuring the net increase (or decrease) in value.

$$\text{NCF} = \text{Revenue} - \text{Operating Cost} - \text{Investment} - \text{Taxes} \qquad \textbf{(2.1)}$$

NCF stands for *Net Cash Flow* and measures the amount of money in the treasury or checkbook at specified points in time, usually a year. The terms checkbook and treasury illustrate the similarity of the process for individuals as well as organizations.

The cost categories – operating cost (*Opex*), investments or capital costs (*Capex*), and taxes, reflect outflows to the treasury. These are costs of doing business. They differ primarily in their tax treatment and spending patterns over the project life. Everyone is familiar with taxes, for example, having paid income taxes, sales taxes, value added taxes (*VAT*), and excise taxes, depending on the country of residence. In addition, extractive industries pay production taxes, like royalties, severance taxes, Petroleum Revenue Tax (*PRT*) in the UK, etc. Production taxes are levied on the volumes produced by the host country. Each taxes is covered in more detail in Chapter 3.

Operating costs have two major characteristics: they occur every year production exists and normally receive 100% tax relief in the year the cost is incurred. If $1 is spent this year, then $1 is deducted from revenue to compute income tax liabilities. Examples of operating costs include electricity, fuel, maintenance, labor, and so on. Some like to consider Opex as items without any lasting value (or no salvage value), or expenditures consumed in the production process.

Capital expenditures or investments (Capex) include costs like factories, buildings, computers, vehicles, wells, production equipment, pipelines, platforms,, etc., which have lasting value. The productive life of each item is expected to exceed one year. Capex differs from Opex in that the bulk of the expenditure occurs before production begins (usually), and only partial tax relief is granted the year the cost is incurred. The first part should be self-evident – a building must be built before it can be rented. Partial tax relief means that $1 spent this year receives only a fraction of a $1 in tax relief when computing income taxes in the same year. A full $1 of tax relief will be received over several years, not one year like Opex. This fraction varies by country, as Chapter 6 illustrates.

The basic process is illustrated in the simple flow diagram of Figure 2.1.

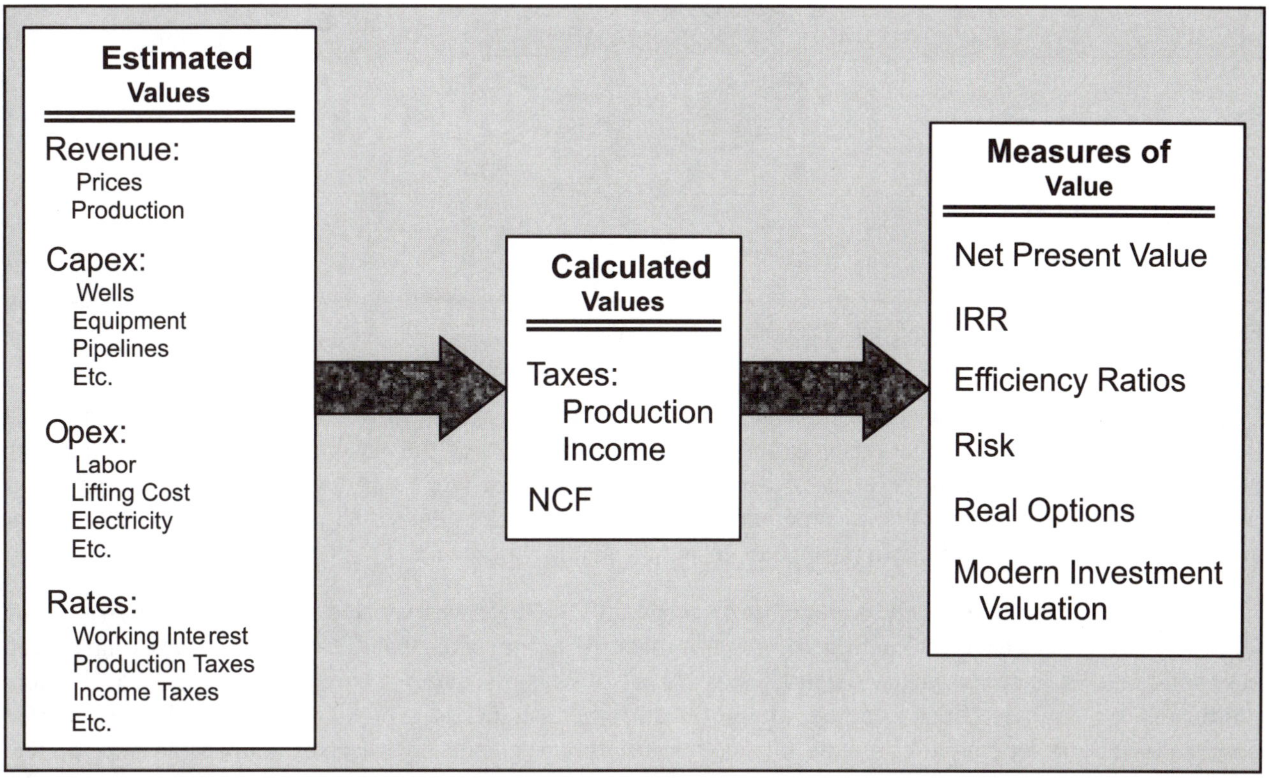

Figure 2.1 Basic NCF flow diagram

This is a simplified version of Figure 1.10. Realistic, expected values for each input, including production volumes, prices, sales, capital and operating costs, working interest (WI), and other tax rates are required. Once the estimated values are generated, taxes and then NCF are derived using Equation 2.1. The NCF form the foundation for the measures of value and risk for the project, like net present value (*NPV* or *PV*), internal rate-of-return (*IRR*) or discounted cash flow rate-of-return (*IRR* or *DCF-ROR*). Chapter 6 summarizes the NCF process and the measures of value are discussed in Chapter 5.

It is important to understand that all profit measures only approximate value, none measures value exactly. Many mistakes occur because the investors misunderstood the initial assumptions that lead to the respective value measures. A common lament by those preparing information for final decision-making is the refrain "my management just wants to rank using one number and doesn't want to understand the interrelationship among the components that comprise project value." Any process that ignores the linkage between inputs and outputs seldom, if ever, adds value to the treasury.

Simple pie diagrams communicate the essential elements of project valuation, quickly and easily. Figure 2.2 summarizes one such example. The revenues from the project are split into various components. Capital expenditures account for 43% of total project revenues, while Opex are 19%, production taxes are 11%, royalty 17% and income taxes are 4%. The remaining 6% is net cash flow. This small profit level surprises many, but 6% on total project revenues of $2.5 billion adds considerable value, although the percentage is quite small. Such values are quite common, primarily because production taxes and royalties absorb a large share of the profit (about 28% here). These taxes are direct reductions of revenue, often before consideration of Capex and Opex costs.

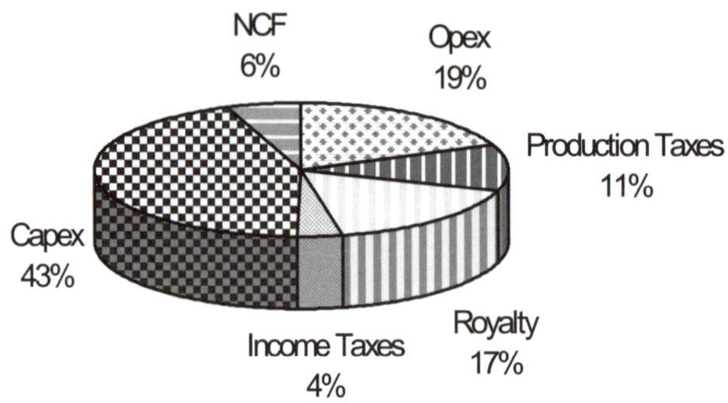

Figure 2.2 Pie diagram of revenue distribution from a project

Some are also surprised by the small income tax percentage, given that the income tax rate in most countries is over 30%. Income taxes seldom take more than 10% of the revenue stream, even in the high income tax countries due to the allowed deductions for expenses, like Capex, Opex, and royalties. After deducting expenses, the effective income tax rate is always less than the stated tax rate. The key to evaluating countries is the combined impact of all costs, not just the income tax.

Figure 2.3 illustrates the variability in corporate tax rates for selected countries. Countries, like Germany and Japan, have the highest income tax rates. It is no secret that Germany and Japan have been economic leaders in recent years. High tax taxes don't always discourage economic performance, as many politicians and lobbyists like to argue. Italy, on the other hand, has a high tax rate, but has performed poorly. Also, just looking at corporate income taxes without considering all taxes distorts the perspective. Norway has the lowest income tax rate at around 29%. The income tax rate was dropped in the early 90's from over 50% as part of their movement into the European Union. They offset the income tax drop by increasing production taxes for petroleum, called the Special Petroleum Tax, from less than 30% to over 50%. It is the total tax burden, not the income tax rate, that's important.

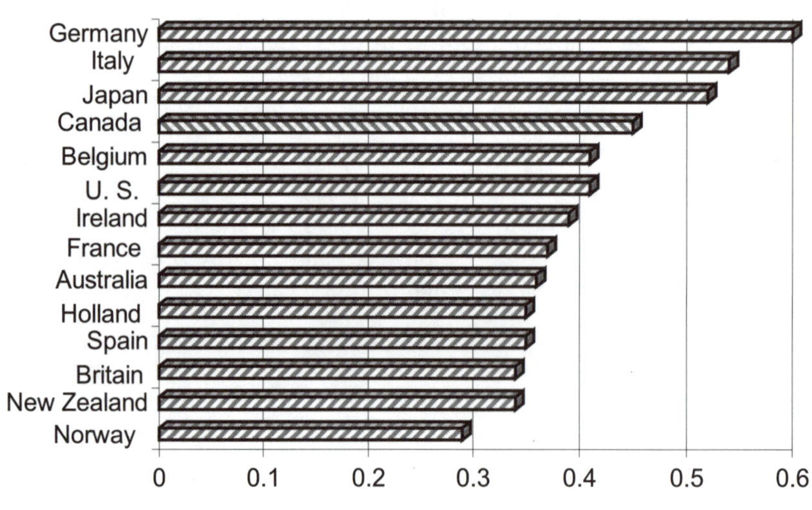

Figure 2.3 Corporate tax rates for selected countries

Figure 2.4 shows the NCF pattern for the same project used to generate the pie diagram in Figure 2.2. The annual cash flows start negative indicating the expenditure of capital as the project begins. Then the slope becomes positive as revenue starts to come in. NCF's declines as production begins to fall off. The cumulative values show a similar pattern but to a greater extreme. The cumulative NCF is about $144M, as in the pie diagram.

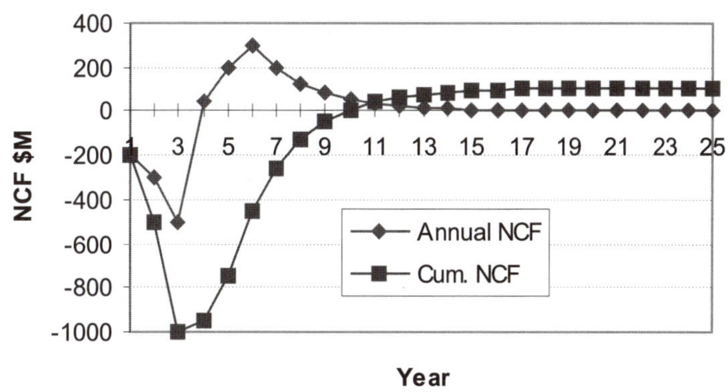

Figure 2.4 Annual and cumulative NCF for a project

Detailed steps for deriving the NCF patterns for different tax regimes are outlined in Chapter 3. The intent here is to give professionals new to the investment evaluation process a feel for the basic concepts. The rest of the book covers the relevant elements in more depth.

PURPOSES AND PROBLEMS OF INVESTMENT ANALYSIS

In order to appreciate the professional judgment required in an investment analysis, the range of uses for investment appraisals must also be understood. Evaluations are used for many reasons, including:

1. Sales and exchange of properties
2. Loans
3. Corporate investment decisions
4. Exploration and development strategies
5. Accounting and tax planning
6. Estate settlements
7. Unitization and joint venture agreements
8. Bid evaluation
9. Evaluating government regulations
10. Play and prospect evaluation

Each topic involves different participants, with unique goals and objectives, often with strong emotional and technical conflicts. Maintaining a professional demeanor, without falling into the associated emotional traps, challenges even the most experienced and knowledgeable.

Because each category has different needs and requirements, selecting the right approach often defies the unwary. The evaluation approach must be tailored to the specific purpose of the client. It is always necessary to convert technical and economic variables into ranges. This means that the analysis must realistically assess geological, engineering, and operations knowledge, consistent with the myriad of other forces affecting value. This is essential when one remembers that the analytical process essentially models future events, often over 50 years, as illustrated by Figure 2.1. Remember: ***the only information known with certainty is that every input variable is measured with error.*** Since it is impossible to know the future with certainty, sound analysis of past events and careful appraisal of possible future events are the basis for any professional analysis. The objective is to minimize the cost or losses from excessive optimism, without forgoing the upside benefits arising from undue pessimism. While it may be true that "only optimists accomplish anything," it is also correct to say that "there are few bankrupt pessimists."

In spite of the precarious nature of modeling uncertain events, investors hire professionals to do just that. If modeling the future was easy, organizations could save considerable salary costs by hiring secretaries and technicians. Trying to understand and anticipate the future justifies the salaries paid to most professionals. As this vision declines, our value to the organization diminishes. Even though the disciplines working in the business environment face a chaotic world, in fact some argue it is so chaotic that predicting anything is impossible, our job is to make the best guesses possible.(2.1) Without entering into the debates of *chaos theory*, our knowledge is an attempt to understand and manage what appears as a chaotic, disordered system by constructing the best models possible, in the time allotted.

Within the confines of uncertainty, the goals and objectives of the participants cited above must be recognized. When buying and selling producing properties, the extreme divergence between the buyers and sellers valuation shocks many. But, buyers and sellers seldom face the same business environment. Differences in cost of money, price forecasts, cost of operations, strategies, interact to influence the valuation. Buyers often view the long term as being more valuable than the sellers, who often need immediate cash.

Seeking loans from a lenders usually suggest capital shortages or budget constraints. The borrower needs capital to complete the project, while lenders are concerned, often overly so, with the ability of the borrower to repay the note plus interest. Lenders require evaluations, but are just as interested in the existence of collateral to back-up the loan. The real question to the lender is "Does the borrower have assets which can be produced at an economic rate for a long enough period to time to repay the debt and interest."

Lenders often apply conservative methods to avoid risk. Common practice includes reducing production or sales estimates to adjust for risk. This rule-of-thumb misdirects the analysis. Those seeking loans learn real quickly to upgrade the initial estimate before the lender reduced the estimate to determine loan value. Better loans emerge when the lender weighs each input, and formally appraises, not discards, risky values. Producing *minimum probable values* (value at risk, VAK®) leads to better loan performance than arbitrarily adjusting values. Chapters 5-10 discuss the necessary procedures, with examples.

More energy and time is probably spent making organization investment decisions than all other categories combined. Most organizations justify their existence as a vehicle for investing money more efficiently than the investor can themselves. This is probably true. Note that neither the term organization or owner is defined, allowing for complete flexibility in capturing different political systems. Organizations have relied on single estimates historically to determine their investments. The continued improvement in technology permits formal recognition of risks. Unfortunately, regardless of the methods discussed in this book and others, organizational politics dominate goals and objectives, often conflicting with making sound investment decisions.

Management uses investment analysis for two basic purposes: first, to determine which projects satisfy basic investment guidelines, and second, to compare the relative attractiveness of alternative investments. The second aspect is often referred to as *portfolio management.* Most professionals spend their entire lives either recording or proposing investments, many without understanding their role in the overall system. Where does the system breakdown? Primarily when the objectives of the individual differ from the organization's objectives. Inconsistent objectives plague most organizations.

The stated objective of publicly traded organizations is the *maximization of shareholder wealth.* Figure 2.5 captures the diversity in objectives. Producing departments are usually more conservative than geological groups. Likewise, the geophysical and legal departments view the problem differently, usually along the tasks they are expected to perform: geophysicists to identify traps and legal to sign contracts.

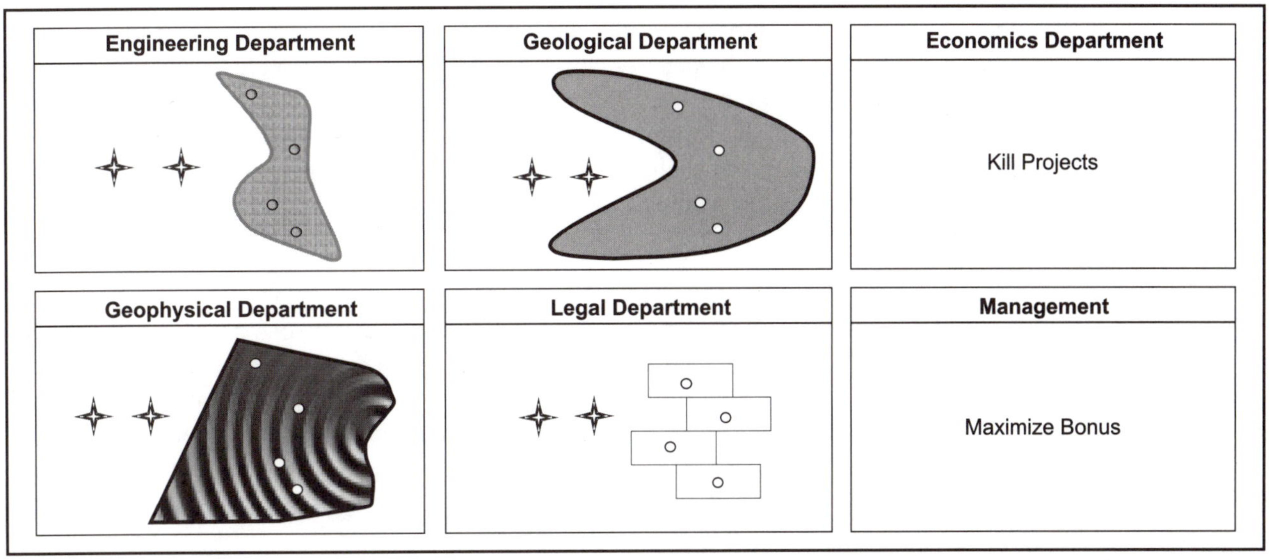

Figure 2.5 Differences in professional perspective

Lastly, most professionals envision the role of the economics or commercial groups to kill their projects, while management is seen to maximize their bonus.

All of these views hold to some extent and illustrate the importance of understanding the purpose of the analysis. Organizations' analyze investments for the stated purpose of maximizing shareholder wealth, but other, often hidden objectives also impact the process. Personal well being is one. In fact, one of the toughest management task is establishing an incentive system consistent with the goals and objectives of the organization, and aligns with the personal objectives of employees.

The wide latitude of interpretation by the respective disciplines creates conflicts since no one can ever be truly unbiased. However, avoiding any conscious, consistent bias enhances the chances of success. One logically wishes to please, and for that reason may be tempted to interpret information as they think a supervisor, client or the incentive system seeks.

While employees work for the organization, and, therefore, must respond to specific assignments, the manner of the response defines the true professional. At some point everyone will have to perform some task or assignment with which they disagree. That is the nature of life. When attitudes like the following emerge, the slide from the path of professionalism has begun.

- We have to be optimistic to get anything through the front office.
- Once the project is approved, we can always explain what went wrong.
- Estimate what management wants to see, then back calculate rate and reserves to satisfy management criterion.

Accounting and tax planning (item 5) reflect the desire to minimize tax payments to the relevant governments. Failure to adequately estimate production and profits (the basis for most taxes) often leads to higher tax burdens and creates conflicts with the taxing authorities. Because taxes are an integral part of the evaluation process, the organization needs good estimates of likely future taxes. These estimates then flow back into the investment decision making process. Estate planning faces the same problem, except it deals with the dead, not the living.

Unitization captures the conflict between various mineral owners with competing views of the best development approach. Reservoirs often underlie surface leases with different owners, with each owner developing the resource in their own way. Unitization seeks to optimize the whole reservoir, not the part under the ownership of each individual. Estimating production volumes and cost of the whole unit, rather than each piece, usually leads to very different investment patterns.

Bidding, whether for assets held by private individuals or governments, is one of the toughest investment decisions to make. The bid process is usually competitive, mostly using sealed bids. The parties submit a bid in an envelope by the specified time and date. The bids are opened at the appointed time and the high bidder wins. The bids may be in the form of actual money, commitments to invest specific sums of money, rates of taxation, or combinations of each. Trying to establish a bid value with imprecise or no information, with the goal of outbidding other competitors, but without paying too much, makes for a very frustrating and inexact process. Anyone who is too critical of performance in this area usually has never participated in the exercise.

Most governments seldom enact legislation without considering the impact on costs and production. In order to balance business promotion with the need for tax revenues, the first step estimates the cost of the regulation. Taxes appear fairly easy at first glance, since the new tax rate times any expected adjustment in production volumes measures the cost change. But, since costs impact economic recovery, higher taxes often reduces ultimate production. How much is the task of the evaluation. Other regulations include safety, abandonment, etc. Each has a cost and a corresponding benefit. The analysis must estimate these costs and benefits as best it can.

Play and prospect analysis is also becoming increasingly important. The increasing movement toward international exploration and operations places all but the very largest organizations in the same financial situation as independents. Smaller organizations face capital constraints daily. Multinationals have greater capital resources, but even this capital is stretched when the world becomes the domain, rather than just one or two countries. Limiting the international search to those countries with the best chance of satisfying objectives is quite difficult. Data is usually marginal, if it exists at all. Meshing goals and objectives, like a gas versus oil strategy, with cloudy information about specific country politics, tax regimes, stability, acreage allocation procedures, complicates the already difficult valuation process. Sound analysis not only requires good engineering, geoscience, economic, tax, legal, political, etc. in the country of residence, but the same information in foreign countries. Obviously, the more countries being evaluated, the greater the expertise and information collection required.

Probably the major mistake made by companies new to the international game can be summarized as cultural bias. Too often, faced with little information about a specific country, professionals revert to attitudes and behavior appropriate for the home country. American companies commonly underestimate the importance of establishing a long presence, basically getting to know the important politicians and bureaucrats in each country. Professionals often fail to appreciate the importance of contacts and friendships in other areas of the world. Huge sums of money change hands regularly, and the parties to the transaction may never meet, because the legal system of property rights protects against fraud and deceit very effectively. In those areas with limited or unclear property rights, people want and demand personal contact with investors and trading partners. Going back to earlier comments about appreciating the contribution of all disciplines, the legal profession imparts this favorable situation.

HISTORICAL INVESTMENT PERFORMANCE: RESULTS & CAUSES

The errors that creep into evaluations arise from several sources – some which may be corrected; others exist due to limited knowledge, data, and processing capabilities, and may never be corrected. Professionals often felt that poor price forecasts dominate sound technical analysis. Some erroneously believe the poor forecasting performance of future prices eliminates the need for good technical work. This section outlines some general industry investment results, and then summarizes the underlying causes. The next section then develops a general approach that tries to overcome these defects.

Four examples of input predictions for actual investment opportunities are reviewed: production profiles, field developments information, plant cost estimation, and price forecasting. The process compares the estimates used to make the investment decision with actual outcome. This process goes by several names in industry – post installation appraisal (PIA), follow ups, investment quality appraisal

(IQA), etc. Looking backwards is a little like evaluating your favorite team the day after the critical match. The purpose is to learn from the mistakes, not cast blame or dispersion on those involved, which is where the sporting analogy falls apart. The active phrase is "learn from our mistakes," since everyone makes poor investment decisions.

Figure 2.6 compares estimated production profiles with actual profiles from 160 different projects from around the world. No values are shown on the y axis to indicate that the estimates have been normalized to reflect very different producing rates. The estimated production profile exceeds actual production for most of the early years, then falling under the actual production around year 8. The area between the two curves prior to year 8 is greater than the area after the intersection, indicating an overestimate of total production, as well.

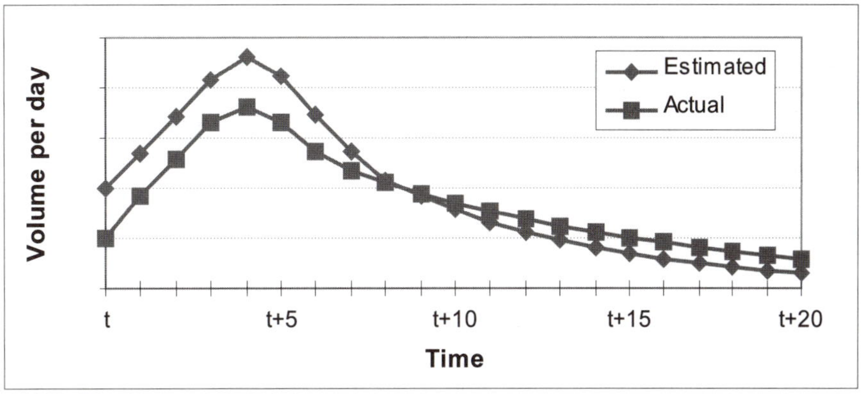

Figure 2.6 Errors in production volume estimates

Out of the 160 profile estimates, actual production was less than the estimated production 159 times. If production estimates were unbiased, about half of the estimated profiles would exceed the actual and half less (assuming a normal distribution). The consistent overestimate of production corroborates the notion of excess optimism introduced in the last section. After presenting summary figures, like these, for more than 30 years, the majority of every class agrees that excess optimism dominates most production estimates for one very simple reason: most professionals believe they are competing for limited capital resources. The person lying, exaggerating, or distorting reality the most (you select the term) obtains the capital requested for their projects. This competitive nature really does exist, but is this professional behavior?

A more detailed study of production and cost estimates exists for the Gulf of Mexico.(2.2) Rising product prices in the late 70's and 80's made higher cost areas much more economically attractive. Geoscience had long speculated on the presence of commercial hydrocarbons in deeper water, but economics limited extensive activity until higher prices emerged. Table 2.1 is divided into two sections: projects begun before 1982, the basis for the original study, and projects commencing after 1982. The latter column covers projects reviewed by the authors of this book, and not the authors of the original article.

TABLE 2.1

Post Evaluation of Selected Offshore Projects

Average for All Projects		
	Before 1983	**After 1983**
Initial Production	–10	0
Reserves	–9	0
Project Time	+29	–10
Development Cost	+33	–5
Present Value	+88	–92
Overrun (+), %	Underrun (–), %	

The dual time frame reflects variation in prevailing technical and cost estimation practices. Prior to 1982 the industry mood was euphoric, believing prices would continue rising forever. Faced with what some believed would be oil prices in excess of $200 per barrel and gas prices over $15 per Mcf by 2000, any cost could be justified. This is the reason that project time (29% longer), development cost (33% higher) cost and present value (88% less) diverge so significantly from the estimated values. The initial production and reserves are also less than estimated, consistent with the information in the previous figure.

The results after 1982 display a significant improvement for most estimations, except for one: present value. Initial production and reserves match the estimated values almost exactly, while project time and development costs are less than the estimated values. The technical staffs obviously improved the accuracy of the estimates once the euphoria of price forecasts was eliminated. The one major failure is really the only one that matters – present value to most investors. For those new to the subject, present value adjusts future cash flows for the time value of money (money is worth more today than in the future). The project added 92% less to the value of the organization than originally estimated. Why?, because price forecasts still reflected recent optimism, not market realities.

Project estimation continues to improve especially in the face of constant, if not declining, resource prices in most industries. Still, some investors estimate that about 75% to 80% of the projects actually funded overestimate the value added to the organization (on a present value basis). Many immediately react with dismay at such figures, and some even try to lay the blame on some professions doorstep. In reality, this figure really isn't surprising if people will stop to think about it, and those casting blame should first look to see if they are living in a glass house.

Attitudes, especially optimism and competition for scarce capital, play a role in generating poor estimates. But, the real cause lies with the nature of the process. Over 100,000 estimated values are generated for even simple projects. When large, frontier developments exist, millions of possible combinations of variable inputs exist. The large number of values are compounded by the sequential process utilized in investment analysis, where geoscience summarizes their work for engineers, then engineers pass forward one case to the commercial group, and so on. Management then decides on the project attractiveness based on one set of values that has been reduced to, usually, a few set of numbers. It is hardly surprising that crucial elements fall between the cracks when making investment decisions. Remember that each of the disciplines cited may have a multitude of sub layers, like petroleum, civil, mechanical, chemical and electrical engineering. The need to adequately convey relevant information at every stage becomes the binding constraint. This process is displayed graphically a few pages later.

Figure 2.7. illustrates errors in cost estimation. Professionals often blame cost overruns on inflation rising faster than anticipated. A study by the Rand Corp. tested the importance of inflation forecast errors for process and manufacturing facilities.[2.3] The motivation behind the argument concerns responsibility for cost overruns. If inflation is the primary cause, engineering cannot be blamed. Figure 2.6 computes that inflation errors accounted for only 11% of the misestimates. Other causes included delays arising from bad weather and strikes, and unanticipated regulatory standards. Of course, one has to always ask how many projects are likely to suffer from bad weather or delays due to regulations. Experts in the field of project scheduling feel that most project schedules reflect they way professionals would like the project to go, not how they are likely to go.[2.4] Optimistic scheduling seriously impacts most cost estimations.

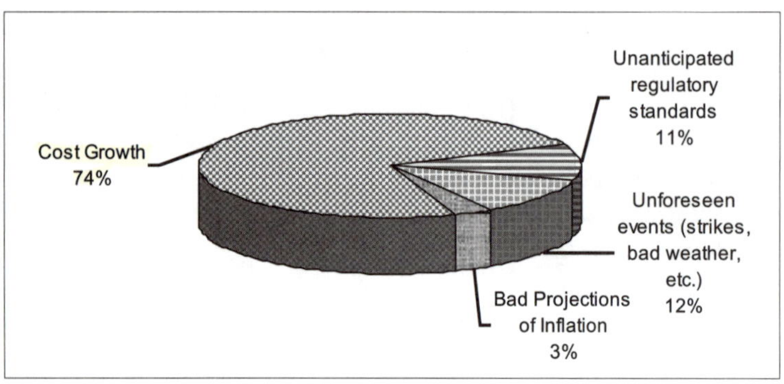

Figure 2.7 Sources of cost estimation error

Cost growth represents the main error source, over 70%. Cost growth in the Rand terminology captures the effect of improperly sizing equipment, omitting important components of the system, and design changes during the detailed design and construction phases. The common phases of project scheduling and cost estimation include: 1. Conceptual design, 2. Detailed design, 3. Construction, and 4. Startup. The cost estimates used in Figure 2.7 come from the conceptual design stage, while the actual costs occur at the end of the project start-up. Figure 2.8 depicts the degree of estimation error by each stage. Note that the errors are largest when the least is known about the project. As the project progresses, the gap between estimated and actual decreases, until the costs match at the end. This relationship holds for virtually all estimations.

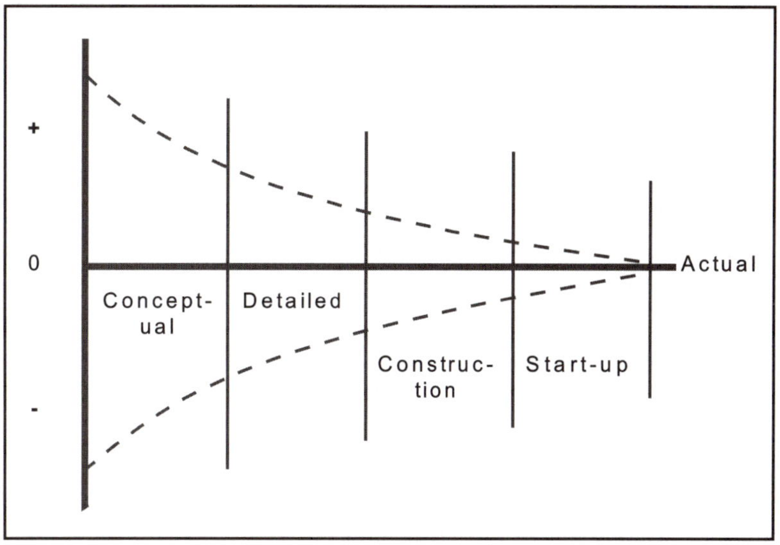

Figure 2.8 Cost estimation by project stage

The last post appraisal concerns price forecasting, a key component of investment valuation. The rise and fall, or cyclical nature of prices, complicates all forecasting efforts, but is extra trouble when dealing with product prices. The huge expenditures invested, based on inaccurate price forecasts, is testimony to the importance of getting these values right. Chapter 7 discusses price and exchange rate forecasting in more detail, but the errors in forecasting are summarized here. Figure 2.9 gives actual and estimated oil prices for several companies between 1970 and 1995. The forecasts for Saudi light indicate the commonality of forecast errors. Four forecast periods are provided, 1970, 1974, 1980, and 1985.

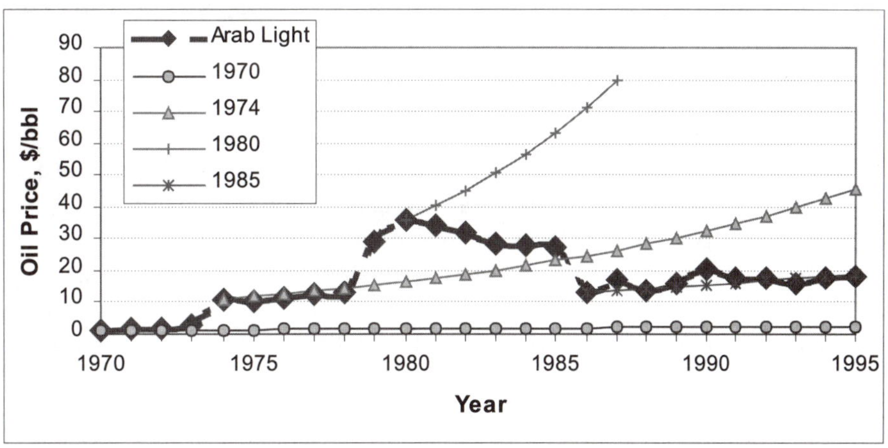

Figure 2.9 Accuracy of oil price forecasts

The 1970 forecast extrapolates from a starting price of $1.21 per barrel to an ending value of slightly less than $3.00 per barrel. This reflects the stability in world oil prices for the years between World War II and 1970. After the first *OPEC* embargo following the Arab/Israeli war in 1973, price rose to over $10 per barrel. Forecasts then assumed that this price jump caused by the war would continue at a constant escalation rate of about 6% per annum. Likewise, the 1980 price jump, motivated by a combination of events – the Iraq/Iran War and the former Soviet Union's invasion of Afghanistan – was extrapolated at over 12% per year. This constant extrapolation generated price forecasts of over $200 per barrel by the end of the century. When Saudi Arabia discontinued their role of acting as a swing producer to comply with the OPEC production quotas in 1986, price dropped almost instantaneously. Price changes since then have kept pace with inflation, except for the brief period in 1990 and 1991 during the Gulf War. The discontinuities returned during the last part of the 90' and early part of the next decade.

These price forecasts, when compared to actual Arab Light prices, signify horrible errors. Since value estimates depend on selling prices, such errors distort value estimates and misdirects investment decisions. This is certainly what happened in the petroleum industry during the OPEC boom and bust periods. Telecommunication and Dot.Coms are more recent examples.

The lessons of the various post appraisals suggest that multiple causes contribute to poor investment decisions. To merely say that bad investments occur misses the point, because bad investment decisions will always exist in an imperfect world. The key issue concerns the willingness to correct those mistakes by learning from the failures. Evidence on the willingness to learn from past failures is mixed: some estimation errors have been reduced, while others still follow the same path. The most dismal area of performance still arises from price forecasting.

Several main themes run throughout the post appraisal process. One summary of common problems outlines the main causes of errors to be:

- Use of invalid inputs
- Omission of important components
- Selecting wrong alternatives
- Wishful thinking

Invalid input occurs most often when the inputs used in the evaluation are unsubstantiated. Undue reliance on computers tends to enhance this problem. Many professionals fail to verify their inputs as long as the output, measured in costs, production profiles, or economic parameters (like MPV, DCF-ROR, NPV/Inv), satisfies investment requirements. Perhaps the simplest illustration is a workover problem we give in our classes. Faced with the same data, the n class members usually get at least n+1 different solutions (because some run the problem more than once). While this divergence diminishes with practice, the problem of multiple solutions to the same data still exists. One organization found that over 80% of the computer runs used to justify projects contained errors, although most were trivial.

Do these errors matter though? Yes, often with disastrous results. Ever investor has at least one story about how they got it wrong. For instance, a company negotiating a producer/processor NGL split inadvertently switched the propane and butane prices (butane was selling for about twice propane, while the propane occurred in a much larger volume). The analysis told the processor that they needed 65% of the NGL's to break-even. The contract was eventually settled at 77% to allow for hedges. After building and starting-up the plant, the processor quickly realized over 85% of the NGL stream was needed for the project to break-even.

Omission of relevant inputs explains most major investment failures. Omissions means important variables are completely left out of the analysis. Our favorite, most extreme case is leaving out the cost of onshore support facilities for an exploratory play in the offshore Atlantic Ocean. Everyone prepared their lease bid evaluations assuming onshore support facilities were available to support offshore activity. Not only did the facilities not exist, the industry paid over $1 billion to rectify the deficiency. This same problem plagues international activities as well. Too often, people wish the environment was like their home area.

A more common, but equally important omission arises in project development plans. The analysis typically addresses only the cost of initial development and operation, totally ignoring the *life cycle costing* aspects of the problem. Major cost and production components, like artificial lift, secondary and tertiary recovery schemes, additional facilities for increasing water cuts, equipment maintenance and replacement, etc., are ignored and left for the operation's staff to worry about. Royal Dutch Shell undertook a major study of their North Sea design and operation standards in the late 1980's.[(2.5)] They concluded that design considerations underestimated the impact of operating costs, significantly reducing the value of the project.

Selection of the wrong alternative reflects the failure to recognize that more than one option exists for each project. Too many evaluations recommend a scheme which only yields a profit when every one or the great bulk of their estimates is correct. This seldom happens, much less being able to balance the risk and return of projects. Most favorable analyses are presented, not the most likely or average outcomes. Yet, the lesson from this section is "what can go wrong, will go wrong." The tendency is to recommend the alternative satisfying ego needs, rather than balancing risk and return optimally. Examples of balancing risk and return are provided in Chapter 5-10.

Wishful thinking dominates most investment analysis. We see this in every aspect of life, not just industry. Punters (investors) in the stock market love to gamble on their favorite areas of interest, regardless of the merits of that interest. The same holds true of organizations; they believe their technical expertise will minimize any damage from random occurrences. Their professionals are so good that they can accommodate any situation that arises. This includes strikes, bad weather, price declines, etc. The key to sound investment planning is anticipating the unexpected. Ignorance may be bliss, but it also leads to the loss of money and careers.

A more detailed taxonomy of errors has been prepared by Dr. Elizabeth Pate-Cornell.[(2.6)] Organizational errors fall into two main categories: gross errors which are like 2+2=5, and judgment errors which reflect both ambiguous or incomplete information. Gross errors are easier to remedy because more time and money can be spent to collect information or check one's analysis. Judgment errors resist corrective actions because they capture the conflicts inherent in the human psyche and limitations of our knowledge.

Judgment error is further divided into poor and good judgment by individuals. These two components could be split even further. Several points stand out, however. First, the bad judgment category is credited with most investment and safety failures. The ovals labeled misuse, reckless, etc. are self evident,

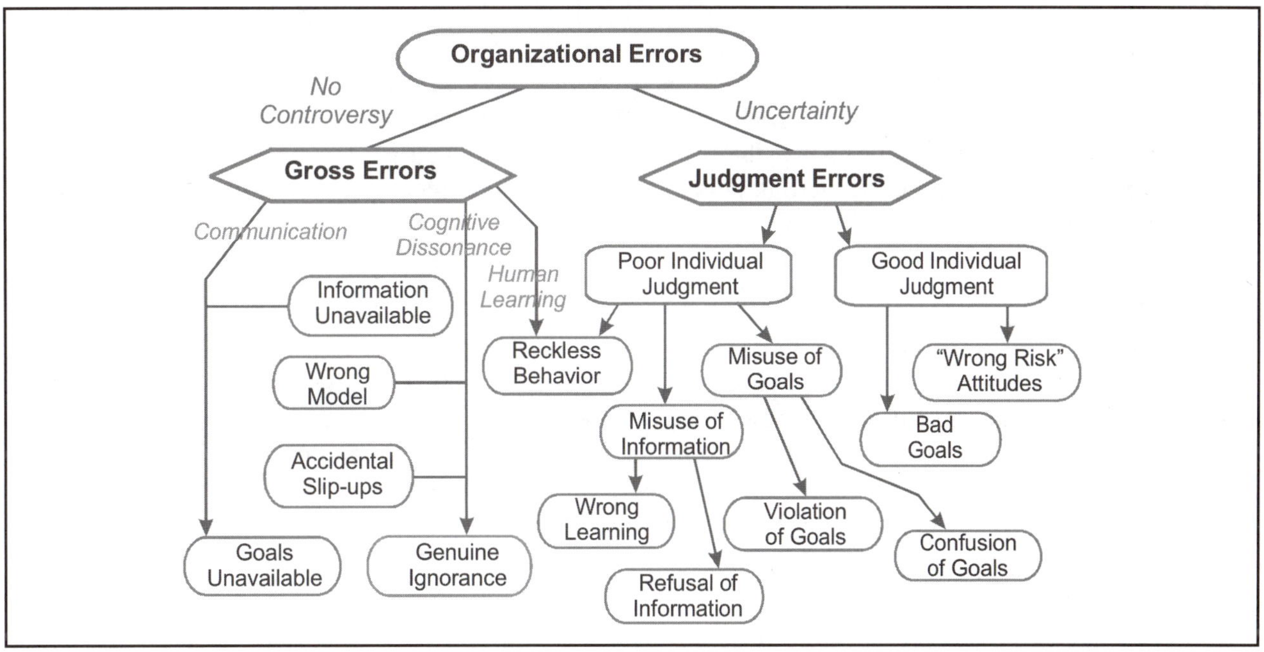

Figure 2.10 A taxonomy of organizational errors

except for the misuse of goals. Organizational goals often conflict with each other and are poorly stated. Examples of conflicts include maximizing NPV without spending any operating or capital costs, while adhering to safety specifications. Even worse, personal incentive systems typically require return on capital employed (ROCE) thresholds before any bonus is paid. Another tier in the typical bonus calculation includes reserve replacement. Well costs needed to replace reserves are included in the denominator of ROCE (See Chapter 4 for the actual definition). So, spending money to replace reserves reduces ROCE. The problem compounds when expenditures on safety and environmental issues are included.

The poor definition of goals, misunderstanding of goals, or the outright violation of goals probably covers the major problem areas in investment analysis. The entire exercise of appraising investments requires a clear statement of goals, and the organizational commitment to carry out this objective. Most of the problems with historical investment performance can be attributed to the failure to achieve this situation.

The experienced reader should carefully review the taxonomy of errors for areas that they can relate to. For the less experienced, ask those who have made investment mistakes for war stories. While war stories are often boring and time wasting, any lessons learnt may help avoid expensive, career threatening errors in the future. In reviewing the taxonomy, however, please reflect on the operating environment at the time the decision was made. Failing to control for, or understand the motivational system of the organization at the time the decision was made ignores perhaps the most critical element. Dr. Cornell states "One can expect a variety of management errors ...caused by organizational factors, such as excessive time pressure or failure to monitor hazard signals. These errors increase the probabilities of component failures either by increasing the probability of some initiating events or by decreasing the system's capacity (to respond to the events)."

The focus on investment decision-making errors in the preceding pages is intended to draw your attention to two elements: one is the need to understand the lessons from past mistakes, and second, is the importance of following a consistent, organized approach. The next section outlines one system that appears to work well in practice, although no system will ever avoid all errors.

MAKING INVESTMENT DECISIONS

Following the five step process summarized in Figure 2.11 increases the chances of achieving investment objectives, however defined. Each cell contains subsections describing the tasks to be completed in each section and the basic methodologies, if appropriate. Each item is discussed in some detail below to illustrate the nature of the questions. Drawing such figures always presents some dilemmas about how to show the relationship, because in reality, the results of one cell influences the subsequent path, which, in turn, redirects attention back to the starting point. This simultaneity must be recognized to implement Figure 2.11 correctly.

Formulate Questions

The first step is also the least understood; for the process of question formulation determines the entire course of action that follows. Many failures observed in the past stem largely from asking the wrong questions at the very outset. Professionals have been known to work very diligently, and very professionally, providing technical and economic answers to irrelevant or unimportant questions. Learning to ask the right questions requires as much art as science, demanding teamwork from all involved. The subcategories suggest that the three basic elements require describing the goals and objectives of the analysis, as well identifying likely problems. As the analysis proceeds, these elements will be modified in light of newer information.

Every investment objective should be formulated broadly in terms that relate to an overall investment strategy, including goals and incentives of the organization. Specification of these goals, objectives,

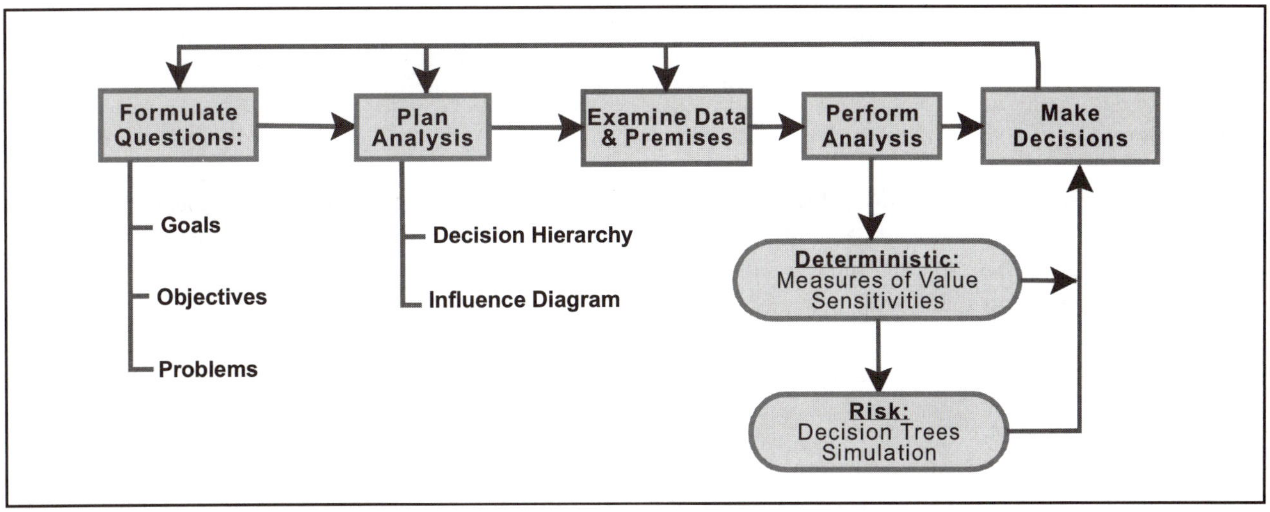

Figure 2.11 One system for analyzing investments

and problems structures the thinking of those involved, since professionals typically work to solve individual pieces of the puzzle. Defining the questions too narrowly often limits or precludes analysis of relevant alternatives. Subsequently, a less than thorough evaluation emerges. For example, the assignment "evaluate the merits of expanding the existing production system" structures thinking. Given this task, many professionals would spend their time analyzing the best size increment, choice of latest technology, scheduling, etc. A more general question, however, is "What can be done to this property to maximize value." Presenting the question in this manner expands greatly the number of possible issues to consider. Some examples include a) doing nothing other than regular maintenance, b) adding capacity, c) sell the asset, or d) retrofit the facility with the latest technology

After agreeing on the goals and objectives of the analysis, the problem should turn to anticipating potential problems. Again, this exercise can never be exact. Without understanding potential bottlenecks before they arise, effective circumvention is almost impossible. This includes every aspect of the analysis: legal and contractual issues, markets for products, available support infrastructure, etc. These items characterize the "omitted variables" in evaluations. Too often the technical staff goes off collecting and analyzing information before such problems are addressed. We have seen a significant amount of time wasted on technical evaluation before the impossibility of the project (usually legal or political), became obvious. In manpower constrained organizations, this expenditure of time wastes valuable resources.

For example, if contract terms are important, be sure to read the existing contract or proposed contract depending on the stage of the project. Are new markets or new transportation facilities required for production? If so, be certain these areas are fully evaluated. Beware of arbitrary price and cost premises. What government regulations impact the venture, or have these regulations even been defined? Many a project has come to grief over regulatory requirements. It is impossible to evaluate what we don't think about.

Problem specification includes organizational impediments and biases. Every organization exhibits it's own culture, built up over time. That culture often has biases against certain types of activities. We are currently trying to get one organization to overcome its bias against countries with service contracts. Management maintains that they have no interest in service contracts; yet, one of their most profitable subsidiaries operates under a service contract. In fact, the service contract adds far more value than concessionary and contractual systems they operate under elsewhere. Other examples include biases against certain technologies, because "we tried it 20 years ago and it didn't work."

Whether the problems arise from internal or external sources, sound investment analysis can only proceed when all participants understand and communicate. Some prefer to call this the diagnostic phase, where the issues and problems are actually diagnosed. Later phases seek to structure remedies based on the diagnosis.

Plan Analysis

Most projects proceed along the path described in the last section in four main stages: conceptual design, detailed design, construction, and operation. Each stage is characterized by the amount of information available and, hence, the technical detail involved. Information and detail increase the further into the life of the project. Two main tools are used to outline the project scope – one is an *influence diagram* and the second is a *decision hierarchy*. Normally we recommend constructing an influence diagram first, followed by the decision hierarchy as the best use of limited resources. Each is discussed in turn with a simple example.

The influence diagram describes the variables involved in the project and their interactions conceptually. The key word here is conceptually. The goal is to develop an understanding of the entire system, not to answer specific questions. Influence diagrams concern themselves more with what questions need answering. They are just a modified flow diagram with the arrows depicting the direction of causality. Note that no physical measures of the actual impact exist. Quantification takes place later.

Figure 2.12 presents a simple influence diagram for a waterflood project. Assuming waterflooding optimizes field performance, the analysis plan follows the path in the influence diagram. Needed data inputs include operating costs, capital costs, reserves, production profiles, prices, etc. In structuring the analysis certain relationships, like between capital costs and production rates, must be estimated. This analytical format structures the thought process, providing directions for filling or, possibly, quantifying the gaps in our knowledge, rather than following a haphazard, uncoordinated path.

Influence diagrams improve analysis in several ways. First, they help outline data needs and possible courses of action to obtain that data. Second, the interrelationship between variables becomes obvious. The choice of the best alternative requires understanding the dependency between capital expenditures and production volumes, and then how the production volumes impact operating costs, in turn. And, these

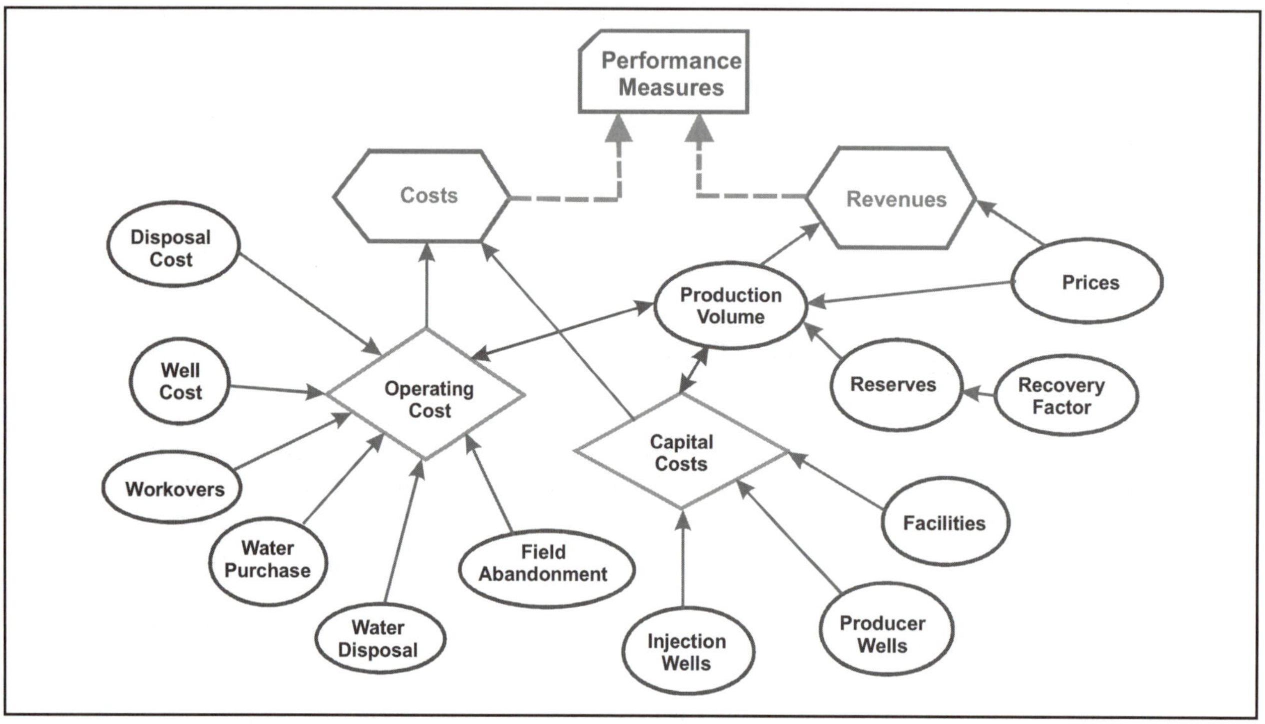

Figure 2.12 Waterflood influence diagram

variables depend on the price received for the product. This framework forces the analysis to consider the goals of the organization in a much more direct manner than just meeting simplified performance standards. Some of the errors specified in Figure 2.10 may be avoided if the system, and interrelationships within the system are identified first.

Probably the main complaint about influence diagrams relates to the increasing complexity as the project increases in scope. What appears to be a very simple diagram can cover hundreds of pages for large projects, depending on the level of detail desired. This situation is actually a good reason to use an influence diagram. Yes, it's more work, but the larger the project, the more likely one or more important elements of the project may be overlooked. Having an effective blueprint of the project, before professionals become engrossed in their areas of expertise, provides better direction and more efficient utilization of time and costs. As a general rule, the level of effort should vary in proportion to the estimated benefit and costs associated with the investment opportunity.

For large projects, employing two levels of influence diagrams reduces complexity to a point where effective judgment is possible. The first level divides the project into discrete element that interact in series or parallel within the total system. The second level would be a diagram for each module, as shown in Figure 2.12.

After generating a project blueprint, the next need is to prioritize the elements in the action plan. Of the hundreds of elements in a project, not all are equally important. The lessons from historical analysis indicates that too much time is wasted generating unimportant values, based on the excuse of being technically accurate. The prioritization process helps especially in interacting with management. Even though the staff may have identified the question accurately, the relative importance of individual variables may differ. Sorting out any differences between technical disciplines or staff and management, and, why, facilitates the orderly decision-making process.

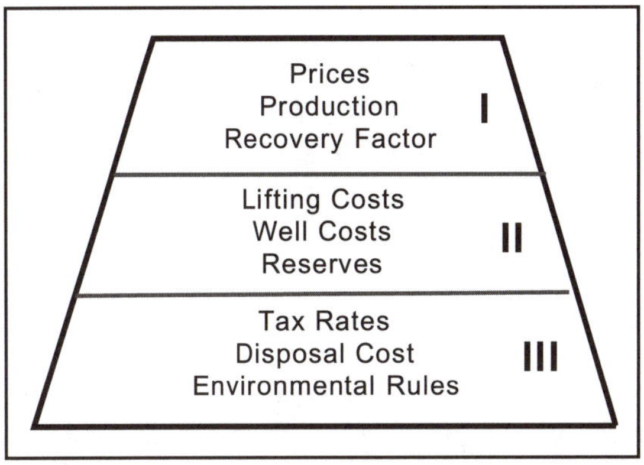

Figure 2.13 A decision hierarchy example

The decisions hierarchy comes in several variants, though each seeks to help the professionals focus on the critical problem elements. The most common approach uses a triangle or pyramid split into at least three levels. The first level specifies the objectives, the second level the questions to be asked, and the last the basic assumptions required. Most texts in Decision Methods recommend this approach. Slightly modified approaches, like the diagram in Figure 2.13 aid decision-making by dividing the input elements into three tiers, labeled I, II and III, for convenience. The Tier I elements are believed to be the most important, Tier II the second most important, and so on. More tiers can be added depending on the circumstances of the analysis.

The time and energy spent on collecting data, the next phase, are specified here. Most importantly, decision hierarchies allow management to input their beliefs. This "check" enhances the prospects for communicating goals and objectives, before the detail work starts. Note how this approach might help resolve some of the organizational errors outlined in Figure 2.10.

The circularity outlined in Figure 2.11 also becomes apparent here. The importance of each variable at this point reflects experience, current understanding of the task, bias, preconceived notions, etc. As later steps are added to the analysis, these classifications should be revised. Variables ranked highly may prove to be unimportant, while the less important increase in stature. A second real benefit of decision hierarchy arises from building a consensus about the analysis among involved disciplines. Technical professionals typically rank their parts higher and downgrade others. Management often views the problem from a totally different perspective. Figure 2.14 outlines one decision hierarchy put together by

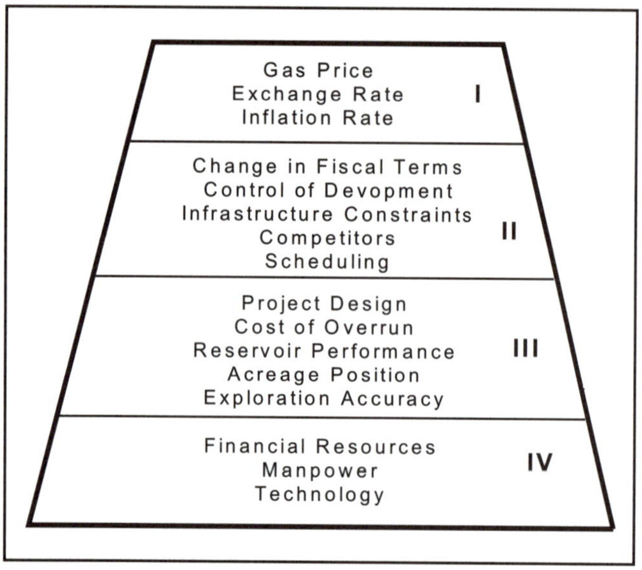

Figure 2.14 Example decision hierarchy for S. E. Asia project

management. The Southeast Asian project involved developing a major gas field, including processing and transportation facilities.

Technical professional typically place their areas of interest in Tiers I and II. Management rankings place three categories – prices, exchange rates, and inflation – highest. The next tier includes other less technical areas: changes in fiscal regimes, cost and likelihood of overruns, control of the development scheme, competitors in the area, and scheduling of the project. The engineering and geoscience disciplines show up in Tiers III and IV, along with several others.

These ranking don't diminish the importance of good technical work; it is trying to balance the relative importance from all the knowledge bases for a specific project. The relative rankings change over the project life-cycle. Also, these rankings usually reflect only the first perceptions. The further into the project we go, the more likely the relative rankings will be rearranged. In fact, if the relative importance fails to vary during the course of the project, something is amiss, and, a good guess is that the staff is providing answers they think management wants to see, not necessarily their professional opinions.

Examine Data and Premises

This phase normally dominates time allocation in project analysis. Begin by gathering required data and confirming the premises under which the analysis will be made. Another term for premises is assumptions. Most organizations maintain entire staffs (See Chapter 1) to develop and communicate the major assumptions used to analyze investment opportunities. For most organizations, these premises include, price forecasts (Chapter 7), exchange rate forecasts (Chapter 7), discount rates (Chapter 4 and 8), overhead rates (Chapter 6), country income and production tax rates (Chapter 3), etc.

Historically, the discussion and appraisal of premises impact on investment metrics, both risk and return, was met with almost complete resistance by everyone. Technical professionals felt they lacked the expertise to alter existing standards, and headquarters argued that the standards guaranteed a consistent appraisal of competing, often mutually exclusive investments. The need for consistency is a fundamental truth; in fact, this entire book seeks to provide a foundation for consistent investment decisions.

Unfortunately, assumed premises influence final project choices as much or more than other variables. To ignore the potential variability of these rates for specific projects virtually guarantees under achieving investment performance, usually in foregoing attractive investments, in favor of low risk, short-lived projects. Ignoring guideline premises isn't necessary, all the same computations can be made with existing guideline premises. The premises designed to provide consistency should be expanded to include information, or knowledge about variability, instead of conveying single, deterministic values. To argue for risk management without allowing professionals to incorporate the variability in these premises into their decision-making framework is a recipe for failure. Progressive investors now allow their staff to include alternative premises as part of their analysis, and some even demand formal recognition of premise variability.

Data exists from a variety of sources. Most countries have either public or private groups who specialize in providing historical information about costs and production rates. U. S. companies like

Dwight's, Petroleum Information, Minerals Management Service, Energy Information Agency, Arthur Anderson, etc. summarize historical financial and economic data in the U. S. Agencies in other countries offer similar services.

All data and premises must be evaluated with a critical eye. For example, if only average capital costs are available, are these costs appropriate? Do they reflect the construction cost environment now, not yesterday? If no, why not? Does the analysis assume a guaranteed market for the products? If so, how variable is the price.? Prices vary significantly among regions depending on local markets, transportation costs, etc. Do your premises account for such individual conditions?

The best advice we can give is to look critically for any tacit assumptions built into the premises. For example, is continued technological advancement being taken for granted? Even the converse, assuming stagnant technology change may be just as bad. Does the premise or data take into account impending regulatory changes? Accurate historical data may mislead the analysis if regulatory changes either improve or exacerbate costs. Every assumption needs to be explicitly considered.

In all cases, be willing to look beneath the surface of the data and premises for an understanding on the impact on the overall system specified in the influence diagram or decision hierarchy. This is especially true of some accounting data, which can be misleading if used in a cash flow model. These expenses measure *sunk costs,* like *depreciation*, not actual flows of money. This situation arises quite often when buying or selling assets.

One test of data and premises is to compare internal values to those reported externally. Prices are, for example, readily available from lenders and in trade publications. The Society of Petroleum Evaluation Engineers surveys it's members every year for price forecasts and publishes the results. Financial markets, like the futures market, also provide checks for short-run price forecasts (less than 7 years). Significant differences should signal important assumptions worthy of being checked. Cost information is also available from most construction companies. Faced with a continuing need to estimate costs around the world, they maintain very good data bases on almost all cost categories. Similarly, a phone call to vendors supplying equipment or services leads to a quick, free check on any cost estimate.

At the core of any effort to generate data is the need to represent the uncertainty in that data. The most common approach assumes each value is known with certainty, when, in reality, estimated data always differs from the best guesses. The data examination phase must then communicate these uncertainties. At the simplest level, suppose someone asked you for the height of the tallest mountain in North America (which happens to be Mt. McKinley in Alaska). How comfortable would you be stating that the height was 20,320 ft. (6,157 meters)? Would it be easier to report, say, 17,000 to 23,350 feet. Using ranges effectively conveys information about uncertainty. The alternative of quoting a single, or deterministic value, then doing sensitivities is subject to a phenomenon called *anchoring,* as explained in Chapter 6.

The push toward ranges of values, rather than single values, is a relatively new phenomenon. Even though Dr. John Campbell Sr. and Dr. Paul Newendorp applied basic statistical principles to the industry as far back as 1968,[(2.7)] the process didn't catch on until the personal computer allowed the concepts to be applied quickly and easily, primarily on spreadsheets; though superb commercial software now exists, as well. Today, these concepts are being applied regularly to almost every facet of investment opportunities.[(2.8)]

The complexity in combining technical and commercial issues to make good investment decisions necessitates establishing ranges when collecting the data and creating premises, as the most effective way to preserve continuity throughout the project. This is not a criticism of the classical, deterministic approach; rather, an expression of the need to overcome the limitations of that system as the pace of technical and commercial changes, nationally and globally, accelerates.

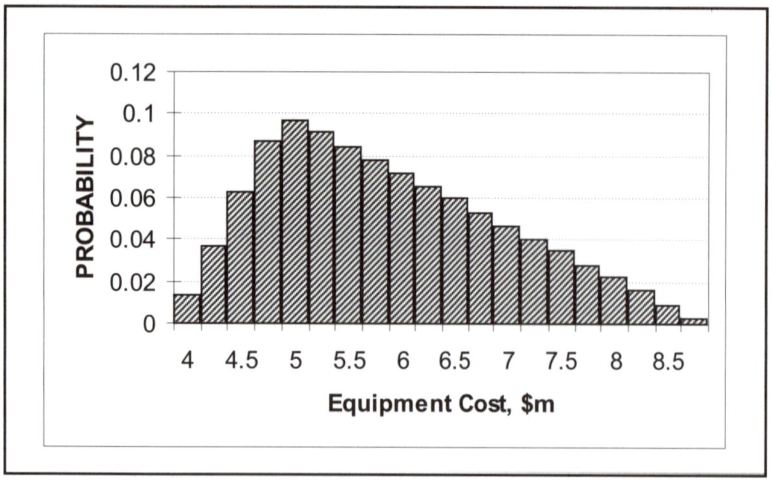

Figure 2.15 Variability in equipment cost

For example, having been assigned the task of estimating the cost to acquire and install some equipment, the deterministic approach yields a single value, like \$5 million. The next level of complexity adds ranges, like plus or minus 20%. So, now the quoted cost might be \$4-\$6 million, with a *most likely* or *base case* value of \$5 million. Although an improvement in communicating real world conditions, the source of the variation must still be conveyed. Applying the knowledge inherent in statistics is probably the best way to capture variability for individual variables. Figure 2.15 illustrates the same equipment cost estimate using a distribution, rather than a single value with ranges, assuming a low value of \$4 m, a most likely of \$5 m, and a high value of \$9 m.

One moment to describe this book's nomenclature. Some engineering literature interchanges the symbol M and MM to represent million. This book follows normal business practice of using m for millions and k for thousands. The quoted values in the previous paragraph represent millions.

The advantage of displaying ranges, like Figure 2.15, is apparent to many, especially when asked for a cost estimate by other groups without sufficient time to analyze the situation in detail. The range or variability passes along your confidence in the estimate; obviously, the wider the range, the less certain the estimate. The primary reluctance to adopting this approach comes from the psychological need to be perfect, and this desire infects all disciplines and knowledge bases. It's hard to conceive of going to school for as many years as we have or are, without knowing more at the end. We don't know of any school or discipline that teaches how to predict the future with certainty, only manage that uncertainty. Risk approaches just formalize the imperfections in our knowledge and experience, and doesn't cast aspersions on anyone's abilities.

Perform Analysis

This phase minimizes the amount of real work, because the computer does most of the arithmetic today. When the authors began their professional careers, the calculations were done with slide rules and desk top calculators, often larger than today's PC's. Aside from dating us, it shows again how technology has changed over the last 30 years. Computer programs, while increasing in sophistication and ease of use, basically are black boxes to most users. The typical user is unclear about what is actually happening, only that if the output values exceed organizational guidelines, their project is approved. Chapters 3-10 provide details about the calculations in the black box. This section describes the outputs from the black box.

Figure 2.1 outlined the basic approach. This phase completes the middle two steps: deriving taxes and NCF estimates, then computing the measures of value. The intermediate tax and NCF estimates help the organization plan for future cash flows and tax liabilities, but most investors rely on summary measures of value to make the majority of the investment decisions.

Deterministic Analysis

The process starts by plugging the estimated values obtained from the previous phases into the computer program. While inputting values into computers seems easy, lack of understanding about variable names and importance probably causes more errors than any other source, although these errors are

TABLE 2.2
Typical Output of Project Evaluation

Parameters	Discount Rate			
	0%	10%	15%	20%
NPV ($M)	89.92	36.68	27.37	16.26
NPV/INV	2.91	1.25	0.95	0.58
SIV ($M)	89.92	76.42	73.95	68.95
DPO-years	2.82	3.21	3.40	3.79
	Risk Weighted NPV = 16.88			
Year	t	t+1	t+2	t+3
AT NCF ($M)	-30.9	18.3	15.3	12.9

usually minor. Once data are input and the computer runs, the first page of output is usually the management summary. Though programs vary, it may look something like Table 2.2.

The value measures, like NPV, NPV/Inv, Strategic Investment Value (SIV), discounted payout (DPO), and risk weighting, measure the value added as the result of investing in a project (See Chapter 7). Each value measure is summarized for different assumptions about the organizations cost of borrowing – called the *discount rate* (See Chapter 3). Also included is the actual cash flows from the project for the first four years. These values estimate the burden to the treasury (cash flows) in the early years. The more negative the NCF, the more money the treasury must invest. For those with extreme capital constraints (very little money), the NCF pattern may be as important as the measures of value.

As long as the deterministic measures of value are greater than zero (value is added to the treasury), then projects usually move on for further comparison with other projects. Before accepting this project, however, the outputs pass a personal reasonable test. That is, do the numbers in the output report make sense to you. If not, go back to the details of the output reports and begin checking values, number by number, until you understand what is happening. The old "garbage in, garbage out" rule applies here.

Since all estimates contain some errors, can the analysis help us understand the relative importance of each input variable and which inputs to concentrate on refining the values. The answer is obviously yes, and involves the brute force approach of *sensitivity analysis,* or some have renamed sources of value. Trying to describe the process of going back to the computer, changing each input one at a time, then rerunning the program wastes time and space, but is the foundation of sensitivity analysis. Although the decision hierarchy provided initial assessments of the most important variables, the sensitivity approach quantifies these assessments.

Historically each sensitivity found it's way into a table. Given the hundreds of variables found in most projects, the sensitivity tables often multiplied the number of pages in the report beyond anyone's comprehension. An easier way to present the sensitivity analysis of the decision hierarchy estimates is via a *tornado diagram.* Like most fancy phrases, a tornado diagram is a graphical representation of the outcomes of the sensitivity, like Figure 2.16. The

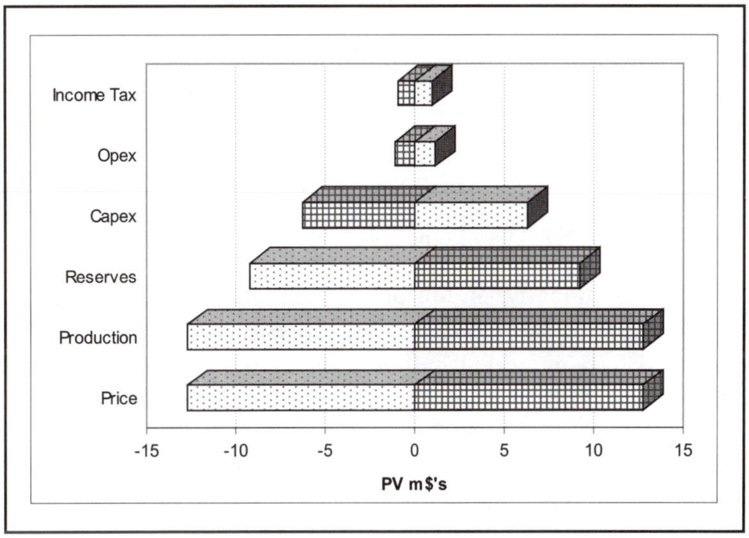

Figure 2.16 Tornado diagram for sources of value

wider the values, the more sensitive the measure of value (PV in this example) is to any change in the input variable. Price and production impact NPV the most, while income tax and Opex alter the project valuation very little.

The hatched area of each bar represents the impact of an increase in each element. A 20% increase in price improvement in the project NPV (about $13M). For the cost categories – Capex, Opex, and taxes – the same increase reduces PV, since these are deductions in NCF (Review Equation 2.1). Increasing a negative number reduces profits. Conversely, the dotted portion shows that a 20% reduction in price, production and reserves decreases value.

Stochastic Analysis

Tornado diagrams communicate the relative importance of variables in the simplest possible way: changing one variable at a time, though some software allows the user to specify multiple sensitivities. When hundreds of changes for each of hundreds of variables, one at a time or in combination, are possible, the number of sensitivities increase beyond the time available or the ability to convey the outcomes meaningfully. The *simulation* process fills this void. It is the ultimate culmination of all the efforts discussed in the earlier phases. Simulation models the interactions described in the influence diagram, along with the variability in the data and premises. With good modeling, even the goals, premises, and potential problems, discussed in phase 1 can be included. Chapter 6 outlines the process and modeling procedures for technical elements, and Chapter 8 integrates the technical and economic components for the complete project evaluation.

The output of the simulation process appears like Figure 2.17, the same development analysis discussed in Table 2.2 and Figure 2.16. Figure 2.17 is the end result of the simulation process assuming that NPV is the desired output variable. Simulation builds on the calculation process outlined in Figure 2.1 by adding the concept of variability for each input, as illustrated with the cost estimate earlier. By allowing each input to vary in a controlled manner, ranges and likelihood's of possible outcomes are documented. Rather than seeing just one deterministic outcome, a fuller set of possible outcome becomes apparent. The graph tells us the *most likely* outcome of the project – an NPV of about $33 m and the spread of outcomes: -$77 m to $94 m. This variability in measures of value, like NPV or NPV/INV, captures most peoples definition of risk. The solid vertical line shows the value of zero, or about 10% of the output values were less than zero, or the project reduced value about 10% of the time.

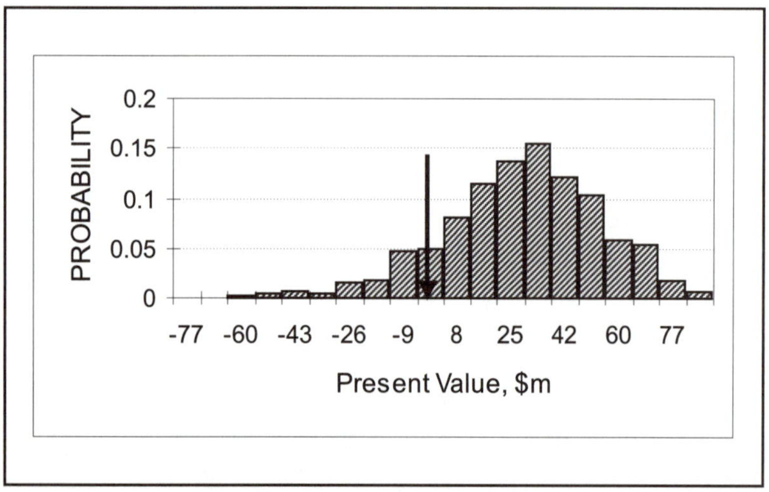

Figure 2.17 Stochastic project results

Traditionally, arguments against simulation focused on the time and computing power required to develop and run the models. With current software and hardware, existing models can be expanded to include risk just by adding information on input variability. The solution time can be as low as a few seconds or several hours depending on the hardware and model complexity. The second complaint deals with the inability to link specific combinations of inputs to each output. Since each output NPV in this case may result from different input combinations, answering such questions wasn't always easy. Most programs now provide output in sufficient detail to answer such questions.

Sensitivities can also be added to the simulations to communicate the relative importance of specific variables. Most software will draw tornado diagrams just like Figure 2.16. The tornado diagram is interpreted just like before.

Chapters 4 and 8 cover these topics in great detail, while Chapter 9 applies the concepts to typical investment decisions. We elected to omit any reference to decision trees, which were referred to in Figure 2.10. Decision trees are just an intermediary between influence diagrams and simulation methods, although are quite useful for novice users of risk methods, and are explained in Chapter 9.

Make Decision

The last step is the culmination of all the previous steps. Defining the goals and objectives, laying out the investment system, collecting data, and processing the information, bring us to the climax of having to actually make a decision to invest or not, and the form of that investment. This book emphasizes that investing is an inexact science. No matter how meticulous the analysis, bad investments, including foregoing good projects, will always take place. The objective is to minimize the number and severity of the bad investments.

Figure 2.17 illustrates the risk and return components of every project. In fact, every project has some risk and return possibilities. Making sound investment decisions means trading off the relative importance of each opportunities risk and return. Viewed at the senior management level, all these projects must be combined to insure that risk and return objectives for the entire organization are met. This is called *portfolio management.* While portfolio management has it's origin in the stock market, most organizations talk today about their portfolio of assets. To make decisions that achieve investor objectives, the complex interaction of all the investment opportunities must be well understood and analyzed, not just the part contributed by each project.

For individual investments, several options usually exist. In an offshore development, a tension leg platform with a pipeline might be one option; whereas, a floating production and storage system with subsea completions could be another option. Various combinations between these two extreme decisions also exist. Likewise, in selecting a production system, high quality, non-corrosive alloys might be considered relative to using carbon steel with corrosion inhibitors. The list of options is almost endless.

The choice of the best option is termed *optimization*. The process is not well understood in industry right now. Again, the omission of optimization methods arose because of the huge time commitment and cost of implementation. Special programs and training were necessary using old mainframe hardware. Now the same analysis can be conducted using existing PC software, by asking the right questions. A typical question arises when sizing facilities to obtain different production volumes . As the influence diagram in Figures 1.10 and 2.12 show, increasing production requires additional capital outlays and impacts Opex. The combination of these factors ultimately determines project value (Figure 2.1). To optimize value or minimize risk implies some understanding of the systematic relationship between inputs, like production and cost.

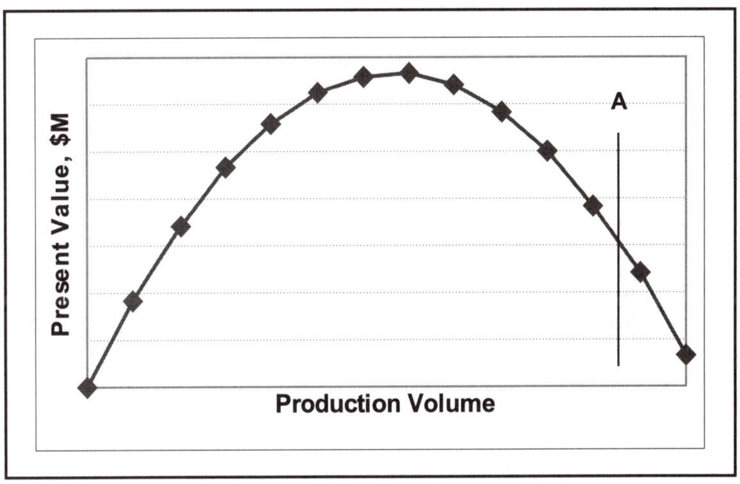

Figure 2.18 Example of suboptimal investment choice

Figure 2.18 highlights a typical tradeoff. Because of the sequential nature of the decision-making process, one group decided on the desired production volume first, and then the facilities, production process and transportation system selected. When the project was finally analyzed for economic contribution, the deterministic solution came out at point A. The y-axis is present value in millions of dollars, and is positive for all values. The project was approved, because the sensitivities showed robustness in the economic values to variations in the initial assumptions.

After further review of other alternatives, the recommended development scheme clearly adds value (in NPV terms), but not as much as it could have with a different development plan. This tradeoff is referred to as a *suboptimal* decision. Decisions that choose the A option may meet other guidelines on economic value (NPV>0), like satisfying cash flow needs in certain years. This is called *satisficing*.

The decision to choose scheme A is called suboptimal, because it was assumed that *maximizing shareholder wealth* is the prime objective of the organization: finding and producing products is merely a means to that end. Avoiding conflicts among stated goals and objectives is the real purpose of the optimization process. Stated another way, what is the tradeoff of placing a higher priority on one goal relative to another? These issues are outlined further in Chapter 10, along with modeling tips on how to set up and run problems using existing software. Examples are also provided for both single and multiple project investment decisions, and for ranking investments in the capital budgeting process.

SUMMARY

Most organizations exist to add value for their stakeholders. Business accomplishes this by investing capital in those investments earning the best returns; governments also try to earn a return on investments, but also have objectives related to quality of life, employment, etc. This chapter outlines the basic process involved in analyzing and managing investment opportunities for those unfamiliar with the concepts, without discussing the details. More importantly, it summarizes some available information about how and why past investments have failed to achieve their objectives. By learning from these mistakes, hopefully future performance will improve. In this spirit we have tried to present an approach that will hopefully limit ones experience with bad investment performance.

The first two chapters have discussed the framework under which investment appraisals are performed. The book now turns to a more detailed analysis of the disciplines and the information contributed by each to the investment decision making process. The goal is to provide enough depth on each topic so that the reader will appreciate the basic concepts, understand how and why they are used in actual practice, and, even better, have a feel for the limitations of each topic. Entire disciplines or areas of specialty exist for each chapter or often subsections of a chapter. Many professionals spend their entire careers without ever mastering the concepts presented here, if there even is such a thing as mastery of a discipline. Good luck and have fun.

REFERENCES

2.1 Capen, Ed, Presentation to the Oklahoma City SPE (Nov. 1995).

2.2 JPT (Feb. 1982), pp. 433-439.

2.3 The Rand Corporation (1983).

2.4 Westney, D., Personal Communication.

2.5 Smulders, B. H. N. , "Reducing the Cost of Offshore Developments," European GPA (1990).

2.6 Elizabeth Pate-Cornell, "Organizational Aspects of Engineering Safety: The Case of Offshore Platforms," *Science* (30 Nov. 1990), pp. 1210-1217.

2.7 Newendorp, P. and J. Campbell, "Decision Methods for Petroleum Investments," John M. Campbell & Co. (Oct. 1968).

2.8 Gutleber, D. S., Heiberger, E. M., and T. D. Morris, "Simulation Analysis for Integrated Evaluation of Technical and Commercial Risk," *JPT* (Dec. 1995), pp. 1062-1067.

CHAPTER 3

ESTIMATING THE FLOW OF MONEY

Net Cash Flow (NCF) provides the foundation for valuing investment opportunities, and, thus, contributes to all investment decision-making processes. NCF converts technical estimates from disciplines, like geoscience and engineering, into the units investors care about: money. Using a common basis, like money, for comparing projects with different revenues, investment costs, risks, and timing allows investors to compare risk (Chapter 8 & 9), and select the best combination of projects (Chapter 10). Public and private organizations exist to enhance the well being of the people they report to; however, one measures that performance. Private organizations maximize shareholder's wealth, since investors buy shares to make money. Public organizations balance spending money wisely with additional, often contradictory objectives of employing people, conservation of national resources, funding government programs, and regulating private companies. Each effort requires accurate estimates of the magnitude and timing of the flow of money to have any hope of achieving these objectives.

The critics of the NCF approach emphasize failures in market economies to adequately price costs and benefits. We agree that the valuation process is imperfect. This book seeks to understand the imperfections in such values. Having incomplete, bad, distorted values, whatever you believe, doesn't eliminate the need for a consistent format for valuing ideas? Critics complain that issues, like life and the environment, exceed any attempt at valuation, and any attempt at valuation demeans life itself. This certainly requires many of the knowledge bases discussed in Chapter 1 to even discuss. This chapter provides a format for discussing such issues, even if the critics opt for an infinite value of a species.

The basic components of the common valuation system, called net cash flow (NCF), are developed first. Like all valuation concepts, alternative names are available: funds flow (FF), cash surplus after taxes (CSAT), then-current cash flow (TCCF), etc. NCF is used here, but the name employed matters not, as long as the basic approach is adhered to; namely, the process accurately models the flow of money to the relevant treasury – yours, the companies, the country, etc.

Timing and magnitude impact every organization, regardless of size or ownership. The term, net cash flow, measures money remaining after all costs, including taxes, are deducted from revenues. NCF, thus, measures revenue available for discretionary spending.

NCF estimates are used to:

- measure the impact of the project on liquidity of the company,
- estimate profitability (Chapter 5),
- assess the risk of the project (Chapter 8 & 9),
- analyze impact of tax regimes on resource development and conservation, and
- optimize the portfolio of projects (Chapter 10).

NCF forms the foundation for all management decisions; be they classical measures of profitability (NPV, IRR, NPV/INV) and risk, or the modern investment valuation process. The old phrase "garbage in, garbage out" applies to every investment decision made, for either your personal assets or your employers.

The penalty for illiquidity is loss of wealth and personal assets, and severe austerity measures, like higher unemployment, inflation, and a reduced standard of living. The perpetual criticism of the World Bank and International Monetary Fund for their lending practices, while containing kernels of truth, ignores the sad fact that the recipients failed to invest the funds in projects that generated cash flows to cover the investment costs.

The failure to understand NCF extends to industries as well. The mergers and acquisitions (M&A) over the last 50 years highlight the conceit of many managers, as they bought firms outside their areas of expertise: auto rental firms, mineral companies, retail stores, breweries, and etc. Different industries and even different projects within the same industry face very different cash flows. Until investors truly understand the variation in NCF, this will be the ultimate "never ending story." You can always tell when this process has occurred, when an organization decides to focus on their "core-competence," after several years of excessive spending. It means the investor realizes that they didn't understand the intricacies of the investment well enough.

NCF CONCEPT

Deriving NCF equates to balancing your checkbook. NCF measures the trade-off between revenues or benefits against expenditures for investment, operating costs and taxes. The volume of money remaining after paying all bills measures discretionary revenue or NCF. Discretionary is the key word; money is available to be spent as desired: cars, vacations, motorcycles, spouse, dividends, medical plans, etc.

Organizations make key investment decisions based on projections about future NCF, be it governments or private firms. Bad estimates of future NCF's, as outlined in Chapter 2, mean investors over commit on future project spending. Inaccurate NCF estimates retard growth and misallocate of scarce capital.

$$\begin{array}{ll} \text{Net Revenue}_t & \sum \text{Net Revenue} \\ \quad -\text{Opex}_t & \quad -\sum \text{Opex} \\ \quad -\text{Overhead}_t & \quad -\sum \text{Overhead} \\ \quad -\text{Capex}_t & \quad -\sum \text{Capex} \\ \quad -\text{Taxes}_t & \quad -\sum \text{Taxes} \\ =\text{NCF}_t & =\sum \text{NCF} \end{array} \tag{3.1}$$

NCF derivation follows a relatively simple logic, as illustrated in Equation 3.1, where the subscript t reflects the desired time period: monthly, daily, yearly, etc. Most of the examples herein use annual NCF, as most analysis does, though exceptions exist. Cumulative NCF emphasizes the basics of double entry bookkeeping: the difference of the sums is the same as the sum of the differences. This notion seems trivial now, but facilitates software development, as shown in Chapter 8.

Equation 3.1 summarizes the simplest NCF format. Conventions vary across organizations, however. Although the different conventions do not influence the final NCF values, they generate inconsistent nomenclature and often confuse, rather than enhance decision-making. A generalized version of common conventions is outlined in Equation 3.2.

$$
\begin{aligned}
&\text{Revenue}_t\\
&\quad -\text{Production Taxes}\\
&\quad -\text{Overhead}_t\\
&= \text{Net Operating Income(NOI)}\\
&\quad -\text{Taxes}_t\\
&= \text{After-tax Income}_t\\
&\quad -\text{Capex}_t\\
&= \text{NCF}_t
\end{aligned}
\tag{3.2}
$$

Equation 3.2 modifies the earlier format by including several intermediate calculations, like net operating income and after-tax income, but the basic components are the same. The examples in this chapter include mineral industries, because they face the same taxes as all other industries, plus an additional tax levied on production; hence, the additions of the production tax component in Equation 3.2. Other industries can ignore this component, but the remaining elements still apply.

Equation 3.1 and 3.2 produce the same NCF values. Regardless of format, avoid using terms with duplicate, conflicting meanings. A classic example is after-tax income. It is used in financial reports, tax reports, and, unfortunately, investment decisions, each time having a different meaning. Examples are presented later. We use the term income to designate values used to compute one or more taxes, like depreciation or capital recovery. Cash flow designates the actual flow of money in a project.

Basic definitions for each component are shown below. The costs and revenues in each definition should be considered when deriving NCF, even if you organization defines a variable differently.

Revenue: Multiplies price and production rate projections. Many projects, like manufacturing and processing produce constant revenue on a real basis. Production in the typical mineral project declines as the resource is depleted to an economic limit, where lifting costs or operating expenses exceed revenues. Technical information needed to estimate reserves and production profiles are covered in a companion book, Petroleum Property Analysis.

Direct Operating Costs: Includes variable expenses (a cost tied to volume) and fixed expenses (costs unrelated to volume). If the operation ceases, these costs become zero. *(Opex, O&M).*

Overhead or General Expenses: Measures fixed expenses such as accounting, management, and professional fees, which are not related to actual operations. Incremental overhead expenses attributed to a project should be included in the evaluation *(OH).*

Overhead recognizes that projects must pay for expenses, like salaries, office rent, accounting and legal services, and vacation and pension plans. Formulas for calculating and distributing overhead involve allocating costs are always arbitrary. The entire discipline of cost accounting addresses these issues. Common examples include saying X% of production must be used to pay for overhead. Others use a fixed percentage of Capex or Opex. Let's say we add a 20% charge for overhead. That means every dollar of Capex reduces the NCF by 1*(1+X). Including OH reduces investment valuation, and should be avoided unless the investment reduces or adds overhead. Brealy and Myers argue that including overhead in NCF totally undermines the entire process.[3.1]

Capital Expenditures (Tangible and Intangible Capital): Defined as initial costs required to develop an investment. Outlays for production systems, buildings, transportation, and land are included. Many capital outlays usually occur in a project's early years, but additional outlays will be required in later years to accelerate or maintain revenues (CAPEX, TCAP, ICAP, IDC).

A common question among technical professionals is "How to differentiate between Capex and Opex?" The answer, which varies by country and professional, is the unequivocal "It depends." This answer depends on the tax code in each country. Accountants define Capex as an expenditure that could have a salvage value (after one year), while Opex has none. Buying a computer might have salvage value, whilst paying for a unit of electricity definitely has none. A more important issue concerns how investors interact with the local tax authority. Aggressive taxpayers classifying expenditures as Opex (vs. Capex) reduce their cost by about \$0.10 for every dollar spent. A \$1 Capex costs about \$0.75 after-tax, while a \$1 Opex costs about \$0.65 because of differences in the timing of tax relief..

Abandonment Value: Part of the investment outlay may be recovered at the end of the project life. Such Projects possess residual salvage values. This value may be negative if the cost of abandoning the asset (like offshore platforms) exceeds the value of the selling the asset.

Taxes: This is the most time-consuming part of developing NCF estimates. Types of taxes include: *production taxes* (*severance, ad valorem, and royalty*), *excise taxes* (sales, special taxes, and PRT), *property taxes*, state or region income taxes, and national *income taxes. Capital recovery* [depreciation, depletion, and amortization (the same as *DD&A* in financial books)] is necessary to compute taxes. Applicable regulations must be determined and proper computations performed to estimate taxes. Just because a law exists does not mean all parties interpret it the same way. This is no different from professionals arriving at conflicting conclusions from phase behavior, and other technical areas. Organizations follow very different practices in applying tax law, just like individuals.

Equation 3.3 summarizes the basic format that works in any country. The top box in Equation 3.3 develops net revenue, which measures money available to an investor for paying investment and operating cost. Gross revenue, while important on a total project basis, includes revenues dedicated to others – the landowner, the state, or a third party, even before the project begins. Gross revenue overstates the value of the project to the investor by the amount of the price or production dependent taxes. Deducting these variables simplifies risk management.

Equation 3.3

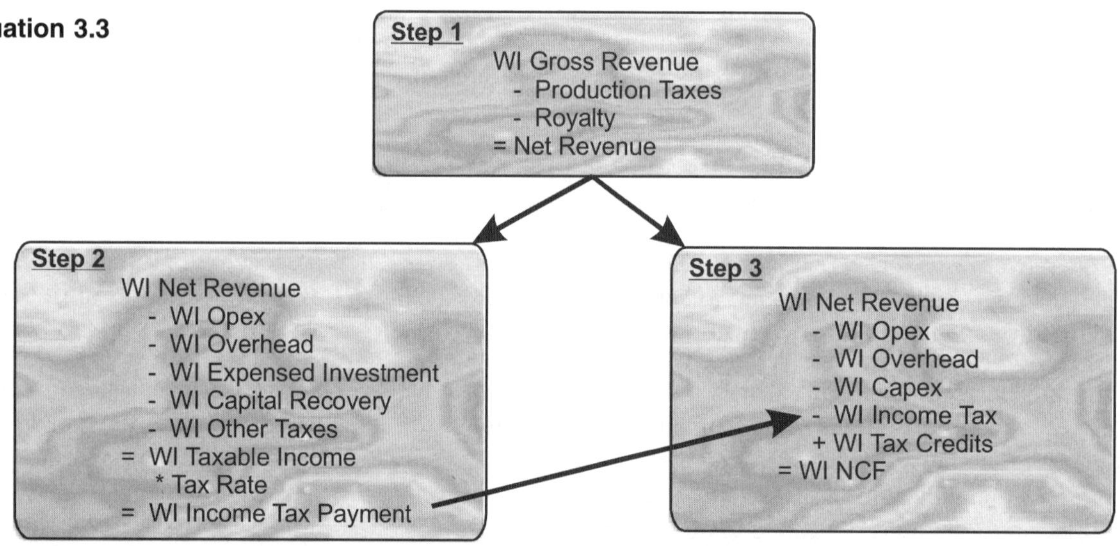

Net revenue flows into Step 2, used to compute income taxes (IT), which then flows into Step 3. Some texts add a category called *After-tax income* (ATI), which differs significantly from NCF. ATI fails to reflect real cash flow, because of the capital recovery line item in Step 2. Local governments specify the capital recovery process, like depreciation and depletion, to achieve their specific objectives.

The NCF derivation in Step 3 captures investment costs and tax impacts of the investment as they occur. ATI, on the other hand, splits investment costs into two categories: capitalized and expensed. Expensed investments correctly reflect the actual flow of money – they recognize the year when the money is spent. Capitalized investments enter ATI through the capital recovery category, including depreciation and depletion. These are called *non-cash charges,* since they exist only on paper for computing taxes.

Computing capital recovery involves various rules governing the type of recovery and the number of years over which recovery is allowed. Capital recovery signifies a process where expenditures are recovered (written off on the tax calculation) over a period longer than one year. Each country defines their own capital recovery process, but all combine one or more of three types: straight-line, sum-of-years digits, and declining balance.

Regardless of the method used, depreciation in any year is computed from Equation 3.4.

$$\text{Depreciation}_t = \text{Depreciation Factor}_t * \text{Depreciation Base}_t \qquad \textbf{(3.4)}$$

The three forms of depreciation differ in the factor and the base subject to depreciation. Each requires total depreciation to equal the capitalized investment over the life of the project. The basic equation for each is:

$$\begin{aligned} &\text{Straight Line (SL):} && D_t = \frac{1}{n}(C - SV) \\ &\text{Sum of Years Digits (BYD):} && D_t = \frac{y}{SYD}(C - SV) \\ &\text{Declining Balance (DB):} && D_t = \frac{DB}{n}(C - SV) \end{aligned} \qquad \textbf{(3.5)}$$

where:

D_t = depreciation in year t
C = original cost of the capitalized investment
SV = salvage value of capitalized investment (usually zero)
n = number of years of depreciation
y = number of years remaining in depreciation
SYD = sum of years digits
DB = declining balance factor

Each method recovers the original investment, but the timing of the recovery varies. Declining balance has the highest present value, meaning the cost recovery schedule yields a higher tax savings than SYD or SL depreciation.

Example 3.1 contrasts the differences in depreciation timing for the three cases. The impact of the time value of money alters the value of each depreciation schedule (Chapter 5). The accelerated depreciation methods – sum-of-years digits and declining balance – show a higher present value, because depreciation is larger in the early years.

NCF varies considerably across industries, and failure to understand these differences is horribly bad management. Trillions of dollars have been spent on M&A over the last few decades with hundred of

Example 3.1: Compute the SL, SYD and 200% DB over 5 years for a $10m investment.

Year	Depreciation Factor	*Depreciation Base	= Depreciation
1	0.2	10.0	2.0
2	0.2	10.0	2.0
3	0.2	10.0	2.0
4	0.2	10.0	2.0
5	0.2	10.0	2.0
Total	1.0		10.0
NPV_{10}			7.58
NPV_{15}			6.70

CHAPTER 3

Example 3.1: *(Cont'd.)* Compute the SL, SYD and 200% DB over 5 years for a $10m investment.

Year	Depreciation Factor	*Depreciation Base	= Depreciation
1	5/15	10.0	3.33
2	4/15	10.0	2.67
3	3/15	10.0	2.00
4	2/15	10.0	1.33
5	1/15	10.0	0.67
Total			10.0
NPV_{10}			8.06
NPV_{15}			7.32

Year	Depreciation Factor	*Depreciation Base	= Depreciation
1	0.40	10.00	4.00
2	0.40	6.00	2.40
3	0.40	3.60	1.44
4	0.40	2.16	0.86
5	0.40	1.30	1.30
Total			10.0
NPV_{10}			8.10
NPV_{15}			7.38

million spent on consultants and internal staff to generate NCF. At the end of the day, the acquiring mangers never really understood the differences across industries or allowed the acquired organizations to operate effectively. Management theory is mostly about handling such diversity effectively, on a timely basis.

Figures 3.1a-c illustrate the differences across industries. Figure 3.1a shows a real estate example, which has a very low NCF during the life of the project. Profits are realized when the property is sold in the last year. The holding period and the risk last until the property is sold. Suppose that the city where this property is located experiences a surplus of space renters and rental rates fall, meaning other revenue sources must exist to avoid bankruptcy.

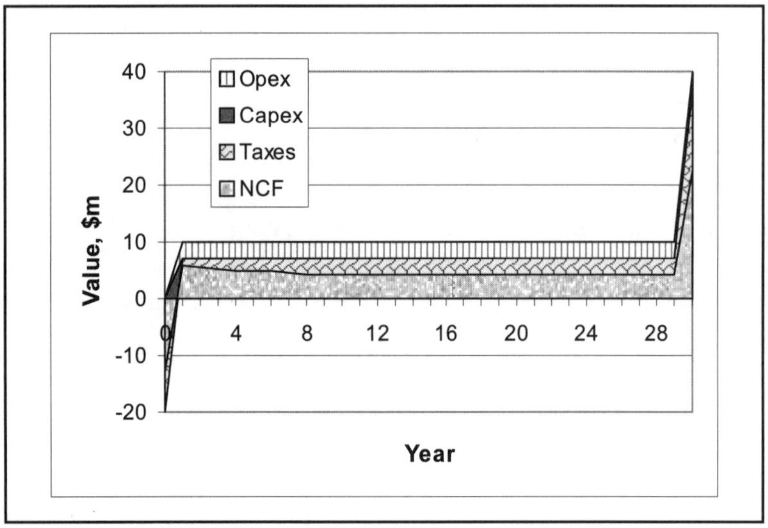

Figure 3.1a Rental Estate NCF

The process plant (refinery) in Figure 3.1b shows a little larger NCF, but also has higher initial investments and production costs. What would happen if production was overestimated, or the market for the product was 10% less than estimated? Manufacturing faces extremely low profit margins, relative to other industries. The NCF is quite high as long as the cost of materials being processed is reasonable. Small feedstock changes often totally erode the NCF value.

Figure 3.1c reflects a typical mineral project. Note that the major risk is finding the mineral. If hydrocarbons, coal, or copper exists, the NCF is large enough to minimize the risk of losing money. Investors experience less operating risk with an oil project than real estate or processing. Once found and developed, mineral projects needs far less attention than mainstream businesses.

National governments use NCF estimates and its source components to assess the impact of tax and licensing regimes. Obviously, governments seek to acquire as much of the revenue as possible for their constituency, the citizens of the country. Conflict arises when private investors feel that the revenues left to them are inadequate to cover the risk and costs of a project. Such laws constantly change to alter the balance between the competing goals of taxing regulatory authorities and investors, and reflect the resulting compromises. And true to such systems, someone is usually unhappy.

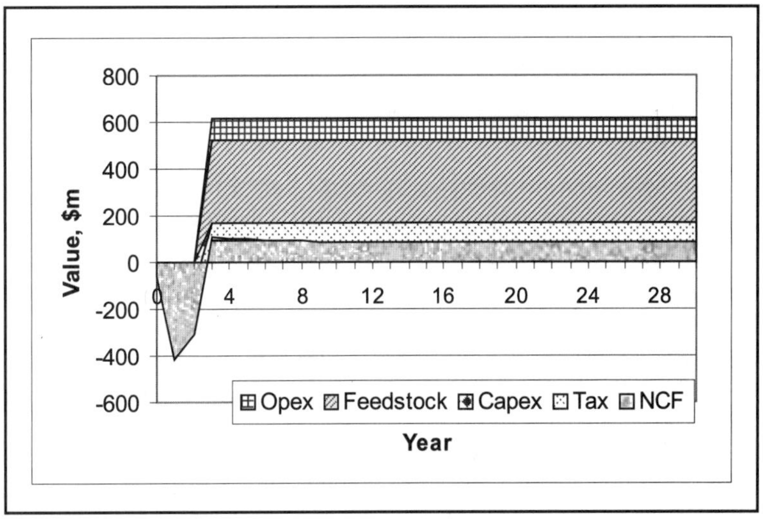

Figure 3.1b Process/Manufacturing NCF

Desire to reap more of the pie, changing economics (a maturing area), and changes in political regimes, all tend to signal changes in taxes and NCF. The perpetual ebb and flow of tax and licensing rules follows naturally from the political/economic climate.

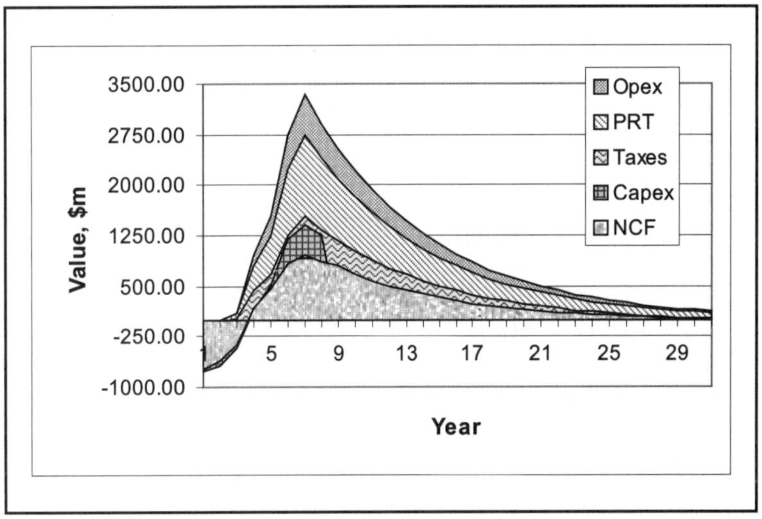

Figure 3.1c Mineral NCF

Including graphs similar to Figure 3.1 for each investment opportunity increases the chances that investors will be able to visualize the fundamental differences. With the computerization of most investment evaluations, such graphs are easy to prepare. Additional methods for presenting project analysis are presented in Chapters 8 and 9

INTERNATIONAL FISCAL AGREEMENTS

Before addressing specific tax details, it is important to recognize that taxes are not associated with fundamental laws, like thermodynamics or plate tectonics. Taxes result from political compromise and, therefore, changing tax laws are unpleasant facts of life. Tax regimes influence investment decisions as much, if not more than physical and economic conditions. Good technical decisions under one tax regime often destroy value in other tax regimes. That is the reason good investors seek to understand the interaction of taxes and their technical decisions.

Countries impose fiscal regimes to optimize the value of their resources and markets for the benefit of the local citizens. New entrants often wonder why the fiscal regimes seem so harsh and uncompromising, or, at least, far stricter than conditions at home. Several reasons exist, but a quick review of history provides the most telling of all: the abuse of less developed countries by more experienced, knowledgeable investors. This abuse goes back centuries and cuts across all cultures. Developing countries established a legacy of detailed control over investors to avoid, both real and perceived, discrimination. Though current multinationals operate far more responsibly than their predecessors, the foundation of mistrust lives on.

Fiscal regimes control more than just tax rates, and, in fact, the non-tax fiscal requirements often bother the operating companies more than the tax burden. By varying the burden of capital investment, distribution of profit, the allocation of risk, and operating and budgetary control, the local country rules either enhance or distort the investment potential to investors. For example, some countries require direct governmental review of the development and operating plans, while others sell the license to operate, and then leave the operator alone. Other countries maintain an interest in the investment, but require the private investor to cover the governments share of the development costs. The dynamics of taxes often makes the knowledge associated with true science and engineering appear to be an exact.

The variability of fiscal agreements worsens when countries change the fiscal requirements, but only for future agreements, leaving the old or existing agreements in place. Two identical investment opportunities, one operating under the old rules and a new one with different rules, experience very different economic performance, forcing the investor to develop and operate differently to achieve their investment objectives. Many countries avoid this dilemma by changing all the fiscal agreements simultaneously, which places all investors on an equal footing.

The tax calculations detailed later represent commonly observed situations in the respective country, based on our experience. Again, the key ingredient is to verify that your entity operates under the assumptions outlined here, since tax regimes change quite often.

Types of Fiscal Agreements

Fiscal agreements allocate the rights to develop and operate specific businesses within a country. As globalization continues to dominate the world market, understanding and implementing the fiscal regimes becomes even more important. As countries open up their telecommunications, water and electrical generation, and mineral industries, the investor capable of seeing the business opportunity in each fiscal regime will win the race to fame and fortune

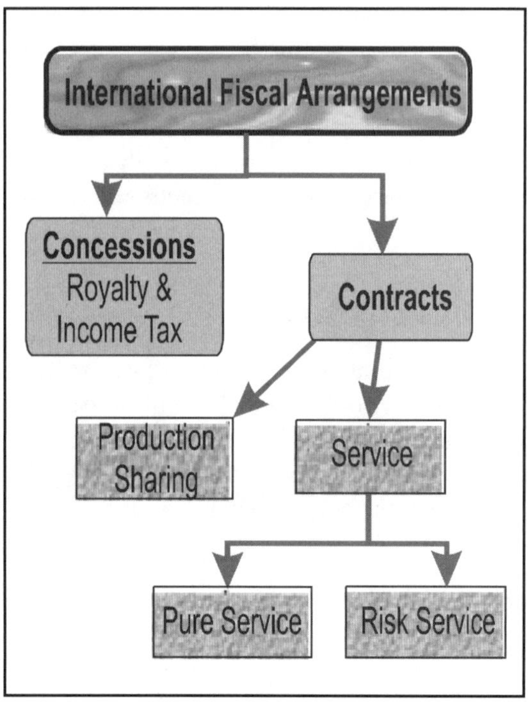

Figure 3.2 Fiscal regimes

The young professional may work under more fiscal regimes in the first few years of their careers than the previous generation did in an entire career. Methods for allocating ownership are as diverse and complex as other aspects of humanity: religion, law, politics, etc. One summary of fiscal regimes is shown in Figure 3.2.[(3.2)]

While most countries follow the basic format, others combine elements of each agreement type. The differences are important for the assessment of the long-term risk associated with developing an investment profile in each country.

Concessions

A common form for allocating business rights is the concession agreement. The local country assigns the right to operate in return for a share of the proceeds. Companies compete for concession rights in a variety of ways: bonus (a front-end payment), royalties, and taxes. The reliance placed on a given technique varies among countries. Most of the countries in Europe and America utilize concessions to various degrees.

Ownership rights are allocated via bonus bidding. The rules are very simple: the highest bidder wins. Minimum bonuses and performance specifications are often established, based on the expected value of future production. The deficiency in the system is that the asset is worthless, if production never occurs. The current example of bonus bidding is the allocation of telecommunication rights, usually for multi-billions of $'s. The government treasury reaps the benefits of the bonus, without incurring any risk.

Observe the frequency of allocating new bandwidth, mobile phones. or television rights in the telecommunication industry based on bonus payments. Bonuses increase the investment cost, since the acquisition cost is not tied to actual production. Similarly, firms paid considerable sums for the right to satellite bandwith, but by the time the satellites were launched, demand switched to other forms, making the investment and bonus worthless.

Royalties are tied to production in most countries, although gross revenue is used to compute royalty in countries like West Germany. The operating company usually produces, processes (if necessary), and pays the local government a fee based on the sales price. Some governments take the royalty in kind, depending on their needs and objectives.

Royalty rates vary significantly between countries: going as low as a few percent and to a high over 40%. Royalty rates also vary as a function of production rates, like in Canada. Variable royalties benefit the host country by tying the royalty to yearly production, where the biggest, and often most efficient producers pay the highest rates. Cash flows increase when rates rise and drop as production falls. Operators and landowners benefit because the economic limit (the time when revenue falls below Opex) is delayed as the royalty drops. This tends to increase total production over the life of the asset. Operators generally lose revenues, because the host country takes a higher percentage of the production from the more profitable ventures.

Income taxes represent the other major form of compensation under the concession agreement. Taxes are computed primarily on before tax income (BT income). BT income typically subtracts royalty, operating cost, allowed overhead, expensed investments, and capital recovery from gross income. The appropriate tax rate, which currently ranges from around 25% to 85%, multiplied by taxable income represents the income tax payment (IT). (See Equation 3.3)

Investment risk falls on the investor almost 100%, especially for a new entrant into the country. The host country typically argues that failed investments can be offset against income taxes. This is true only when the investor has other revenue producing assets. If no other revenue exists, the investment tax relief is delayed until revenue does occur, which oftentimes never happens. Then, the investor bears the full burden of the cost. This situation takes place all to often.

A similar situation arises when countries create *ring-fences* for the tax computation. Most concession countries define the entire country as a ring-fence, so a loss in manufacturing reduces the tax burden from a tax paying retail activity. The U. K. specifically exempts losses from refining and transportation from exploration and production profits, as an example of one type of ring-fence.

Contractual Systems

The host country retains ownership of the asset under the contractual fiscal regime, which is just the opposite of the concessionary system. Business rights are allocated based on a bonus, work program, or combination of each. Again, the most optimistic or high bidder wins the contest. The worst situations occur when the bidding is by invitation and hidden from public view. The opportunity for bribery, deceit, etc. destroys value in most cases.

Production Sharing (PSC or PSA)

Production sharing began in Indonesia with the decision to split production between the operator and the host country, usually in the form of a state owned firm. The method for computing the split varies, as do the percentage going to each party. Splits vary from 85/15 for oil and 35/65 for gas in Indonesia to 81/19 in Libya. The host country receives the first value in each instance. These splits also vary within a country depending on when the concession was obtained and the location.

The host country/operator split is multiplied by the difference between revenue and cost recovery, which are costs, like operating costs, expensed investment, and a portion of capital investments. Defining cost recovery influences risk considerably in a PSA. Most PSA arrangements exist in developing countries, with limited investment capital; hence, the country tries to get the private investor to fund the states share of the appraisal and development cost. Then, the country allows the investor to recover these extra costs from future production: thc cost recovery category. The investor's risk increases owing to the time lag between initial cost and cost recovery. The possibility also exits that the project will be a complete failure, and the investor will absorb 100% of the initial cost, while receiving only 15% of the revenues. This is risk.

Operators also pay taxes to the local country. Between the splits and income taxes, contractors pay up to 95% of project revenue to the host country in a few cases.

Some question the wisdom of operating in areas where 95% of the gross revenue goes to the host country. The incentive arises because the local country pays 95% of the costs after construction and operation commences, thus reducing operating risk. A more important issue concerns when the host country starts sharing the costs, because the state partner is carried through exploration and some or all of the initial development phase. Another unique feature occurs when the state oil companies pay operators taxes out of their share. Egypt, Vietnam and Libya follow this approach.

Full assessment of tax burdens is important when comparing countries. Another reason is scale: 5% on billions of dollars adds more value than 100% of a few cents. Multinational organizations have overheads that prevent them from effectively identifying, investing in and operating small projects; so, the lower margin, but higher volume assets often become relatively more attractive, even with high tax regimes.

Service Contracts

Local governments occasionally negotiate service contracts, where the operator performs services in exchange for cost reimbursement plus a predetermined profit. The profit is usually a percentage of the costs incurred. Argentina and some concessions in Indonesia use a service contract, as well as many Middle East countries. The fee, which is negotiated with the host country, is normally subject to local income taxes.

Sometimes the operator funds all investment and operating costs initially, and then recovers the expenditure by taking the production in kind, say 10 units of production. Some countries prefer these contracts, because the investor incurs both the risk of spending the money and the risk in selling the product. If the market price drops dramatically or no market exists, the operator loses.

The *risk service contract* often allows for a sliding scale. Countries, like Ecuador and Russia, employ an "R" factor, where the allowed profit varies with the overall profitability of the producing area. These contracts resemble the PSC format very closely.

Summary

International agreements for producing oil and gas vary considerably. Countries seldom follow the same pattern, preferring to set the standards to achieve their specific needs, even in the basic categories outlined above. Certain countries even vary according to when the agreements were signed. A commonly asked question is, "Are the differences really important?" The ultimate profitability of an investment varies according to the effective tax rate.

UNITED STATES NCF

Taxes and NCF in the U.S. exemplify the concession fiscal regime. The U.S. possesses more different types of taxes than most countries, because private citizens own water and mineral rights, whereas the state owns all natural resources in most other countries, although two exceptions are Canada and Germany. With private ownership of resources, states feel they have the right to collect taxes and the Federal Government levies a like number of taxes.

Net Revenue Derivation

Gross revenue less royalties, severance and ad valorem taxes equals net revenue, as illustrated in Equation 3.6. Each item in the equation is explained below.

$$\text{WI Gross Revenue}_t - \text{WI Royalty}_t - \text{WI Severance Tax}_t - \text{WI Ad Valorem Tax}_t = \text{WI Net Revenue}_t \quad \textbf{(3.6)}$$

Royalties: The percentage of gross production allocated to the original owner of the asset rights defines royalty. Typical owners include federal and state governments, Indian tribes, and private citizens. Royalties are expressed on a fractional basis, like 1/6, 1/8, or 3/16, as determined by negotiation with the asset. The federal government may also allocate land using royalty bidding. Royalty rates over 90% have been bid when royalties are used to determine the winner. Example 3.2 shows the basic methodology.

Example 3.2: Given the price and production data, compute gross revenue and royalty, assuming a 1/6 royalty. All values in M = million.

	(1)	(2)	(3)	(4)	(5) = (3)*(4)
Year	Production (M bbls)	Price ($/bbl)	WI Gross Revenue	Royalty Rate	Royalty
0-1	5.35	18	96.3	0.1667	16.05
1-2	10.60	18	190.8	0.1667	31.8
2-3	8.60	18	154.8	0.1667	25.8
3-4	6.10	18	109.8	0.1667	18.3
4-5	3.30	18	59.4	0.1667	9.9
5-6	1.60	18	28.8	0.1667	4.8
6-7	0.30	18	5.4	0.1667	0.9
Total	35.85		645.3		107.55

Another form of royalty, the overriding royalty interest (ORI), extends the basic royalty concept. Royalties normally reflect terms between the landowner and the initial contracting company. The contracting company may then sublease the rights (farm-out) to a third party. The original company retains an overriding royalty. Overriding royalty is computed after the original royalty, but it overrides other claims to revenue, hence its name. Independents often compensate their staff with overriding royalties (often called overrides).

Some companies modify this example by using the net revenue interest (NRI) concept. NRI is defined as NRI = WI*(1 – royalty rate), where WI is working interest. At a 100% working interest and the 1/6 royalty rate, NRI = 1.0 (1 – 1/6) = 0.833. Multiplying 0.8333 by gross revenue yields the same royalty amount in Column 5 of Example 3.2

Production Taxes: Severance and ad valorem taxes generate revenue for state and local governments. Severance taxes are levied by the state and ad valorem taxes by the county, in general, though some states like Alaska allocate part of the ad valorem revenues to the state as well as the borough. Severance taxes exist only in the U.S. Though individuals own the bulk of the minerals, the state assumes minerals belong in part to the public. Rates may vary from 0 to 35% and are handled like the royalty example.

Ad Valorem taxes are levied mostly against the assessed value of equipment and buildings, though some areas include inventories of raw material, like paper for publishing or hydrocarbons in the ground. Counties, parishes, or boroughs typically appraise the equipment, and then established the assessed value, normally a fraction of the true economic value. Assessed value times the assigned tax rate defines the ad valorem tax. This process is very similar to the way governments assess property taxes or rates on personal housing.

Some companies simplify the calculations by assuming ad valorem taxes are a fraction of the equipments original cost. The fraction is determined by dividing estimated ad valorem tax payments by total equipment value, giving an effective ad valorem tax rate averaged over the state. Some distortion exists since counties levy different ad valorem taxes, according to their individual needs and composition of industries.

The second approach assumes that counties use ad valorem taxes to collect revenue, and, as such, really take a certain percentage of production (like a severance tax). Taking the ratio of ad valorem tax revenues to total production in a state yields an effective rate for ad valorem taxes, which is similar to a royalty. The product of this effective rate and production approximates the ad valorem tax.

Both approaches produce errors in ad valorem tax estimates. The degree of error varies by state, by county in each state, and estimates of the effective rate. Always review this procedure to insure that it yields the desired results. These errors in the ad valorem assumptions pale in comparison to other inputs, and seldom impact investment decision making significantly. The fraction of production is used in Example 3.3 for convenience.

The product of the tax rate and after royalty income yields the severance and ad valorem payments. Royalty owners normally pay their own production taxes, though this is negotiable. The royalty owner's cash flow from the project is computed from (0.1667)*(96.3), or $16.05 in year one.

Example 3.3: Using gross revenue and royalty from the previous example, compute the severance and ad valorem payments for the project. All values in $m=million.

	(3)	(5)	(6)=(3)-(5)	(7)=(6)*.06	(8)=(6)*.08
Year	WI Gross Revenue, $m	Royalty, $m	After Royalty Income	6% Severance Tax, $m	8% Ad Valorem Tax, $m
0-1	96.3	16.05	80.25	4.82	6.42
1-2	190.8	31.8	159.00	9.54	12.72
2-3	154.8	25.8	129.00	7.74	10.32
3-4	109.8	18.3	91.50	5.49	7.32
4-5	59.4	9.9	49.50	2.97	3.96
5-6	28.8	4.8	24.00	1.44	1.92
6-7	5.4	0.9	4.50	0.27	0.36
Total	645.3	107.55	537.75	32.27	43.02

Year 0-1: Severance Tax = (96.3)*(1 - 0.1667)*0.06 = 4.82

Severance taxes vary in most states depending on the mineral involved. Texas, for example, levied a 4.6% severance tax on oil and 7.5% tax on gas. States publish the respective current tax rates, so uncertainty about current rate poses no problem. States amend the tax rates, however, as their financial needs change. Assuming a constant tax rate over the life of the project biases the cash flows of the project. The bias is accepted, because detailed predictions of future severance and ad valorem tax rates seldom possesses the accuracy to improve individual investment decisions.

A slightly different format exists in California, which taxes the present worth of reserves. Companies estimate recoverable reserves and the likely production profile, and then compute gross revenue using prices mandated by the state. Yearly gross revenue is then discounted at 10% to the present. The value of reserves in the ground is taxed at the specified rate. It is really a tax on the inventory of oil (called a Mineral Properties Tax).

Table 3.1 shows severance tax rates for several states.

TABLE 3.1

State Severance Rates as a % of Revenue

State	Oil	Gas
Alabama	8.00%	8.00%
Alaska	15.00%	15.00%
Arkansas (1)	5.00%	0.00%
California	0.00%	0.00%
Colorado	1.10%	1.10%
Kansas (2)	0.00%	0.00%
Louisiana (3)	12.50%	0.00%
Mississippi	6.00%	6.00%
Montana	5.50%	3.20%
Nebraska	3.00%	3.00%
New Mexico (4)	6.30%	6.30%
Oklahoma	7.10%	7.10%
Texas	4.60%	7.50%

(1) Gas severance tax = \$0.03/Mcf
(2) Oil severance tax = \$0.04/bbl and \$0.09/Mcf for gas.
(3) Gas severance tax = \$0.07/Mcf
(4) Gas severance tax = \$0.139/Mcf and 2.55% of revenue.

The most complicated severance tax exists in Alaska. Geographical areas dependent on one resource, especially hydrocarbons, tend to tax that resource to extremes. Like most of these areas, taxing the best and most prolific sources, while offering tax breaks to marginal areas, is paramount. The oil severance is computed as follows:

$$\text{Severance Tax}_t = \text{Rate}_t * \text{ELF}_t \tag{3.7}$$

where: rate = 12.5% for the first five years of production and 15% thereafter, and
ELF = economic limit factor

$$\text{ELF} = \left(1 - \frac{300}{\text{Production / Well / Day}}\right)^{\left(\frac{150{,}000}{\text{Field Production}}\right)^{(460/200)}}$$

The goal in formulating ELF, which has become more complex over time, was to tax the large fields, like Prudhoe Bay, and reduce taxes on marginal fields. The concept was that the economic limit of a well in Alaska was 300 bopd. In the first parenthesis, a well operating at 300 bopd would have a ratio of 300/300, making ELF equal to 0, meaning no severance tax would be paid. For high productivity wells, say 5,000 bopd, the ratio of 300/5000 means ELF is slightly less than 1. Again the philosophy is: tax the prolific wells and minimize taxes on marginal wells.

The first exponent shifts the tax burden to the large producing fields, such as Prudhoe Bay. A field producing 150,000 bopd has a coefficient of 1. When daily production falls below 150,000, the exponent becomes greater than 1,which causes ELF to approach 0 faster. Fields, like Prudhoe Bay, which produced in excess of 1 million barrels a day, resulting in a fraction less than 1, slows the rate at which ELF declines toward zero.

The exponent, 460/300, emerged from political battles in Alaska. A fraction squared approached zero faster than when raised to a power of 1. As the staff in Alaska related the story to us, the House of Representatives wanted a ratio of 300/300 (an anti-business bias), and the Senate wanted a ratio of 600/300 (a pro business bias). Normal political compromise systems would dictate a compromise to 450/300. As the story is told, the governor, a pro business advocate, upped the ratio to 460/300. Whether this accurately depicts the situation or not, it is still interesting. Whatever the reality, the net effect is that the ELF calculation looks like Figure 3.3, where the lines reflect daily production per well.

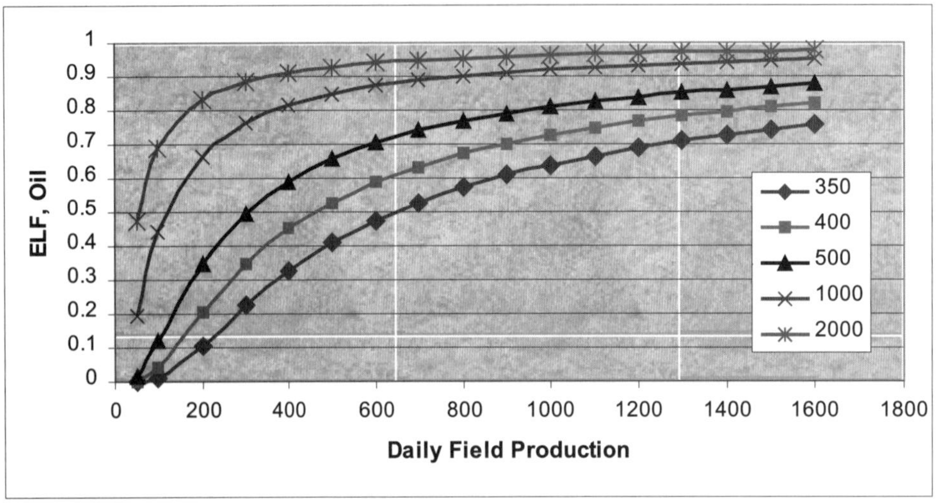

Figure 3.3 Alaskan ELF for different daily well production rates

Net revenue, which measures monies actually available to pay investment, operating expenses, and income taxes, are derived in Example 3.4. The state, county, landowners, and the federal government receive 29% of total gross revenue, while the investors receive the remaining 71% (= 462/645). This reflects the split before paying for the costs and income taxes, however.

Example 3.4: Derive the Net Revenue for the project using the information in the previous examples.

	(3)	(5)	(7)	(8)	(9)=3 – 5 – 7 – 8
Year	WI Gross Revenue, $m	Royalty, $m	6% Severance Tax, $m	8% Ad Valorem Tax, $m	Net Revenue
0-1	96.3	16.05	4.82	6.42	69.02
1-2	190.8	31.8	9.54	12.72	136.74
2-3	154.8	25.8	7.74	10.32	110.94
3-4	109.8	18.3	5.49	7.32	78.69
4-5	59.4	9.9	2.97	3.96	42.57
5-6	28.8	4.8	1.44	1.92	20.64
6-7	5.4	0.9	0.27	0.36	3.87
Total	645.3	107.55	32.27	43.02	462.47

Tax and Income Derivation

The apparent illogical nature of tax laws frustrates most professionals. Tax laws in democracies originate from compromises made by executive leaders and hundreds of legislators, each with different goals and philosophies, then modified, often just slightly, over time. Tax laws, at any point in time, reflect the outcome of these compromises and the proximity to the next election. Tax laws are tedious, but not mathematically challenging. Keeping the terminology straight and remembering to complete all of the calculations, in the right order, causes most of the problems.

Computing income taxes requires splitting investment costs into two basic categories – capitalized and expensed. The capitalized (tangible) and expensed (intangible) categories differ in the timing of the tax write-off or tax relief. Expensed items receive tax relief immediately – in the year the money is spent. Capitalized items obtain tax relief over several years, with the method of tax relief varying for the type of expenditure. Table 3.2 summarizes typical capitalized/expensed splits by category of investment.

TABLE 3.2

Typical Tax Categories

Category	Expensed	Capitalized	Capital Recovery
Dry Holes and R&D	100%	0%	
Producing Wells: Tangibles	0%	100%	MACRS 7
Intangibles	70% for majors, 100% for independents	30% for majors, 0% for independents	5 Year SL
Drilling Platforms	0%	100%	MACRS 7
Production Platforms	0%	100%	MACRS 7
Equipment	0%	100%	MACRS 7
Bonus and Leasehold	0%	100%	Depletion
Lease Rentals	100%	0%	

Seven year Modified accelerated cost recovery (*MACRS 7*) rates are specified in Table 3.3.

TABLE 3.3

Taxable Depreciation Values by Year

Year	MACRS 5	MACRS 7
1	0.20	0.143
2	0.32	0.245
3	0.19	0.175
4	0.12	0.125
5	0.11	0.089
6	0.06	0.089
7	0.00	0.089
8	0.00	0.045
Total	1.00	1.00

Producing wells combine several categories of capitalization. Tangible costs, including some casing, tubing, wellheads, submersible pumps, etc., use the MACRS7 schedule. Intangible costs include drilling rig rental, mud, drill bits, etc., are 70% expensed and 30% capitalized by law, for majors. The capitalized portion is recovered using a 60-month or 5-year straight-line (SL) depreciation. Most expenditures up to the time the well is logged and the completion decision is made are intangible. Observe that wells have three different tax treatments: MACRS7, 5 year SL, and expensed.

Depreciation

Capitalized items subject to depreciation include casing, tubing, flow lines, tank batteries, cementing production platforms, etc. This covers expenditures with a life likely to exceed one year. Depreciation write-offs depend on the type of expenditure. Most investments fall into two basic categories: 5 and 7-year lives, though other categories exist. The depreciation schedule for each project life is presented in Table 3.3, along with common examples of each in Table 3.4.

TABLE 3.4

Typical Examples of Investment Classes

5 Year Life:	Automobiles, trucks, & drilling equipment
7 Year Life:	All production and exploration equipment
10 Year Life:	Crude oil refining equipment
15 Year Life:	Transmission pipelines & equipment
31.5 Years:	Buildings

The five-year values under the 1986 law are derived from a 200% declining balance over five years, often referred to as a 40% declining balance in Europe and Canada. Depreciation in the seven-year category converts to a 28.6% declining balance in these areas. The seven-year

CHAPTER 3

category covers virtually every petroleum investment except for drilling equipment (5 year), oil refining equipment (10 year), and transmission pipeline and related equipment (15 year). Buildings and manufacturing facilities go on as long as 31.5 years. The process is illustrated in Example 3.5.

Example 3.5: Tangible investments of $28.8 and 86.4 occur in year 1 and 2, respectively. Using the 7 year MACRS rates, derive the depreciation schedule for the project. All values $m.

	(10)	(11)	(12)	(13)=(11+12)
		Depreciation for:		
Year	Tangible Investment	Year 0-1	Year 1-2	Total Depreciation
0-1	43.2	6.18	0.00	6.18
1-2	19.1	10.58	2.73	13.32
2-3	0.0	7.56	4.68	12.24
3-4	0.0	5.40	3.34	8.74
4-5	0.0	3.84	2.39	6.23
5-6	0.0	3.84	1.70	5.54
6-7	0.0	3.84	1.70	5.54
7-8	0.0	1.94	1.70	3.64
8-9	0.0	0.00	0.86	0.86
Total	62.30	43.20	19.10	62.30

Year 0-1 Investment = 0.143*43.2 = 6.18

Year 1-2 Investment = 0.245*43.2 = 10.58

Depreciation begins when the project is classified as ready for service. The definition of ready for service varies among companies. Some define ready for service as capable of producing, while others require production to actually take place. Gas wells and manufacturing plants, for example, are often completed, but sales delayed until the transportation system is constructed. Process plants take several years to build and start-up. Offshore platforms are constructed and wells drilled, but production cannot commence until the transportation system is connected. Delays between the completion of the project from a technical perspective and initial sales raise doubts about the specification of ready for service.

The question is whether a tangible investment capable of working, but not active, is ready for service and can be depreciated. Opinions and practice vary. Some argue that capable of working is the same as ready for service; others take a more conservative position and begin depreciation only when sales begin. Decisions regarding the correct approach depend on the legal staff's opinion about what can be justified in tax court. Aggressive interpretation of ready for service and beginning depreciation one year early reduces the AT NPV of project cost by about 2%.

Example 3.5 continues depreciation through year 8-9 as per the MACRS 7 schedule. Yet, the previous examples of net revenue stop the project in year 6-7. Computer software handles the conflict in short life projects in several ways. The most common approach truncates the depreciation schedule in the last year of production and take remaining write-offs in that last year. Another assumes that tangible investments generating depreciation will be moved to another location, so depreciation continues for the specified life of the asset class. Neither assumption always reflects the actual disposition of equipment.

Cost and Statutory Depletion

Most industries have some experience with cost depletion. Natural resource industries, whether renewable or non-renewable, must replace the depleting asset. The government encourages reinvestment of profits via cost or statutory depletion. Mineral production, for example, depletes the primary asset. Depletion provides capital for the replacement of natural resources like petroleum, coal, forests, CO_2 and the like. The form taken by the depletion write-off varies according to whether a company is classified as a major or independent and the resource involved. Majors take cost depletion on bonus payments only for petroleum products, while independents select the better of cost depletion or percentage (or statutory) depletion. For non-petroleum products, percentage depletion is available for everyone. Percentage depletion improves the economics of a project by increasing the magnitude of the tax write-offs.

Other industries utilize cost depletion as the result of mergers and acquisitions. When a firm buys another, the tax code splits the purchase price into two components: the value of actual physical assets, and non-physical assets, like the name, trademarks, etc. The former items are depreciated, and the later depleted. Some accountants will also refer to this process as amortization.

The bonus, or non-tangible cost recovery is matched to the expected future production profile using a revenue matching principle, called units of production (UOP). Bonus recovered in a year equals the percentage of total production expected to occur each year. The equation is:

$$UOP_t = \frac{P_1}{TP} * (\text{Bonus \& Leasehold Cost}) \quad \textbf{(3.8)}$$

where:

UOP_t = portion of bonus recovered in year t

P_t = production in year t

TP = total production over life of project

The UOP calculation requires estimates of annual production volumes and total production over the life of the project. The UOP schedule contains some errors, since P_t and TP are unknown. These errors, however, have little impact on investment decisions. Example 3.6 shows that the total $25m spent is recovered exactly over the expected 7-year production.

Example 3.6: Derive the cost depletion schedule assuming a $25m bonus and production from a previous example.

	(14)	(1)	(15)	(16)=(14)*(15)
Year	**Bonus, $m**	**Production**	**UOP Factor**	**Cost Depletion, $m**
0-1	25.00	5.35	0.15	3.73
1-2		10.60	0.30	7.39
2-3		8.60	0.24	6.00
3-4		6.10	0.17	4.25
4-5		3.30	0.09	2.30
5-6		1.60	0.04	1.12
6-7		0.30	0.01	0.21
Total	25.00	35.85	1.00	25.00

Since total production varies considerably over the project life, questions arise as to how to handle such changes. First, the analysis depends more on the actual production values in column 1. The errors from mis-estimating the revenue are far more important than the timing of the cost depletion schedule in column 16. Second, in actual practice, if the total production estimate is altered during the project life, the accountants will use the future production to create a new UOP schedule that is then applied to the remaining depletable amount.

Small producers receive additional tax relief in the form of *percentage depletion*. Percentage depletion chooses the lesser of the product of the appropriate tax rate and taxable income or 15% of net revenue. Taxable income equals gross income less lease operating expense, overhead directly assignable to the

CHAPTER 3

lease, and depreciation. The larger value of cost depletion and percentage depletion reflects the depletion write-off.

Allowable Depletion = The greater of cost depletion or percentage depletion **(3.9)**

where: Percentage Depletion = the lesser of:

1. 15% of Depletable Income, or
2. Tax Rate times Taxable Income

Column 17 is just 15% of Net Revenue. The second part, 35% of taxable income, comes from first subtracting the major costs, like depreciation and Opex from Net Revenue, then multiplying by the tax rate. The minimum percentage depletion in year 0-1 is negative, because of the expensed Capex. This revenue is marginal enough so that the 15% of net revenue never dominates. The last column, allowed depletion, is the greater of cost depletion and percentage depletion. Since total cost depletion was $25 m, percentage depletion confers a small economic advantage to independents in this example. The gap between the two forms of depletion can be much larger in actual practice.

Example 3.7: Determine the percentage depletion schedule using the following information, and then compute the allowed deduction for an independent producer. All values in $m.

	(9)	(17)	(18)	(20)	(21)	(22)	
Year	**WI Net Revenue**	**15% of Net Revenue**	**Deductions**	**Taxable Income**	**35% of Taxable Income**	**Percentage Depletion**	**Allowed Depletion**
0-1	69.02	10.35	91.34	-32.67	-11.44	-11.44	3.73
1-2	136.74	20.51	100.61	15.62	5.47	5.47	7.39
2-3	110.94	16.64	76.69	17.61	6.16	6.16	6.16
3-4	78.69	11.80	55.69	11.20	3.92	3.92	4.25
4-5	42.57	6.39	33.58	2.60	0.91	0.91	2.30
5-6	20.64	3.10	19.26	-1.72	-0.60	-0.60	1.12
6-7	3.87	0.58	8.04	-4.75	-1.66	-1.66	0.21
Total	462.47	69.37	385.21	7.89	2.76	2.76	25.17

Other minerals using depletion include carbon dioxide, nitrogen, and iodine. Bonuses for leases, advance royalty payments, and other payments made without regard to production are excluded from percentage depletion. Also, now percentage depletion will be granted on properties, which were developed by majors, but later sold to independents.

For marginal production defined as less than 15 stb/day on a calendar and property basis, the statutory depletion rate will be increased by 1% (subject to a maximum of 10%) for each whole dollar the average domestic price is less than $20 for the previous calendar year. This proviso holds only for stripper and heavy oil wells owned by independents and royalty holders.

The terms major and independent relate to the scale of operation. Anyone with pipelines or other downstream operations is classified as a major. We know of several cases where end users bought gas production, only to realize the considerable benefits of operating them as separate legal entities (no direct ties, hence, it preserves the independent status). Percentage depletion only applies to the first 1,000 bopd for the year. Those producing in excess of 1,000 bopd have been known to assign some of the rights to their spouse, children, dog, cat, etc. until everyone falls below the threshold.

Intangible Depreciation

Intangible depreciation defines the schedule of recovery for capitalized intangible costs (IDC's) and some seismic expenditure. As far as we know, only the petroleum industry uses the 5-year SL process outlined in Table 3.3. Normally, a 5-year SL would seem simple. Most software, however, assumes that the investment occurs in the middle of the year. Since there are 60 months in 5 years, the software takes a 6/60 (=10%) ratio to indicate this half-year assumption. This is followed by 4 years at 20%, ending with the remaining 10%. Example 3.8 illustrates the process.

Example 3.8: Given the investment classified as intangible, use the standard capitalized/expensed split and 5 year SL depreciation schedule to derive the tax relief. All values in $m.

(23)	(24)	(25)		(26)		(27)
Intangible Cost	70% Expensed	30% Capitalized	5 Year SL Schedule	Investment in Year 0-1	Investment in Year 1-2	Intangible (IDC) Depreciation
57.60	40.32	17.28	0.10	1.73	0.00	1.73
13.20	9.24	3.96	0.20	3.46	0.40	3.85
0.00	0.00	0.00	0.20	3.46	0.79	4.25
0.00	0.00	0.00	0.20	3.46	0.79	4.25
0.00	0.00	0.00	0.20	3.46	0.79	4.25
0.00	0.00	0.00	0.10	1.73	0.79	2.52
0.00	0.00	0.00		0.00	0.40	0.40
70.80	49.56	21.24		17.28	3.96	21.24

Before 1982, intangibles were expensed for everyone. Only independents expense intangibles now, while majors follow the splits described here. In 1984, 20% of the IDC's were amortized over three years. Beginning in 1987, 30% of the IDC's are capitalized and recovered using a five-year straight-line capital recovery. Most software begins depreciation in the year an investment is made, though some permits the user to delay depreciation based on the ready for service issue.

Income Taxes

Estimated tax payments emerge from the process of splitting investments into tangible and intangible, and then developing the capital recovery schedules. Payments to Federal and state governments may take up to half of the total cash flow. Depreciation and depletions themselves are not cash flows; they merely influence the NCF process via the income tax calculation.

The federal income tax rate fell from 46% in 1986, to 40% in 1987 and 34% in 1988 as part of President Reagan's effort to reduce government intervention in the economy via his 1986 tax reform. Raging debates took place over the merits of lowering the tax rate. Ignoring the distributive aspects of taxes, investors keep more of the project's revenues with lower taxes. However, investors also absorb more of the impact of failed investments. In general, lower tax rates force the investor to face the consequences of bad investments, and reap the benefits of successful investments, the hallmark of market economics.

States also levy income taxes, which range in value from 0 to 16%. Those operating in multiple states often elect to use an average state tax rate, based on the states they operate in. Rather than compute state taxes separately, most software combines the Federal tax rate (FTR) with the state rate. Since state income taxes can be offset against federal taxes, the effective rate is:

$$ETR = FTR + STR * (1 - FTR) \quad \textbf{(3.10)}$$

where: FTR = federal tax rate and STR = state tax rate

With modifications in the tax laws over the last decade, most corporate investors use a rate of 35-38%. Common state rates for national firms average 2-5%. Assuming a 3% STR, the ETR is about 37% (= 0.35 + .03*(1 – 0.35). Assumptions about ETR values may go as high as 43%, depending on the geographical dispersion of activities.

Prior to 1987, *investment tax credits* (ITC's) acted as a stimulus to investment by directly reducing income taxes payments, thus, increasing NCF. A tax credit reduces income taxes payments directly, rather than just reducing taxable income. Most tax credits for business have been reduced, if not totally eliminated. Emphasis is currently on tax credits for individuals.

Equation 3.11 defines the computation of the investment tax credit. Later examples assume a zero investment tax credit.

$$\text{ITC} = \text{ITC Rate} * \text{Qualifying Expenditures} \tag{3.11}$$

The main tax credits available on minerals include a tight gas credit, an alternative fuels credit, and an enhanced oil recovery (EOR) credit. The tight gas credit has virtually phased out, and the alternative fuels credit, primarily in the form of coal bed methane, attracts far less interest now.

Producing reservoirs receive a 15% ITC for new EOR projects with first injection after 31 December 1990, or for significant expansion of existing EOR projects. The credit classifies expenditures for equipment, IDC's and injectants as qualified costs. Acceptable projects include all of those originally listed in the now defunct Windfall Profits Tax (WPT) plus immiscible non-hydrocarbon gas injection. These processes include:

TABLE 3.5

Enhanced Oil Recovery (EOR) Methods Qualifying for ITC

• Miscible fluid displacement	• Cyclic steam injection
• Steam drive injection	• Alkaline flooding
• Polymer waterflood	• Carbonated water floods
• Micro-emulsion	• Immiscible (CO_2)
• In-situ combustion	• Any IRS approved project

As capital recovery reflects 100% of CAPEX, adding a 15% ITC would permit companies to recover 115% of actual cost. When electing to use the 15% ITC, only 1 - 0.15 or 0.85 of the CAPEX is subject to capital recovery.

Tax credits also exist for tight sand gas ($0.52/Mcf flat) and coal seam gas ($0.848 in 1990 escalating at annual inflation rates). These tax credits begin to phase out when the average annual U.S. crude price exceeds $37.76. This amount is adjusted annually for inflation.

Taxable income (29), as derived in Example 3.9, is net revenue less all costs. Column (30), federal income tax, is 0.35 times taxable income (column 29). ITC and state taxes are ignored in this example. Taxable income less federal taxes plus ITC yields AT income (31 = 29 –30).

Total income is $31.04 million, which appears fine at first glance. These results, especially the yearly ATI pattern, are illusory, however, because tangible and intangible depreciation and depletion distort the cash flow pattern. NCF strives to model the flow of money entering and leaving the treasury. The presence of the *non-cash charges*, like depreciation, leads to incorrect measurement of cash flow timing. AT income recognizes major cash expenditures over 5 to 7 years, instead of the year the costs are actually incurred.

Example 3.9: Derive the income tax schedule using the previous data. All values in $m.

Year	(9) WI Net Revenue	– (28) Opex	– (13) Depreciation Tangible	– (27) Depreciation Intangib.	– (21) Expensed Capex	– (24) Cost Depletion	= (29) Taxable Income	– (30) Income Tax	= (31) After-Tax Income
0-1	69.02	43.11	6.18	1.73	40.32	3.73	-26.05	-9.12	-16.93
1-2	136.74	74.20	13.32	3.85	9.24	7.39	28.74	10.06	18.68
2-3	110.94	60.20	12.24	4.25	0	6.00	28.26	9.89	18.37
3-4	78.69	42.70	8.74	4.25	0	4.25	18.75	6.56	12.18
4-5	42.57	23.10	6.23	4.25	0	2.30	6.69	2.34	4.35
5-6	20.64	11.20	5.54	2.52	0	1.12	0.26	0.09	0.17
6-7	3.87	2.10	5.54	0.40	0	0.21	-4.38	-1.53	-2.85
7-8	0	0	3.64	0.00	0	0.00	-3.64	-1.28	-2.37
8-9	0	0	0.86	0.00	0	0.00	-0.86	-0.30	-0.56
Total	462.47	256.61	62.30	21.24	49.56	25.00	47.76	16.71	31.04

Net Cash Flow

Measuring money flows accurately drives the NCF computation. The distortion in AT income becomes obvious when NCF in Example 3.10 is compared to AT income. Columns 9, 28, and 30 are copied from the previous example, while the investments reflect actual expenditure patters for investments. NCF is WI Net Revenue less the other columns.

Example 3.10: Derive the NCF for the project used in the previous examples. All values in $m.

Year	(9) WI Net Revenue	– (28) Opex	– (10) Investments Tangible	– (23) Investments Intangible	– (14) Investments Bonus	– (30) Income Tax	= (31) NCF
0-1	69.02	43.11	43.20	57.60	25.00	-9.12	-90.78
1-2	136.74	74.20	19.10	13.20	0.00	10.06	20.18
2-3	110.94	60.20	0.00	0.00	0.00	9.89	40.85
3-4	78.69	42.70	0.00	0.00	0.00	6.56	29.43
4-5	42.57	23.10	0.00	0.00	0.00	2.34	17.13
5-6	20.64	11.20	0.00	0.00	0.00	0.09	9.35
6-7	3.87	2.10	0.00	0.00	0.00	-1.53	3.30
7-8	0.00	0.00	0.00	0.00	0.00	-1.28	1.28
8-9	0.00	0.00	0.00	0.00	0.00	-0.30	0.30
Total	462.47	256.61	62.30	70.80	25.00	16.71	31.04

Observe that total NCF equals total AT income. The cash flows indicated by NCF vary significantly from AT income: large, significant negative cash flows occur in the early years, followed by large positive values toward the middle and end of the project life. These timing differences impact project evaluations greatly. This contrasts sharply with the money flows in the AT income table. Equally as important, AT income displays negative values in the last three years, while NCF has positive values. Depreciation in Column 13 causes taxable income to go negative. The negative taxable income multiplied by the inverse of the tax rate yields a negative ATI. Is this correct? No, because depreciation is merely a reduction in taxable income, not a true measure of money flows. Column 31 in Example 3.10 shows a positive cash flow owing to the tax relief.

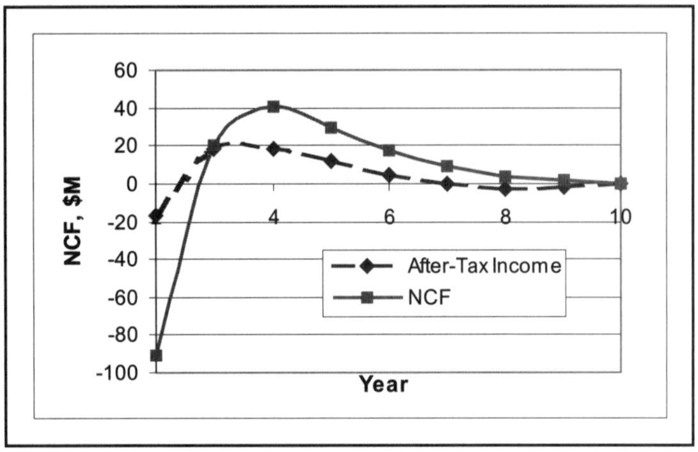

Figure 3.4 Net Income vs. NCF

Figure 3.4 compares NCF and ATI graphically. The wider swings in NCF values are easily discernible, the result of measuring the actual flow of money. Since the NCF and ATI produce the same total, the area underneath the curves are the same, but the timing implications are quite different.

NCF total indicates that the treasury grows from the project by \$31.04 million, ignoring the time value of money. Liquidity and, hence, default risk exists, because of large capital outlays in the early years; whereas. ATI suggests that project risk (taken as negative values) occurs in the last years of the project.

Does NCF indicate that this project adds value to the treasury? As Chapter 1 indicated, this is a modeling process to answer that question, by asking if any important information is missing from the analysis. For those with some experience, the immediate answer is yes! The investor borrowed money, as represented in the WACC, as derived in the next chapter, and NCF ignores the repayment of interest to the bank and dividends to the equity owners. Chapter 5 presents methods for valuing profitability.

Validation of NCF Values

An essential feature of successful investment analysis requires verifying that values used in computing the profitability measures and assessing risk are accurate, and reflect the professional's original assumptions. Several approaches may be used. First, check to see if the NCF pattern shows unusual patterns, like small initial negative values or negative values at the end of the project life. Evaluations are often erroneously redone when NCF is negative because the economic limit is assumed to have been reached. Economic limit is determined from columns 1 and 2, not NCF. Good software packages do likewise.

The proper treatment of taxes can be assessed by determining if the sum of tangible depreciation, intangible depreciation, depletion, and expensed IDC's equal total investment. For example, summing these values gives \$158.1, which equals total investment. Since capital recovery forms the basis for tax calculations, estimated taxes in column 30 should be correct if the two values match.

Other tests for validating are possible, but the key feature of all tests involves avoiding the assumption that if the computer prints results, the values must be correct. Take time to verify that your inputs generate the proper output. Probably 30-70% of all evaluations possess errors that could have been caught if the professional had validated the results. Errors of validation are seldom caught in most instances, but are very embarrassing when a supervisor, manager or competitor finds the mistake.

NORWEGIAN TAXES AND NCF

Norway made its entrance into the club of producing countries in 1971, with initial production from the Ekofisk Field. Since then Norway has continued to be a major area of interest for exploration and production. E/P occurs offshore, because of the absence of sedimentary rock onshore; moreover, most of the recent finds suggest that gas will dominate oil in the near future. Existing production and recent exploration success indicates that Norway will be a leading producer for years to come.

Several discoveries have since been made in the northern areas, although no commercial production has yet taken place. The areas north of the 62nd parallel include by far the largest portion of the

Norwegian continental shelves. The discoveries to date have been made in two regions: in the Haltenbanken (around 65th parallel, mid-Norway) and in the Tromsoflaket (southwestern corner of Barents Sea north of Norway). Development has started one of the Haltenbanken fields, but further developments depend on the establishment of a feasible gas offtake solution. This is even more of a problem in the far north, for which reason major developments are not expected until after the year 2000.

The developments so far have concentrated on fields that are large by U.S. standards. Developments are normally very costly: the Ekofisk, Statfjord and Gullfaks development costs are each in the order of \$10 billion. The main technological challenge is water depth, ranging from 200 feet (Ekofisk) to 1000 feet (Troll) and beyond. While these depths are now quite common in many areas, the severity of the weather, especially ice flows complicates the problem immensely.

Development concepts have favored very large integrated platforms, especially in the northern North Sea. The Statfjord and Gullfaks fields use each three Condeep platforms, where the base structure is made of reinforced concrete that contains crude oil storage cells and also is used to float the platform out to sea. The Gullfaks C platform, standing on the bottom in 700 feet of water, is the largest object ever moved by man.

Ekofisk and most other fields in the southern North Sea have been developed using platforms on steel jackets. More recent development concepts include subsea structures (Tommeliten, several satellite fields), floating systems (Snorre, Heidrun, Frigg, Hod) and combined solutions (Veslefrikk). There is a marked trend towards smaller and cheaper concepts as development focuses on smaller fields. In addition, several small fields are being developed as satellites to larger ones, using their facilities for processing and off take.

Most fields and pipelines in Norway are owned jointly by several oil companies. Companies that are active in Norway include majors (Shell, Exxon/Mobil, BP), other international oil companies (Phillips Petroleum, Conoco, Amerada Hess, TotalElf, Fina, Agip and others), and the Norwegian companies (Statoil, Norsk Hydro and Saga Petroleum).

Norwegian Petroleum Policies

The general objective of Norwegian petroleum policies has been to derive maximum benefits for the Norwegian society from petroleum reserves. The Government takes an active role in controlling various aspects of the petroleum activities, using a variety of instruments:

- Taxation
- Granting licenses for exploration and production
- Government approval of development plans
- Statoil, the Government owned petroleum company
- Regulations covering operations, safety and environmental control, and
- Procurement preferences

Petroleum policies do not tend to change much as a consequence of changing governments, although there are differences between the parties on some petroleum related issues. Policies concerning petroleum activities are generally controlled by the national government - not the regional or local bodies.

Awarding Licenses and Changing Policies

Before 1987, most licenses required the private companies to pay for Statoil's share of the exploration costs, with the exception of other Norwegian companies like Saga and Norsk Hydro. Carried exploration lasted until the field was declared commercial. This proviso was dropped in 1987 for a variety of reasons.

Statoil also can increase its share of the field working interest, at the expense of the other licensees, once the field is approved for development. The extent of the future State share partially depends on projected future production rates. License awards are influenced by sliding scale rates proposed by the applicant.

While the sliding scale rate is usually exercised by the legislature (Storting), they recently elected to forgo the higher rate for the Snorre Field. In the early 1990's, the Storting removed this feature from the license rounds, forcing Statoil to compete for acreage with everyone else.

Statoil's, the government's commercial E/P arm, position has also changed over time. Initially Statoil was guaranteed a 50% working interest. In the mid-1980's Statoil's holdings were split into a Statoil share and a direct State share. Statoil only votes and receives cash flow from their share. They act as an agent for the State on the remainder. Increases in the sliding scale WI benefit the State, not Statoil.

Most North Sea developments require a development to be submitted to specified agencies. The State tries to control a reasonably even level of field development by deferring acceptance of development plans. The Storting approves the plan in Norway.

The development plan includes plans for established offtakes, market sales, flaring, timing, etc. Since Norwegian gas is normally sold as life-of-field contracts to Continental buyers, gas sales involve very large and long contracts.

Norway impacts field values also by encouraging the use of Norwegian supplies and limiting production. Foreign suppliers are not excluded from bidding on services, but face major obstacles, especially if a branch office doesn't exist in Norway. This tends to increase the cost of developing and operating fields. The impact of higher costs is impacted by production limitations imposed in conjunction with OPEC. A 7.5% forced reduction was applied in 1987 to the biannual production plans submitted by the companies. This rate was later reduced to 5% and finally abolished in 1990. The government has clearly expressed a willingness to control production for price stabilization.

Net Cash Flow (NCF) Derivation

Project value is altered in Norway by the impaction of three basic taxes:

- Special Petroleum Tax (SPT)
- Corporate Income Tax (CT)
- Royalty

Royalty and income tax are similar to those in other parts of the world, although the details vary slightly in the computation. The special petroleum tax (SPT) is similar to the Petroleum Revenue Tax (PRT) in the U.K. and the old Windfall Profits Tax (WPT) in the U.S. Each was designed to tax away the "excessive" profits being made by the oil companies during the 1970's.

The NCF derivation follows the format in Equation 3.3.

In countries outside of the U.S., gross revenue is not simply sales price times production. Crude sales are booked in Norway at the "norm" price. The norm price is established by a governmental committee based on observed and reported market prices for crude. "Posted prices" perform the same function in other countries. No norm price exists for gas and NGL as the companies report their actual sales revenues. Internal transfers must be recorded on an arms-length basis.

The norm price exists to prevent companies from selling crude oil to their non-Norwegian affiliates at artificially low prices to avoid payment of taxes. Other countries use posted prices for the same reason. Until the advent of posted or norm prices, international companies minimized their tax burden by manipulating internal transfers to record profits in the country with the most favorable taxes. Project evaluations seldom consider this issue, although daily operating decisions are affected.

Royalty

The royalty measures the portion of the field's production that is transferred to the Government at the source, or alternatively, the Government can elect to receive the equivalent value in cash. Normal practice is that the royalty for gas and NGL is accounted for in cash terms; whereas, the crude is sold on the Government's behalf by Statoil.

Royalty rates were adjusted following the crash in oil prices in 1985. Newer fields, defined as a field receiving development approval after 1985, pay no royalty. Fields receiving development approval before 1985 pay a sliding scale royalty on oil, a 12.5% rate for gas, and NGL's at the gas rate if landed in gaseous form. Oil's sliding scale rate is defined in Table 3.6.

Once field production exceeds 100,000 barrels per day, a floor of 12% is set on the royalty rate of 12%. Fields producing more than 100,000 bopd will, thus, pay a 12% royalty rate even after field production falls below this schedule. Moreover, the tax rates apply to total field production, not incremental production. Total field royalty rates complicate investment decisions because each incremental barrel may alter the royalty burden for the entire field. See Chapter 9 for a more detailed discussion of constrained investments.

TABLE 3.6

Royalty Rates for Crude Oil

Production Rate, bpd	Royalty Rate
0 to 40,000	8%
40,001 to 100,000	10%
100,001 to 225,000	12%
225,001 to 350,000	14%
> 350,000	16%

Royalty volumes are credited at the field export point, usually entry into the pipeline. Paid on a quarterly basis, it is based on gross value less any transportation and handling expenses associated with pipeline tariffs, loading buoys, tankers, etc.

In Example 3.11, net revenue is WI gross revenue less royalty. Observe that royalty rises from 10% in Year 1-2 to 12% in Year 2-3 because production exceeded the 100 000 stb/day threshold, raising the royalty rate to 12%. Thereafter, the royalty rate does not decline back to 8% because the field exceeded the 100,000 stb/day level.

Example 3.11: Assuming a 25% WI in the following Norwegian field, compute the royalty and net revenue. All values in $m, except as indicated.

	(1)	(2)=(1)*365	(3)	(4)=(3)*(2)*0.25	(5)	(6)=(5)*(4)	(7)=(4)-(6)
Year	Daily Production, stb/day	Gross Production, M bbl	Price , $/bbl	WI Gross Revenue	Royalty Rate, %	Royalty	WI Net Revenue
0-1	0.00	0.00	0.00	0.00	0.00	0.00	0.00
1-2	58,630	21.40	18.00	96.30	0.10	9.63	86.67
2-3	116,164	42.40	18.00	190.80	0.12	22.90	167.90
3-4	94,247	34.40	19.00	163.40	0.12	19.61	143.79
4-5	66,849	24.40	20.00	122.00	0.12	14.64	107.36
5-6	56,164	20.50	21.00	107.62	0.12	12.91	94.71
6-7	37,538	13.70	22.00	75.36	0.12	9.04	66.31
7-8	23,288	8.50	23.00	48.88	0.12	5.87	43.01
Total		165.30		804.36		94.60	709.76

Small royalty changes impact valuations considerably. It is common to argue over equity issues to the 8-9th decimal place in the North Sea. These decimal places often seem unimportant, but do relate to large sums of money.

Special Petroleum Tax and Income Tax Derivation

The special petroleum tax (SPT) and income tax (CT) are based on taxable income, like most other countries. The basis for the tax is income, less deductions, incurred in the entirety of Norway. Revenues and tax deductions from all Norwegian activities are pooled for the SPT and CT calculation. The "ring-fence" for these taxes is, thus, the Norwegian national boundary, just like the U.S. and most other countries except the U.K. and Indonesia.

In this discussion, as in the presentation of the other countries in this chapter, it is assumed that companies possess tax paying producing fields to offset exploration and early development cost. In actuality companies entering Norway initially do not have revenues to offset their costs. The law allows these costs to be carried forward automatically 15 years, and even longer carry-forwards may be applied for (like the Esso exemption). A carry-forward reduces profits in future years, thus lowering taxes, although the company loses the time value of money.

For computing SPT and CT, taxable income is first derived. The equation for taxable income in Norway is given in Equation 3.12.

$$\begin{aligned}\text{Taxable Income}_t = {} & \text{Net Revenue}_t \\ & - \text{Opex}_t \\ & - \text{Abandonment Cost}_t\,(\text{Opex}) \\ & - \text{Exploration Cost}_t \\ & - \text{Depreciation}_t \\ & - \text{Interest Payments}_t\ (\text{if applicable})\end{aligned} \tag{3.12}$$

Operating (OPEX), abandonment, and exploration costs may be deducted in the year the money is spent if revenues exist, or carried forward if needed. The exploration tax relief does not depend on finding commercial reserves.

Abandonment costs present a problem since the salvage value of recovered equipment is expected to be less than the cost. The tax system does not allow companies to deduct monies set aside for abandonment on their taxes. Instead, the State reimburses companies for a portion of the actual abandonment costs. The reimbursable portion is computed as the abandonment cost times a factor, where the factor equals total taxes divided by total revenue. The remaining abandonment costs are not tax deductible.

Interest costs are treated differently among companies. Many elect to ignore interest costs directly by building this cost into the discount rate, explained in Chapter 4. Others prefer to evaluate interest costs directly. Actual tax calculations include interest.

Should interest costs be considered directly, interest is treated as an expensed item, like OPEX. The actual deduction depends on how the money is borrowed. If interest arises on debt incurred by a Norwegian affiliate, 100% of the interest is deducted. International companies, however, often loan money to the Norwegian company from non-Norwegian sources. Only 75% of the funds forwarded may be classified as debt and only that portion may generate interest. Working interest is ignored in these examples.

Capital recovery (depreciation) is based on a 6-year straight-line basis; hence, 1/6 of all development expenditures are recovered each year. Capital recovery begins the year the money is spent, with no delay for project start or first production. Example 3.12 shows a simple cost recovery schedule.

Example 3.12: Compute the 6 year SL depreciation for the 25% WI, based on the Capex schedule. All values $m.

	(8)	(9)	(10)	(11)
		Capital Recovery In:		Total
Year	Capex	Year 0-1	Year 1-2	Depreciation
0-1	48.00	8.00	0.00	8.00
1-2	144.00	8.00	24.00	32.00
2-3	0.00	8.00	24.00	32.00
3-4	0.00	8.00	24.00	32.00
4-5	0.00	8.00	24.00	32.00
5-6	0.00	8.00	24.00	32.00
6-7	0.00	0.00	24.00	24.00
7-8	0.00	0.00	0.00	0.00
Total	192.00	48.00	144.00	192.00

Development costs occur in years 1 and 2. Since depreciation begins in the year the money is spent, 1/6 of $48 million, or $8 million, offsets revenues from year 1 to year 6. A similar pattern follows for the $144 million expenditure in year 2. Total depreciation is the sum of each year's depreciation values.

Income Tax

Income taxes in Norway are levied at the rate of 28% currently. This combines both a national and local tax, but for evaluation purposes this distinction is unimportant. Example 3.13 illustrates the income tax computation using the values from previous exhibits and assuming the project incurs $75 million in exploration and delineation costs.

Example 3.13: Using the information from previous examples, derive the income tax schedule for the project. All values $m.

	(7) = (4)–(6)	(12)	(11)	(13)	(14)	(15) = (14)*0.28
Year	WI Net Revenue	Opex	Capital Recovery	Exploration Cost	CT Taxable Income	Income Tax
0-1	0.00	0.00	8.00	75.00	-83.00	-23.24
1-2	86.67	37.45	32.00	0.00	17.22	4.82
2-3	167.90	74.20	32.00	0.00	61.70	17.28
3-4	143.79	60.20	32.00	0.00	51.59	14.45
4-5	107.36	42.70	32.00	0.00	32.66	9.14
5-6	94.71	35.87	32.00	0.00	26.83	7.51
6-7	66.31	23.98	24.00	0.00	18.34	5.13
7-8	43.01	14.88	0.00	0.00	28.14	7.88
Total	709.76	289.28	192.00	75.00	153.48	42.98

Taxable income, as defined earlier, is net revenue less deductions. Taxable income times the tax rate yields the income tax payments. Total taxes paid on the project are $42.98 million.

Special Petroleum Tax (SPT)

The SPT uses taxable income tax as the starting point. To minimize the impact of SPT, two other deductions from taxable income are allowed. The first and most important allows the company to offset 15% of WI revenue, while the second permits an uplift of 6.67% on investments made before 1986. The latter offset is only important for older fields.

Equation summarizes the SPT computation.

$$SPT_t = 0.50 * (\text{CT Taxable Income}_t - \text{SPT Deduction}_t - \text{Uplift}_t) \quad \textbf{(3.13)}$$

Special taxes are computed at a rate of 50% currently. The rate started at 35%, but dropped to 30% as t oil prices fell in the 1980's, but was later revised as Norway became more involved with the European Union. Prior to this change in the early 90's, the CT rate was around 50%. To help Norwegian business compete, the CT was dropped to 28% and the SPT rate raised to 50%. This change allowed the treasury to receive about the same amount of tax revenue, and taxed other Norwegian businesses at one of the lowest rates in the EU.

Example 3.14 shows WI gross revenue (Column 4), as the before royalty revenue of the project. The SPT deduction rate of 15% (Column 16) times WI revenue yields the SPT deduction (Column 17). The SPT deduction used to be called the production allowance, but it was dropped for all fields in 1992. SPT taxable income is the CT taxable income reduced further by the SPT deduction or relief. The SPT owed comes from the SPT taxable income times the appropriate SPT rate, a 50% rate used here.

Example 3.14: Compute the SPT using values from the previous examples and an SPT rate of 0.48. All values in $m.

Year	(14) CT Taxable Income	(29) Uplift	(18) = 14 – 17 – 29 SPT Income	(19) SPT Paid
0-1	-83.00	0.00	-83.00	-41.50
1-2	17.22	7.20	10.02	5.01
2-3	61.70	7.20	54.50	27.25
3-4	51.59	7.20	44.39	22.20
4-5	32.66	7.20	25.46	12.73
5-6	26.83	7.20	19.63	9.82
6-7	18.34	7.20	11.14	5.57
7-8	28.14	0.00	28.14	14.07
Total	153.48	43.20	110.28	55.14

Uplift reduces SPT payments by allowing an additional write-off. It was 6.66% on fields developed before 1987, then dropped until 1992. After 1992, a 5% uplift is allowed on development expenditures beginning with depreciation and lasting for 6 years. Negative SPT obligations are carried forward in time. Development expenditures begin with the Plan for Development and Operations (PDO) is approved by NPD.

These illustrations assume that income and special petroleum taxes are paid in the year the obligations occur. Many computer programs actually try to anticipate when the taxes are paid. Norwegian taxpayers submit estimates of income in the early fall of the tax paying year. They then pre-pay the estimated and final taxes for year t according to the following schedule:

- October of Year t: 50% of estimated taxes
- April of Year t+1: 50% of estimated taxes
- October of Year t+1: Adjustment for actual taxes.

The unique component of the Norwegian tax regime is the non-deductibility of the SPT in computing income tax. Other countries with taxes similar to SPT deduct the SPT when computing income taxes, which lessens the SPT burden. Because the two taxes are independent, some see the total tax take of the government as 78% [= 0.28 + 0.50], but this overstates the real burden because of the 15% deduction and uplift. No income is paid since allowed deductions exceed revenues (see the $-10.37 SPT Income).

NCF

Valuation of the project follows the format in Equation 3.14. Revenues less actual costs, accounted for in the year the money was actually spent, measure the value of the project. In Norway revenue is composed of the valuation of the production stream plus often processing and transportation tariffs levied on other fields using these facilities. Costs fall generally under four main categories: operating, exploration, development, and taxes. Each of these may be sub-divided as needed.

The basic format for estimating NCF in Norway is given in Equation 3.14.

$$\begin{aligned} NCF_t = WI\ & \text{Net Revenue}_t \\ & - \text{Opex}_t \\ & - \text{Exploration Investments}_t \\ & - \text{Development Investments}_t \\ & - \text{Income Tax}_t \\ & - \text{Special Petroleum Tax}_t \end{aligned} \tag{3.14}$$

The project incurs negative cash flows in years 0-2 due to exploration and development capital costs. Years 3-7 show positive cash flows. Total NCF is $55.37 million (Net Revenue less deductions).

The negative income tax and SPT values imply tax relief. Since the basic equation subtracts income tax and SPT as costs, a double negative augments NCF. Example 3.15 assumes the company is currently paying taxes in Norway. Had this been the initial or an early project, the negative values would have been carried forward until the tax relief was depleted.

Example 3.15: Derive the NCF schedule using the previous information. All values in $m.

	(7) = (4) – (6)	– (12)	– (13)	– (8)	– (15)	– (19)	= (20)
Year	WI Net Revenue	Opex	Exploration Cost	Capex	Income Tax	SPT Paid	NCF
0-1	0.00	0.00	75.00	48.00	-23.24	-41.50	-58.26
1-2	86.67	37.45	0.00	144.00	4.82	5.01	-104.61
2-3	167.90	74.20	0.00	0.00	17.28	27.25	49.17
3-4	143.79	60.20	0.00	0.00	14.45	22.20	46.95
4-5	107.36	42.70	0.00	0.00	9.14	12.73	42.79
5-6	94.71	35.87	0.00	0.00	7.51	9.82	41.50
6-7	66.31	23.98	0.00	0.00	5.13	5.57	31.63
7-8	43.01	14.88	0.00	0.00	7.88	14.07	6.19
Total	709.76	289.28	75.00	192.00	42.98	55.14	55.37

The example project earns money for the treasury and would be acceptable to most companies on the basis of undiscounted cash flow. The project also pays out (cumulative NCF=0) in year 5-6, which is also quite good for a project in the Norwegian sector. Incorporating the time value of money principles (See Chapter 5) will not alter the decision to accept this project. The ranking of this project relative to other profitable projects may change, however.

Example of a Longer-Life Norwegian Project

Offshore projects typically have longer exploration and development lead times than the simplified examples used to illustrate the Norwegian tax regime. Also, in Norway as in every other country a complicating feature of project evaluations arises from exchange rate differences. Non-Norwegian companies must compare investments at the home office. Whether the relevant currency unit is dollars, sterling, francs, etc., Norwegian kroner are usually converted to the home currency using exchange rate forecasts. These exchange rate forecasts are subject to the same uncertainties as production prices, and cost estimates, as explained in Chapter 5.

Example 3.16 summarizes the NCF for a longer-life project using Norwegian kroner (NOK) as the base currency. Like the simpler example, the NOK NCF in Column 26 is the difference between net revenue and the estimated costs of the project including taxes. The first four years display negative cash flows due to development costs. Abandonment costs also cause the last year to be negative. In between NOK NCF is positive. This is a common profile.

Example 3.16: Analyze the NCF pattern for the following project. All values in $m.

Year	(21)	– (22)	– (23)	– (24)	– (25)	= (26)	/ (27)	= (28)
	Net Revenue	Opex	Capex	Income Tax	SPT	NOK NCF	NOK/$ Exchange Rate	NCF
0-1	0	0	0	0	0	0	6.50	0.00
1-2	0	0	171	-14	-9	-148	6.50	-22.77
2-3	0	0	409	-49	-29	-331	6.75	-49.04
3-4	0	0	567	-97	-57	-413	7.00	-59.00
4-5	255	85	340	-39	-35	-96	7.25	-13.24
5-6	893	161	179	231	96	226	7.50	30.13
6-7	1,219	169	94	385	172	399	7.50	53.20
7-8	1,280	177	20	424	193	466	8.00	58.25
8-9	1,344	186	21	485	226	426	8.00	53.25
9-10	1,303	195	22	506	240	340	8.00	42.50
10-11	1,026	205	23	387	182	229	7.50	30.53
11-12	599	216	24	177	78	104	7.25	14.34
12-13	503	226	25	129	54	69	7.00	9.86
13-14	396	238	26	69	23	40	7.00	5.71
14-15	277	977		-386	-221	-93	7.00	-13.29
Total	9,095	2,835	1,921	2,208	913	1,218		140.45

A dollar denominated company converts the NOK NCF to dollars by dividing the exchange rate forecast (Column 27) into the NOK NCF estimate. Column 28 shows the value of the project NCF in dollars. Had a different currency been relevant, the appropriate values would have been substituted into Column 27.

Summary

The important characteristics of Norway as a place for making petroleum investments:

- Norway is a high cost environment, both due to the extraordinary technical challenges to extraction and high labor and service costs.
- Projects require considerable financial strength due to the long duration of exploration and development phases. Quick return, low risk projects are very rare on a stand-alone basis.

- The tax regime optimizes the financial return to Norwegian society, while providing incentives to attract and keep outside investors. The tax regime varies as world prices and business climate goes through various business stages.
- The nominal tax rate may rise up to around 78%.
- High tax rates absorb some of the financial risks failed investments. In a failed investment, the government offsets the 78% as per the tax rate. Projects often look much better on an after-tax basis than a before-tax basis.
- Investment returns favor those with existing projects in Norway, relative to new entrants in the market place.

UNITED KINGDOM NCF

The fiscal terms in the U.K. are both complex and in a continual state of revision. The specific terms regulating the allocation of public assets, like telecommunication and minerals, vary by license round and location. The terms specified today often contrast quite significantly from previous rules used to allocate resources. These terms generally follow the rise and fall of expected changes in product prices.

Resources used to be allocated by a governmental department assigned to a specific industry, like the old U.K. Department of Energy's (DEn), but now such activities fall under the jurisdiction of the Department of Trade and Industry (DTI) assessment of the partnerships' qualifications. Early rounds emphasized characteristics like:

1. Technical qualifications of consortium,
2. Experience
3. Financial attributes,
4. Composition of joint venture
5. Work program (money to be spent, including seismic and number of wells drilled to specific depths, or miles of new circuits created), or a bonus (up front payment).

An early goal during the license rounds, in part, was to build U.K. technical expertise for creating employment and building expertise that can eventually be marketed in other countries. The Labour government that implemented the policy was vilified for these ideas, but this led to organizations, like BBC and BP, which are world-class.

Recent bidding for telecommunications employed a bonus bidding process. In the ninth license round for petroleume, bonus bidding was added, producing a bid of over $34 million by Amoco (now BP) for a 100% working interest (WI) in three blocks. The highest bid for a single block (15/18b) was $28.33 million. (Note: the dollar was valued at $1.10 per pound at this time). A bonus merely gives the winner the right to conduct further exploration efforts. Later rounds focused on work programs to allocate blocks.

To date, the specific terms that regulate the development of a particular field vary depending on location, license, date of development approval, and in the case of natural gas fields, the nature of the gas sales contract. Three fiscal elements currently impact profitability. These are:

1. a royalty to the U.K. government
2. the *Petroleum Revenue Tax* (*PRT*), and
3. the Corporation Tax (CT)

These provisions, when combined, enabled the Government to retain as much as 85.7% of revenues at various times. Government's share of the revenue split may also be as low as 30% under the current tax regime.

Background

The first four license rounds took place between 1964 and 1972, and today the majority of U.K. production comes from the blocks awarded in these initial rounds, even though roughly 30% have yet to begin producing. The fifth and sixth rounds held between 1977 and 1979 revised the tax and royalty regulations and initiated the program, which enabled the now defunct British National Oil Company (BNOC) to acquire a 51% interest in any new license. BNOC was also carried through the project's exploration program. License rounds conducted after 1980 eliminated such participation rights, but did make a provision for BNOC to purchase up to 51 percent of production at market prices. Following the ninth round, this provision was eliminated. BP purchased BNOC in the late 80's.

Because of difference in the various licensing rounds, three distinct fiscal regimes govern the petroleum fiscal regime. These subgroups are applicable to prescribed hydrocarbon development and specifically regulate:

1. New oil and gas fields: defined as fields approved for development after 1 April, 1982, but excludes projects in Southern North Sea areas between latitudes 52°6N and 55°N;
2. Old oil and gas fields, new onshore fields, and those fields in the Southern North Sea (excluded in 1), and
3. Gas fields whose contracts were approved prior to June 1975. (Primarily Frigg and Brent)

U.K. Ring Fence

In the discussion of U.S. and Norwegian tax regimes, the basis for the tax computations was income and costs incurred in the country, regardless of source. Pooling of incomes and costs at a national level dominates tax regime formulation, worldwide. Other countries define the ring-fence (the basis for a tax computation) in finer divisions. These divisions may be by field (U.K.), concession area (Indonesia), business, or company. The intent is to keep profitable ventures from subsidizing poor or marginal entities.

U.K evaluations are complicated by the use of different ring fences for royalty, PRT, and income tax. Figure 3.5 outlines the ring fences for each tax.

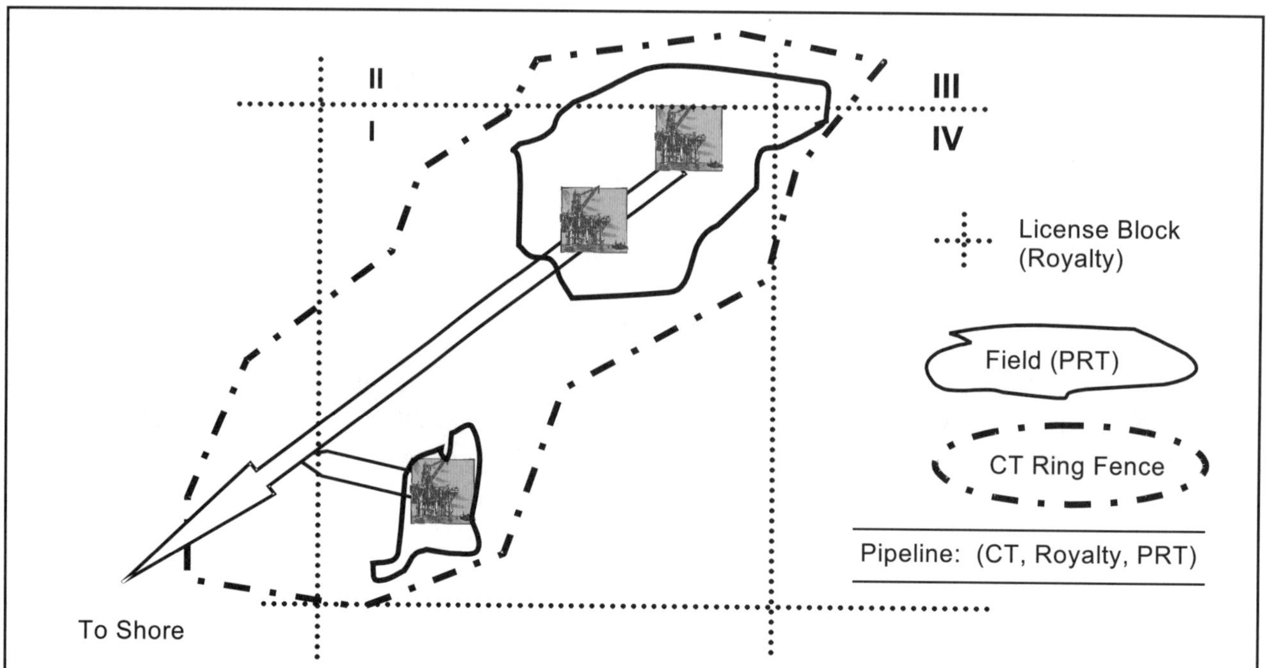

Figure 3.5 Geography of U. K. taxes

Royalties are based on the license block. The larger reservoir in the example actually overlaps four different license blocks. If the four blocks had been assigned under different regimes, different royalty rates would apply to the production stream depending on the original source of the molecules.

PRT applies to each distinguished reservoir, and may cover one or more license blocks. Different reservoirs within the same license blocks may face unique, effective PRT rates. The U.K. DOE defines the PRT ring fence for each, non-communicating reservoir. Differential reservoir pressure data alone is insufficient evidence to create separate ring fences. The concept of *blue water* also applies. Geological information must also be submitted to establish that the reservoirs have different oil/water or gas/water contacts. Negotiations are critical in establishing PRT ring fences.

As explained in the PRT discussion below, the PRT rate is either 0% or 50%, depending on when the DTI approved the field development plan. The smaller field may pay a 0% PRT rate if classified as a separate ring fence, and a 50% PRT rate if part of an existing, producing field. Significant economic impacts arise from the ring fence classification.

Table 3.7 summarizes the basic elements of the UK tax regime as it varied over time. Each element is discussed in detail later. Several features complicate the tax regime. First, fields pay rates based on when the license was awarded or field development approved, not the current rate. Therefore, some fields pay PRT, while the adjacent field may not. This complicates the software for estimating taxes greatly. Second, the record keeping varies considerably from field to field.

TABLE 3.7

Summary of Basic Royalty, PRT and CT Rates

Central and Northern North Sea Area			
		Petroleum Revenue Tax	
Fields Awarded Between:	Royalty	Tax	Volume Allowance
1967 and 1976	12.5% less deductions	50%	5 M tonnes
1976 to 1982	12.5% with no deductions	50%	10 M tonnes
1982 to 1993	0%	50%	10 M tonnes
After April 1993	0%	0%	-
Souther Gas Basin			
		Petroleum Revenue Tax	
Fields Awarded Between:	**Royalty**	**Tax**	**Volume Allowance**
Pre-July 1975 contracts	12.5%	0%	–
June 1975 to 1988	12.5%	50%	5 M tonnes
1988 to 1993	0%	50%	2.5 M tonnes
Post 1993	0%	0%	–

Most countries consolidate gains and losses from all ventures to determine income tax. The U.K. differentiates between upstream and downstream income, however. The UK government adopted this distinction in the early 1970's to prevent the oil industry, which was expected to be highly profitable from subsidizing losses in other industries, like steel and manufacturing.

Royalty

Royalties are paid to the DTI based on the volume of production. Most government's reserve the right to take the hydrocarbons in kind, or collect revenue based on a fair market value of the hydrocarbons.

Currently, three methods of calculating oil and gas royalties exist. Oil fields discovered in blocks awarded in the first four rounds compute royalty as 12.5 percent of the wellhead value of production, after

TABLE 3.8

Allowable Royalty Deduction (Rounds 1-4)

	Expenditure	Deduction
A. Oil Fields	Production & drilling platforms	70% over 8 years SL
	Flare structures	100% over 8 years SL
	Platform Opex	60%
	Transportation costs	100%
	Onshore terminal costs	95%
	Interest	100%
B. Gas Fields	Production platforms	100% on 15% DB
	Drilling platforms	70% on 15% DB
	Pipelines, compression, etc.	100% on 15% DB
	Opex	100%

deducting initial transportation and treatment costs. Gas royalties use the same rate, after deducting the cost of compression, treating, storage, and the like. The specific allowances for both oil and gas fields are outlined in Table 3.8.

Blocks awarded in the fifth, sixth, and seventh rounds, calculate royalties as 12.5 percent of the products landed value, and therefore, permits no deductions.

Onshore royalty rates follow a sliding scale royalty scheme. Table 3.9 summarizes the sliding scale rates assuming 30° gravity crude.

TABLE 3.9

Onshore Royalty Rates

Production		
Tonnes/Yr	bbls/day	Royalty Rates, %
<100,000	< 2,008	5
100,000 to 150,000	2,008 to 3,012	7.5
150,001 to 200,000	3,013 to 4,016	10
> 200,000	> 4,016	12.5

Licenses granted between 1967 and 1976 deduct processing and transportation costs when computing the royalty payment, while licenses granted between 1977 and 1982 eliminate the tariff allowance. Assignments of licenses between 1983 and 1988 pay a flat 12.5%. After 1988, royalty was eliminated for all fields, an attempt to encourage development of marginal fields.

Royalties are paid every 6 months with payment due two months after the end of the period. The first period extends from January – June with payment due 31st of August. The second period ends 31 December with payment due 28 February of the following year.

The complicated variations in the royalty rate have minimal impact on investment decisions, because royalty payments receive tax relief in the more important PRT and CT computation. For fields that pay full PRT and CT, the effective royalty rate falls below 4% for larger fields, owing to these allowances.

Petroleum Revenue Tax

The U.K. Government introduced PRT in 1974 to capture the majority of the windfall profits that resulted from rapidly rising world oil prices. The basic PRT rate was set at 45 percent in 1974 and later increased to 75 percent of eligible PRT taxable income. The tax is paid to the Inland Revenue. The PRT is computed half-yearly on a field basis. The following examples employ a yearly convention for simplicity.

The U.K. uses a field or reservoir ring fence for PRT computations; thus, costs for new field developments cannot offset PRT liabilities from older, profitable fields, like Forties or Brent. The field ring-fence concept effectively prevents companies from using expenditures for exploration and development to lower PRT payments among producing fields. Companies can recover these costs, but the recovery is delayed until the reservoir actually begins production.

With exploration declining as world oil prices declined in the early 1980's, the UK government introduced cross-field allowances to stimulate future expenditures. Cross-field allowances symbolize how a well intended tax regime distorts investment patterns. Exploration, appraisal, and a portion of the development expenditures (10% for fields receiving development approval after April 1987 from non-producing fields) were used to offset PRT payments in existing fields. These expenditures lose the uplift benefit as explained below, however.

The intent – to encourage more exploration – was reasonable and well intentioned. The government unfortunately forgot that tax relief only matters to those paying taxes. Companies with fully PRT paying fields reduced their exploration and appraisal (E&A) cost to around 15% of every dollar spent, with the government paying the other 85% via reduced PRT and CT receipts from these fields. Firms with no producing fields got no PRT relief, so they paid about $0.65 for every dollar of E&A expenditure. The cross-field allowance, thus, encouraged the sale of producing fields to new country entrants, with sale price being far higher than normal to integrate the tax savings. This exemption died an honorable death in the early 1990's.

Subsequent discoveries or extensions of producing horizons greatly complicate ring-fence determination and valuation. If the new horizon is classified as a separate reservoir, the DTI specifies a separate ring-fence; thereby, delaying the offset of expenditures against PRT. Establishing the new horizon as part of the same reservoir (some communication) allows the exploration and development expenditures to be deducted immediately against PRT. The economics may be reduced or improved depending on the status of the existing field, i.e., depending on its uplift and/or oil allowance deductions.

For example, the Ninian PRT ring fence encompasses the C, D and E Terraces and about half of B Terrace (Columba & West Ninian reservoirs). The existing ring fence was drawn to include the reservoirs identified when Ninian's Annex B (development plan) was approved. See Figure 3.6. Although the reservoirs are not in communication with Ninian, as established by pressure isolation and structural separation, the government would not agree to draw a new ring fence around

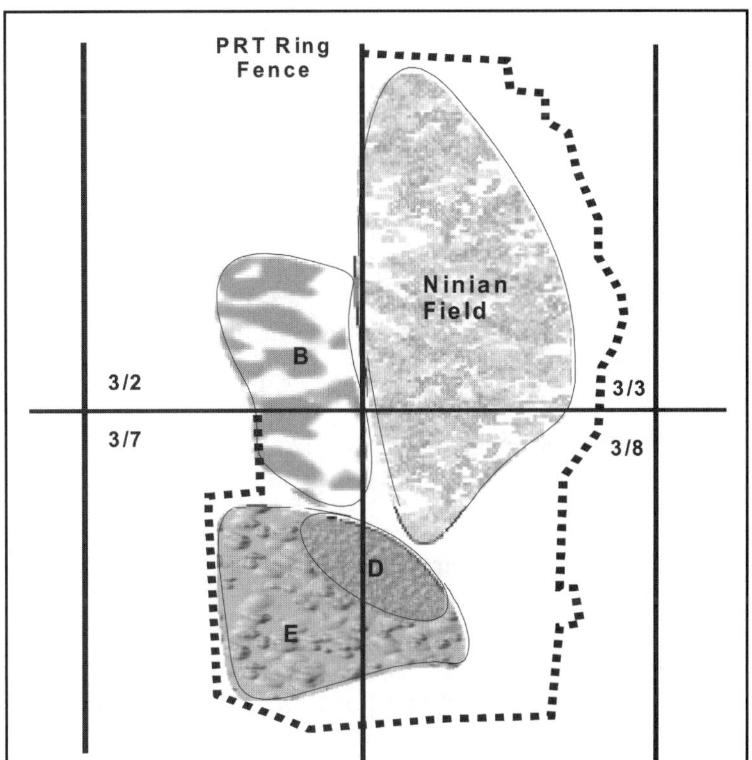

Figure 3.6 Columba and West Ninian block interests

CHAPTER 3

Columba/West Ninian. They cite "a series of precedents which establish a policy" of requiring *blue water* separation between the reservoirs." This appears to require that Columba's oil lie entirely below the original oil/water contact at Ninian, which cannot be demonstrated in all areas. This has a major impact on the economics of developing the Columba/West Ninian reservoirs. The economics of these satellites for various ring fence status is given in Table 3.10.

TABLE 3.10

Impact of Ring Fence on Economics

Economics	IRR	Payout
Inside ring fence	20%	6.9 years
Separate ring fence	39%	4.3 years

The government takes a much higher percentage of project revenues if the project remains within the existing ring fence and if the project is successful. However, if producers and injectors fail to perform as expected, the government would be subsidizing the project through tax credits. Some advantages and disadvantages of a separate ring fence are listed below:

Advantage	Disadvantages
Royalty is not paid on new fields (post 1984)	Initial Capex exposure due to lower tax rates
No PRT is paid until payout and uplift are exhausted (often never)	Project economics are poorer in the event of a bust due to small reservoir blocks or lack of reservoir continuity between injectors and producers
Uplift is received on Capex to help defer payout	

Equation 3.15 defines the PRT computation, with t indicating yearly values.

$$\begin{aligned} &\text{WI Net Revenue}_t \\ &\quad -\text{WI Opex}_t \\ &\quad -(0.35)*(\text{WI Qualifying Expenditure}_t) \\ &\quad -\text{WI Capex}_t \\ &\quad -\text{WI Oil Allowance}_t \\ &= \text{WI PRT Income}_t \\ &\quad *0.50 \text{ } or \text{ } 0.0 \\ &= \text{WI PRT}_t \end{aligned} \tag{3.15}$$

Operating costs (OPEX) includes lifting and overhead costs associated with production, workovers, and maintenance and overhaul of equipment. Revenues reflect cash inflow from sales of petroleum products or tariffs from leasing platform or pipeline equipment. Should PRT become negative, it is set to zero unless the costs may be used to offset PRT payments in another field. A major element in future North Sea platform revenue is the tariffs from processing satellite field production. These tariffs are exempt from PRT up to about 10,000 barrels per day, regardless of the monetary value, as outlined at the end of the section.

PRT is further complicated by the different stages, which operate over the life of the field, as Figure 3.7 illustrates. Between project start and first production, all costs receive uplift. No PRT is paid during this stage since no revenue is received. First production is often classified as the first barrel after 100,000 bbls (15,900 m^3). The allowance allows for well testing and auxiliary reservoir analysis, though considerable leeway exists based on negotiations with DTI.

Between first production and payback, PRT is computed but is still negative because cumulative costs, including uplift and oil allowance, still exceed revenue receipts. Qualifying expenditures are defined below, as are the safeguard period and oil allowance.

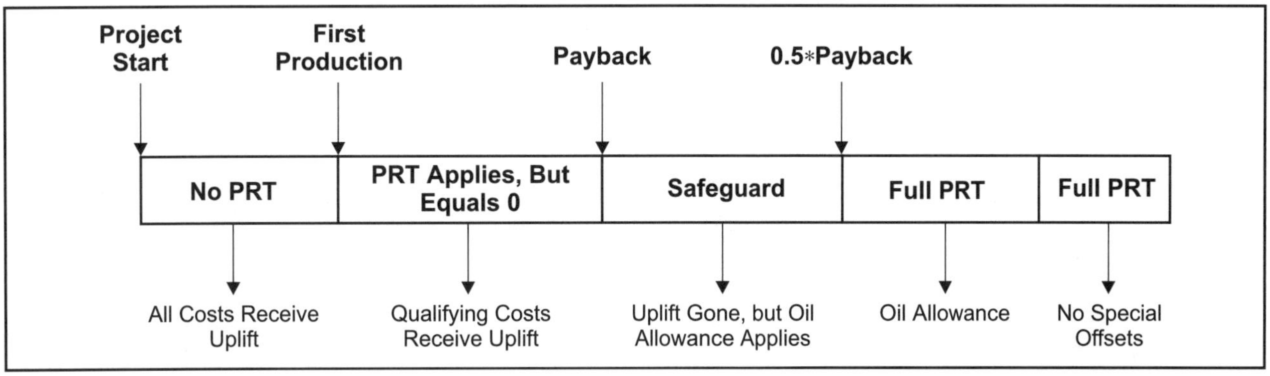

Figure 3.7 Stages of PRT

Uplift Deduction

Qualifying expenditures are uplifted (the 0.35) to enhance the value of eligible write-offs. The uplift is intended to offset, in part, exclusion of interest payments, and to provide an incentive for production. Uplift, like other taxes, has evolved over time, starting at a 75% rate, but later falling to the current 35%.

Uplift only applies to qualifying expenditures made during the net profit period (payback period). Project payback is defined as the time when cumulative cash flows equal zero (total revenue less total cost equals zero), inclusive of the uplift deduction.

Uplift is discontinued after the field reaches payback. Projects occurring later in the field's life, like infill drilling or EOR, lose potential tax savings associated with uplift. More importantly, significant PRT saving may arise from altering production and investment schedules to delay reaching the net profit period. Several fields were significantly modified just before the payback period to reduce PRT payments, again indicating distortions in engineering practice to mange tax burdens efficiently.

Qualifying expenditures vary depending on the stage of field development. Before first production, all expenditures receive uplift. After the net profit period is reached, uplift no longer applies. Between first production and the net profit period, only certain expenditures qualify. Operating and maintenance costs are excluded from uplift in this period, for instance. Table 3.11 summarizes eligible and disallowed expenditures during the net profit period.

TABLE 3.11

Eligible and Disallowed Expenditures for Uplift Between First Production and Payback

Qualifying Expenditures	Non-qualifying expenditures
Expenditures under old AFE's	Safety
Correcting design faults	Replacements
Items in original design	Other improvements
Improvements to water injection	
Improvements to direct production (win more oil)	

Example 3.17 demonstrates the derivation of uplifted capital for the PRT derivation. Capex in column 4 is augmented by the 35% to yield total uplifted capital in column 5. The concept of adding 35% as a PRT deduction seems trivial to some, but when projects cost hundreds of millions or billions, uplift represents a considerable sum of money.

Example 3.17: Given the revenue, Opex, and Capex schedules, derive the royalty and uplift obligations assuming a 12.5% royalty rate. All values in $m.

	(1)	(2) = (1) * 0.125	(3)	(4)	(5) = 1.35 * (4)
Year	**WI Revenue**	**Royalty**	**Opex**	**Capex**	**Uplifted Capital**
0-1	0.00	0.00	0.00	1,106.00	1,493.10
1-2	1,586.00	198.25	83.00	663.00	895.05
2-3	1,393.00	174.13	99.00	0.00	0.00
3-4	1,086.00	135.75	136.00	0.00	0.00
4-5	684.00	85.50	128.00	0.00	0.00
5-6	532.00	66.50	122.00	0.00	0.00
6-7	391.00	48.88	111.00	0.00	0.00
7-8	307.00	38.38	109.00	0.00	0.00
Total	5,979.00	747.38	788.00	1,769.00	2,388.15

Oil Allowance

Projects also benefit from an *oil allowance*, which reduces PRT payments, but really refers to all hydrocarbon production, not just oil. The allowance exempts part of the production from the PRT calculation, essentially preventing smaller, marginal producing fields from ever having to pay PRT. Oil allowance was part of the government's strategy to tax the most productive producers as much as possible, and still encourage development of marginal fields.

The allowance applies only to PRT (not to CT), and varies by type of field, location, and the time when the field development plan was approved by the government. After 31 December 1978, the maximum exemption was 250,000 metric tonnes (about 1.832 million barrels or 5,000 barrels per day) each six-month period. The allowance is discontinued when total exemptions reach 5 million metric tonnes of production (36.5 million barrels). This ceiling prevents the field owners from producing less than 10,000 barrels per day forever, though the loss in time value of money would far exceed the reduced tax burden. These rates also applied to onshore fields until 1988 when the volume allowance was reduced to 2.5 million tonnes.

The allowances increase for new fields. For those fields, which the government approved for development after 1 April 1982, and fields north of 55° N and south of 52° N, the oil allowance is doubled. The allowance is increased to 500,000 metric tonnes per half-yearly period (≈3.65 million barrels per half year or about 10,000 barrels per day) with a field maximum of 10 million tonnes (≈73 million barrels).

Figure 3.8 demonstrates a simple example of the daily and total oil allowance. The x, daily rate, might be 10,000 bpd, with the total area of the curve indicating the total reserve limit. Production above x and outside the box area pays a full PRT rate

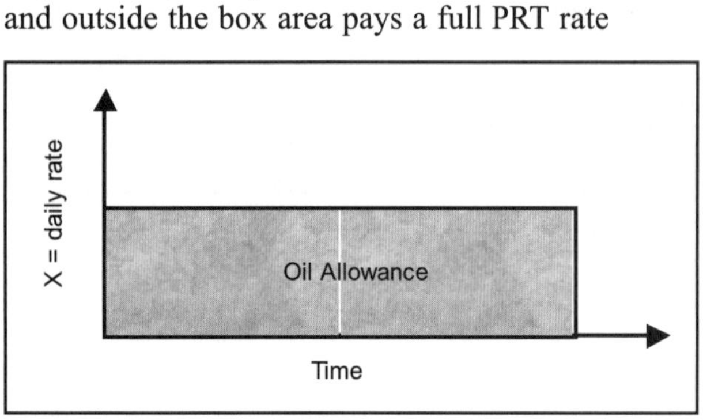

Figure 3.8 Daily and total oil allowance

The oil allowance prices production at the prevailing market price when it is produced, even though the rates are specified in tonnes. The allowance is particularly important for marginal fields. Fields considered part of existing fields might lose the allowance and, thereby, pay the full 50% PRT rate on all production. Those outside of the ring fence and below the ceiling values would pay no PRT.

PRT is paid every 6 months, with payment due two months after the end of the period. The first period extends from January to June, with payment due on 31 August. The second period ends 31 December, with the payment due 28 February of the following year. This lag provides considerable opportunity for managing ones tax burdens. Pictures exist of tankers going in circles in the North Sea until the day after the ending period. By landing the oil on 1 July, the company keeps the proceeds of the sale, which can be invested in an interest bearing account, until payment is due almost 8 months later. Again, when hundreds of millions of £ are involved, the interest earned may be considerable.

Equivalent allowances exist for gas. The allowance was originally set at 20 billion cubic feet (BCF) and later reduced to 10 billion cubic feet. For gas fields approved for development after March 1982, the allowance went back to the original 20 BCF, except in the Southern North Sea. Gas contracts written before the middle of 1975 are exempt from PRT, including the Brent and Frigg fields.

Fields producing gas and oil are integrated using one of two methods to compute PRT and the appropriate allowance. One method converts gas to oil on Btu equivalence, which is essentially a unit of production weighting scheme. The second method applies the allowance against oil production initially, and the remainder to gas if any allowance remains.

Example 3.18 displays a common software approach. If the field qualifies for a maximum of 7.3 million barrels per year, the product of price and production yields column 8, the maximum possible yearly value of the oil allowance. This column should be interpreted as the maximum possible, not the amount used.

Example 3.18: Compute the maximum allowance in each period and assuming a new field allowance of 7.3 million barrels per year.

	(6)	(7)	(8)=(6)*(7)
Year	Price, $/bbl	Allowable Production, MM bbls	Maximum Yearly Oil Allowance
0-1	0.00	0	0.00
1-2	18.00	7.3	131.40
2-3	18.00	7.3	131.40
3-4	19.00	7.3	138.70
4-5	19.00	7.3	138.70
5-6	20.00	7.3	146.00
6-7	21.00	7.3	153.30
7-8	22.00	7.3	160.60
Total			1,000.10

The sequencing of allowed deductions complicates the PRT computation far beyond any measure of reasonableness. The oil allowance, for instance, is taken after all other deductions. Should the other deductions produce a negative or zero PRT in a specific year, the allowance is ignored for that year. If, for instance, other costs totally offset PRT revenue in year 1-2, the calculation ignores the oil allowance of $131.40. In cases where the oil allowance is ignored, the total field allowance of 73 million barrels remains intact, but had the field used the oil allowance, the remaining field allowance is now 73 – 7.3 = 65.7 million barrels available for use in future years. Because oil allowance continues until used, investors use actual costs to reduce or minimize PRT first.

Example 3.19 illustrates the fairly length, often-complicated PRT derivation. The first box subtracts the sum of expenses from revenue. Example 3.19a recognizes that the PRT basis in column 13 (–$1,493.10) is negative in the first year due to expenses. Since the ring fence is the field, the cost of

CHAPTER 3

Example 3.19: Using the data from the previous examples, derive the PRT owed to the government. All values in \$m = million.

Year	(1) WI Revenue	(9) Opex	(2) Royalty	(5) Uplifted Capital	(10) = 9 + 2 + 5 Total Expenses	(11) = 1 – 10 Revenue – Expenses
0-1	0.00	0.00	0.00	1,493.10	1,493.10	-1,493.10
1-2	1,586.00	83.00	198.25	895.05	1,176.30	409.70
2-3	1,393.00	99.00	174.13	0.00	273.13	1,119.88
3-4	1,086.00	136.00	135.75	0.00	271.75	814.25
4-5	684.00	128.00	85.50	0.00	213.50	470.50
5-6	532.00	122.00	66.50	0.00	188.50	343.50
6-7	391.00	111.00	48.88	0.00	159.88	231.13
7-8	307.00	109.00	38.38	0.00	147.38	159.63
Total	5,979.00	788.00	747.38	2,388.15	3,923.53	2,055.48

Example 3.19a:

Year	(11) Revenue – Expenses	(12) Carry Forward Relief	(13) PRT Basis	(8) Oil Allowance	(9) PRT Income	(14) 50% PRT
0-1	-1,493.10	0	-1,493.10	0.00	0.00	0.00
1-2	409.70	-1,493.10	-1,083.40	131.40	0.00	0.00
2-3	1,119.88	-1,083.40	36.47	131.40	0.00	0.00
3-4	814.25	0.00	814.25	138.70	675.55	337.78
4-5	470.50	0.00	470.50	138.70	331.80	165.90
5-6	343.50	0.00	343.50	146.00	197.50	98.75
6-7	231.13	0.00	231.13	153.30	77.83	38.91
7-8	159.63	0.00	159.63	160.60	0.00	0.00
Total	2,055.48				1,282.68	641.34

–\$1,493.10 is carried forward to Year 1-2, in Column 12, as the arrows indicate. The revenue in Year 1-2 exceeds expenses, but the PRT basis is still negative because of the prior years cost carry forward.

PRT paid in Year 2-3 is still zero, even though the PRT basis is positive, because of the combination of the oil allowance deduction. PRT payments begin in the fourth year, but oil allowance reduces the amount paid. Finally, the PRT payments again become zero because of oil allowance. PRT taxable income becomes positive starting in year 3-4, with the resulting 50% PRT payments.

Payback and the Safeguard Period

The impact of PRT in the initial phase of production is further abated by the application of safeguard. *Safeguard* acts as a buffer against excessive PRT payments, especially early in the field life after incurring extensive investments. Full PRT payments are effectively delayed via "safeguard." *Payback* and safeguard are effective tax planning tools at the disposal of investors.

Payback marks the starting point for switching to the full PRT rate, and is defined as the point in time when cumulative field income equal expenditures. Expenditures include all construction and operating costs. Royalties are also included when dealing with gross revenue, but excluded when using net revenue.

Figure 3.9 illustrates payback and safeguard for a sample field. Revenues begin as zero and accumulate until equaling cumulative cost at the end of four periods. The safeguard period is half of the payback period, so 2 (= 0.5 * 4) periods define safeguard. Investors have historically invested additional capital to reap the best advantages from the safeguard calculation. The optimal time to influence safeguard occurs just before payback.

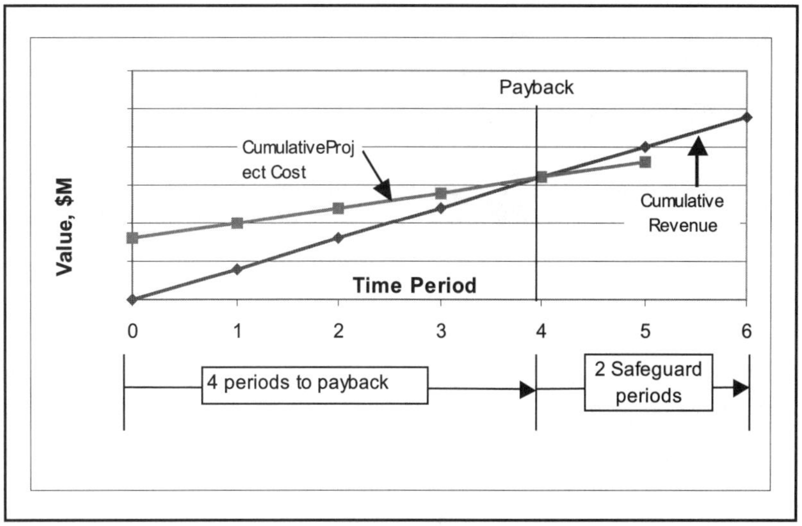

Figure 3.9 Payback and Safeguard

Safeguard protects smaller, less profitable investments from paying the high PRT tax early in the field life, but it greatly complicates the software used to analyze investment opportunities for two reasons. First, detailed histories of revenues and expenditures must be kept. Second, safeguard requires two computations for each field. The first computes PRT as in the last example, while the second compares the full PRT against the safeguard PRT. The actual PRT payment is the lesser of the full PRT and the safeguard PRT. The safeguard equation is defined in Equation 3.16:

$$\text{Safeguard PRT} = 0.80 * \left[\text{adjusted profit} - 0.30 * \sum(\text{ae})\right] \quad (3.16)$$

where: ae = accumulated expenditure eligible for uplift, and

Adjusted profit = revenues less allowed deductions (see the following example)

Equation 3.16 defines the situation for yearly computations. Half yearly analysis reduces 0.30 to 0.15. The other values remain the same. Safeguard only applies for 0.5 times the net profit period (payback or payout). After the safeguard period expires, the calculation reverts to the regular PRT computation. For fields in which safeguard is important, the net profit period is often extended to maximize safeguard benefits. This can be achieved by accelerating costs, like workovers, delaying production, or a combination of each.

Example 3.20 continues the previous examples. Payback, or the net profit period, occurs in year 2-3, where the cumulative net profit goes positive. Safeguard then applies for another 1.5 years or 3 half-year periods, if the half-year convention is employed. Since the example assumes yearly data, the safeguard period is 0.5 times 3 or 1.5 years. The government lets the investor round up to 2 years to define to define the safeguard period, which is year 4-5 for this example. To compute safeguard PRT, derive adjusted profit and the portion of accumulated capital, which can be deducted. The difference is safeguard profit. Multiply 80% by safeguard profit to estimate PRT under safeguard.

Adjusted profit, column 17, is derived by subtracting Opex, and royalty from WI Revenue. Adjusted profit then subtracts column 18, 30% of the original Capex (excluding uplift) to get safeguard profit in Column 19. Column 21, actual PRT paid, is the lesser of column 20 and column 14 (Example 3.19a) in years 3-4 and 4-5, and PRT at 50% from column 14 in all other years. Note that in periods when PRT becomes negative, zero is used, indicating that the tax never causes a negative cash flow to the government. Observe that safeguard lowers the ultimate PRT payments from $641 million to $364 million. Clearly, paying attention to safeguard matters to investors trying to maximize shareholder value.

Example 3.20: Compute the net profit period, safeguard PRT and the actual PRT paid. All values in $m.

	(1)	(9)	(2)	(5)	(10)=9+2+5	(15)=1–5	(16)
Year	WI Revenue	Opex	Royalty	Uplifted Capital	Total Expenses	Net Profit	Cumulative Net Profit
0-1	0.00	0.00	0.00	1,493.10	1,493.10	-1,493.10	-1,493.10
1-2	1,586.00	83.00	198.25	895.05	1,176.30	409.70	-1,083.40
2-3	1,393.00	99.00	174.13	0.00	273.13	1,119.88	36.47
3-4	1,086.00	136.00	135.75	0.00	271.75	814.25	850.73
4-5	684.00	128.00	85.50	0.00	213.50	470.50	1,321.23
5-6	532.00	122.00	66.50	0.00	188.50	343.50	1,664.73
6-7	391.00	111.00	48.88	0.00	159.88	231.13	1,895.85
7-8	307.00	109.00	38.38	0.00	147.38	159.63	2,055.48
Total	5,979.00	788.00	747.38	2,388.15	3,923.53	2,055.48	

Example 3.21: Using a net profit period of 3 years, derive the safeguard PRT and actual PRT payments for the project. All values in $m.

	(1)	- (9)	- (2)	= (17)	- (18)	= (19)	(20)=19*.8	(21)
Year	WI Revenue	Opex	Royalty	Adjusted Profit	30% of Total Capex	Safe-guard Profit	Safeguard PRT @ 80%	Actual PRT Paid
0-1	0.00	0.00	0.00	0.00	331.80	0.00	0	0
1-2	1,586.00	83.00	198.25	1,304.75	530.70	774.05	619.24	0
2-3	1,393.00	99.00	174.13	1,119.88	530.70	589.18	471.34	0
3-4	1,086.00	136.00	135.75	814.25	530.70	283.55	226.84	226.84
4-5	684.00	128.00	85.50	470.50	530.70	0.00	0	0
5-6	532.00	122.00	66.50	343.50	530.70	0.00	0	98.75
6-7	391.00	111.00	48.88	231.13	530.70	0.00	0	38.91
7-8	307.00	109.00	38.38	159.63	530.70	0.00	0	0.00
Total	5,979.00	788.00	747.38	4,443.63		1,646.78	1,317.42	364.50

$$331.8 = 0.301 * 1106.0$$

$$530.7 = 0.30 * (1106.0 + 663.0)$$

U.K. Corporate Tax

The U.K. income tax (CT) differs between upstream and downstream, as shown earlier. Upstream losses can be used to offset downstream profits, but downstream losses cannot be used to reduce upstream profits. This non-linearity was implemented by the Labour government in the early 1970's to prevent loss making industries, like British Steel, from using the petroleum industry to recover their losses. This legal stipulation has minimal impact on investment decisions.

The U.K. corporate tax was lowered to 35 percent in 1986 and 33% in 1990, and today some use 30%. Operating losses may be carried back one year or ahead indefinitely, and no corporate taxes are paid until previous losses are recovered. Companies issuing dividends pay 25/75's of the likely tax bill in advance, based on the dividend amount (called *advance corporate tax*, ACT). Most evaluations ignore dividend payments, since this is a management decision. Corporate income taxes are paid on profits for the financial year beginning on the 1st of April and final payment is normally due nine months after the end of the accounting period.

$$\begin{aligned} \text{WI Revenue}_t &- \text{WI Royalty}_t \\ &- \text{WI Opex}_t \\ &- \text{WI PRT}_t \\ &- \text{WI Expensed Capex}_t \\ &- \text{WI Capital Allowance}_t \text{ (Depreciation)} \\ &- \text{WI Interest}_t \text{ (if relevant)} \\ &= \text{WI Taxable Income} \\ &* 0.33 \\ &= \text{WI Corporate Income Tax}_t \end{aligned} \tag{3.17}$$

All of the items except capital allowance and expensed investment were outlined above. Expensed investments correspond to intangible expenditures, primarily exploration costs. Tangible investment expenditures, primarily development costs are depreciated using a 25% declining balance. Annual capital allowance equals 25% of the value of the undepreciated investment at the beginning of the year. Undepreciated investment measures the difference between the original cost of the asset less accumulated depreciation. Capital uplift does not apply when computing depreciation for U.K. corporate tax.

Observe the difference between the timing of the tangible spending and capital allowance in Example 3.22. The money is spent in the first two years, but is recovered over the life of the project. This distorts the measured flow of money and is the reason after-tax income (or net income) fails to adequately measure money flows for investment decision-making.

Example 3.22: Assuming the investment schedule used to derive uplift and a 50/50 split among tangible and intangible, determine the expensed Capex and capital allowance for the project. All values in $m.

	(4)	(22)=(4)*0.5	(22)=(4)*0.6	(23)	(24)=(23)*0.25
Year	Investment	Intangible (Expensed)	Tangible (Capitalized)	Undepreciated Capital	Capital Allowance
0-1	1,106.00	553.00	553.00	553.00	138.25
1-2	663.00	331.50	331.50	746.25	186.56
2-3	0.00	0.00	0.00	559.69	139.92
3-4	0.00	0.00	0.00	419.77	104.94
4-5	0.00	0.00	0.00	314.82	78.71
5-6	0.00	0.00	0.00	236.12	59.03
6-7	0.00	0.00	0.00	177.09	44.27
7-8	0.00	0.00	0.00	132.82	132.82
Total	1,769.00	884.50	884.50		884.50

The timing impact of declining balance depreciation in most projects is understated by this example. Because depreciation is calculated as 25 percent of the book value, the book value never reaches zero. This example, like most software, assumes that any remaining book value is written off in the last year of production.

Example 3.23: Derive the UK CT and after-tax income schedule for the project. Assume a 33% CT rate. All values in $m.

	(1)	– (9)	– (2)	– (22)	– (24)	– (21)	= (25)	– (26)	= (27)
Year	WI Revenue	Opex	Royalty	Intangible (Expensed)	Capital Allowance	PRT	Taxable Income	Income Tax	AT Income
0-1	0.00	0.00	0.00	553.00	138.25	0.00	-691.25	-228.11	-463.14
1-2	1,586.00	83.00	198.25	331.50	186.56	0.00	786.69	259.61	527.08
2-3	1,393.00	99.00	174.125	0.00	139.92	0.00	979.95	323.38	656.57
3-4	1,086.00	136.00	135.75	0.00	104.94	226.84	482.47	159.21	323.25
4-5	684.00	128.00	85.5	0.00	78.71	0.00	391.79	129.29	262.50
5-6	532.00	122.00	66.5	0.00	59.03	98.75	185.72	61.29	124.43
6-7	391.00	111.00	48.875	0.00	44.27	38.91	147.94	48.82	99.12
7-8	307.00	109.00	38.375	0.00	132.82	0.00	26.81	8.85	17.96
Total	5,979.00	788.00	747.375	884.50	884.50	364.50	2,310.12	762.34	1,547.78

Net Cash Flow Derivation

Owing to the distortions arising from depreciation (called a *non-cash charge*), the best measure of the true cash flows in a project is defined by Net Cash Flow. The basic equation is:

$$\begin{aligned} \text{WI Net Revenue}_t &- \text{WI Opex}_t \\ &- \text{WI PRT}_t \\ &- \text{WI UK CT}_t \\ &- \text{WI Capex}_t \\ &= \text{WI NCF}_t \end{aligned} \quad \textbf{(3.18)}$$

Example 3.24 derives NCF from the data in the previous examples by subtracting the costs from WI Revenue. The normal cash flow pattern, with negative values followed by positive NCF, emerges here as well, yielding a total NCF of $1547.78. Observe that total AT income equals the total NCF of the project. The value of $1,547.78 indicates that it does not matter which is used if only the totals are used to make investment decision. Comparing the timing of the cash flows in each produces a totally different picture, however. After-tax income shows smaller negative values (roughly a $400 million difference in the first year) and larger positive values in the early years of the project. NCF makes up the difference in the later years of the project.

Example 3.24: Compute the NCF for the project. All values in $m.

	(1)	- (9)	- (2)	- (4)	- (21)	- (26)	= (28)
Year	WI Revenue	Opex	Royalty	Capex	PRT	Income Tax	NCF
0-1	0.00	0.00	0.00	1,106.00	0.00	-228.11	-877.89
1-2	1,586.00	83.00	198.25	663.00	0.00	259.61	382.14
2-3	1,393.00	99.00	174.13	0.00	0.00	323.38	796.49
3-4	1,086.00	136.00	135.75	0.00	226.84	159.21	428.20
4-5	684.00	128.00	85.50	0.00	0.00	129.29	341.21
5-6	532.00	122.00	66.50	0.00	98.75	61.29	183.46
6-7	391.00	111.00	48.88	0.00	38.91	48.82	143.39
7-8	307.00	109.00	38.38	0.00	0.00	8.85	150.78
Total	5,979.00	788.00	747.38	1,769.00	364.50	762.34	1,547.78

Accountants and lawyers, often use after-tax income for various legal and accounting purposes, not for investment decision-making. AT income distorts the cash flow projects by ignoring the timing of tangible investment expenditures. Using non-cash charges, like depreciation and amortization, compounds this distortion. For these charges, no money actually changes hands. Depreciation and amortization are required to compute taxes and financial book earnings, not NCF.

Integrating and Timing of Taxes

Government revenue collections from royalty, PRT and corporate taxes involve some complicated interactions. The net impact is not as complicated as first appears, however. Even though the sum of the taxes (0.125 + 0.50 + 0.33) equals 0.955, the government does not actually take 95.5% of revenues from a project. Because royalty is a deduction against PRT and CT, and PRT against CT, the real burden for any combination of U. K. taxes can be found by solving Equation 3.19.

$$\text{AT Value} = (1 - \text{Royalty Rate}) * (1 - \text{PRT}) * (1 - \text{CT}) \quad \textbf{(3.19)}$$

For the values cited above, the effective value of production is (1 – 0.125)∗(1 – 0.50)∗(1 – 0.33) or 0.2931. Companies keep 29.31% of revenues and the government takes the rest when facing full tax rates. Conversely, with expenses like a dry hole, the company only pays 29.31% of the cost, and the remainder shelters income generated by other projects. The relationship can be illustrated with the table at right. For every pound sterling or dollar earned on a project, the following holds.

TABLE 3.12

Derivation of AT Value of Revenue

Revenue	$1.0000
∗ 0.125	– 0.125
= After-royalty revenue	= $0.875
∗ 0.50 PRT rate	– 0.4375
= After-PRT revenue	=0.4375
∗ 0.33	– 0.1444
= After-tax revenue	= 0.2931

The same relationship applies for any combination of taxes. Dropping royalty, as provided in later tax regimes, provides less tax relief than often believed. Dropping royalty increases AT revenue to the investor to 33.5% [=(1 – 0)∗(1 – 0.50)∗(1 – 0.33)]. Therefore, dropping a 12.5% royalty only adds to the investors take by about 4%.

Another, often neglected element of tax management concerns the timing of payment. As indicated earlier, PRT is paid two months after the close of the chargeable period. A tax on revenue received in December is paid two months later, while the PRT obligation incurred on revenue received in January flows out of the treasury eight months later. Such delays offer considerable opportunity for scheduling inflows and outflows to add value to the treasury. For instance, money received in January can be invested in interest bearing accounts for the remaining 7 months. Though the amount of interest earned may be small at the project level, when combined with revenues from all projects may amount to millions in interest earnings.

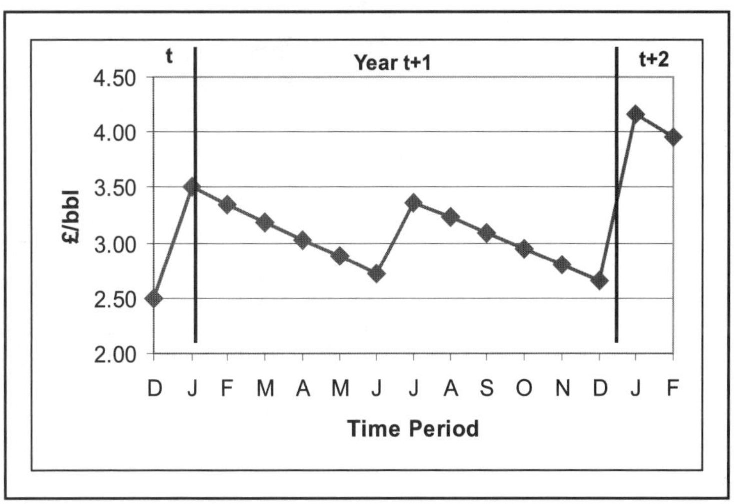

Figure 3.10 Income per barrel from the U. K. sector over a three-year period

Figure 3.10 illustrates the basic concepts for a three-year period. The line reflects the changing value over the year, adjusted for the time value of money. The January price in year t + 1 is worth less than the same value next year, due to the falling corporate tax rate. More importantly, the price in June is worth less than January due its immediate payment to the government. The time varying value of production is the reason some effort is made to minimize revenues at the end of the chargeable period, while maximizing revenues early in the chargeable period (scheduling of plant shutdowns for maintenance and de-bottlenecking). This takes the form of maximizing production in Jan., Feb. and Mar., then shutting the platform in for maintenance the last three months. The max and min values vary between year t, t+1, and t+2 because of changes in the income tax rate taking place at the same time.

Tariff Receipts

The concept of tariffs is becoming a more important issue in the North Sea. As major, existing platforms decline and marginal fields become more prominent, excess capacity is created in existing process and transportation (conveyance) facilities. Developers of marginal fields may install their own production facilities or lease them from existing systems. Smaller, marginal fields often cannot sustain the high cost of installing separate facilities. Owners of existing facilities can benefit by leasing their extra capacity to these fields in the form of a tariff.

Tariff receipts, or tariff payments in the case of a satellite field, can have a major impact on net cash flow. The added profits arise from agreements between field groups for the processing of the satellite's produced and/or injected fluids on an existing host platform. Tariff Receipts Allowance (TRA) allows the tariff income on the first 250,000 metric tonnes of produced fluids per PRT period (10,000 barrels/day) to be free from PRT – regardless of the monetary value of the tariff. While this income is still subject to Royalty and Corporation Tax, the overall tax burden on this revenue is much lower than that on a barrel of oil production (assuming the host field is beyond the PRT safeguard period). This income may offset operating costs significantly and could defer abandonment by lowering the host platform's economic limit.

Figure 3.11 shows a situation where a company has a significant interest in the host platform, but has no interest in a satellite field. The value on the remaining reserves at the platform will be increased by about 40% by the tariff income. The realization that controlling production and transportation mechanisms added value began with the Forties Field. BP management has publicly commented that tariff receipts from the Forties production system and pipeline would add more value than producing the Forties reserves (over 4 billion barrels). This motivated a furious effort in the UK and other worldwide locales to lock-up the production and transportation system. Some called this focusing on "core assets."

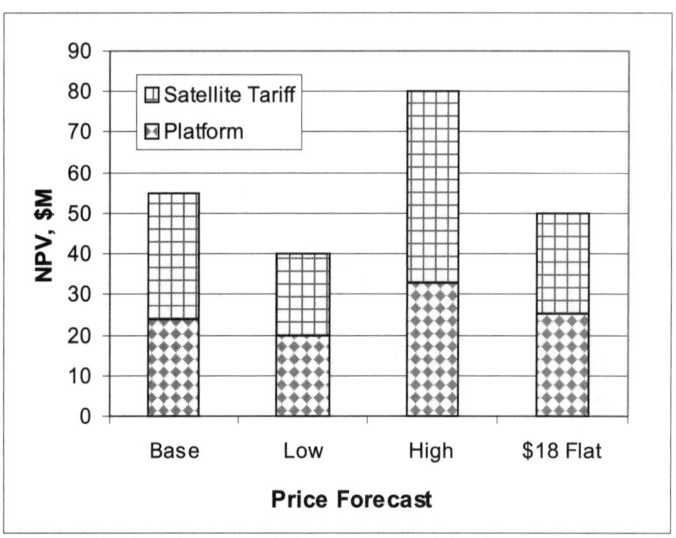

Figure 3.11 Share of platform NPV, with and without satellite tariff

Figure 3.12 illustrates the potential benefits of controlling the infrastructure in an area. The figure represents a scenario where a greater interest is held in the satellite field (25%) than in the host platform (17.1%). The satellite pays a £100 tariff to the platform. The tariff is a deduction to the satellite platform and revenue to the platform. Classical analysis treats each legal entity separately, and, as such, fails to capture the real value to the treasury.

£100 Tariff at 33% CT rate

	Satellite @ 25.0% WI	**Platform @ 17.1%**
Pre-tax Payment or Receipt	-25.00	17.10
Post-tax Effect	-16.75	11.46

Total Cost = -16.75 + 11.46 = -5.29

or

= (25% - 17.1%)∗(100)∗(1 - 0.33) = -5.29

Figure 3.12 Satellite and platform tariff computation

The £100 expenditure creates a post-tax lost of £-16.75 to the satellite, and post-tax gain of £11.46, yielding a net loss of £-5.29. The value to the treasury is negative, but not as negative as just looking at the satellite fields alone. Looking at the whole, not the pieces, is called *downstream benefits*. Ignoring the downstream benefits of an asset typically understates the real value to the treasury.

The simple summation of the individual asset values misses several critical points. First, the satellite field may make important investment decisions, totally independent of the downstream. Again, this partial analysis distorts, often seriously, important investment decisions. Second, the process of consolidating and tracking multiple satellites going through several platforms, each with several transportation options, complicates the analysis to the extent that most investors elect to ignore the problem. Simplifying the analysis to avoid the complexity ultimately loses money for the investor.

The current problem arose because analytical tools had difficulty integrating separate assets accurately and easily in the past. This process can now be achieved; though, not with the mainframe software designed in the 70' and 80's that has been converted to the PC. The process of understanding the complex interaction between assets is termed *value chain analysis*. The process is no more complicated than your corner grocery store owner trying to understand which product adds value to their treasury. Chapters 8 and 9 cover this topic in more detail.

Summary

The U.K. tax regime wins the dubious award of being the most complicated mechanism for collecting taxes. Most professionals have a difficult time understanding the relationship amongst the taxes, much less altering technical decisions to maximize the value of projects for the company. This complexity arises from 1) varying rates depending on receipt of a license, 2) sequencing of allowances, and 3) conditional provisions (safeguard).

Even with this complexity, the current tax regime appears quite effective at taxing larger fields while encouraging smaller field development, at least now. As the U.K. sector of the North Sea matures, benefits for smaller, more marginal field developments will be needed even more.

INDONESIA NCF

Indonesia, the only OPEC member in Asia, is a senior producing country, having produced oil for more than 100 years. It contains very mature producing areas and also relatively unexplored areas. Like most mature areas, Indonesia faces problems with replacing production, especially as newly discovered reserve sizes decline (roughly 20 million barrels onshore and 40-50 million barrels offshore). One problem plaguing successful investment activities stem from delays due to governmental bureaucracy, and the political uncertainties that arose after the fall of the Suharto government. The government claims to recognize this and is making overtures to correct the problem. With the long production history in Indonesia, the present infrastructure with existing services, markets, and procedures can produce attractive investment results once the bottlenecks are eliminated.

The right, both Signature and Production, to develop and explore is acquired primarily through bonus bidding, where the high bidder normally wins the right to produce. PSC's are awarded based primarily on Signature Bonus (which includes 3 parts) – 1: Compensation for Information, 2: Equipment & Services and 3: Educational Grant) and Work Program (bid in $). A production Bonus is bid, but that item is usually negotiated upwards by Pertamina to conform to other PSC's in the area, where the high bidder normally wins this right. The term of a PSC is for 30 years, with an initial exploration period of 6 years and an option by the contractor to extend for an additional 4 years. If commercial quantities are not discovered during the initial 6 years or the extension, then the contact terminates in its entirety. Acreage is typically consolidated into concession areas. Each concession area is treated as a separate ring fence like the reservoir for the U.K. PRT (i.e., a separate company).

Operations and taxes are governed by the specific terms of the *Production Sharing Contract* (*PSC*) or *Production Sharing Agreement (PSA)*. Each PSC is initially negotiated with the government oil company – Pertamina, and then approved by the Minister of Oil and Gas (after authority is given by the President of the Republic of Indonesia). The President must give authority for each PSC to be awarded. Because the PSC's are negotiated separately and independent of each other, significant variations often arise. Pertamina has a model contract based on the Terms existing at the time the contract is signed (Incentive Package). They do not vary (except for bonus amounts) from the model for the original contract period (30 yrs) for PSC's signed during a particular vintage. When contracts are extended past the initial period, then variations in splits and other items may exist. This is highly dependent on the PSC area and the remaining potential in the block; moreover, the nature of the PSC may vary as the life of the PSC ends. Caltex, for instance, effectively switched to a service contract at the end of the life of their PSC.

Even though each PSC has unique features, common elements apply to all. Aside from the Signatory and Production bonus, Indonesia was compensated in two basic ways: profit hydrocarbons, and income tax. These items are outlined more completely below.

Background on PSC's

Because of the growing popularity of PSA's, Figure 3.13 compares the Indonesian and Egyptian PSA's to highlight common differences. The picture of a barrel of oil is split into two categories: *cost oil* and *profit oil*. Cost oil represents the volume of production allocated to the producer to recover Capex and Opex costs. In most countries, the operator carries the state or pays 100% of these costs, though the state may elect to invest directly. Setting the percentage allocated to cost recovery impacts the investing process greatly. Too low a percentage and the investment costs can't be recovered. Too high a percentage and the state loses money.

Indonesia

First Tranche Production:
20% of Hydrocarbons.

Cost Recovery:
As much as needed up to 80%.

Profit Hydrocarbons:
Varies, but common split to investor is 28.8% oil and 42.31% gas.

Egypt

Cost Recovery:
Allocates 30% of production for cost recovery.

Excess Cost Recovery:
Production exceeding that neededto recovery costs is split between state and investor.

Profit Hydrocarbons:
15-20% of oil to investor depending on production volume.

Figure 3.13 Cost and Profit Oil for two PSA's

One solution, practiced in Egypt, sets cost recovery at 30%, and then specifies a formula for handling the excess cost recovery. One adaptation forces the investor to give back 100% of the excess cost oil, while another splits the excess cost recovery 85/15% to the state. This effectively bounds cost recovery at an upper level of 30%, and it may be less. In practice, this works well when new fields come on line because the 30% adequately covers investment. As fields decline, the 30% amount fails to cover Opex and additional Capex, which often forces premature abandonment because of adequate investments. Indonesia solves the problem by allocating 80% of the production for cost recovery.

Only 80% of production flows into cost recovery, because in August 1988 the First Trance Production (FTP) contracts were introduced. FTP's applied to all new contracts and extensions of existing owners. Under the FTP, the first 20% of production is allocated between the government and the WI owners, regardless of costs incurred to produce the oil. Typically, the government receives 71.2% of the 20% or 14.23% of the first production. The remainder goes to the investor and is exempt from cost recovery, but is subject to income tax. At a 48% income tax rate, the investor keeps roughly 3% of the FTP.

Some prefer to think of FTP as a 14.23% royalty, but it is really places a limit of 83% [= 80% + 3%] on cost recovery.

Profit hydrocarbons determine the respective shares of the remaining production. Again, considerable variation exists. Some countries opt for a sliding scale, like Egypt, with the percentage going to the state rising as production increases. Indonesia opts for a different split between oil and gas. In virtually every country, the profit hydrocarbons pay income tax

The basic format for computing the elements of Figure 3.14 is presented in Figure 3.12. While the computations are straightforward, the right sequence is essential. The product of price and production gives gross revenue. FTP is touched on above. The cost recovery and investment credits are deductions that compensate the contractor for their Capex and Opex. The remainder, Profit Hydrocarbons, is divvied up between Pertamina and the contractor according to a set formula. The contractor percentage becomes their taxable income, less an allowance for the *Domestic Market Obligation (DMO)*. After paying income tax and deducting Capex and Opex, yields the NCF for the contractor. Each element is expanded below.

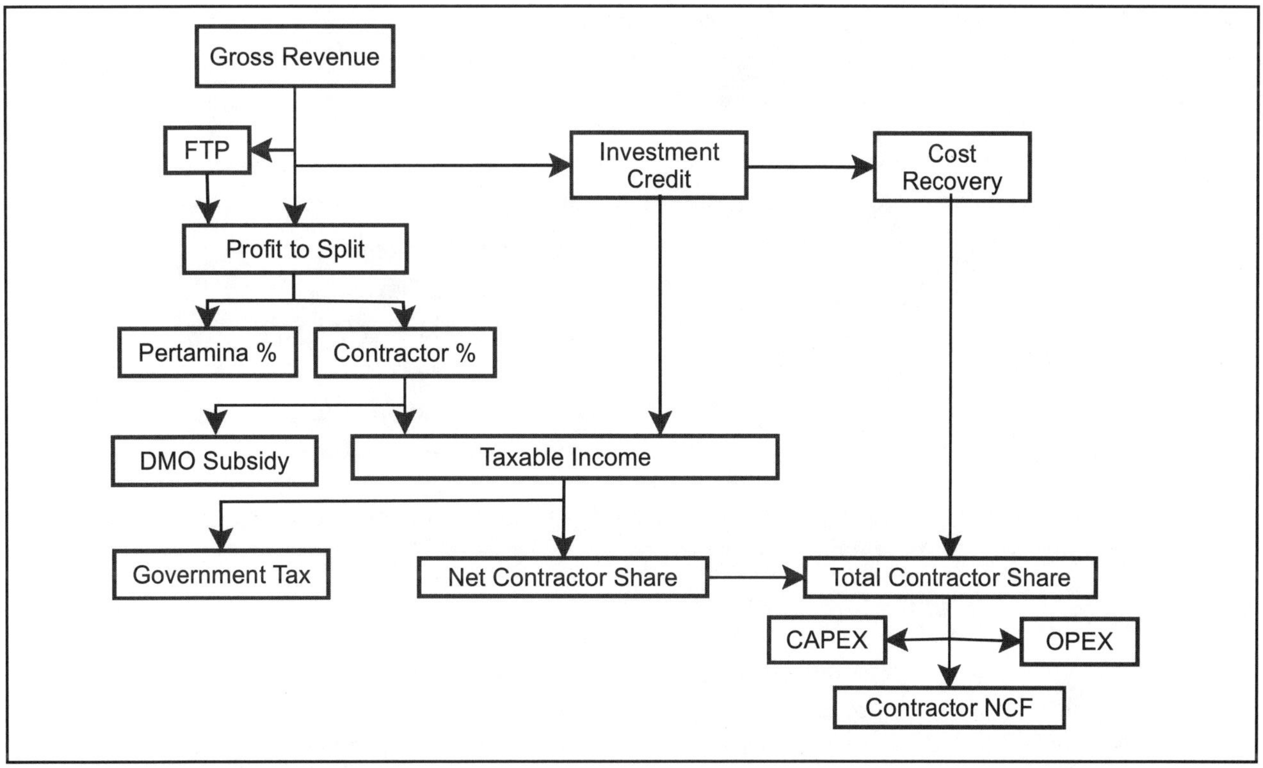

Figure 3.14 Graph of tax calculations in Indonesia

The vast array of different % splits, write-off provisions, cost definitions among the PSC's complicates the analysis. To help understand the variability in the terms, Table 3.13 summarizes the basic inputs needed to generate NCF, along with ranges in the values observed currently and in the past. The reader can see that considerable variation exists. The process is generally the same, regardless of the actual rates used. The following examples use specific values without reference to specific areas.

TABLE 3.13

Inputs for NCF Derivation with Ranges

Category	Range
First Tranche Production	0% to 20%
Investment Credit	0 to 127% of Capex spent
Pre-production Costs	Expensed or amortized over 5 years
Depreciation: Oil	5 or 7 year at a 25% DB or double declining balance with option to shift to SL
Depreciation: Gas	10% to 25% DB over 4, 5, 7 or 8 years
Pre-Tax Profit Split - Contractor %	19% to 71%
DMO obligation	10% to 25% of market
Income tax rate	44% to 48%

To facilitate the understanding of the NCF process, the basic NCF equation is presented first, and then the specific elements addressed in more detail. Equation 3.20 outlines the NCF derivation.

$$\begin{aligned} NCF = & \text{Effective Cost Recovery Hydrocarbons}_t \\ & + \text{Domestic Market Revenue}_t \\ & + \text{Contractor Revenue}_t \\ & - \text{Opex (including over head)}_t \\ & - \text{Pre-Production Costs}_t \\ & - \text{Capex}_t \\ & - \text{Income Taxes}_t \end{aligned} \tag{3.20}$$

The side calculations needed to generate the components of Equation 3.20 are one for Pertamina share and one for the income tax. These are summarized in Equation 3.21.

$$\begin{aligned} & \text{Net Revenue}_t \\ & \quad - \text{Cost Recovery}_t \\ & = \text{Profit Revenue}_t \\ & \quad * \text{Pertamina \%} \\ & = \text{Pertamina Share}_t \end{aligned} \qquad \begin{aligned} & \text{Contractor Revenue}_t \\ & \quad + \text{DMO Revenue}_t \\ & \quad + \text{Investment Credit}_t \\ & = \text{Taxable Income}_t \\ & \quad * \text{Income Tax Rate}_t \\ & = \text{Income Tax}_t \end{aligned} \tag{3.21}$$

The DMO subsidy forces the contractor to sell a portion of their hydrocarbons in the local market at below the going price for the product. This effectively reduces the NCF because of the lost revenue.

First Tranche Production (FTP)

FTP applies only to PSC's formed after 1988. Those created before 1988 ignore the FTP calculation. One big difference between a concession and PSC emerges here. In a concession, the ownership of the minerals transfers to the contractor. Under the PSC format, ownership remains with the local government and is subject to the jurisdiction of the State. Profit sharing and cost recovery merely compensate the contractor for their expenditures.

Example 3.25 demonstrates the derivation of FTP. Of the total Gross Revenue of \$672 million, slightly more than \$134 million is exempted from the cost recovery process. The contractor receives \$26.90 million that is subject to income tax.

Example 3.25: Use the price and production schedules to generate the FTP and Net Revenue for the project assuming a 20% rate, with 80% going to Pertamina. Values in \$m.

	(1)	(2)	(3)=(1)(2)	(4)	(5)=(3)*(4)	(6)=(3)–(5)	(7)=(3)*0.04
Year	Production M bbls	Price, \$/bbl	Gross Revenue	FTP Oil%	FTP	Net Revenue	Contractor FTP
0-1	0.00	0.00	0.00	20	0.00	0.00	0.00
1-2	5.35	18.00	96.30	20	19.26	77.04	3.85
2-3	10.60	18.00	190.80	20	38.16	152.64	7.63
3-4	8.60	19.00	163.40	20	32.68	130.72	6.54
4-5	6.10	19.00	115.90	20	23.18	92.72	4.64
5-6	3.30	20.00	66.00	20	13.20	52.80	2.64
6-7	1.60	21.00	33.60	20	6.72	26.88	1.34
7-8	0.30	22.00	6.60	20	1.32	5.28	0.26
Total	35.85		672.60		134.52	538.08	26.90

Cost Recovery Hydrocarbons (CRH)

Cost recovery hydrocarbons is the summation of the following items:

$$\begin{aligned}\text{Cost Recovery Hydrocarbons}_t = &\ \text{Opex}_t \\ &+\text{Expensed Investment}_t \\ &+\text{Depreciation}_t \\ &+\text{Amortization}_t \\ &+\text{Investment Credit}_t\end{aligned} \tag{3.22}$$

Operating expenses, including overhead are items likely to have no future salvage value. Indonesia defines Opex like other countries. Depreciation includes casing, tubing, platforms, pipelines, etc. Pre-1990 licenses used a double declining balance depreciation based on either a 7 or 14-year life. So, a 7 year investment would use a (1/7)*2 = 0.2857 DB schedule. After 1990, the basic depreciation schedule follows a fixed DB rate, like 10 to 25% for a specified number of years. Any remaining depreciation is written-off in the last year. The life and percentage varies between oil and gas Capex.

Example 3.26 illustrates the capital recovery process assuming that the project qualifies for a 25% DB over a 5-year period. The Capex in column 8 is depreciated for the two-investment periods in column 10. Observe that the total recovery equals the initial expenditure with the remainder being written-off in the fifth year. The sum of the two capital recoveries equals the original Capex.

The expensed investment category in Equation 3.22 covers several different elements. One is the actual Capex that is expensable, like rig rate, mud, drill bits, etc. Dry holes and seismic expenditures may also fall into this category depending on when the expenditure is made.

A more complicated aspect of expensed investments concerns the category called – *pre-production costs*. Costs incurred after the PSC is signed and before production begins cannot be charged to Pertamina. The CRH process accumulates these pre-production costs until production begins. Once production commences, the costs are included in the CRH. The actual handling of the pre-production costs depends on when the PSC was signed. Before 1988, the pre-production costs were included in amortization, using a

Example 3.26: Assuming all Capex qualifies for a 25% DB rate over a 5 year period, determine the capital recovery schedule for the project. Values in $m.

	(8)	(9)	(10)=Capex * (9)		(11)
			Investment in Year:		
Year	Capex	DB Factor	1-2	2-3	Total Depreciation
0-1	0	0.25	0.00	0.00	0.00
1-2	48	0.25	12.00	0.00	12.00
2-3	112	0.25	9.00	28.00	37.00
3-4	0	0.25	6.75	21.00	27.75
4-5	0	0.25	5.06	15.75	20.81
5-6	0	0.25	15.19	11.81	27.00
6-7	0	0.25	0.00	35.44	35.44
7-8	0	0.25	0.00	0.00	0.00
Total	160		48.00	112.00	160.00

5-year SL method. After that time, they are expensed if revenues are sufficient to offset them. Pre-production costs may be carried forward under the new system.

CRH cannot make Pertamina's share negative. The contractor funds all the costs until commercialization. This is sometimes called carrying the State. When declared commercial, Pertamina has the right to demand a 10% undivided interest in the project for themselves or another Indonesian firm. The Indonesian participant must compensate the contractor for 10% of the pre-production costs by writing a check, or can opt to pay the 10% out of future entitlements (with a 50% penalty applied). This is another example of the State being carried by the investor. After electing to participate, the Indonesian partner pays 10% of all future costs.

The last category is the *investment credit (IC)*. The IC applies to fixed facilities, such as platforms, pipelines, processing equipment, etc., but excludes drilling and completion costs. If costs exceed revenues, the IC must be carried forward. With the restriction of a 2-year carry forward, the IC is deducted before Opex and other costs, which have an unlimited carry forward provision. With IC rates of 17-20% for most PSC's, but as high as 110% for joint-operating agreements (JOA's), IC effectively alters the share splits. The IC is computed when the asset is declared ready for service.

Example 3.27: Given the following costs and a 17% IC rate and assuming that all Capex and $23M of pre-production costs qualify for IC, determine CRH. Values in $m.

	(12)	(13)	(14)	(15)	(16)=12+13+14+15	(17)
Year	Opex	Pre-Production Cost	Capital Recovery	Investment Credit	Cost Recovery Hydrocarbons	Cumulative CRH
0-1	0.00	65.00	0.00	3.91	68.91	68.91
1-2	51.50	0.00	12.00	8.16	71.66	140.57
2-3	63.50	0.00	37.00	19.04	119.54	260.11
3-4	43.00	0.00	27.75	0	70.75	330.86
4-5	30.50	0.00	20.81	0	51.31	382.17
5-6	12.50	0.00	27.00	0	39.50	421.67
6-7	8.00	0.00	35.44	0	43.44	465.11
7-8	1.15	0.00	0.00	0	1.15	466.26
Total	210.15	65.00	160.00	31.11	466.26	

Several features complicate the IC. First, the PSC agreements stipulate that Pertamina must always receive 25% or more of the production (it was 49% before 1988). If IC causes that number to fall below 25%, the IC is disallowed. Any cost included in the Plan of Development is eligible for IC. What makes this difficult is the movement to secondary and tertiary production, which is seldom recognized in the Plan of Development. Costs designed to win more oil normally qualify for IC, but rate acceleration projects do not.

The CRH totals $466 million. The real test, however, will be when the analysis matches revenues and costs. Again, the fundamental rules governing the calculation prevent the Pertamina share from ever going negative. When that happens, cost recovery must be deferred until revenue covers the costs.

Profit Hydrocarbons

The end of the OPEC period that led to a major price decline forced Indonesia to adjust the profit split, just like the UK, Norway and US adjusted their tax regimes. For most of the life of the PSC concept, Pertamina received 85% of the oil and 70% of the gas. After prices fell, the split was increased for the contractor to encourage exploration and development.

The split takes place after certain costs are allowed. These cost recovery hydrocarbons (CRH) include operating costs, maintenance/overhaul costs, depreciation, amortization, and an investment credit, as defined in Equation 3.22.

Example 3.28 displays the timing problems that complicate the calculation. Gross revenue less CRH from the previous example results in negative hydrocarbons in years 0-1 and 6-7. The first negative arises because of capital investment in the first years. The second negative stems from the depreciation write-off. Since Pertamina's share must be positive, the negative values are carried forward until revenue exists to offset the costs. Column 19 gives the timing changes in PRH arising from these carry forward provisions.

The last column, Column 22, modifies the computed CRH to reflect the timing changes in actual cost recovery due to the mismatch between expenditures and revenues. Observe that the total effective CRH of $461.87 is less than the actual expenditure of $466.26. The gap is caused by the inability to recover all costs. The negative $9.84 M in year 6-7 in Column 18 comes from the depreciation write-off, which is greater than revenue. Profit hydrocarbons in year 7-8 are only $5.45 million, so the project fails to recover $4.39 million (= –9.84 + 5.45). The failure to recover all costs occurs in many PSC arrangements.

Example 3.28: Assuming 72% of the profit oil goes to Pertamina, calculate Pertamina's and the contractor's profit shares. Values in $m.

Year	(3)=(1)*(2) Gross Revenue	(16) Cost Recovery Hydrocarbons	(18) Profit Hydrocarbons	(19) PRH with Carry Forward	(20)=(19)*0.72 Pertamina Share	(21)=19 – 20 Contractor Share	(22) Effective CRH
0-1	0.00	68.91	-68.91	-68.91	0.00	0.00	0.00
1-2	96.30	71.66	24.64	-44.27	0.00	0.00	96.30
2-3	190.80	119.54	71.26	26.99	19.43	5.44	163.81
3-4	163.40	70.75	92.65	119.64	86.14	24.12	70.75
4-5	115.90	51.31	64.59	64.59	46.50	13.02	51.31
5-6	66.00	39.50	26.50	26.50	19.08	5.34	39.50
6-7	33.60	43.44	-9.84	-9.84	0.00	0.00	33.60
7-8	6.60	1.15	5.45	0.00	0.00	0.00	6.60
Total	672.60	466.26	206.34	114.70	171.16	47.92	461.87

CHAPTER 3

Income Tax

Indonesian income taxes range from 44% to 58%, again depending on when the PSC was approved. The most common and recommended rate is 48%. This rate is a combination of an actual income tax rate of 35% and a 20% dividend rate [0.48 = 0.35 + (1 – 0.35) * 0.2]. The 48% rate is applied to taxable income, defined as gross revenue less allowed deductions. The investment credit is excluded in the derivation of taxable income.

Example 3.29: Derive the DMO obligation for the project. Values in $m.

	(23)	(24)	* (25)	= (26)	(27) = (23) – (24)
Year	Contractor Production	Local Market Production	DMO Price	DMO Revenue	Contractor Production – DMO
0-1	0.00	0	18.00	0.00	0.00
1-2	1.50	0	18.00	0.00	1.50
2-3	2.97	0	18.00	0.00	2.97
3-4	2.41	0	19.00	0.00	2.41
4-5	1.71	0	19.00	0.00	1.71
5-6	0.92	0.092	5.00	0.46	0.83
6-7	0.45	0	21.00	0.00	0.45
7-8	0.08	0.008	5.50	0.05	0.08
Total	10.04	0.101		0.51	9.94

Equation 3.21 defined taxable income as the sum of DMO revenue, contractor revenue (without DMO revenue, and investment credit. This differs from other countries, where costs are considered directly. However, in a PSC, where costs are recovered before the profit split, multiplying profit production by the contractor share effectively deducts those costs without having to consider them again. Investment credits are added back because they are deductions for CRH only, not taxable income.

Example 3.30: Derive the income tax schedule for the project using a 48% tax rate. Values in $m.

	(26)	+ (27)	+ (15)	= (28)	(29) = (28) * 0.48	(30) = (28) – (29)
Year	DMO Revenue	Contractor Revenue	Investment Credit	Taxable Income	Income Tax	AT Income
0-1	0.000	0.00	3.91	3.91	1.88	2.03
1-2	0.000	26.96	8.16	35.12	16.86	18.26
2-3	0.000	53.42	19.04	72.46	34.78	37.68
3-4	0.000	45.75	0.00	45.75	21.96	23.79
4-5	0.000	32.45	0.00	32.45	15.58	16.88
5-6	0.462	16.63	0.00	17.09	8.21	8.89
6-7	0.000	9.41	0.00	9.41	4.52	4.89
7-8	0.046	1.66	0.00	1.71	0.82	0.89
Total	0.508	186.30	31.11	217.91	104.60	113.31

The domestic market obligation complicates the calculation. The DMO volume is 25% of the total oil liftings multiplied by the contractor's pre-tax profit split, with the total DMO volume limited to the total contractor production volume. DMO production is valued in several ways: $0.20 per barrel in old fields to 25% of the actual market price. Some fields us 10% of market price. DMO terms change over time, with the contractor receiving full market rates for the first 60 months from the date the field is placed on production. This effectively exempts them from the DMO.

Taxable income is positive, even in the first year, because of the investment credit. To be correct, the IC should be carried forward until revenues actually exist. Column 29 is the payment to the Indonesian government, and is a part of the NCF calculation.

Project NCF

NCF for the project is derived from adding the revenue sources and then subtracting all costs, as given in Equation 3.20 earlier. Example 3.31 shows the derivation.

Example 3.31: Derive the NCF schedule for the project. Values in $m.

	(22)	(26)	(27)	(12)	(13)	(8)	(29)	(30)
Year	Effective CRH	DMO Revenue	Contractor Revenue	Opex	Pre-Production Cost	Capex	Income Tax	NCF
0-1	0.00	0.00	0.00	0.00	65.00	0.00	1.88	-66.88
1-2	96.30	0.00	26.96	51.50	0.00	48.00	16.86	6.90
2-3	163.81	0.00	53.42	63.50	0.00	112.00	34.78	6.95
3-4	70.75	0.00	45.75	43.00	0.00	0.00	21.96	51.54
4-5	51.31	0.00	32.45	30.50	0.00	0.00	15.58	37.69
5-6	39.50	0.46	16.63	12.50	0.00	0.00	8.21	35.89
6-7	33.60	0.00	9.41	8.00	0.00	0.00	4.52	30.49
7-8	6.60	0.05	1.66	1.15	0.00	0.00	0.82	6.34
Total	461.87	0.51	186.30	210.15	65.00	160.00	104.60	108.93

Total NCF for the project is $108.93 million. This value is slightly less than the AT income, which the examples for other countries in this chapter showed were equal. The difference results again from the inability to recover all the costs, as shown in the previous examples.

Summary

The effective profit from this example is about 16% of the gross revenue (= 108/672), which is low by international standards now. Contractors keep almost double this amount in most other countries. This problem is compounded by the aging nature of the Indonesian area, though some new areas are being opened up, especially in deep-water

PSC's attract investment when potential production is large enough to make values like 16% quite meaningful. However, when the area has limited or unproven production capability, PSC's discourage new entrants to take the risk of entering the country.

VALUE OF INVESTMENTS IN SELECTED COUNTRIES

Investment value varies depending on its location, quantity, cost of finding and developing, chemical characteristics, and equally as important, the quantity kept by the local government and the timing of the tax computation. Historical objectives of maximizing producing rates just do not work in a world of complicated tax systems, and as seen in the four country examples, significant differences in the form, content, and timing of taxing exist.

Technical professionals often ask, "Does the impact of taxes really matter?" Table 3.14 summarizes the economic performance measures from several countries. These measures are explained in detail in Chapter 5. It is only important to realize that significantly different results occur in various countries.

TABLE 3.14

Comparison of Performance Measures for Selected Countries

Country	NPV_{10}	IRR	NPV_{10}/INV_{10}	DPO	$SIV_{10/4}$
U. S.	60.08	13.41	0.15	9.18	117.88
U. K.	165.02	18.75	0.42	6.87	343.61
Norway	68.74	14.81	0.17	8.35	75.21
Trinidad	-25.79	-0.31	-0.10	none	-25.79
Egypt	283.13	20.6	0.65	6.84	791.45
Canada	7.25	11.21	0.44	16.38	45.28
Indonesia	81.99	13.55	0.17	7.9	167.55

In addition, the relative ranking of countries varies with the size of the project. For larger or smaller projects, with different timing characteristics, the relative attractiveness may change dramatically.

The profit estimates depend on length of exploration, first production, flow rates, size of investment, and so on. Changing just one item often shifts the preference to another country. Variation in the valuation across countries is the only message in Table 3.14. The investment performance measures are discussed in Chapter 5 in detail. DPO stands for discounted payout, and SIV for strategic investment value. The same values for production, price, Opex and Capex were used, with only the effective tax regime accounting for differences in the results.

CHAPTER 3

SUMMARY

Monetizing investment opportunities frustrates many owing to the arduous, time-consuming nature of the task. The classic phrase, "garbage in, garbage out" applies at every step in the process. Every input, including the tax elements, face considerable risk. The lesson from historical appraisal of investment decisions is that the major cause of poor investments results from ignoring or omitting important variables. The variables we consider formally, no matter how accurate the estimates, seldom destroy a significant amount of the investment value. Only a sound assessment of the money remaining to the investor, after all costs are recognized, gives them a chance of achieving their goals.

For many investments, the tendency is to look at before-tax profits and assume that taxes take care of themselves. The examples demonstrate that this is not true. Taxes are designed and implemented to shift the burden of risk and timing to the investor and away from the local country.

Tax variation among countries also demonstrates that investment opportunities vary in value, depending on whose country they are located, and the type of producing conditions. Just a few of the many tax regimes existing around the world are presented. The following chapters transform the NCF's into measures of profitability (Chapter 5), and then assess the impact of risk on the project (Chapter 8). The key assumption throughout this chapter is that the input numbers were valid. Keep in mind the imperfection of every number that goes into an assessment of an investment opportunity. The question is how imperfect (risk assessment) and what can be done to mitigate the risks (risk management).

REFERENCES

3.1 Brealy and Myers, *Principles of Corporate Finance*, McGraw Hill (1996).

3.2 Daniel Johnston, *Petroleum Fiscal Systems and Production Sharing Contracts*, Penwell Press (1994).

CHAPTER 4

THE MANAGEMENT SETTING: GOALS AND ISSUES

The knowledge required to conduct business, along with a simple overview of common organizational perspectives and roles of each group, were highlighted in Chapter 1. The second chapter provided some perspectives on the process for making investment decisions, with summary measures of historical performance. This chapter expands on these general processes and the NCF derivation in the last chapter to include greater details on approaches used to achieve management objectives. Figure 1.6 showed arrows flowing from the headquarters to the operating units. This chapter looks at the elements that go into those arrows.

Two issues dominate the management decision-making process: identifying and successfully implementing the best investment opportunities that satisfy the objectives and goals set by management, and communicating that performance to interested parties, both within and outside the organization. Like most knowledge, simple statements of the theory disguise the complexity inherent in the successful execution, and this complexity increases with the size of the organization. One person organizations hopefully can communicate with themselves exactly, but every employee added increases the chances of miscommunication dramatically. Multinational organizations, with thousands of staff, operating in vastly different cultural, religious, geographical, products, etc. climates, face enormous challenges in trying to build a cohesive, unified team.

One of our colleagues argues that the single most important issue is defining the objectives, and matching the performance measures closely to those objectives.[4.1] The most commonly used phrase to define objectives is "maximize shareholder value." This reflects a market orientation, and defines shareholders as the beneficiaries of the organization. The nominal performance measure is the share price of the organizations stock: rising share prices satisfy the objective. Modern investment theory expands the concept to include share prices rising faster than inflation and/or the market as a whole or competitors. If all shares increase 10% in value, and your company goes up by 7%, the perception is that management failed.

Others complain the market based approach ignores equally as important issues; opting for the phase "maximizing stakeholder value." Stakeholders include citizens of the country or world, purchasers of the product, employees, etc. Companies that build defective nuclear power plants, or emit harmful chemicals or gases certainly impact a larger target area. Others continuing to sell defective tires, or hiding evidence of medical damage from smoking certainly draw the ire of many. Employees probably reflect the stakeholder with the greatest contradiction, benefiting from the increase in share price, but less so if the increase is achieved by laying them off or retiring them.

Much of the revolt against globalization revolves around the feeling that shareholders are getting preference over stakeholders. Each reader has to determine their own feelings on these matters, but observe that, going back to Figure 1.1, any decision must include knowledge from philosophy, ethics, religion, etc. The focus here assumes that management sets goals and objectives, not whether these goals are the right ones. In fact, much of the controversy over governmental and business activities reflects just this point.

The strategic planning process tries to anticipate changes in the business environment, and investment decision-making seeks to implement that vision. Dominating changes include, shifting demand for product(s), supply shifts across countries, legal and environmental restrictions, changing cost structures, etc. Organizations respond by changing organizational structures, cutting employees, adopting different incentive systems to motivate the remaining staff, etc. The business to business (B2B) aspect of the Internet captures the essence the change culture, for example.

This chapter outlines the system for measuring and communicating performance. Understanding the management perspective, and how they interact with outside investors (shareholders and stakeholders) helps technical professionals perform their jobs efficiently and correctly. Far too many disciplines fail to convey the roles and responsibilities of their students within the organizational environment. The attitude seems to be that following the scripted set of procedures learned in school defines successful professionals. Unfortunately, this is a misleading impression. Being good is important, but being good requires adaptability to the organizational objectives. What works well in one organization may differ in another, and both will change over time.

The intended audience is non-business professionals, who need an overview of the business environment. The growing emphasis on financial reporting for comparison with competitors, and implementation of employee incentive systems increases the importance of understanding the systems used by organizations. As the discussion unfolds, the abuses, as well as the proper uses, of the system will be defined.

Overview

Defining the exact starting point for the modern business perspective remains elusive, though one candidate that appeals to us, began with John D. Rockefeller starting Standard Oil of Ohio in the 1870's, eventually leading to the founding of Standard Oil of New Jersey in 1899, combined with innovations made by Mr. Ford in automobile manufacturing. The original 18 companies of Standard Oil of New Jersey became over 39 companies with the break-up of Standard Oil of New Jersey by the U. S. Supreme Court for breaches of anti-trust law. Rockefeller and Ford realized that *economies of scale* can be achieved by increasing the size of the organization. Larger firms produce at lower average costs, in essence. Assuming the product sells at that same price, a lower cost means higher profit margins.

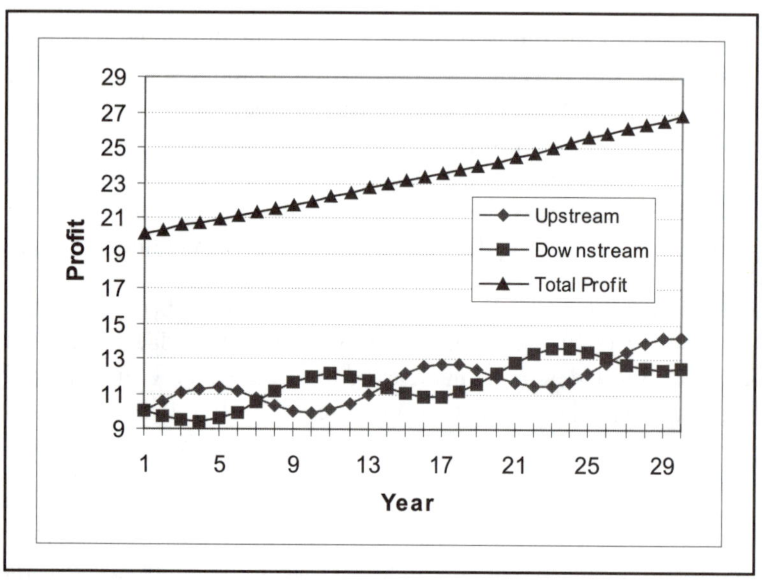

Figure 4.1 Effect of vertical integration between different segments of organization

The real innovation, however, was vertical integration. A comparable buzzword now is *portfolio management.* Messer's Rockefeller and Ford realized that the simplest vehicle for reducing risk was to make a profit at every stage of production (this ignores their in depth understanding of monopoly control as well). Figure 4.1 illustrates the simple relationship between vertically integrated activity. Vertical integration occurs when one unit sells their product to another unit owned by the same company. With Ford, they manufactured the rubber, which was sold to the tire company, that was sold to the automotive company. Rockefeller sold crude oil at the wellhead to his refinery, which sold the gasoline to his filling station. Rising wellhead prices increase upstream profits, but reduce downstream profits, since raw materials reflect a major cost to refiners and retailers. Declining prices reverse this process. By mixing upstream and downstream components properly, the organization shows a stable profit, even though each segment follows a definite business cycle, with downstream countercyclical to upstream. Investors concentrating entirely on one side of the business will experience more volatility in their profits. The stable profitability generated from vertically integrating the portfolio of businesses allows for more aggressive, riskier investing patterns.

Horizontal integration achieves the same stabilization. By having upstream and downstream activity in as many countries of the world as possible, the organization can take advantage of gains in the local business environment. Conversely, risks, like business recessions and expropriation, are offset partially by profits from other countries. Chua and Smith show that effective, worldwide diversification reduces risk, just the opposite of many professionals view of international political risk.[4.2] Royal Dutch Shell is viewed by most financial analysts as having the best mix of horizontal and vertical integration, for this reason.

As industries mature, the growth potential indicated by the rising line in Figure 4.1diminishes. The shift in Bill Gates strategy for Microsoft into other communication mediums indicates a maturing of the computer industry. Petroleum similarly shifted it's investment focus into other minerals like coal and copper, and other lines of business, like retailing (Montgomery Wards), brewing (Miller Brewing), automotive (Avis), office supplies (Reliance Electric), etc.

The conglomerate stages seldom last long, not because the primary industry begins to decline, but because the management skills required to provide the knowledge and experience to properly manage conglomerates faces *diminishing returns*, though there have been several outstanding exceptions.

The shift in required management skills, combined with the ultimate decline of the primary industry, usually leads to massive sales of low performing sectors, and radical retrenchment in the remaining business, called the *core business* in current jargon. This is happening in several industries today. Daimler Benz, the automotive giant, radically restructured the empire built up during the mature stage.[4.3] Likewise, the petroleum industry continues to retrench, often leaving the older, more mature areas entirely. British Petroleum, now Beyond Petroleum, sold it's U. S. onshore operations entirely, while UNOCAL sold it's California operations. The quest is to define and concentrate attention on the core business.

Part of the shifting business environment originates in the age of rapid communication. Rockefeller's vertical integration appeared attractive when the ability to communicate globally was limited. Today, with instantaneous communication around the world, 24 hours a day, 7 days a week, it makes less sense for automotive firms to make radios, tires and other parts. Others can concentrate on making radios and respond to changing market conditions far faster and cheaper than large, integrated firms. So the shifting skill set is motivated by technology as much as industry life-cycle.

Figure 4.2 shows demand growth by region for the last 35 years to illustrate the impact of change. The traditional large consumers, notably Western Europe and North America consumed about 2/3's of the world consumption in 1966. After almost 30 years of flat consumption, the rest of the world was consuming considerably more. With flat or declining populations, companies based in Western Europe or North America are unlikely to achieve high profits in the traditional areas. This prompted the shift in focus from domestic markets into the international arena, both in exploration and production, and refining and retailing. Historical data were taken from the BP Review of World Energy.[4.4]

Perhaps the most intriguing question concerns the continuation of demand growth in the rest of the world for the new century. If global warming and other environmental issues continue to grow in importance, will alternative energy sources become higher priority? Conversely, could abatement of pollution issues and resurgence of the economies in Russia and Asia fuel an even greater growth? Whatever

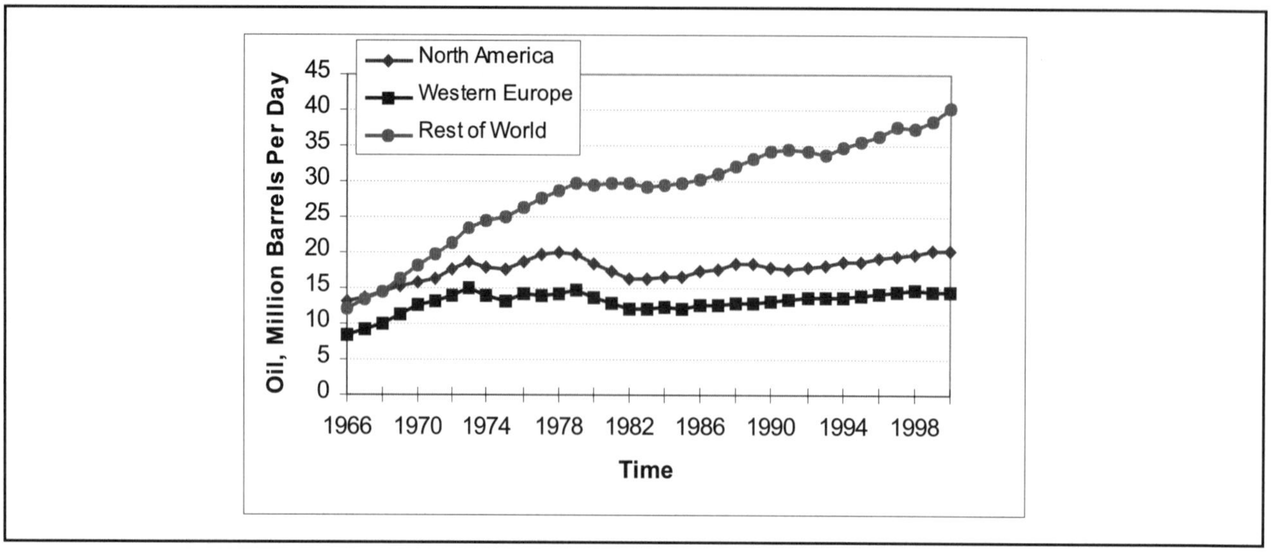

Figure 4.2 Historical World Oil Demand, 1966-2000

transpires, changing demand will control future business conditions. To make a profit in the coming years, companies must manage their assets far more efficiently.

The Basics of Business

Perhaps the best starting point follows from the simple question – Why do businesses exist at all? This question really addresses the issue of what can a business do that an individual cannot? The discussion of the general economy in Chapter 1 showed business or industry as purchasing raw materials and labor in order to produce goods and services for consumers. This promotes the efficient allocation of capital and labor between suppliers and users. Organizations provide a vehicle for combining knowledgeable professionals with sufficient capital to invest in projects earning higher returns than individuals, alone, could achieve. Individuals are limited by knowledge, experience and ability to raise capital. By combining these resources in one entity, a business achieves *economies of scale.*

Figure 4.3 illustrates the management perspective, which views organizations as essentially intermediaries. Firms acquire investment capital from lenders and other investors through various markets – primarily stocks, bonds, and bank borrowings. With other people's capital, the organization applies funds to *overhead*, *working capital,* investments, tax payments, loan repayment, dividend payments, etc. When the investments are successful, *cash flow from operations* are generated, thus, becoming a further inflow of money into the corporate treasury. Another name used for cash flow from operations is *net cash flow* or sometimes just *cash flow.*

The net cash flow or cash flow from operations controls the size of the capital budget for new investments. Since few organizations issue stocks or debt every year, the yearly capital budgets come from profits or cash flows generated from existing projects. When these cash flows fall below projections, for whatever reasons – bad production estimates, poor price forecasting, etc. – insufficient funds exits to finance future projects. Faced with cash shortfalls, most management reacts by cutting expenses. Since most of us can't fire our spouses or children in personal cases, we seek other ways to reduce budgets. But, the two biggest controllable items in most organization's budgets are people and investments; hence, they are the natural places to reduce costs. In fact, cash flow from operations account for 75-85% of new money flowing into the organizational treasury on an annual basis. The lessons from the past are very simple: misestimate cash flows, for whatever reason, and future staffing and spending suffer the consequence.

The top half of Figure 4.3 summarizes the sources of capital – basically loans (or debt) and equity capital. Both components are legal descriptions about ownership of the firm, financial benefits, and voting

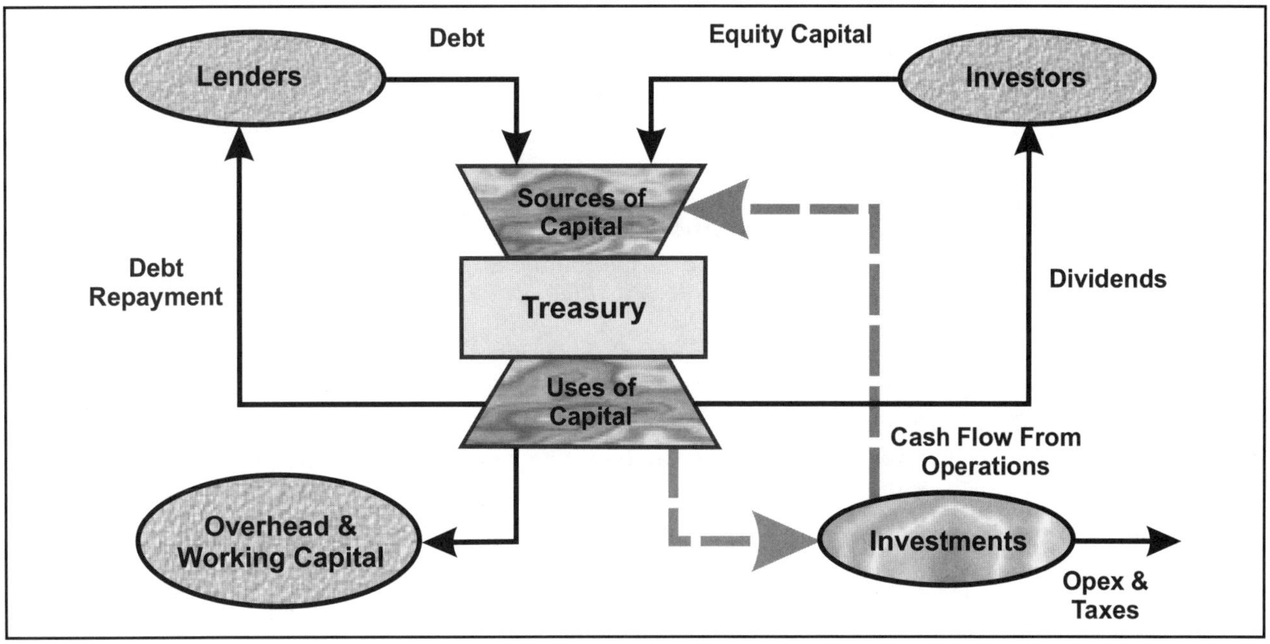

Figure 4.3 Business model of cash flow

privileges, which are discussed further in the *cost-of-capital* discussion. The owners of an organization are investors who purchase shares of private sector corporations or the citizens of a country for state owned entities. Management technically work for the equity holders or shareholders.

Most people prefer more wealth to less wealth. Shareholder value was traditionally viewed as being maximized by satisfying the following performance measures:

1. Making a profit each year,
2. Achieving growth in earnings, assets, equity, etc.
3. Stabilizing growth and profit.
4. Maintaining liquidity and solvency, and
5. Being socially responsible.

The first, and probably most important, task to most management is earning a profit each year. Failure to earn a profit has cost many an executive their job. Profit is necessary for paying dividends and meeting other obligations. Growth satisfies the need to cover the loss of purchasing power due to inflation and to compete with alternative investments. Inflation measures increases or decreases in the cost of goods and services, as explained later in the chapter. If inflation rises by 5% and profits remain constant, the value of the organization erodes. Likewise, since a wide range of investment mediums exist, firms must provide a comparative return to similar investments to attract any capital. For instance, if a risk free savings account paid 8% and an organization's share price increased 6%, where would you invest your money?

Item 3, stability, is important because of the growing dominance of pension plans in the market place. Some estimate that as much as 50-60% of the world stockmarkets or *bourses* share value is held by pension plans. Because pension plans have monthly cash flow obligations to their pensioners, stable dividend streams are crucial to the pension plans cash flow planning. Erratic dividend payments complicates pension plan management; hence their desire to invest in stable dividend streams. Stability appeals to others as well, but pension plans seem to place a great premium on stable dividends.

Liquidity and *solvency* concern future ownership of the organization. Bankruptcy begins with the inability to pay claims, usually salaries, raw material purchases, etc. Highly liquid firms have large volumes of cash or marketable assets, like stock, and low liquidity exists when assets are held in a form difficult to convert into cash, like property, transportation systems, plants for manufacturing, etc. Cash allows immediate payment of obligations, while the more illiquid assets often take time to convert to cash.

Liquidity sounds like a good idea and generally is. Putting too much into illiquid investments reduces the ability to pay claims. Keeping just enough money in cash or very liquid forms to pay claims plus a little extra for errors in estimating cash flows is a tough balancing act. Any money in cash earns less than money invested in long term assets. Most importantly, investors don't need organizations to place their money in account earning minimal interest.

Insolvency becomes the next stage after liquidity. Firms normally become insolvent by failing to pay their debts at the specified time. The creditors have the option under most legal systems to ask for immediate payment. If the firm cannot pay the debt, a *bankruptcy* petition is filed by the creditors. The company is usually placed in receivership, or managed by an outside party named by the court until the firm pays its debt or is liquidated (assets sold to pay the debt). This is called Chapter 7 in the U. S. An intermediate step in the U. S. is called Chapter 11, where the company can legally avoid paying debts while it reorganizes. Solvency, at the extreme, involves transferring ownership of assets from the shareholders to the debtors.

Modern management views items 1-5 above as being too narrowly defined. The typical firm expands the goals and objectives to include phrases like:

- Generating excellent financial results
- Creating a superb environment for people to work,
- Behaving in an ethical and responsible manner
- Giving superior service to customers, and
- Working in partnership with suppliers and contractors.

Quantifying such objectives faces serious difficulties. For most organizations, the real meaning shows up in their incentive systems for staff and management. The incentive system should motivate actions consistent with organizational objectives. Although staff and management often feel the incentive system is out of sync with the real objectives, most also agree on the difficulty, if not impossibility, of matching a simple set of incentives with the complex interaction of goals and objective of major organizations.

These objectives are often quantified as:

- replacing assets
- earning a reasonable profit (defined as *return on capital employed (ROCE)* for most companies or *return on capitalized cost (ROCC)* as defined later)
- earning decent growth of profits and dividends
- lowering operating and development costs
- outperforming the competitors on these measures

How these items are measured is quite important. Every country prescribes certain principles and rules governing measuring and reporting of performance. Though variations exist, the principles outlined below exist in all. One key feature is the reliance on financial reporting, as prepared by financial accountants or *auditors.*

Defining the objectives becomes an art in actual practice. Achieving some performance standard for the shareholders implies that some knowledge of shareholder desires exist. It is quite common for companies to have hundreds of millions of shares or, for the very largest, even a billion shares outstanding. Moreover, these shares are held by rather diverse groups of individuals. Figure 4.4 provides a pie diagram of shareholder distribution for one company. Note that institutions dominate the percentages, while individual and employees, though smaller, have a significant share. This pie diagram is based on roughly 500 million shares outstanding. Most of the institutions, like Wells Fargo Bank, hold the shares in their trust departments for someone else. The single largest shareholder, as it is in many organizations, is the employee savings plan.

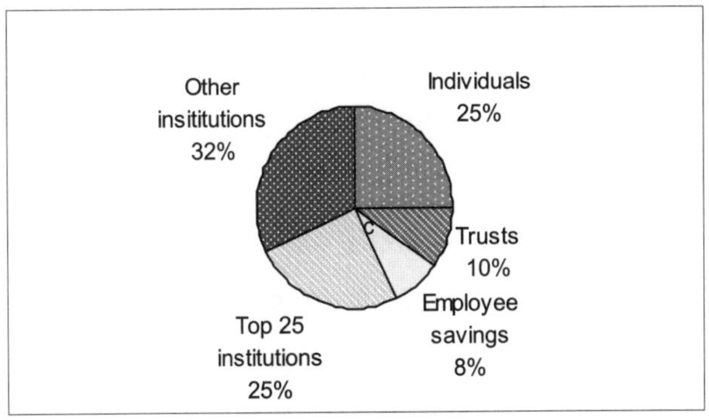

Figure 4.4 Pie diagram of share ownership distribution

To achieve success, the objectives must be defined relative to the interests of the current shareholders and also prospective shareholders. Management practice involves balancing the likely conflicting interests of, say the trusts and institutions, relative to individuals and employee savings plans. Employees, for instance, certainly desire profits and stability, but most would also like to a job. Institutions and trust need stable dividends to fund the cash flow needs of their pensioners.

The information outlined in the next few sections describes the basics of auditing and financial reporting. Like most disciplines professionals can spend years of study and practice to master the detailed intricacies of auditing. A detailed understanding of financial reporting practice is not critical for performing investment comparisons or competitor analysis, but it helps to realize the basis of the reported values and the assumptions under which the values were derived.

FINANCIAL REPORTING: THE BACKGROUND

Like all professional societies, financial reporting involves the interaction of regulatory authorities and professionals in accounting and finance. Most countries require companies offering debt and shares publicly to meet certain reporting and operating requirements. The Securities and Exchange Commission (SEC) in the U. S. and the Department of Trade and Industry (DTI) in the U. K. exemplify such organizations in two countries. The increasing globalization of economies has lead to more international standards of financial reporting, like the 4th directive of the Economic Union (EU), which seeks to consolidate the financial reporting practices of member countries.

The actual implementation of financial reporting rules is left to the accounting professions, like the American Institute of Certified Public Accountants (AICPA) in the U. S. and the Institute of Chartered Accountants (ICA) in the U. K. and Canada. Though the names vary in specific countries and over time, these groups form committees to establish consistent guidelines for financial reporting. These committees go by different names, like Standard Financial Accounting Standard (SFAS) in the U. S. and Certified Chartered Accounting Board (CCAP) in the U. K. Both prepare guidelines and enforce compliance of standard accounting practice (SAP). In some countries, the rules are equivalent to law; other countries treat the rules as guidelines. International accounting firms specialize in counseling investors on the specific procedures in specific countries.

Country variations in financial practices creates problems for anyone trying to operate a truly global organization.. As an attempt to provide consistency amongst countries, the International Federation of Accountants (IFA) meets annually to discuss and understand rule variations internationally. Consistency is important, because of the cost of complying with these rules. Large, international organizations often pay \$5 to \$200 million a year to comply with financial reporting standards in a single country. This number multiplied by several countries and thousands of publicly traded companies implies a significant sum of money is being spent annually to provide financial information.

Why do organizations spend such sums to provide accounting information? Because the reporting is required to access the financial markets of each country. Firms listed in more than one country reconcile the differences between the reporting requirements in each annual report, which adds to the cost of preparation. This dual or multi country reporting will probably increase in the future.

Though *maximizing shareholder value* captures the essence of an organization's objectives, reporting this information necessary for investors to determine the extent wealth is being maximized is the goal of the annual report and associated documents (like the 10K in the U. S.). Financial books are designed to achieve several main tasks:

1. Measurement of costs, profits and asset distribution,
2. Communication of item 1 to interested parties,
3. Comparability of information among companies, and
4. Verifiability of information for accuracy and honesty.

Each task is important in its own right, but collectively provide the mechanism that has helped fuel the globalization of commerce. To achieve efficiency in capital markets, suppliers of capital (banks, shareholders, etc.) require assurance that their capital is being used wisely. Capital users, likewise, need a vehicle for reporting their performance relative to their competitors. The four goals, taken together, provide an avenue for capital users and lenders to make intelligent investment decisions.

Measurement seeks to quantify performance with regard to profitability, growth, stability, liquidity and other issues, which varies, depending on country reporting requirements. Each of these items is explained later as the individual elements of financial reporting are explained in more detail. The report tries to quantify the values associated with the elements of business activity outlined in Figure 4.3. Having hired the auditors to quantify the values, communication arises when the annual report is sent to all shareholders and filed with the designated regulatory authority, and most report are available on the firms web sites now. Some countries require additional reports, like the structure and amount of management salaries and bonuses, in the 10K report filed in the U. S.

Comparability is a critical, yet often misunderstood, task of financial reporting. Companies in different industries, different product lines, and varying geographical areas have various options for reporting their activities. Two basic options were considered by the auditors: report events as they actually happened and let the reader decipher the meaning, or standardize the reports using specified guidelines. Developers of financial reporting understood full well that both systems had advantages and disadvantages. The first option requires detailed knowledge of local country income tax regimes, which few people possess.

CHAPTER 4

The second option was chosen for two basic reasons: it reduced the volume of information needed to compare company performance, and allowed for direct company comparison with less additional analysis. This advantage comes at the cost of users having to learn the basic principles and assumptions underlying the standardized approach.

Perhaps the most critical need is verifiability. The value of financial reporting depends directly on the quality of the information provided. Unscrupulous management could easily manipulate the information to present a distorted image of the organization. Auditing, the branch of accounting responsible for preparing and validating financial reports, developed from the need to guarantee the accuracy of the information. Auditors are hired to insure that the financial reports are a *fair representation* (U. S.) and a *true and fair view* in the U. K. The auditors signature on the financial report implies that the information contained therein accurately reflects the companies performance.

Alas, this assumption of complete integrity seems more doubtful each year. Historical failures, such as the Penn Square bankruptcy, the BCCI collapse, and Rupert Murdoch siphoning funds out of employee pension schemes, suggest severe shortcomings in the system. Several estimates show auditors facing worldwide lawsuits of over $30 billion for failure to find and report management misdeeds.

Financial reports originated in the collapse of the City of Glasgow Bank in 1870 and was later expanded to include all U. K. companies by 1900. The U. S. followed suit almost immediately. Shareholders and lenders used the information to estimate the chance of bankruptcy initially. Since these early days, the list of financial users has expanded to include the following:

- Company management
- Industry competitors
- Investors and investment analysts
- Lenders
- National governments (Department of Energy
- International agencies (World Bank)
- Suppliers (credit analysis)
- Industrial groups (API, UKOOA)
- Special interest (Greenpeace, etc.)
- Incentive schemes

Companies increasingly compare performance of each group using financial reports. The decision to sell, buy, allocate capital, reduce staff, etc. revolves around reported financial performance. Similarly management incentives track financial performance; higher bonuses following improved performance and vice versa. Though well documented abuses of this incentive/performance relationship exist, which has been compounded by the arrogance of individual managers, especially in the entertainment industry, the pay for performance concept dominates in most countries.

One of the fastest growing trends involves using financial indicators for formal comparison of relative company performance. This is called *competitor analysis*. The objective: to identify relative strengths and weaknesses. Used properly, the analysis provides interesting, useful information. Problems occur when the analyst or management places too much weight on one or two years performance, especially when strategies are changing to respond to a new business environment. Dropping or altering a strategy on the basis of last years performance normally indicates a lack of faith in that strategy, and creates confusion and, often uncertainty, during implementation. The benefits from establishing good, consistent strategies outweighs the short-run underperformance.

The other users of financial information, like the Energy Information Agency in the U. S. Department of Energy, compare the performance of groups of companies over time, or more of an industry perspective. International bodies use the information to determine responses to bid requests and other credit evaluations. Special interest groups in the U. S. used financial reports to justify the *Alternate Minimum Tax (AMT)*. These groups convinced Congress that many organizations failed to pay their fair share of income taxes. The AMT requires everyone to pay a minimum tax rate even if they incurred large, legitimate tax deductible expenses that offset their revenues. This is a classic case of abusing a reasonable system designed for another purpose (financial reporting) to achieve the selfish objectives of special interest groups.

ELEMENTS OF FINANCIAL REPORTING

Technical professionals spend considerable effort learning the nuances of the physical system that governs their knowledge base. The financial reporting system is very similar. It attempts to describe annual flows and stock of money or assets held by an organization on a yearly basis. Though financial reporting has no scientific basis, except the rules of elementary math, the basic quest is the same. The general system of financial reporting comprises four main elements. They are:

1. Income statement (flow of money, assets or liabilities)
2. Balance sheet (stock of money, assets or liabilities)

3. Sources and uses statement (or cash flow statement although we dislike this phrase)
4. Supplementary information.

Several points emerge from these components. First, the income statement and balance sheet are linked together. The stock of assets or money as measured by the balance sheet cannot change unless the flow of money or assets (the income statement) varies. A simple diagram illustrates the relationship between the balance sheet and income statement. Figure 4.5 shows the change in company value over time.

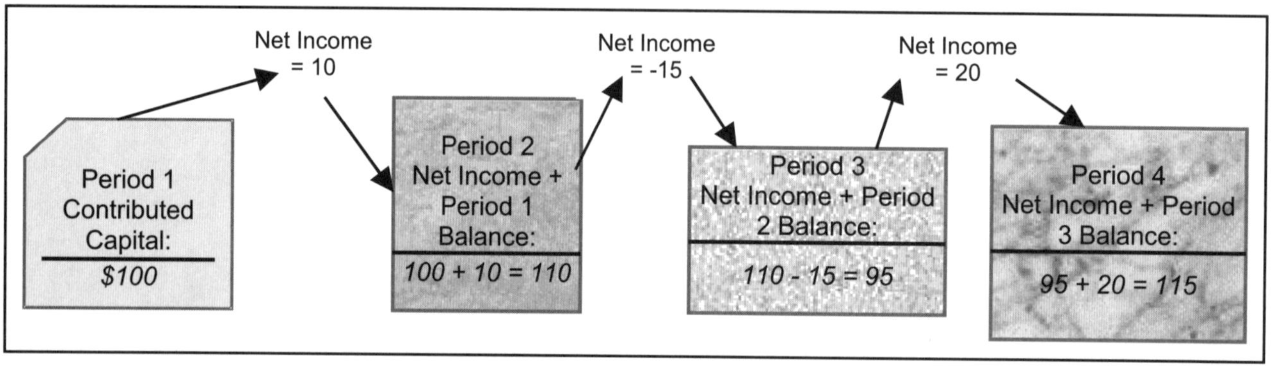

Figure 4.5 Change in company value over time

Period 1 reflects the starting point of an organization when the value arises from capital input by the owners, normally by purchasing shares as part of the original stock offering, called contributed capital. The company uses the capital to buy equipment and other fixed assets to produce their product. If this leads to a positive net income, the total value or year end balance increases by this amount. In the example, the $100 contributed capital led to production levels that generated a $10 net income. Assuming all the monies are reinvested, the stock of money at the end of Period 2 becomes $110 Likewise, negative net income of $-15 in year 3 reduces the total balance to $95. Year 4 shows another profit, hence an increasing balance again.

The net income value (or net profit as some call it) and its components for the companies fiscal year (365 days) are reported on the income statement. The balance sheet measures the sum total of the value at the end of the fiscal year, usually 31 December of the year. Again, the balance sheet also reports information about the distribution of the values. The sources and uses statement measures the change in the balance sheet components between years. Accountants use this statement to reconcile changes over time.

Supplemental information forms the basis for much of the competitor analysis. It includes the footnotes, which describe the basis for the values reported in the income statement and balance sheet, and, as such, contain useful information. The examples provided later illustrate specifics for the petroleum industry on reserves, production, costs, etc. because of its unique reporting requirements.

Income Statement

The income statement measures the flow of money over a one year period. The profit or loss from these activities goes by various names: net income, results of operations, profit contribution, etc. This book uses net income as the basic phrase. Net income provides insights into the relative magnitude of costs and revenues for the entire organization and major operating divisions. Major categories of information include: revenues, costs and expenses, taxes, net income, and earnings per share. Careful analysis of changes in each category allows analysts to predict where the company may go financially in the future.

Though income statement reports vary across countries, and companies choose different formats within individual countries, the basic elements are the same. Table 4.1 summarizes common income

TABLE 4.1

Sample Income Statements from Two Countries

United States	United Kingdom
Total Sales	Turnover
– Production taxes	– Production taxes
± Other income	– Cost of sales (Opex + DD&A)
= Total Revenue	= Gross Profit
– Purchased products	– Distribution and administrative expense
– Operating expenses	– Exploration write-offs
– Exploration expenses, including dry holes	± Other income
– Selling and administration costs (overhead)	= Operating Profit
– Taxes other than income taxes	– Interest expense
– Interest expense	= Profit before taxes
– Depreciation, depletion & abandonment (DD&A)	– Taxation
= Income before income taxes	= Profit after taxes
– income taxes	± Extraordinary items
= Income before accounting adjustments	± Minority interest
± Extraordinary items	= Net income
= Net Income after extraordinary items	

statements for the U. S. and the U. K. The U. K. format is similar to the system being followed in most European Union (EU) countries.

Both formats capture the same basic information, and if two organizations had the same costs and revenues, the net income values would be within a percent of each other, although the intermediate steps differ greatly. For instance, the cost of sales category in the U. K. includes purchased products (the cost to a refinery or chemical plant of buying hydrocarbons as feedstock), operating expenses, taxes other than income taxes (sales tax, property tax, etc.), and DD&A, while the U.S report breaks these items out separately.

The "± other income" category causes some confusion. Total sales and turnover reflect revenues arising from ongoing activities, a business activity that will take place next year. Other income indicates revenues from one time events, like the disposition of assets. Since selling assets can only take place once (legally), other income measures revenues received in one year that cannot be earned in subsequent years.

Several other important elements of income statements include first the category of exploration write-offs. Two, accepted methods exist for reporting exploration expenditures: the *successful efforts method* and *full cost accounting*. Most multinational companies use the successful efforts method, while smaller, mostly domestic firms employ full cost accounting. The difference impacts the handling of property acquisition and R&D efforts, like exploration, primarily. An unsuccessful exploratory well or (R+D) is expensed when drilled under full cost accounting, but capitalized until the property is determined to be non-productive under the successful efforts method. For example, suppose a well was drilled on a lease with other drillable prospects. The lease may still be productive, even though the well was dry. If the lease is abandoned after drilling several more dry holes, then all the dry holes will be written-off in the year the property is abandoned. Several years may pass between drilling the dry hole and actually reporting the cost on the income statement. Costs are reported only when the property is classified as a success or failure, hence the name successful efforts method. The only impact is a delay in reporting actual exploration expenditures on the income statement.

Second, depreciation, depletion and amortization (DD&A) refers to *capital recovery* using the units of production method over the life of the project. For non-petroleum capital costs, a straight line DD&A method for the life of the asset is normally employed. Chapter 3 explains the various capital recovery methods in detail. Discussion of DD&A often raises questions about the exact meaning of *capitalize* and *expense*. Expense is easiest, because it reflects immediate cost recovery. A $1 spent this year is deducted against this years income when computing taxes. Expensed items include operating costs, electricity, corrosion inhibitor, maintenance, labor, etc.

Cost are capitalized when they are expected to be in operation longer than one year. Typical examples include pumps, compressors, plants, pipelines, and vehicles. Accountants sometimes express this longer life concept differently; they say the expenditure could have a salvage value in the future. Costs for assets with an economic life greater than one year are capitalized, then written off against income over time. The choice of capital recovery method (depreciation, depletion and amortization) depends on the industry, country, and management choice.

Capitalizing or expensing a cost impacts only the timing of reporting actual costs on the income statement, not the total expenditure. Example 4.1 illustrates the difference between capitalizing and expensing a cost. Both recovery methods recover the actual $5 million expenditure, just over different time frames.

Example 4.1: A $5 million expenditure can be treated as capitalized or expensed. Assuming a five year straight line life for the asset, derive the write off for an expensed and capitalized income statement. Which method reflects the year of actual expenditure and which improves reported profits?

Year	Opex	Capex
1	$5	$1
2		$1
3		$1
4		$1
5		$1
Total	$5	$5

Table 4.2 shows a sample income statement for one organization. The income statement measures the flow of money during the year by category. Revenues less expensed costs, capital recovery and taxes yield net income, which is also called *net earnings* or *profit contribution* by others. The heading uses the term consolidated statement of income. Consolidations sum categories from all business lines or operating groups in the organization.

Analyzing income statements requires more analysis than just looking at the net income figure of $1,789 in year t. Noting that net income rose from $(74) or –$74 million to a plus $1,789 distorts the actual performance of the company for several reasons. First, –$74 million arises from an accounting change, meaning that the accountants decided to report the figures differently. Observe that the –$74 is the result of a deduction of –$924 million accounting change in year t-2, called "cumulative effect of accounting change." The firm did not actually spend $924 million in t-2. This sum is an accounting entry designed to correct a deficiency in previous accounts and was required by the SEC.

This accounting correction reflected the omission of liabilities associated with pension plans. Other issues aside, the organization really made $850 million in year t-2, which would increase the value of shareholder equity by a like amount assuming no other changes. The SEC pension regulation said, in effect, that shareholder equity was historically overstated by $924 million by omitting pension liabilities. Recognizing pension liabilities reduces shareholder equity by a net amount of –$74 million, after

TABLE 4.2
Income Statement for the Example Corporation

Consolidated Statement of Income			
millions of dollars, except per share values	Year		
	t	t-1	t-2
Revenues			
Sales and other operating revenues	$26,048	$25,336	$25,280
Production taxes	3,409	2,824	2,738
Other income	905	457	201
Total Revenues	30,362	28,617	28,219
Costs and Expenses			
Purchased crude oil, gas and other products	13,558	12,878	12,495
Operating expenses	4,743	4,688	5,309
Exploration expenses, including exploratory dry holes	633	529	662
Selling and administrative expenses	2,227	1,849	2,319
Taxes other than income taxes	4,153	3,648	3,744
Depreciation, depletion, amortization and retirements	2,239	2,193	2,440
Interest expenses	318	325	247
Total costs and expenses	27,871	26,110	27,216
Income before Income taxes	2,491	2,507	1,003
Income taxes	702	687	153
Income before accounting change	1,789	1,820	850
Cumulative effect of accounting changes			(924)
Net Income	$1,789	$1,820	$(74)
Net Income per share, excluding accounting changes	$3.60	$3.66	$1.71

recognizing the positive net income. The $924 million is not real money; it is a vehicle for reducing shareholder equity on the balance sheet, as discussed next. How shareholder equity declines is explained in the discussion of the balance sheet.

This seemingly arbitrary adjustments to the income statement arise from the linkage between the income statement and balance sheet shown in Figure 4.5, and from regulatory fiat, like the pension adjustment, and company recognition of historical errors. A classical example of historical error follows a major acquisition. The price paid to acquire an asset is split between the accounting value of actual physical assets, like plant and equipment, and the difference between purchase price and the accounting value of physical assets, called *goodwill.* Because *market value* usually exceeds *book value*, goodwill is a positive number. When the buyer realizes that they over paid for the asset, they *write down* the value of the goodwill, resulting in a form of accounting change similar to the pension adjustment.

The other major concession to the comparability objective shows up in the two non-cash charge categories. The term non-cash charge means the reported deduction against income doesn't reflect actual expenditures in that year. The money was actually spent, but in a another year from that reported in the annual report. The items include exploratory dry holes and DD&A in Table 4.2. DD&A reduces taxable income by over $4 billion in year t, and exploration expenses reduces it a further $633 million.

These two distortions – allowances for extraordinary items and non-cash charges – so distort the perceptions of organization performance that some ignore financial reports for making investment decisions entirely; others modify the reported values to adjust for these distortions. We address this issue in greater detail after the primary components of financial reporting are outlined. But, this does provide a good point to reiterate important terminology. The analytical process defined here is called *financial book* analysis, as opposed to the performance measures generated from *tax books* (See Chapter 3). The two approaches often generate conflicting performance measures, which confuses and warp investment patterns in practice. Since most incentive systems and competitor analysis use financial books, professionals receive conflicting signals over the organization's goals and objectives.

Because of the characteristics of financial reporting, which arise from the desire to compare one firm versus others, the best way to analyze net income (before accounting changes) is over time. Since financial reporting rules emphasize relativity, not absolute measurement, the key question is "How has your company done relative to others?" This is the real foundation of financial reporting. Figure 4.6 shows net income for the firm and the 23 largest integrated companies in the same industry. The data has been transformed into percentage changes to adjust for different scale effects, a common approach when comparing organizations of different size. The FRS stands for the Federal Reporting System, as published by the U. S. Energy Information Agency in the Department of Energy.

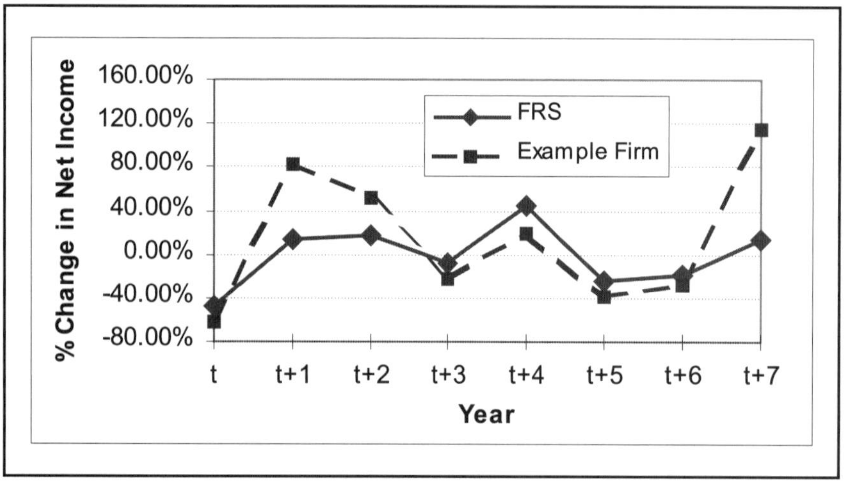

Figure 4.6 Percentage change in net income

Balance Sheet

The balance sheet indicates the stock of money, rather than a money flow. Balance sheets measure the wealth of the firm at a specific point in time, usually the end of the year (31 December), and are similar to material balance equation in engineering, except the balance being estimated is money. The basic process is provided in Equation 4.1.

$$\text{Assets} = \text{Liabilities} + \text{Shareholder Equity}$$
$$\textit{or} \qquad \textbf{(4.1)}$$
$$\text{Assets} - \text{Liabilities} = \text{Shareholder Equity}$$

Assets are anything which has value or the power to generate revenue, while liabilities reflects any obligatory payment. The identity says that the assets of an organization always equal its liabilities plus equity ownership. In the event the firm was ever liquidated, the proceeds of the sale (assets) would be sold, and the proceeds split between liability obligations and shareholder equity.

Balance sheets, and the process of deriving a balance sheet confuse many, especially accounting students, even though the math used is just addition, subtraction and multiplication. Everyone who has applied for a loan has prepared their own balance sheet. Table 4.3 shows the basic loan application form. The term net worth is normally substituted for shareholder equity for individuals, but the process is the same. Just add the value of short-term and long-term assets, and then subtract total liabilities to estimate net worth. Shareholders, like individuals, own everything left over after paying off all liability obligations. Long–term is defined as any obligation or asset expected to extend beyond a year. The 12 month or year definition distinguishes between short-term and long-term.

TABLE 4.4

Illustration of Personal Balance Sheet

	Assets	Liabilities
Short-term or Current (< 12 months)	• Cash	• Credit card • Utility bills • Bank overdrafts
Long-term (> 12 months)	• Car • House • Furniture • Company stock • Saving	• Mortgage • Car loan • School loans
Total		
Net Worth = Assets – Liabilities		

The format for presenting balance sheets for publicly held companies varies considerably around the world. Table 4.4 compares the traditional textbook U. S. approach with the British system, each with a simple example. Both follow the logic of double entry accounting, they just proceed in a slightly different order. The U. S. format begins with the near money or short-term assets listed first, followed by the long-term assets. The U. K. example illustrates the procedures adopted under the Companies Act of 1985, which are designed to bring U. K financial reporting in harmony with the Economics Union (EU) procedures. The EU format emphasize long-term values first.

TABLE 4.3

Example U. S. and U. K. Balance Sheets, $million

United States			
	Assets		Liabilities
Current	25	Current	16
Investments	5	Loans	10
Property	40	Equity	44
Total	70	Total	70

United Kingdom		
Fixed Assets		45
Current Assets	25	
Current Liabilities	16	
Net Current Assets		9
Total Assets less current liabilities		54
Loans		10
Capital and Reserves		44

The two simple balance sheets yield the same values, only the order of presentation differs. In the U. S. example, total assets of $70 million are first summed, then, current liabilities ($16) and loans $(10) are subtracted to obtain shareholder equity of $44 million. The test of double entry bookkeeping is when total liabilities plus equity equals total assets ($70 million).

The U. K. or EU system begins with long term assets of $45 million and then adds the difference between current assets of $25 and current liabilities of $16 million to compute $54 million. Outstanding loans of $10 million are then subtracted to obtain the capital and reserve accounts (shareholder equity) of $44 million.

An example balance sheet is given in Table 4.5. Long-term assets earn higher returns than current assets so the less allocated to current assets increases yields. Some money must be kept in current assets to pay bills and prevent illiquid situations or even bankruptcy. The decision on the allocation of funds between current and long-term assets depends on current and expected investments and short-term obligations. The firm expects to pay out $5,024 m in year t and has amassed $6,642 m to pay for it. The difference between current assets and current liabilities is *working capital*, or $1,618 million.

TABLE 4.5

Example Balance Sheet

Consolidated Statement of Financial Condition			
	millions of dollars	**t**	**t-1**
Assets			
Current Assets –	Cash	166	103
	Marketable securities - at cost	1,623	1,114
	Accounts and notes receivable less defaults	3,180	3,196
	Inventories	1,042	1,110
	Prepaid expenses and income taxes	631	571
Total Current Assets		6,642	6,094
Long-term Assets –	Investments and related advances	470	318
	Long term receivables and related advances	661	705
	Properties - at cost less DD&A	21,543	21,369
	Total Assets	29,316	28,486
Liabilities and Shareholder Equity			
Current liabilities –	Current portion of long term obligations	24	53
	Short term obligations	224	1,007
	Accounts payable	2,759	2,473
	Accrued liabilities	1,162	974
	Taxes payable (including income taxes)	855	836
	Total Current Liabilities	5,024	5,343
Long-term debt		4,387	4,037
Deferred income taxes		2,961	2,995
Deferred non-current liabilities		2,547	2,425
Minority interest		15	21
Shareholders equity –	Common stock	2,166	2,147
	Retained earnings	12,223	11,557
	Foreign currency adjustment	(7)	(39)
	Total shareholder equity	14,382	13,665
	Total Liabilities + shareholder equity	29,316	24,846

Most of the categories in current assets and liabilities are obvious, as most people can relate to cash. Marketable securities measure the cash on hand, which is unlikely to be needed for several months, so it is invested in interest bearing accounts. Accounts and notes receivable indicate the sale of commodities, like oil or gas, or an asset like a pump, where a bill has been sent, but payment has not been received. This float is like the gap between buying something with a credit card, but not having to pay until the credit card statement is received. *Inventories* estimate the value of unprocessed and processed items, like crude oil or jet fuel, sitting in a tank or pipeline waiting to be sold. *Prepaid expenses* indicate costs paid in advance, like income taxes paid every paycheck by individuals and quarterly by companies, or money placed in escrow for contractors to draw from. This occurs primarily on very large projects where contractors spend millions each month on behalf of the company. Having an escrow account eliminates the need to bill the client and then waiting for payment.

Long-term investments normally take place at the parent or holding company level, because it indicates investments in assets like debt instruments, equity securities, real estate, or joint ventures with other companies. Actual physical assets like equipment, wells, lease acquisition etc. fall into the properties category. The remaining item, *long-term receivables*, usually indicate sale of an asset like a producing property or building that will be repaid over a period longer than one year.

This liability and equity section reverses the asset process to measure the amount owed to others. Current portion of long-term debt is the principal amount of the debt maturing in the coming year, while short-term obligations reflect short-term debt, like bank and commercial paper borrowings. *Accounts payable* are just the opposite of accounts receivable, measuring money owed to others. *Accrued liabilities* measures expenses used before actual payment. The best example is an electricity bill; where the electricity is physically used before the bill is received, and then paid, so the obligation is considered an accrual. Salaries fall into the same category since you have to work before receiving a paycheck. Taxes payable accounts for all taxes, production, real estate, and income, owed by the firm.

In the long-term categories, debt is something most of us can relate to – the sample company has incurred over \$4,387 million in debt, up about \$300 million from the previous year. *Deferred income taxes* are a purely accounting entry to indicate distortions arising from reporting rules. The actual rules for computing income tax in most countries differ from the financial reporting rules, because of the comparability issues discussed earlier. Deferred tax is a name created to measure the difference between actual payment of income taxes (called *current taxes)* relative to income taxes reported on financial books (*financial income taxes).* The equation is:

$$\text{Deferred Taxes} = \text{Financial book income taxes} - \text{Current taxes} \tag{4.2}$$

Balance sheet deferred taxes measure the sum of every years deferred tax amount from the day the firm was chartered or incorporated. This concept is addressed later in the chapter.

Non-current liabilities is often broken down into two main categories – reserves, and provisions and contingencies. Both indicate events that could impose a cost on the firm in the future, or the actual amount of the cost is unclear. Examples include litigation, uncollectible receivables, self insured risks, catastrophes, warranties for performance, employee retirement and medical compensation, etc. The \$2,547 m in the example is obviously a significant sum of money.

Shareholder equity divides the amount owed to the shareholders into three main components. The first, common stock, specifies the amount the firm received from the initial purchase of the stock. Retained earnings indicates the sum of yearly profits, net income, retained by the firm for reinvestment in new assets. The foreign currency adjustment indicates that the example company operates in foreign currencies, and these currencies fluctuate against the currency used in the financial report – the US\$.

Several main points dominate discussion of the balance sheet. First, look for major changes in categories between years. The almost \$500+ m increase in marketable securities (45%) is a tremendous leap. Historically, such changes reflect hoarding cash for possible acquisitions, an increase in risk, or major capital needs. Though one can only guess about the reason, just asking the question helps compare competitors.

Many observe the total asset value of \$29,316 m, and conclude that number indicates the value of the company. Unfortunately, this is wrong. The total asset value is dominated by the category, called properties, or \$21,543 m. Only the cost for acquiring the properties, structures and equipment is included, less accumulated capital recovery or DD&A. The value received from producing from those assets is totally ignored.

An almost immediate response is "What is the point of valuing something at cost instead of the value received from production?" Auditing seeks to accurately measure actual historical events, not guess the future. The value realized from selling products generated by the assets can only be guessed at, and is, thus, ignored. So, the total asset number of \$29,316 m assumes that the firm could only be sold for the *book value* of its assets. In reality, its value as a going concern is higher; called the *market value,* which is inferred from stock or share prices.

Remembering that shareholder equity, computed by subtracting liabilities from total assets, suggests that the equity value of $14,382 m also underestimates the value to the shareholder. That's the reason people talk about the book value of equity, $14,382, versus the *market value.* Multiplying the number of shares outstanding (which can be found in a news paper or trading service) by the share price yields the market value of the firm. Assuming $68 per share market price for the firm and 496 m shares outstanding, the market value is about $33,728 m (=68*496,000,000). The $19,346 m differential (33,728-14,382) reflects the gain in valuing the firm as a viable, going concern, rather than at the liquidation book value. This bias is a conscious part of financial reporting.

Sources and Uses Statement (Consolidated Cash Flow)

Figure 4.3 presented the highly simplified view that assets (hence shareholder equity) increase as net income rises. This is true as long as all other monetary items remain constant, which seldom happens. The allocation of money within the organization is captured by the sources and uses statement, or as some prefer – consolidated cash flows. Three major categories exist – operations, investing and financing. The last category, financing, exists solely in the domain of corporate management. The typical professional

TABLE 4.6

Example Sources and Uses Statement

Consolidated Sources and Uses			
millions of dollars	**t**	**t-1**	**t-2**
Cash flow from operations			
Net income (loss)	1,789	1,820	(74)
Depreciation, depletion, and amortization	2,239	2,193	2,440
(Increase) decrease in receivables	(137)	(18)	476
(Increase) decrease in inventories	68	(89)	130
Increase (decrease) in payables and accrued liabilities	492	(371)	(788)
Deferred taxes and other items	(122)	(44)	(88)
Cumulative effects of accounting changes	0	0	924
Net cash provided from operating activities	4,329	3,491	3,020
Cash flow from investing activities			
Capital expenditures	(2,572)	(2,817)	(2,334)
Proceeds from disposition of property and other assets	335	594	452
New investments, advance and business acquisition	(91)	(200)	(126)
Proceeds from sale of investments	176	256	8
Other	(18)	(2)	18
Net cash used in investing activities	(2,170)	(2,169)	(1,982)
Cash flow from financing activities			
New long-term obligations	438	1,313	3,061
Repayment of long-term obligations	(138)	(2,286)	(3,147)
Cash dividends paid	(1,092)	(1,092)	(1,091)
Issuance of common stock	29	27	25
Acquisition of common stock	(41)	(32)	(29)
Increase (decrease) in short-term obligations	(783)	677	(152)
Net cash used in financing activities	(1,587)	(1,393)	(1,333)
Increase (decrease) in marketable securities	572	(71)	(295)
Cash and marketable securities - beginning of year	1,217	1,288	1,583
Cash and marketable securities - end of year	1,789	1,217	1,288

involved in operations influences only capital expenditures in the investing category and net income in the operations category.

Before exploring the details of each row, note that the total cash and marketable securities at the end of the year t of $1,789 m equals the sum of cash and marketable securities in the balance sheet. This form provides the background information about why marketable securities increased by $500+ m in the balance sheet, as discussed previously. Net income comes from the income statement and just duplicates previous values. Net income distorts the real flow of money for reasons presented in the income statement section. The categories following net income seek to correct these deficiencies.

The most important corrections from the perspective of size are DD&A and deferred taxes, both non-cash charges, and cumulative effect of accounting change. DD&A measures current year tax write-offs, which occurred in previous years. Adding this amount back corrects the deficiency. Likewise, the arbitrary, but required accounting change is added back to reflect that the company did not really spend $924m in year t-2. The interpretation of the other working capital categories follows the sign interpretation in each row, and seldom impacts the analysis significantly.

Of the remaining categories in the investing and financing sections, most should be self-evident. The two biggest are capital expenditures and dividends. The key element is change over time relative to other companies. Dividends, for example, failed to grow with even the inflation rate, forcing investors to downgrade the stock price. The prudent reaction was to announce an increase in dividends which management did in year t+1.

Traditional financial analysis fails to measure the real cash flows generated from operations. Some analysts favor adjusting financial values to compute *financial cash flows (FCF)*, which is closer to the format used in specific project analysis (See Chapter 3). The basic equation is:

$$\text{Financial Cash Flow} = \text{Net income} + \text{DD\&A} + \text{Deferred taxes} - \text{Capital expenditures} \quad \textbf{(4.3)}$$

Compare the FCF values with the reported net income. Both the relative change over time and the magnitude differ significantly. The importance of having the FCF alternative to net income arises from the critical role net income plays in the comparison of companies, and in establishing individual company incentive systems. Investment decisions are made using NCF; yet, professional are rewarded and compared using net income, which bears little or no relationship to cash flow, as Example 4.2 indicates. This inconsistency contributes to the communication gap between strategic planning and actual investment decision-making, which is expanded on later, after more of the details of financial reporting are covered.

Example 4.2: Construct the NCF for years t, t-1, and t-2 and compare to net income for the same years.

Category:	t	t-1	t-2
Net Income	1,789	1,820	(74)
+ DD&A	2,239	2,193	2,440
± Deferred taxes	(122)	(44)	(88)
– Capital expenditures	(2,572)	(2,817)	(2,334)
± Cumulative effect of accounting changes	0	0	924
= Financial cash flow (FCF)	1,334	1,152	868
Net Income	1,789	1,820	(74)

Footnotes and Supplemental Information

The supporting, most interesting details for the income statement, balance sheet and sources and uses statements are provided in the footnotes. The income statement, balance sheet, and sources and uses reports cover at most 3 pages, while the footnotes and supplemental information often run up to 30 pages. Details about actual income tax paid (*current taxes*) in domestic and foreign countries, as well as details of outstanding litigation, compensation plans, etc. exist in the footnotes. We recommend a quick reading of the footnotes when comparing a firm to others.

For the mineral industry, the supplementary information values producing properties on the basis of expected future revenues and costs. Since investments are undertaken to find and produce minerals, knowing the volume of hydrocarbons helps value the company. The supplemental information describes the financial performance of the exploration and production sector (upstream), with all the transportation, refining chemical, and marketing components (downstream) removed. The major difference between companies concerns the transportation segment, where some companies include pipeline gathering systems in upstream, while others place them in downstream.

Upstream supplemental information follows the same general format as the income statement, with most companies computing *results of operations,* usually broken down by geographical region. Table 4.7 gives one example.

TABLE 4.7

Example of Results of Operations

Results of Operations for Oil and Gas Producing Activities					
millions of dollars	**U. S.**	**Canada**	**Europe**	**Other**	**Worldwide**
Revenues from consolidated subsidiaries	2,497	323	2	877	3,699
Revenues from unaffiliated entities	460	412	668	603	3,699
Other revenues	263	186	100	69	618
Total Revenues	3,220	921	770	1,549	6,460
Production costs					
Taxes other than income taxes	242	17	21	65	345
Operating Costs	788	265	278	401	1,732
Exploration expenses	113	117	178	225	633
DD&A	629	261	215	340	1,445
Other related costs	412	27	130	151	720
Total Costs	2,184	687	822	1,182	4,875
Operating Profit	1,036	234	(52)	367	1,585
– Income tax expense	188	113	11	290	602
= Results of Operations	848	121	(63)	77	983

CHAPTER 4

The first two revenue rows, consolidated and unaffiliated, indicate ownership of the revenues. Consolidated subsidiaries exist when the parent owns more than 50% or more of the shares, thus effectively controlling management and investment activity. When less than 50% of the shares are held by the parent, it is called an unaffiliated company. Other revenues measure one-off activity, like sales of properties, and litigation settlements with other companies or governments.

Taxes other than income taxes include production taxes, royalties, sales taxes, property taxes, etc. Operating costs are standard lifting costs. Exploration expenses include geological and geophysical costs, along with amortization of unproductive properties and exploratory dry holes believed to condemn the acreage. Non-cash charges include DD&A as before, as well as part of the exploration expense, and other related costs. Other related costs are the upstream equivalent to extraordinary items in the incomes statement; it includes cost expected to occur only once. A classic example would be writing-off all or part of the purchase of a producing property when the reserves are determined to be less than anticipated.

Analysis of the results of operations follows the same procedures discussed earlier – changes over time and relative to other companies. Most analysts also evaluate the distribution of income worldwide, since diversifying results of operations reduces risk. Expropriation of assets in one country should impact a diversified company less than one with all of their assets in one country.

The next supplemental table represents a complete, radical departure from the basic tenets of financial reporting. The future net cash flow (FNCF) or standardized measure of oil and gas reserves (SMOG) tries to forecast upstream performance making some very critical assumptions. Guidelines for assumptions are found in SFAS 69 and include the following items:

- year end prices and costs per BOE are held constant for the life of the production, except when contractually allowed.. (Oil selling for $16/bbl at the end of last year will sell for $16/bbl every year production exists)
- current income tax, production tax, and other taxes are constant over the project life,
- a 10% discount rate is used since prices and costs are held constant,
- only proved developed reserves are considered, and
- a registered professional engineer must determine the production profile.

The FNCF effectively assumes no change from the conditions under which the results of operation data was presented. These static conditions, plus the sensitivity in reserve and production estimates, prevents the FNCF from being a true estimate of fair market value. Some companies refer to FNCF as NPV_{10}, as if it was a real present value calculation. Nothing is further from the truth, because of the assumptions cited above. Because of these shortcomings, some authors recommend ignoring FNCF altogether.[4.5]

Table 4.8 shows the FNCF for one year. Future cash flow or revenue is the year end constant price multiplied by the estimated production profile based on proved reserves. Development and production costs assume the same constant rate, as does income tax, on a barrel of oil equivalent basis, and the discount rate of 10% is specified by SFAS 69. If these assumptions reflected the markets belief about the future, the market value for worldwide upstream activity would be $10,991 m.

To augment the FNCF information, the supplemental information includes detailed information about reserve estimates, broken down by oil, gas, and NGL's, by geographical region and by year. This allows analysts to look at reserve changes over time by location and type, and to compare them to production (reserve replacement). Unlike many of the other values in financial reports, the auditors seldom prepare the reserve estimates; normally, the reserve estimates come from in-house staff or outside reserve consultants, who are then liable from lawsuits that may (and do) arise. Coordinating the use of

TABLE 4.8

Future Net Cash Flow Example

Future Net Cash Flow					
millions of dollars	U. S	Canada	Europe	Other	Worldwide
Future cash flows	33,605	8,135	6,736	10,951	59,427
Future development and production costs	16,922	3,686	3,939	4,207	28,754
Future income taxes	3,999	1,471	950	2,776	9,196
Future net cash flow	12,684	2,978	1,847	3,968	21,477
10% annual discount rate	7,189	1,324	538	1,435	10,486
Discounted net cash flow	5,495	1,654	1,309	2,533	10,991

assumptions and methods to insure consistency among the reserve estimates in multinational organizations becomes quite time consuming.

Table 4.9 shows the proved reserve estimate in one year for the U. S. and worldwide. The annual report also provides the information for Canada, Europe, and Other, like the FNCF, but they are omitted here for space reasons. Analysts look for several events: are reserves increasing or decreasing, and what is the worldwide reserve distribution? In this case oil reserves declined, gas reserves increased, and NGL's stayed the same.

TABLE 4.9

Estimated Proved Reserves by Country and Type

	Estimated Proved Reserves					
liquids in M barrels, gas in billion CF	United States			Worldwide		
	Oil	NGL	Gas	Oil	NGL	Gas
Beginning of year t-1	813	443	11,767	1,714	509	17,650
Revisions of previous estimates	(20)	18	220	13	18	484
Improved recovery applications	16	3	1	56	3	4
Extensions, discoveries, & other	48	6	555	139	10	1,857
Purchases of reserves in place	5	–	117	9	–	124
Sales of reserves in place	(5)	(1)	(39)	(37)	(2)	(93)
Production	(71)	(22)	(893)	(198)	(29)	(1,505)
End of year t	786	447	11,728	1,696	509	18,521
BTU Equivalent			2,022			3,193
Value Equivalent			1,173			1,852

One of the main measures for comparing companies is their reserve replacement ratio, or the change in reserves divided by production. Production is listed in the next to last row and reserve additions are the sum of each reserve category. Worldwide oil experienced an 91% reserve replacement =(13+56+139+9-37)/198. Most incentive systems and analysts like to see at least 100% reserve replacement each year; otherwise, the firm is liquidating reserves, which is slowly going out of business.

Always be very careful about using reserve estimates, especially when someone has combined liquids and gases into one reserve number, the BOE equivalent. Gas and oil can be combined using several means, with the physical entity – energy – being merely one approach. For financial reports, which try to value assets and liabilities, the relative value of gas and oil should be recognized. The last two rows in Table 4.9 show the impact of alternative conversion methods. The BTU equivalent row uses a conversion factor of 5.8 MCF to get one barrel, while the value row recognizes that it takes about 10 MCF to realize the same revenue (See Chapter 7). We prefer the value based approach since gas rarely sells on a BTU equivalent basis with oil at the wellhead. The net effect of converting gas to oil on a BTU basis is an overstatement of reserves.

The second major deficiency stems from the habit of combining all reserve categories, effectively ignoring the relative contribution by category. This is important because no one ever asks the purpose of the reserve replacement measure. If reserve replacement provides a guide to the most effective exploration programs, do the categories of revisions, improved recovery or sales contribute meaningful information? Probably not, only extensions and discoveries indicate the fruits of exploration.

Suppose a firm completely replaced reserves by buying another firm? Is this an indication of exploration acumen? One of the premier reserve replacers over the last decade did so by running 3D seismic on its two largest fields and then upgrading the reserve estimate. This is not a criticism of the 3D seismic.

Should a firm replacing this way be considered equal with one replacing reserves with new discoveries? Not when comparing competing investment opportunities!

The reserve replacement distortion compounds when analysts and management focuses on *finding cost.* The concept of finding cost is like a margin analysis for most firms. If it costs $4 to obtain the product and it sells for $16 a unit, a healthy profit margin exists. Like many oversimplified measures, finding cost has little relevance to anything. Computing finding cost uses reserves from Table 4.9 and upstream costs reported in the supplemental information. Table 4.10 gives exploration and development cost by category and geographical region for one year.

TABLE 4.10

Exploration and Development Costs by Year and Region

	Upstream Costs				
	U. S.	**Canada**	**Europe**	**Other**	**Worldwide**
Property Acquisition					
Proved	52	11	9	1	73
Unproved	50	51	3	2	106
Exploration	245	116	185	291	837
Development	614	246	193	446	1,499
Total Cost	961	424	390	740	2,515
Exploration finding costs, $/bbl					4.06
Development costs, $/bbl					2.42

Table 4.10 captures actual expenditures, even though administrative expenses (overhead) are included. The slight deviation arises from the inclusion of depreciation on support equipment, like research and development, but this amount is so small it can be ignored for any analysis. The exploration finding cost which is the value reported in the press is derived by taking total reserve change (ignoring production) from Table 4.9, converting gas to oil on a BTU basis and then dividing total BOE into the sum of acquisitions and exploration. The value of $4.06 {=(73+106+837)/618.6} indicates that every BOE cost about $4.06 to acquire and develop, in most interpretations.

Does this value reflect a god or bad result? The answer depends on the change over time and comparable competitor costs. Finding costs fail to capture the real cost per unit (or efficiency of exploration), because of the mismatch in timing. The denominator, change in proved reserves, is divided into exploration costs for the same year. By definition, proved reserves exist only when production commences. Very few exploration expenditures result in production in the year the money is spent. The lag between acquisition and exploration expenditures and the booking of proved reserves exceeds five years in major exploration efforts, with the lag almost always exceeding at least a couple of years. Matching one years cost with reserve change misses the point. Those companies who have bothered to correlate exploration expenditures with proved reserve changes find an average value of 3.5 to 5 years. The best way to reduce finding costs is to stop exploring and liquidate the company.

The last major component of upstream supplemental information is the capitalized cost section. This is the equivalent of the properties row in the balance sheet. It measures the original cost of a capitalized cost less accumulated depreciation, and is the *book value* of upstream assets. Table 4.11 gives the capitalized costs for one example. Most of the capitalized costs belong to proved properties, as expected.

The information presented so far captures the essence of financial reports. At this point, most professionals (outside of accounting and management) delight in their career choice to be technical professionals. Whatever the limitations of the information, financial reports provide the only readily available basis for comparing firms and tracking performance over time, without detailed inside information. This was the

TABLE 4.11

Example of Capitalized Costs

	U.S.	Canada	Europe	Other	Worldwide
Unproved properties	252	133	102	170	657
Proved properties	6,406	1,830	1,361	1,248	10,845
Support Equipment and facilities	299	43	42	108	492
Net capitalized cost	6,957	2,006	1,505	1,526	11,994

intent. None of the deficiencies mentioned or, even some omitted from the discussion, are unknown. It is a little like listening to a presentation on 3D modeling, compositional reservoir modeling, or project scheduling – inherent assumptions exist, and these must be understood to make good decisions.

FINANCIAL RATIOS

The most common approach used in *financial statement analysis* employs the information discussed in the last section to form *financial ratios.* These ratios are dimensionless numbers, and seek to generate consistent, relative measures of performance. Though other methods exist for analyzing companies, like comparative and commons size financial statements, ratio methods dominate.[4.6]

Some of the most commonly used ratios are summarized in Table 4.12, along with the equation and brief description of each.

TABLE 4.12

Common Financial Ratios

Financial Ratios		
Ratio	**Equation**	**Summary**
Profitability		
Return on Assets (ROA or ROI)	$= \frac{\text{net income}}{\text{total assets}}$	Measures operating efficiency of return on capital. Maximize value.
Earnings per share (EPS)	$= \frac{\text{net income}}{\text{outstanding stock}}$	Indicates allocation of net income to each share. Maximize value.
Return on Equity (ROE)	$= \frac{\text{net income}}{\text{shareholder equity}}$	Rate earned on resources provided by stock owners. Maximize value.
Profit Margin	$= \frac{\text{net income}}{\text{total revenue}}$	Shows margin on each unit of sales. Maximize but limit is 1.0.
Price-Earnings Ratio (P/E)	$= \frac{\text{share market price}}{\text{earnings per share}}$	Indicates markets capitalization of assets. Maximize value
Return on Capital Employed (ROCE)	$= \frac{\text{net income}}{\text{capital employed}}$	Another profit efficiency ratio using different values. Maximize value.
Return on Capitalized Cost (ROCC)	$= \frac{\text{results of operations}}{\text{capitalized cost}}$	Profit measure using supplemental information for upstream. Maximize value.
Liquidity		
Current Ratio (CR)	$= \frac{\text{current assets}}{\text{current liabilities}}$	Indicates ability to meet current obligations as going concern. Should be >1.
Capitalization		
Debt/Equity (D/E)	$= \frac{\text{total debt}}{\text{shareholder equity}}$	Shows relative capital contribution by source. Value depends on industry & country.
Debt/Total Capitalization	$= \frac{\text{total debt}}{\text{equity + debt}}$	Another measure of capital contribution with same goals.

These ratios and many others not shown here are commonly used to measure the relative performance and changes over time. *Efficient market* advocates argue that ratio information is redundant since financial information has already been fully reflected in the current stock price. We counter that financial reporting enhances the ability of an efficient market to operate. Regardless of ones viewpoint, most investors and lenders, worldwide, utilize financial ratios as part of the investing and lending process. The ratios, using the previous financial reports, are shown in Example 4.2.

Example 4.3: Compute the financial ratios using the example financial reports.

	Industry	Example Company
Return on Assets (ROA)	9.6%	$=\frac{\text{net income}}{\text{total assets}}=\frac{1,789}{29,316}=0.061\ \textit{or}\ 6.1\%$
Earnings per share (EPS)		$=\frac{\text{net income}}{\text{outstanding stock}}=\frac{1,789}{6,440}=3.6$
Return on Equity (ROE)	12.0%	$=\frac{\text{net income}}{\text{shareholder equity}}=\frac{1,789}{14,382}=0.124\ \textit{or}\ 12.4\%$
Profit Margin	4.2%	$=\frac{\text{net income}}{\text{total revenue}}=\frac{1,789}{30,362}=0.0589\ \textit{or}\ 5.89\%$
Price-Earnings Ratio (P/E)	15.3	$=\frac{\text{share market price}}{\text{earnings per share}}=\frac{58}{3.6}=16.11$
Return on Capital Employed (ROCE)		$=\frac{\text{net income}}{\text{capital employed}}=\frac{1,789}{19,023}=0.094\ \textit{or}\ 9.4\%$
Return on Capitalized Cost (ROCC)		$=\frac{\text{results of operations}}{\text{capitalized cost}}=\frac{983}{11,994}=0.082\ \textit{or}\ 8.2\%$
Current Ratio	0.97	$=\frac{\text{current assets}}{\text{current liabilities}}=\frac{6,642}{5,024}=1.322$
Debt/Equity	41.8%	$=\frac{\text{total debt}}{\text{shareholder equity}}=\frac{4,387}{14,382}=40.8\%$
Debt/Total Capitalization	29.5%	$=\frac{\text{total debt}}{\text{equity+debt}}=\frac{4,387}{4,387+14,382}=23.37\%$

The numerator in most ratios is net income, with all of the associated problems discussed in the income statement. We prefer to compute these ratios using net cash flow, as calculated in Equation 4.3. as well. This measures return on the profit from just operations and project investment, ignoring management financial decisions. Of all the ratios, ROCE dominates. ROCE combines debt and equity, but not working capital to derive the capital employed denominator. In the example, capital employed is the sum of all debt (short-term and long-term), capitalized lease obligations, shareholder equity, and minority interest. Another common adjustment adds after-tax interest expense to net income to form the numerator. Such numerator adjustments impact the computed value only slightly in actual practice.

The last measure, ROCC, is used to compare upstream operations. The results of operation numerator and capitalized cost denominator come from the supplemental information section. The real difference between ROCE and ROCC is that capitalized cost in ROCC excludes deferred taxes, while ROCE includes deferred taxes.

The example firm under-performed the industry in return on assets, but had higher profit margins, P/E ratio, and return on equity. Similar findings emerge for most companies: they are better in some areas, but worse in others. The easiest analysis occurs when a firm consistently beats or under performs the competition, but most companies are like the example shown here.

The P/E ratio furnishes interesting information about the markets assessment of a firm relative to internal assumptions, primarily the cost-of-capital. The P/E ratio measures the value per share of a viable, going concern relative to book value. The larger this value, the greater the markets expectation of future results. Some actually compute a rough measure for a market discount rate by dividing the P/E ration into one, or 1/(P/E) = 1/16.11 = 0.062 or 6.2%. The market values the shares at a discount rate of about 6%. The higher the P/E ratio, the lower the market discount rate.

Comparing organizations or plotting changes over time is a simple process requiring time, data and graphics software. Technical professional have more questions about which ratio best measures performance, and how one measure compares to another. The dominant profitability measure for determining incentive goals is ROCE. Since all profit measures use net income in the numerator, with only the denominator varying, the profit ratios should vary in a consistent pattern. Figure 4.7 illustrates ROCE, ROA, and ROE for the last 30 years using the data from the federal reporting system.(4.7) The three return measures track each other quite well except for 1992, which is due to the write-off of extraordinary items.

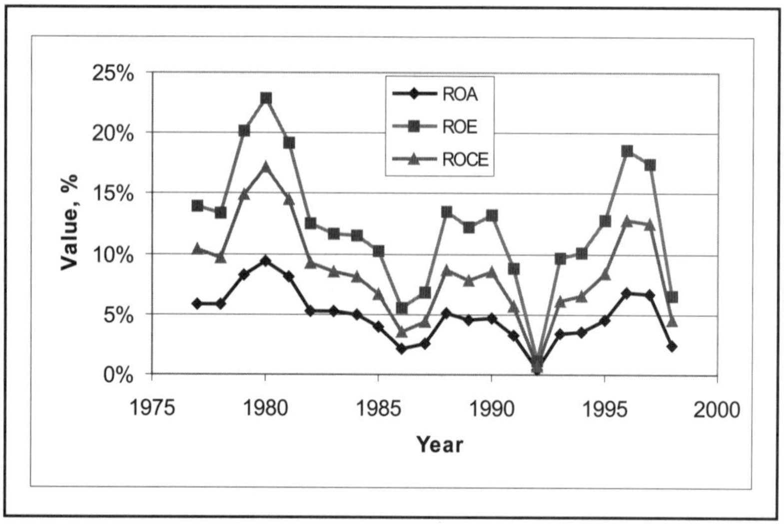

Figure 4.7 Comparison of financial performance measures

The key element in every profit measure is the specification of the numerator – net income in the usual case. A good profit measure should indicate the real profitability to the company. Profits really arise from two distinct components: profits from actual operations and general corporate decisions. FCF reflects operating profits the best, while net income captures the profit from all activities: still with the limitations noted earlier.

Figure 4.8 illustrates the divergence between FCF and net income over a 20 year period. We prefer FCF, because it accurately measures the flow of money better than net income. Since money flows form the foundation of investment analysis, having similar measures of financial profitability would help reduce the gap between the two, as explored later in this chapter. Figures such as these can be very misleading using visual inspection. It appears that FCF moves opposite of net income, because of the increasing gap starting in the early 70's and continuing to the mid 80's. Remember that this coincides with the OPEC boom period, when increasing prices encouraged major investment expenditures world wide. In the late 80's, the two measures appear to move together. The simple correlation (Chapter 6) between the two is 39%, indicating a slight, but positive relationship.

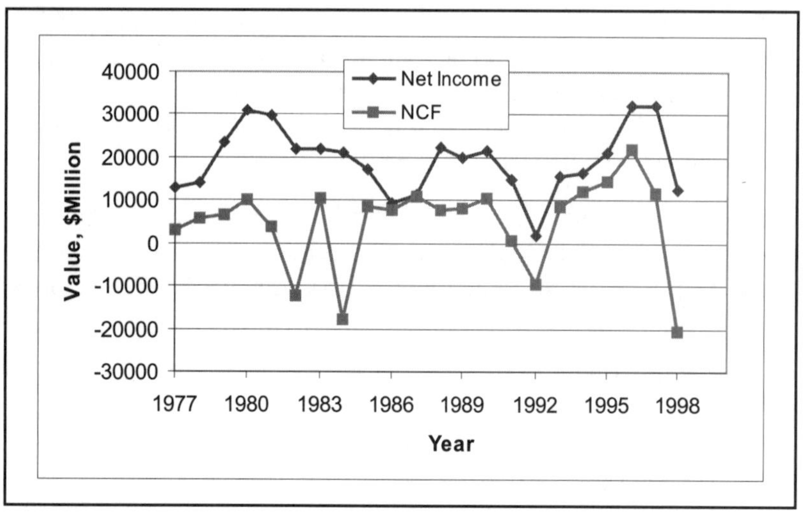

Figure 4.8 Comparison of net income and NCF

Individual companies normally show more variability between the two profit measures. The equivalent correlation for the example firm is about 10%. Aggregate examples tend to disguise the variability in relationships as part of the aggregation process.

The other significant ratios are various debt measures. These reflect the distribution of borrowed capital between debt and equity. The choice of the debt/equity or debt/total capitalization matters not in an evaluation, because only the scale changes. Figure 4.9 provides a historical summary of the FRS measures for both debt ratios, but a more detailed discussion of the relative importance of debt and equity is deferred until the cost-of-capital is discussed.

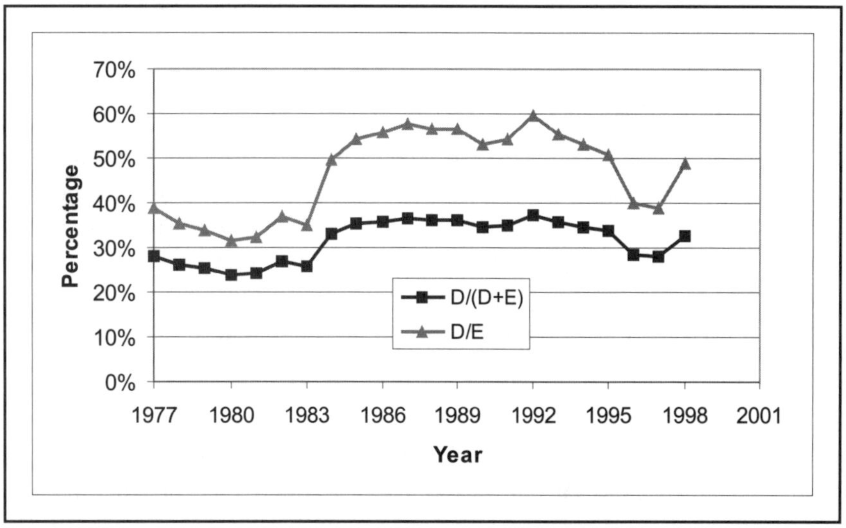

Figure 4.9 Historical debt and equity ratios

Many authors have tried to link financial measures to shareholder value, with complete failure. The next section focuses on why they failed to link financial and economic performance. Since most readers of this book will never study financial markets formally, a simplified version of research demonstrates the relationship between a common ratio, like ROE, and shareholder returns. Figure 4.10 plots the percentage change in ROE against the percentage change in share price for 20 companies for a selected year. If share price responded to changing financial information, a positive relationship should occur.

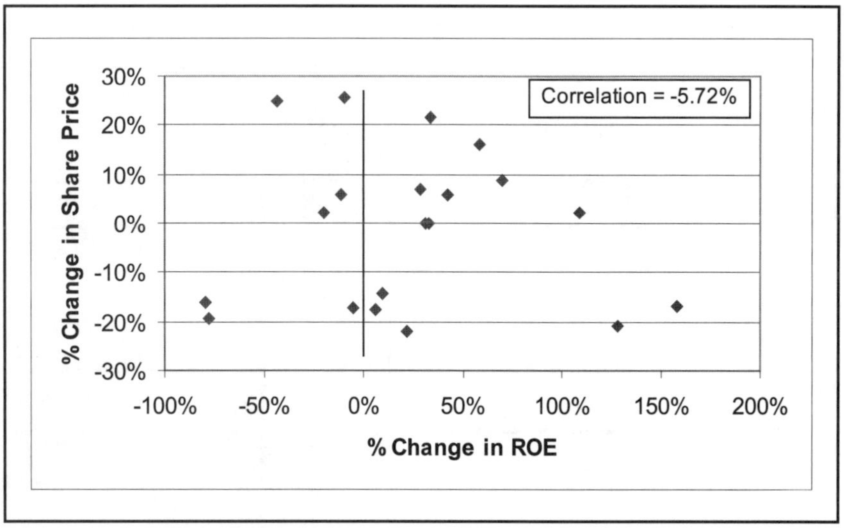

Figure 4.10 Relationship between financial and market performance measures

The actual results appear to be fairly random, as supported by the correlation coefficient of -5.72%, or effectively zero relationship. Of the 20 observations, 8 are in quadrants where an increase in ROE leads to a reduction in share price. Another 10 values have a positive relationship between ROE and share price, and 2 values show ROE increasing by 32 and 31% with no change in share price.

This section depicts common usage of financial information. Though highly abbreviated, it does present the essence of the purpose of and methods for utilizing financial reports. At this point in our classes, technical professionals often cheer when asked if they would like to move on. While much of what has been discussed seems arcane, irrelevant, misguided, etc. at first glance, financial book information plays a critical role in decision-making, though, not for the reasons many believe.

Financial information supplies information about an organizations performance. Critics often blame financial reporting for the perceived short-run orientation of firms. Every chief executive, we have known, views themselves as taking a long-run perspective. The ability to match their financial targets with actual performance, which is measured quarterly and annually, gives them credibility with the investment community. Matching short-run expectations with performance enhances the investment communities faith in the CEO's vision for the future. Once a CEO loses this credibility, share prices normally fall dramatically, and can seldom be redeemed, without changing senior management. The short-run really acts as proxy information about long-run performance.

Accounting vs. Economic Analysis

The preceding discussion acts as if the financial book approach adequately measures shareholder value, and financial analysts would like this to be so. Unfortunately, investors utilize a decision process, which differs significantly in nature and scope from the financial approach. In fact, it is quite easy to show that investors using a financial approach seriously under-perform a project based approach. Of great concern is the increasing reliance on financial based investment decisions, with little understanding of the relationship between the two approaches and the resultant consequences.

Figure 4.11 highlights the difference between financial and investment analysis. Financial analysis sums historical information for the entire organization in a backward looking, aggregate process. Project or economic analysis estimates future actual cash flows for each investment opportunity. Financial books sum the values from current activities at a specific point and time, as shown by the vertical dotted area. This yields the ratios and financial information, like net income, ROCE, ROE, etc. Project valuations look forward, predicting by predicting future prices, production, costs, taxes, etc. The project performance measures, like NPV, IRR, and NPV/INV, dominate investment decision-making.

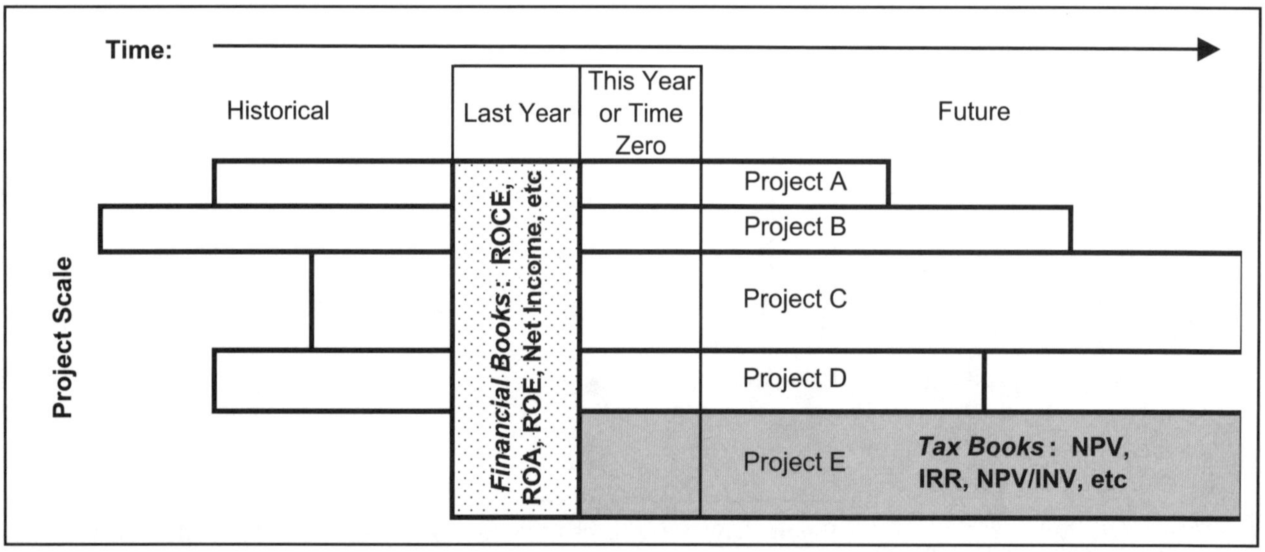

Figure 4.11 Financial versus project analysis

Financial and project analysis differ considerably in the reported timing of money flows and the number of projects. These differences are critical when analyzing investment opportunities. The summation of historical results often fails to indicate future performance, and creates serious misconceptions about the performance of management and professionals within a firm. Probably the extreme indication of the limitations of financial information is highlighted in Figure 4.12.

The explosion of the Internet dot.com companies raised serious questions about the market valuation of investments. Amazon.Com exhibited a very interesting relationship between the historical based financials and market valuation. The almost inverse relationship is explained by the market basing their valuation on future expectations, not historical valuations. Whether the market is right is a totally different question, and beyond the scope of this discussion.(4.8)

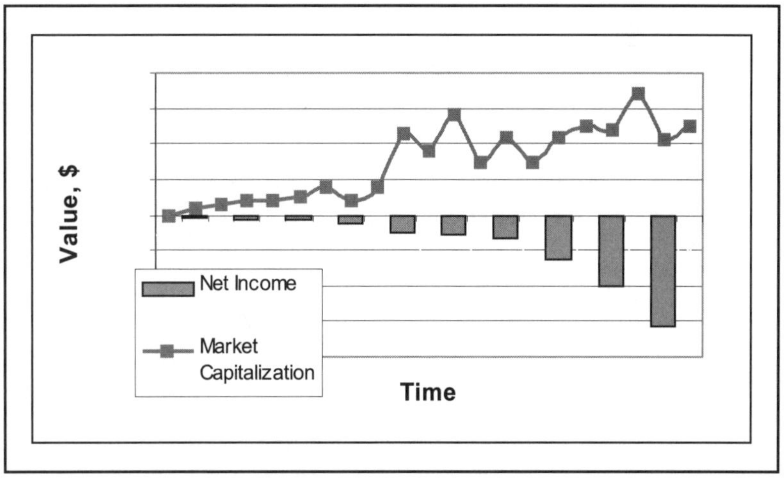

Figure 4.12 Financial versus market capitalization for Amazon.com

The conflict between financial and market valuation has existed for decades, and comes as no surprise to finance professionals. To others this result is surprising, but, whether it is a surprise or not, the differences are crucial to the operation of organizations. At several places in this section, the term, *maximizing shareholder value*, has been used. Management creates value when decisions provide benefits greater than costs. As simple as this sounds, measuring benefits and costs is fraught with danger, because each occurs at different times in the future. This also creates havoc for compensation schemes when performance measures ignore future benefits arising from current investments.

To close the gap between financial and economic valuations, financial theorists have extended the traditional ratios discussed to date. The three discussed here include Tobin's q, economic value added (EVA), and market value added (MVA). Each seeks to correct financial accounting deficiencies by adding market based information. EVA and MVA are explained later after some additional, required material has been added.

Tobin's q originated with James Tobin.(4.9) He sought to provide a better measure of the value created by management, including that from intangible assets, like market power, goodwill, and future investment opportunities. The larger q, the greater the value of the firm. Comparing firms based on q is tantamount to predicting future cash flows, or moving away from the historical approach. The original equation is defined in Equation 4.4.

$$q = \frac{\text{Market value of assets}}{\text{Replacement cost of assets}} \quad \textbf{(4.4)}$$

While the equations appears simple, determining both elements of the equations are quite difficult. A number of researchers have experimented with proxies to simplify the calculation.(4.10) Equation 4.5 illustrates one suggestion.

$$\text{Proxy for } q = \frac{\text{Book Debt} + \text{LV of PS} + \text{MV of CS}}{\text{Total Assets}} \quad \textbf{(4.5)}$$

where:

LV = liquidating value
PS = preferred stock
MV = market value
CS = common stock

The numerator essentially estimates the market value of debt and equity, and the denominator comes directly from the balance sheet. The main difference from traditional ratios arises from the use of the market value of the common stock. This effectively incorporates future expectations of the market in place of the backward looking book values. Example 4.4 demonstrates the process.

Example 4.4: Estimate Tobin's q for the sample company assuming that 500 million shares are outstanding and currently selling for $60 per share. No preferred stock exists. Also compute the BV to MV ratio. Use the financial reports for the other data.

$$q = \frac{4{,}387 + 0 + 30{,}000}{29{,}316} = \frac{34{,}387}{29{,}316} = 1.17$$

The 1.17 is a dimensionless number and must be compared to other companies, like all ratios. This value indicates a profitable, but fairly conservative investment relative to other investments.

$$\frac{BV}{MV} = \frac{14{,}382}{30{,}000} = 0.4794$$

A simpler, but more accurate correction for accounting information combines the book value of equity (BV) information with market equity information (MV) to create a ratio, BV/MV or some use MV/BV. Research suggests that the ratio explains future stock performance better than any other measure available.[4.11] Little theoretical justification exists for the explanatory power of the ratio, but several speculations exist.

One explanation ties the BV/MV ratio to risk: as the ratio gets larger (MV falls relative to book value), risk rises because the market perceives little future benefit. According to *the efficient market hypothesis (EMH),* the market is correcting historical information to reflect its expectations of the future. A second explanation focuses on BV/MV as a proxy for future growth in returns. The greater the BV/MV value, the lower the firm's expected future growth.[4.12] The value of 0.4794 would be considered low, indicating a higher expected future growth or relatively low risk.

FORWARD LOOK FINANCIAL REPORTING

Financial reporting plays an important role in decision-making at all levels of the organization, regardless of any perceived or actual limitations. One driving reason for the significant role occurs because of the formal relationship between executive and employee compensation schemes and financial information, like ROCE, either alone or relative to ones competitors. Another linkage exists via the planning process. Setting strategies, budgets, manning levels, etc. all hinge on the expected future consequences of those expenditures. By predicting future financials, management can match spending patterns to likely consequences. Management is essentially anticipating its future financial reports. While many professionals lament what they perceive as undue emphasis on financials, any management that ignores financial information altogether faces even greater perils. The key is finding the right balance.

One common approach asks individual business units to compute both the financial and economic implications for each investment opportunity. The accepted projects are then rolled up to get a consolidated view of future business performance. This approach effectively makes accounting information forward looking, just like traditional economic analysis. Unfortunately, different answers emerge from the two approaches, because of several fundamental differences in the underlying process, and, these differences go back to the basic notion of accounting, as explained in the first part of this chapter.

Accounting follows the *revenue matching* process, which seeks to align revenues and expenditures over the life of an investment. Another aspect refers to the *accrual* process. This means accounting recognizes costs when the obligation for payment is incurred, not when the bills are actually paid. The combination of revenue matching and accruals causes the timing of the reported numbers in financial books to differ significantly from traditional project (or tax) analysis.

The major difference between tax and financial analysis are outlined below. Each is discussed in turn. The first three impact the timing of money flows, and the last item affects the reporting mechanism.

- Capitalized vs. Expensed split
- Capital Recovery Process
- Tax Calculation
- Financial Performance

Of the four categories, the combination of the capital vs. expense split and different capital recovery (or depreciation) cause most of the gap between financial and project analysis to occur. Table 4.13 summarizes the major differences for petroleum projects, because they exhibit the most dramatic differences. Since drilling wells involves the risk of failing to find economic minerals, the tax regime allows the investor to expense much of the cost. Only after commercial deposits are found and the well is completed are most of the costs capitalized. On financials, all costs are capitalized, regardless of the nature of the expenditure.

TABLE 4.13

Differences Between Financial and Tax Calculations

Categories	% Capitalized On	
	Financial	**Tax**
Producing Wells	100	15 to 30
Developmental Dry Holes	100	0
Geological & Geophysical (G&G)	0	50 to 70
Depreciation Method: Financial Books: Combination of units of production (UOP) and straight line (SL) Tax Books: Depreciation specified by country tax authority (7 year MACRS in US)		

The developmental dry hole category best epitomizes the difference between accounting and economic analysis. Drilling a dry hole has no lasting value to the investment, since nothing will ever be produced, and tax regimes allow expensing of the expenditure. Because financial accounting follows a revenue matching process, it capitalizes any expenditure, which impacts future revenue streams. Since developmental dry hole are associated with producing fields, financial reporting capitalizes the entire amount. Financial practitioners argue that the expenditure provides information about the existing reservoir (where it isn't), and that information will be used to make future decisions. This is consistent with similar situations in manufacturing or real estate when buildings are constructed, but never used. Unused or unrented buildings are like dry holes.

Chapter 3 explains units of production and tax depreciation in detail. This discussion emphasizes the different results that emerge from financial and economic analysis. Example 4.5 demonstrates the capital recovery differences for simple project in the U. S. UOP is derived by dividing annual production by total production over the life of the project.

Capital recovery impacts the timing tax payments directly, and the subsequent cash flows indirectly through the tax stream. Such timing differences change then alter all of the subsequent performance measures. Example 4.5 continued constructs the net income for the same project outlined in the U. S. section of Chapter 3.

The net revenue and Opex are forecasts, while DD&A comes from the previous table. Taxable income is merely revenue less Opex and DD&A. Taxable income times the assumed tax rate of 35% measures financial book taxes. Subtracting financial book taxes from taxable income yields project net income, the equivalent to the net income in the financial reports.

Example 4.5: Derive the DD&A and net income for the following project. All values in $m.

	(1)	(2)	(3)	(4)	(5)	(6)	(7)=6+5
			UOP		DD&A		
Period	Investment	Production	Year 0-1	Year 1-2	Year 0-1	Year 1-2	Total
0-1	125.80	5.35	0.149	0.000	18.77	0.00	18.77
1-2	32.30	10.60	0.296	0.348	37.20	11.23	48.42
2-3		8.60	0.240	0.282	30.18	9.11	39.29
3-4		6.10	0.170	0.200	21.41	6.46	27.87
4-5		3.30	0.092	0.108	11.58	3.49	15.07
5-6		1.60	0.045	0.052	5.61	1.69	7.31
6-7		0.30	0.008	0.010	1.05	0.32	1.37
7-8		0.00	0.000	0.000	0.00	0.00	0.00
Total	158.10	35.85	1.000	1.00	125.80	32.30	158.10

UOP in column 3: $0.149 = \frac{5.35}{35.85}$ and $0.296 = \frac{10.60}{35.85}$

DD&A in column 5: $18.77 = 0.149 * 125.8$ and $37.20 = 0.296 * 125.8$

Year	(9) WI Net Revenue	– (28) Opex	– (6) DD&A	= (7) Taxable Income	(8)=7*0.35 Financial Book Taxes	(9) Net Income	(10) NCF
0-1	69.015	43.11	18.77	7.13	2.50	4.64	-90.78
1-2	136.74	74.2	48.42	14.12	4.94	9.18	20.18
2-3	110.94	60.2	39.29	11.45	4.01	7.45	40.85
3-4	78.69	42.7	27.87	8.12	2.84	5.28	29.43
4-5	42.57	23.1	15.07	4.40	1.54	2.86	17.13
5-6	20.64	11.2	7.31	2.13	0.75	1.39	9.35
6-7	3.87	2.1	1.37	0.40	0.14	0.26	3.30
7-8	0	0	0.00	0.00	0.00	0.00	1.28
8-7			0.00	0.00	0.00	0.00	0.30
Total	462.47	256.61	158.10	47.76	16.71	31.04	31.04

Column 10 repeats the NCF derivation for the same project from Chapter 3. First, observe that two different methods produce the same total value, $31.04, or the area under the curves is the same. This should come as no surprise since both methods allow 100% cost recovery, just the timing of the recovery varies. Second, observe that the yearly patterns between net income and NCF vary considerably. Net income almost always displays positive values, because all of the investment is capitalized and excluded from the valuation (via DD&A) until production commences. NCF typically begins with negative values, since it recognizes expenditures as they occur, and then becomes positive until the end of the project. Figure 4.13 demonstrates the typical relationship between NCF and Net Income in forward looking reporting.

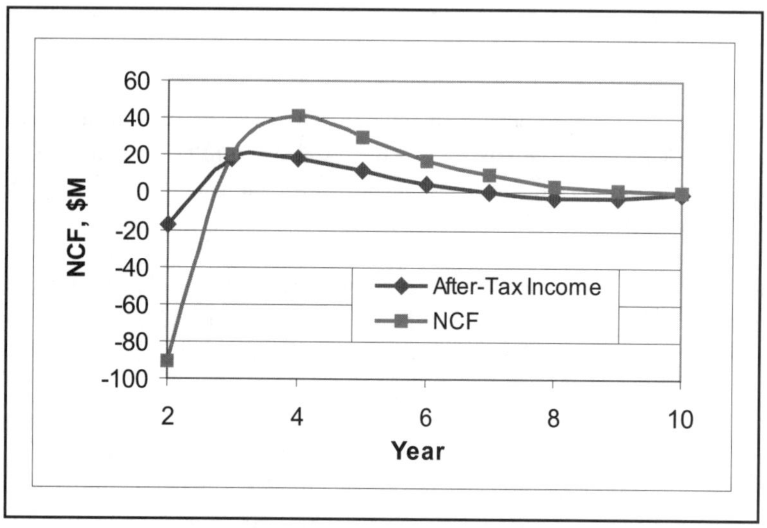

Figure 4.13 Comparison of Net Income and NCF

Deferred Taxes

Several other aspects emerge from the differences between NCF and Net Income. One critical factor for computing accounting ratios is *deferred taxes*. The example computed financial book taxes assuming the specified capitalized and expensed split, and then applied a UOP depreciation schedule. Since NCF uses a different split for capitalized and expensed items, and a country specific depreciation schedule, like 7 year MACRS in the U. S. or 6 year SL in other countries, a different tax schedule occurs.

Like most disciplines, accounting names these conflicting values – deferred taxes. Equation 4.2 defined deferred taxes for historical financials, and the same definition applies to forward looking financials. Example 4.6 continues the previous example to illustrates deferred taxes.

Example 4.6: Derive the deferred tax schedule using the current tax values for the U. S. from Chapter 6 and the financial book taxes from the last example. All values in $m.

	(8)	– (30)	= (32)	(33)
Year	Financial Book Taxes	Current Tax	Deferred Tax	Cumulative Deferred Tax
0-1	2.50	-9.12	11.61	11.61
1-2	4.94	10.06	-5.12	6.50
2-3	4.01	9.89	-5.88	0.62
3-4	2.84	6.56	-3.72	-3.10
4-5	1.54	2.34	-0.80	-3.90
5-6	0.75	0.09	0.66	-3.25
6-7	0.14	-1.53	1.67	-1.58
7-8	0.00	-1.28	1.28	-0.30
8-7	0.00	-0.30	0.30	0.00
Total	16.71	16.71	0.00	

Again, the summation of financial book taxes and current tax (actual tax paid to the local tax authority) produces the same value because both methods allow 100% cost recovery. Deferred tax, the difference between the two, sums to zero, but with an entirely different schedule.

Figure 4.14 displays yearly and cumulative deferred taxation over the project life. This example follows a common pattern: positive deferred taxes in the early, investment years, followed by negative values when tax depreciation occurs faster than the UOP depreciation. Toward the end of a project, tax depreciation has been used up, but UOP depreciation still occurs because of the revenue matching process used in financial accounting.

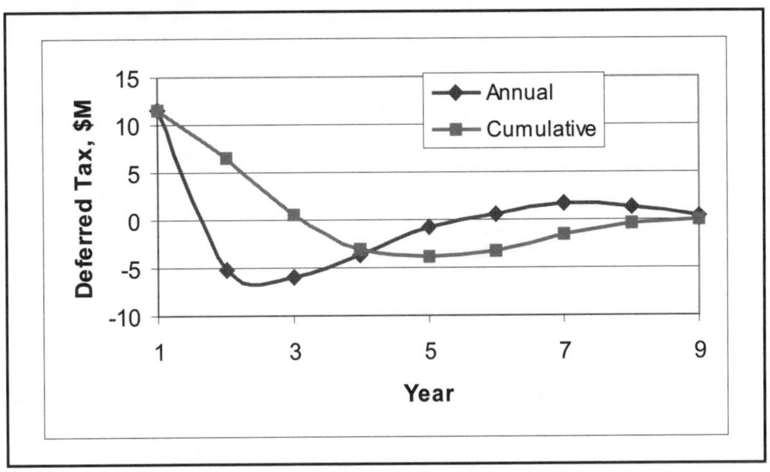

Figure 4.14 Annual and cumulative deferred taxes

An often asked question is "Who cares." Certainly, making intelligent investment decisions is independent of the deferred tax number, but just a little exposure to industry practice will produce reference to the deferred tax term. People without a formal understanding of deferred tax hear references to it, and assume that deferred tax impacts shareholder value. In reality, the current tax column reflects the actual payment to the local tax authority, and is the true measure of tax cash flows. Financial taxes measure a reported number, not an actual cash flow. Deferred tax, thus, captures the deferral of truth (just kidding) in financial accounting. Deferred taxes matter because it is a component of the project ROCE computation.

Financial Performance

The final difference between accounting and economic valuation measures arise in the use of ROCE or other traditional ratios, relative to NPV, IRR, etc. Organizations employ ROCE standards on performance contracts for senior executives, employee compensation schemes, and contracts with managers of specific operating entities (business units). People behave the way they are rewarded.

Return-on-capital employed (ROCE) was defined earlier as:

$$ROCE = \frac{\text{Net Income (NI)}}{\text{Average Capital Employed (ACE)}} \qquad ACE = \frac{CE_{BOY} + CE_{EOY}}{2} \tag{4.6}$$

where:

CE_{BOY} = capital employed at beginning of the year

CE_{EOY} = capital employed at end of the year, or

CE_{EOY} = CE_{BOY} – DD&A – Deferred Taxes + Capital Expenditures

NI follows financial accounting practice, while the ACE approach is fairly common in accounting. Since balance sheets are normally constructed for the end of the year (31 December), the averaging process converts the denominator to a mid-year concept. In the great majority of cases, using end of year or mid-year has little impact on computing ROCE. The primary exception arises when a significant capital outlay occurs relative to previous years, or a firm chooses to stop investing entirely. In these cases, the ROCE could be impacted greatly.

Example 4.7 derives the ROCE and ACE using the information from the previous examples. Net Income is repeated from the earlier example. CE_{BOY} starts at zero because no money has been spent. In the first year, the project spends $125.8 million but recoups $11.61 in deferred taxes and $18.77 in DD&A, leaving an ending balance of $95.41. The ending balance at the end of year 0-1 becomes the starting

Example 4.7: Compute the ROCE using the data from the previous example. All values in $m.

	(9)	(34)	+ (1)	– (32)	– (6)	= (35)	(36)	(37) = 9/36
Year	Net Income	CE_{BOY}	CAPEX	Deferred Taxes	DD&A	CE_{EOY}	ACE	ROCE
0-1	4.64	0	125.80	11.61	18.78	95.41	47.71	9.72%
1-2	9.18	95.41	32.30	-5.12	48.42	84.41	89.91	10.21%
2-3	7.45	84.41	0.00	-5.88	39.29	51.00	67.71	11.00%
3-4	5.28	51.00	0.00	-3.72	27.87	26.86	38.93	13.57%
4-5	2.86	26.86	0.00	-0.80	15.07	12.58	19.72	14.49%
5-6	1.39	12.58	0.00	0.66	7.31	4.62	8.60	16.10%
6-7	0.26	4.62	0.00	1.67	1.37	1.58	3.10	8.38%
7-8	0							
8-7	0							
Total	31.04		158.10	-1.58	158.10			

$CE_{EOY} = 0 + 125.80 - 11.61 - 18.78 = 95.41$ $\qquad ACE_{0-1} = \frac{0+95.41}{2} = 47.71$

balance for the start of the next year. ACE is the average of the starting and ending balance. ROCE is net income divided by ACE.

Now that ROCE has been generated, what do we do with it? For making investment decisions, absolutely nothing. For aggregating with other projects to see if our portfolio reaches the threshold needed to earn our compensation package, it helps immensely. This sounds crass and cynical to some, but remember Figure 4.10, which showed no relationship between ROE and share price, the normal measure of shareholder value.

Limitations and Abuses of Accounting Performance Measures

A dangerous problem has cropped up in the interpretation of financial information. Several knowledgeable, experienced professionals with different companies have uttered phrases like "we approve projects with IRR's of 18-20%, but the company ROCE never achieves these values." Referring back to Figure 4.11, it is hopefully apparent that financial profit measures, like ROCE or ROA, are unlikely to ever match project profit measures, like IRR or NPV. Aggregating all projects in a single year using financial net income should never produce the same value as a single project NCF evaluated over time. The total number of projects involved, the number of years, and the monetary values all differ. If all inputs differ, why should the outputs be the same, except by accident.

Even worse, they are comparing estimated values with actual values, without first asking what the actual IRR for the project was. This is comparing apples to oranges.

In spite of this logic, some of the professionals mentioned above are from Missouri (the Show me state). Figure 4.15 illustrates the difference between IRR and ROCE for a single project on a forward looking basis. The numbers are generated from an investment which generates a 10% IRR based on a $50 million Capex. Next, the net income and ACE were calculated, which then generates ROCE. Observe that ROCE for the project exceeds the 10% return objective only in the first year (18.77% ROCE). The highest ROCE occurs in the first year because, as shown in Example 4.6, ACE is the average of the starting investment (zero) and the additional Capex during the year. The ROCE calculation effectively uses only half the investment in the first year. Thereafter, ROCE uses a higher denominator, and ROCE falls below the return objective of 10%.

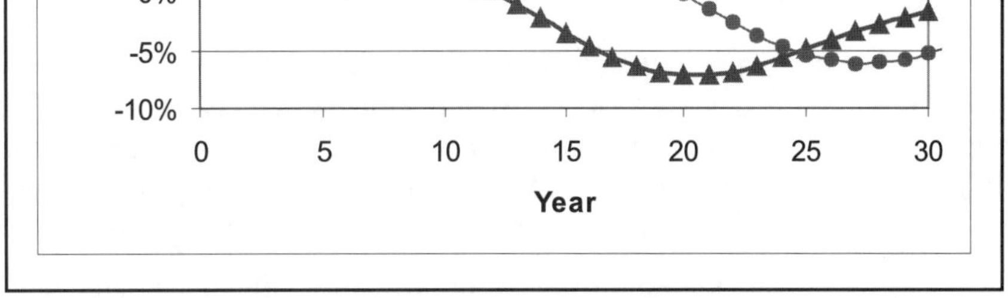

Figure 4.15 Comparison of accounting and economic performance measures: ROCE vs. IRR

So, even if a project inputs were totally accurate, a project earning a 10% IRR would never have an ROCE above 10%, except in the first year. The negative ROCE values occurring in the later years fascinated us even more. They occur because the *revenue matching* principle used in financial accounting spreads DD&A over the life of the project, actually causing the Net Income to go negative toward the end of the project life. Projects with negative ROCE certainly retard efforts to achieve the desired compensation.

CHAPTER 4

The misguided belief in the equivalence between financial and economic performance measures ignores the underlying differences between the two. First, the sources of the valuation, Net Income for ROCE and NCF for IRR, differ dramatically over time, as Figure 4.13 demonstrates. Second, IRR adjusts NCF for the time value of money concept, while ROCE ignores time value of money completely.

The response to this education is another misguided perception that somehow these problems cancel out when all the projects are aggregated. To illustrate this fallacy, the same investment used in Figure 4.15 was repeated for 10 more years. The consolidated ROCE schedule is shown as the enterprise ROCE. Again, note that even aggregating the projects over an 11 year period, the ROCE falls below the desired 10% standard.

As an interesting experiment, we asked the question "What does IRR need to be for the project before the ROCE for the first 10 years of the project exceeded 10%?" The answer found using goal seek was about a 23% IRR, or a value significantly greater than the 10% return objective. This explains why many firms may specify a 10% return objective, but then add the constraint that IRR must exceed 20% to be accepted.

Figure 4.15 portrays another of the problems with ROCE. At the end of the project life, ROCE goes negative, even though positive economic profits exist, due to the historical non-cash charges. Because of this problem, companies have made some incredibly silly decisions using ROCE. One example involves selecting assets for sale. DD&A is a financial book value, bearing no relationship to depreciation used to compute income taxes. Selling a profitable property to eliminate a fictional DD&A value seldom adds value, and may reduce shareholder value. Another recent example was a company selling spare equipment, because they added to the capital cost (reduced ROCE) without improving revenue; yet, a year later they had to buy new equipment at several times the value of the old equipment. Almost $40 m was spent that reduced ROCE even more in that year. Financial performance measures have absolutely nothing to do with shareholder value.

Improving Financial Performance Measures

Financial books provide the bulk of information about the performance of organizations. Like any report, the reader must exercise caution; otherwise, gross errors may plague the decision-making process. The process of preparing financial reports involves considerable time and cost. The information can be useful, just be sure to understand its strengths and weaknesses.

The problems plaguing financial measures have been well documented and methods for improving the information are underway. *Economic value added* (EVA) adjusts traditional financial analysis to better approximate actual economic profit. Firms, like Coca-Cola, CSX Corp., and AT&T, use EVA to evaluate and reward their management. Though relatively new in its implementation, the concept has been around over 100 years.[4.13] The EVA process follows the following steps:

- Calculation of operating profit from financial statement data by adjusting accounting profit for some of the distortions discussed earlier.
- Calculation of the cost-of-capital. and
- Comparison of operating profit to the cost-of-capital.

EVA adjusts accounting measures by formally including the cost of using other peoples money, and correcting the accrual based accounting measures to reflect the actual flow of money. This format is expressed in Equation 4.7:

$$\text{Economic Profit} = \text{Net Operating Profit after taxes} - (\text{Cost of Capital} * \text{Capital}) \tag{4.7}$$

The methodology requires considerable time and energy reviewing and editing annual reports, which is one reason it is so popular with people who know how and like to do that. The second addition is formal consideration of the cost-of-capital, like the project return standard used in economic analysis. Determination of the cost-of-capital is discussed in the next section.

Without going into detailed examples of EVA, because it requires more detailed knowledge of financial reporting than can be adequately covered here, several excellent references exist.[4.14, 4.15] New books on value management are published everyday that pursue these topics in great detail.[4.16. 4.17]

While most of the value management approaches try to convert financial information to economic compatible approaches, another approach, called *market value added* (MVA), appeals to the information available in the market place relative to book values. Equation 4.7 defines the basic format for MVA.

$$\text{MVA} = \text{Market Value of Firm} - \text{Capital} \qquad \textbf{(4.8)}$$

where the market value of the firm is the sum of the market values of debt and equity and capital is the book value of debt and equity. Also, to handle scale effects, practitioners normally work with percentage changes over time. Example 4.8 shows the calculations for a two year period for the example company used earlier.

Example 4.8: Compute the MVA for the example company using the previous data, and assuming that the share price was $55 in year t and $60 in year t+1 for 500 million shares outstanding.

	Book Value			Market Value			MVA
Year	Debt	Equity	Total	Debt	Equity	Total	Total
t	4,037	13,667	17,704	4,037	27,500	31,537	13,833
t+1	4,387	14,382	18,769	4,387	30,000	34,387	15,618
Change	350	715	1,065	350	2,500	2,850	1,785
							12.90%

The data under the book value heading comes from the financial reports presented earlier. The market value information is the stock price times the number of outstanding shares. The example also assumes that the debt book value fairly represents the market debt value. The last column, MVA Total, captures the change over the two year period. Finally, the percentage change of 12.9% is the ratio of $1,785 to the starting value $13,833. MVA increases almost 13%. Note that this compares to a historical ROE of 12%.

Financial Summary

This section summarizes the basic format associated with financial reporting, along with considerable discussion of the uses of the information. Like all professions, care must be exercised when using such information, for the potential for misuse and abuse runs rampant. Failure to understand the assumptions and principles behind the generation of the data exacerbates the problem, just as in a technical discipline.

In analyzing organizations for investing, determining performance standards or incentive schemes is a complicated process. Two choices currently prevail: extrapolate from historical information, or trust that the market data conveys the right answer. Our feeling is that both approaches can create as much harm as good when used improperly. Be careful.

ESTABLISHING THE DISCOUNT RATE

One of the main applications of financial information is to establish criteria for accepting or rejecting projects – the discount rate. Effective standardization of investment analysis often separates the successful from the failed organizations. The entire subject of investment analysis assumes money is spent to make more money. To properly analyze an investment alternative, the cost of the invested money must be estimated. If the project fails to recover the cost of the investment plus cost of borrowing, it destroys value. Chapter 2 outlined evidence about profit performance historically.

Management controls investment patterns via several avenues: establishing hurdle or discount rates, commodity price forecasts, inflation forecasts, and exchange rate forecasts for international firms. This section addresses methods for establishing hurdle rates, while Chapter 7 covers the other topics. Like other areas relating to project analysis, alternative terms describe the same process; such as project return standard, cost-of-capital, etc. Whatever the logic used to justify the number, every project must earn enough money to cover the capital outlay, or investment cost plus provide the desired return to the investors (debt and equity).

Investors express required discount rates in percentages, like 10% or 15%. If the hurdle rate is 15%, an investment earning 20% exceeds the required value and earns more than it costs, or adds value to the treasury. A 5% return earns less than the hurdle and is normally rejected unless mitigating circumstances, like safety or environmental concerns exist.

TABLE 4.14

Alternative Methods for Selecting Hurdle Rates

1. Cost of Debt	20.5%
2. Cost of Equity	1.7%
3. Weighted Cost-of-Capital	31.6%
4. Subjective Measure	27.3%
5. Expectations for Growth	2.6%
6. Risk Adjusted Rate	9.5%
7. Other	6.8%
Total	100.0%

A variety of methods exists to establish hurdle rates for individual projects. A survey by Boyle and Schenk found that firms used several methods to compute the hurdle rate.[(4.18)] The alternative methods are summarized in Table 4.14.

Slightly less than 80% of the surveyed firms employ method 1, 3, or 4. Most privately held companies and governments use method 1, while larger, publicly owned organizations use method 3 or 4. The difference lies in the resulting values, cost of debt may vary from 3-8%, while methods 3 and 4 normally yield values from 9% to 25%. Taking extreme cases, more projects can pass a 3% hurdle rate than a 25% hurdle rate. Between methods 3 and 4, we prefer 3, the weighted cost-of-capital. Adding subjective elements commonly takes two forms.

First, the cost-of-capital is increased to reflect risk. The error in artificially adjusting the cost-of-capital is illustrated in Chapter 5 in some detail. The cost-of- capital already captures all costs including the markets perception of risk. A bank, for instance, adjusts the interest rate to reflect their perception of extra risk. Likewise, investors purchasing shares carefully assess future risk. Adding an artificial premium for risk effectively counts risk twice in the hurdle rate. Most of the financial theorists demonstrate that this follows from the *efficient market hypothesis*. We personally agree with those who believe that the efficient market hypothesis is generally true, but heed the advice of those who see its limitations.[(4.19)]

The second adjustment arises when management wants to encourage certain types of projects, usually labeled strategic investments. Most of the chemical industry was justified using different hurdle rates than traditional lines of business. Today, the same approach is being used for building electricity power plants to use natural gas production, and to compare lease versus purchase decisions. Changing the hurdle rate to accommodate specific investments is management's prerogative, but care should always be exercised to avoid expensive mistakes.

Modern asset valuation (MAV) recommends using the after-tax cost of debt, and handling investor risk by quantifying the impact of risk in the actual cash flows. Adding value means generating a positive inflow of money. Direct analysis of these cash flows goes straight to the heart of the issue rather than burying it the often little understood, hodgepodge of factors called a hurdle rate. Since cost-of-capital dominates the current investment process, the discussion turns to explaining this concept.

Weighted Average Cost-of-Capital (WACC) – The Traditional Approach

The *weighted average cost-of-capital* means exactly what the name implies. A firm borrows money in the form of debt and equity, each with its own distinct cost. Combining the various costs using a weighting scheme yields an average or weighted cost-of-capital. If every project earns at least the average cost-of-capital, the lenders recovers their investment plus earn the specified return. Equation 4.9 summarizes the simplest format. Review Figure 4.3 to see where this fits into the organization.

$$WACC = (E)*C_e + (1-E)*C_d*(1-TR) \tag{4.9}$$

where:

E = percentage of equity in the capital structure
$(1 - E)$ = percentage of debt of in the capital structure
TR = effective tax rate
C_e = cost of equity
C_d = cost of debt

Other types of borrowing, like preferred shares, can be added, but the process is exactly the same. Besides, all other borrowing types just mix the properties of debt and equity. Debt has two main features: a fixed payment (interest) is due every year, and the debt owners have seniority in the case of bankruptcy. Equity reverses this relationship: no payments are guaranteed, shareholders are last to receive compensation during bankruptcy, and, in exchange for giving up any guarantees, the shareholders get to vote for management and receive a free copy of the financial report.

Debt and equity costs vary to compensate investors for differences in risk. Measuring the cost of debt is easier and more accurate than equity cost estimation. The cost of debt, C_d, is the weighted average of outstanding debt times the effective interest rate. These required numbers are reported in the footnotes of many annual reports, so the calculation is a simple averaging process. The financial report gives before-tax interest rates, so the (1-TR) element of Equation 4.9 converts the value to an after-tax basis in those countries that allow deduction of interest on income taxes. When interest is not deductible for income tax purposes, ignore the 1-TR term.

Example 4.9: The financial report of a company shows that they issues $100 million in bonds five years ago at an interest rate of 12%, and $300 million in bonds last year at 10%. A note from the local bank on $50 million at 8% also exists. Assuming a tax rate of 40%, what is the after-tax cost of debt, C_d, for the $450 million in debt?

$$C_d = \left[\left(\frac{100}{450}\right)*0.12 + \left(\frac{300}{450}\right)*0.10 + \left(\frac{50}{450}\right)*0.09\right](1-0.40)$$
$$= (0.0267 + 0.0667 + 0.01)*0.6 = (0.1033)*0.6 = 0.062$$

Debt costs about 10% before-tax and 6.2% after-tax. The borrower pays an effective rate of 6.2%. Most major borrowers have an effective cost of debt between 4-7%, depending on when the debt was issued and the relative magnitude of the borrowings.

Calculating the cost of equity, C_e, is tougher, for several reasons. First, shareholders are a very diverse group as shown in Figure 4.4. Pension plans may not expect the same returns as individual investors, and even if they do, determining this value is quite difficult. Shareholders also receive their return in two forms: dividends and equity appreciation. Paying dividends yearly appeals to retirees and others involved with pension schemes, while younger, more aggressive investors may prefer higher capital appreciation, and no dividends. For companies with millions or billions of shares outstanding, surveying shareholders for information on desired returns could be cost prohibitive. The high cost of acquiring desired return information forces management to employ some simplifications. Different tax regimes for dividends and capital gains further complicate the problem.

The simplest approach to estimating the cost of equity assumes that the share price includes all information about the markets desired returns (another outgrowth of the efficient market hypothesis). Handling dividends is easy since every firm announces dividends, so this number is known. Extrapolating this value forever gives one estimate of the future dividend stream. Estimating the length of time investors will hold their shares presents serious problems, however. With about 500 million shares outstanding, for the example company, some shares will be sold this year, more the next, and so on. Estimating the timing and magnitude of these sales involves some complicated modelling. Companies have historical information on the length of the holding periods (10% < a year, 20%< two years, etc.). Assuming historical patterns hold, an annualized estimate can be generated.

Rather than go through the more complicated process, assume that stock holders hold their shares forever. This convenient assumption eliminates capital gains, since dividends are the only way to earn a return when shares are never sold (called a perpetuity). This called the *dividend valuation model,* as derived in Equation 4.10.*(4.20)*

$$P = \sum_{t=1}^{\infty} \frac{D(1+g)^t}{(1+C_e)^t}$$

$$C_e = \frac{D}{P} + g + \frac{g*D}{P} \Rightarrow \frac{D}{P} + g \qquad \textbf{(4.10)}$$

where:

P = price of the stock
D = dividends paid during the year
t = time measured in years
g = expected growth rate in dividends over time (usually greater than inflation) and the other variables are defined earlier

Values for the share price, P, and current dividends, D, can be found anywhere stock quotations are available, while dividend growth is usually assumed or taken from speeches by management. A common value for g is around 10% or the inflation rate plus 4-6%. Historical growth can also be used, but most investors look to the future, not the past. The only unknown in Equation 4.5 is the cost of equity, C_e. Solving the infinite series gives the second part of the equation (we did this on MathCAD© owing to too many years away from math class). Of the three terms in the second part of the equation, the (g*D)/P is normally dropped because the value is so small. Assuming a $2 dividend and a 10% growth, taking 10% of the dividend stream (= $0.20) contributes little to the final value.

Paying a $2 dividend on a $60 stock price yields a dividend return of 3.33%. The remaining 10% cost comes from the growth target.

Completing Equation 4.10 requires allocating capital between equity (E) and debt (1-E). The financial report contains values for long term debt and equity; moreover, the debt to total capitalization ratio gives this percentage directly. In the example company annual report, debt comprised 23.37% of total capital (= 1- E), so equity is the remaining percentage, 76.63% (= E). Historical debt and equity percentages are available for any publicly traded company.

Example 4.10: A company pays a $2 per share dividend on a stock selling for $60 per share and is expected to grow at 10% per year. Compute the cost of equity, C_e.

$$C_e = \frac{2}{60} + 0.10 = 0.0333 + 0.10 = 0.1333 \quad or \quad 13.3\%$$

CHAPTER 4

Choosing between debt and equity is a complex decision, because changing the ratio alters the cost of each. Debt is cheaper than equity, as the example shows, owing to the deductibility of interest and the lower risk to the lender. Lenders of debt are guaranteed interest payments (dividends don't have to be paid), and debt holders recover their investment first when a company liquidates and shareholders receive what's leftover. Figure 4.16 depicts the risk/return tradeoff for various sources of funds.

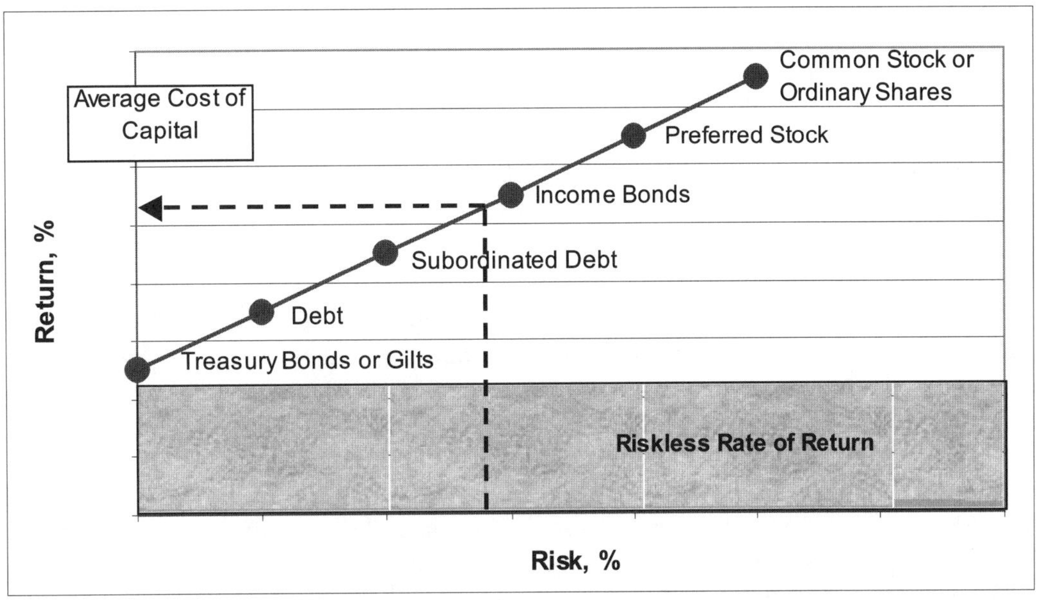

Figure 4.16 Risk/return trade-off for sources of capital

Government backed securities, like treasury bills in the U. S. and gilt's in the U. K, offer the lowest return because of lower risk. Why, because governments can either raise taxes, print more money, or borrow more if they run a short of cash. Debt has the next lowest return due to the guarantees in the loan agreements. Risk and return rises with other instruments until common or ordinary shares are reached. The actual value varies by industry, firm within an industry, and over time as market forces change, like inflation and exchange rates.

At first glance, the optimal course of action would be to fund the organization entirely with debt because of the lower cost (this called going private or a leverage buyout, LBO). Alas, it isn't that simple. As debt increases, the coverage ratios get worse, meaning the ability to repay interest and principal declines. Take the situation for the example firm. Net income in year t was around $1,820m, with long-term debt and equity being $4,024m and $30 billion, respectively. The equity figure is based on 500m outstanding shares times the market price of $60 per share. Now, suppose management decides to buy out the shareholders. Added to the present debt, the company would have to pay interest on over $34 billion, which at a before-tax rate of say 8%, requires about $2.72 billion annually in interest payments. With a net income of less than $2 billion, most lenders would perceive an increase in risk, and demand an even higher interest rate.

The relationship between the amount of debt and the cost of funds is shown in Figure 4.17. Up to some debt percentage, the market seldom demands a higher risk premium. The threshold for starting to increase the risk premium depends on a variety of factors, but a crude rule-of-thumb for international firms is around 30%. For this figure the cost of debt and equity computed in the examples were extended from 0% to the 30% threshold, then increased thereafter.

Companies like Moody's, Standard and Poors, Value Line and others provide estimates of these curves, for a fee, of course. If the firm has no plans for major expenditures, it can operate around the

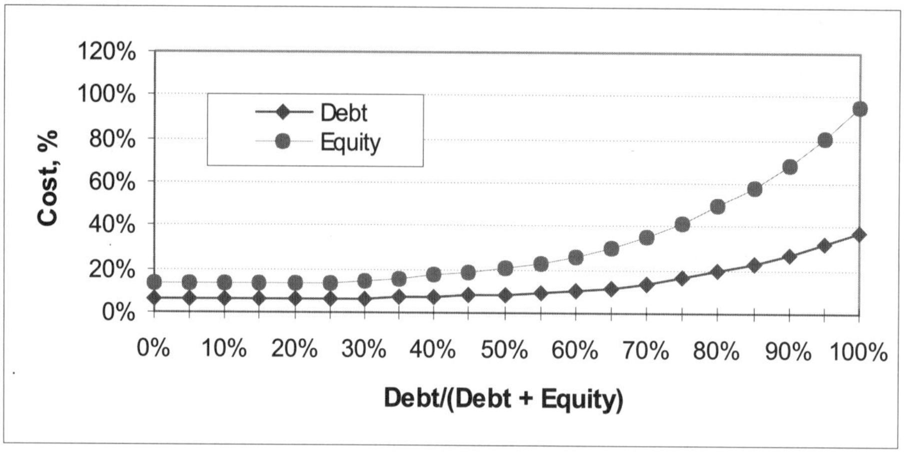

Figure 4.17 Effect of capital structure on the cost of funds

relevant threshold value, say 30%. The problem with operating near the threshold is the lumpiness of most investments, When borrowing money for a major acquisition or development, large sums of capital are involved, often billions. During a mega acquisition, spending $50-200 billion is quite common. Borrowing the entire amount impacts the capital structure considerably, as companies like Chevron and UNOCAL, discovered. Figure 4.18 shows the same industry debt to debt plus equity ratio displayed earlier, along with similar values for UNOCAL and Chevron. Both firms had debt levels near or below the industry, but the large borrowing jumped them far above the industry average, at for a brief period. The jump in debt ratios increases the cost of capital for both firms.

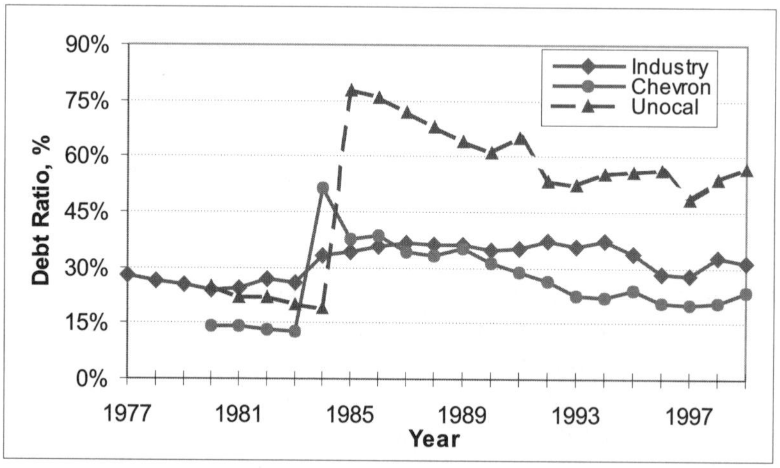

Figure 4.18 Sample capitalization ratios

CHAPTER 4

Optimal debt/equity ratios vary with the competitive environment internationally. Figure 4.17 differs around the world, allowing firms in some countries to borrow more than other countries. In particular, the threshold before borrowing costs increase may be as high as 50-60% in Germany and Japan because of borrowing rules set-up to assist them to recover from WWII. Part of the difference arises from the higher domestic savings rates, which increases the supply of investment money relative to demand, causing interest rates to fall. Another, perhaps more important element emerges from the close working relationship between the primary lenders, banks, and the firms. Filings by Daimler Benz for listing on the New York stock exchange under U. S. accounting rules demonstrated the strong relationship with prominent German and Swiss banks. By having detailed insights into Daimler Benz's financial condition, risk is reduced and, thus, interest rates fall.

Example 4.11 combines the cost of debt and equity, and the portion of equity used from the previous examples. The example assumes 70% equity and 30% debt to derive the weighted cost-of-capital. The calculated cost-of-capital of 11% replicates a common industry value. WACC values for industry range from 8 to 20%, depending on firm size and expectations about equity.

Example 4.11: Management decides to use 70% equity and 30% in their capital structure. With a 13.33% cost of equity and 6.2% cost of debt, compute the weighted cost-of-capital.

$$WACC = (0.7)(0.133) + (0.3)(0.062) = 0.091 + 0.0186 = 0.1119\% \quad or \quad 11.2\%$$

The WACC example includes historical estimates of the cost of debt, cost of equity and capitalization structure. Any mixture of debt or equity can be handled with this structure. The WACC forms the starting point for establishing the investment discount rate. If every project earns exactly 11%, the debt and equity holders receive the expected interest and dividend return. Returns in excess of 11% permit complete repayment of interest and dividends, plus generating surplus funds for reinvestment in the new projects. If a project earns less than 11%, someone will be unhappy, and that unhappy person is usually the shareholder. Debtors always get their interest payment, since defaulting on a loan causes bankruptcy. The shareholders will forgo their dividend or growth in dividend.

Two complaints revolve around this discussion. One concentrates on the use of historical information, to the exclusion of future cost estimation. Adding estimates of future costs actually is embedded in the equity cost, so this complaint misses the point to a certain extent. The second and more relevant objection stems from the growing trend toward managing risk directly. The numbers for debt and equity reflect actual borrowing, or what accountants called *paid-up capital*. This means the numbers are reported directly in the financial reports. One firm may borrow money to hedge against fire or other calamities, while another may buy insurance. The first firm shows debt with the associated interest payment, while the second shifts the burden into its operating cost and therefore removes it from WACC.

Analysis of actual project performance, like those shown in Chapter 2, indicate that around 70-80% of all projects earn less than the WACC. Poor predictions of price, production, reserves, costs, etc. cause this failure. Many assume that this means the organization is going out of business. Not necessarily. First, the remaining projects (which are usually the largest ones) often earn enough to offset the losers. Second, even if the aggregate performance still falls under the WACC, only the shareholders dividend growth expectations are impacted. This may cost management their job if the shareholders get too upset, but it shouldn't make the firm insolvent.

Capital Asset Pricing Model for Equity Valuation

The *capital asset pricing model (CAPM)* tries to overcome the limitations in the dividend valuation model by relying on market information. By comparing the historical movement in individual firm share prices relative to the market, like S&P 500 in the US or FTSE in the UK, Equation 4.11 first estimates β, or the slope of a line. Then, with estimates of future market returns and the appropriate risk free rates, the cost of equity is derived.

$$C_e = R_f + \beta * (\overline{MR} - R_f^*) \quad \textbf{(4.11)}$$

where:

R_f = risk free investment (30 year treasury bonds = 5%)

β = volatility of company stock versus market, usually S&P 500 index (= 0.8)

$\overline{MR}$ = expected market return on equities (historical market risk investment (10 year return on S&P 500 = 18.21%)

R_f^* = historical risk free investment (10 year return on US long-term bond = 8.6%)

Beta measures the sensitivity of the returns on the firms stock to changes in the returns from the market. A beta of 1 means the firm returns move in unison with the market, and beta < 1 implies the firms returns change less than the market, or are less risky.

Various methods exist for determining the risk premium ($\overline{MR} - R_f$). Stewart advocates a 6% market premium, based on the historical spread between the S&P 500 returns and the return on long-term government bonds.(4.21) Copeland, et. al. advocate the use of the difference between the geometric mean return on the market (S&P 500) and long-term government bonds, both computed over a long time frame.(4.22) They argue for a number around 5%.

Example 4.12: Use the CAPM model to determine the WACC assuming $\beta = 0.8$, $\overline{MR} = 0.15$, and the risk free rate is 5% as argued by Copeland, and 8.6% as given in the definition of Equation 4.10.

Risk Free Rate = 5%	Risk Free Rate = 8.6%
$C_e = 0.05 + 0.8 * (0.15 - 0.05) = 0.13$	$C_e = 0.05 + 0.8 * (0.15 - 0.086) = 0.1012$
$WACC = 0.7 * 0.13 + 0.3 * 0.62 = 0.1096$ *or* 10.96%	$WACC = 0.7 * 0.1012 + 0.3 * 0.62 = 0.0894$ *or* 8.94%

The left hand column uses the same risk free rate of 5%, while the right hand column uses 5% for the risk free rate and 8.6% to reflect the value of bonds as an alternative investment. Both methods are used in practice. The 5% value comes from averages over the last 50-100 years, while the 8.6% reflects the last 10 years. The choice of time frame is quite important, obviously. We prefer the longer time frame, or at least a time frame that matches the longest investment opportunity being considered by the investor.

The CAPM approach provides an alternative measure of the cost-of-equity. Some authors are concerned that it adds as many problems as it solves.(4.23, 4.24) Estimation of WACC is fraught with risk, regardless of the model used to generate the estimate. Anyone who uses one number without recognizing the inherent risks is both likely to miss value adding investments, and should avoid addressing risks in prices, production, costs, etc. The reason: the choice of the discount rate is the single most important input into the investment valuation process.

Inflation Adjusted Discount rate

The WACC computed above goes by several names: *nominal* WACC, *money-of-the-day* WACC, and *current* WACC. These synonyms mean that estimated inflation is included in the cost of debt and equity. Observe that the cost of debt values cited were 12%, 10%, and 9%. When a bank lends you money, numbers like these are quoted. These values include the banks estimate of inflation. If the bank thought inflation was going to be 15%, they wouldn't loan money at 10%. Similarly, The estimate for the cost of equity indicated that dividend growth, g, should be greater than inflation.

An alternative approach used by many international firms considers inflation directly, rather than burying it in the discount rate. Anyone operating internationally understands the impact of the variability of inflation. In the U. S. inflation reached 15% in the early 80's, while some Latin American and former Soviet Union countries have exceeded 20% per month. A second, equally important issue recognizes the variability of inflation over time. Most people expect inflation rates to vary, so the question becomes what inflation assumption to use in calculating the cost-of-capital.

The *inflation adjusted discount rate* goes by several names: *real* discount rate, *deflated* discount rate, or *constant* discount rate. These synonyms mean inflation is taken out of the cited value to reflect the purchasing power or value in a reference year, like 2001. The basic equation is:

$$\text{Nominal WACC} = (1 + \text{Inflation Rate})(1 + \text{Real Rate}) - 1$$

$$or$$

$$(1 + \text{Real Rate}) = \frac{1 + \text{Nominal WACC}}{1 + \text{Inflation Rate}} \qquad \textbf{(4.12)}$$

$$or$$

$$(1 + \text{Real Rate}) = \frac{1 + 0.11}{1 + 0.04} = 1.067 \quad or \quad 6.7\%$$

Normal practice begins by estimating the nominal WACC, as before and then adjusting WACC using the average expected inflation rate. If a 4% inflation rate is predicted, an inflation adjusted hurdle of 6.7% gives the same investment decisions as an 11% nominal discount rate. This equivalence disappears, however, when inflation rates change over time. The real difference between the two approaches is that the nominal approach implies constant inflation rates, while the inflation adjusted method allows inflation to vary. Chapter 7 discusses inflation forecasting.

Figure 4.19 compares the nominal and inflation adjusted or real discount rates historically. The dotted part of the bar chart indicates the real discount rate used, while the upper part of the chart indicates the estimated inflation rate. The values on top each bar are the nominal discount rate or the product of the values within the bar using Equation 4.12. The period covers the OPEC boom between 1973 and 1981 as well as the bust after 1986.

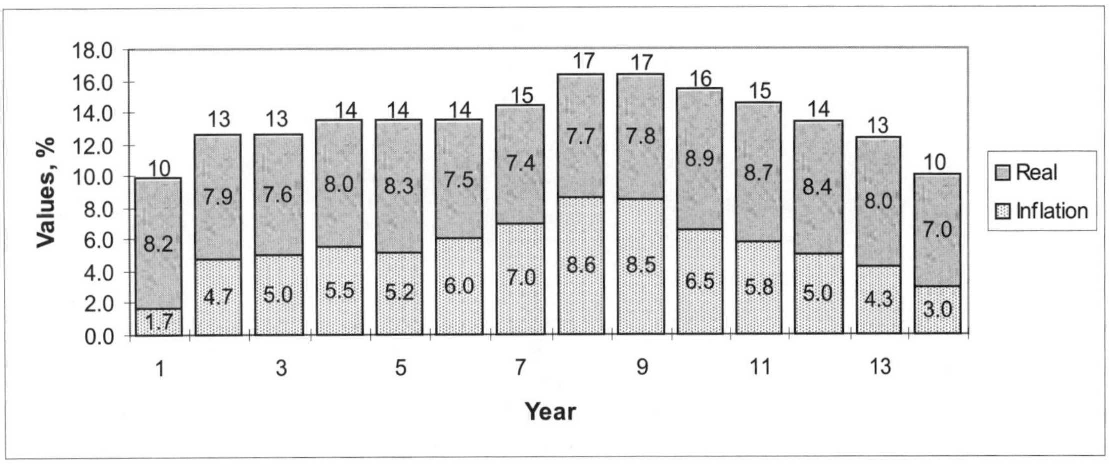

Figure 4.19 Nominal versus inflation adjusted discount rate

In the early 70's the inflation rate was less than 2%. As inflation rose during the boom period, the company adjusted both the estimated inflation rate and required real discount rate until peaking in years 8 and 9, after which the values began to decline. By the last year the values were back to the same nominal rate as the starting discount rate in year 1. This is where most companies are now and will likely stay unless another shock occurs.

For firms adjusting their nominal discount rates to reflect inflation, the equivalence between the two approaches is hopefully obvious. Reality is a different matter though. Investors using nominal discount rates seldom change the value and then with a great deal of reluctance. However a discount rate is established, it is viable as long as it is consistent with the organizations overall strategy. Unfortunately, some firms ignore the need for consistency.

Like many aspects of investment analysis, one can never say something is absolutely wrong, but using high discounts in low inflation periods runs counter to most investor requirements. Refer back to the risk and return line in Figure 4.16. The major determinant of the risk free rate is inflation. As inflation falls the intercept of the line shifts down, implying a falling real rate. Even if this logic is ignored, just be aware that the logic described in Equation 4.12 produces very different investment decisions than decisions based on discount rates used in Equation 4.11. We prefer equation 4.12.

The major objection raised about the formal specification of inflation concerns the ability to project inflation accurately. In truth inflation has little impact on investment decisions. Investment analysis proceeds by first estimating the value of an item in this year, say year t. Then, most computer programs escalate that item to generate future values. For instance, if operating costs are \$2 m this year and the *escalation rate* is 4% per year, operating costs in the future are computed as follows:

Year	1	2	3	4	5	6	7	8	9
Opex	2	2.08	2.16	2.25	2.34	2.43	2.53	2.63	2.74

Operating costs increase by 4% a year. Escalation captures the same process as inflation – the change in cost over time, but is slightly different. Inflation measures the change in the cost of all goods and services in an economy, while escalation refers to specific elements of the economy. Combining the escalation of all commodities produces the inflation rate. (See Chapter 7)

Each escalation rate though can be split into two components: that specific to the item (the real or inflation adjusted component) and the general inflation rate. Equipment costs rose more than 20% in years when the inflation rate was about 14%. The real component would then be 5.26% {=(1.20/1.14)-1}. Once an item is escalated, it is then discounted using either the nominal or inflation adjusted discount rate. The basic relationship is outlined in Equation 4.12.

$$NPV = \frac{Opex*(1+i)*(1+r_e)}{(1+i)*(1+r_p)} \qquad \textbf{(4.13)}$$

where:

- NPV = net present value
- Opex = operating cost
- r_p = real discount rate
- i = inflation rate
- r_e = real escalation rate

Observe that inflation cancels out in the process of compute present value. What really controls the valuation of projects is the real escalation rate, r_e, relative to the real discount rate, r_p. If $r_e > r_p$ the item increases in importance over time and the opposite if $r_e < r_p$. But it should be apparent that errors in the inflation forecast cancel out when computing present values.

Most computer programs have the capability to handle escalation rates for each commodity which differs from the inflation rate. Most companies assume that individual commodities increase at the inflation rate, meaning the value of $r_e = 0$.

SUMMARY

This WACC computation and the variants discussed so far reflect item 3 in Table 4.14. Some use this value as the discount rate; others add or subtract from it to reflect subjective factors. Probably the most common subjective factor is risk. We have heard people say that exploration is riskier than other business lines, so add 2-15% to the WACC. Conversely, some lower the rate when risk appears to be less, like in a pipeline or manufacturing. Another, more cynical explanation, heard far too often, is that "technical professionals can't predict their input values accurately, so this just corrects for poor data input."

The limitations of WACC should be self-evident from the discussion. All models make limiting assumptions and WACC is no exception. Arbitrarily adding or subtracting subjective risk values contradicts the entire process. Debt and equity costs include the markets perception of risk, and these risk estimates vary with the capitalization rate. Financial reports describe each firms lines of business and economic performance and analyst scrutinize the ability to meet their debt obligations. So, the market knows what is happening in all business lines. Believers in efficient markets must also accept that the market incorporates this information into their lending decisions

No reasonable, logical framework has ever been presented to justify changing the discount rate for risk. The problem arises from an era of limited computing power (we call it the slide rule era, even though main frame computers might be included). Early capital budgeting decisions focused entirely on using WACC to value projects. Later the need to reflect risk in the inputs, like price, production, costs, taxes, etc., became apparent. Since analyzing input variability took considerable time, the easiest solution was to add a few percentage points to WACC. This allowed usage of existing programs without having to perform detailed risk assessment. This process is very understandable, since every discipline faces unknowns that are difficult to handle.

This approach simplifies risk beyond reason with today's computational tools. Business and intermediate school texts only use this approach because it is easy to demonstrate the concept of risk. Most texts very carefully emphasize the limitations of such approaches. Experts in the field of capital budgeting have very strong opinions about using the discount rate to include risk, like: Bierman and Smidt showed as far back as 1971 that the proper way to discount was with the after-tax cost-of-debt.[4.25] With the growth of the efficient market hypothesis and the capital asset pricing model, experts in the field shifted to the belief that the risk free rate was the proper discount rate.[4.26]

Furthermore, current technology allows direct, detailed risk analysis. To continue to use a slide rule mentality ignores the opportunities to add value by tackling risk directly, rather than informally.

On another point about the value of financial books, recent discussion by Jensen notes that the debate about the relationship between financial and project profit measures goes back as far as 1918.[4.27] Whether one likes or dislikes financial reporting, it is here and required by law and people find it easy to use. The best approach it to use understand financial reports, and use them as wisely as possible.

REFERENCES

4.1 Howell, J., Personal Communication.

4.2 Chua, J. and R. Woodward, *JPT* (Apr. 1992), pp. 502-505.

4.3 *The Economist* (27 Jan., 1996), p. 17.

4.4 *BP Statistical Review of World Energy*, various years, and the Arthur Anderson, *World Oil Trends* (1995 edition).

4.5 Campbell, J., *Petroleum Evaluation for Financial Disclosures,* Campbell Petroleum Series (1982).

4.6 Bernstein, L., *Financial Statement Analysis,* Richard Irwin Inc. (1974).

4.7 *Performance Profiles of Major Energy Producers*, Energy Information Administration (Jan. 1995).

4.8 "Amazons's Amazing Ambition," *The Economist* (26 Feb., 2000), p. 24.

4.9 Tobin, J., "A General Equilibrium Approach to Monetary Theory," *Journal of Money, Credit, and Banking* (Feb. 1969), pp. 15-29.

4.10 Lindenberg, E. B. and S. A. Ross, "Tobin's q Ratio and Industrial Organization," *Journal of Business* (Jan. 1981), pp. 1-32.

4.11 Fama, E. and K. French, "The Cross-Section of Expected Stock Returns," *Journal of Finance* (June 1992), pp. 427-65

4.12 Harris, R. and F. Marston, "Value versus Growth Stocks: Book-to-Market Growth and Beta," *Financial Analysts Journal* (Sept. 1994), pp. 18-24.

4.13 Marshall, A., *Principles of Economics*, McMillan Press (1890).

4.14 Stewart, G., *The Quest for Value*, Harper Collings (1991).

4.15 Stewart, G., "EVA: Fact and Fantasy," *Journal of Applied Corporate Finance* (Summer 1994), pp. 71-84.

4.16 Knight, J., *Value Based Management: Developing a Systematic Approach to Creating Shareholder Value*, McGraw-Hill (1997).

4.17 Rappaprot, A., *Creating Shareholder Value: A Guide to Managers and Investors*, Free Press (1997).

4.18 Boyle, H. and G. Schenck, *JPT* (Sept. 1984), p. 680.

4.19 Edgar Peters, *Chaos and Order in the Capital Markets*, John Wiley and Sons (1991).

4.20 Gordon, M., "Dividends, Earnings and Stock Prices." *Review of Economics and Statistics* (May 1959), pp. 131-155.

4.21 Stewart, *ibid.*

4.22 Copeland, T., Keller, T., and J. Murin, *Valuation: Measuring and Managing the Value of Companies,* John Wiley and Sons (1994).

4.23 Fama and French, *ibid.*

4.24 Haugen, R., *The New Finance: The Case Against Efficient Markets*, Prentice-Hall (1995).

4.25 Bierman, H. and S. Smidt, *The Capital Budgeting Decision*, McMillan Press (1971).

4.26 Robert Jensen, "A Modern Theory of Finance Analysis Difference Between Accounting and Economic Rates of Return," in Raj Aggarwal, *Capital Budgeting Under Uncertainty*, Prentice-Hall (1993).

4.27 Jensen, *ibid.*

CHAPTER 5

MEASURING VALUE: ASSUMPTIONS AND LIMITATIONS

Accurate comparison of investment opportunities probably causes more problems than any other decision-making activity; yet, few fully appreciate the inherent complexities and limitations of the process. The preceding pages describe the inputs into the process for generating NCF and financial accounts. Before reading this chapter, please realize that most investments require professionals to estimate values for hundreds, if not thousands, of variables. After deriving the initial estimates, forecasts are generated for each variable, often up to 50 years in some cases. The combination of these thousands of inexact numbers somehow comes together to define the value of an investment.

This chapter defines the process of converting the myriad of estimated values into a value format that investors can use to achieve their investment objectives. Even with pure intentions, any process faces several risks. One critical component is the imprecision in the numbers, since errors tend to compound, rather than cancel out. Second, the process faces the problem of reducing the complex interaction of variables to a manageable size, with the potential for losing or missing important issues. Even if a value measure could overcome these serious issues, conflicts in defining profitability and inconsistent objectives, often within the same organization, but certainly across organizations, complicate the ultimate decision-making. These are not mathematical issues, but decision-making problems. Should profits be measured using financial books (like ROCE) or cash flows? Most organizations move back and forth between financial and cash reports without regard for the impact on investment decisions, often leading to inconsistent and unstable investment patterns.

Consistency in defining profit is desirable, but organizations have goals other than profit. Chapter 4 outlined the basic goals of organizations. They are:

- Profitability
- Stability
- Growth
- Liquidity, and
- Solvency.

Governmental agencies add employment, fiscal responsibility, and the like to these objectives. Observe that investing to make a profit today may reduce growth and stability in the future, not to mention liquidity and solvency. Undertaking investments to create employment opportunities may reduce profitability in the near term, and so on. Industry, in fact, often reduces employment to enhance short-term profitability, but at the cost of future growth. Some firms now define their scarcest resource as manpower, not capital

None of the value metrics captures the trade-off in the conflicting objectives. Most investors focus entirely on profitability, to the complete exclusion of growth, stability, etc. Decision-makers then subjectively modify the investments to accommodate stability, growth, etc. This approach is flawed, because clear guidelines never exist about the proper treatment of the other objectives, or the proper balance among the objectives. This causes huge swings in investment patterns from year to year to correct for historical errors. Chapter 10 covers realistic methods for effective portfolio management that address these trade-offs.

With this understanding of the limitations in measuring profitability, the basic tenet of all profit models is the *time value of money.* Science has thermodynamics and plate tectonics that form the foundation of the respective disciplines. Time value of money is the essence of economic analysis. It says, "money today is worth more than money in the future." Ask yourself if you prefer $1 today or $1 in twenty years. Most people would opt for the $1 today, though cultures exist which weight their grandchildren's interest as much as their own. All profit measures used to select investments are based on the time value of money principle.

BASIC VALUE EQUATIONS

Many formulas exist which incorporate time value of money into profit measures, and are reviewed here for the reader who has not been exposed to the material, or needing a refresher.

Simple Interest: Simple interest rates are usually quoted as the percentage of the principle for a period of one year. With simple interest, the amount repaid depends on the length of time of the loan. This type of loan may be for any period, and is usually obtained by an individual from a bank. Borrowing $1000 for one year at 8% simple interest requires repayment of $1080 (= 1000 x 1.08) one year later. Simple interest is computed on the principal amount of the loan.

Compound Interest: With compound interest, the amount of interest paid is based on the principal plus interest, not just the principal like simple interest. Compound interest always exceeds simple interest due to the inclusion of interest previously earned or paid.

The following example illustrates compound interest. Assume you borrow $2000 with no payments due until the end of year 4. Since both principal and interest is due at the end of 4 years, the total amount due is $2720.98, as shown in Table 5.1, at an interest rate of 8%.

TABLE 5.1

Illustration of Compound Interest

Year	Principal at Start of Year	Interest @ 8%	Amount Owed at end of Year
1	$2000.00	$160.00	$2160.00
2	$2160.00	$172.80	$2332.80
3	$2332.80	$186.62	$2519.42
4	$2519.42	$201.55	$2720.98

Performing these calculations becomes quite tedious as the number of years increases. Equation 5.1 simplifies the calculation.

$$FN_n = PV_i * (1+i)^n = 2000 * (1.08)^4 = 2720.98 \tag{5.1}$$

where:

n = number of interest periods between the present and a future specified time

i = interest rate (expressed as a fraction)

PV_i = principal sum of money subject to interest (loaned or invested)

FV_n = future sum of money, n years away from the principal investment

CHAPTER 5

The amount of interest at the end of the first year is $PV_i*(1 + i)$, at the end of the second period $PV_i*(1 + i)^2$ and so on. Equation 5.1 sums the terms for n interest periods.

Equation 5.1 says that, if a sum "PV_i" invested at the present is compounded at interest rate "i", the future value at the end of "n" years is "FV_n." "FV_n" is the future value n years in the future and "PV_i," a present value at i discount rate. Most investment analysis estimates future NCF, which are equivalent to FV. To compare investments, normal practice computes PV by rearranging Equation 5.1, as shown in Equation 5.2.

$$PV_8 = \frac{FV}{(1+i)^n} = \frac{2720.98}{(1.08)^4} = 2000 \quad \textbf{(5.2)}$$

The time reference distinguishes "PV_i" from "FV_n". "PV_i" values money now and "FV_n" values money in the future. The difference between PV and FV reflect interest earnings between now and time "n". The two sums are equivalent, for anyone regarding 8% interest (i = 0.08) as fair would be willing to pay \$2,000 to receive \$2,720.98 four years hence or vice versa.

Equations 7.1 and 7.2 are often simplified by converting the values in parenthesis to a measure called a *discount factor* or *compound factor,* where

$$\begin{aligned} CF &= (1+i)^n = (1.08)^4 = 1.3605, \textit{and} \\ DF &= \frac{1}{(1+i)^n} = \frac{1}{1.3605} = 0.7350 \end{aligned} \quad \textbf{(5.3)}$$

where n and i are defined as before. Present value "PV;" times the compound factor "CF" gives the future value "FV_n," or \$2,720.98 = 2,000*(1.3605); conversely, \$2,000 = \$2,720.98*(0.7350). Discount and compound factors simplify calculations since numerous tables exist for different values of "i" and "n," as illustrated later in Appendix 5A.

Discount and compound factors also help explain time value of money. Choosing the right measure of time value of money was discussed in Chapter 4 in the cost-of-capital section. Texts historically tie the choice of factor to the cost of money or opportunity cost. In reality, the discount factor is merely a weighting scheme, reflecting that money is worth more today than money received in the future. Figure 5.1 demonstrates the relative impact of money as time and rate varies.

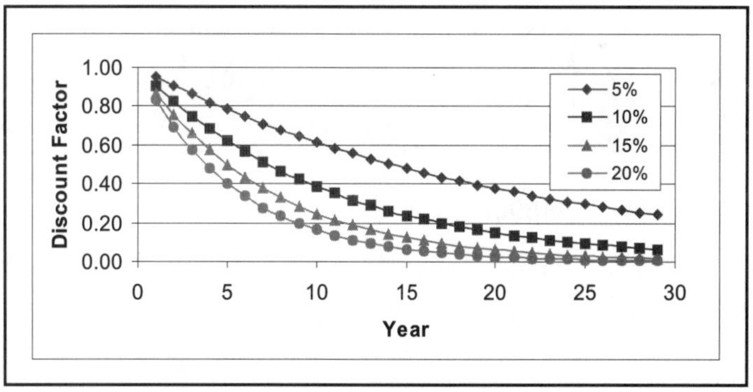

Figure 5.1 Discount rates over time

The discount factors decline over time, as expected, although the rate of change depends on the discount rate used. At a 5% discount rate, the value of \$1 at the end of 30 years is worth more than \$0.20. At a 20% discount rate, money is worthless at the end of 30 years. The value of money depends both on the discount rate used and on the length of time in the future. Higher discount rates impose a steeper slope on the lines.

Another way to approach time value of money determines the number of years before \$1 diminishes to some value, like \$0.10. At a 5% discount rate, more than 45 years must pass, while the same values for a 10% rate is 24 years, 16 years for a 15% rate, and 12 years for 20%. The choice of rate then influences investors' perspectives on the future. Said another way, investors using a 20% discount rate have a much shorter investment horizon than one using a 5% rate. For those new to the subject, investors use considerably different investment rates.

The profit models build on the time value of money weighting. One problem in the traditional models stems from the focus strictly on profit. Organizational goals – like liquidity, growth, stability, etc. – require money coming in on a regular basis. Adopting a discount of 15% says money adds little value after about 15 years; yet, most investors realize that the inflow of money has some value for achieving liquidity, stability, and growth objectives. This conflict between traditional profit measures and other objectives distorts investment patterns in actual practice.

Traditional value measures are explained first, and then alternative models, which seek to balance the multiple investment objectives better. No simple model can accurately combine all objectives into one value. This requires the tools outlined in Chapter 10.

Nominal and Effective Interest Rates

Equations 5.1 thru 5.3 assume that interest is paid once a year. Most lenders, whether it is a bank, a credit card agency, the corporate treasury or the local government, compound more often than once a year. The *nominal interest rate* is the quoted rate. The *effective interest rate* is a function of the nominal rate and the number of compounding periods each year. Most bank loans are paid monthly, for instance. Equation 5.4 gives the basic relationship for one year (n=1) and multiple years (n>1).

$$i=\left[1+\left(\frac{j}{m}\right)\right]^{m}-1 \quad or \quad i=\left[1+\left(\frac{j}{m}\right)\right]^{m*n}-n \qquad \textbf{(5.4)}$$

where: m = the number of interest periods per year (monthly, quarterly, daily, etc.)
j = the nominal interest rate, a fraction and the other variables are defined as before

Example 5.1: A bank advertises an interest rate of 8%, compounded quarterly. What is the effective rate? How would the effective rate change if the bank went to daily compounding? Assume n = 1.

$i=\left[1+\left(\frac{0.08}{4}\right)\right]^{4}-1=0.082$	$i=\left[1+\left(\frac{0.08}{365}\right)\right]^{365}-1=0.083277$

Continuous Compounding

The variable m can be measured in days, hours, seconds, nanoseconds, etc. As m $\Rightarrow \infty$, the exponential function emerges in Equation 5.5:

$$i=e^{j}-1 \quad or \quad i=e^{j*n}-n \qquad \textbf{(5.5)}$$

where: e = logarithm base e. *(Warning: Never use log base 10)*

Example 5.2: Compute the effective interest rate using an 8% nominal rate and continuous compounding.

$$i=e^{0.08}-1=0.0083287$$

BASIC VALUATION MODEL

Chapter 4 defines the discount rate (DR) used in the time value of money equations. The task now turns to meshing the cost of money with the cash flows generated in Chapter 3. Like most models, however, the assumptions greatly impact the investment analysis. The basic money model followed by most organizations (including governments) looks like Figure 5.2.

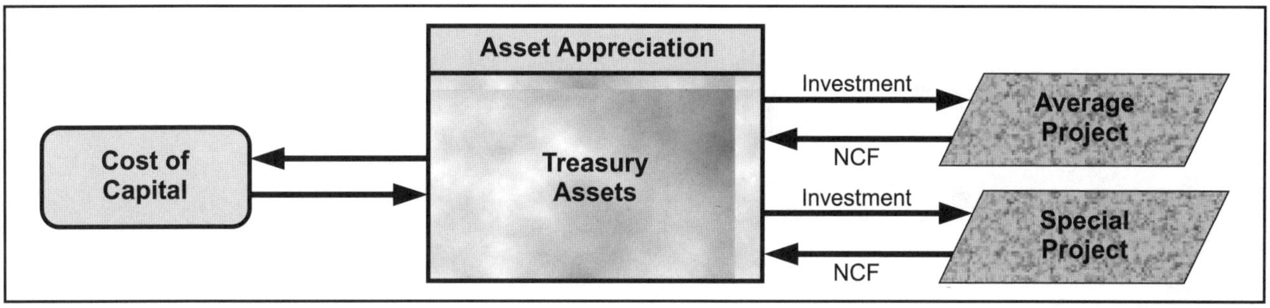

Figure 5.2 Basic valuation model

Organizations are intermediaries, raising capital then investing the capital in projects. The box labeled cost-of-capital refers to any source of capital, be it shareholders, bondholders, taxes or formal debt. They provide money, receive dividends, and interest in return. The overall cost of capital or the cost of the loan becomes the discount rate used to compare investment alternatives (ignoring risk and opportunity costs, as was explained in Chapter 4.

Organizations seek to satisfy the owners by maximizing the size of its treasury. This asset appreciation becomes the growth in value, or value added in current management jargon. This growth comes from the NCF generated by the average and special projects. The treasury borrows money from outside, incurring an obligation to pay the dividends and interest. It then invests the capital in projects that hopefully generate enough NCF to pay the required dividends and interest, while still leaving enough money for asset appreciation.

Every organization follows this basic format, whether a private firm or national government. Where investors differ is in the usage of the average and special project concepts. Graphically the difference is minimal: each receives capital from the treasury and generates NCF in return. Important differences emerge when trying to quantify the relative attractiveness of investment alternatives. Those using only the average project concept, employ a single discount rate for every project, regardless of type, risk, location, duration, product yield, etc.

Figure 5.1 illustrates why discounting is just a weighting scheme that quantifies the greater value of money today than in the future. Critics of this philosophy argue that it destroys the discounting process. This is incorrect. Discounting accurately weights the present more than the future. The question missed by many is whether the weighting scheme properly reflects a proper balance between all the goals and objectives of the organization. For example, exploration exists to replace current production to insure profitability in the long run. Yet, a $1 spent today to add production in 10-15 years would be valued quite low. Adopting a strategy to expand and then valuing future producton close to zero, highlights a common contradiction in valuation metrics.

The average project approach, illustrated in Figure 5.2, is the simplest possible format. It assumes that comparing every project with the same discount rate produces no distortions in the investment portfolio. This is a questionable assumption and attacked quite vociferously by anyone trying to model investment opportunities accurately. Most organizations actually modify the discount rate to reflect special circumstances; what varies among investors is the frequency and formality of the notion of a special project.

Investors using the strategic concept believe the set of investment opportunities cannot be captured accurately with a single, WACC, discount rate. Some projects provide liquidity and slower growth, at the expense of current profits. Some use the word strategic to describe those investments, and value the strategic part by lowering the discount rate to increase the values forthcoming in future years.

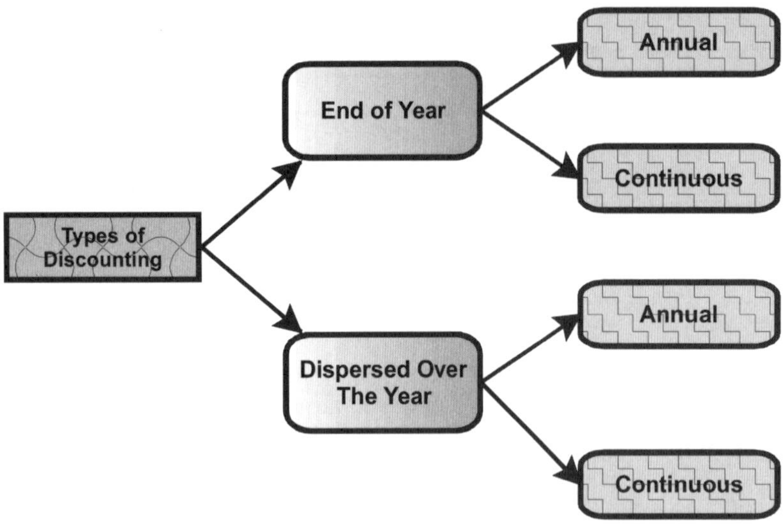

$$DF = \frac{1}{(1+i)^t} \quad (5.6)$$

$$DF = \frac{1}{e^{i*t}} \quad (5.7)$$

$$DF = \frac{1}{(1+i)^{t-0.5}} \quad (5.8)$$

$$DF = \frac{1}{e^{i*(t-1)}} * \left[\frac{1-e^{i}}{i}\right] \text{ or } \frac{1}{e^{i*(t-0.50)}} \quad (5.9)$$

Figure 5.3 Typical discounting assumptions

There are several assumptions inherent in models like these that are realistic from a practical viewpoint.

1. Money entering the treasury from a given project loses its identity with that project. The project NCF is used to pay general treasury obligations and invest in new projects at the average opportunity rate. This rate varies, but 10-25% nominal is common.
2. When computing the time value of money by an interest formula, the time at which the cash flow is received or disbursed does not need to coincide with the timing of the interest periods. Continuous compounding might be used, although the cash flows are assumed to be daily, monthly, or lumped at the midpoint of the year. So long as a system consistent with company fiscal policy is employed, the timing factors will not affect the basic investment decision within the same organization.

Ignore item 2 when dealing with other companies, however. The increasing trend toward using joint ventures, partnerships, alliances, etc to reduce cost and risk highlights the need to recognize the importance of timing differences among companies. More often than ever before, professionals interact with their counterparts from other organizations to select the best investment. Assumptions about cash flow timing and discounting influence the investment decision-making process, often dramatically.

Figure 5.3 summarizes the basic differences in deriving the discount factors for most investors. Other variations actually exist, but Figure 5.3 captures the main differences. Cash flow pattern refers to the inflow and outflow of money from the treasury during a year – once a year or over the year. Cash flow dispersed over the year may be uniform, exponential, hypergeometric, etc. Most investment evaluation programs assume uniform (or mid-year); whereas, general computer programs, like spreadsheets and databases, adopt the end of year convention.

The difference between point-in-time and uniform cash flow patterns is illustrated in Figure 5.4. Point-in-time (PIT) cash flows move into or out of the treasury every 365 days; roughly $4000 in year 2. With the uniform system, money begins flowing into the treasury on the first day of the year, accumulating until $4000 is realized 365 days later. Both assumptions yield equivalent totals at the end of 365 days, only the timing of the money differs. Most investors us the uniform approach.

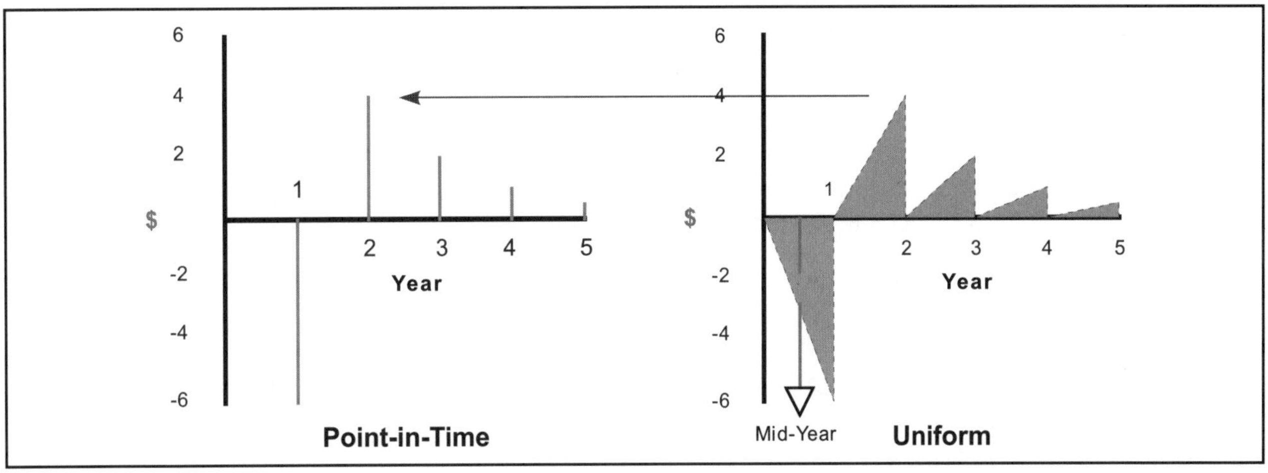

Figure 5.4 PIT versus uniform cash flow

The second column in Figure 5.3, Interest Periods, defines the number of discounting periods each year. Annual interest periods charge interest against the project once a year, or m = 1 in Equation 5.6, which is another way of writing Equation 5.4. Continuous calculates interest on the unpaid loan amount instantaneously. Multinationals tend to use Equation 5.8, and generic computer programs, like spreadsheets, default to Equation 5.6.

Most textbooks use alternative labels to describe the Equations shown in Figure 5.3. One common alternative uses reinvestment rate as a substitute for interest periods. While reinvestment of project cash flows is easy to visualize when compounding, such as used Table 5.1, it makes less sense when discounting. Others, notably Daugherty, prefer the term *return on unamortized investment*[(5.1)], which reflects the cost to the project of borrowing money from the treasury that is levied on the unpaid balance. All such terms, including ours, seek to place Figure 5.3 into a format that one can relate to everyday experience. They are, thus, analogies and, like all analogies, incorrect in certain instances. Generating a realistic example, which makes little sense for each of the terms, is quite easy. One should select the terminology, which they are comfortable with as long as the limitations of that label are understood.

The equation column defines the computation of the discount for each combination. Equation 5.8 and 5.9 assume uniform (or mid-year) cash flows. The equations would change if cash flow varied over the year, like in an exponential or hyperbolic function. Examples in the present value section show that the choice of equation may produce conflicting investment decisions for marginal projects.

CLASSICAL INVESTMENT VALUATION (CIV)

The classical approach, used by the majority of investors today, began over 100 years ago, but evolved into the dominant investment tool in the 1950's and 60's. Understanding the mechanics of the classical system, often referred to as the discounted cash flow (DCF) approach, is critical to understand and participate in the investment decision-making process of most organizations. However, the process contributes significantly to the under performance of many organizations. The so-called "winner" generally finds a way to circumvent the limitations of the classical DCF process, either by appealing to the concept of "strategic investments," or by engaging in mergers and acquisitions. Both solutions provide only temporary solutions to the under performing investments associated with CIV, however. Only a fuller grasp of the shortcomings inherent in the classical investment process, with some appreciation for better techniques, can improve our chances of making better investment decisions.

This section outlines the classical DCF that dominates the investment decision process currently. Several intelligent, organizationally successful professionals have accused us of trampling on the sacred DCF process. We believe in the classical investment process, but also recognize the deficiencies. As technology progresses, the limitations can and should be, surmounted. Ignoring sound, logical improvements is neither prudent management nor a solid foundation for making investment decisions.

The next section outlines the classical process, including the basic tenets that underlie it. This includes a discussion of performance measures, like NPV, IRR, NPV/Inv, payback or payout, etc. Then, the modern improvements to the classical system are outlined, ending with a comparison of the performance measures that result from the adopting the modern approach.

Classical DCF sought to achieve two objective: 1) identify investment opportunities that would add value to the organization, and 2) select the combination of value adding investments that would achieve the stated goals and objectives (called ranking). These objective still exist today, only the toolkit to address the details of each question has improved. What required a Ph.D. with outstanding programming skills previously can now be done with most spreadsheet or commercial software today. The ability to answer the questions has improved several orders of magnitude; the willingness to ask the right questions has lagged behind.

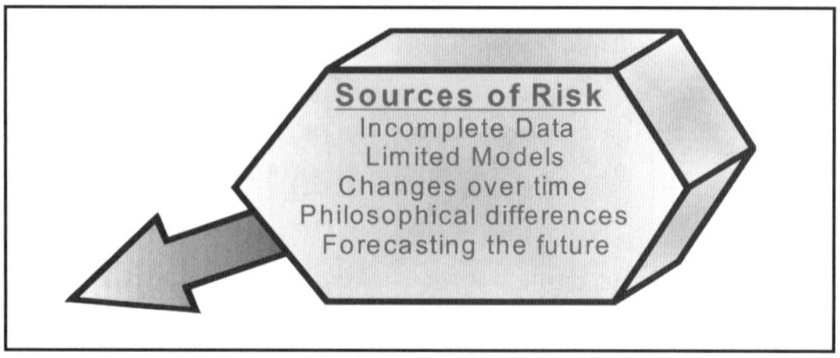

Figure 5.5 Sources of risk in investment decision-making

Figure 5.5 summarizes a few of the sources of risk that exist when making investment decisions. It results from a much larger discussion of technical decision-making, but captures the salient issues. In the classical DCF, the data are bad; the models for deriving any number an abstraction of reality; forecasts are imprecise, and then everyone changes their mind over time.

Were the professional who developed the classical DCF ignorant of these problems? Absolutely not. In fact, they probably understood the deficiencies of the classical system better than the practitioners today. But, when the slide rule, the desktop calculator, and even a mainframe computer with 32k of ram are the primary tools, addressing these issues effectively prohibits successful implementation of an investment decision system. The only recourse was to simplify the investment system to a manageable scale. That was achieved by stipulating that all numbers would reflect the average or expected values.

By mandating the use of expected values, variability or risk in the entire process was assumed away. Secondly, many believed this system insured consistency across the organization, so management could simply compare the performance measures to insure maximum investment performance.

Before the classical DCF approach is outlined in detail, a simple review will help understand the problem. Equation 5.10 combines the cost-of-capital with the NCF formulation from Chapter 3 into the classical DCF.

$$\text{Value} = \sum_{t=1}^{n}\left[\frac{\overline{\text{Price}}*\overline{\text{Production}} - \overline{\text{Opex}} - \overline{\text{Capex}} - \overline{\text{Taxes}}}{(1+\text{WACC}+?)^{(t-0.5)}}\right] \tag{5.10}$$

The value measure is the average of all the components of NCF (the numerator) divided by the WACC, plus the question mark for those desiring to add another risk component. The denominator is merely the discount factor, as derived in the previous section.

Equation 5.10 can easily be computed with old technology. Does it provide the information needed to make good investment decisions? Probably not in a global world. What causes the system to break down and to under achieve in investment performance? First, the average inputs aren't really averages; they are the most optimistic values provided by the professionals to justify their projects (See Chapter 2). One review of the last 11 projects in a major multinational found that actual production fell below expected production by 50%. Second, the inputs are related to each other, not independent, as the numbers assume. Production volume influences Opex, Capex, and taxes. The inputs generated, assuming independence, overstate the real value of the investment, in all cases. Third, WACC is derived based on assumptions about future investment performance, so is it really independent of the numerator and problems one and two?

Modern investment valuation addresses the concerns mentioned here plus adds far more condemning criticisms of the classical system. The classical system buried variability of the inputs into the expected value because it couldn't handle risk formally and logically. Next, the classical approach assumes that the investor puts up their capital, and then ignore all subsequent events through the project life, called options analysis.

The modern approach addresses risk in a formal, logical and orderly process, and measures the impact of dependencies easily and directly. It also accurately acknowledges that investing requires constant review and involvement to respond to the dynamic business environment. Changing prices, markets, tax laws allow the investor to change the scale of the operation, the location, and other operating characteristics. These options add value that the classical approach ignores. Valuing risk and options demands more effort from the investor, but the rewards adequately compensate one for work.

The classical investment system provided the foundation for the modern, global world, and should be given respect for its successes. The modern approach seeks to improve investment decisions by directly analyzing the previously ignored risks and options, not to discredit the classical approach. This process is akin to modern investors using the Internet and email, rather than the teletype or smoke signals to communicate in their business. The classical system will continue to add some value, but the premier investor in the future will be the one the grasps and applies the improved toolkit.

Net Present Value (NPV or PV)

The measure of value used most often is referred to by several names – net present value (NPV), present value (PV), present worth (PW), net present worth (NPW), etc., depending on the user's convention. Each may be treated as equivalent to the others in most instances, though some use net to indicate after-tax and PV to suggest before-tax. NPV measures the present value of project discounted to a common reference point, usually the current year. NPV is defined as:

$$NPV = NCF_1 * DF_1 + NCF_2 * DF_2 + ... + NCF_n * DF_n$$

or **(5.11)**

$$= \sum_{t=1}^{N} NCF_t * DF_t \quad \text{or} \quad \sum_{t=1}^{N} \frac{NCF_t}{(1+DR)^{(t-0.5)}}$$

where: DF = discount factor as defined in Figure 5.3

t = year

N = life of project

NPV yields a measure of value with the same units as the NCF – dollars, sterling, kroner, etc. When NPV > 0, the treasury earns more from the project than by investing in the average project (Figure 5.1). Asset appreciation occurs and the treasury achieves its basic objective: maximizing shareholder wealth.

Investment decision-making is really a staged affair, because most investors can identify more investment opportunities than their budget can accommodate, referred to as a "capital constrained" environment. Investment analysis using NPV or any other measure follows three basic steps.

1. Identify those projects meeting the hurdle rate (NPV > 0)
2. Select among project alternatives that maximizes NPV, and
3. Choose the combination of projects that provide the organization with the desired risk/return portfolio.

This section addresses the first item and later sections discuss 2 and 3.

Example 5.3 shows that a series of NCF's at a 10% hurdle rate meets the requirement of NPV>0. The function in Excel is = NPV (discount rate, data_array). All values in the data array command are discounted, so include only year 1-4 values in the function and then add –51,785 to that total to get $11,612.31.

Example 5.3: Use the following NCF's and a 10% discount rate with Equation 5.6 to compute the project NPV.

Year	Discounting Equation	(1) Discount Factor	(2) NCF, \$m	(3)=(1)*(2) NPV, \$m
0	$1/(1.1)^0 =$	1.000	-51,785.00	-51,785.00
1	1/(1.1)1 =	0.909091	20,000.00	18,181.82
2	1/(1.1)2 =	0.826446	20,000.00	16,528.93
3	1/(1.1)3 =	0.751315	20,000.00	15,026.30
4	1/(1.1)4 =	0.683013	20,000.00	13,660.27
Total			28,215.00	11,612.31

The project increases the size of the treasury by the amount of $28,215, which is often labeled NPV_0, meaning NPV at a 0% discount rate. The NPV column total of $11,612 is often shown as NPV_{10}. The NPV_{10} is less than the NPV_0 for stand-alone projects, because of the weighting scheme assumed in the discounting process. Understand that the key word in the last sentence is stand-alone projects. Many investment decisions involve comparisons of alternatives or trade-offs. When comparing incremental or alternative economics, the relationship between NPV_0 and any $NPV_{>0}$ varies according to the timing and magnitude of NCF. Later examples illustrate this point.

The reduction in value from $28,215 to $11,612 confuses many people. They ask "if the project actually adds $28,215 in value to the treasury, why is the project only credited with increasing the treasury by $11,612. The explanation goes back to the reason for deriving the discount factor given in Chapter 4 and the NCF in Chapter 3. NCF measures benefits less all costs; yet, a major cost of any project includes the cost of borrowing debt and equity (and alternative investment opportunities). The NCF format ignored repayment of dividends and interest. One approach is to think of the difference between NPV_0 and NPV_{10} as the additional cost of paying dividends and interest.

This explanation works when the discount rate reflects the cost-of-capital. Others prefer to think of the discount rate as analogous to one's investment options. If an organization can earn a return of, say 12% (which is usually the cost-of-capital plus several percent, the $NPV_{12}>0$ reflects the earnings of the project over and above the earning of the hypothetical return from another project. Note also that this analogy requires a higher discount rate than the cost-of-capital analogy for discount rates, because most investors desire a return greater than the cost-of-capital.

Both analogies for NPV are correct up to a point. The real reason for the format of discount factors reflects the limitations of the primary calculation tools when it was developed – the slide rule. Slide rules handle multiplication quite easily, but not addition. Converting the analogies used above into a factor to be multiplied by NCF eases the computational process. It is important to realize that the analogies were developed to justify the computation, not vice versa.

Several other, more understandable methods exist for explaining NPV. One approach builds on the compounding principles illustrated in Table 5.1. The compounding approach seeks the value of the positive cash flows plus the amount earned in from reinvesting the proceeds from the project. Given the cash flows from above, the value of the cash returns at the end of year four can be computed as follows.

TABLE 5.2

One Derivation of Discounted Value

Year	NCF	Interest Earned	Total
1	20,000	0	0
2	20,000	2,000	2,000
3	20,000	2,000 + 2,000 +200	4,200
4	20,000	2,000 + 2,000 + 2,000 + 200 + 200 +200 + 20	6,620
Total	80,000		12,820

At the end of year 4 the project generates $80,000 plus the interest from reinvesting this sum over four years. In year 2, the interest on $20,000 at 10% is $2000. In year 3, 10% is earned from the cash flows in year 1 and year 2 plus interest on the interest earned in year 1 of $2000. A similar situation holds in year 4.

The total value of the positive cash flows at the end of year 4 sums the basic receipts of $20,000 per year or $80,000 plus the interest earned on re-investing the NCF in alternative projects, which equals $92,820 ($80,000 + 12,820). This value at the end of year 4 must still be compared to the initial cost of the project of $51,785 in year 0. Discounting the future value back to now and then, subtracting the project cost, gives:

$$NPV = -51{,}785 + \frac{80{,}000 + 12{,}820}{(1+0.10)^4} = -51{,}785 + 92{,}820 * 0.683 = 11{,}612$$

The NPV, whether computed using discount factors or by estimating the returns from reinvesting the cash flows, yields the same answer.

Deriving NPV values by including reinvestment cash flows directly only partially explains the discounting process. Another approach computes NPV by modifying the NCF's directly. Effectively, each cash flow is charged an amount equal to the hurdle rate. Taking the same example, the NPV computation is illustrated below.

TABLE 5.3

Another View of Discounting

Year	NCF	Borrowing or Opportunity Charge	NPV
0	-51,785	0.0	-51,785.0
1	20,000	–1,818.2	18,181.8
2	20,000	–1,818.2 – 1,652.9	16,528.9
3	20,000	–1,818.2 – 1,652.9 – 1,502.6	15,026.3
4	20,000	–1,818.2 – 1,652.9 – 1,502.6 – 1,367.2	13,659.1
	28,215		11,611.13

This approach deducts from NCF a charge that could reflect either the cost of borrowing or opportunity charge. The value of $1,818.2 comes from the product of $20,000 and 1-(1/1.1), which is the effective interest rate for one year at a 10% discount rate. Deducting the yearly borrowing or opportunity charges yields the same sum as the NPV_{10} derived in Example 5.2.

Regardless of how one derives NPV, the same number emerges. Discount factors just simplify the process. Imagine how many calculations are needed to derive NPV when the cash flows cover 30 to 50 years.

Impact of Alternative Equations

The importance of the different equations for computing time value of money profit models is often questioned. Like any model, different equations yield different results. The main concern is the magnitude of the resulting difference and when the choice of equation matters. In summary, for time value of money equations, this divergence seldom matters for very good or very bad projects. For marginal projects (which are the most common), the various DF equations are critical. NPV describes a procedure (model), which yields different results depending on the equations used. This divergence arises most often in meetings with partners, or when selling or buying properties. NPV quoted by one company may be quite different than those computed by another, even when inputs, like production and cost, are the same.

Example 5.4: Given the following NCF, compute NPV using the four equations in Figure 5.3 using 10% and 15% discount rates. A year value of 0 means the discount factor equals 1.

Year	0	0-1	1-2	2-3	3-4	4-5
NCF	-2000	0	1000	800	600	600

Equation	5.6	5.7	5.8	5.9
@10%	209.86	177.49	317.72	290.99
@15%	-76.49	-136.37	62.90	10.66

As an example, the value of $62.90 is found by summing the products of:

$$2{,}000*1.0 + 0.0 + 1{,}000*0.811 + 800*0.706 + 600*0.613 + 600*0.533$$

where the discount factors are from the tables at the end of the book.

At 15%, the end of year cash flow equations produce negative values, and the uniform equations yield positive NPV's. Conflicting signals arise because money is worth more when received early in the year rather than the end of the year. The continuous interest assumption lowers NPV, because the opportunity costs are higher when money is reinvested continuously. The same set of net cash flows produce conflicting estimated values depending on the discounting assumptions employed. Such differences occur frequently.

Nominal vs. Deflated NPV

Countries experiencing highly volatile inflation rates need an approach that captures the impact of inflation directly. The NPV equations examined so far embed inflation in the discount rate and are quite adequate for stable inflation periods. Volatility in inflation must be considered to accurately value an investment in countries with unstable inflation rates.

Example 5.5 illustrates a common extension of the NPV methodology used by international investors, operating in highly inflation regimes. Column 1 duplicates the NCF used earlier. Assuming an inflation rate of 4%, column 3, the deflated NCF, captures the decline in purchasing power due to inflation. To demonstrate the equivalence between the nominal discounting approach and real discounting, the discount factor of 5.77% in column 4 was computed by dividing 1.04 (the inflation rate) into the nominal 10% discount rate. Unsurprisingly, the discounted NCF in column 5 equals the nominal value of $11,612 determined above, as it always will when the inflation rate is constant over the life of the investment.

Figure 5.6 shows the bias arising from using constant inflation rates. The flat inflation line, indicated by the triangle symbol, shows the common assumption found in the valuation process. The other lines – indicating rising inflation, declining inflation, or just variable inflation over time – depict the real world better.

Example 5.5: If the inflation rate is expected to be 4% over the project life, compute the deflated and discounted values using Equation 5.6.

Year	(1) MOD NCF, \$m	(2) Deflation Factor @ 4%	(3)=(1)*(2) Deflated NCF, \$m	(4) Discount Factor @ 5.77%	(5)=(3)*(4) Discounted NCF, \$m
0	-51,785	1.00	-51,785	1.00	-51,785.00
1	20,000	0.96	19,231	0.95	18,181.82
2	20,000	0.92	18,491	0.89	16,528.93
3	20,000	0.89	17,780	0.85	15,026.30
4	20,000	0.85	17,096	0.80	13,660.27
Total	28,215		20,813		11,612.31

where 5.77 = 1.10/1.04

In high inflation periods, the rising inflation curve is the most appropriate. Similarly, declining inflation fits some countries where governments implement fiscal austerity packages to control inflation. Inflation forecasts are notoriously inaccurate, and often considered to be as poor as price forecasts. In situations where inflation is reasonably expected to change dramatically, the deflated/discounting process is preferred. The trade-off balances accuracy versus the possible danger arising from forecast errors. Most multinationals, in most countries today use inflation forecasts that are almost flat, or change so little, the forecast is essentially flat. Others prefer to assume that the exchange rate shifts in the opposite direction to inflation, negating the impact.

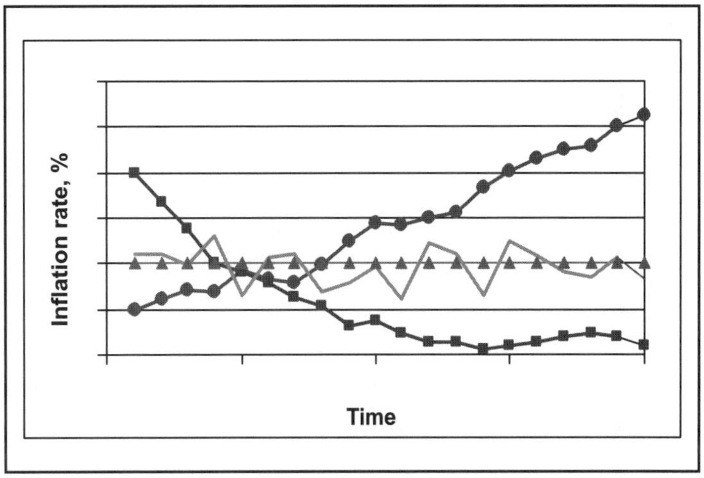

Figure 5.6 Illustration of different inflation rates

Characteristics of NPV

1. *Provides consistent decisions among alternative investments*
2. *Gives greatest weight to early NCF*
3. *Continues to charge interest after investment capital is recovered*
4. *Biased in favor of larger projects (IRR and NPV/Inv).*

The valuation process hinges on using comparable assumptions for generating NCF and then converting NCF to NPV by adopting a time value of money convention. This approach allows comparison of projects of different sizes, locations, life, etc. Assuming the inputs accurately reflect reality, organizations realize consistent decisions among alternative investment opportunities.

The NPV computation involves some biases, however. NCF depends on predicting production volumes, prices, exchange rates, operating and capital costs, and so on. These estimates, often thousands of values, generate a NCF, including taxes, and then, the time value of money methodology reduces these hundreds, if not thousands of estimates to one value – called NPV. Collapsing the predicted values for each variable to one number introduces the possibility that important elements will be ignored or analyzed improperly.

The bias toward early returns arises from the time value of weighting scheme (Characteristic 2). Characteristic 4, the large project bias, simply means that larger projects have higher NPV's. Adjusting for project size is the objective of a ratio like NPV to investment or breakeven discount rate, as explained next.

Characteristic 3 presents a more difficult task, because it challenges the core assumptions of traditional investment models. In the NPV examples, the NCF's were discounted at 10% over the 4-year life of the project. Figure 5.2, the basic valuation model, shows the project borrowing money from the "bank" and then repaying that money plus the cost of borrowing. Once the borrowed money (*principal*) and cost of borrowing is repaid, the traditional model continues to pay the "bank." In reality, the project would cease paying to the "bank" once the principal and costs are fully repaid. A later section explores the problems with the traditional models more fully and proposes several alternative solutions. This bias merely asks users to understand the limitations of traditional profit models, not to discard them.

Several other, common time value of money models exist in investor's toolkits. These include the internal rate of return approach. and a ratio of NPV to investment. Each is discussed in turn.

Efficiency Measures

NPV/Inv corrects the scale bias in NPV by adjusting NPV for the size of the investment. Since the magnitude of NPV partially depends on the size of the project, with larger projects having higher NPV's, some investors measure the efficiency of capital usage in the investment. Two projects may yield the same NPV, say \$600 million, but if one spends \$300 million and the other \$0.10 to achieve that NPV, the lower cost project uses capital more efficiently. Some believe an efficiency ratio is the only profit measure needed to make sound investment decisions.*(5.2)*

The efficiency ratios go by several names: discounted return-on-investment (DROI), profitability index (PI), capital efficiency (CE), and NPV to investment (NPV/Inv). Some users place their organizations name in front of the phrase. Regardless of the name employed, the efficiency ratios follow the format in Equation 5.12. or 5.13.

$$\frac{NPV_i}{Inv_i} = \frac{\sum_{t=1}^{n} NCF_t * DF_t}{\sum_{t=1}^{n} Inv_t * DF_t} = \frac{NPV_i}{\sum_{t=1}^{n} Inv_t * DFt} \tag{5.12}$$

where all the values were defined in the NPV section, except for Inv, which is covered below.

$$\frac{NPV_i}{Inv_i} = \frac{NPV_i}{\sum_{t=1}^{n} Inv_t * DF_t} + 1 \tag{5.13}$$

Equation 5.13 just adds the value of one to Equation 5.12.

The efficiency ratios yield a dimensionless number, since the numerator and denominator use the same currency. Dividing \$'s by \$'s yields a dimensionless figure. For accepting a project, the NPV value in the numerator controls the decision. When NPV > 0 (Equation 5.12) or NPV > 1 (Equation 5.13), the project adds value or just breaks even, and should be accepted. Conversely, the efficiency ratio duplicates the NPV value for the basic decision to accept the project or not. The next step of ranking projects under a capital constraint is where the efficiency ratio really helps investors.

Example 5.6 shows a simple ranking, with Project A having an NPV/Inv of 2, and Project B a ratio of 0.75. The number actually means that Project A recovers all project costs, plus an additional \$2 for every \$1 invested. Since that number exceeds the 0.75 for Project B, users of such ratios select Project A,

Example 5.6: Given the values for NPV and Inv, derive the efficiency ratios and interpret the results.

	Project	
	A	**B**
NPV	600	600
Inv	300	800
NPV/Inv	2 = 600/300	0.75 = 600/800

and call it the more efficient. Most projects yield values slightly in excess of 0 to 0.6 in practical circumstances (for Equation 5.12), and 1.0 to 1.6 for Equation 5.13.

Although NPV/Inv provides useful information in some circumstances, it does possess limitations, just like every other performance model. Efficiency measures are most useful when comparing alternative investment decisions, like size of the production system, etc.

Difficulty with NPV/Inv arises when the alternatives include Capex (or Inv) versus Opex alternatives. Most users of the efficiency measures define Inv as some form of Capex. If the choice is to purchase equipment (a Capex) or lease the equipment (Opex), the denominator goes to 0 for the Opex option, making it impossible to compute the ratio, because of the division by zero error that occurs. Technically, the ratio is undefined, but some software avoids the division by zero error by printing out NPV/Inv = 249,999,999.49 or something like, -1. Both values just convey the division by zero error. The same problem arises when one option has no cost at all, like selling an asset versus expanding the production system. Selling only generates revenue with no cost, so the efficiency metric is distorted.

The best way to handle situations without investment or just Opex expenditure is to derive the incremental benefit of the two alternatives, and then compute the ratio. If the incremental NPV/Inv exceeds the firm specific threshold, the capital expenditure option should be accepted.

Some advocates argue that the real merit of the efficiency ratios occurs when ranking projects. Some use a ranking system where the projects are sorted from highest to lowest, based on NPV/Inv, and then the projects accepted until the capital budget is exhausted. This approach provides satisfactory results only when other constraints or objectives are ignored. Secondary constraints might be to achieve a financial objective, like ROCE, market share in sales, or a minimum level of investment activity in each of the organizations geographical business units. Even without secondary objectives, Mao argues that efficiency ratios should never be used to rank projects when any, single project exceeds 5% of the capital budget.[5.3] The formal optimization methods, as discussed in Chapter 10, correct for the secondary considerations and budget limitations.

Another variation in the efficiency ratios seen in actual practice concerns the precise definition of investment, or Inv. Some common definitions include:

1. Inv = before-tax, undiscounted investment over the life of the project.
2. Inv = after-tax, undiscounted investment over the project life.
3. Inv = before-tax, discounted investment over the project life.
4. Inv = after-tax, discounted investment over the project life.
5. Inv = before-tax capital investment plus after-tax expensed investment.
6. Inv = each of the first 4 options, but only including costs until a positive NCF occurs (often called *maximum cash outlay* or MCO).
7. Inv = each of the first 4 options, but only including costs until payout.

The choice of the definition influences the investment decisions that actually take place. Managements often set NPV/Inv constraints above zero, like 0.5, when facing cash flow or budget crunches. This approach seeks to insure that only the very best projects are approved. Alas, in the real world, the investment opportunities are restructured to meet these hurdles or metrics. For example, in a large development, using definition 4 for Inv, the technical staff leased the equipment (making it an Opex) until production began, when they structured a purchase arrangement from the leasing company, such that the NCF never went negative; hence, no significant investment ever occurred, allowing them to satisfy the 0.5 NPV/Inv ratio

Others opt for the maximum cash outlay approach to circumvent the problem. Figure 5.7 shows a simple example of MCO. The values go negative in the early years because of the Capex outlay, and then develop a positive slope as production and sales begin. The cumulative curves reaches a crest at the end of the project life, declining in the last year when decommissioning of the asset takes place.

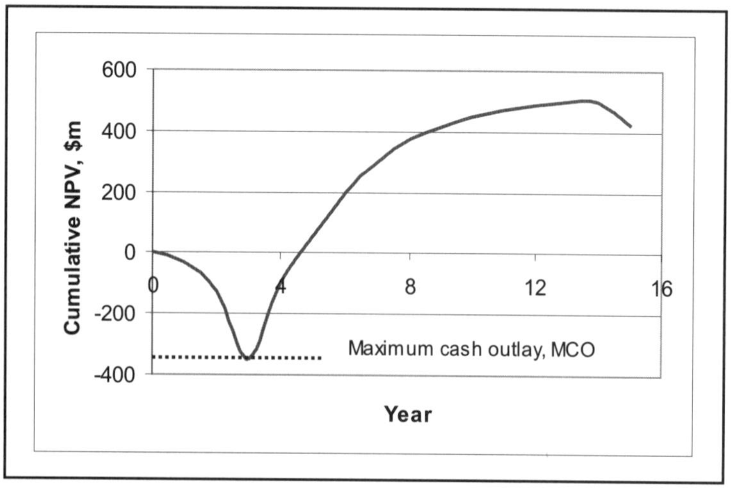

Figure 5.7 Example of maximum cash outlay

Because the y-axis is NPV, the MCO relates to after-tax, discounted values. Had the graph used NCF instead of NPV, MCO would relate to AT, undiscounted values. MCO may relate to several different computational processes, depending on how the organization chooses to define it. Be careful when bandying such a term about, especially when dealing with representatives from different organizations.

One of the major problems with MCO occurs when a project recovers all its investment costs in the first year, called payback, as defined below. If the cumulative value never goes negative (Figure 5.7 never enters the negative quadrant when dealing with annual data), most software faces the division by zero problem. One solution computes MCO using monthly data, instead of yearly numbers. If that is too difficult for the software, option 2 is to take the larger of MCO or the first year investment cost, appropriately discounted and taxed to meet corporate metrics.

The efficiency ratios solve one bias in NPV, but add others, which is standard for all metrics and not a criticism of NPV/Inv. Cautioning users to use the metric with care is the same advise parents give their children "drive carefully." Chapter 10 introduces and illustrates methods for correcting several of these problems.

Characteristics of NPV/Inv

1. *It adjusts NPV for size of investment.*
2. *It favors investments with low initial capital outlay and large NPV's.*
3. *It measures the efficiency of capital usage.*

Breakeven Discount Rate (BDR or IRR)

The breakeven discount rate preceded use of NPV and was the dominant model for evaluating projects in the 50's and 60's. I. Fisher developed the concept in the 1890's, calling it *internal rate of return (IRR)*. The first usage in the petroleum industry was in the early 50's,[(5.4)] but didn't catch on until Campbell introduced it into the forerunner of this text.[(5.5)] IRR is measured as a percent or decimal fraction, just like the discount rate. The ease of use – just compare it to the discount rate – accounts for the popularity of IRR. Accept a project when IRR is greater than the discount rate, plus saying that the project earns 20% is familiar, and comfortable.

From the inception, debate has raged over the proper name and its interpretation. In the economic world, names like *effective yield to maturity, marginal productivity of capital,* and *IRR* are used interchangeably. Names like *profitability index (PI), discounted return on investment (DCF-ROR), rate-of-return (ROR),* and *IRR* exist in software today. Though the names differ, they use the same equation for computing IRR. Because of the naming conflicts, and inconsistencies in defining exactly what IRR means (below), we coined the phrase *breakeven discount rate (BDR)* as a compromise. BDR = IRR without the interpretation problems.

Textbook IRR or BDR Solution

IRR or BDR modifies the NPV equation presented earlier. NPV sums of the product of NCF and discount factor, where the discount rate is normally the WACC. IRR or BDR changes the unknown by solving for the discount rate that sets the NCF equal to zero. Equation 5.14 describes the basic relationship.

$$0 = NCF_1 * DF_1 + NCF_2 * DF_2 + ... + NCF_n * DF_n \quad \text{or} \quad = \sum_{i=1}^{n} NCF_i * DF_i \tag{5.14}$$

which is the NPV equation set equal to 0. The actual solution depends on the equation for computing DF. For example, if DF = $(1 + i)^t$, then Equation 5.14 becomes:

$$0 = \sum_{t=1}^{n} \frac{NCF_t}{(1 + BDR)^{t-0.5}} \tag{5.15}$$

IRR equals the discount rate that sets the cash flow values equal. Because the equation is non-linear, most computers use trial-and-error algorithms, which provides the most accurate results. Attempts to take the derivative and then solve for IRR will fail more than it succeeds. The iterative approach is used by most spreadsheet and calculator software, because it is quick and accurate. The function in Excel for computing BDR is = IRR(array values, guess). The array values are the cells with the data and guess is the starting condition for the iteration, usually 0.

TABLE 5.4

Values for Generating the NPV Profile

Discount Rate	0%	5%	10%	15%	20%	25%	30%
NPV	28,215	19,134	11,612	5,314	-10.3	-4,553	-8,460

Software usually finds BDR by drawing a curve like the one in Figure 5.8. The NPV at different discount rates are computed. When the NPV changes sign, usually positive to negative, the software interpolates between these two values. The answer is reported as BDR. The calculation uses the same data as the NPV example, where NPV_0 is \$28,215, NPV_{10} is \$11,612. The values for NPV_5 = \$19,314, NPV_{15} = \$5,314, NPV_{20} = -\$10, and NPV_{25} = \$-4,553 repeated the NPV calculation at these discount rates. At $NPV_{20,}$ the value becomes slightly negative, indicating that the line crosses the x-axis just before 20%.

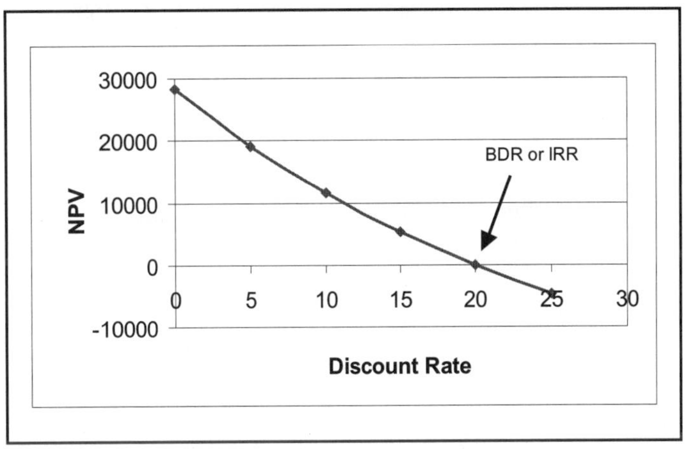

Figure 5.8 Example BDR or IRR calculation

CHAPTER 5

Most software would report a value, like 19.99%. A BDR of 20% would be good enough given the accuracy of the input values. At a 20% percent discount rate, the NPV of the project equals 0. If the WACC is 10%, the project returns more than the cost-of-capital. Some go another step and say, "the project earns or contributes 20% to the treasury."

IRR gained popularity because users interpreted the number to be the rate-of-return on the project. So, a 20% return could easily be compared to alternative investment. For someone earning a 5% percent return on a savings account, or 10% in the stock market, this project earned more. Or, if borrowing money costs 10%, a 20% BDR was higher, again implying a good investment. Decision-makers never had to worry about the size of the investment. The decision came down to accepting investments whenever BDR exceeded the discount rate. This was easy and simple.

Like many models, the assumptions of the calculation got lost in the interpretation. I. Fisher very carefully explained that the word, internal, in IRR means that the computed value is specific to the project and has no relationship to the corporate treasury.[5.6] A 20% value means that if the project borrows money at 20% or the project reinvestment rate is 20%, the final NPV is equal to 0. We underline the word, project, to emphasize Fisher's point: the calculation assumes the project IRR has no impact on the treasury. Yet, the entire approach of capital budgeting seeks to model the impact of a project on the organization. Does an inconsistency arise if we use an IRR number specific to a project to make organizational decisions? You bet they do, and often-bad decisions.

IRR (or BDR) was never intended to measure a project's impact on the treasury. Mathematically, BDR simply computes the discount rate at which NPV = 0. In many disciplines, the point where a value equals 0 is called the breakeven point. Hence, our uses of the term breakeven discount rate. IRR or BDR is nothing more than the mathematical solution of an equation to find the discount rate that sets NPV = 0. The goal here is to eliminate the use of the idea that a project actually earns 20%, because it does not.

If IRR or BDR measures only the breakeven point, why use it. BDR has more value than once thought by academics. Besides including the time value of money, it offers a crude measure of risk, or, as some prefer, an estimate of project robustness. The greater the gap between BDR and the discount rate (DR), the more robust the project economics are to changes in the initial assumptions about the input variables, like production, price, Capex, taxes, etc.

Whenever IRR > DR, the project earns more than the minimum hurdle rate and is accepted. At IRR < DR, reject the project, and when IRR=DR, the project recovers the initial investment and the interest needed to repay the treasury. Note that most stand-alone projects follow a pattern similar to Figure 5.8, with a negatively sloped line, implying that NPV and BDR give the same accept/reject decision.

IRR or BDR values in excess of 25 to 30% are meaningless, because such rates seldom occur in actual practice. For one thing, regulating governments tend to regard profits that generate profitability above this level as "excessive" and alter taxes accordingly. For a number of reasons, making investment decisions from among the pool of satisfactory projects should be based on additional considerations than just their IRR or BDR.

The iterative process used in computing BDR or IRR creates some significant problems if the user isn't careful about interpreting the output. Most programs start at 0%, raise the discount rate at each iteration, and then test for a sign change between the last two values. If no sign change ever occurs, as often happens in many maintenance and least cost investments, the program prints out something like "IRR exceeds 100%", or "IRR equals 800%". The values for >100% and 800% are always the largest value for the discount factor considered in the iterative process. These statements do not mean that IRR equals these values, just that there was no sign change between 0 and this value. The better programs will indicate that the iterative process was unable to find a unique IRR or BDR, defined again as a sign change in the NPV profile.

Computer programs, however, vary in quality. Many fail to check for implicit characteristics in the rate of return calculation that govern its applicability, as specified below. It is the users responsibility to verify that such programs produce meaningful measures of IRR or BDR.

When computing or interpreting the breakeven discount rate, one must be aware of its fundamental limitations. When making the basic accept/reject decision, these characteristics seldom cause a problem. Choosing among the best alternative or ranking projects, however, faces serious potential for bad investment decision if these characteristics are ignored.

Characteristics of breakeven discount rate (BDR or IRR)

1. *It provides a profit indicator, independent of the absolute size of the investment.*
2. *The estimated return is sensitive to errors in estimating investment requirements and NCF in the early years.*
3. *IRR or BDR cannot be computed if NCF contains all positive or all negative values, or the project does not payout.*
4. *It is biased in favor of projects with low initial investment and early cash returns because revenue early in the project life influences it the most.*
5. *No direct measure is supplied regarding the absolute size of the profit generated, particularly in long-life projects.*
6. *The project is charged a cost at the IRR or BDR value, not the average discount rate, DR.*
7. *Multiple rates of return are possible. A solution may exist for every sign change. If two sign changes occur, two values of IRR or BDR may satisfy the equation.*
8. *It will give meaningless results in many acceleration projects.*

The following section discusses each item in more detail, but collectively, the characteristics lead investors to misuse BDR or IRR more than any other single performance measure – many use the term, but few understand it. The classic misuse is to raise the return standard to adjust for risk, especially in foreign country projects. Most companies pursue foreign investments in order to satisfy long-run strategies. Since BDR or IRR biases decisions in favor of projects with early cash returns, practitioners of this strategy are being inconsistent. They are saying, "We invest to be premier in the future," but adopt procedures that guarantee that they will never accept the projects needed to achieve the objective.

Probably the best use and, actually, the way knowledgeable users apply BDR is to measure project sensitivity. The closer BDR or IRR comes to the DR; small changes in the initial price, production, cost, and taxes may lead to a destruction of value, rather than adding value from the investment. Conversely, the larger the IRR or BDR, the less chance the investment has of losing money. Some interpret this as a crude measure of risk. The closer BDR is to the required discount rate, the greater the risk of losing money (or not meeting the desired return to the treasury).

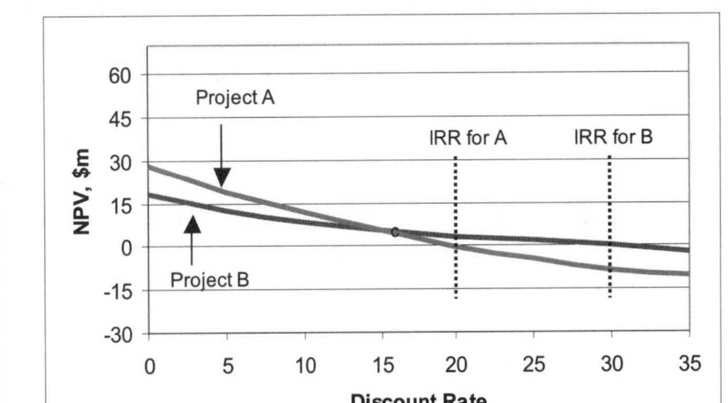

Figure 5.9a NPV profiles for competing projects

Figure 5.8a illustrates two competing investment opportunities. Project A is repeated from Figure 5.7, while Project B reflects an alternative. Observe that the NPV_{15} is the same for each, but the BDR is higher for Project B, about 30% relative to the 20% for project A. With the same NPV and a higher BDR, Project B would by preferred by most, but not all, investors, because of its greater robustness to changes in the initial assumptions. Other investors, with a 10% discount rate, correctly note that the NPV from project A is higher. This example illustrates, once again, the sensitivity in investment decision-making to the choice of the discount rate. In addition, the investor must make some choices about trading-off the greater risk in project A (less robust) with the higher return at a 10% discount rate.

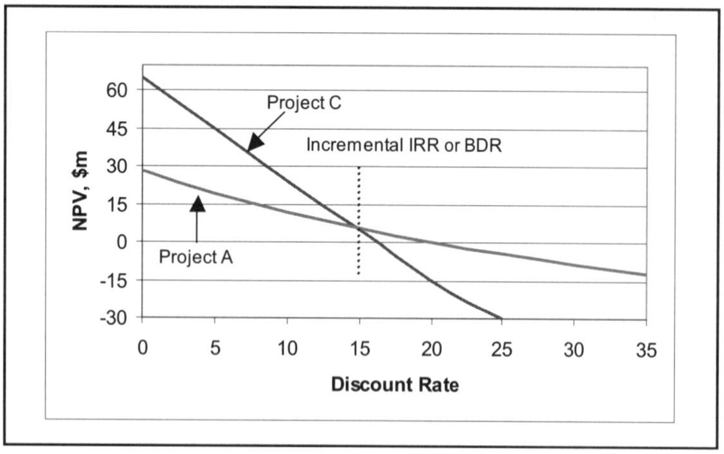

Figure 5.9b NPV profiles for competing projects

Figure 5.9b extends the same situation for a project C relative to project A. Project C also has a higher NPV_{10}, but a lower IRR or BDR. Should the investor take the higher growth in treasury value (NPV) or greater robustness to input values (BDR)? It depends. Those blessed with large treasuries and good cash flows would take Project C. More risk averse or those needing cash flow immediately would probably elect Project A. Chapter 8 introduces tools for incorporating the wealth position in the determining the proper risk and return trade-off.

One common approach used in industry tries to answer the question by taking the difference between the two alternatives (called incremental analysis). Professionals will be asked to quote the incremental IRR or BDR at some time in their career. In this simple illustration, the incremental IRR or BDR is highlighted by the vertical, dashed line. Why? Because, the definition of BDR seeks the discount rate that achieves a zero NPV. At a 15% discount rate, $NPV_A = NPV_C$, so the IRR is 15%. Does this mean that the one project earns 15% more than the other? This situation probably best illustrates the limitations of IRR. At 15%, both projects contribute the same amount to the treasury, or the investor should be indifferent between the projects (hence our name, breakeven discount rate). At a discount rate less than 15%, project C adds more value to the treasury, while A adds more value at discount rates higher than 15%.

This simple example of problems arising from incremental analysis worsens as the investment opportunities become more complex. The next section demonstrates the problems with using IRR in many real world investments.

IRR with multiple solutions

The problems with IRR arise from the non-linearity in the generating equation, and the mistaken belief in the simple interpretation of the output. In truth, IRR works well when a large number of low, similar risk and similar cost investments exist. That was probably true when investment decisions dealt with local or national investments, but globalization destroys these premises.

With greater usage and increasing complexity in investments, problems emerged that confounded the people presenting the recommendations to management, and managements ability to interpret the numbers. The traditional textbook example conveys a typical investment as starting with a negative NCF, followed by a series of positive values, leading to the common NPV profile, like Figure 5.8. Table 5.5 compares three different NCF patterns. The first NCF column continues the example from NPV. The second NCF column adds abandonment costs, while the third columns allows for a Capex upgrade of the production system in year 2-3 of the project. The last two columns reflect the normal investment pattern, not column 1.

Just looking at the numerical results disguises the fundamental differences in the metrics associated with each cash flow pattern. The textbook NCF shows an NPV_{10} of $10.56 and an IRR of 20%. This is

TABLE 5.5
Comparison of Different NCF Patterns, all $ amounts in million

Year	Textbook NCF	Abandonment NCF	Ongoing NCF
0-1	-51.78	-41.78	-21.78
1-2	20.00	20.00	25.00
2-3	20.00	20.00	-20.00
3-4	20.00	20.00	30.00
4-5	20.00	20.00	20.00
5-6	0	-30.00	-20.00
NPV_5	18.22	5.36	10.08
NPV_{10}	10.56	2.71	7.45
NPV_{15}	4.62	0.35	5.26
IRR or BDR	20%	16%	33%

consistent with the negatively sloped line shown earlier. The metrics include the negative first year investment in Excel's NPV, instead of excluding it, like before. That is the reason the NPV value falls from the previously reported number of $11.61.

The abandonment NCF has an NPV_{10} equal to $2.71 m, with IRR declining to 16%. A lower NPV should have a lower IRR, if the original curve is correct. The first hint of a possible problem exists in the last column, with an NPV_{10} of $7.45, but IRR increasing to 33%. Figures 5.10a-c demonstrate the differences and contrasts between the three investment patterns.

Figure 5.10a follows the previous pattern with no surprises. Figure 5.10b demonstrates the beginning of the problem. Two intersections with the x-axis exist, one at the reported 16% and the other at around –28%. This parabolic shape exists because of the two sign changes in the abandonment NCF pattern. The first negative is due to the initial investment, and the second negative occurs because of abandonment cost.

Better software reports both IRR values, which causes enormous consternation when reporting the results. Should 16%, or –28% go on the reporting form? Which would be harder to explain to a group of people?

Figure 5.10c demonstrates an even more radical process, because of the 4 sign changes in the NCF. The additional Capex in the 3rd year that typifies an upgrade in the production system confuses the results even more. With a reported result of 33%, but a lower NPV creates even more

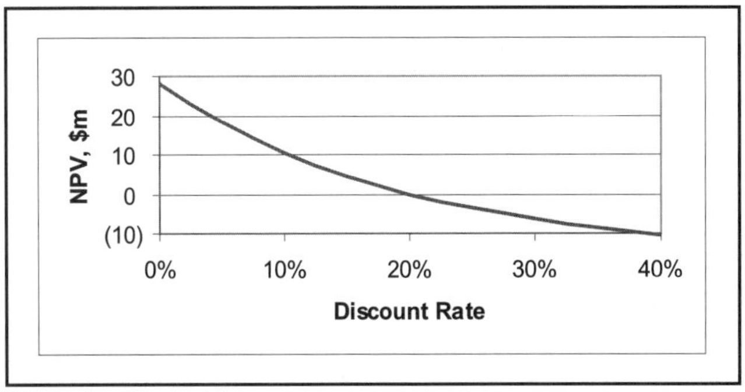

Figure 5.10a NPV profile for textbook NCF

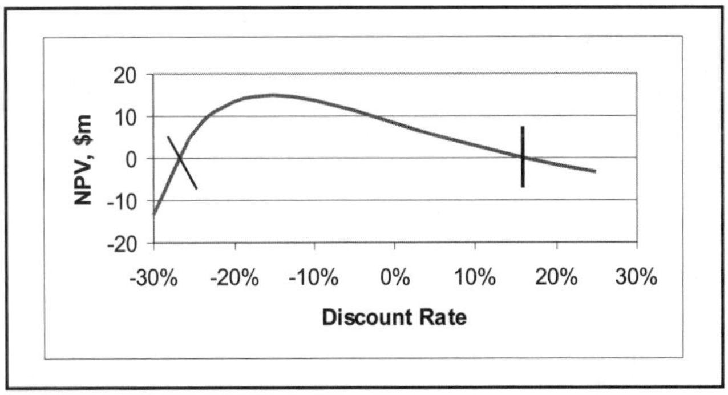

Figure 5.10b NPV profile for abandonment NCF

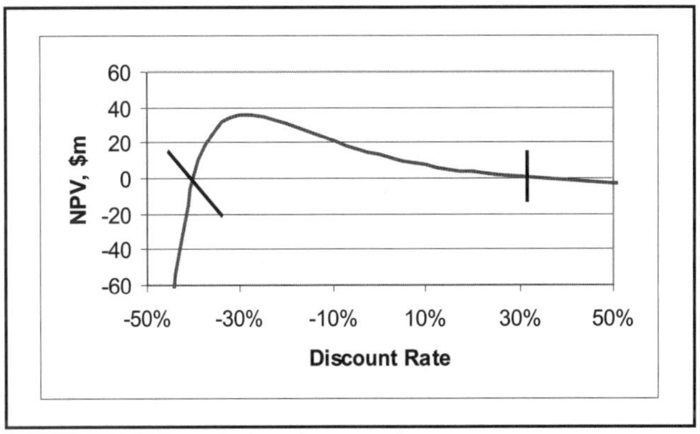

Figure 5.10c Ongoing investment NCF

CHAPTER 5

discussion in the investment committee. Probably the best practice is to show these graphs to illustrate the contradictory results.

The odd shaped curves occurs because of the polynomial solution in Equation 5.14 and 5.15. BDR is the largest real root solution of the equation. Furthermore, with N years in the project, N real root solutions are possible. The necessary condition for real roots is a sign change, so a NCF profile with 4 sign changes could experience 4 real roots. In addition, if real roots exist, imaginary root solutions could also exist. Reporting the imaginary IRR makes for interesting discussions during meetings. The solution depends upon both necessary and sufficient conditions, which are summarized as follows:

"A real root may exist for every sign change in NCF."

"The sufficient conditions hinges on the magnitude of the values associated with the sign changes."

Most software ignores these complexities when solving for IRR or BDR. The most common situation finds the program quitting when the first solution occurs. Some software will continue the search for specified intervals, and then reports both values. This is better technically, but quite disconcerting to the unaware professional. Most investment metric summaries contain one box for IRR, but with two reported, choosing between 2 or more numbers presents a dilemma. The easiest and best approach is to type in "See Figure x.xx" and then add the NPV profile to the report. This lets the reviewer see the situation, rather than having to sort out a number they may not understand.

Probably the most common experience with these problems arises from incremental analysis. A common term for incremental is acceleration projects, where a production system already exists, and the investor seeks to increase or expand production for whatever reason. The analysis requires comparing the option of continuing production as is, versus spending additional capital to increase production. Like the discussion of NPV/Inv, many investors prefer to look at this situation on an incremental basis. However, when using the IRR or BDR profit metric, more problems are often created than solved.

Investors typically choose to accelerate production because they have cash flow needs. The reasons they need cash are vast and variable, but we have spent considerable time during our careers redesigning projects to accommodate these cash needs than actually optimizing profit metrics. This is an important and common issue in the investment world.

Example 5.7 presents a typical, though abbreviated example of an acceleration project. The NCF's for the base case, which means do nothing but normal maintenance, and the acceleration case are shown in the first two columns of numbers. The Incremental NCF is the difference between the base and acceleration NCF's. The NPV profile for each case is reported below. Ignoring the time value of money, the base case yields a higher return, \$163.75 to \$158.75, so why would investors ever spend money to get less money. Because the investor needs the higher cash flow in the first 3 years of production. The sum of the incremental values in the first 3 production years shows roughly \$137 M more (the sum of the first 3 positive NCF years in the incremental column), which for a \$90 M investment contributes a considerable sum to the treasury. Over the respective lives of the alternatives, the acceleration case lowers the treasury value by \$5 million to obtain more NCF in the early years. Note that the incremental NCF has two sets of negative values: in the first year and in the last 3 years.

Valuing the acceleration option using the classical metrics shows positive NPV's from a 10% to 55% discount rate. If the investor adopts the 10% discount rate, the acceleration option adds more value to the treasury because of the early NCF receipts. This incremental valuation also illustrates the proper way to compute NPV/Inv, as discussed in that section.

Two sign changes exist: one between 5% and 10%, and the other between 55% and 60% for the incremental case. Which one should be reported? Neither one reflects the common interpretation of IRR or BDR. Both merely indicate the discount rate where the investor would be indifferent between the "do nothing" and the "acceleration" option.

Example 5.7: A current production system can be accelerated by investing additional money. Given the NCF for the base, acceleration and incremental system, compute the NPV and IRR (BDR) values for the investment proposal. Use mid-year, annual discounting.

NCF			
Year	**Base Case**	**Acceleration**	**Incremental**
0	0.00	-90.00	-90.00
0-1	45.00	145.00	100.00
1-2	36.25	70.00	33.75
2-3	30.00	33.75	3.75
3-4	22.50	0.00	-22.50
4-5	20.00	0.00	-20.00
5-6	10.00	0.00	-10.00
Total	163.75	158.75	-5.00

NPV Profile			
Discount Rate	**Base Case**	**Acceleration**	**Incremental**
0%	163.75	158.75	-5.00
5%	146.83	146.44	-0.39
10%	133.03	135.52	2.49
15%	121.61	125.77	4.17
20%	112.03	117.01	4.98
25%	103.92	109.10	5.18
30%	96.98	101.91	4.94
35%	90.98	95.36	4.38
40%	85.75	89.36	3.61
45%	81.16	83.84	2.67
50%	77.11	78.74	1.64
55%	73.49	74.02	0.53
60%	70.26	69.64	-0.62
65%	67.35	65.56	-1.79
70%	64.72	61.75	-2.97

Figure 5.11 explains the incremental IRR process graphically. The first graph plots the profiles for the two cases separately, and the second graph the incremental NPV profile. The happy faces indicate the intersection of the NPV's for each project, about 5.5% and 57%, respectively. The vertical arrows con necting the two figures verify that the incremental BDR equals the discount rate where the difference between the two options is zero.

The IRR or BDR in incremental economics usually establishes the boundaries for the economic metrics. Below 5.5% and above 57%, the metrics prefer the base case. At discount rates between 5.5% and 57%, the acceleration option maximizes value. What should the investor do? Answering such questions depends on the investor's perspective of future events (prices), need for increased cash flow, and wealth position. The classical asset valuation process struggles when trying to answer these questions, and this failing drives the demand for more flexible metrics.

The most practical interpretation of these results reverts to the notion that BDR indicates robustness or risk. Recommend the incremental option when the spread between the high and low BDR's satisfies the investor's risk perception. One common rule requires the lower of the two BDR's to be at least

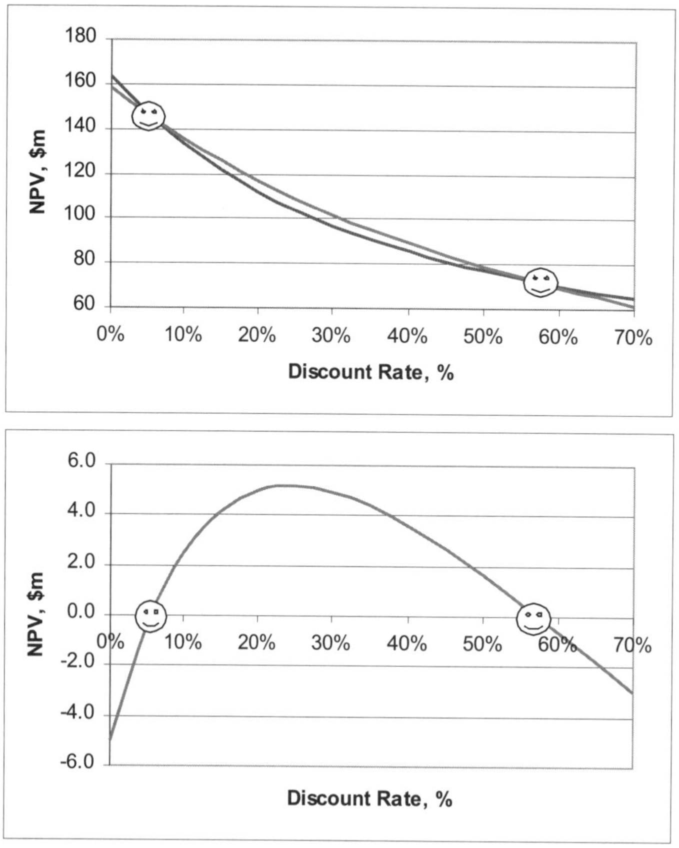

Figure 5.11 NPV profiles for acceleration project

half of the required discount rate; so an investor using a 10% DR would seek lower BDR's of less than 5%, which implies rejecting the acceleration option, in this example.

Use all IRR or BDR numbers with caution, since they just solve an equation, and that solution does not always fit neatly with common usage. Further complications arise when the incremental investment accelerates production, and also increases ultimate production. A pure acceleration example and an acceleration case with increased production, either because of growing markets, increasing market share, or enhanced reserves in the mineral industry, are shown in Figure 5.12. The solid line reflects the base or do nothing production profile, while the highlighted areas illustrate higher production in the early years, followed by a steeper decline. In the first curve, the highlighted areas are equal; implying the change in total production is zero. In the second curve, the area of the top portion exceeds the area of the lower portion,

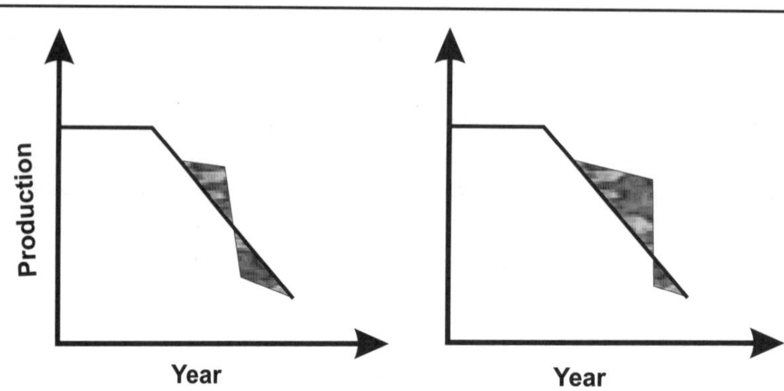

Figure 5.12 Pure acceleration and acceleration with additional production

meaning that total production increases over the life of the project. Figure 5.12 is based on a pure acceleration case.

The acceleration with additional production scenario produces an NPV profile similar to Figures 5.10b and 5.10c. One unique feature of both is that the curve has a negatively sloped line starting at a 0% discount rate and moving to the right. Unless extreme care is exercised, the analyst might mistakenly believe that the normal, single IRR value exists. The second IRR exists; it is just hidden from normal software.

Growth-Rate-of Return (GRR) or Modified IRR (MIRR)

For as many years as decision theorists rejected IRR and BDR as an important metric for analyzing investment opportunities, it still probably dominates all other metrics in applied settings. Many of the reasons for this dominance were addressed earlier in the IRR or BDR section. For those reporting to die hard IRR users, the best solution to the problems mentioned above is to use the GRR or MIRR metric. Both names are encountered in the literature, but more articles have been written using GRR.[5.7] MIRR is the function name found in Excel and Lotus 123 that computes GRR.

The function is MIRR(data array, finance rate, reinvestment rate). Some have objected to the use of the term reinvestment rate, preferring the term *return on unamortized capital.*[5.8] The choice of terminology matters not, though it does impact the way people think about the numerical process.

Both metrics solve the dual IRR problem by eliminating the multiple sign changes. Equation 5.2 defined the process for computing present value from a given future value. The NPV section extended the format to include multiple cash flows, which cause the problem. GRR rectifies the problem by adopting Equation 5.16.

$$PV_{FR} = \sum \frac{-NCF}{(1+FR)_t}$$
$$FV_{RR} = \sum (+NCF)*(1+RR)^t \tag{5.16}$$
$$PV*(1+GRR)n = FV$$

where:

FR = the finance rate in the MIRR function (cost-of-capital in most cases)
RR = the reinvestment rate in the MIRR function (opportunity cost)
GRR = the growth rate-of-return
n = number of years in the project

GRR compounds the positive NCF values to a specified point in time, usually the last year of the project (N). Then, the negative NCF values are discounted to the present using the finance rate, which is the normal discount rate in most applications. This leaves the solution equation with one positive value and one negative value, or one real root solution. Figure 5.13 illustrates the process.

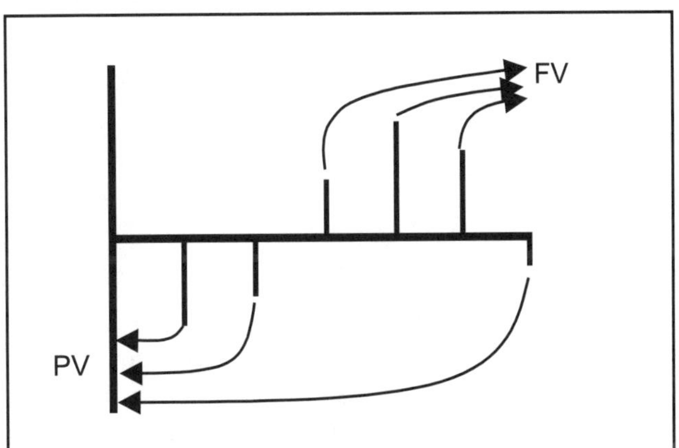

Figure 5.13 GRR and MIRR process

Computing MIRR solves a world of problems in a practical setting. The emphasis here is the word – practical. Ideally, it would be outstanding to communicate the limitations and impractical interpretation of BDR. Professionals, young and old, often have neither the time or training to communicate the problem, and discussion of BDR deficiencies detracts from the real purpose of making sound investment decisions. Quoting the MIRR and going on with the discussion about the merits of the project saves time and does little harm. In fact, enlightened software automatically switches to MIRR when multiple sign changes exist in the project NCF.

Example 5.8 continues the acceleration example to demonstrate GRR or MIRR. Columns 1 and 2 show the year and NCF for the incremental NCF. Column 3 repeats the yearly 10% discount factors assuming a mid-year cash flow and annual interest (Equation 5.8). Column 4 is the product of the negative NCF's and the appropriate discount factors, yielding a total negative amount of -$117.68. The FV computation is slightly more complicated, because the positive NCF numbers are compounded to the end of the project life, assumed to be at the end of year 6.

Example 5.8: Compute the GRR or MIRR for the incremental NCF investment options in Example 5.7. Assume that the finance rate and reinvestment rate are both 10%.

(1) Year	(2) ΔNCF	(3) Discount Factor @ 10%	(4) PV = – NCF*DF	(5) FV=NCF/DF	(6) NCF for GRR Calculation
0	-90.00	1.000000	-90.00	0	-117.68
0-1	100.00	0.953463	0	168.91	
1-2	33.75	0.866784	0	51.82	
2-3	3.75	0.787986	0	5.23	
3-4	-22.50	0.716351	-14.65	0	
4-5	-20.00	0.651228	-11.84	0	
5-6	-10.00	0.592025	-5.38	0	225.96
Total	-5.00		-117.68	225.96	

$$FV = NCF_0 - 1*(1+0.10)^6 - 0.5 + NCF_1 - 2*(1+0.10)^6 - 1.5 + NCF_2 - 3*(1+0.10)^6 - 2.5$$
$$= 100*1.1^{5.5} + 33.75*1.1^{4.5} + 3.75*1.1^{3.5}$$
$$= 100*1.689 + 33.75*1.536 + 3.75*1.395 = 225.96$$

Solving for the GRR equation gives 10.36% by plugging the values in column 6 into the Excel IRR function. Using the MIRR function on column 2 produces a value of 9.73%, but that assumed end of year discounting and the example uses mid-year. To approximate the process, divide 9.73% by the half-year value of 0.9753 to raise the MIRR to 10.2%, which is accurate enough.

MIRR or GRR eliminates the unrealistic elements that plagued the traditional BDR, and also adds several other interesting features into investment decisions. First, Seba[(5.9)] and Daugherty[(5.10)] show that GRR gives the same rankings as NPV/Inv, eliminating one source of ranking conflicts. When the reinvestment and finance rate in MIRR are equal, MIRR and NPV/Inv can be approximated by Equation 5.17:

$$GRR = (1+DR)*(NPV/Inv+1)^{1/N} - 1$$
or
$$GRR = (1.10)*\left(\frac{2.49}{90}+1\right)^{1/6} - 1 = 0.105 \quad or \quad 10.5\% \qquad \textbf{(5.17)}$$

The second important addition arises from the explicit distinction between the finance rate and the reinvestment rate. For the first time in the classical valuation process, a metric differentiates between the cost of borrowing money and the reinvestment opportunity from the cash thrown off by the project. Today, the great bulk of the investors assume that these two numbers are equal, but modern asset valuation expands on this idea in a formal, logical manner. To support the notion that MIV just builds on the classical system, Mao argued in 1969 that every opportunity is a mixed investment: composed of investment outflows and inflows to repay the investment, and additional cash receipts (overdrafts in Mao's terminology) that provide stability, liquidity, and growth potential, and, as such, should be handled differently from the investment component.[(5.11)]

One problem with GRR and MIRR relates to the definition of N in Equation 5.17. In the example, N depended on the life of the project. Defining N as the project life works fine when dealing with the question of whether the project satisfies the profit metric for acceptance. When moving to the ranking of competing alternatives or limited budgets, Capen emphasizes the need to establish the same value for N in all projects. A constant value for N across all projects is needed, because the magnitude of FV is a function of N, with longer-life projects having a larger FV. Capen recommends using a value of 7 or 10 years for consistency.

Characteristics of GRR or MIRR

1. *It consistently handles different project lives when ranking.*
2. *It corrects for the multiple root problem in IRR or BDR.*
3. *It provides a more realistic measure of the rate-of-return from the project than IRR, and*
4. *It introduces the importance of differentiating between the components of NCF and their relative risks in analyzing investment opportunities.*

Discounted Payout or Payout

A traditional investment metric, which began, probably, with the first investment and still used extensively today, is payout (PO) or discounted payout (DPO). Some use the term payback or discounted payback as a synonym. Payout is just DPO when the DR equals zero, or the time value of money is ignored. In both cases, the metric computes the length of time (years or months) needed to recover the investment or initial outlay of capital. As a crude risk measure, the investor prefers smaller payout times, like several months. Many investors associate longer payouts with greater risk exposure. A common application of payout is in the sale or purchase of small producing assets, where the participants have neither the technical staff or time to complete formal DCF analysis. Maximum purchase price depends on the value that can be recovered at current NCF (often before tax) in 20 or 24 months time. The approach works well for small, relatively stable investments, as witnessed by its continued popularity by many investors.

Payout is the length of time needed for cumulative NCF to reach zero. Figure 5.14 shows two cumulative NCF curves, one undiscounted (DPO_0 or PO) and one discounted at 10% (DPO_{10}). The payout period is the intersection of the cumulative curve and the x-axis. The undiscounted PO (PO_0) intersects the x-axis in 4.6 years, while DPO_{10} has a larger value of 5.1 years. The project takes 4.6 years to recover all the Capex, Opex, and taxes incurred up to that point in time. At PO, the investor is neutral in the investment, essentially having recovered all costs.

Regular PO conveys information about the time the investment capital is at risk, ignoring a critical piece of the puzzle – time value of money. DPO at the designated discount rate corrects the flaw in PO. Computing the time needed to recover all the previous costs, plus the time needed to earn the desired return (10% in the example) means DPO will always be greater than undiscounted PO. The figure shows that another half year is needed to

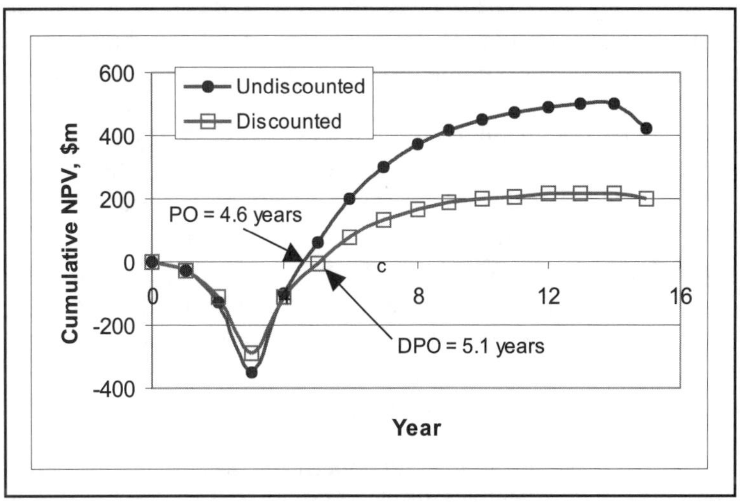

Figure 5.14 Payout and undiscounted payout

Example 5.9: Compute PO and DPO_{10} using the following NCF. $ values in millions.

Year	NCF	Cumulative NCF	NPV	Cumulative NPV
0	-51,785.00	-51,785.00	-51,785.00	-51,785.00
1	20,000.00	-31,785.00	18,181.82	-33,603.18
2	20,000.00	-11,785.00	16,528.93	-17,074.25
3	20,000.00	8,215.00	15,026.30	-2,047.95
4	20,000.00	28,215.00	13,660.27	11,612.32
Total	28,215.00		11,612.32	
PO		4.59		
DPO				5.15

$$DPO = 4 + \frac{-(-2,047)}{11,612 - (-2047)} = 4.15$$

earn the specified 10% return. At DPO, the project has recovered all costs plus paid the lenders their required return or matched the opportunity cost. The project has broken even from this risk perspective.

In the simple example, the project might go on for another 10 years, but the DPO ignores all NCF after that point in time. By ignoring the subsequent NCF, DPO focuses on the risk perspective to the exclusion of total value added to the treasury. Modern asset valuation corrects part of that problem. But, one critical question investors must ask themselves concerns whether the riskiness of the project NCF's differs after DPO relative to before. If the investor borrows the money for the project from the bank at 10%, the loan has been repaid at DPO, and 10 years of NCF is still to come. Would you perceive a change in risk? How you answer that question will impact the way that you respond to MIV!

Characteristics of DPO and PO:

1. It ignores NCF after payout, thus fails to provide a metric of total value.
2. It favors investments with low initial outlays and early cash returns.
3. Defines the point where investment risk changes in the project.

Comparison of Classical Profit Measures

Example 5.10 represents a typical tabular format for three simple projects. The NCF pattern is followed by the calculated values for NPV, IRR, DPO, MIRR, and NPV/Inv. All three projects satisfy a discount standard of both 10% and 15%. Suppose, however, these are mutually exclusive projects or the budget only allows a commitment to one project. Which one would you recommend?

Investors using NPV, as the dominant criteria, would select project A, while those using IRR would go for B. NPV/Inv opts for C. Three partners in the same project, each using different metrics, would have considerable discussion, often acrimonius, about the preferred alternative. This happens quite often. Rather than dwell on the differences right now, a more important question concerns the characteristics of the ranking process relative to the final decision. Project A comes top using NPV, because it is the largest project, one of the major biases of NPV. BDR or IRR prefers project B, because of the lower initial capital outlay and the quicker cash returns, as seen by payout. Project C wins with NPV/Inv due to the low initial capital outlay. In looking at the results of the three traditional profit metrics, they are consistent with the biases discussed in each individual section.

Well, which is the right metric? Like all investment decisions, "it depends on the business environment and financial condition of the investor." Large, multinational corporations generally use NPV, owing to their huge asset base. Alternatively, individuals, like Bill Gates of Microsoft, use NPV, because of

Example 5.10: Three investments with the following NCF's have been prepared by the technical staff. Make a recommendation as to the acceptability of each project assuming 1) you have enough funds to accept all three, and then 2) budget restriction limit you to only one project. Assume a 10% discount rate or standard.

	Investment		
Year	A	B	C
0-1	-51,785	-31,785	-29,180
1-2	20,000	22,500	0
2-3	20,000	20,765	0
3-4	20,000	0	20,000
4-5	20,000	0	35,320
Total	28,215	11,480	26,140
NPV_{10}	11,612.31	5,830.70	9,970.33
NPV_{15}	5,314.57	3,481.54	4,164.65
NPV_{20}	-10.31	1,385.14	-572.75
BDR	20%	24%	19%
NPV/Inv	0.224	0.183	0.342
PO	3.59	2.45	4.26
DPO	4.15	2.66	4.59
MIRR	16%	15%	18%

their wealth. Small individuals with few assets or limited wealth normally opt for IRR. Any project failure or delay may severely damage their financial well-being, hence, emphasizing low risk exposure and quick payouts fits their economic situation. Investors employing an efficiency measure are usually facing large capital expenditures relative to their budgets and assets. Adopting NPV/Inv provides an incentive to lower the initial capital burden.

The results also provide interesting feedback on IRR, as seen via the MIRR metric. IRR was chastised for using the IRR number as the reinvestment rate, not the opportunity cost of money. When the MIRR values use 10% for the finance and reinvestment rate, observe the dramatic shift in project B. Now project B moves to the bottom of the table from the top (using IRR). This verifies the notion by Seba and Daugherty that MIRR can be derived from the NPV/Inv value.

This brief, simple illustrates the most common method investors use to choose the final combination of projects. Rank them from high to low on some criteria until the budget is exhausted. Then, see if that portfolio fits the secondary or other strategic objectives, like meeting the incentive plan ROCE value, or entering and maintaining exposure in a new country. Failing to satisfy these objectives requires replacing the lowest priority projects until all objectives are satisfied. This is ranking and has little in common with risk assessment and management, except by accident.

Comparison of Traditional Profit Metrics

An old, but useful display of the relationship among the classical metrics plots one measure against another for a portfolio of projects.[(5.12)] Example 5.11 illustrates several common performance measures plotted against each other for 25 different projects. The project portfolio differs from many investors by being heavily weighted toward large, international projects. In this portfolio, about half of the projects were such, and the remainder was smaller, incremental projects, like maintenance and expansion of existing assets. Most investors probably have over 2/3's of their projects in the smaller category, by number.

Example 5.11: Plots of NPV, IRR, and payout against each other, along with a fuller correlation matrix for all the traditional metrics.

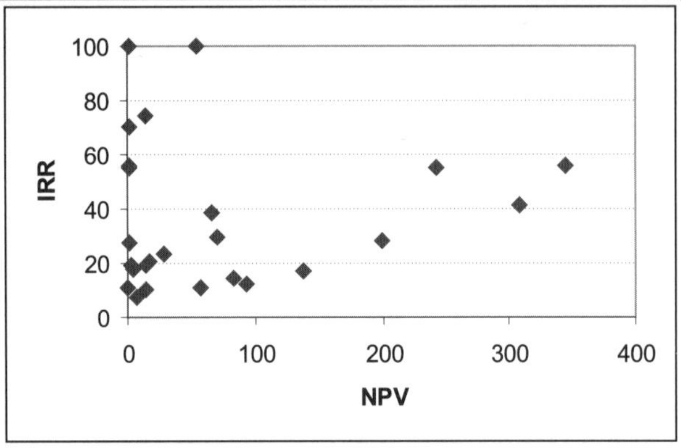

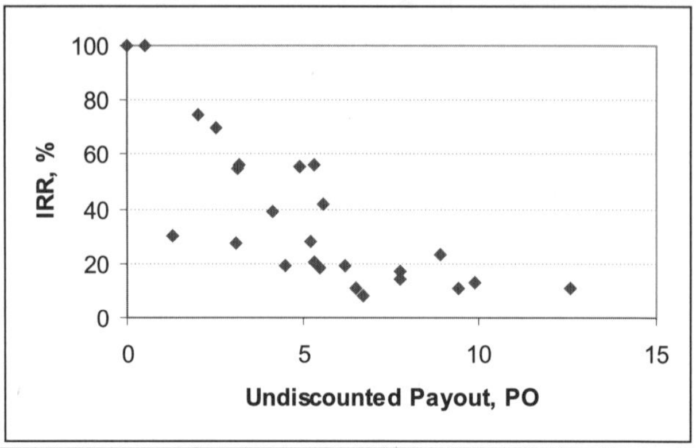

	NPV	IRR	NPV/Inv	PO	DPO	Invest
NPV	1					
IRR	0.075132	1				
NPV/Inv	0.503942	0.062565	1			
PO	0.119255	-0.7672	-0.00567	1		
DPO	-0.00724	-0.73428	-0.06803	0.929072	1	
Invest	0.151024	-0.37509	-0.00226	0.744217	0.665056	1

IRR and NPV show almost no relationship primarily as the result of the lower valued projects near the origin. All the high IRR projects had very low NPV's, being associated with maintenance of production systems and equipment, and least-cost analysis (See Chapter 9). Common wisdom suggests that IRR is inversely related to payout, as the second of the two figures indicates. In fact, in this sample, achieving a high IRR requires a payout less than about 5 or 6 years. This explains why investors in projects with long lead times for construction, but long producing lives, like electrical generation and steel plants, seldom use IRR to rank alternative investment options. The long lead-time that causes the high payouts favors incremental investments of existing assets, and, thus, one never builds for the future.

Most of the pertinent relationships among the traditional metrics come through in the correlation table. NPV and IRR have almost no relationship, while the NPV and NPV/Inv have a correlation of about 50%, for obvious reasons. Similarly, the negative relationship between IRR and PO (and DPO) is around –70%, with the investment magnitude also being fairly high and negative. This supports the statement that IRR favors low investment projects. The short-run bias compounds when the correlation between investment magnitude and PO reaches almost 75%. To maximize IRR, never invest!

Summary of Classical DCF Valuation

The preceding pages outline the basic metrics and logic for analyzing investments under the umbrella of the classical system. NPV, BDR, NPV/Inv, MIRR, and DPO provided the decision-tools that most of the modern world was founded on, at least from an investment perspective. The discussion of each metric identified the respective strengths and weakness, and the role other metrics provided in correcting those limitations. None of the discussion undermines the potential contribution each metric makes to efficient investment decision-making. Neither are they perfect, and the real issues concern how to improve the metrics while keeping the desirable elements. That is the quest of modern investment valuation (MIV).

MODERN INVESTMENT VALUATION (MIV)

The modern approach to investment decision-making has been going on for over 30 years. The founders and proponents of the classical system were very aware of the limiting assumptions for practical implementation. What's important to remember is that the investment model used by the majority of investors was never intended to be the dominant profit model, just a special case to be used until the calculation tools improved enough to handle the analysis in the desired detail. With current computer technology, the barrier to change is the knowledge and will of the investors, not the toolkit. When all the reasons for keeping the old system are presented and analyzed, they all break down to a psychological motive – the discomfort that change brings. Most human beings, up to 90% by some accounts, experience discomfort, often to the point of depression, when forced to abandon an old, comfortable system, in favor of the new and unknown. This emotion underlies all disciplines, not just investment decision-making.[(5.13)] Or, as Mark Twain said ""I'm all for progress; it's change I don't like."

Before jumping into the particulars of MIV, several words of caution are in order. To those desiring theoretical correctness, we apologize up front for failing to do so. The discussion seeks to demystify the jargon, with no intent to teach the details of *arbitrage pricing theory* (APT), *certainty equivalent value* or *capital asset pricing model* (CAPM), though elements of each are introduced, here and in Chapter 8, to make the necessary point. To the practical person, some jargon and new concepts has to be included. In both instances the discussion seeks to enhance the awareness of why the classical system distorts the performance metrics of investment opportunities, and provide a motivation for overcoming the "depression" of expanding the investment toolkit.

Expanding on the classical DCF or CIV process would draw less attention if the deficiencies in the investment deficiencies weren't so painfully obvious. A huge body of literature shows that "the use of standard DCF methods can induce systematic, and possibly misleading, biases into the analyses that lie behind project design and selection."[(5.14)] This section starts with a cursory review of these criticisms. The following two sections – decomposing the sources of risk and value into finer detail, and real options – illustrate the defects in the classical DCF in more detail. The chapter concludes with some simple applications to highlight the differences in the various approaches. Before you even begin reading the section, remember the opening comments by a professor friend who always says, "I am going to discuss the best, most up to date, but still imperfect knowledge."

Before jumping into the details, the vocabulary in this area, as in most disciplines, use conflicting terminology. Some use the term *real options* to signify all deviations from the classical system. We follow the arguments of David Laughton.[(5.15)] He effectively argues that real options is a subset of the MIV process, as the following discussions address.

Criticisms of Classical DCF

The valuation process estimates future NCF, broken down by component, like price, production, Capex, Opex, taxes, etc. Then, the time value of money component computes a metric like NPV, BDR, etc. This modeling process forgets that NCF is a commodity with characteristics that vary by time and risk. The classical process, owing to a restricted toolkit, buried the timing and risk issues into the WACC or DR. MIV allows the investor to split these components into the desired level of detail with significant impact on the perception and, ultimate, performance of investments.

Perhaps the best way to introduce MIV is to quote the experts, though some of the comments duplicate the same point.

Flaw 1: *Businessmen have tended to make capital budgeting decisions using their intuition, rules of thumb, or investment criteria with faulty theoretical foundations, and, thus, are apt to give incorrect answers in a large percentage of decisions.*(5.16)

Flaw 2: *Although they certainly understand the arithmetic of calculation, they may not understand the logic of the method deeply enough to trust it or use it without mistakes.*(5.17)

Flaw 3: *Some projects are unusually risky at start-up but only of normal risk (or less risk) once the start-up is successfully passed.*(5.18)

Flaw 4: *Classical DCF assumes uncertainty (or risk) increases at a constant discount rate (geometrically) over time.*(5.19)

Flaw 5: *Single discount rates improperly account for the changing nature of risk over time and among the elements of a project.*(5.20)

Flaw 6: *Students are generally taught that the correct discount rate is simply the opportunity cost-of-capital for the particular project, e.g., the expected rate-of-return that could be earned from an investment of similar risk. In principle, the opportunity cost should reflect the non diversifiable or systematic risk that is associated with the particular project. The risk might have characteristics that vary from the company's other individual projects or from its average investment activity. In practice, however, the opportunity cost of a specific project may be hard to measure. As a result, students learn that a company's WACC is a reasonable substitute. The WACC offers a reasonable substitute as long as the company's projects do not differ greatly from one another in their non-diversifiable risk.*(5.21)

Flaw 7: *The constant discounting used to produce values for large classes of projects is based on the false premises that: 1) the risks in the different projects are of the same magnitude; and 2) these risks are resolved at a constant rate over time.*(5.22)

Flaw 8: *Classical DCF assumes that each investment decision is irreversible. Once management makes a decision, no changes or responses to future business conditions are possible.*(5.23)

Other authors support these references, and a full reporting of the worthwhile quotes in books and journals would go on for pages. Most of the authors provide detailed examples that the flawed classical system produces biases against long-term and strategic investments by discounting the future excessively, and by undervaluing the opportunity for project managers to respond to changes in future business environments. The collective effect of these biases probably lowers the estimated profit by at least 1/3 over what they could have earned by understanding risk and options better.

There exists the danger of simplifying the issue too much, but the undue reliance on averages or expected values to create a workable investment system distorts the distribution of investments, causing both greater risk and lower returns to the investor. Several simple analogs might help. Suppose educational programs designed the training curriculums around the notion that the average human being had an IQ of 100, and then taught everyone, whether they had an IQ of 60 or 180, exactly the same way. Likewise, suppose the government designed their health and welfare programs using just the average income. Would this practice distort the dissemination of required services to those individuals, especially to those most in need?

The last two questions merely reiterate the distributional issues ignored in mathematical averages, but that is what the classical DCF does. In fact, some professionals believe that they can just impose formal risk methods, like decision-trees and simulation (Chapters 6 and 8) on top of the classical DCF and get better decisions. This perception is correct up to a point. Better understanding of variations in projects and the sources of value do emerge from formal risk assessment, but the bias against long-term investments and the under valuation of options still exists.

The Principle of Additivity or Decomposition

Rather than trying to summarize the process in the last 4 chapters verbally, a quick duplication of the relevant process serves to illustrate the improvements resulting from implementing MIV. Figure 5.15 reproduces the corporate perspective from Chapter 4.

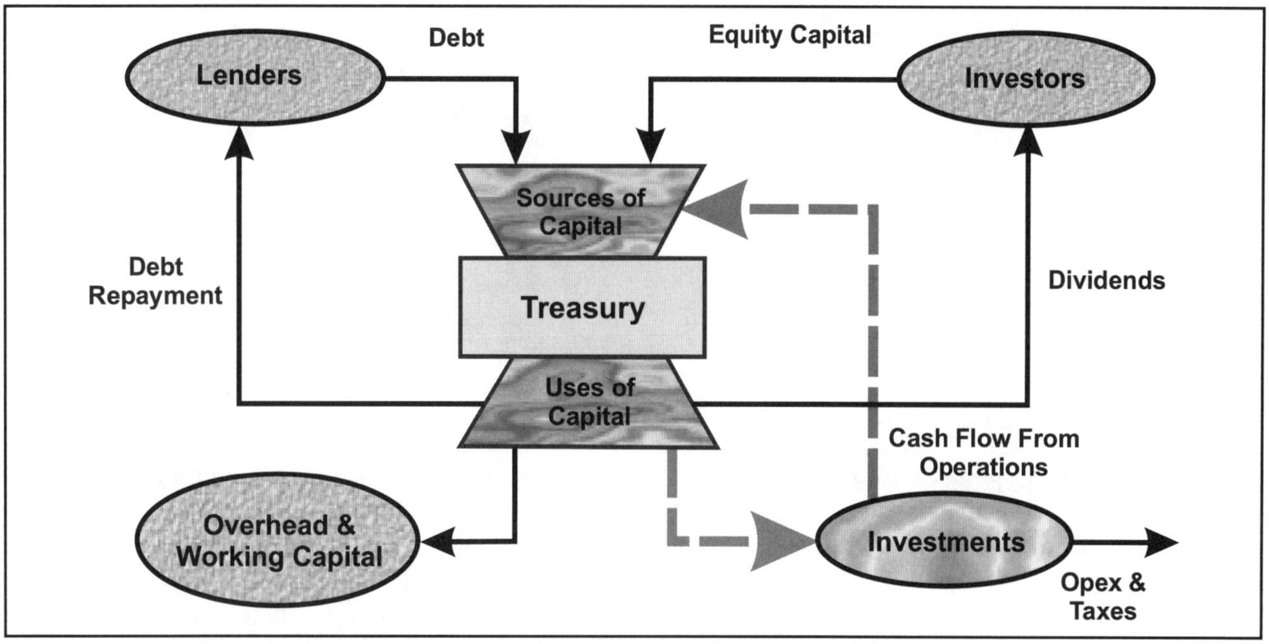

Figure 5.15 Corporate perspective in Figure 4.3

The process of acquiring capital, led to the generation of the weighted average cost-of-capital (WACC). The critical element in the computation was the averaging of the various sources of funding, via a variety of schemes. The one approach that captures the risk and return trade-off, which helps explain MIV, was the capital asset pricing model (CAPM). That figure is duplicated in Figure 5.16. Observe that the risk free rate box adds the words, systematic risk, and the top section refers to unsystematic risk. The WACC was derived from the risk free rate or systematic risk, R_f, plus a risk premium to reflect unsystematic risk, R_P. Systematic risk, which is tied to the entire economy, cannot be diversified away, while unsystematic risk, which relates to individual entities, can be diversified away.

Another term for diversifiable is "non-macroeconomic," meaning it's movement over time is uncorrelated with the overall economy, as measured by GNP or GDP (See Chapter 7). A classic example would be an individual oil or gas reservoir. A 10% change in a single reservoir will neither destroy the world economy nor improve it. Likewise, a change in an individual stock (the top of the curve) has risk, but that risk can be reduced or eliminated by also purchasing a stock with an opposite characteristic. Hence, the terms – diversification by engaging in portfolio management – exist. If the world economy crashes, every investment opportunity will fall with it. That portion of an asset is called systemic risk, or non-diversifiable risk.

The classical system ignores the variability in the choice of investment options. It takes the WACC generated by Figure 5.15 and applies it to all investments, as Figure 5.16 shows.

The classical approach follows a top down logic, like the military structure in Chapter 2. The corporate WACC or opportunity cost (Review Flaw 6) mandates that all asset units must earn 10%, and then

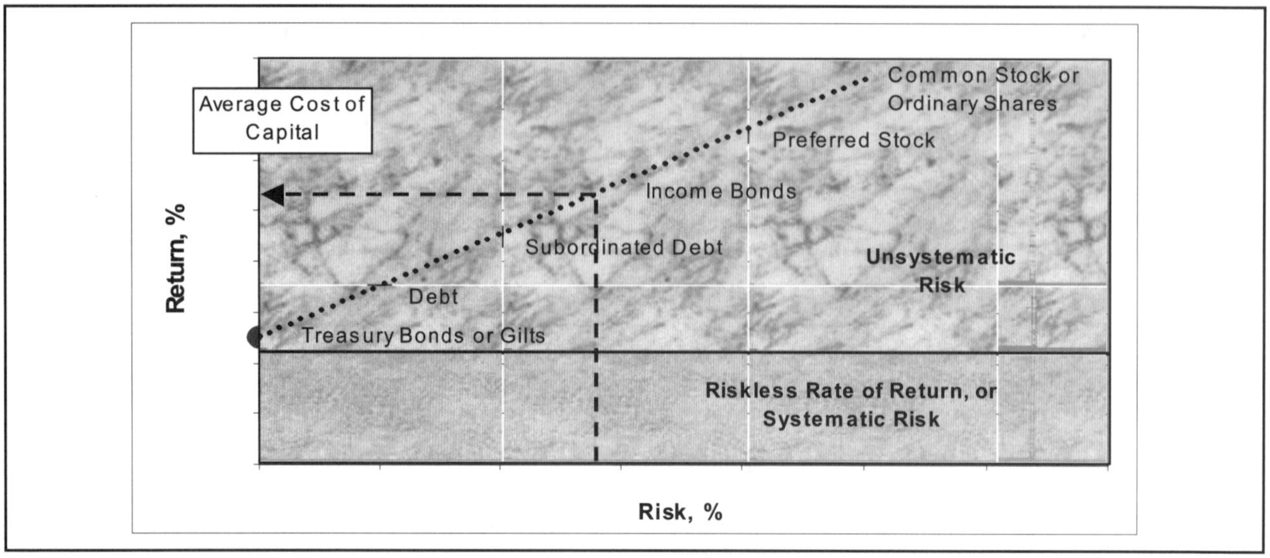

Figure 5.16 Risk and return trade-off from Figure 3.16

each project within each asset faces the 10% hurdle. Investors using the top down approach recognized the distortions in investment patterns caused by this simplification, especially when it made emerging technologies, like computers, broadband mediums, etc., uncompetitive with old, established industries. The solution was to declare the new investment opportunities, strategic, and apply a lower discount rate.

The modern approach formally recognizes that the risk and return patterns differed across assets, and projects operating under specific business conditions. Figure 5.17 assumes an equal allocation of money to the assets and projects. With an equal weighting, the total for all projects sums to the 8% return required by asset B, and the sum of the assets equals the 10% return objective of the corporation. This is still top down in that the corporate office determines the required return and the budget allocation to the assets. But, it is bottom up in allowing the specific assets to determine the risk and return portfolio to achieve the stated objectives.

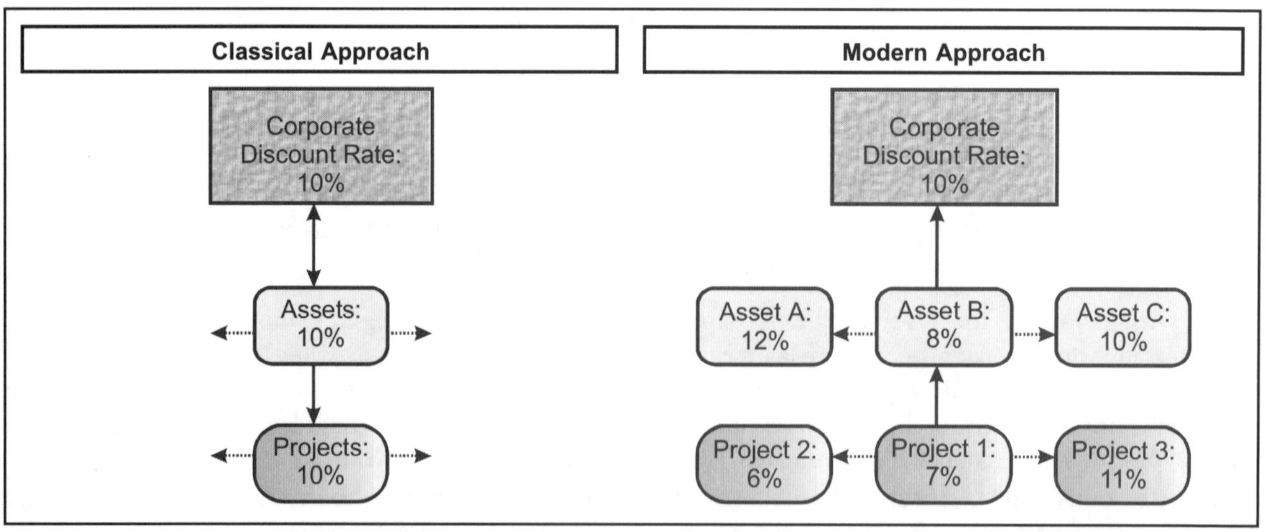

Figure 5.17 Comparison of classical and modern valuation systems

Figure 5.18 illustrates that the modern approach continues the risk and return trade-off established at the corporate level. Instead of reporting debt, equity, and other sources of capital, the positively sloped line reflects different asset and project risk/return relationships. The Asset A-E labels are followed by project examples. The 'or" between the asset and project type just indicates that the same process could be used at each level.

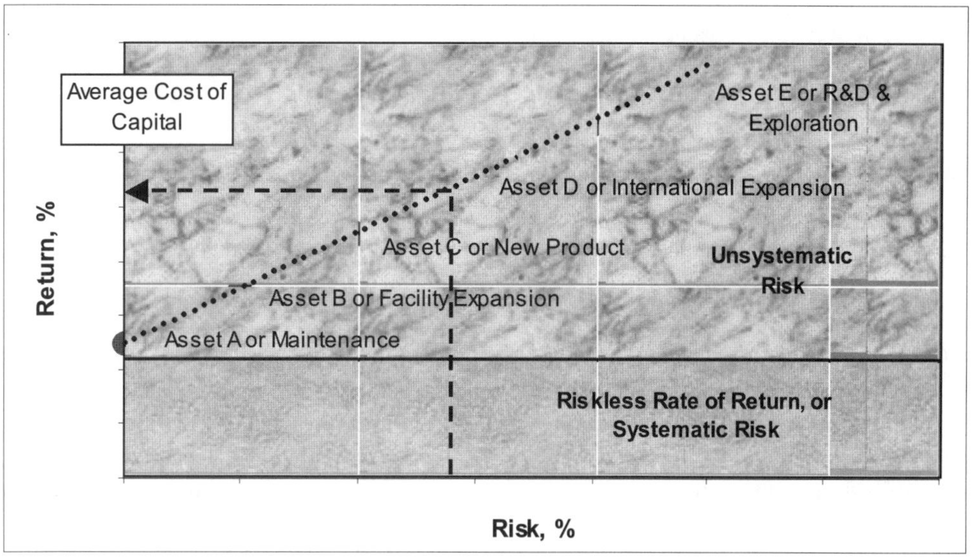

Figure 5.18 Asset and project risk/return profiles

Organizations, like Siemans,[5.24] realized that using one or an average discount rate caused them to miss or forego attractive investments. Their solution: adopt a different return standard for their 16 divisions, as indicated by Figure 5.18. The corporate office then allocates capital to each division to achieve their corporate WACC or opportunity cost perspective, reproduced in Figure 5.15.

At the project level, Royal Dutch Shell performed a lookback on their offshore platform design and operations, worldwide, over several decades.[5.25] They found that the design staff minimized the importance of Opex during operations, and focused almost entirely on reducing initial Capex. The authors realized that the design engineers responded to the classical investment valuation process, using the same discount rate, and intentionally reduced front end costs (Capex) by increasing future costs (Opex). Because both were discounted at the same discount rate, the future costs impacted project value significantly less.

The recommended solution was to adopt the risk and return trade-off in Figure 5.18. Opex expenditures were treated as lower risk, like the maintenance example, and Capex, being riskier, moved along the line to the right. Formally recognizing the risk differences allowed them to justify correcting for the Capex bias in the CIV process, by spending more on initial capital to reduce Opex over the life cycle of the project.

The CIV favoritism towards spending Opex in the future is well documented in the literature. Several of the quotes in the Flaws section earlier made reference to the bias. Salahor[5.26] and Laughton[5.27] provide extensive lists and examples of other literature that supports the same notion.

The industrial based solutions disaggregate the corporate view to lower levels. Though an improvement in the recognition of variability or risk at lower levels, the theoretically correct solution under MIV follows the format in Equation 5.18, which decomposes Equation 5.10 into finer detail.

$$\text{Value} = \sum_{t=1}^{n}\left[\frac{\overline{\text{Price}*\text{Production}} - \overline{\text{Opex}} - \overline{\text{Capex}} - \overline{\text{Taxes}}}{(1+\text{WACC}+?)^{(t-0.5)}}\right] \qquad \text{Eq. 5.10}$$

CHAPTER 5

becomes:

$$\text{Value} = \sum_{t=1}^{n}\left[\frac{\text{Price}_t}{(1+R_f+R_p^{\text{Price}})^{(t-0.5)}} * \frac{\text{Production}_t}{(1+R_f+R_p^{\text{Prod}})^{(t-0.5)}} - \frac{\text{Opex}_t}{(1+R_f+R_p^{\text{Opex}})^{(t-0.5)}} - \frac{\text{Capex}_t}{(1+R_f+R_p^{\text{Capex}})^{(t-0.5)}} - \frac{\text{Taxes}_t}{(1+R_f+R_p^{\text{Taxes}})^{(t-0.5)}}\right] \tag{5.18}$$

where: R_f = the risk free rate,

R_p = the risk premium for the variable name in the superscript.

Equation 5.18 seems like a very simple expansion of the classical model, and, it is. Decision sciences originally began with Equation 5.18, but quickly encountered the practical problem of how to establish the R_p for each component of the equation. To get investors to adopt the methodology, the process actually flowed from starting with Equation 5.18 and reducing it to Equation 5.10, which given WACC or DR, becomes easily applicable, although heavily biased owing to the treatment of each component as if it was the same.

MIV and real options focus considerable attention on measuring and understanding the risk elements in investment decisions. In most projects, for instance, the Capex occurs in the first few years and falls off dramatically thereafter. Furthermore, the Capex faces greater risks in that a production system may be built, and then never used or under utilized relative to its specification. The reasons are varied: no market for the product, supply constraints, obsolete technology, etc. Opex, conversely, exists mainly when production takes place, and is partially controllable by the operator, e.g., if Opex gets to high, the operator has the *option* to shut the plant down, change the operating characteristics, sell it, abandon it, etc. This option reduces the risk for the Opex, which is totally lost when using the classical system.

The format for Equation 5.18 follows from the capital asset pricing model. One deficiency of this instructional format arises from the interdependence (correlation) among the variables. Taxes, for example, vary with the other variables, but CAPM ignores that relationship. Real applications of MIV and real options (RO) must address such relationships.

The analog to applying CIV in the technical world would be to say that the average heat load for a piece of equipment is some number. Then, that value would be applied worldwide, totally ignoring the individual equipment characteristics. Or, suppose the weatherman told you the average worldwide temperature at that moment was z, would you then use z to make travel plans for a destination thousands of miles away. CIV effectively does this for investment decisions.

MIV and RO exist to provide tools for generating R_p for each variable. Chapters 8 and 9 cover that element in greater detail. This section addresses just the biases in CIV that current tools can overcome, if implemented.

Risk and Time Diversification

Even the MIV discussed to date faces some inaccuracies. Once R_p is set, the framework assumes risk follows the same path for the rest of the project. The validity of this assumption is a raging debate in the literature today. Time diversification is a simple notion, closely related to the general principle of diversification, a key concept underpinning modern portfolio theory. The basic idea is that you should never put all of your eggs in one basket. In the stock market, this means that holding a portfolio of securities reduces risk relative to holding just one or two individual securities by spreading the risk. If the returns to the securities in the portfolio are independent, then the volatility of the overall portfolio will be lower than in the volatility of the stocks that comprise the portfolio. This occurs because independent price movements of the securities in the portfolio offset each, reducing risk in the portfolio.

Modern portfolio theory uses the standard deviation of annual returns as a numerical proxy for risk. Over the last 70 years, the annual rate of return to the stock market as a whole has averaged about 11 percent. During the same period, the annual standard deviation of returns has been about 20 percent. It is generally recognized that stock returns are log normally distributed. Standard statistical analysis suggests that over a one-year time horizon, there is about a two thirds chance that returns will range from about minus 9 to plus 31 percent (plus and minus one standard deviation). Notice that there is a significant probability (roughly one chance in three) of actually losing money over a one-year time horizon. The possibility of losing money defines risk in the stock market.

Modern Portfolio Theory concentrates on a one-year investment horizon. The common conception of risk is that increases the further into the future the investment is held. This is the essence of flaw 2 cited earlier, and is captured in Figure 5.19. This is certainly the typical view in a capital budgeting context. However, this short-term perspective may be wrong since there are cogent arguments to suggest that the risk of holding an investment decreases, on average, with a lengthening of the investment horizon. (Note: MIV just maintains that the discount rate changes without prescribing the direction of change.)

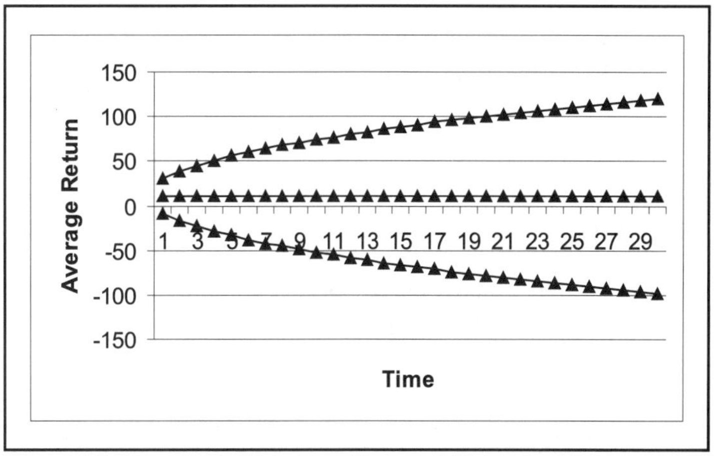

Figure 5.19 Classical view of risk over time

For marketable securities, the intuition is straightforward. If stock market returns are independent from one year to the next, then good years in the market will be offset by the bad years, and the risk of holding equities over long periods will be lower than the risk associated with holding them for just one year. If the investment is to be held for more than one year, the probability that periods of low returns will be followed by periods of high returns increases significantly. In other words, it is possible to diversify across time, i.e. time diversification.

This notion is the foundation for the advice given to young people to commit significant amounts of money to the stock market, and those near retirement age to buy fixed income securities, because they are less risky over short time horizons. Commitments of funds to stocks may be volatile over short periods, but, as long as they are held for a long time period, the actual average return will eventually converge to the mean.

The diminution of risk over longer time horizons may be quantified. The standard deviation around the actual N period average return will be equal to the standard deviation around the one- year return divided by the square root of N. Returning to the stock market example above, the standard deviation around the average annual return of 11 percent over a 10 a ten-year horizon will be about 6.3 percent. Thus, there will be about a two-thirds chance (plus and minus one standard deviation) that the average return over the ten-year period will range from 4.7 to 17.3 percent. Notice how the range of possible outcomes has tightened considerably as returns are diversified across time.

The principle of time diversification is illustrated graphically in Figure 5.20 using the stock marker data example. Notice that the vertical axis is average return and the horizontal axis is time. The diversification is more dramatic for longer time periods. Using the stock market example, the standard deviation around the expected return over a 25-year horizon becomes 4 percent (20% divided by the square root of 25). Thus, there is a two third chance that actual average returns will range form 7 to 15 percent and a 95% chance (+/– 2 SDs) that actual average returns will range from 3 to 19 percent. Over a 25-year hori-

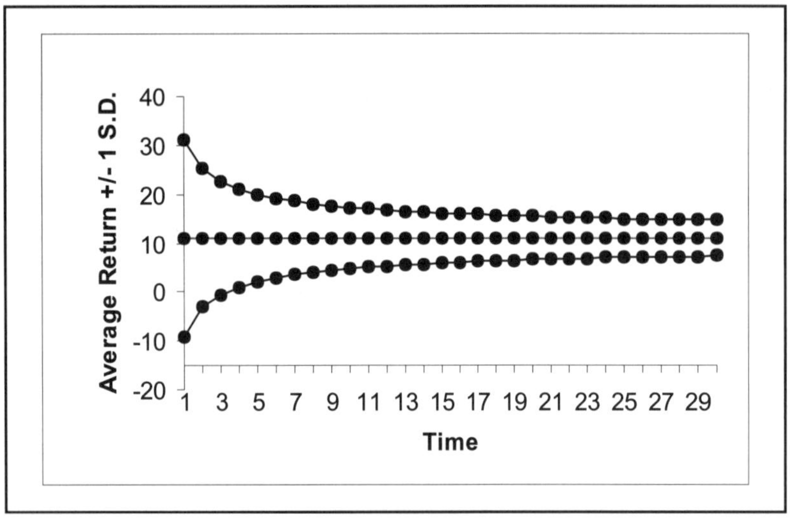

Figure 5.20 Time diversification

zon, there is essentially no chance of losing money in the stock market. Over long enough time horizons, the probability of under-performing a riskless asset becomes essentially zero.

The principle of time diversification applies to MIV. Consider two projects with equal risk. Risk in this context is the volatility of cash flows. One project has a relatively short time horizon, say 5 years and the other a relatively long horizon, say 25 years. Conventional wisdom would view the 5-year project as less risky. But, is it? Over 5 years, the probability that a sequence of poor outcomes could cause the project to lose money is significant. The 25-year project, on the other hand, has a longer period for the law of averages to work out, and a sequence of poor initial cash flows could eventually be overcome by a series of above average cash flows. The 25-year project has a greater strategic value than the 5-year project. Instead of penalizing the 25-year project with a higher discount rate as is typically suggested, time diversification applies a lower discount rate to projects with greater strategic value, or time diversification potential.

The strategic value of time diversification is quantifiable by adjusting the discount rate for the diversification benefits of longer time horizons. Breaking out the relevant components of Equation 5.18 gives:

$$DR_a^i = R_f + R_p^i \tag{5.19}$$

where: the values are defined as before, except the superscript i relates to the *ith* variable in the NCF equation. The risk premium may be adjusted for the average period over which cash flows are received from the project. Notice that this is slightly different from the stock market where the total time horizon is considered. The difference is that for marketable investments like stocks, the primary benefits are only realized when the investment is sold. Cash flows benefits are received over time and thus the average time period over which cash flows are received is relevant. The appropriate adjustment is to divide the risk premium by the square root of the average period for benefits:

$$DR_a^i = R_f + \frac{R_p^i}{\sqrt{\frac{N}{2}}} \tag{5.20}$$

where DR^a is the adjusted discount rate, and N is the time horizon of the project.

For example, suppose that the riskless rate is 5% and a company normally adds a risk premium of 10%, so that the normal discount rate for risky projects is 15%. Using the above formulation, the strategic discount rate for a 20-year project or individual cash flow (average period = 10 years) would be

$$DR_a^i = 5\% + \frac{10}{\sqrt{\frac{20}{2}}} = 5\% + \frac{10}{3.16} = 8.2\%$$

This format justifies the explanation given by Siemans at the operating level, and can be extended to the Royal Dutch Shell example. For a project with major Capex occurring over a 4 year period and Opex over a 50 year period, the respective discount rates become:

$$DR_a^{Capex} = 0.05\% + \frac{0.10}{\sqrt{\frac{4}{2}}} = 0.05 + \frac{0.10}{1.414} = 0.1207$$

$$DR_a^{Opex} = 0.05\% + \frac{0.10}{\sqrt{\frac{50}{2}}} = 0.05 + \frac{0.10}{5} = 0.70$$

Simple Improvements to CIV

The first part of this chapter developed the CIV investment process used by most investors, then discussed the limitations in the classical DCF. Chapters 8 and 9 discuss the details of real options and MIV far beyond the interest of some readers. This section demonstrates simple, yet, effective changes in the CIV that capture some of the most critical improvements to the classical system, without resorting to complex theories; however relevant those may be to successful investing.

The next two sub-sections introduce two modifications to the classical measures, as introduced by the authors in other publications.[5.28, 5.29] The first, called Strategic Investment Value (SIV), combines the time diversification issue with the classical system. The second new approach, Venture Capitalist Value (VCV), challenges the traditional funding decisions as a measure of opportunity cost. Neither approach claims to be a theoretically correct application of MIV or RO, but does illustrate the benefit to correcting some of the CIV deficiencies.

Strategic Investment Value (SIV)

SIV follows exactly the same format as traditional DCF, except for including a basic rule for determining when the discount rate should change. The model assumes all the cash flows are paid to the treasury until discounted payback (DPO) is reached. At DPO, the treasury has recovered all costs, including charges for the implied discount rate. Or, the treasury has recovered the principal and interest on the entire project. Equation 5.21 defines SIV.

$$SIV = \sum_{t=1}^{DPO} \frac{NCF_t}{(1+DR)^{t-0.5}} + \sum_{t=DPO}^{N} \frac{NCF_t}{(1+DR^a)^{t-0.5}}$$

or **(5.21)**

$$SIV = 0 + \sum_{t=DPO}^{N} \frac{NCF_t}{(1+DR^a)^{t-0.5}}$$

SIV uses two discount rates in valuing real assets. First, the project is discounted until the treasury recovers all principal and interest. Project NCF received after DPO is discounted at the rate DR^a, as obtained from Equation 5.20. SIV still doesn't resolve many of the criticisms of traditional DCF, but does simply address the bias associated with a constant discount rate, consistent with the notion of time diversification.

SIV ignores risk in the individual components of NCF, which is often captured in simulation methods. It does highlight one of the major deficiencies of simulation practice though. Simulation measures include risk directly in the components of NCF – production, price, Opex, Capex, taxes, scheduling, etc. This is the purpose of the risk premium component in the equation for computing DR^a. If a complete simulation is performed and the resulting NCF is discounted at the normal DR, risk is effectively counted twice. Only the risk free rate, R_f, should be used to discount the NCF when a complete simulation is performed.

Venture Capitalist Value (VCV)

The VCV approach shifts the focus of the analysis to the source of the investment capital. Instead of applying for a loan from the corporate treasury, VCV assumes that a venture capitalist supplies the funds. Rather than relying on discounting, this format assumes the venture capitalist dictates an amortization schedule for recapturing principal and capital. At termination of the amortization period, the venture capitalist receives an equity position in the project. This is an excellent reality check on the entire concept of time value of money metrics.

With VCV, the emphasis shifts to measuring the cash flows differently, rather than focusing on discounting. This is important, because, as earlier sections illustrate, the discount rate combines the time value of money with risk. The distinction between the two becomes lost, even though they vary quite differently over time. This approach separates the two issues. The equation for computing VCV is:

$$VCV = \sum_{t=1}^{n} \frac{NCF_t - Amort_t}{(1+R_f)_t - 0.5} + \sum_{t=n+1}^{N} \frac{NCF_t * (1 - VCWI)}{(1+R_f)_t} \quad \textbf{(5.22)}$$

where:

Amort = the interest payments to the venture capitalist based on the defined interest rate and duration of repayment schedule, like a home amortization schedule,

n = the length of the amortization schedule, and

VCWI = the working interest received by the venture capitalist at the end of the repayment period.

The risk premium is incorporated into the amortization schedule in the first part of Equation 5.22. This amount is then discounted at the risk free rate, which we take here to be the inflation rate (though actual data suggests inflation plus 1 to 3%). The second half of the equation splits the cash flow after period n between the venture capitalist and the investor, which is also divided by the time value of money. The reduction in purchasing power resulting from inflation lowers the value of the future cash flows, as usual.

The main benefit of VCW is the handling of the risk premium by reducing the NCF via the amortization schedule, a linear process rather than a non-linear one. Once the lender is repaid the interest and principal for the investment, the cash flows are split according to the term VCWI.

The value used in determining the amortization schedule and the working interest to each party is negotiable. The examples cited below arbitrarily assume a 10% interest rate and a 20% working interest to the venture capitalist.

Sample Applications

In this section, the traditional DCF and the partial movement to MIV are applied to investment opportunities from the petroleum industry. The results are summarized in Table 5.6. The investments considered include the following:

- The workover of an existing well with a production life of 10 years.
- The drilling of a single oil well with a producing life of 15 years.
- A gas field development scheme where drilling occurs over a 6 year time frame and project life is 25 years.
- Rate acceleration of an existing reservoir covering a 30 year time frame, and
- The valuation of three options for developing an offshore oil field: build platform, use FPSO, and tie back to existing platform and paying for transportation and treating via a higher tariff.

TABLE 5.6

Profit Measures for Selected Projects

					Offshore Development Options		
	Workover	Single Well	Rate Acceleration	Multi-Well Develop.	Fixed Platform	FPSO	Subsea with Tieback
Years in project	10	15	30.	36	50	50	50
Risk Premium	.034	.027	.018	0.018	0.015	0.15	0.15
NPV_5	2.41	2.4	-17.98	65.92	474.0	384.7	339.6
NPV_{10}	2.11	1.57	6.52	29.2	57.1	92.64	137.1
NPV_{15}	1.88	0.97	12.27	12.01	-156.6	-56.3	27.9
IRR (BDR)	None	27.4	7.9%	23.2%	11.05%	12.7	16.9
SIV	2.5	2.29	-61.8	99.5	289.1	415.8	427.2
VCV_{10}	2.1	0.86	-110.2	113.5	520.4	746.6	543.3
DPO_{10} (yrs)	<1 year	3.89	2.8	10.3	15.8	13.0	9.5
NPV/Inv	4.42	0.48	0.43	1.71	0.13	0.21	0.44
Project Investment	0.5	6.0	27.7	124.9	2,208.0	980.2	666.0

Each example assumes a 10% discount rate and a 2.5% inflation rate. The risk premium is computed for SIV and VCV using Equation 5.20. For VCV, the examples assume the same 10% return for the venture capitalist and a 10-year amortization schedule. The inflation rate for VCV is assumed to be 2.5% per annum and a 20% working interest going to the venture capitalist after the amortization period. The results are quite sensitive to the choice of these parameters. SIV gives the same answer as NPV_{10} if the risk premium after discounted payback equals the pre discounted payback number. These values can be changed to fit other assumptions, but do highlight the relative differences between the value measures.

The risk premium values follow the path indicated in the time diversification section. The assumed 10% discount rate and 2.5% inflation rate (risk free rate) implies a risk premium of about 7.5%. As project life increases, the risk premium falls quite a bit. A 10-year project has a risk premium of about 3.4%, decreasing to 1.5% for a 50 year project.

The nuances of the various value measures are quite intriguing. The gap between NPV_{10} and SIV, for instance, increase as the life of the project lengthens. For the 10-year life of the workover, the SIV of \$2.5 million exceeds the NPV_{10} by \$0.40 million. The single well example shows a similar relationship, though the gap is larger because of the longer life. For the remaining projects, the SIV is 2-6 times larger than the NPV_{10}, indicating that the longer life projects contribute more to the treasury when the risk premium is adjusted. The objective is to value the strategic contribution of long-life projects to the treasury.

An interesting contrast between the NPV and SIV shows up in the acceleration project, where the NPV_{10} of \$6.52 million has the opposite sign of the SIV_{10} of \$-61.8. The reduced value in SIV emerges because the future production pushed up to the earlier years is valued at the lower discount rate, more than offsetting the benefits of early production. This is a classic example of how traditional DCF is heavily biased in favor of the early years.

VCV follows a different pattern. Assuming a 10-year amortization schedule and a 20% working interest, the VCV values are actually less than the NPV for the workover and single well investments. This is consistent with notion of the venture capitalist approach, which focuses on long-term, strategic investments. Receiving a return on investment is important, but the cash flow objectives of investing are better reflected in VCV.

A similar disparity between NPV and VCV arises for the rate acceleration project, as it did for SIV, because of the change in the risk premium over the life of the project. The loss of shifting of future production is valued higher than classical DCF. For the multi-well gas project and offshore development, the VCV value exceeds NPV by again 3-10 times.

In comparing the SIV to the VCV value for the last four columns in Table 5.6, observe that VCV is larger for all the projects, with the difference varying by the nature of the project. VCV exceeds SIV because of the nonlinear nature of the risk premium after discounted payback relative to the linear WI used in VCV after discounted.

Perhaps the most intriguing difference emerges in the selection of the best offshore development scheme. NPV prefers the tieback to an existing platform, because of the reduced front end Capex and the higher Opex over the life of the project. SIV also favors the tariff option over the FPSO, by a slight amount. This is due to the low inflation rate used in the example. (Note that if inflation rises by less than one-half percent the FPSO is favored.)

VCV opts for the FPSO primarily because of the lower initial Capex. It rejects the tariff approach because of the greater impact of the higher tariff over the 50-year life of the project. It thus balances the Capex versus Opex differently than the other measures.

A recent article in Business Week expounds on just this same point.[5.30] Several contributors using options analysis indicate they elected to invest in larger, less efficient development schemes (as indicated by classical DCF), because of the options that arose over the longer life of the projects. For an illustration of the broader applications of options analysis, this article is recommended reading.

SUMMARY

Growing awareness that traditional DCF fails to capture the complexities of the modern investment environment has motivated an extensive effort to improve the decision-making process. Many practitioners understand the methodology and computation of DCF based measures of value, but few ever knew or remembered the underlying premises of CIV. This chapter outlined the classical approach, including emphasizing its strengths as well as limitations.

The two main focal points raised by MIV are: risk and the proper discount rate. Trying to understand the impact of variability on investment decisions hinges on the concept of time. Bernstein, a leading writer on risk issues states: "Time and risk are opposite sides of the same coin, for if there were no tomorrow, there would be no risk."[5.31] Real investment opportunities display all the characteristics discussed so far, but with greater complexity. Figure 5.21 illustrates the complexity.

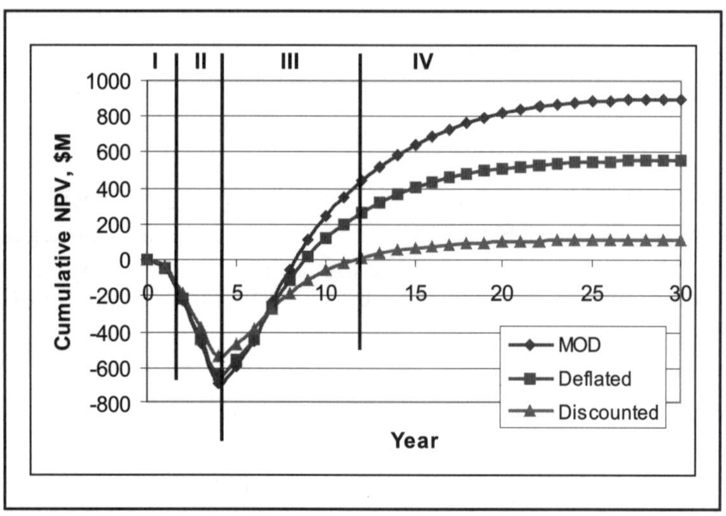

Figure 5.21 Complexity in investment opportunities

The cumulative NPV is divided into MOD, deflated and discounted values, and 4 vertical lines are added to reflect the changing nature of risk over time, or phases of a project. The major limitation of just changing the risk premium is the implication that the risk factor is constant with time. Phases I-IV in the figure suggest otherwise. The phases correspond to the categories in Table 5.7. The nature of risk changes over time, and none of the methods outlined so far handle the discrete, changing nature of risk. Only the format outlined in Equation 5.16, where

TABLE 5.7

Phases of Major Investments

Phase	Activity	Main Risks
I	R&D or Exploration	Success or failure, and size
II	Development & Construction	Production volume and development cost & timing
III	Operation	Volume/Price/Opex/Market
IV	Project reaches DPO	Virtually none because of options

the risk premium varies by variable and by time, adequately captures the complexity needed to make sound investment decisions.

This chapter sets the stage for the need to improve decision-making. Chapter 8 formally introduces risk assessment and real options methods, followed by example applications in Chapter 9. Then, Chapter 10 combines all the concepts into examples of portfolio and project optimization. Those working for classical companies, with no desire to improve, can quit reading the book at this point.

REFERENCES

5.1 Daugherty, E., *JPT* (1985).

5.2 Seba, J., "Proceedings of the SPE Hydrocarbon Economics and Evaluation Symposium" (1987), pp. 173-180.

5.3 Mao, J., *Quantitative Analysis of Financial Decisions*, MacMillan Press (1969).

5.4 Brons, F. and M. Silbergh, *JPT* (Mar. 1954).

5.5 Campbell, J., *Oil Property Evaluation*, Prentice-Hall (1959).

5.6 Fisher, I., *The Theory of Interest*, Yale University Press (1930).

5.7 Capen, E., Clapp, R., and Phelps, W., *JPT* (May 1976), pp. 531-543.

5.8 Stermole, F., *Economic Evaluation and Investment Decision Methods*, Investment Evaluation Corp. (1980).

5.9 Seba, R., Proceedings of the 1987 Hydrocarbon and Economics Evaluation Symposium, pp. 173-180.

5.10 Daugherty, E, *ibid.*

5.11 Mao, *ibid.*

5.12 Norther, I. G., *JPT* (July 1964), p. 727.

5.13 Kuhn, T., *The Structure of Scientific Revolutions*, University of Chicago Press (1996).

5.14 Salahor, G., "Implications of Output Price Risk and Operating Leverage for the Evaluation of Petroleum Development Projects," *The Energy Journal*, Vol. 19 (1998), pp. 13-46.

5.15 Laughton, D., Sagi, J., and J. Samis, "Modern Asset Pricing and Project Evaluation in the Energy Industry," *The Energy Journal* (2000).

5.16 Bierman, H. and S. Smidt, *The Capital Budgeting Decision, 3rd Edition*, The McMillan Co., New York (1971).

5.17 Myers, S. "Finance Theory and Finance Strategy," Interfaces (Jan-Feb, 1984), pp.126-137.

5.18 Myers, *ibid.*

5.19 Robicheck, A. and S. Myers, "Conceptual Problems in the Use of Risk Adjusted Discount Rates," *Journal of Finance* (Dec. 1977), pp. 727-730.

5.20 Trigeoris, L., *Real Options: Managerial Flexibility and Strategy in Resource Allocation*, MIT Press (1996).

5.21 Dixit, A. and R. Pindyck, *Investment Under Uncertainty*, Princeton University Press (1994).

5.22 Laughton, D., *ibid.*

5.23 Campbell, J., Campbell, R., and S. Brown, "Measuring Strategic Investment Value." *SPE* 56453 (Oct. 2000).

5.24 "How High a Hurdle Rate," *The Economist* (8 May, 1999), pp. 82.

5.25 Smulders, A., "Reducing the Cost of Offshore Developments," European GPA (1990).

5.26 Salahor, *ibid.*

5.27 Laughton, *ibid.*

5.28 Campbell, J. and R. Campbell, *SPE* Paper 6322, Hydrocarbon Economics Evaluation Symposium (1977).

5.29 Campbell, J., Campbell, R., and S. Brown, *SPE* Paper 56453, Fall Annual Meetings (1999).

5.30 "Exploiting Uncertainty," *Business Week* (7 June, 1999), pp. 118-123.

5.31 Bernstein, P., *Against the Gods*, John Wiley (1996).

NOTES:

APPENDIX 5A

The basic equations for computing the time value of money are often extended to facilitate certain types of problems; namely, when money flows in equal payments. Before the advent of the spreadsheet, these equations accelerated the computational process. This section demonstrates several of the common equal payment situations that arise in the real world.

Equal Payment Series, Compound Amount Factor

Investors have the option of using their own money to fund investments or to use someone else's money. Probably, the most common form of project financing occurs when the asset is leased. Leasing benefits the treasury by being an Opex, rather than a Capex. Formal comparison of the lease versus purchase decision is covered in Chapter 9. The leasing company typically quotes their terms in terms like $2 million a year for 10 years, an equal payment series.

The equation for determining the present value of a series of equal payments is:

$$PV_i = CF\left[\frac{(1+i)^n - 1}{i}\right] \qquad \textbf{(5A.1)}$$

Example 5A.1: You are asked to analyze the benefits of upgrading production equipment for an asset. Because of a budget constraint, you negotiate a 10-year lease for $2 million per year as an alternative to buying the equipment for $20 million. What is the NPC of the leasing cost assuming a 10% discount rate over the life of the lease.

$$NPC_{10} = \$2*\left[\frac{(1+0.10)^{10} - 1}{0.10}\right] = \$2*15.94 = \$31.87$$

The net present cost of a $2 million lease for 10 years at 10% is $31.87 million, before-tax.

Equal Payment Series, Sinking Fund Factor

When the investor knows that an investment or expenditure will occur in the future, they may opt to accumulate the necessary sum over a period of time rather than take the funds out of that years cash flows. One example concerns the cost of abandoning or decommissioning an asset. The equal payment measures the yearly contribution to the sinking fund necessary to generate sufficient funds to pay for the abandonment costs. For individuals, determining the amount of money put into savings each year to realize a certain amount at retirement certainly is relevant.

The equation is:

$$SF = FV_n*\left[\frac{1}{(1+i)^n - 1}\right] \qquad \textbf{(5A.2)}$$

Example 5A.2: Determine the sum of money to place into a sinking fund each year in order to accumulate $40 million at the end of 5 years. Assume that money can be invested at 10% per annum.

$$SF_5 = \$40*\left[\frac{0.10}{(1+0.10)^5 - 1}\right] = \$40*0.1638 = \$6.55$$

The investor must set aside $6.55 million yearly for 5 years to have enough to fund the decommissioning of the asset. Similarly, if you want to have $40 million for retirement in 5 years, you must invest the same amount in an account earning 10%.

Equal Payment Series, Capital Recovery Factor

This equation helps immensely when considering investments with unequal lives. When developing a production system, vendors often confuse the analysis by arguing that their equipment has a 10-year life, and their competitor's equipment only as an 8-year life. Because of the longer life, they try to charge more for the equipment. The easiest and best way to compare the two alternatives is to compute the annual charge for each option. The results can be compared directly, with the low cost option being preferred.

The equation is:

$$CF = PV_i * \left[\frac{i*(1+i)^n}{(1+i)^n - 1} \right] \qquad \textbf{(5A.3)}$$

> **Example 5A.3:** A production system needs a compressor. Two vendors respond to the bid request. Vendor A's compressor costs \$450 k with a 6 year life, and Vendor B charges \$500 k for a compressor with an 8 year life. Which is the cheaper alternative at 10%?
>
> $$CF_6 = \$450 * \left[\frac{0.10*(1+0.10)^6}{(1+0.10)^6 - 1} \right] = \$450*0.2296 = \$103.3$$
>
> $$CF_8 = \$500 * \left[\frac{0.10*(1+0.10)^8}{(1+0.10)^8 - 1} \right] = \$500*0.1874 = \$93.72$$
>
> The longer life compressor is cheaper, if the asset produces over an 8-year period.

Equal Payment Series, Present Value Factor

This equal payment series compares directly the value of an immediate expenditure or an equal payment over a specific time period.

The equation is:

$$PV_i = CF * \left[\frac{(1+i)^n - 1}{1*(1+i)^n - 1} \right] \qquad \textbf{(5A.4)}$$

> **Example 5A.4:** Compare the NPC of leasing a pump at \$300 k per year for 5 years to the cost of purchasing the same pump for \$850 k using a 10% discount rate. Both values are after-tax.
>
> $$NPC_{10} = \$300 * \left[\frac{(1+0.10)^5 - 1}{0.10*(1+0.10)^5} \right] = \$300*3.79 = \$1,137.2$$
>
> Leasing cost about \$250 thousand more than an outright purchase, allowing for taxes and the time value of money.

CHAPTER 6

MEASURING VARIABILITY

The previous chapters demonstrated the classical DCF process, and some of the distortions that take place in the investment valuation process. The end of the last chapter introduced some of the criticisms of the classical process, and simple methods for addressing the biases. This chapter addresses tools for measuring the variability in specific inputs, directly and accurately, rather than approximating risk indirectly via the discount rate.

Experienced professionals know that every numerical value used to analyze investment opportunities faces the risk that the actual value will differ, perhaps significantly, from the one used to make the decision, as discussed in Chapter 2. The odds of that difference occurring, and the consequences of the deviation, working either for or against the investor, comprise the knowledge base, called risk assessment. Whatever the source of the risk, – incomplete information, imprecise equations, bad data sampling, evolving technology, changing market shares, etc. – understanding the chances of the risk occurring and the resulting impact on actual investment performance provides the insights that ultimately determines the investors ability to achieve their objectives. This chapter outlines the basic tools and techniques for identifying and quantifying risk for the basic components that underpin the investment process. Later chapters (8 and 10) review procedures for incorporating risk assessment information into risk management, along with detailed examples (Chapter 9).

Figure 6.1 displays an influence diagram characterizing the classical *deterministic* investment analysis discussed so far. The figure expands primary inputs to the valuation process – production, scheduling, costs, prices and taxes, as introduced in Chapter 2 to capture more specific details. Generally, a single value estimate for each input is generated, and those values fitted into the calculation process for NCF and profit measures, like NPV. Classical investment analysis recognized the existence of variability in the inputs. Owing to computational limitations, handling risk formally greatly increased the complexity of the analysis, without adding any real value to the decision-making process. In fact, most multinational organizations specifically stipulate that the input values should be the expected value (or average or mean) of each variable. This approach ideally standardizes the process for generating the input values across all units around the world, permitting management to make consistent decisions.

The one unique aspect of Figure 6.1 revolves around the symbol, labeled reserves. This segment introduces the issues faced in the mineral industry, where below ground, or sub-surface issues associated with geoscience knowledge plays a critical role in decision-making. Porosity (the volume of the mineral "lake" with pores or spaces to hold minerals), trap size (the overall volume of minerals), and recovery factor (what can be produced) determine the volume of production. This is important because the geoscience disciplines have probably adopted formal risk methods to a greater extent than any other knowledge group.

Change, unfortunately, requires a motivating force.[6.1] That force resulted from globalization of business, forcing professionals to move outside their comfort zone of knowledge. Traditional, informal risk assessment worked well when the experience and working knowledge of an area spawned good

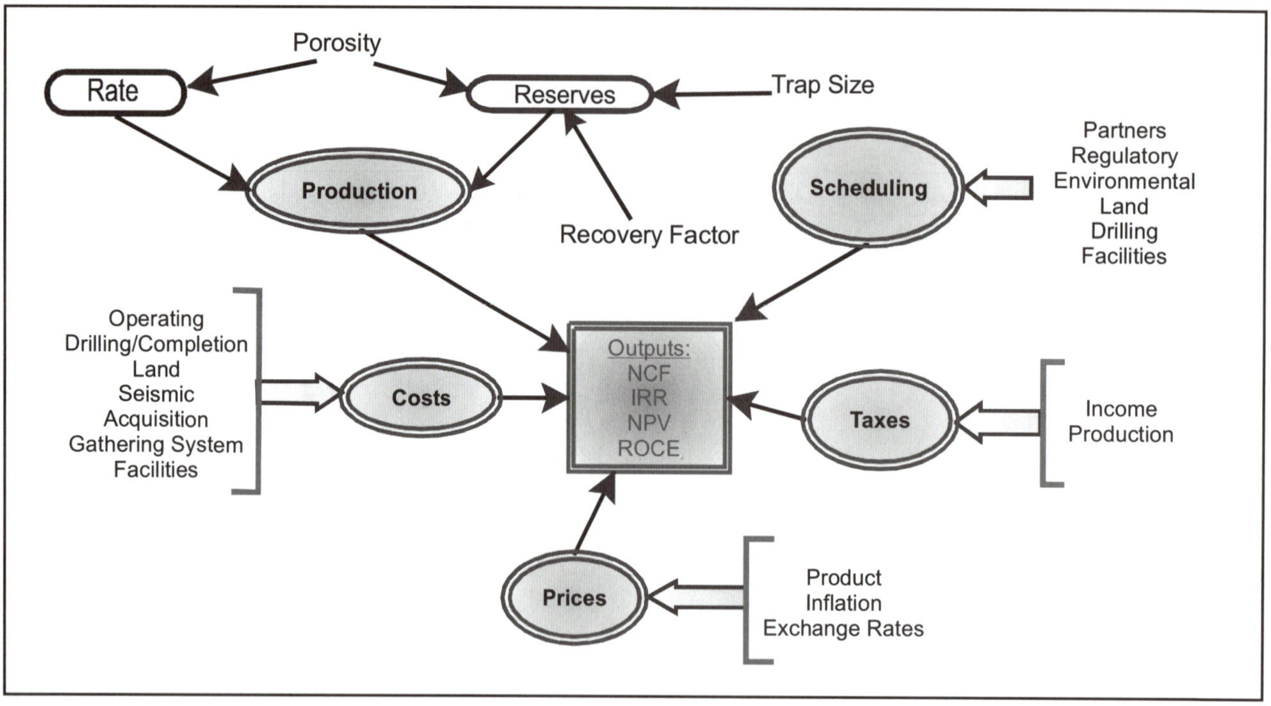

Figure 6.1 Deterministic influence diagram

expected value inputs. As the cultural, legal, religious, customs, infrastructure changed, the informal approach based on experience requires more detailed analysis. In engineering terms, the constants to the equation or thought process became variables. Some investors handle this transition better than others.

Figure 6.2 illustrates the extension of the deterministic model to include partial risk assessment. Formal risk assessment only changes the way the inputs are viewed, not the underlying decision process. By recognizing the *variability* in the porosity input to the rate and reserve components, risk assessment

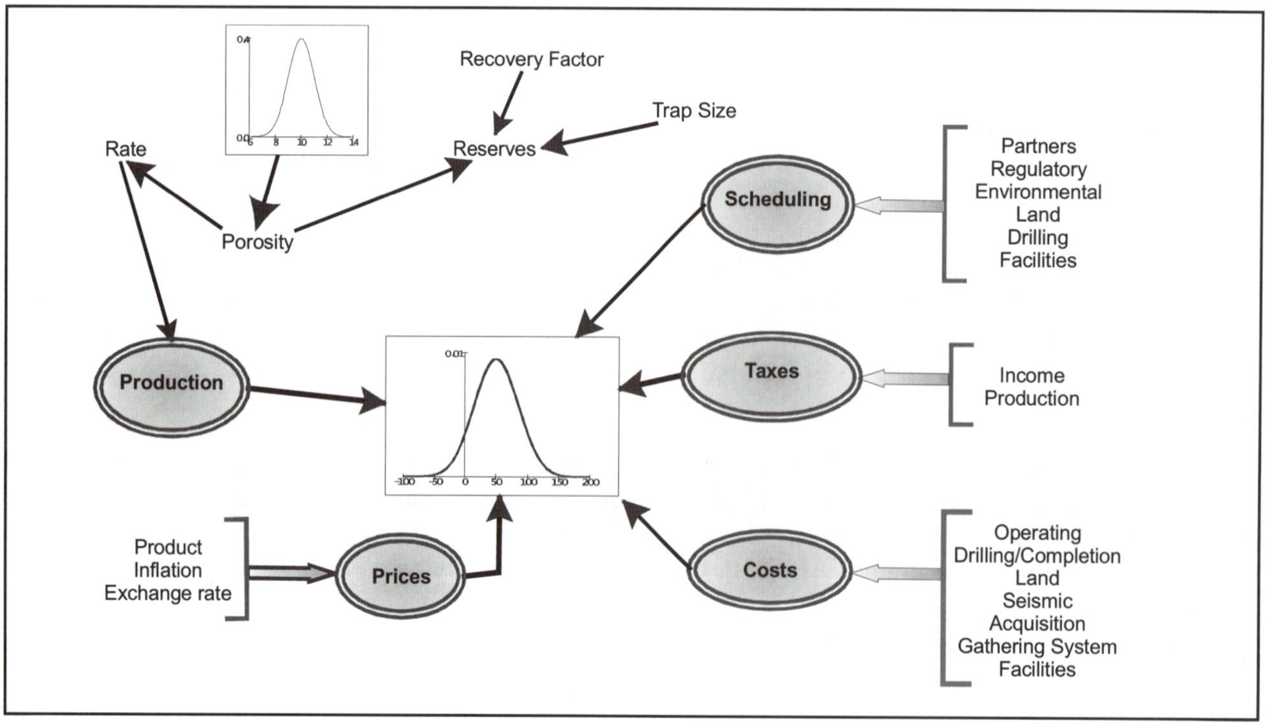

Figure 6.2 Influence diagram with one risk element

allows the analysis to stipulate ranges of outcomes for the measures of value. Variability in outputs captures the essence of investment risk. Observe that the distribution in the center of the graph has a solid vertical line thru the origin. All outcomes to the left of the vertical line indicate the money lost from the investment, and the area to the left indicates the chances or probability of a loss occurring.

The quantitative understanding of risk dates back several centuries with the application of mathematical principles to gambling. Bernstein even argues that risk assessment principles, as developed through statistical procedures, helped demystify the world to the open minded.[(6.2)] The concepts eventually migrated to specific applications in the technical area. For instance, the atomic bomb was developed using formal risk assessment, because any mistake would have disastrous consequence to the builders. Quantum mechanics, the study of micro physics, deals in probabilities. Even the most basic elementary particle, the Higgs boson (believed to give mass to all basic units), originated in statistical applications. In the late 1960's, Dr. Campbell Sr. adapted the basic statistical concepts to petroleum applications.[(6.3)] In spite of the fact that the techniques have proved useful in identifying and understanding risk, applications have been limited. Historical analysis shows conclusively that poor or improper risk assessment has contributed to bad investment decisions

Since about 1990, however, interest in applying risk assessment concepts has grown exponentially. Even with this growth, the applications are often incomplete, failing to fully address all salient risk issues. Why have statistical applications failed to become more common? For two reasons, first, the computer software was difficult and cumbersome, so few had the time or resources to utilize the risk principles, without extending the analysis time by often at least an order of magnitude. Mainframe computer programs existed in the late 70's and early 80's that analyzed risk, but only PhD's or those with the time to learn the process used them.

Second, few understood or were motivated to understand the concepts. A variety of reasons exist for ignoring formal risk assessment, including:

- it removes professional judgment from the analysis,
- good data don't exist,
- our staff has more important things to do, and time spent analyzing risk is wasted,
- why base decisions on subjective values that may not occur, and
- I'm not going to risk my career on values based on "smiles, mirrors, and black magic."

Risk assessment addresses understanding, organizing and reducing potential problems, not eliminating professional judgment, no matter what the condition of the data. Prudent application of statistical principles should be welcomed by professionals. It is a formal, organized approach for presenting professional judgment. With the continued movement to push responsibility down to the lowest professional levels and adoption of incentive systems that reward initiative, effective communication of risks is essential.

Perhaps the core reason for employing formal risk assessment concerns the very nature of the respective disciplines. Most disciplines preach the gospel that applying the specified equations in the right circumstances yields good decisions. This *reductionism* process has been going on since the Renaissance. The essence is very simple – by reducing every issue to its basic components, humanity can eliminate variations. Statistics, on the other hand, is about understanding, describing, and communicating, variations. To adopt statistical features forces an admission that each disciplines possess limitations. While most of us know this, admitting it is another thing, especially when handling difficult problems. We have made this point to the statistics profession to explain the reason for the unpopularity of statisticians.[(6.4)]

Applying statistics to risk assessment is a difficult subject to address in a clear, yet concise manner. Part of the difficulty arises from the lack of exposure as part of technical training. Those exposed usually encountered a mathematician who wanted to present the mathematical purity and unique language, not the practical applications. This accounts for the tendency of most stat students to sell their book as soon after the final exam as possible. Statistics has it's own language. The first part of this chapter tries to demystify the language and provide some concrete examples. Later sections summarize risk assessment applications working primarily with technical data.

Like most other disciplines, statistics, ala risk assessment, has benefited from the PC revolution. Software exists today that allows analysis to be done in minutes, if not seconds, that took hours on the mainframe. Most spreadsheets, like Excel and Lotus 123, perform detailed statistical applications. Add on software, like @Risk and Crystal Ball, expands these analytical options significantly. Combined with PC databases, tools exist for good data storage and retrieval, statistical analysis, and communication. The tools are cheap and easy to use; the real question concerns the will to use them.

Figure 6.3 reflects the best risk assessment process, in our opinion. At the start of the project, every input should be considered as variable; hence, subject to risk. Figure 6.2, which predominates in many settings, grossly understates the real risk in the project. Only by starting with Figure 6.3 as the basic concept will the analysis have the slightest chance of capturing the risk essence in each investment opportunity.

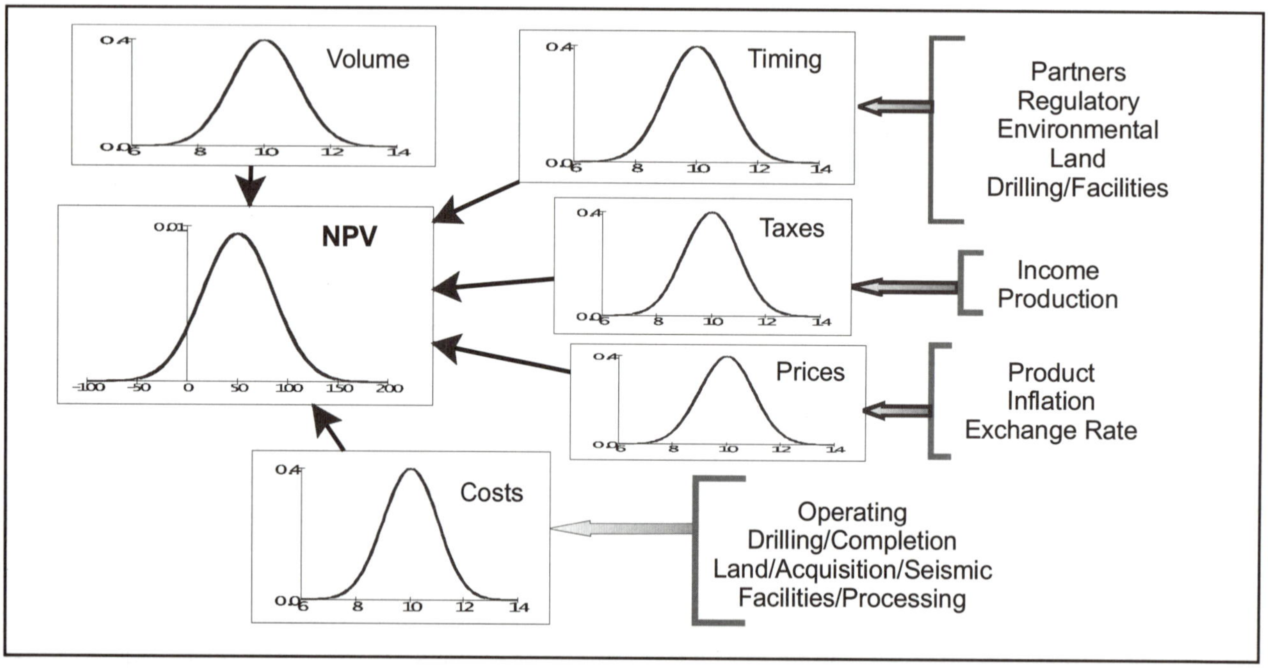

Figure 6.3 Preferred influence diagram for risk assessment

One legitimate criticism of Figure 6.3 concerns the amount of work, and the possibility that considerable time and energy will be wasted risking the unimportant. That "risk" of risk assessment is true. By beginning with Figure 6.3, the trivial risks with no chance of losing money, while other risks, which can damage profitability, are identified. Chapter 2 clearly illustrated that the ignored elements cause most investment failures. The complexity in identifying, quantifying, and reporting risk effectively challenges everyone, much less those trying to establish general standards for multinational organization with thousands to staff. This and later chapters present the tools needed to perform the analysis, and emphasize the lessons learned from the process of assessing risk, not just the calculations. Well organized, formal risk assessment greatly improves the decision-making process, just by helping to define the problem, even before the first computation is made.

Figure 6.3 disturbs us in one important way: it ignores the dependency between the input elements. Each input element correlates with the other, and ignoring this dependency produces flawed results.

THE CURRENT PROBLEM

Before jumping into the quagmire of statistic jargon, a quick review of the current system is necessary. Ingrained in the investment process are many calculations and concepts in use since 1959, when the first book on quantifying value was published.(6.5) The primary computational tools – the slide rule and desk calculator – limited data handling. The developers of the classical valuation concepts minimized the numbers needed to perform the analysis by using correlations, short cut methods and rules-of-thumb. The process combined hard to measure or unmeasurable variables as empirical constants, and given names like recovery factor, damage factor, water drive constant, heat transfer, PVT equations, etc. Most equations were limited to raw or interpreted numbers, using readily measured variables like pressure, temperature, flow rate, and system physical properties.

Correlations, consisting of a family of lines or nomographs with no confirming data points, dominated most engineering training. Some were the only correlations available and therefore were accepted (by default). A portion of the correlations proved quite useful, if one understands their limitations; others were just flat wrong or were so limited that they had no legitimate applications. The ordinary professional had no way to distinguish among them.

Such limitations forced the analytical process to compartmentalize knowledge into distinct skill areas, a deficiency that is still being corrected. Industry developed narrow specialty areas, like mechanical and chemical engineering, geosciences, economics, tax, etc. Some were so narrow, they specialized in a single piece of equipment (compressors, pumps, etc.). The guru's role was to translate and extend limited technology into good decisions using their practical experience. Successful practitioners incorporated correction factors (essentially probabilities), considered to be their intellectual property and never entered into the public domain. The technology in print was a sanitized version of the technology being practiced.

Concerns about economics and risk were minimal and usually limited to achieving a short payout time or internal rate or return. Political, environmental, and regulatory matters were a nuisance, but seldom formally considered in investment decisions.

Many mistakes were made, but this approach was both familiar and satisfactory as long as the following general conditions prevailed:

- The systems were simple and involved a fairly narrow technological base,
- The specialists necessary to make the system work were familiar with the system's actual needs and could informally modify the theoretical model to match the real needs.
- Most investments represented a small part of the investor's total capital. The amount of money at risk was so small *gambler's ruin* was insignificant and the reward to risk ratio was favorable.
- Prices were relatively stable and unlikely to change much, particularly during the short payout period.
- Periods of product oversupply existed, but the product demand curve continued to trend upward. No one expected prices to fall below the current levels.

These factors have changed and eroded with time, but the incentive to change was limited as long as profits were satisfactory (called *satisficing*). The traditional approach governs most analysis today, even though it is disguised within the confines of much fancier software. Fortunately, newer tools are forcing the entire system to radically change.

Current software eliminates the need for simplicity and ease of use, at the expense of accuracy. Unfortunately, it also far outstrips the ability of most professionals to implement modern valuation processes. Such software can be improved to make it more user friendly, integrate different risk concepts easier, and interact with other programs, especially databases. Too much of what is calculated is merely old, familiar, outdated technology dressed up in new attire.

Making intelligent investment decisions without formally addressing risk is impossible, or requires a very intelligent or lucky decision-maker. So, why do investors ignore the modern valuation system? Evidence suggests that individual investors and small businesses can effectively retain the deterministic system, because the small scale of both the number and magnitude of investment opportunities simplifies their task. As these scales increase, the need for consistency across geographical and operating divisions dominates the thought process. Establishing the same process becomes the dominant objective, though achieving consistency, while promoting individual creativity, challenges everyone. This process often becomes merely a means to rank alternatives, not value risk and return trade-offs, which is how to add value to the treasury.

Most organizations psychologically prefer a defective, but known process, to a new, unfamiliar concept. This is the nature of human beings, regardless of race, sex, culture, nationality, religion, etc. A favorite notion is: "How does one stimulate risk averse people to formally consider risk in their decision-making?" Maybe this explains why the adoption of formal risk and return valuation processes has been so slow in coming.

A word of warning: applying statistical procedures, effectively, requires a detailed knowledge of the real system to which they are applied. When used as a mere calculation exercise, without the control of experience or sound judgment, formal risk assessment produces bad results, just like any other poorly or misapplied procedure.

ABOUT RISK AND UNCERTAINTY

This chapter summarizes the basic principles needed to understand the variability in the technical elements of investments. The optimal time to combine professional judgment with formal risk assessment occurs when the initial data assumptions are established, not after the economics are run. This achieves several goals. First, it forces professionals to recognize the dependence between inputs related to economics and those that are not. Completion programs and timing, size and nature of facilities, investment scheduling, etc. varies with economic conditions, for example. The variability inherent in the business environment should be established before economics are computed, as illustrated in Figure 6.4.

Second, establishing agreement on a reasonable range of values for all inputs at the outset reduces the tendency to change initial estimates to obtain management approval (Chapters 1 and 2). Reaching a consensus over the variability of each input minimizes distortions caused by professional optimism to win project approval.

Third, it encourages detailed analysis of methods for altering controllables, like the development and operation schemes, to achieve optimal performance. An easy way to improve project economics is to increase areal extent or other geological variables. This deflects the real attention away from controllable elements, like facility sizing, number of production units, etc.

References to risk exist in many professional articles, in professional meetings, and in everyday conversation. Yet, debate still rages over what does *risk* mean and does it really differ in meaning from *uncertainty*. One can always find references to support any position. Our favorite statement occurred at a professional meeting where the speaker invoked risk throughout the entire lecture. The first question at the end inquired as to their definition of risk. The response was quick and to the point. "Whatever you want it to mean." Many definitions exist, which often contradicts the next persons. The one risk definition, which captures the essence of the issue without appealing to statistical jargon, is "risk is uncertainty that matters."[(6.6)]

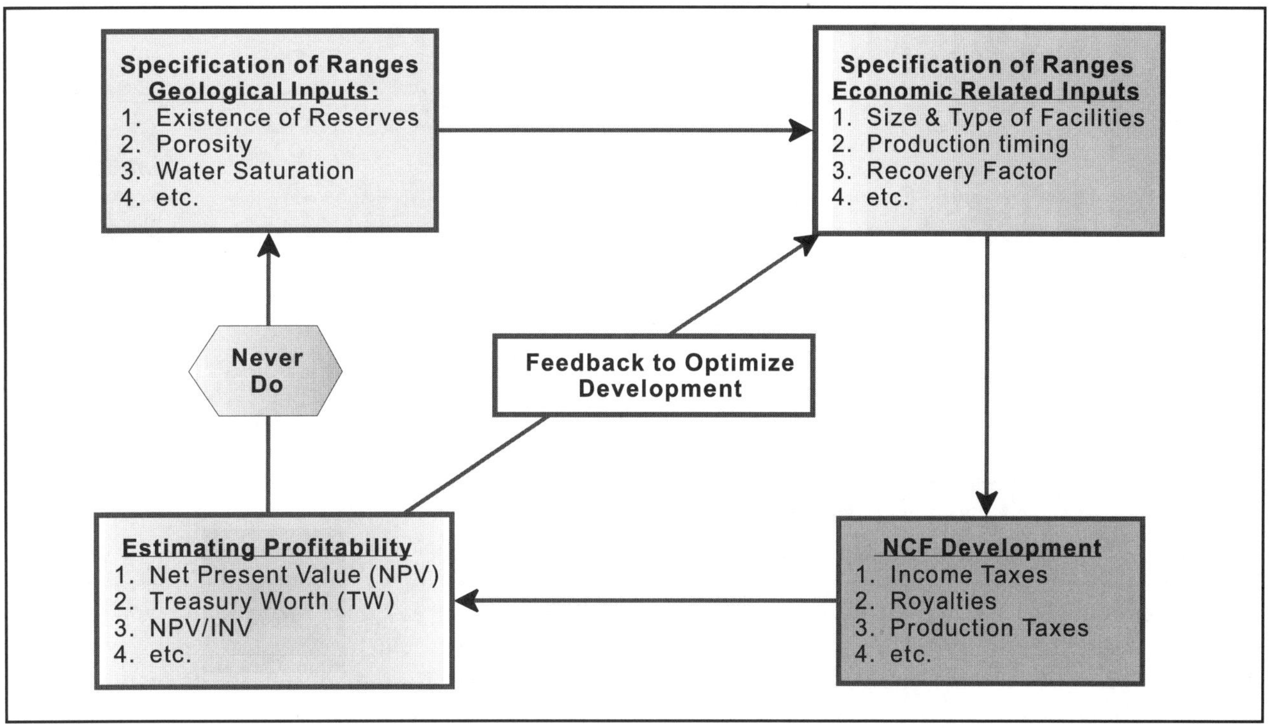

Figure 6.4 Relationship between inputs and outputs

This statement just defines risk as the existence of incomplete knowledge. Others like to separate the lack of knowledge into two different categories: risk and uncertainty. Four common definitions are found in the literature. They include:

1. Risk and uncertainty are synonyms (this seems to be the most prevalent).
2. Uncertainty relates to a condition where the probabilities of events are unknown, and risk exists when probabilities are defined.
3. Uncertainty exists when no gains or losses exist depending on the outcome, whereas risk reflects either the loss of money if an investment turns sour or money foregone by not investing in a project. See Figure 6.5.
4. Risk covers geological risk (dry hole versus commercial reserves) and uncertainty deals with economic, technical and political issues. See Figure 6.5a.

Definition 1 in Figure 6.5 is probably the most common in industry, while definition 2 occurs most often in statistical and business texts. We prefer to tie risk to both gains and losses, like Figure 6.5. Being

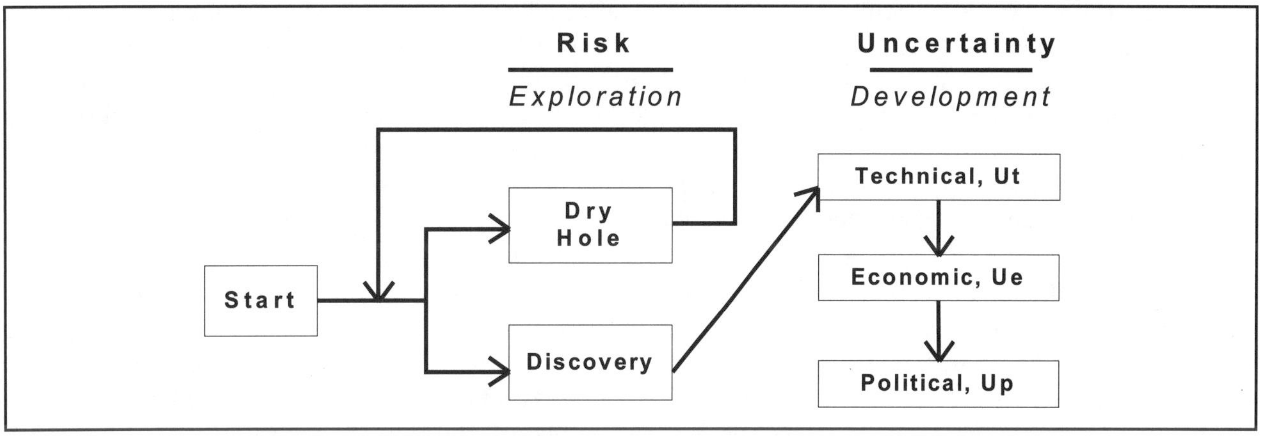

Figure 6.5 Risk vs. Uncertainty, definition 1

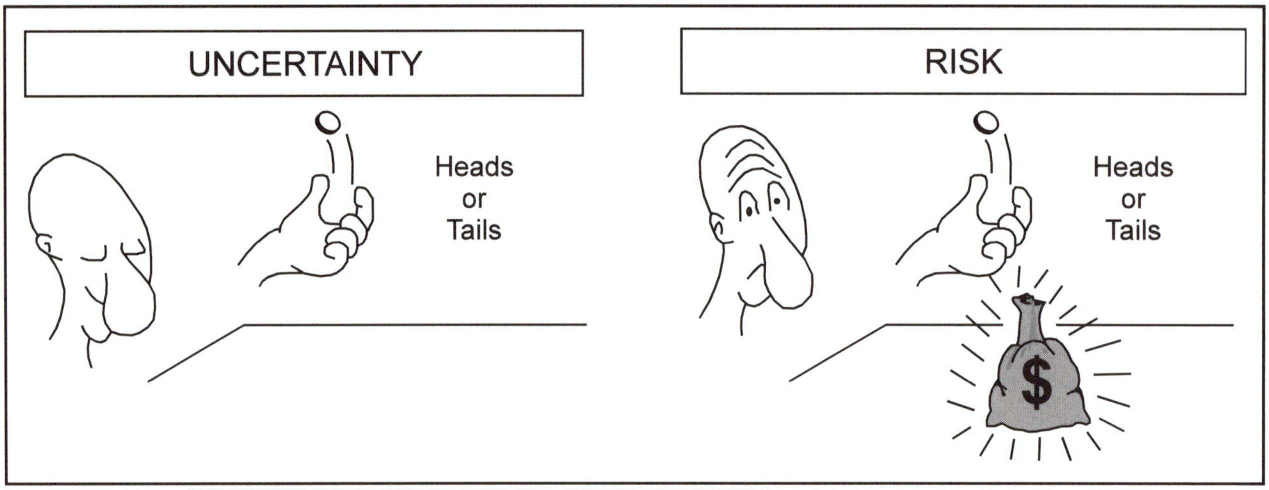

Figure 6.5a Risk and Uncertainty, definition 2

uncertain about the outcome of the throw of a dice occurs every time the die is thrown, but risk only exists when a bet is made. We may be uncertain about the likelihood of rain in Outer Mongolia or you might be uncertain about the movement of a particular stock, but if the rain in Outer Mongolia has no impact on you, or you don't own that share of stock, most people neither care nor are interested in the outcome. Our interest is stimulated only when a gain or loss may arise.

By virtue of training and experience, the professional develops a series of *cause-effect* relationships. An engineer attempts to define these in the form of correlations and equations, which, although inexact, provide the relationship of dependent and independent variables necessary to implement the judgment process. Geoscientists develop theories about mineral formation, evolution of the earth's crust, and observed patterns as the basis for judgment decision. Physicians apply their own cause-effect relationships to diagnose illness. The principle is the same in all professions, even though details vary.

In developing laws, concepts and theories the professional samples from actual events and then using the *inductive reasoning process* – develops a relationship that fits their interpretation of the samples. The better professional is aware that his sample is incomplete and imperfect. A *hypothesis* only becomes a *law* by successfully passing the test of time and usage. Thermodynamics is a superb example. As more samples (data) are obtained, existing laws are modified and/or discarded.

Most training (and ego needs) dictates that professional's overcome imperfection by the application of personal judgment. The necessity for exercising a significant amount of personal judgment in arriving at a meaningful answer is the primary element that separates the true professional from those just trained in a discipline. The need for good judgment is obvious and cannot be compromised by unfounded optimism. When properly applied, statistics and probability do not compromise the judgment process; they provide a tool for organizing and assessing the importance of judgment. Applying risk principles makes decision-making tougher, not easier; because it forces decision-makers to formally recognize the trade-off between risk and return, not hide behind superficial indicators. Those seeking to make all decisions using one, simplistic variable become quite frustrated with statistics.

This frustration is compounded by the manner in which statistics and probability are presented. A simple system (in concept) is obscured by vague language and an inordinate amount of what appears trivial. Persons using statistical tools with limited expertise find it difficult to separate the wheat from the chaff. This problem arises in the study of most disciplines. Has the geoscientist ever become confused by engineering terms, or the engineer with geoscience concepts, or both groups in dealing with economics. The answer is an emphatic, yes.

STATISTICS, PROBABILITY AND SAMPLING

Statistic is the name given to a process for collecting, analyzing, summarizing, and presenting data. *Descriptive statistics* measures the variability in the data, because all data possesses the characteristic of *randomness.* Random means that values change depending on when and how it is collected. Those watching the U. S. Presidential elections in 2000 observed this process directly. Causes of randomness include imprecision of data gathering devices, the non-uniformity of nature, and human error in interpreting the results. In logging a well to determine porosity and water saturation, for example, the logs provide a range of values. A portion of the variation arises from the response of the logging tool and it's interpretation. Also, porosity and water saturation truly vary at different points. In using such data, understanding the characteristics of the data before making inferences about the nature of the system becomes critical. More problems occur in real applications of statistics from using the methods improperly than because of weaknesses in the methods themselves.

Methods for analyzing data obviously depend on the source of that data. Geoscience, for instance, possesses less concrete data, depending mainly on physical or conceptual analogs. This data limitation forces usage of more subjective statistical applications. Engineering, on the other hand, relies more on actual production or cost histories.

Figure 6.6 outlines the basic statistical process. The diagram concentrates on the primary application areas in statistics, and hardly exhausts all topics. What is the most realistic way to use statistical data? Take a simple reservoir volumetric equation. Is it realistic to compute *average* porosity and water saturation, and then plug the values into a volumetric equation to find *average* hydrocarbons-in-place? Would it be better to use other outputs, like *median* or *most likely values?* The values differ and the results impact valuations significantly. Statistics seeks to answer these questions.

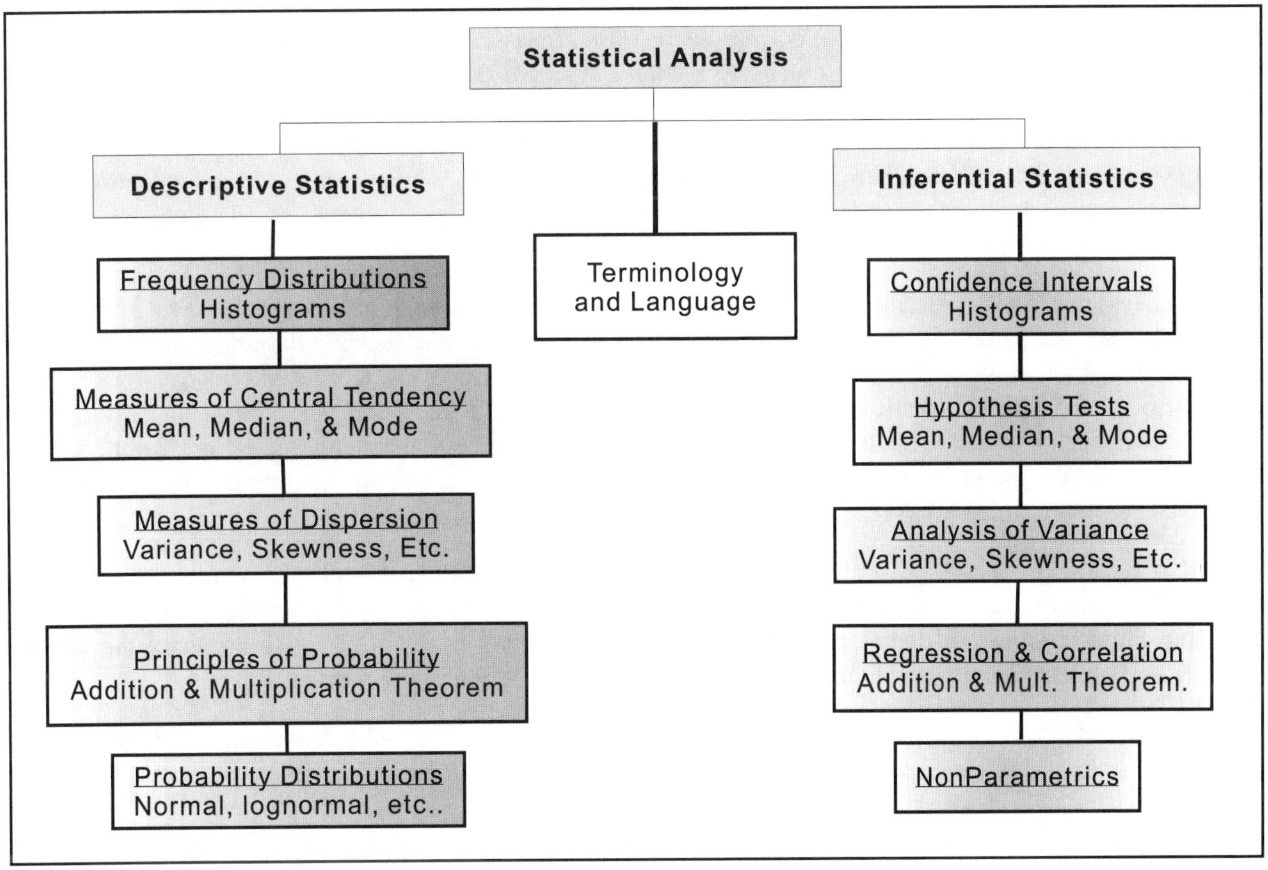

Figure 6.6 Outline of statistical analysis

The next sections focus on the language, terminology and basic methodologies used in statistics. Those who remember their formal stat education can skip them. Following the review is the *descriptive statistic* overview, followed by selected topics in *inferential statistics.*

Language of Statistics

Like all professions, statistics has its own language. Learning the basics of statistics is probably easier and quicker than most technical systems, because nature is not an issue. The statistical system seeks a format for describing unknown or variable events that can be generalized to use the same language for communicating the information. Statistics seeks one language for describing all the forces impacting investment decisions. Once the basic notions are learned, statistics merely repeats or offers a different twist on the same idea.

Several key words dominate the language of statistics. The basic format for the words is:

Population (Sample Space): the range of all possible outcomes or events that can possibly take place, expressed as a whole finite number or assumed to be infinite in size. Specific physical entities, like a reservoir or manufacturing plant, are considered a *population,* even though its size is unknown.

Sample: a single value or group of values of the elements within the total population obtained by tests, interpretation of test results, or from direct counting.

Raw Data: data collected which have not been organized in some numerical fashion. Statistics is the methodology of ordering of raw data to answer specific questions. Statistics does nothing more than provide a process for analyzing raw data to draw inferences about the population.

The population (sample space) defines all possible, measurable outcomes. Classical illustrations of the basic concepts use gambling examples. Consider a standard deck of 52 cards. The population size is 52, composed of 52 elements (cards). By shifting to elements rather than cards, the language has essentially normalized the terms. Populations relate to elements, mass, volume, velocity, density, costs, etc. In rolling a standard pair of dice, there are 6^2 or 36 possible outcomes (36 elements). These are *a priori* populations, where the total size and description of the population is known in advance. The objective is understanding and predicting the relative outcomes of specific events.

Investment valuations increase in complexity, because the population is never known in advance. Collecting and analyzing raw data seeks to provide information about the population where the sample space is ill defined or unknown. An infinite number of sub-surface maps, development costs, prices, etc. exist for even the small projects. The absolute size, shape, and value of the population can only be surmised, but never known absolutely. This is one reason why sound subjective judgment is so important in the application of these techniques. This situation requires taking a *sample* of the population, then organizing the sample data to draw *inferences* about the unknown *population* values.

The basic process is illustrated simply in Figure 6.7. Three wells collect information about the reservoir. The data are collected into a category called descriptive statistics, which are then utilized to infer reservoir characteristics. Statistics and the base unit of statistics – probabilities – characterize the sample data. Based on tests of the sample data, the variability in the reservoir can be inferred.

Elements comprising the sample space, whether finite like cards or infinite like most real investment situations, are either discrete or continuous. Counting the number of pumps or compressors, hopefully yields whole numbers like 1, 2, 3, ..., and not 3.5 or 4.68. This sample data is *discrete*. In measuring variables like porosity, values between 0 and 1 could occur. The sample data is continuous. As a rule, measurements result in continuous data and counting gives discrete data. Most valuation variables encompass infinite sample spaces with continuous variables. Exceptions include equipment counts and

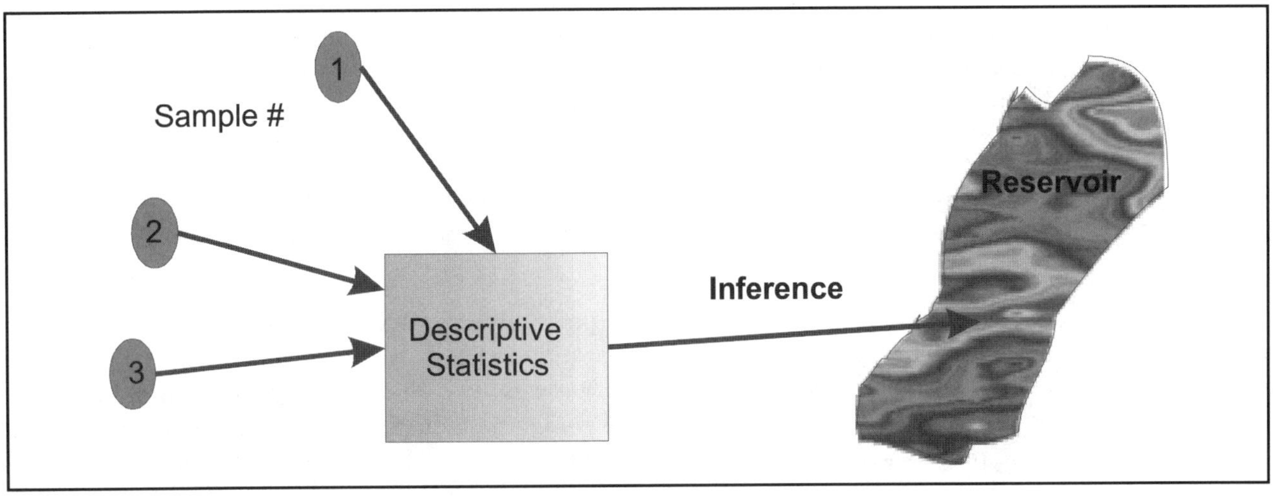

Figure 6.7 Illustration of the descriptive and inferential process

geoscience information on chance of closure, chance of source rock, etc. – which are similar to flipping a coin.

Units of Statistics: Probabilities

Probabilities are the basic units of statistics and are expressed as a fraction between 0 to 1 or as a percentage ranging from 0 to 100%. Probabilities provide a standardized way of describing any variable from any population, regardless of the units of the variable. Density, volume, pressure, temperature, costs, years, etc. are covered by one format. Standardized formats promote communication among those versed in the language, but retards communication and confuses those less well versed.

Figure 6.8 outlines the basic probability range with simple examples. If the probability is 0, the event cannot occur, witness the chance of swimming the Atlantic Ocean without stopping. The physical world will not allow liquids to exist at a temperature of 1,000 degrees F, for most instances. If the probability is 1, the event occurs with certainty. Mortal people are 100% sure that they will die someday (unless

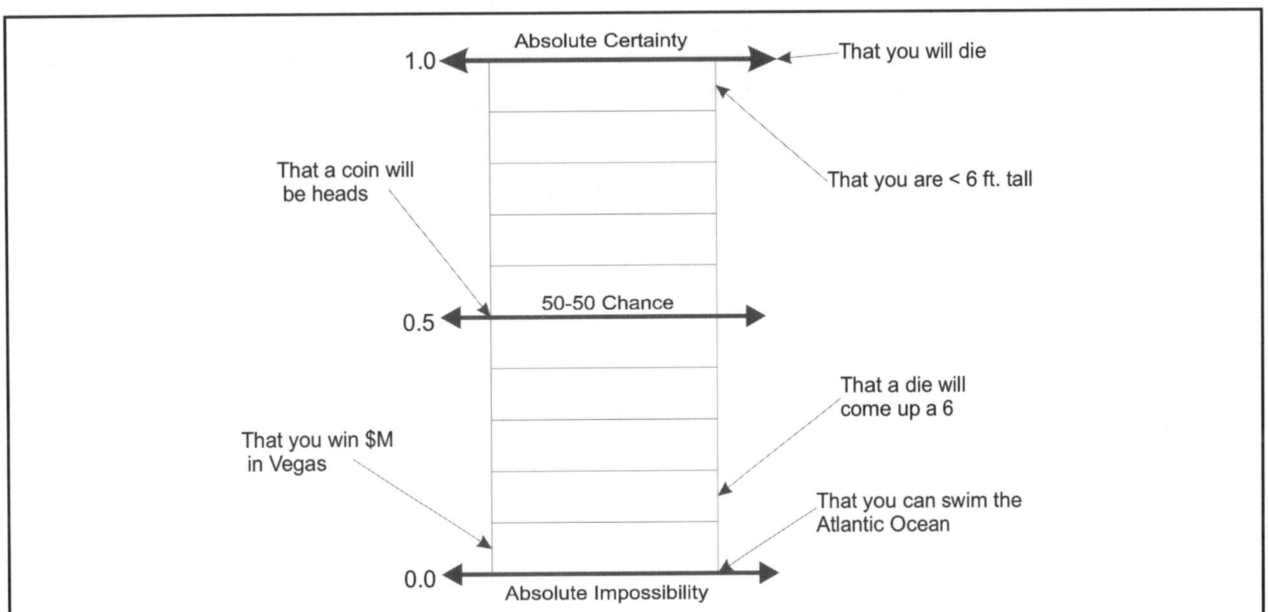

Figure 6.8 Probability, the language of risk

one believes in reincarnation). Most real world systems never reach exact values of 0 or 1, even though they may approach these limits close enough to use these values.

It is important to recognize that statistics and its language – probability – originate in the axioms assumed by the developers, not on any physical or observed truths. Like most axioms, any range of values would have worked, such as a lower value of – (3.14) and an upper bound of e (=2.71). The limit values have little impact, because the probabilities are normalized assuming the area under the curve is 1.0 (or 100%).

Three basic types of probabilities exist: a priori probabilities, subjective probabilities, and empirical probabilities. Each type has different characteristics and applications. More importantly, the ability and accuracy of inferences varies according to the type of probability. With *a prior* probabilities, the entire population of outcomes is known before hand. With subjective probabilities, so little is known that many prefer to describe these probabilities as a statement of degree of belief. Finally, empirical probabilities are computed from actual data. These formats are outlined in Table 6.1. This classification deviates from traditional definitions in order to capture the types of data available and usage in the practical setting.

TABLE 6.1

Different Types of Probabilities

Type of Probability	Characteristic	Example
A Priori	The population elements are known beforehand	• Deal of Cards • Roll of Dice • Flip of Coin
Subjective	Little or no data exists and the population is unknown. Applied to unique events	• Outcome of football game • Possibility of Rain • Discovering oil in frontier area
Empirical (descriptive stat)	Calculated from historical or current data	• Batting average • Winning percentage • Decline curve

A Priori Probabilities: This type exists only with complete knowledge of the physical system, such as gambling. The odds of an outcome in any game are known exactly. Gambling establishments compute the odds of winning and losing based on the rules of the game and the *law of large numbers*. By altering the rules about when the house has to hit in blackjack or by changing the payoffs, the house determines their profit.

In tossing a fair coin, only two possible outcomes exist (heads and tails). The probability of obtaining either is known with certainty. In a standard deck of cards, there are 52 possible outcomes. On the initial draw, the probability of getting any suit is 13/52 = 0.25; the probability of drawing any card is 1/52 = 0.019; the probability of getting a red king is 2/52 = 0.038. Similar examples exist for all games of chance. What they have in common is Equation 6.1.

$$\text{probability} = \frac{\text{number of occurences}}{\text{total number of outcomes}} \tag{6.1}$$

Once the number of occurrences and total possible outcomes are known, simply divide one number by the other to create a dimensionless value. The arithmetic is very simple; the complexity arises when defining the number of occurrences and total possible outcomes – the realm of sampling.

Sampling

Sampling is the process of obtaining data on a given system to develop an understanding of its behavior. A sample is just a subset of the population. The most common purpose is to predict future behavior based on the assumption that sufficient samples have been obtained to define the population or sample space. This assumption, restated, is "the future is like the past or the population mirrors the data" Insuring the validity of this assumption is the weak link in most applications.

Common sampling questions include:

- How many cores must be taken to determine the composition of a given fluid for a specified error margin.
- Several chromatographic analyses of a gas indicate different results. Are the differences significant or the result of chance fluctuations?
- What is the likely future variation in production rates based on the sampling distribution, so that plant sizes can be determined, contractual guarantees given, etc.?
- Was the change in production a result of operations or merely a chance fluctuation?

Sampling, like most other subdisciplines, has evolved to the point where it has become an area of specialization within statistics, and worthy of entire books. Two separate approaches reflect the complexity of the area. Both issues address computing sample space size (the denominator of Equation 4.1). Defining the sample space or population must reflect variations over time as activity takes place. Second, defining the population involves counting the number of members. The task here is determining whether the order of occurrence is important. These topics have several choices, each with unique terms. The order of counting is split into permutations and combinations, while the variation over time is reduced to sampling with replacement and sampling without replacement. Each is covered in turn.

Sampling with Replacement: The total sample space remains constant as different observations are taken from the population. For the card games cited above, asking the probability of two red kings in a standard 52 card deck is computed to be 2/52 = 0.0385. This sampling issue concerns the question of how the probability changes on the next draw of a card. If the card drawn the first time is replaced (hence sampling with replacement), 52 total cards still exist. Since the total sample space is still 52, the probability will not change on the next draw.

Sampling with replacement applies to most production, plant and economic decisions. Trying to determine downtime of equipment, the price of oil and gas, and plant size does not change the population size as samples are drawn from the sample space. Distributions of workover and completion program, reliability of mechanical systems, safety performance, etc. do not reduce the number of members in the population. This makes the probability estimation process far easier.

Sampling without Replacement: This format recognizes that the number of members in the population changes with the sampling process. By removing a member of the population, the population size falls by the corresponding amounts. If the numerator of Equation 6.1 remains the same, the probability must increase. In the card example, suppose the first card drawn is discarded, leaving 52 -1 = 51 cards left. The probability of getting two red kings on the second draw is 2/51 = 0.0392, so the probability increases with the reduction in the number of sample members.

The key lesson is that probabilities of any event changes when no replacement occurs. This is important. Most exploration and reservoir evaluations are exercises in sampling without replacement. If a 100 million barrel (15.9 million m^2) field is discovered, one less field exists – the field cannot be replaced (in our lifetime). Summaries of reserves in exploration trends often assume a lognormal distribution (defined later). While lognormal distributions approximate basins in the early stages, each discovery removes one member from the population and therefore alters the odds of the next discovery. This problem is compounded by the tendency to find the larger fields first, leaving the remaining population to be more heavily weighted toward small and medium size fields. The distribution and probabilities of reserves must change to reflect sampling without replacement. The hypergeometric distribution formally accounts for non-replacement of reserves.

Combinations, Permutations and Multiple Choice Arrangement: To establish the size of the population or the number of events in Equation 6.1, being able to count the total number of outcomes becomes essential for larger problems. In the a priori gambling examples, organizing a standard deck of cards to count the number of members is easy. The terms permutation and combination are fancy terms for quick counting techniques. The primary difference is that the order in which the members are observed is important in permutations, and not in combinations. Multiple choice arrangement extends permutations, because order is important, but also allows for duplications.

The equations for the three counting methods are given in Equation 6.2

$$\text{Combination} = {}_{n}C_{r} = \frac{n!}{r! * (n-r)!}$$

$$\text{Permutation} = {}_{n}P_{r} = \frac{n!}{(n-r)!} \tag{6.2}$$

$$\text{Multiple Choice} = {}_{n}M_{r} = n!$$

where: n is the number of elements, r is the number selected at a time, ! indicates factorials, C is for combinations, M for multiple choice arrangements and P for permutations.

Example 6.1 demonstrates the counting principles. These formulas provide some insights into the number of sensitivities needed to fully describe all possible events. This inherent complexity is the reason for the growing popularity of simulation techniques, explained later in this chapter, and optimization techniques discussed in Chapter 10.

Example 6.1: You have been asked to select 4 pumps out of 10 well field for maintenance. How many alternatives will you have to analyze to cover all possible options?

If order is unimportant, the combinations are:

$${}_{n}C_{r} = \frac{n!}{r!(n-r)!} = \frac{10!}{4!(10-4)!} = \frac{3{,}628{,}800}{24 * 720} = 210$$

If order is important, the permutations are:

$${}_{n}P_{r} = \frac{n!}{(n-r)!} = \frac{10!}{(10-4)!} = \frac{3{,}628{,}800}{720} = 5{,}040$$

If order matters and duplication is allowed, the multiple arrangement is:

$${}_{n}M_{r} = n_{r} = 10^{4} = 10{,}000$$

DESCRIPTIVE STATISTICS

Descriptive statistics organize the relationships found in samples or in populations. Analysis of sample data provides information, which provides crucial inputs into the decision-making process. One step concerns analyzing the range of possible values in the variable. Establishing the high and low values helps focus subsequent technical effort on the important issues, like reducing or defining these ranges better. Cost data from similar projects yields information about the range of future costs (after adjusting for inflation and technical changes). Sampling pressures and temperatures leads to the expectations that future values will be similar to these values. The calculations define a sample space that hopefully includes future values of each element in the system being examined.

The basic problem is to collect sample data so that the statistics adequately describe the population. If too few samples exist, the descriptive statistics must be extended using judgment and experience (typically the situation). From a practical standpoint, the decision maker is faced with a question of how much data is needed before risking large amounts of capital. Extended well testing and seismic studies, and polling more voters, etc. are classic examples of trying to get better descriptive statistics.

If data exists, the first step is to organize the data in some manner, as shown in Example 6.2. Remember the objective is to generalize, organize and communicate. The first, easiest, and still most commonly used approach classifies data into groups of data, called *classes*. Each class consists of an array of data varying in value between an upper and lower bound.

Example 6.2: The Opex per unit for 20 different producers is shown below ($ per unit).

0.17, 0.16, 0.10, 0.12, 0.18, 0.14, 0.16, 0.19, 0.15, 0.14
0.12, 0.16, 0.17, 0.19, 0.15, 0.16, 0.11, 0.21, 0.15, 0.19

The first and critical decision concerns the number of *class intervals* to use to summarize the information. The number of classes is always arbitrary and depends on the nature, type and importance of the variable in the analysis. Various rules-of-thumb have appeared over the years. The simplest approach selects the number of intervals so that each interval could have 4 to 5 data points or elements. Here, 20 data point would suggest about 4 (= 20/5) or 5 (= 20/4) intervals. Other suggestions are included in Equation 6.3.

$$\text{Number of Interval (C)} = 1 + 3.3*\log(n) \quad \textit{or} \quad 2^{C} \geq n \tag{6.3}$$

where: C is the total number of class intervals, and n is the number of data points.

Equation 6.3 solves for the first value of c such that the function 2^c exceeds the number of data points. With 20 data points, 2^4 equals 16 while 2^5 is greater than 20. Note that each approach yields a class interval values around 5. Equation 6. effectively limit the maximum number of intervals to a range of 5 to 12. For example, twelve class intervals occur with 2, 154 observations, which is more data than usually exists.

The number of class intervals affects the results. Most computer software, as described later, allows the user to select or vary the number of class intervals. Always be willing to vary the number of intervals, regardless of the classes stipulated by the formulas.

After selecting the number of classes the, *class interval width* is selected using Equation 6.4, assuming widths of equal size, and illustrated using the cost values.

$$\text{Class Width} = \frac{\text{Largest Value} - \text{Smallest Value}}{\text{Number of Intervals}} = \frac{0.21 - 0.10}{6} = 0.18 \tag{6.4}$$

Table 6.2 organizes the sample data into six class intervals. The first interval is 0.10-0.12, the second goes from 0.12-0.14, etc.. The computed interval width of 0.18 is rounded up to 0.02. Most computer software reports the width in the same manner. The upper bound of one interval (0.12-0.14) appears to overlap the lower bound of the second bound (0.14-0.16). The way to interpret the bound is that 0.14 is really 0.13999 or 14.0001, depending on which interval is chosen. The choice is unimportant as long as one is consistent.

The second column, labeled *class mark,* indicates the midpoint of the class interval. The class mark could occur at any point within the interval, but tradition dictates using the midpoint. When the data

TABLE 6.2

Class Intervals for Cost Example

Class Interval	Class Mark	Members	No. of Members
0.10-0.12	0.11	0.10, 0.11	2
0.12-0.14	0.13	0.12, 0.12	2
0.14-0.16	0.15	0.14, 0.14, 0.15, 0.15, 0.15	5
0.16-0.18	0.17	0.16, 0.16, 0.16, 0.16, 0.17, 0.17	6
0.18 - 0.20	0.19	0.18, 0.19, 0.19, 0.19	4
0.20 - 0.22	0.21	0.21	1

is spread unevenly within the interval, give some thought to changing the class mark to the average of the data points in the interval. Intervals 0.14-0.16 and 0.16-0.18 are good candidates for choosing another end point since the values occur more frequently at the low end of the interval. It is important to vary the number of intervals and class mark to insure the summary information mirrors the original data.

Table 6.3 transforms the raw data into three statistical measures – *relative frequency, cumulative frequency, and relative cumulative frequency.* These are fancier words, but are just transformations of the raw data.

TABLE 6.3

Class Inverval for Cost Example

(1)	(2)	(3)= (2)/20	(4)	(5)=(4)/20
Class Interval	Frequency	Relative Frequency	Cumulative Frequency	Relative Cumulative Frequency
0.10-0.12	2	0.10	2	0.10
0.12-0.14	2	0.10	4	0.20
0.14-0.16	5	0.25	9	0.45
0.16-0.18	6	0.30	15	0.75
0.18-0.20	4	0.20	19	0.95
0.20-0.22	1	0.05	20	1.00
Total	20	1.00		

Column 1 is repeated from Table 6.2 and Column 2, Frequency, is just the number of members column. The term *relative frequency* is the number of class members divided by the size of the sample (20). Converting from the units of the sample data creates a dimensionless number, relative frequency, which is associated with the word probability. If the sample data mirrors the population, costs fall between \$0.14 – \$0.16 per unit, about 25% of the time. Relative frequencies are just the weighted average of Column 2, with the total summing to unity. This normalization to a dimensionless value achieves the standardization objective in statistics.

Cumulative frequency is the sum of the observations possessing values less that the maximum (upper) boundary in a given class interval – the sum of the frequencies of that class and all lower classes. Column 4 sums the current and past values of column 2. The cumulative frequency of 9 is the sum of 2 + 2 + 5, which says cost was less than \$0.16 per unit in 9 out of the 20 samples.

The *relative cumulative frequency* converts the cumulative frequency into a percentage by dividing Column (4) by the total sample size. In the example, the measured cost of \$0.14 – \$0.16 was less than \$0.16 in 9/20 = 0.45 or 45% of the measurements. Computer software actually labels Column 5 *ascending relative cumulative frequency,* because the total is increasing, Taking 1 minus Column 5 generates the *descending relative cumulative frequency* column. The choice of format is one of convenience; once one set of values are reported, the others can be easily generated.

Histograms and Frequency Polygons

Figures 6.9 and 6.9a graphically depict Table 6.3. All the values are presentable in a graph using the class mark as the x-axis, be it the relative frequency values (Column 3, called a *histogram*) or the frequency data (Column 2, called a *frequency polygon*). The cumulative values can be presented in the same manner, if desired. The frequency data is superimposed on the right hand side y axis for illustration.

In the histogram, 30% (0.3) of the cost values fall between \$0.16 and \$0.18. From the cumulative frequency curve, 75% of the values were less than \$0.18. The relative cumulative frequency curve plotted refers to less than values. It can also be plotted as more than values if desired by taking 1 minus the values.

Notice in Figure 6.9 that the line was extended beyond the histogram to the cost values of 0.9 and 0.23. This is customary. It merely assumes that the adjoining class mark has a zero frequency. The polygon in Figure 6.9(a) is a distribution curve, the typical way for presenting variable data. It specifies the likelihood of the cost that would be obtained from any future measurements on the system from which the curve was obtained, if the first 20 values constitute a valid sample and the forces affecting cost were independent of time. From the curve, the 21st cost value would have a 30% chance of being between \$0.16 and \$0.18; it would likewise have a 75% chance of being less than \$0.18. The distribution serves as the basis for the likelihood of occurrence of possible values of the random variable being considered.

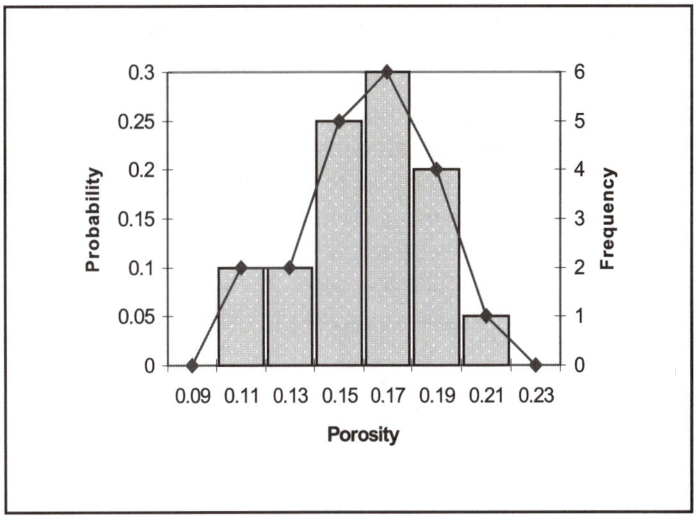

Figure 6.9 Example of porosity histogram

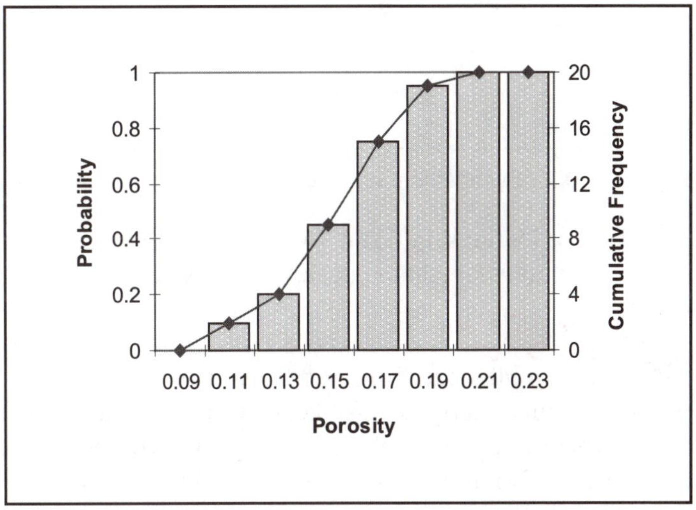

Figure 6.9a Example of porosity cumulative histogram

The process described here is called *stochastic variation*; each observation possesses a random value. Successive observations are not related by a known, fixed rule or relationship. Only information on the sample space is provided. This situation arises often in geoscience, production, costs, and other variables used in evaluations. Thus, the *frequency distribution,* which measures the fraction of the observations in a given class interval, furnishes the *probability distribution*, the basis for most risk assessment and management decisions. The *probability distribution* estimates the chance (likelihood) that a future observation will fall in a given interval.

The shape of these curves varies with the nature and type of data. When insufficient data are available to develop a distribution curve, standard or generic distributions have evolved over time. Some of the more commonly used distributions are described later.

The quality and quantity of data available and used determines the accuracy of the distribution curves. Too often field personnel fail to appreciate the importance of good data and fudge the reported values to minimize their work. Obviously everything that follows is in error. A classic example was the field person measuring water cuts by flowing fluid into their bucket, swirling it, and then estimating water percentage that settled out. When queried about the inaccuracy in the process, they replied "the engineers don't know what to do with the data anyway." Always check the data for possible *measurement errors.*

Measures of Central Tendency and Dispersion

Each distribution may be summarized by a variety of terms. These terms are called *moments* in mathematical statistics. Each distribution has as many moments as data points: 20 sample points could have 20 moments. To simplify the process when computing power was nonexistent, statisticians define unique distributions using as few moments as possible. Some of the summary values are terms like *mean, median, mode, standard deviation, variance, skewness, kurtosis, etc.* This section addresses the definition and computation of these terms.

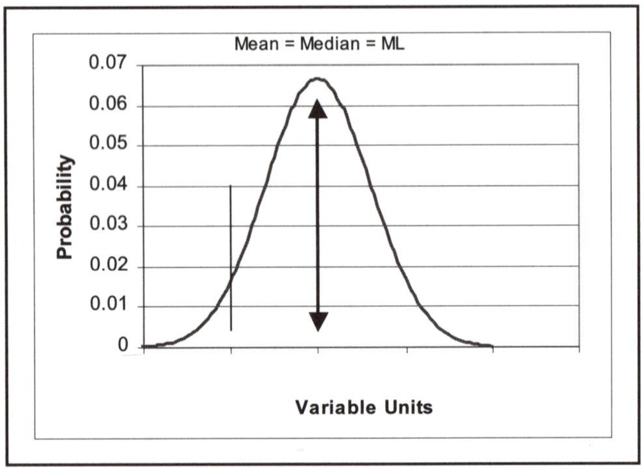

Figure 6.10 Symmetric distribution

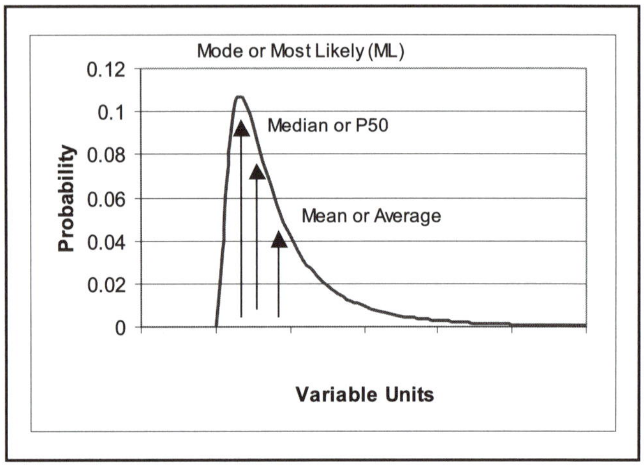

Figure 6.10a Skewed distribution

Distributions fall into two main categories: symmetrical and skewed. Fortunately, these terms match common thought processes. The symmetrical and skewed curves are shown in Figure 6.10 and 6.10a.

A symmetrical distribution occurs when the mean, median, and mode values equal each other. One half of the curve appears just like, or is a mirror image of the other half. Skewed curves display an asymmetry where one half of the curve appears different, often much different from the other half. The long sloping tail of Figure 6.10a is skewed to the right, indicating that the mean is larger than the most likely or mode value. Each term is defined in turn.

Mean: Arithmetic, Weighted, Geometric and Harmonic

The mean is the most often used parameter in a distribution and is the first moment. Other synonyms include average and expected value. The mean is a measure of central tendency, which weights each data value in the sample or population according to its size. Most statistical texts differentiate between a sample mean and the population mean. Although the equations for computing each mean is the same. The Greek symbol, μ, usually represents a population mean and represents every value in the population exactly. The mean, $\overline{X}$, is based only on the sample data. It is then used to make inferences about the population mean. Most statistical texts follow this format, as shall we. You will see very few Greek symbols, however, because industry draws samples from nature and business environment to make inferences; hence, our data are usually sample data.

Means can be computed several ways: on actual data, on grouped data, weighted to reflect sources of data, and so on. Equations 6.5 thru 6.9 summarize the various ways to compute the term called a mean. The formulas are obviously quite different and yield different values. When hearing the term mean or one of it's synonyms, Equation 6.5 is probably being referred to.

Arithmetic Mean	$\overline{X} = \frac{1}{n}\sum_{i=1}^{n} x_i$	**Equation 6.5**
Grouped Mean	$\overline{X} = \sum_{i=1}^{n} cm * n_c$	**Equation 6.6**
Weighted Mean	$\overline{X} = \frac{1}{n}\sum_{i=1}^{n} x_i * w$	**Equation 6.7**
Geometric Mean = P_{50}	$\overline{X} = \sqrt[n]{x_1 * x_2 * \ldots * x_n}$	**Equation 6.8**
Harmonic Mean	$X_h = \frac{n}{\frac{1}{x_1} + \frac{1}{x_2} + \frac{1}{x_3} + \ldots + \frac{1}{x_n}}$	**Equation 6.9**

Where: the mean values are specified in each block, x_i indicates the ith observation taken from sample x, cm is the class mark, n_c is the number of values in the class, and w is a weight given to each observation.

The weighted mean is used mostly in computing grades, and correcting for data sampling errors. If a particular test is more important than others, w might be set to 2, rather than 1. The weighted mean gives the same solution as the arithmetic mean when w=1 for all values. Selection of w > 1 allows the professional to impart judgment into the statistical framework.

Example 6.3: Compute the arithmetic mean for the 20 cost values shown previously using both the class intervals and individual values.

$$\overline{X} = \left[\frac{1}{20}\begin{pmatrix} 0.17+0.16+0.10+0.14+0.12+0.18+0.16+0.19 \\ +0.16+0.12+0.16+0.17+0.19+0.15+0.16+0.11 \\ +0.21+0.15+0.19 \end{pmatrix}\right] = \frac{3.12}{20} = \$0.156$$

The *arithmetic mean* just divides the sum of values by the sample size. Example 6.3 illustrates the mean computation using the original values. Total cost equals 3.12, divided by the sample size of 20, gives an average cost of $0.157.

Example 6.4 extends the computation to the class data used to draw the histogram earlier. Columns 1-3 repeat previous data, while columns 4 and 5 perform the arithmetic. Column 4 multiplies the class mark (by the probability or relative frequency. The sum of column 4 is 3.23, which when divided by the sample size yields a mean value of $0.161, slightly higher than the mean obtained from the raw data

Ignoring the actual data in each interval causes the grouped mean to diverge from the raw data mean. The sum of group data relies solely on the class mark, which may or may not accurately reflect the data within that interval. A quick check of the accuracy of the class mark can be obtained by comparing columns 4 and 6. The class mark equals the actual average only in the last two intervals. The class mark is higher in every other interval, which is the reason the group mean is higher than the raw mean. By shifting to an average of the data in each class (column 5), the average is very close to the raw data average. The better computer software work with column 5, not the class mark.

The *geometric mean* is applied primarily to computing average percentage changes. It is also useful for deriving the median. Some use median and geometric mean as interchangeable terms. The geometric mean is just the n-th root of the product of x values, and measures the midway point between all values.

Example 6.4: Calculate the mean cost using grouped data.

(1)	(2)	(3)	(4)=(2)*(3)	(5)	(6)=(5)/(2)
Class Interval	Class Mark	Frequency	Mark* Frequency	Average of Class Data	Average* Frequency
0.10-0.12	0.11	2	0.22	0.105	0.21
0.12-0.14	0.13	2	0.26	0.125	0.25
0.14-0.16	0.15	5	0.76	0.146	0.73
0.16-0.18	0.17	6	1.02	0.163	0.98
0.18-0.20	0.19	4	0.76	0.19	0.76
0.20-0.22	0.21	1	0.21	0.21	0.21
Total	1	20	3.23		3.14

$$\bar{X} = \frac{3.23}{20} = 0.161 \text{ using class mark, and} = \frac{3.138}{20} = \$0.157 \text{ using class average}$$

Fifty percent of of the values exceed the geometric mean, and 50% fall below the value; hence, some refer to the geometric mean as the P_{50} or 50th percentile.

Example 6.5 compares the various means using initial production data from 42 different producers in the same area. The objective is to determine the initial production rate to use for an evaluation.

Example 6.5: Initial production data from 42 producers are summarized below. Based on this information compute and compare the various means.

Raw Data					
Units/day	Units/day	Units/day	Units/day	Units/day	Units/day
20	67	116	202	411	690
21	72	120	222	480	740
31	73	152	227	482	747
35	73	159	242	532	817
43	102	162	342	576	849
58	107	169	362	589	856
66	113	176	397	671	1,139

Histogram		
Class Interval	Class Mark	Frequency
0-100	50	11
100-300	200	14
300-500	400	6
500-700	600	5
700-900	800	5
> 900	1000	1

$$\bar{X} = \frac{20 + 21 + \ldots + 1{,}139}{42} = \frac{13{,}507.2}{42} = 321.6 \text{ units per day}$$

$$\bar{X}_{cm} = \frac{50*11 + 200*14 + \ldots + 1*1{,}000}{42} = \frac{13{,}750}{42} = 327.4 \text{ units per day}$$

$$\bar{X}_g = \sqrt[42]{(20*21) + \ldots + 1{,}139} = \sqrt[42]{1.39*10^{96}} = 194.6 \text{ units per day}$$

The arithmetic mean indicates a production rate of 321.6 units per day, while the group data is slightly higher at 327.4 units per day. The geometric mean is significantly different, falling to about 195 units per day. The geometric mean indicates that the curve is highly skewed to the left because of the big difference from the arithmetic mean

Median or P_{50}

The median or 50th percentile is the middle observation after the data have been ordered from low to high. When an odd number of values exist, the median is just the mid point. If an even number of values occurs, use the average of the middle two points. Having 20 data points, suggests that we average the 10th and 11th numbers. Since both values are \$0.16, the median or P_{50} is then \$0.16. For the initial production data a similar situation arises. The mid point in Example 6.5 is the 21st and 22nd values. Those values are 176 and 202 for an average of 189 units per day.

The point was made earlier that the geometric mean approximates the median value. The geometric mean is the median when a distribution is truly lognormal (this means perfectly symmetrical when the data is viewed in $\log_{10}$ form). The geometric mean value of 194 is close to the computed value of 189. Differences occur because of the size of the sample and shape of the curve.

Median values can be computed for grouped data as well. By the time the data gets into a spreadsheet, it is just as easy to sort the information as in grouping the data. Formulas for computing medians exist in most statistical text.[6.7] Constructing grouped data takes more time to present and implement than using the sort feature in most spreadsheets.

Using the geometric mean for project analysis creates some serious problems, as explained later. The closer the median is to the mean, the more symmetrical the curve; likewise, the further away one is from the other, the more asymmetrical the curve. Some companies have adopted median reserves as an indicator of the base case, and it is this value, which forms the derivation of the so called *base case* evaluation. One can never say that one number is always better than another, especially since statistics is intended to capture the variability in values – something one number cannot achieve. Users of the median should realize that it is primarily a counting measure, not an indicator of a likely result. A median value of 189 units just says that half the sample had values above this number and the other half were below, without any consideration of the relative likelihood of any specific value.

Mode or Most Likely

The value or group occurring with the greatest frequency is the mode. On a continuous distribution, the mode is the value at the peak of the curve. For the cost data in Example 6.2, a value of \$0.16 occurs four times while \$0.15 and \$0.19 occur three times; thus, \$0.16 is the mode using sample data. Had another value occurred with the same frequency of four, a bimodal situation exists. Like the example, sorting the data in order, then determining which value occurs most determines the mode. Example 6.5 underscores a dilemma for the mode computation, however. Note that every value occurs just once, meaning that no mode exists. This is an example of a uniform distribution where no value occurs any more often than any another. This situation occurs quite often when working with measured data.

A mode can always be obtained by using a histogram, however. For the cost histogram, the modal value is computed by observing the largest class interval and then averaging the values in the interval. Figure 6.9 shows the highest interval to be the \$0.16 to \$0.18 interval. The average of the values in the interval is \$0.167, which is slightly higher than the mean and median porosity values. One could also use the class mark. Please recognize that the modal value is very sensitive to the number of intervals used to construct the histogram.[6.8]

Standard Deviation and Variance (2nd moment)

The previous measures identify alternative ways to indicate the central tendencies of the data. Comparing the mean, median, and mode provides information about the general shape of the curve – the greater the difference, the more asymmetrical the curve. A direct measure of variability is called the *standard deviation,* and it's companion *variance.* The move toward more formal risk assessment and management demands a good understanding of these terms, since they are the direct measures of variability. Interestingly enough, while many have adopted risk methods, most ignore this measure, preferring to believe that using mean, median or modal values somehow adjusts for risk. They don't!

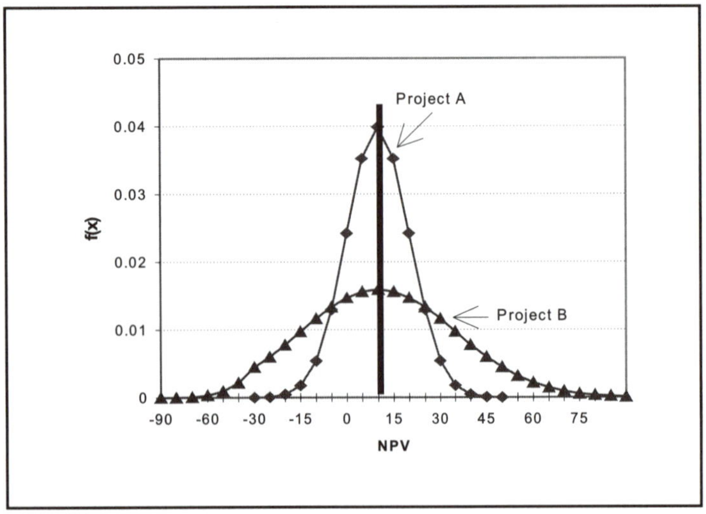

Figure 6.11 Distributions with different standard deviations

Figure 6.11 illustrates three projects, each with the same mean, but different standard deviations. The example relates to project economics, NPV. All curves are symmetric distributions. Each curve has a mean value of $10 million, and a standard deviation of $10 million for Project A, $25 million for Project B, and $0 for C. First, observe that Project B goes further out than Project A. This *dispersion* is the direct result of the standard deviation. Larger standard deviations mean that Project B will go further to the right and left than A.

When data has no variation (the certainty case), the curve would be a straight line like the solid vertical line rising from the $10 value on the x-axis. As variability increases to $10, the project A curve arises. Increasing standard deviation to $25 yields Project B. Knowledge of standard deviations is one way to formally assess and manage risk, as Chapter 8 explores.

The equations for standard deviation and variance are split into population and sample values like the mean. Since population information is seldom known, only the sample formulas are presented. In stat texts the population standard deviation is designated σ, while sample standard deviation is s or s_X. The equation for raw and grouped sample data are given in Equation 6.10 and 6.10a. The standard deviation first takes the difference between each individual value and the sample mean, and then squares the difference. This squaring is the critical step. If a distribution is truly symmetrical, like in Figure 6.11, the negative values exactly match the positive differences, resulting in a zero sum. Squaring prevents this offset from occurring. The sum of the square differences is divided by n-1 to give the standard deviation, s_X. Variance equals s_X^2 or is obtained by eliminating the radical when computing s_X.

Variance and Standard Deviation Equations			
Raw Data	$s_X = \sqrt{\frac{1}{n-1}\sum(x_1 - \bar{X})^2}$	Variance = s_X^2	**Equation 6.10**
Grouped Data	$s_X = \sqrt{\frac{1}{n-1} * \sum f * cm^2 - n * \bar{x}^2}$	Variance = s_X^2	**Equation 6.10a**

where:

s_X = standard deviation,
s_X^2 = variance,
n = sample size,
x_i = ith data sample,
cm = class mark,
f = the frequency number in a class, *and the other values are defined earlier.*

A common, frustrating question asks why the equations divide by n-1, rather than n. The value n-1 reflects the concept called *degrees of freedom (df)*. Textbooks often explain degrees of freedom as the number of observations (n) less the number of constraints without ever defining how to determine the number of constraints. The degrees of freedom really reflect the number of times the data is used to construct a summary variable, like the mean. Since all n observations were used to compute the mean, only n-1 values are left to indicate variation. After computing the standard deviation or variance, only n-2 variations remain. Computer software computes standard deviations for population data using n, and n-1 for samples.

Example 6.6 computes the standard deviation for the production data in the previous example. The value of 293.6 indicates that initial production varies ± 293.6 units from the mean value, on average. The grouped data s_x is smaller at ± 272.4, because of the way the data was grouped. We prefer using the raw data whenever possible to reduce potential bias from the grouping process. Standard deviations are the best measure of variability, however obtained.

Example 6.6: Compute the standard deviation & variance for the production data in Example 6.4.

Raw Data	$s_x = \sqrt{\frac{(20-321.6)^2 + (21-321.6)^2 + ... + (1{,}139-321.6)^2}{42-1}} = \sqrt{\frac{3{,}534{,}636}{42-1}} = 293 \text{ units}$
Grouped Data	$s_x = \sqrt{\frac{11*50^2 + 14*200^2 + ... + 1*1{,}000^2 - 42*327.4^2}{42-1}} = 272.5 \text{ units}$

Standard deviation is measured in the same units as the raw data, whether pressure, temperature, initial production, money, etc. Compare the standard deviation with the mean value provides one measure of risk. An old approach for integrating standard deviation with the mean is called the *coefficient of variation (CV)*. Equation 6.11 defines CV as the ratio of the standard deviation to the mean. The ratio yields a dimensionless value. If two means are roughly the same, this compares the standard deviations directly. The smaller the CV, the less the dispersion around the mean.

$$CV = \frac{s_x}{\overline{X}} = \frac{293.6}{321.6} = 0.913 \qquad \textbf{(6.11)}$$

Indicators such as CV are useful, but graphical displays are more informative. Once the mean and standard deviation are known, the likelihood of outcomes can be computed. Each distribution has a density function that can be solved, but graphs are far easier to interpret. For example the symmetric curve in Figure 6.11 can be extended to formally display the standard deviation. Figure 6.12 shows Project A with the standard deviation indicted.

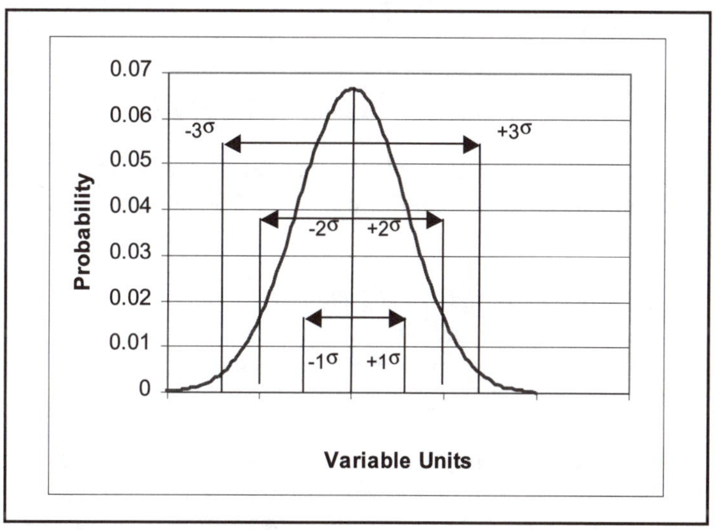

Figure 6.12 Standard deviation

Figure 6.12 was constructed assuming a mean of 10 and a s_x of 10. One standard deviation covers a range from 0 (= 10 – 1*10) to 20 (= 10+ 1*10). This is indicated with the s_x that lies between the first two vertical lines. Moving out to $2s_x$, the range shifts to -10 to 30. Going to $3s_x$ just shifts the values out another 10 in each direction. In normal distributions the s_x range covers about 68.8% of the area under the curve, $2s_x$ captures about 95.45%, and $3s_x$ almost 99.7% of the area. Manufacturing used to use the $3s_x$ rule until Jack Welch made the $6s_x$ rule famous. This means that products coming off the assembly line are tested to insure that 99.997% are defect free. Of course, we always buy the remaining 0.3%.

Skewness: (3rd moment)

The difference between symmetric and asymmetric curves was illustrated previously. Most software compute the *coefficient of skewness (P)*. The coefficient is zero when the mean and median are equal (P = 0). If the mean is greater than the median (P > 0), the curve is skewed to the right, and skewed to the left when the mean is less than the median (P < 0). Equation 4.12 defines the basic relationship using the initial production data from Example 6.5. The median value in Eq. 4.12 could be replaced with the mode depending on one's preference.*(6.9)*

$$P = \frac{3*(\bar{X} - \text{median})}{s_x} = \frac{3*(321.6 - 189)}{293.6} = 1.35 \qquad \textbf{(6.12)}$$

The larger the P value, the more skewed the curve. Like most statistical values, the significance of the P value is easier to understand after plotting a number of curves.

A more generalized version of skewness is represented in Equation 6.12a. This is the format employed by most stat software packages. The value of 0.983 was calculated using the descriptive statistic option in Excel. Though the value is smaller than the Pearson value, this arises from the different formulation. Regardless of the equation used, the ± sign of P indicates the direction of the skewness.

$$P = \frac{n}{(n-1)(n-2)} \sum \frac{(x_i - \bar{X})^3}{s_x} = 0.983 \qquad \textbf{(6.12a)}$$

Kurtosis: (4th moment)

Kurtosis measures the relative peakedness or flatness of a distribution relative to a normal distribution. The equation is the 4th moment of a distribution and is based on the information generated in the first three moments. The resultant, K, is zero when the peak of the curve is the same as a normal distribution. When K > 0, the curve is more peaked than a normal curve, and flatter when K < 0. Equation 6.13 shows the standard equation used by Excel and a value generated from the initial production data in Example 6.5.*(6.10)* A value of -0.005 is so close to zero that the peak of the initial production data appears very similar to a normal distribution, even though it is more skewed.

$$K = \left[\frac{n(n-1)}{(n-1)(n-2)(n-3)} \sum \left(\frac{X_i - \bar{X}}{S_x}\right)\right] - \frac{3(n-1)^2}{(n-1)(N-2)} = -0.005 \qquad \textbf{(6.13)}$$

Basic Types of Events and Probability Theorems

Each of the examples discussed so far assumes that events are independent of each other, or each value does not depend on any other value in any known or presumed measure. Events are classified in three basic ways.

Independent Events: All events (outcomes) are independent if the occurrence of one event has no effect on the occurrence of other events. Suppose one is sampling natural gas to see if it meets contract specifications. Each measurement is independent of all other measurements from different samples. Dependence arises when this condition fails.

Equally Likely Events: Two or more events have an equal probability of occurring if the probability is the same. Flipping a coin exemplifies equally likely events. On any flip of a fair coin the chances of a head equals the odds of a tail – 50%. The current flip is independent of previous flips (independent). This approach is seldom used in industry.

Mutually Exclusive Events: When the occurrence of one event precludes the existence of all other events defines a mutually exclusive event. Common examples include:

- waterflooding and staying on primary recovery at the same time
- capital intensive, low operating cost versus high Opex, low Capex facilities
- types of completion programs or facilities (refrigeration versus cryogenics).

Many investment decisions focus on weeding out less desirable alternatives like these.

Two basic probability theorems govern the computation of the likelihood of these events. The two theorems, the *addition theorem* and *multiplication theorem*, are expressed in terms of two events A and B. The *addition theorem* is written as:

$$f(A+) = f(A) + f(B) - f(AB) \qquad \textbf{(6.14)}$$

where: f represents a probability (likelihood), expressed as a fraction
A is one event, and B is another
(A+B) signifies that A and or B occurs
(AB) signifies that both A and B occur

Equation 6.14 reads as, "The probability of event A and/or B occurring equals the probability of A plus the probability of B minus the probability of both A and B occurring.

The term f(AB) = 0 because a single ball cannot contain two numbers. It only comes into play if Event A and Event B share a common sample space.

Examples of the addition theorem from investments are difficult to create easily because few cases of joint probabilities exist. When those events overlap, the sample space is not as straightforward as the example implies. Finding the probability of success in a prospect with multiple zones is a good example of one application, as Chapter 9 discusses. The probability that A and B occur in sequence or simultaneously drives most analysis.

Example 6.7: A box contains 100 balls, each ball bearing a number from 1 to 100. One ball exists for each number. What is the probability of drawing a 10, 20, or 30 (Event A) or a 70 or 80 (Event B)? From Equation 6.14.

$$f(A+B) = \frac{3}{100} + \frac{2}{100} = 0.05$$

Many investment variables are dependent to a certain degree. If y is dependent on x, then the probability of an event y occurring depends on an event x taking place. *Conditional probability* defines the probability of an event given that some other value occurs. The *multiplication theorem* defines the equation for determining the conditional events. Equation 6.15 specifies the multiplication theorem.

$$f(ABC) = f(A)f(B|A)f(C|AB) \qquad \textbf{(6.15)}$$

where:
f(ABC) = the probability of A, B, and C occurring in sequence or simultaneously, %
f(A) = the probability of A occurring
f(B|A) = the probability of B occurring given that A happens
f(C|AB) = the probability of C occurring if both A and B happen

The multiplication theorem dominates industrial probability applications, because most projects deal with sequential or simultaneous situations. Equation 6.15 is the basis for the use of decision trees, as shown in Chapter 8.

Example 6.8: If production volume of 10 million has a probability f(A) of 0.4, a cost of $2 million has an estimated probability of 0.7 [f(B)], and the specified price probability is 0.3 [f(C)], what is the chance of all three events occurring simultaneously.

$$f(ABC) = (0.4)(0.7)(0.3) = 0.084$$

COMMON PROBABILITY DISTRIBUTIONS

With the foundation of statistics defined, an extensive armada of distributions, with well defined characteristics have been formulated based on these concepts. This section outlines commonly used distributions. Past editions of this book spent a considerable number of pages outlining details of each distribution. Most software now has the functions built in, be they spreadsheets, graphs, or databases. With the ready availability of such software, this section focuses more on applications, uses and examples than formulas.

The distributions discussed in the main body of the text include:

Normal	Rectangular
Log Normal	Triangular
Truncated Distributions	Chi Square
Binomial	Gamma
Hypergeometric	

Other references describe more distributions.[(6.11)]

Very specific distributions comprise the foundation of most discussions of statistical applications. The original objective in creating continuous distributions was to apply statistical concepts using the tools of the day – typically the slide rule and graph paper. Tabular distributions were created to determine confidence intervals and form hypothesis tests once the standard values, usually the mean and standard deviations, were computed. Even the developers of the distributions, however, emphasized their limitations to simplify the application. Probably the best summary of continuous distributions came from Karl Pearson, a prominent statistician, who said in 1935, "I have never found a normal curve fit anything if there was enough observations."[(6.12)] Our experience is the same, but applies to every one of the distributions outlined here. There is no substitute for good data; every distribution is just an approximation.

Normal Distribution

The Normal, Gaussian or Bell Curve Distribution was (supposedly) developed by Carl Gauss to explain variability in predictions of planetary orbits. The normal distribution is used to introduce and explain most statistical concepts for several reasons. First, during the calculator and slide rule eras the normal distribution could take advantage of the myriad of tables designed to simplify the calculations. The Z and t-tables, presented later, are good examples.

Second, normal distributions accurately describe linear systems. The *Law of Large Numbers* stipulates that linear systems, like NCF, approximate a normal distribution. This holds regardless of the shape of the other variables (Opex, Capex, taxes, etc.). Appealing to this property circumvented the need for excessive repetition and tabulation. Unfortunately, real world investment opportunities are seldom large enough to appeal to the law of large numbers.

A third attractive trait emerges from the equivalence of the mean, median, and mode; thus, eliminating the necessity to decide among the parameters. Reference to the *base case* is common practice in industry. Equivalence of the mean, median, and mode reduces inconsistency and avoids the difficult task of defining the *base case*.

Density equations define the probabilities plotted on the y axis and are labeled f(x). Most spreadsheets have already coded the density equations into the formula section if you ever want to check the probability computations. They are shown here for future reference.

Normal Distribution Equations		
Density, f(x)	$= \frac{1}{\sqrt{2\Pi\sigma^2}} e^{-(x-\mu)/2\sigma^2}$	**Equation 6.16**
Mean, μ	$= \frac{1}{n}\sum_{i=1}^{N} x_i$	**Equation 6.17**
Standard Deviation, σ	$= \sqrt{\frac{1}{n-1}\sum_{i=1}^{N}(x_i - \bar{X})^2}$	**Equation 6.18**

The equations mix population and sample parameters. The Greek symbols relate to population values, but the sample values could be substituted for the Greek values. The mean and standard deviation equations are repeated from previous discussions and the variables are defined as before. The sample size is N, the mean is given by μ and the standard deviation by σ. To describe a normal distribution, computer software requires input like =Normal(*mean, standard deviation*).

Figure 6.13 illustrates a normal distribution. The advantages of the normal curve can be illustrated by using the mean and standard deviation to create a standardized normal curve, labeled N(0, 1). The N(0, 1) stands for a normal curve with a mean of 0 and a standard deviation of 1. Equation 6.19 defines the standard normal curve, Z., using population and sample values as:

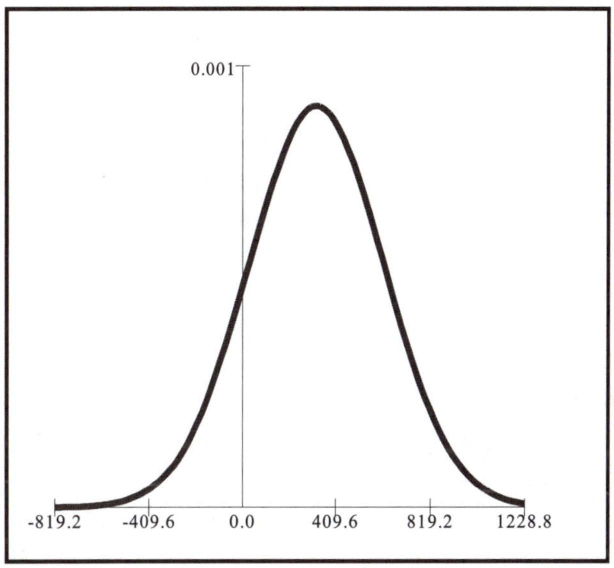

Figure 6.13 Graph of normal distribution for production data

$$Z = \frac{x - \mu_x}{\sigma_x} \text{ or } \frac{x_i - \bar{X}}{\sigma_x} \tag{6.19}$$

Once Z values are computed, the probability of an event taking place can be read from the Z table at the end of the book. The same values can be found by using the appropriate Excel functions, which is NormDist(x value, 0, 1, True). You should duplicate the Z table printed to see how the probabilities are generated.

The plot of the normal distribution using the production data is shown in Figure 6.13. The mean is 321.6 and the standard deviation is 293.6. Applying the normal distribution to the production data illustrates a common pitfall in using distributions. Users often adopt a suggested distribution without understanding the consequences. Here, the mean and standard deviation are applied without any attention given the results. The vertical line goes thru the origin, indicating a significant chance that the production might be negative. Just inserting Normal(321.6, 293.6) into software gives this curve. Unsurprisingly, when negative production is allowed, project economics are usually bad. The easiest way to check a distribution is to plot it, and determine if the range fits your understanding of the physical or economic system.

Example 6.9 illustrates the use of the Z table in the appendix at the end of the book. The probability of any event occurring can be computed, based on the sample mean and standard deviation.

Example 6.9: Using the production data from Example 6.5, estimate the probability of production being greater than 100 less than 800, and between 400 and 800.

1. From the Z table, the value of Z for -0.755 is 0.2236. Production was less than 100 about 22.36% of the time. Conversely, production exceeded 100 about 77.64% (= 1 – 0.2236) of the time.

$$Z = \frac{100 - 321.6}{293.6} = 0.755$$

2. The value of 1.63 has a probability of .9484 from the Z table, or a 94.84% chance of being less than 800.

$$Z = \frac{800 - 321.6}{293.6} = 1.63$$

3. The value of z_1 for 400 is 0.6064 and is 0.9484 for z_2. The difference between z_1 and z_2 measures the portion of the curve between 400 and 800. The value is |0.9484 – 0.6064| = 0.3442 or 34.42%; therefore the probability of a producing rate between 400 and 800 is 34.42%.

$$z_1 = \frac{400 - 321.6}{293.6} = 0.27, \quad z_2 = \frac{800 - 321.6}{293.6} = 1.63$$

LogNormal Distribution

This distribution is used quite often to describe naturally occurring events, like reservoir size, permeability, formation thickness, recovery, etc., the stock market, and to correct for negative production like that in the previous example. Lognormal distributions extend the basic premises used in the normal distribution, since the name means that the logs of the raw data are normally distributed. Lognormal distributions are constrained to positive values due to the nature of logarithms. This works quite well with natural phenomena, which cannot be negative. Another reason for the extensive use of lognormal curves is again the *Law of Large Numbers*. Multiplicative relationships move toward a lognormal curve (a skewed to the right curve). With limited computational power, assuming a lognormal relationship was better than using single point estimates.

Even if nature is truly lognormal two problems arise: first, an investment may not have enough samples to achieve the benefits of the Law of Large Numbers, and second, nature samples without replacement. History demonstrates that small accumulations outnumber large ones. Distributions of worldwide reserves are definitely skewed to the right. To our knowledge, no one has ever established that lognormality best characterizes limited accumulations. The second element, sampling without replacement, undoes the first, even if nature did produce lognormal reserve distributions. Large reservoirs tend to be found first, so as basins mature, the large reservoirs are removed from the population until only the smaller reservoirs are left. Even though the original distribution might be lognormal, development appraisals must reflect the greater dominance of the remaining, smaller accumulations. These are called *truncated distributions*, and discussed next.

Lognormal Distribution Equations		
Density, f(x)	$=\frac{1}{\sqrt{2\Pi\sigma^2}}e^{-(\ln x-\mu)/2\sigma^2}$	**Equation 6.19**
Mean, μ	$=\frac{1}{N}\sum_{i=1}^{N}\log(x_i)$	**Equation 6.20**
Standard Deviation, σ	$=\sqrt{\frac{1}{N-1}\sum_{i=1}^{N}[\log(x_i)-\overline{X}]}$	**Equation 6.21**

Lognormality proved quite popular in the slide rule and calculator eras because of its well behaved and easily defined functional relationships. Several authors have developed procedures for computing reserves, assuming the lognormal distribution is appropriate.[(6.13)] Buckee developed a similar approach.

Computer software requires two inputs to develop a lognormal distribution – the mean and standard deviation. Most software assumes the data is in it's original format and converts it to log, as the equations used here. Others allow insertion of ln data. In Excel and @Risk the formula is Lognorm (*mean, standard deviation*) and Lognorm2 (*mean, standard deviation*). Lognorm uses the input values as is, while Lognorm2 takes the exponential of the input data.

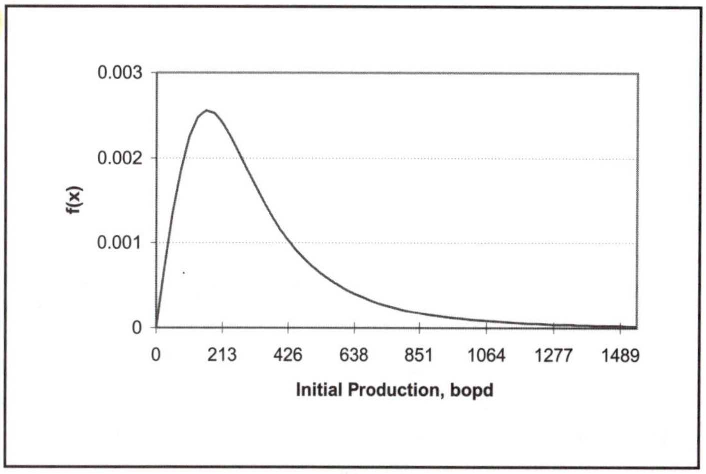

Figure 6.14 Lognormal distribution of production

Figure 6.14 illustrates the lognormal curve based on a mean production of 321. and a standard deviation of 293.6. The origin now becomes the lower limit and the upper value is around 1500 barrels. The most likely value is around 123. At issue is whether the lognormal curve is appropriate for this data. The easiest method is to look at the curve and use professional judgment. Formal tools for making this decision are presented following discussion of the basic distributions.

Truncated Distributions

Discussions of distributions are usually limited to complete distributions like normal and lognormal. Most distributions describe complete populations and fail to address the sampling without replacement as the project proceeds. Reserves may be lognormal before drilling commences. After drilling begins, the discovery of larger fields leaves the smaller fields to be found. At the other end of the reserve distribution, smaller fields, which cannot be economically produced, also may be irrelevant. Removal of upper and lower values illustrates *bounded distributions*.

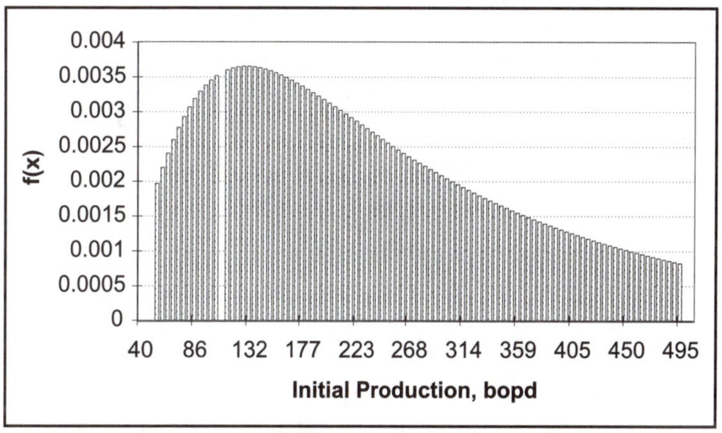

Figure 6.15 Truncated lognormal distribution

Figure 6.15 extends the production data to consider the possibility that the best producing sites had already been used. On the downside, costs in the area require a minimum production rate of 50 units per day to justify the investment. At the upside, the professional believes production cannot exceed 500 units per day.

The fundamental limitation of most analysis is the assumption of *sampling with replacement.* Manufacturing or processing may replace itself, but investments involving Nature don't replace themselves. Gathering historical statistics assumes the future looks like the past. The past is only a guide or starting point for anticipating the future. The crucial element in working with distributions is developing ranges and shapes based on what the professional thinks the future will hold.

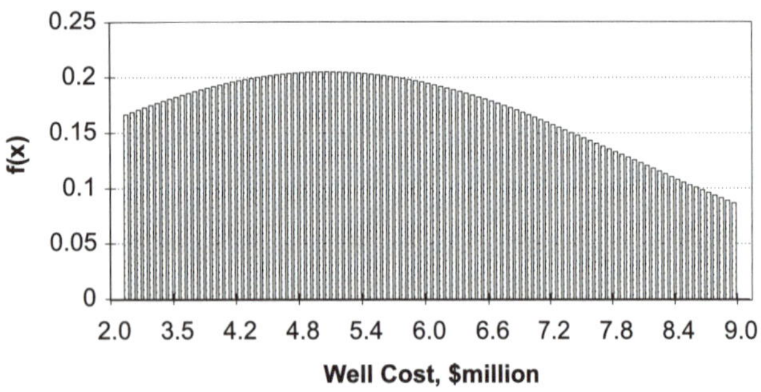

Figure 6.16 Truncated normal distribution

Economic data, like costs and prices, exhibit a *sampling with replacement* reasonable process when specifying distributions. The actual outcome of an investment cost doesn't preclude that cost from occurring again. However, costs and timing issues may still be reflected by truncated issues. The general shape of a curve might be appropriate, but the boundary estimates may be constrained by system conditions. For instance, some cost estimates appear remarkably like a normal distribution (in some locales). Figure 6.16 displays investment cost with a mean of $5 million and a standard deviation of $3. The engineering department is fairly certain that costs cannot go below $3 million nor above $9 million.

The cost estimate looks nothing like a normal distribution with the truncations. The upper tail would have asymptotically approached the x-axis if the maximum value was increased. Such truncated distributions often reflect the complexities of the real world better than simplified distributions, because these boundaries govern the success of projects.

Incorporating truncated curves is easy in both Crystal Ball and @Risk. In Crystal Ball you choose the curve and then drag and drop the end point to match the boundaries. @Risk specifies the equation directly into the formula by specifying "=riskTlognorm (*mean, standard deviation, min value, max value*)." The riskTlognorm tells Excel or Lotus to select the @risk function, while the italics designate the input values to produce the curves in the last two figures. We highly recommend this option for anyone. @Risk only allows truncation of exponential, normal and lognormal curves, while Crystal Ball permits almost all distributions to be truncated.

Binomial Distribution

The binomial distribution is often described as a special case of a *Bernoulli process*, which means absolutely nothing to most people. Bernoulli, one of the founders of modern statistics, described a process for determining probabilities. Since the binomial distribution follows this process so closely, some people use binomial and Bernoulli distribution interchangeably. The binomial distribution has three main conditions:

- only two outcomes are allowed, usually success or failure,
- each trial is an independent event, and
- the probability of each event is constant over all trials.

The last premise implies *sampling with replacement*, which is the primary way to hold the probability constant. Investing in the stock market or new manufacturing may comply with these assumptions. Investing in non-renewable resources doesn't work this way since only a finite number of trials exists. The probability must change with each trial. The *hypergeometric distribution* corrects this problem next. Equipment failure rates, however, are truly independent. Examples of each are provided below.

Binomial Distribution Equations		
Density, f(x)	$=C_x^n(p)^x(1-p)^{n-x}=\frac{n!}{x!(n-x)!}(p)^x(1-p)^{n-x}$	**Equation 6.23**
Mean, μ	$=n*p$	**Equation 6.24**
Standard Deviation, σ	$=\{n*p*(1-p)\}^{0.5}$	**Equation 6.25**

The problem with using P_s is that it is difficult to define, highly uncertain, and subject to variation. Suppose 10 investment opportunities, each with a 1/5 chance, are available. Very seldom do exactly 2 successes exist; instead the successes take on a range of 0, 1, 2, 3, 4, etc.

The binomial distribution was first used in games of chance – flipping a coin, since only two outcomes are permitted. The density function combines the combination formula with the probability of each event. The ! designates factorials. Computing the probability of an event increase in complexity as the number of trials, n, increases. Tables in the Appendix summarize the probability for various values of n and p, for cumulative and density curves.

Example 6.10: In the toss of a fair coin (p=0.5), what is the probability of getting exactly 2 heads in 6 tosses.

$$f(x)=\frac{6!}{2!(6-2)!}(0.5)^2(1-0.5)^{6-2}=\frac{720}{2*24}(0.25)(0.00625)=0.234$$

What is the chance of obtaining 20 success if we invest in 25 projects with a P_s =0.8

$$f(x)=\frac{25!}{20!(25-20)!}(0.8)^{20}(25-20)^{25\text{-}20}=\frac{1.55*10^{25}}{2.43*10^{18}(120)}(0.0115)(0.00032)$$

$$=(53{,}150)(0.0115)(0.00032)\;=\;0.195\quad or\quad 19.5\%$$

Figure 6.17 shows the success rate for n = 25 and p = 0.8. At an 80% success rate, the number of successes, actually observed, could range from about 13 to 25, with the most likely outcome being 20. Note that 19 and 21 have greater than a 15% chance of happening. As important as knowing the likelihood is the issue of other investment decisions which depend on knowing this number. Would it make sense to design other production facilities, plants and platforms based on a certainty of 20 occurrences? Most investment analysis assumes exactly 20 occurrences, but that outcome is less than 20% of the total outcomes.

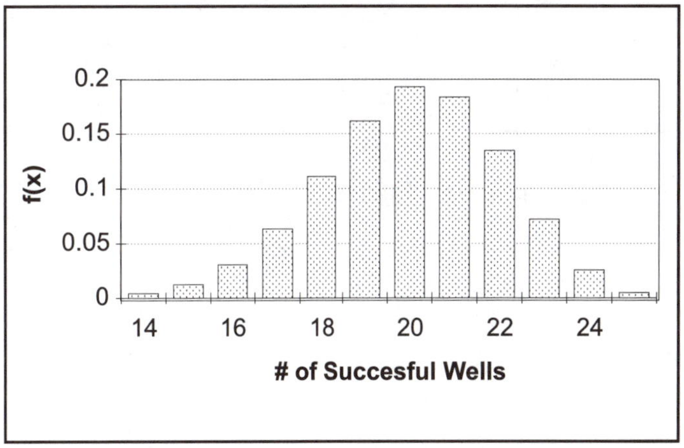

Figure 6.17 Binomial distribution of well success

The binomial distribution is also used extensively in evaluating the reliability of operating equipment. The form of the analysis goes by several names – reliability, redundancy, etc., but the objective is to weigh trade-offs in the cost of excess equipment versus the value of spare capacity. Correct assessment of downtime or uptime and the respective values of the size and amount of equipment impact the overall project assessment. Common applications include:

- power generation facilities on offshore platforms or remote locations
- injection pumps for waterflood or gas cycling projects,
- pumps for pipelines, and
- comparing the value of labor intensive operations versus heavy capital utilization

Example 6.11: Assess the reliability of a system requiring 10,000 KW (3600 kJ/hr). Three alternatives are being considered: 2 - 5000 KW generators, 3 - 5000 KW generators, and 3 - 4000 KW generators. The manufacturer rates each generator at 95% reliability (5% failure rate).

	2 -5000	3 - 5000	3 - 4000	
Available Power	Pi	Pi	Power	Pi
10,000	0.0925	0.9928	12,000	0.8574
5,000	0.0950	0.0071	8,000	0.1354
0	0.0025	0.0010	4,000	0.0071
				0.0010
Total P_i	1	1		1
Average Reliability	0.95	0.9963		0.9685

where: $$0.9685 = \frac{(12{,}000)(0.8754) + (8{,}000)(0.1354) + (4{,}000)(0.0071)}{10{,}000}$$

The 3 - 4000 KW generators will be available about 97% of the time on average. The values under the probability heading, P_i, for the 2 - 5000 KW and 3 - 4000 KW cases are obtained from the binomial tables. To find these value use n = 2 or 3 and p = 0.05.

Computing the 3 - 5000 case requires further manipulations because redundancy is sufficient to stand one generator failing. The power demand is achieved when either none is down (0.875) + one is down (0.1354) = 0.9928. The other values are determined in a like manner.

Hypergeometric Distribution

The hypergeometric distribution corrects the assumptions in the binomial distribution by explicitly recognizing *sampling without replacement* and a *finite sample space*. Hypergeometric is ideal for answering questions like:

- how many wells to drill to meet contract thruput requirements,
- meeting safety specifications,
- determining the number of slots to add to the platform, and
- sizing plants, etc.

In each case a tradeoff between incurring an expense and an opportunity cost of losing production, etc. exists. These costs can only be assessed with information on monetary costs and benefits. These issues are addressed in later chapters.

Hypergeometric Distribution Equations		
Density, f(x)	$= \frac{n!n_p!(N-n_p)!(N-n)!}{n_s!(n-n_s)!(n_p-n_s)![(N-n_p)-(n-n_s)]!N!}$	**Equation 6.26**
Mean, μ	$= \frac{n*n_p}{N}$	**Equation 6.27**
Standard Deviation, σ	$= \left[\frac{n*n_p(N-n_p)(N-n)}{N^2(N-1)}\right]^{0.5}$	**Equation 6.28**

The equations used in the hypergeometric get complicated with the factorials. N indicates the size of the population and n_p the number of successes in the population. A small n refers to the sample size and n_s the number of estimated successes in the sample. The real world seldom conforms exactly to the equation format so some modification is often in order.

Example 6.12: Ten independent prospects have been identified for investing. The goal is to test 5 of the opportunities by drilling one well in each prospect. What is the probability of 2 discoveries if 30% of the prospects in similar areas proved commercial. For these conditions N=10, n_s = 2, n = 5, and n_p = 3 (= 0.3*10).

$$P(2) = \frac{5!3!7!5!}{2!3!1!4!10!} = 0.417$$

The difference between the binomial and hypergeometric distributions is best illustrated by identifying the actual combination of events. Ten mutually exclusive ways of achieving two successes exist. Column 2 in Table 6.4 shows the sequence associated with 5 successes, and column 3 computes the probability of each event. Note that the probability at any stage changes to reflect the sequence, while the total is the same.

The major difference between the hypergeometric and binomial curves occurs in the denominator of each sequence. Since the binomial assumes replacement, the denominator is 10 at each point; whereas in Table 6.4 the denominator falls with each well. In sequence 1, seven failures occur first out of 10, but the value declines as the failure is removed from the population, reducing the next chance of a failure to 6/9. If the same sequence is treated as a binomial the probability for sequence 1 is (7/10)(7/10)(7/10)(3/10)(3/10) = 0.3087, the same value as reported for the binomial distribution in the previous section. Hypergeometric distributions always produce larger probabilities, because of the smaller denominators, which occur because of *sampling without replacement*.

TABLE 6.4

Illustration of Hypergeometric Distribution

(1) Sequence	(2) Occurrence	(3) Probability
1	FFFSS	(7/10)(6/9)(5/8)(3/7)(2/6) = 3/72 =00.417
2	FFSFS	(7/10)(6/9)(3/8)(5/7)(2/6) = 3/72 = 0.417
3	FSFFS	(7/10)(3/9)(6/8)(5/7)(2/6) = 3/72 = 0.417
4	SFFFS	(3/10)(7/9)(6/8)(5/7)(2/6) = 3/72 = 0.417
5	SFFSF	(3/10)(7/9)(6/8)(2/7)(5/6) = 3/72 = 0.417
6	SFSFF	(3/10)(7/9)(2/8)(6/7)(5/6) = 3/72 = 0.417
7	SSFFF	(3/10)(2/9)(7/8)(6/7)(5/6) = 3/72 = 0.417
8	FSFSF	(7/10)(3/9)(6/8)(2/7)(5/6) = 3/72 = 0.417

Example 6.13: You have a contract to deliver a required volume of gas to the market. With an estimate that you need 2 additional wells to satisfy the contract, how many wells do you need to drill to maximize your chances of finding the 2 additional wells?

Wells Drilled	f(x)
5	0.417
6	0.500
7	0.525
8	0.467
9	0.300

Another common application estimates the number of times an event must be performed to achieve a specified result. Fixed objectives, including volume thruputs, are common in today's environment. At issue is how many producing units must be brought on line to achieve these objectives. Example 6.13 shows how the probability of achieving the objective changes with the number of wells drilled. By drilling 7 wells instead of 5, the probability of finding 2 successful wells increases from 41.7% to 52.5%.

Uniform (Rectangular) Distribution

When detailed data or limited knowledge precludes application of more precise (not necessarily better) distribution formats, common practice falls back on subjective distributions; primarily triangular and uniform distributions. These are the simplest distributions, requiring the least data and input. Oftentimes the professional only knows or can guess the minimum, most likely, and high (triangular) or just a minimum and high (uniform) values.

Uniform Distribution Equations		
Density, f(x)	$= \frac{1}{x_{max} - x_{min}}$	**Equation 6.29**
Mean, μ	$= \frac{x_{max} - x_{min}}{2}$	**Equation 6.30**
Standard Deviation, σ	$= \sqrt{\frac{(x_{max} - x_{min})^2}{12}}$	**Equation 6.31**

Only two values, a high, x_{max}, and a low, x_{min}, are needed. This is the reason the uniform is the simplest of all distributions. Don't confuse the simplicity with imprecision. The uniform distribution fits a lot of empirical data as well as any other distribution. To input a uniform distribution in software, enter a formula like uniform(*maximum, minimum*) or choose the figure like the one in Figure 6.18.

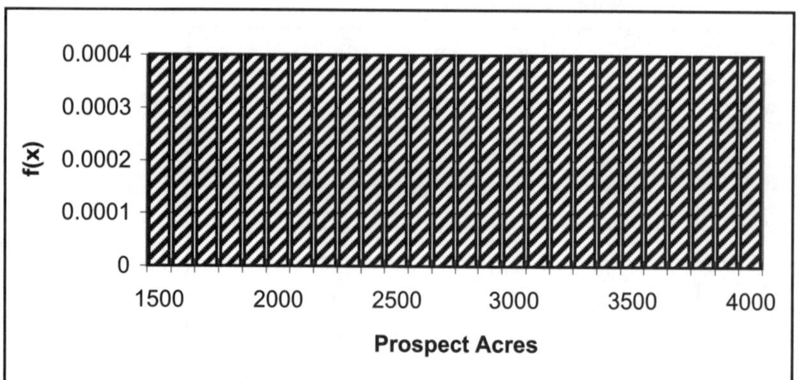

Figure 6.18 Uniform distribution

Figure 6.18 addresses areal extent in a mineral prospect. Based on mapping. the professional believes the area could cover 1500 to 4000 acres (1 acre = 4048 m^2). The figure is a straight line with each value having an equal chance of occurring. Dividing the difference between the high and low values into 1 gives the probability. Many professionals dislike the straight line of a uniform distribution because of "lack of commitment."

By not specifying a most likely value or more complex value, some feel impure and/or a failure. Sometimes data limitations and/or restricted knowledge prohibits stronger statements. The uniform distribution performs quite well in these situations. Disciplines facing data limitations must rely on the uniform. Remember: the distribution should effectively communicate our knowledge.

Triangular Distribution

The triangular distribution extends the uniform distribution by adding a *most likely* value. The professional designates three values – low, most likely, and high. Most software requires the data to be entered in this order or an error message is encountered. The basic format is Triang(*low, most likely, high*). Some software allows the low and high to be the absolute low and high, while others allow flexibility in specifying the low and high as percentiles, like the 10th and 90th percentiles. @Risk allows this flexibility by insertion of a function called RiskTrigen(*bottom, most likely, top, bottom percentile, top percentile*).

Triangular Distribution Equations		
Density, f(x)	$= \begin{cases} \dfrac{2(x-min)}{(ml-min)(max-min)}, & \text{if } min \le x \le ml \\ \dfrac{2(max-x)}{(max-min)(max-ml)}, & ml \le x \le max \end{cases}$	**Equation 6.32**
Mean, μ	$= \dfrac{min+ml+max}{3}$	**Equation 6.33**
Standard Deviation, σ	$= \sqrt{\dfrac{(max-min)(max^2-max*min+min^2)-ml*max*(max-ml)-min*ml(ml-min)}{18(max-min)}}$	**Equation 6.34**

To permit complete flexibility in describing all forms of triangles the density function comes in two variants: one for the portion to the left of the most likely value and the other above the most likely value. The max and min values refer to the absolute maximum and minimum.

Figure 6.19 shows a triangular distribution for a development cost with a minimum value of $100 m, a most likely value of $130 m, and a maximum value of $200 m. The triangular distribution contacts the x axis at 100 and 200. The probability of 0.02 is highest at the most likely point. By changing the most likely value, the curve can take on almost any form of triangle the user desires.

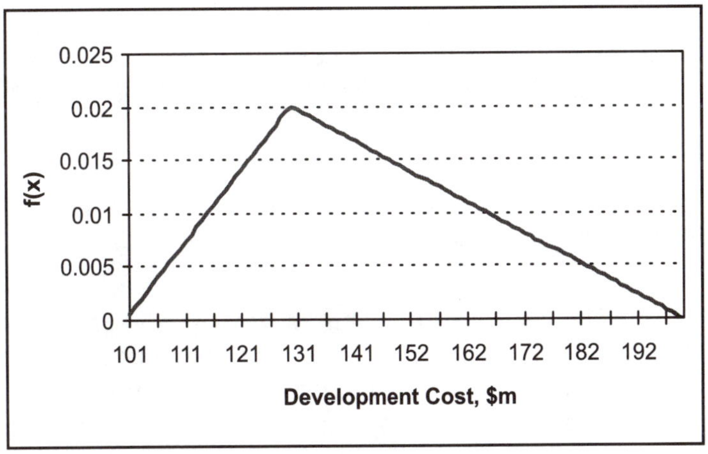

Figure 6.19 Triangular distribution of cost

Some have difficulty accepting the triangular distribution, just like the uniform distribution. What credence can be given to any output based on so little input? This is logical as far as it goes. The limitations of the input are obvious. With limited data, reliance must be place on professional judgment in some form. The proper question to ask is, "What is the advantage of using these distributions relative to available alternatives? About the only alternative is to guess a single value. It is far more reasonable to bound the range of plausible values than to pick a single value. Others rely on established distributions, like normal or lognormal.

Example 6.14: Assuming annual production may be as low as 20, as high as 1139, and have a most likely value of 150, compute the mean, and standard deviation assuming a triangular distribution.

$$\overline{X} = \frac{20+150+1139}{3} = 436.3$$

$$s_x = \sqrt{\frac{(1139-20)(1139^2-1139*20+20^2)-150*1139-150)-20*150(150-20)}{18(1139-20)}} = \sqrt{62{,}421} = 243.9$$

Gamma Distribution

Certain distributions are called *conjugate* distributions, since they have the flexibility to approximate other distributions. The benefit of such curves is the flexibility to approximate a vast array of other curves. The limitation arises from the difficulty in specifying the required input parameters. The gamma distribution needs two inputs, a shape parameter and a scale parameter. The basic function is Gamma (*shape, scale*). Some programs label the shape parameter, alpha and the scale parameter, beta. To utilize this function, the professional must have some knowledge of the shape and scale parameter, which may be difficult when data are limited.

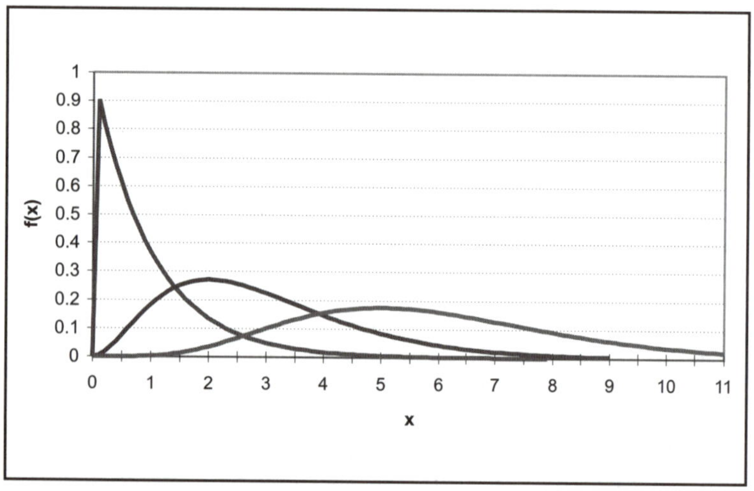

Figure 6.20 Three different gamma distributions

Figure 6.20 summarizes the gamma distribution for three different values of the shape parameter. The three curves are drawn using Gamma(1,1), Gamma(3,1) and Gamma(6,1), respectively. Note that the first curve looks like an exponential curve, the second is slightly skewed to the right, and the third becomes almost symmetric. By choosing different shape and scale parameters many different shapes can be approximated, including highly skewed curves. We would recommend changing the values for both parameters until you feel comfortable with the choice of the shape, scale parameters.

The gamma distribution becomes very useful when experimental data or detailed samples exist. One area of use has been in the area of gas processing, especially in the approximation of heavier ends of the hydrocarbon streams. Prior to the application of the gamma distribution, common practice used a lognormal distribution to approximate C_6+ for PVT matching and prediction. The gamma curve proves especially useful for volatile oils and gas condensate reservoir modeling, and black oil simulations where high percentages of heavier hydrocarbons are present.

The equations for the density function, mean and standard deviation, are provided below. The density function is determined by the interaction between the x values and the selection of the shape and scale parameters. The flexibility in the distribution arises from the interaction of the shape and scale parameters in Equation 6.35. The density function is presented in altered form to simplify the equation. This form works only for cases where α is a positive integer.

Gamma Distribution Equations		
Density, f(x)	$=\dfrac{\beta^{-\alpha}\,x^{\alpha-1}e^{-x/\beta}}{(\alpha-1)!}$, when α is a positive integer	**Equation 6.35**
Mean, μ	$=\alpha*\beta$	**Equation 6.36**
Standard Deviation, σ	$=\sqrt{\alpha*\beta^2}$	**Equation 6.37**

One study has established the empirical relationships needed to approximate the shape and location parameters for applying the gamma distribution.[6.14, 6.15] The values for the shape (α) and scale (β) are defined by the following equations assuming α is unknown.

$$\alpha=\frac{1}{y}(0.5000876+0.1648852*y-0.0544274*y^2)$$

$$\beta=\frac{M_{n+}=\eta}{\alpha}, \quad and \quad y=\ln\left(\frac{M_{n+}-\eta}{M_g}\right) \qquad \textbf{(6.38)}$$

where:

M_g = the geometric mean of the molecular weights

M_{n+} = the average molecular weight of the fractions

η = the minimum molecular weight expected to occur in the system, like 92.14 for heptanes

Other conjugate distributions are available in existing software. These distributions include the Beta distribution and Weibull distribution. Several people swear that the beta distribution is the only distribution that they use. The beta distribution is based on the gamma distribution and works quite well in many applications. Like all distributions, the user must be aware of the limitations and pitfalls arising from misapplying any curve.

Example 6.15: From the following gas analysis, develop the parameters for a gamma distribution using the following information:

$M_g = 81.9 \qquad M_{n+} = 192.7 \qquad \eta = 78.1$

$$\alpha=\frac{1}{\ln\left[\frac{192.7-78.1}{81.9}\right]}*(0.0050+0.1648*0.336-0.0544*0.336^2)=1.631$$

$$\beta=\frac{192.7-78.1}{1.631}=70.26$$

Chi Square Distribution

The chi square distribution serves a different purpose than the previous distributions. Most distributions are used to determine the nature and type of variability. The chi squared distribution, χ^2, determines if data matches any specific type of distribution. This is actually a very important issue. Professionals commonly assume lognormal or normal distributions based on the law of large numbers. The chi square distribution allows formal testing of the accuracy of these assumptions.

Testing for compatibility of data with a formal distribution is called *goodness of fit*. Evaluating the relationship of data to a distribution is called *hypothesis testing*. Saying that multiplicative equations generate lognormal distributions is a testable hypothesis than can be confirmed or denied, provided reasonable data exists. The first step constructs the following formal relationship:

Null Hypothesis: H_o = the data comes from a lognormal distribution

Alternative Hypothesis: H_a = the data doesn't come from a lognormal distribution

Chi Square Distribution Equations		
Density, f(x)	$=\frac{x^{v/2-1}*e^{-x/2}}{2^{v/2}*\Gamma^{(v/2)}}$	**Equation 6.38**
Mean, μ	$=v$	**Equation 6.39**
Standard Deviation, σ	$=\sqrt{2*n}$	**Equation 6.40**

Rejecting the null hypothesis means the data fits some other distribution, although the formulation doesn't identify the alternative distribution.

The chi square distribution is actually a gamma distribution with a shape parameter of $\upsilon/2$ and a scale parameter of 2, where $\upsilon = n-1$ and n is the sample size. The basic equations for a χ^2 are summarized in Equations 4.38 to 4.40, where $\Gamma(\upsilon/2)$ is the shape parameter of a gamma distribution. With the value of υ, the sample size and values for x, a complete distribution is formed.

Equation 6.38 tests the hypothesis that data comes from a specified distribution. The extension makes more sense to most people than the original equations.

$$\chi^2 = \sum_{i=1}^{n} \frac{(O_i - e_i)^2}{e_i} \qquad \textbf{(6.41)}$$

where: O reflects the original data, e the estimated value from the hypothetical distribution density function, and i is the ith data point. The variable e comes from the density function of the distribution specified in H_o. Computing the χ^2 value requires the original data and computation of what the data would look like if it came from the stipulated distribution.. Once χ^2 is computed, it is compared against a table value to determine if H_o or H_a is accepted. Example 6.16 illustrates the process.

Calculating a χ^2 value like 0.787 is meaningless until compared to a standard or reference value. The standardized values capture the variability in the data; most users seek 90-95% accuracy. This means that the analysis accepts that the data comes from a normal distribution when it really does come from a normal distribution 95% of the time. Conversely, the analysis accepts the alternative hypothesis that an-

Example 6.16: Use the cost data in Example 6.2 with a mean of 0.161 and a standard deviation of 0.026 to determine if the normal distribution represents the data.

	(1)	(2)	(3)=20*(2)	
Cost Interval	**O_i**	**f(x)**	**e_i**	**i**
0.10-0.12	2	0.0479	0.0958	0.257
0.12-0.14	2	0.1522	0.3045	0.344
0.140.16	5	0.2750	1.3751	0.032
0.16-0.18	6	0.2829	1.6973	0.011
0.18-0.20	4	0.1657	0.6626	0.134
0.20-0.22	1	0.0552	0.0552	0.009
Total	20	0.98	4.1905	0.787

The values in column 2 are derived from the difference between the cumulative normal percentages, like:

$$f(x) = f(0.12 < x < 0.14) = N\left(\frac{0.12-0.161}{0.026}\right) = N\left(\frac{0.14-0.161}{0.026}\right) = N(-1.58) - N(-0.087) = |-.057-.209| = 0.152$$

other distribution explains the data 5% of the time, when a normal distribution really does fit the data. This is also called a Type I error.

The full table for the χ^2 distribution is given in the table section. A reduced version is reproduced in Table 6.5. The left most column specifies the *degrees of freedom* in the data and is computed by taking the number of classes or data points less one, or df = 6 – 1 = 5. Reading down the leftmost column to a value of 5 then across the row to the 5% column gives a value of 11.07. If $\chi^2 <$ 11.07, the null hypothesis that the data comes from a normal distribution is accepted. If $\chi^2 >$ 11.07, then the alternative hypothesis that the data fits another distribution is accepted. Note that the value changes as the degrees of freedom and significance level varies.

TABLE 6.5

χ^2 Table Values

df	0.05	0.025	0.01
3	7.81	9.35	11.34
4	9.49	11.14	13.28
5	11.07	12.83	15.09
6	12.59	14.44	16.80
7	14.07	16.01	18.47

The computed value of 0.787 is less than 11.07, so the null hypothesis that a normal distribution with a mean of 0.161 and standard deviation of 0.026 matches the data is assumed. As always, some thought must be given to the nature of the quality and accuracy of the sample data. With the small sample size, the values can, and often do, change as additional data is acquired. If other investments in the same area have shown normally distributed costs, then judgment suggests accepting the normal distribution approximation.

Software Options

The selection of the appropriate distribution causes more frustration and concern than almost any all other categories combined. Fortunately, a useful guide is readily available to assist in the selection of the best distribution to a data set. Palisades Corp. markets a program called BestFit™, and Crystal Ball includes a similar, but more limited version. The BestFit program enters data in raw form, as class intervals, or as cumulative density functions. Once that data is entered, the program curve fits the desired distributions to the data and then computes three of *goodness of fit* tests: the χ^2 statistic, the Anderson-Darling (AD) statistic, and the Kolmogorov-Smirnov (KS) test. The data are then ranked according to the best fit, hence, the name of the program. The AD and KS tests are explained in the users manual.[(6.16)]

While additional information is provided about the best distribution to use, the different measures produce conflicting rankings. The question still concerns the best distribution to use. The answer depends on the purpose of the evaluation. Each *goodness of fit* method makes different assumptions. When three

Example 6.17: The rankings and parameters for selected distributions generated by BestFit for the cost data are specified below. Evaluate the results.

(1)	(2)	(3)	(4)	(5)
Distribution	Fitted Values	χ^2 Rank	Anderson-Darling	Kolmogorov-Smirnov
Triangular	(0.0908, 0.16, 0.21)	1	6	10
Normal		2	1	1
Weibull		3	7	4

Three distributions – triangular, weibull, and normal – are shown in column 1. The parameters determined by Bestfit for each distribution are shown in column 2. The χ^2 ranked triangular as the best fit, followed by the normal and Weibull (Column 3). AD and KS ranked the normal distribution as the best fit with triangular ranked 6 and 10 respectively.

different, often conflicting assumptions, accept a normal distribution, accepting the normal distribution is very reasonable. If the output proved to be extremely sensitive to cost, then trying the other distributions would be in order.

Summary of Descriptive Statistics

Trying to describe raw data for making better decisions involves adding a considerable number of terms to ones knowledge base. Hopefully, a better feel for the terminology now exists. Feeling comfortable with distributions takes time and practice, however. There are some distributions in the software that we have never used.

Always remember that using the general histogram function in decision making may be just as good as selecting more popular and common distributions. Most distributions were created because of limited computing power to simplify the calculations. With current tools and resources, both hardware and software, now available, the need for the simplifications may be unnecessary. Always start the data analysis with a histogram, which works quite well as an indicator of variability when large amounts of data exist, most of the time. Precise distributions, like those discussed here, work best when the data is limited, the discipline knowledge provides some guidance, and the results must be communicated to others.

INFERENTIAL STATISTICS

Inferential statistics builds on the foundation laid in *descriptive statistics*. Most investment decisions involve the complex interaction among variables. Descriptive statistics tries to understand the individual variability, while inferential statistics tries to establish the relationship among those variables, or dependence. The first part of this section explores simulation techniques for building simplified systems and measuring the variability in those systems based on individual variable distributions.

The initial simulations first assume that the individual variables are independent of each other. After the concepts of simulation are addressed, discussion turns to establishing dependence among the variables. Simple tests for dependency, and measures are explored and combined with simulation techniques.

Monte Carlo Simulation

Understanding and measuring variability among the individual variables merely begins the risk assessment process. Integrating the information about the variability in the individual elements into the entire system still lies ahead. The basic process for combining individual components to understand system variability is called *simulation* or, the original term, *Monte Carlo simulation*. Simulation is the process of defining relationships that describe system performance, together with formal consideration of the variability in each input element impacting the system. Many assume the name derives from some gaming application. In reality, it was one of a series of code names employed during W. W. II in the development of the atom bomb.

Monte Carlo simulation often invokes a feeling of mysticism when first encountered. Some describe it as a process of mental masturbation; others feel like that it takes too long to perform. Simulation methods merely extend the common "what if" approach. Everyone has rerun programs to answer what if questions, oftentimes for hours or days. It is fair to say that "what if" questions are being run until the final meeting time, at which time more, unanticipated questions arise. Simulation organizes and collects the "what if" answers in an organized, collective process. It just asks "What if" questions more efficiently and logically.

A Graded Slide.

The basic simulation process follows a simple format:

1. Specify the equation or equations of interest, like reserves, production, permeability, price forecasts, phase behavior, NCF, or NPV.
2. Divide independent variables into those known with certainty and those that vary,
3. Specify distributions for the independent variables,
4. Sample repetitively from all varying independent variables,
5. Compute values for each dependent variable on each sample run, and
6. Convert individual values of each dependent variables into a distribution or histogram.

The distributions for the independent variables comes from the descriptive statistics section. Developing distributions is actually easier than building the system of equations. Chapter 2 outlined a process for planning the analysis and building the guidelines that is critical in designing the model.

Equations can be generated for every aspect of an investment analysis. Several examples are given below.

$$\text{Reserves} = 7758 * \text{Acres} * \text{feet} * \phi * \frac{1 - S_w}{B_{oi}} * R_f$$

$$\text{Project Cost} = \text{Daily Rate} * \text{Number of Days}$$

$$\text{Revenue} = \text{Price} * \text{Production}$$

$$\text{NCF} = \text{Revenue} - \text{Opex} - \text{Capex} - \text{Taxes}$$

A dependent variable (reserves, cost, and revenue) is a function of several independent variables in each case. The output of one equation often becomes an input into another equation, as revenue and cost above flow into the NCF equation. Much of the rest of the book builds on this section to derive the variability in specific values, like price, production, etc., along with examples of more detailed applications.

With the available toolkit, simulation of any of these equations is quite simple mathematically. The difficulty comes in building the system to model. Reserves, the volume of minerals available, are a simple volumetric equation, including acre-feet, porosity, water saturation, recovery factor, etc. Acre-feet derives the volume of the mineral, porosity defines the percentage of the volume holding the mineral, water saturation allows for some of the space to be filled with a non-marketable commodity (water), and B_{oi} allows for compressible minerals to change volume as pressure and temperature change, and R_f recognizes that technology won't allow economic recovery of 100% of the minerals.

The volumetric equation appears quite simple and easy, and it is. The problem arises from the need to acquire good data and understand the interrelationship between the input variables, i.e., the dependency between the variables. Available correlations and experience suggest that some of the variables are quite dependent on each other. Water saturation often depends on porosity, and recovery factor will also vary with porosity and water saturation. Since these variables are seldom independent in the real system, they should not be treated as independent statistically.

To illustrate the importance of dependencies, the simulation example first begins with the assumption that the values are independent and adds the dependencies later, to contrast the differences in the results.

Step 1: Defining the Equation

In order to illustrate simulation simply, the reserve equation is reduced to one where all variables are independent. Rewrite the above reserve equation as:

$$\text{Reserves} = \text{Acres} * \text{thickness} * \text{Bbl/Acre Feet}$$

where: h = in feet (= 0.3048 m)
A = in acres (= 4047 m^2)
Bbl/Ac-ft = a net recovery factor based on experience and analogy (= 1233 m^3/m^3)

Recovery factor may not be completely independent, but for early decisions, this may be a satisfactory assumption. Step 1 defines reserves as a function of three variables.

Step 2 & 3: Specifying the Distributions

In step 2 and 3, assume thickness, area, and recovery vary across the formation. In actual applications data on each variable would be used to establish the distribution. The following distributions illustrate the concept: thickness is triangular (100, 130, 200), area is uniform(1500, 4000), and Bbl/Ac-ft is Uniform(300, 600)

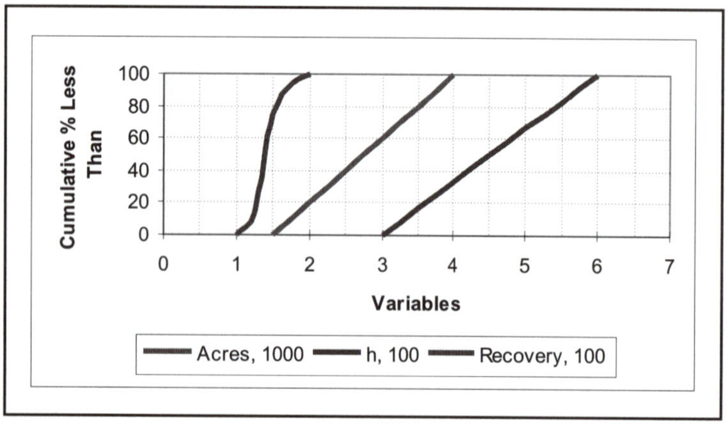

Figure 6.21 Distribution of independent variables for reserve determination

Figure 6.21 converts the equations for each independent variable into a relative cumulative frequency curve, using the equations for the distributions discussed earlier. The x axis has been normalized to plot the three curves on one graph. The recovery and area lines are straight lines, because of the assumption of a uniform distribution. The triangular thickness distribution is the curved line. All distributions, except for uniform, display curvature in the cumulative distribution to varying degrees.

Step 4: Repetitive Sampling from Independent Distributions

Computing reserves requires selecting individual values from Figure 6.21 for thickness, area, and recovery. The critical element is how to select the values. The simplest approach would be to choose values at the users discretion. Unregulated selection of values will reflect the bias of the person performing the analysis, whether obvious or disguised, no matter how well intentioned. To minimize the danger of personal bias, most software uses a *random number* generator to select the percentiles on the y-axis. Once the percentile is selected a unique numerical value for each distribution can be selected.

TABLE 6.6

Example of a Random Number Table

0.2629	0.8779	0.0414	0.7406	0.9822
0.6712	0.9431	0.7066	0.5550	0.5363
0.4651	0.5728	0.5578	0.4398	0.4506
0.4221	0.0927	0.7656	0.9939	0.1958
0.5223	0.7763	0.9788	0.8923	0.2144
0.7224	0.3749	0.8487	0.3204	0.0761
0.6811	0.1552	0.2633	0.9531	0.2324
0.2847	0.1610	0.3599	0.1905	0.3960
0.9212	0.8560	0.7792	0.7209	0.6735
0.3983	0.9128	0.2205	0.9251	0.0574
0.2952	0.1892	0.6283	0.7938	0.8445
0.7755	0.0951	0.2799	0.7746	0.5001
0.6556	0.3355	0.5384	0.1378	0.4316
0.3373	0.6551	0.9372	0.1283	0.3157

A typical random number table looks like Table 6.6. The software generates random numbers based on algorithms to insure that each number has the same probability of being chosen to eliminate biases. The random number generator is essentially based on the use of a uniform distribution with a min value of 0 and a max value of 1. These values were generated using the Rand() function in Excel. A function called Random() extends this simpler format to allow for insertion of nine different distributions into the random number generator instead of the uniform curve.

Inspection of Table 6.6 reveals a dramatic variability in the sequence of values and no discernible pattern; that is, no repetition of values. Statistical formulas exist for testing formally whether undesirable sequences or patterns occur, but that is beyond the scope of this book.

The random numbers are interpreted as a cumulative percentage. The first value of 0.2629 is interpreted as a probability of 26.29%. With this probability, go across from this value on the y axis in Figure 6.21a to the line representing the thickness distribution, then read down to the value on the x axis. The number obtained (about 130 ft.) would be one pass of the simulation. Using the next value of 0.671 in a like fashion would give a value for area of 3100 acres. Applying 0.4651 produces a value of 445 barrels of acre feet. With these three estimates of the independent variable, reserves can be computed from the equation defined in step one.

Figure 6.21a illustrates the traditional Monte Carlo process of sampling. Values are drawn from each input distribution as many times as desired. Each pass then combines the results into the equation(s) of interest defined in Step 1 to produce one estimate. *Sampling* defines how the values of the independent variables are chosen. The process described here continues for the specified number of iterations or trials. This process can take a long time to achieve stability in the simulation (stability is defined below). An alternative to random sampling is *Latin Hypercube Sampling* (LHS).[6.17, 6.18]

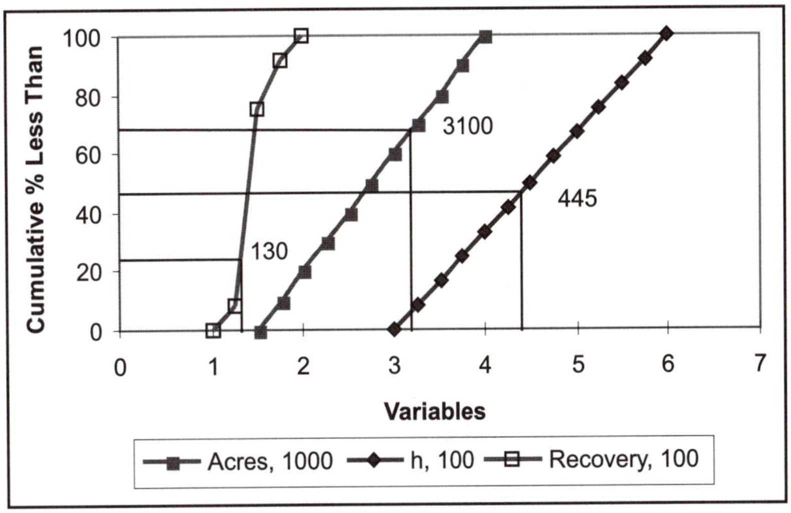

Figure 6.21a Value for one pass of simulation

The Monte Carlo approaches samples from the distribution with no constraints, which permits sampled values to cluster around certain probabilities. The probabilities shown in Figure 6.21a all fell between about 30 and 70 percent. The presence of clustering means more passes are needed to fully capture the full range of values for each input distribution. LHS improves sampling efficiency by splitting each input distribution into segments or intervals and then samples, each one without replacement. The number of segments (called *stratifications*) depends on the number of iterations to be run. For instance, if five passes are made, the number of strata would be 5; likewise, 100 passes would produce 100 strata, n passes gives n segments. The five strata case is shown in Figure 6.21b.

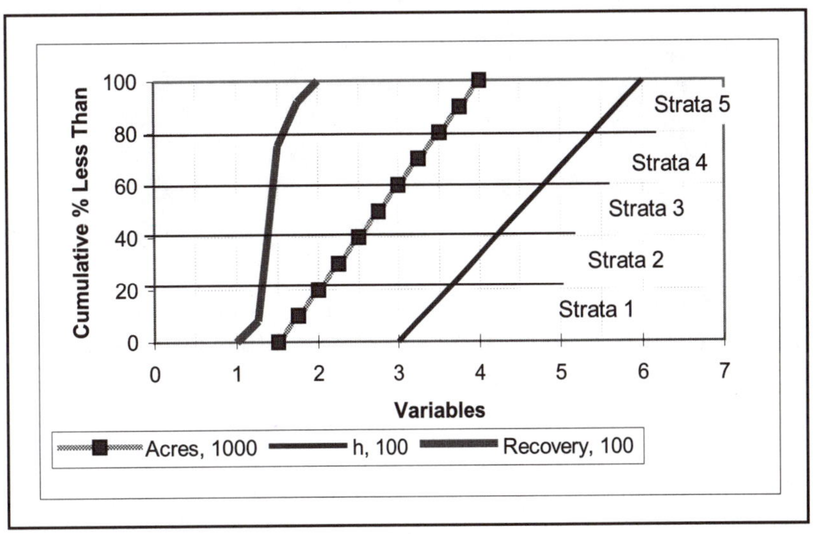

Figure 6.21b Latin hypercube sampling

Each cumulative distributions is split into five segments. Then, each segment is sampled once, independently from the other variables. By sampling without replacement, the input distributions are approximated faster. LHS selects acres from one stratum, thickness from another, and recovery from a third stratum, and then multiplies the values to obtain reserves. The computer never samples again from the same strata.

LHS samples the input distributions more efficienctly, significantly reducing the time required to reach a stable solution. LHS often converges twice as fast for large simulations relative to the Monte Carlo approach. By stratifying the intervals, LHS also has a better chance of capturing inputs with low probabilities of occurring than Monte Carlo. The potential pitfall with LHS concerns the relationship between variables. If the input distributions are correlated, LHS often fails to adequately describe the input distributions. When dependency between variables exists, the developers of LHS recommend using the Monte Carlo approach.

A common question concerns the number of iterations to run. Most software allows as many iterations as desired. The number of runs depends on each individual model. The basic principle, though, is to make enough runs, so that the output distribution converges. By convergence, statisticians mean that key parameters, like the mean, standard deviation, etc., change very little with additional runs. The old rule-of-thumb used to recommend making 300 to 500 runs for each independent variable. In the reserve example, that would mean 900 to 1500 trials. Crystal Ball and @Risk test for convergence differently, but each also monitors the percentage change in the mean, standard deviation, and other components, like percentile distribution. If all the components change very little, the software assumes convergence. Both programs have nice graphics to illustrate the process and keep you informed of the progress. The convergence choices and criterion may be changed according to user specifications.

Step 5: Calculating the Dependent Value

Computing the dependent value follows the logic of the model formulation, as specified in Step. 1. For this example, the calculation is just the product of the three values. Example 6.18 summarizes three iterations in the Monte Carlo Process. Step 5 is the easiest, because the computer runs the specified number of trials and accumulates the results, while the analyst drinks their beverage of choice.

Example 6.18: Use the random numbers in Table 6.8 to compute 3 reserve estimates using the volumetric equation in Step 1.

Random Numbers	Thickness	* Area	* Recovery Factor	= Reserves
0.2629	130			
0.6712		3100		
0.4651			445	179.3
0.4221	140			
0.5223		2850		
0.7223			540	215.5
0.6811	148			
0.2847		2250		
0.9212			580	193.1

The process described in the example follows the same format as the sensitivities commonly applied in evaluating investments. The main difference is that the use of random numbers avoids the bias that creep into most sensitivities, but the same equation(s) and logic is used. The primary deficiency of sensitivities – an organized reporting of results – is corrected in Step 6.

Step 6: Summarizing the Results

The real benefit of the simulation process arrives when the results are summarized in a distribution. After running the desired number of trials, most software plots the results in almost any desired format:

histograms or lines, as either relative or relative cumulative frequencies. The results of the example run for 1000 passes are summarized in Figure 6.21c.

Reserves range from a low value of 64 million barrels to a high value of 440 million barrels. The curve is obviously skewed to the right, as expected (but is not a lognormal distribution). The chance of higher reserves is smaller than for lower reserves. This is consistent with the Law of Large Numbers for a multiplicative calculation. The frequency of occurrences is shown on the left y axis and the probability on the right y axis, just like the first example histogram. The most likely value is about 140 million.

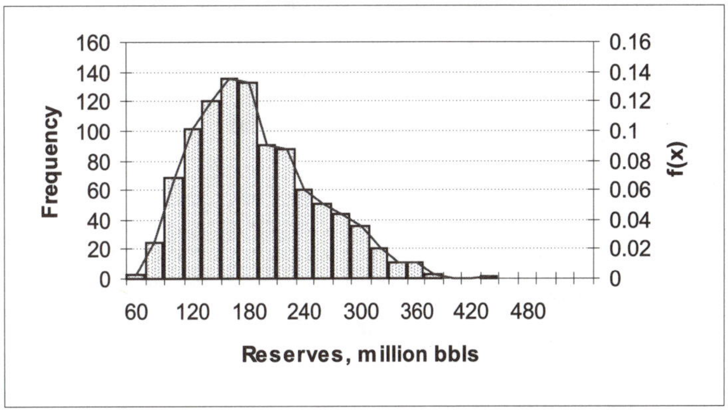

Figure 6.21c Reserve distribution

The curve probably doesn't follow any standard distribution shape, so making a definitive statement about the appropriate distribution would be misleading. Professionals often ask why bother with the extra work to get this figure. Wouldn't just multiplying the low, mean and high values together provide the same information? The answer is no, nor would the additional probability information generated be available. Chapter 8 discusses this issue in some detail.

Just multiplying the low values would give 45 million barrels (=100*300*1500) and high would be 480 million barrels (=200*600*4000). The average of the three inputs gives a mean of 177 million barrels (= 143.3*450*2750). Note that the computed low value is about 14 million barrels lower than the simulation low value, and the high is about 56 million barrels higher (=480-424). The upper value misleads a little because one *outlier* at 440 occurred. The last class interval with more than one value is 380 to 400 million barrels, or about an 80 million barrel differential. Multiplying the low values and then the high values together overstates the actual results. The reason: the chance of three extreme values occurring simultaneously is almost zero.

A second benefit of running the simulation is the detailed output, though the details differ significantly among software. What follows is a common format of the simulation results. The output variable lists the mean result: 177.35 million barrels in Example 6.19. Observe that 177.35 equals the manual calculation in the last paragraph. Means are additive or multiplicative in distributions, but not the other parameters. Each input variable is summarized by cell reference, name, distribution, worksheet (multiple

Example 6.19: Sample output from the reservoir simulation.

Output Variables:		
Cell	**Name**	**Current**
D7	Reserves	177.37

Cell	Name	Current	Worksheet	Formula in Cell
D3	Area	Uniform(1500,4000)	[Book1]Sheet1	'=Uniform(1500,4000)
D4	Thickness	Triang(100,130,200)	[Book1]Sheet1	'=Triang(100,130,200)
D5	Recovery	Uniform(300,600)	[Book1]Sheet1	'=Uniform(300,600)

sheets are permitted), and the actual formula. This a useful summary of the assumptions used in the reserve calculation.

Other reports also help summarize the assumptions and outputs. Example 6.19a specifies the number of iterations (1000), the number of simulations (1), the number of input variables (3) and the lone output variable. For the developer of the model this information is just a repeat, but for others evaluating the information, this provides a quick insight into the details of the analysis. The sampling type, LHS, and the time to run the simulation, 21 seconds, are also reported.

Example 6.19a: Continuation of reserve simulation reports.

Iterations = 1000
Simulations = 1
# Input Variables = 3
# Output Variables = 1
Sampling Type = Latin Hypercube
Runtime = 00:00:21

Summary Statistics				
Cell	**Name**	**Minimum**	**Mean**	**Maximum**
D7	Reserves	58.26357	177.314	428.8875
D3	(Input) Area	1500.31	2750.013	3999.842
D4	(Input) Thickness	101.7048	143.3328	197.4192
D5	(Input) Recovery	300.1031	449.9987	599.9504

Even though the run time was quite quick, the most useful information is still the summary statistics for each input and output variable. The reserve min, mean and max values are reported again. The variation in the input values is also quite interesting. First note that the means are very close to the calculated means. Second that the minimum and maximum values are close to the specified lows and highs, but not quite. Multiplying the low inputs will not give the low reserve value, because the low values won't occur at the same time. The same situation holds for the high values.

Further output reports summarize the characteristics and cumulative percentiles of the input distributions and the output distributions. Example 6.19b shows the report for the reserve example. The far left

Example 6.19b: Reservoir simulation data continued.

Name	Reserves	Area	Thickness	Recovery
Description	Output	Uniform(1500,4000)	Triang(100,130,200)	Uniform(300,600)
Cell	D7	D3	D4	D5
Minimum =	58.26357	1500.31	101.7048	300.1031
Maximum =	428.8875	3999.842	197.4192	599.9504
Mean =	177.314	2750.013	143.3328	449.9987
Std Deviation =	64.36269	721.6611	20.94719	86.59867
Variance =	4142.555	520794.8	438.7848	7499.33
Skewness =	0.64884	1.10E-04	0.3554602	1.41E-04
Kurtosis =	2.973582	1.80012	2.397425	1.800022
Errors =	0	0	0	0
Mode =	160.1851	1562.799	132.812	412.5458
5% Perc =	88.13448	1623.849	112.1435	314.7907
10% Perc =	100.8518	1749.259	117.2933	329.8672
15% Perc =	111.4533	1874.245	121.191	344.9663
20% Perc =	120.3357	1998.889	124.4511	359.8101
25% Perc =	128.8179	2124.894	127.3563	374.9681
30% Perc =	137.272	2249.321	129.9978	389.8583
35% Perc =	144.2664	2374.83	132.5168	404.8745
40% Perc =	152.972	2497.552	135.1422	419.9574

column gives the label for specific categories, like min, max, mean, standard deviation, skewness, etc. The bottom rows labeled 5%, 10%, and so on are the cumulative percentiles for each variable. These values are used to plot the distributions if desired. The actual values go to 95%, but are omitted to minimize space.

One last issue concerns the sensitivity of the output to the choice of input distributions and values. For any equation, some variables are more important than others. Investors like to know which variables impact output the most. Both Crystal Ball and @Risk provide a tornado chart of the correlation between the outputs and inputs.

The Regression column measures the relationship between each input variable and the output variable. The values can range from -1 to 1. Area has the biggest impact with a value of 0.72 and thickness the least at 0.40. The Corr. Coeff. column is based on the Spearman rank correlation coefficient. The traditional correlation coefficient is explained next. The Spearman correlation coefficient bases the calculations on ranks, not absolute values like the traditional measure.[6.20] Although the details of the calculation are covered elsewhere, the interpretation is like the correlation coefficient: the closer either value gets to 1 or -1, the better the *goodness of fit*.[6.19] The Spearman correlation coefficient is called a *non-parametric* test because it works for all distributions. Non-parametric means that the test or equation doesn't require parameter inputs to utilize, like a mean or standard deviation. This makes it more flexible, but also less precise when parametric information is available.

Example 6.19c: Reserve distribution sensitivity.

Simulation Sensitivities for Reserves in Cell D7			
Cell	**Name**	**Regression (Std B)**	**Corr Coeff**
#1	D3 Area	0.7238264	0.7305103
#2	D5 Recovery	0.5327937	0.5149626
#3	D4 Thickness	0.4028285	0.4055009

The output of simulation is extensive and exhaustive. The real benefit is the ability to better approximate the range of possible outcomes in a project. Every professional knows that variability plagues all project estimates. Accurate quantification of variability probably determines success or failure. Other methods, including traditional investment criteria, exist to evaluate variability, but current simulation techniques are the most organized and easy to use.

One limitation of the reserve example is the assumption of independence between the input variables. The simple volumetric equation was selected to minimize dependency. With other relationships, the requirements for independence are harder to achieve. The next section explores ways to incorporate dependencies into the simulation process.

Measuring Degree of Dependency

This section drops the assumption of independence and discusses methods for including dependency. Establishing whether – and the extent to which – variables interrelate is probably more important than deciding on the distributions. Assuming independence, when a dependency really exists, biases the results, often quite significantly. The reserve simulation circumvented the dependency problem by collapsing the dependent variables (porosity, water saturation, etc.) into one recovery factor. As investment analysis becomes more complex, combining geological, engineering design and timing, cost estimates, and economics (like price forecasts), establishing the degree and type of dependency gets quite complicated, very quickly. Sound risk assessment requires reasonable estimates of dependencies.

Two separate aspects of dependency are important.

1. Determining the degree to which variables are interrelated, and
2. Estimating whether the relationship between variables is physically meaningful or just a random error.

Current software allows easy determination of answers to both questions. Again, the issue is knowing what questions to ask and how to interpret the output.

As one example, consider the application of pressure measurements. If all pressure change is attributed to reservoir performance, when it is, in fact, mostly random, the error in conclusions and recommendations are often astronomical. When using or preparing empirical correlations for any analysis, always ask, "What is the reliability of the correlation." Correlations exist for equations of state, cost per unit, mobilization and demobilization time, and inflation vs. product prices. The same question must be asked in all of these areas.

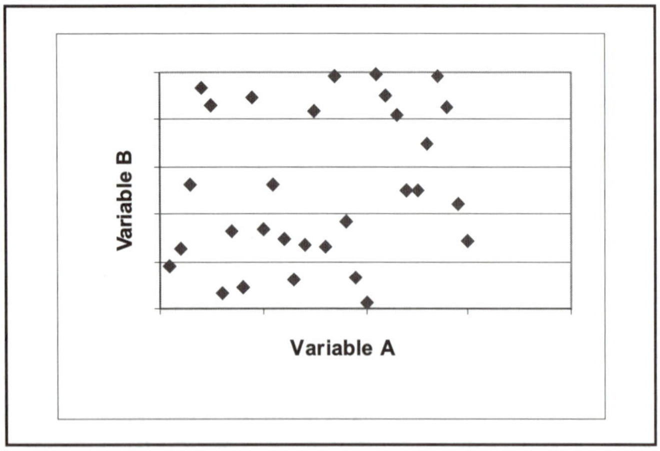

Figure 6.22 Two independent variables

The various degrees of correlation or relationship are shown in Figures 6.20, 6.20a, and 6.20b. The first shows two variables which are totally unrelated with each other, or uncorrelated. No discernible pattern exists between variable A and B. Figure 6.20a displays the typical relationship where every change in C produces an exact change in variable D, or perfectly correlated. The last display, Figure 6.20b, shows a partial correlation between variables E and F. Every change in E impacts the value of F, but not exactly. Variable F is *partially dependent* on E.

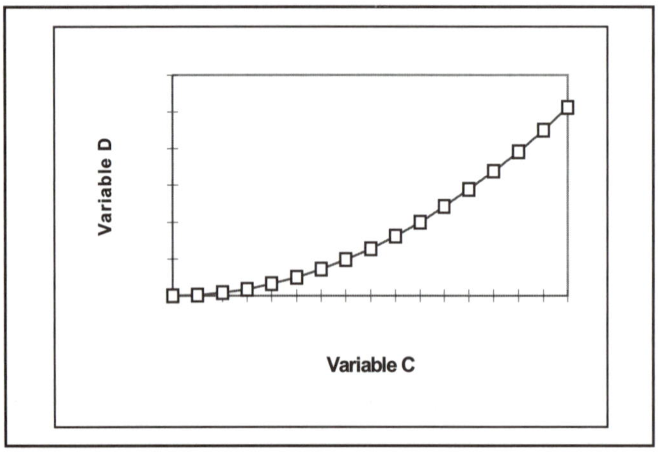

Figure 6.22a Perfectly correlated variables

Figure 6.22b is the proper representation of the real physical and economic world. Most data vary or changes in conjunction with other variables, but measuring the degree of these relationships is difficult, if not impossible. Relationships can be presented in several ways. Probably the easiest approach begins with some very simple notions of relationships, and then expands the concepts. Correlation is defined and illustrated first, and then continuing on to the equations for curve fitting.

Examples of partial relationships include the following:

- porosity and permeability
- porosity and water saturation
- density and molecular weight
- oil density and viscosity
- formation thickness and productivity
- ultimate recovery and product price
- price and design choice
- equipment downtime and maintenance

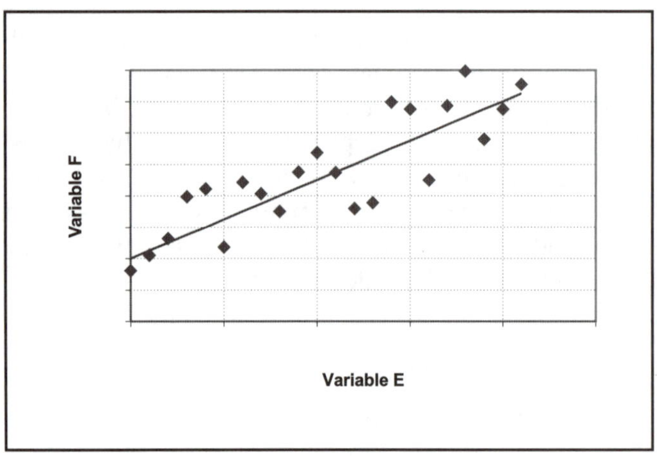

Figure 6.22b Partially correlated variables

Correlation

The Pearson correlation coefficient measures the degree and kind of relationship between two variables. The goal is to measure the extent to which the selected variables vary together, called *covariance* (the product in the numerator), relative to the individual variable standard deviations. The basic correlation equation is:

$$r = \frac{\sum\left[(x_i - \bar{X})(y_i - \bar{Y})\right]}{n*s_x*s_y} = \frac{\sum xy - n*\bar{X}*\bar{Y}}{n*s_x*s_y} \quad \textbf{(6.42)}$$

Where: s_x is the standard deviation of variable x, s_y is the standard deviation for variable y, and the other values are defined as before. The first ratio is the formal definition and the second ratio is the shortcut used by most software. The software first sums the product of the two variables x and y, then subtracts the product of the sample size and the two means.

The denominator defines the total amount of variation within the data. Since the standard deviation is the square root of variance, multiplying two standard deviations yields the variance of the two variables. If the numerator equals the denominator, the ratio is one, so the correlation coefficient is also one. A zero covariance (zero numerator) implies zero correlation. Also note that the correlation coefficient takes on the sign of the numerator, the covariance. If the covariance is positive, so is the correlation coefficient and vice versa.

Example 6.20: Use the initial production rate and facility cost data to determine the correlation coefficient. Rate is in thousands of units and cost in $million.

Initial Rate	Cost	Initial Rate	Cost	Initial Rate	Cost
29.06	737.1	8.27	309	30	1476.4
30	1218.2	17.23	627.2	30	1166.3
21.61	670.7	16.90	1028	30	1413.4
10.08	419.9	30	1528	24.38	2093.1
30	988.3	7.95	563.3	30	1815.3
30	1255.5	30	1431.1	26.22	982.7
30	3225.8	7.23	440.5	30	1661.7
17.70	785.4	14.47	1343.1	16.23	633.5
30	1050.7	23.38	849.5	15.12	336.6
30	1131.9	25.72	603.4	30	899.5

The following input values were obtained by inputting the data into Excel and then using the descriptive statistics option: mean rate = 23.38, standard deviation rate = 8.049, ΣXY = 847,291.32, mean cost = 1089, standard deviation cost = 604.52, n =30

$$r = \frac{847{,}291.32 - 30*23.38*1{,}089.50}{30*8.047*604.52} = \frac{82{,}951.03}{145{,}954.50} = 0.5683$$

Having obtained a correlation, the oft asked question is "what do I do with this number." First, 0.5683 indicates that initial rate and facility cost are partially correlated. The exact interpretation creates considerable confusion in some settings, but is quite simple. A correlation of 0.5683 means that 32.3 % (= 0.5683^2) of the variation in initial rate is associated with the variability in facility cost. Squaring the correlation coefficient converts it back to the variability term used to construct the correlation value.

Be careful, when using the built in statistical functions in Excel. The correlation function assumes that the values come from a population, not a sample, and use 7.94 for s_x and 594 for s_y, which generates a correlation value of 0.587, rather than the sample based values of 0.5683 cited above.

Correlations are an easy way to build dependencies into a simulation. Reverting to the reserve simulation, the same correlation analysis was performed on actual data, and yielded Table 6.7. Thickness and area had a correlation of around 50%, while recovery and thickness produced a correlation of 75%. The third combination in the 3×3 matrix, area and recovery, was found to be so close to zero that the value was set to zero. The main diagonal in the matrix shows a value of 1.0, indicating that each variable is perfectly correlated with itself.

TABLE 6.7

Sample Correlation Output

	Thickness	Area	Recovery
Thickness	1	0.50	0.75
Area	0.50	1	0.0
Recovery	0.75	0.0	1

Adding correlations or dependencies to simulations impacts the output, often significantly. The following table compares different reserve simulations for different types of correlations. The first column repeats the calculations assuming independence between thickness, area, and recovery. The values differ slightly from the previous simulation, because a different set of random values was selected. The second column applies the correlation matrix in Table 6.8. The third column uses the same correlations, but reverses the signs.

TABLE 6.8

Impact of Correlation on Output

	Reserves: Independent	Reserves: Positive Correlation	Reserves: Negative Correlation
Minimum =	52.78	46.95	92.12
Maximum =	405.33	471.65	271.92
Mean =	177.40	184.19	170.35
Std Deviation =	64.73	84.09	38.20
Variance =	4190.85	7071.80	1459.44
Skewness =	0.67	0.80	0.10

When positive correlations are used, the low and high values get further apart, as indicated by the standard deviation rising to 84 million barrels. This should make sense because a high area is associated with high thickness and recovery, with a positive correlation. With a negative correlation, the process is reversed; low thickness leads to high area, etc. The net impact is that the reserve distribution becomes narrower, with the standard deviation falling to 38.2 million barrels.

Some will draw the inference that positive correlations increase deviations and negative ones reduce deviations. That conclusion is correct for this example, but only this example. Simple, multiplicative equations generate such results, but additive, ratio, and non-linear, etc. equations yield very different results. Every simulation differs in the number and type of relationships postulated.

Two problems arise from using correlation coefficients. First, most people cannot relate intuitively to terms like 0.56 and often ask, "What does this mean." Second, and more serious, the correlation coefficients computed in the more basic software packages are always *simple correlation coefficients*. The term "simple" means that the correlations are computed two at a time, totally ignoring all other variables. This exclusion means that the correlation may understate or overstate the real relationship between variables. Better statistical software computes the partial correlation coefficient to correct this problem. Another corrective approach applies regression or a curve fitting method.

Regression

Traditional math education uses equations for a linear line: Y = m*X + b. Statistics extends this relationship by formally recognizing that the relationship is imperfect, so the term called a residual (e) is added: Y = m*X + b ± e. The residual, e, is the vertical difference between the estimated line and the actual values of Y.

Figure 6.23 illustrates residuals as the difference of each value from the estimated line. Regression is the process of finding a line that minimizes the sum of the absolute differences between the actual values, Y, and the line. This means finding value for m and b to minimize the residuals. When the residuals are all zero, a perfect linear correlation (r = 1.0) exists.

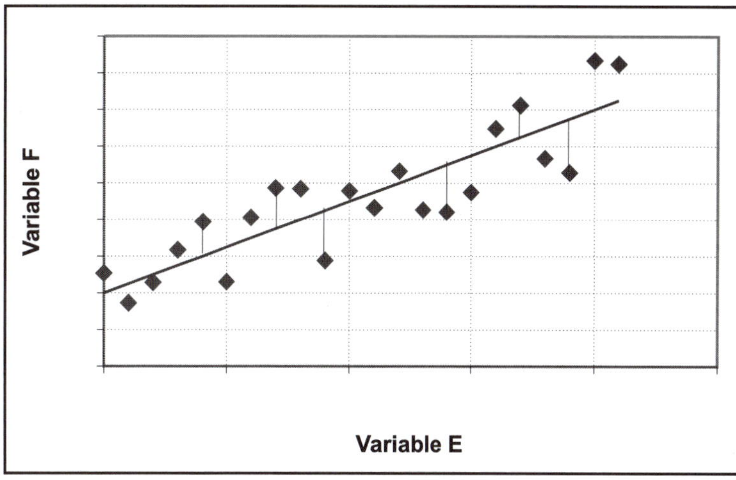

Figure 6.23 Illustration of minimizing residuals

Solving the equation for the slope and intercept values requires finding answers for several equations subject to the constraint that the residuals are minimized. The solution solves the slope equation first, then the intercept formula as illustrated in Equation 6.43.

$$\text{slope (b)} = \frac{\sum xy - n*\overline{X}*\overline{Y}}{n*s_x^2}, \quad \text{and} \quad \text{intercept (a)} = \overline{Y} - b*\overline{X} \qquad \textbf{(6.43)}$$

where the values were defined in the correlation coefficient equation.

Example 6.21: Use the initial rate and cost data from the last example to determine the equation for a line.

$$b = \frac{847{,}297.3 - 30*23.38*1{,}089.5}{30*7.91^2} = \frac{82{,}951.03}{1{,}878.29} = 44.16$$

$$a = 1{,}089.5 - 44.16*23{,}37 = 56.75$$

A one unit increase in rate requires additional capital outlay of $44.16 million.

An often asked question addresses how the correlation coefficient relates to the equations for linear or nonlinear lines. Everyone has dealt with equations of lines and most have heard reference to variables being correlated, but few understand that equations for a line and correlation are the same thing, just expressed differently. Correlation generates a dimensionless relationship between variables, while a regression preserves the units of x and y. Pearson created the correlation coefficient as a vehicle for comparing relationships totally independent of the units used.

The relationship follows from the equations used so far, as summarized below.

$$r = \frac{\sum x*y - n*\overline{X}*\overline{Y}}{n*s_x*s_y} \quad \text{provides input to} \quad b = \frac{\sum x*y - n*\overline{X}*\overline{Y}}{n*s_x^2}$$

The previous example on reserves input r into the simulation. Once r is specified, the computer also knows the sample size, n, and the standard deviations for the input distributions. With information on r, n, s_x, and s_y, the numerator of r can be calculated. The numerator in both equations is the same. With a known n and s_x, the slope coefficient, b, can be derived once the correlation and input distributions are specified. The only difference between r and b in a *univariate* relationship is the units. Slope parameters carry the units of the variables, capital cost per unit of initial production rate in the example, while r is dimensionless. This interpretation becomes more complicated with multivariate models, but the same principle holds.

Software solutions for a regression also provide details of *the goodness of fit*. Excel finds the best fit by inputting the data in rows or columns, then applying the regression package in the Analysis Tools or Data Tools depending on the version. Lotus offers a similar option The output comes out like Example 6.21a.

Example 6.21a: Regression results for initial production rate on capital cost.

Regression Statistics	
Multiple R	0.587933
R Square	0.345665
Adjusted R Square	0.322296
Standard Error	497.661
Observations	30

	Coefficients	Standard Error	t Stat	P-value
Intercept	56.75334	283.482953	0.20020019	0.842771
Depth	44.16297	11.4829079	3.845974372	0.000634

Multiple R, at 0.587, repeats the correlation coefficient. Multiple R normally relates to multivariate regressions, while correlation coefficient is limited to two variables. Most software uses this one label to capture both univariate and multivariate relationships to save space. R^2 converts the Multiple R to a domain of 0 to 1 and is computed by squaring the Multiple R ($0.345 = 0.587^2$). R^2 defines the total variation in Y (cost) explained by the independent variable X (initial rate). Adjusted R^2 modifies the R^2 to reflect the sample size. Because smaller samples have less variability, sample size can be very important in computing R^2. The adjusted R^2 is always smaller than the R^2 value, and the greater the gap between the two, the more important sample size is in the evaluation.

Another common question is "what is a good R^2 value?" The correct answer is that it depends on the nature, amount and type of data, and model. For time series data, like price forecasts, production profiles, cost escalation, etc. R^2 often falls in the 50-95% range, because each value is correlated with other time periods. For physical data where time is irrelevant, good or acceptable R^2 values might fall in a range from 20 to 50%. These are just rough rules of thumb. Every model is different and must be assessed individually. Remember: R^2 may be too high as well as too low.

Example 6.21b: Residuals, e, for cost versus rate regression.

(1)	(2)	(3)	(4)=(2)–(3)
Observation	Cost	Predicted Cost	Residuals =e
1	737.1	1,340.292	-603.192
2	1218.2	1,381.642	-163.442
3	670.7	1,011.115	-340.415
4	419.9	501.829	-81.929
5	988.3	1,381.642	-393.342
6	1,255.5	1,381.642	-126.142

Standard Errors of Regression

The standard error value of 497.61 is important for simulations, because it defines the standard deviation of the errors, e. The residual is defined as the difference between the actual cost and the estimated cost, based on the equations for the estimated line. The vertical lines in Figure 6.23 measure the residual for each observation or data point. Example 6.21b summarizes the first six data points. Column 2 is the actual cost, predicted cost from the regression is in column 3, and column 4 measures the difference.

The residuals are measured in the same units as the dependent variable, cost in this example. With an array of residuals, the usual parameters, mean and standard deviation, can be computed. The slope and intercept parameters are computed so the mean value of the residuals equals 0. Because the residuals measure the error in estimating Y, the term *standard error* is used instead of standard deviation. The standard error is interpreted just like the standard deviation: if the mean value of X is substituted into the regression equation, about 66.6% of the time, Y would take on the following interval values:

$$Y = 55.75 + 44.13*23.38 - 497.66 = \$591.84 \text{ million}$$

to

$$Y = 55.75 + 44.13*23.38 + 497.66 = \$1{,}587.16 \text{ million}$$

To capture this variation within a spreadsheet simulation instead of using the correlation coefficient, enter the equation with a distribution for the error term in the following format. The Normal distribution will select random values for the error term which will be added or subtracted from the estimated value depending on the sign.

$$Y = a + b*X + \text{Normal}(0, e) = 55.75 + 44.13*X + \text{Normal}(0, 497.66)$$

The plot of residual values for cost is given in Figure 6.24. Calculating residuals is very easy; interpreting the importance and validity is much harder. To insure that the coefficients are unbiased, understanding the residuals is crucial. Biases in the residuals influences estimation of the slope and intercept coefficients which alters any forecasts in turn. Various texts describe more detailed methods for evaluating residuals.[6.21, 6.22]

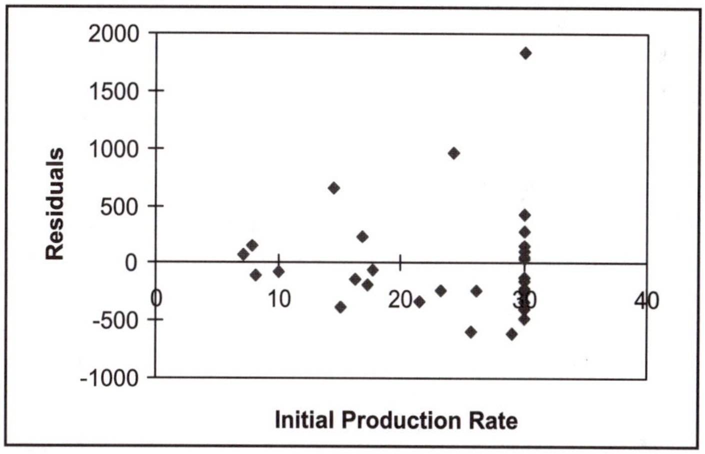

Figure 6.24 Residual, e, for cost estimation

Interpreting residuals depends on two basic types of data: order and unordered. Ordered data includes times series like prices and costs where the data follows a natural progression. Product price in one year is expected to vary relative to another year. Thus, a natural order exists for presenting and analyzing data. Cost is unordered, because the choice of input order is a matter of choice. The ideal in either case is for the residuals to vary randomly. With unordered data, this is more difficult since the data points can be rearranged arbitrarily to achieve the appearance of randomness. The residuals in Figure 6.24 appear random and don't generate major concerns, until the very last x values, which occur about 30 thousand units. The concentration of residuals around 30 thousand indicates that an upper bound exists in the data. This raises questions about the cause of the upper constraint and how and if, it can be overcome. This suggests that a careful review of the model is in order to determine these causes, and possible solutions. This exercise is beyond the scope of this section.

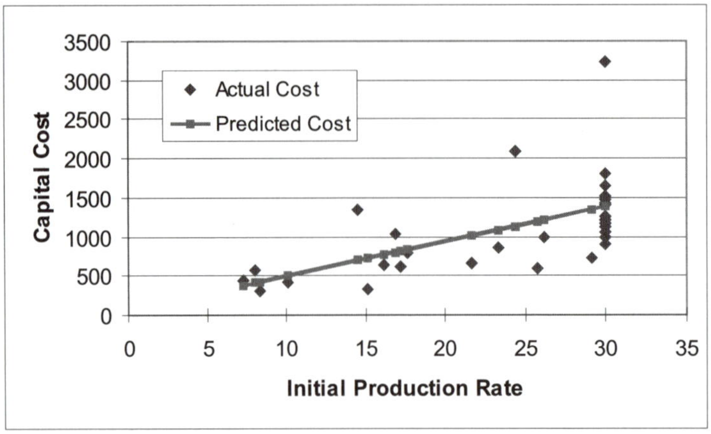

Figure 6.25 Actual versus estimated cost values

Another equally valid approach for reaching the same conclusion graphs the actual values and the regression line together, as shown in Figure 6.25. The vertical difference between each value and the line is the residual, as shown in Figure 6.24, with the same interpretation. Some prefer to see Figure 6.25.

Hypothesis Testing

Other information provided in the regression output is geared toward testing a single hypothesis: does the regression really explain variation in the data or is the relationship an illusion. Two basic relationships are tested: one is whether the $R^2 = 0$, and the other is a test of the coefficients a = 0 and b = 0. The tests are summarized as:

$$H_o:\ R^2 = 0,\ a = 0,\ b = 0$$

$$H_a:\ R^2 \neq 0,\ a \neq 0,\ b \neq 0$$

The basic tools for testing the hypothesis are the Student t test and the F test. For larger samples, the F test is just the Student t test squared. This is an oversimplification, but captures the essence of the issue. The Student t-test is used primarily to evaluate the individual coefficients, and the F-test to appraise R^2. These tables are listed in the tables section at the end of the book. The tables were generated using the F-text and t-test modules in Excel's Analysis Toolpack, which can be found under the menu Tools and Add Ins.

The formula for the t-statistic is shown in Equation 6.44. The numerator is the coefficient, b or a, minus the hypothesized population value, normally assumed to be 0, but other values could also be used. The second division shows the standard b – 0 assumption. The value for e is the residual, and the portion under the radical is the sum of squares of the variable x.

$$t = \frac{b-\beta}{\dfrac{e}{\sqrt{\sum x^2 - n*\bar{X}^2}}} = \frac{b-0}{\dfrac{e}{\sqrt{\sum x^2 - n*\bar{X}^2}}} \quad \textbf{(6.44)}$$

where all the values are defined as before.

The first ratio summarizes the information for the regression in Example 6.21a. The denominator coincides with the information under the Standard Error column and the t value of 6.52 for b and 8.11 for a fall under the t statistic column.

Example 6.22: Compute the t statistic for a and b in the gravity versus depth regression example.

$$t = \frac{b-\beta}{\dfrac{e}{\sqrt{\sum x^2 - n*\bar{X}^2}}} = \frac{44.169}{\dfrac{497.66}{\sqrt{1,878.29}}} = \frac{44.169}{11.48} = 3.84$$

$$t = \frac{56.75}{283.48} = 0.20$$

Numbers like these are meaningless unless compared to a standard reference. At the start of the chapter, the notion that statistics merely normalizes data to dimensionless units was presented. That normalization process allows the creation of standard tables for comparison. An abbreviated Student t table is shown in Table 6.7, with the full table is presented in the table section at the end of the book.

df	$t_{0.75}$	$t_{0.90}$	$t_{0.95}$	$t_{0.975}$	$t_{0.99}$	$t_{0.995}$
27	0.684	1.314	1.703	2.052	2.473	2.771
28	0.683	1.313	1.701	2.048	2.467	2.763
29	0.683	1.311	1.699	2.045	2.462	2.756

The standard is to accept the alternative hypothesis, H_a, when the computed $t > t_\alpha$. This means that the coefficient differs significantly from 0. To select t_α choose the significance level (a common value is 95%), which means the test correctly accepts the right hypothesis 95% of the time, or errs 5% of the time, and the degrees of freedom, df. The degrees of freedom is the sample size less the number of computed parameters, two in this case: a and b. At 28 degrees of freedom (28 = 30 – 2), $t_{0.95} = 1.701$. The most important parameter, the slope coefficient, has a t-value of 3.84, which is greater than 1.701, indicating that the slope differs significantly from 0, with a 5% error margin. The 5% also means that the statistics will accept the alternative hypothesis of a significant difference, when the value really equals zero, 5% of the time.

The intercept value of 56.75 leads to a t-value of 0.20, which is less than 1.701. Accepting the null hypothesis fits expectations, since a project with no production should avoid all costs. Graphically, the estimated line goes through the origin. As an aside, the choice of the critical value, 1.701 assumes a one-tail hypothesis test, or the 5% is just on the right side of the distribution. For a two-tail test, use half the error amount, or 0.025 and the column at 0.975. This means the error is 2.5% on either side of the distribution.

Hypothesis tests on the R^2 also could also be performed, but the exercise only confirms the slope coefficient hypothesis when only one independent variable is involved. The F-value is 14.52 and the critical F value is 3.37, so R^2 also differs significantly from zero. When multiple variables are involved just follow the same principles as outlined with the t table using the F table in Excel.

One last output in Example 6.21a is the column labeled P value. The value for the intercept, a, is 0.834, and 0.000634 for the slope, b. This indicates the α value at which the null hypothesis would be accepted, 0.06% error, or 0.9994 significance. This is a sensitivity on the choice of α. Since value like 0.05 or 0.10 are common, these are sufficiently small to worry about spurious correlations. The value is found by the software searching the t table for the df and significance level when the null hypothesis is accepted.

Prediction Intervals

The traditional simulation equation is built on the relationship $Y = a + b*X \pm e$, where e is assumed to be a Normal(0, e) distribution. The problem is that the values were obtained from sample data, and predictions often extrapolate beyond the ranges of the sample data. This formula works when predictions are limited to the data range. When extrapolating beyond the data, the formula must recognize that extension. The equation for computing forecast or prediction intervals is:

$$P_{y|x} = \hat{Y} \pm t_{\alpha} * e * \sqrt{1 + \frac{1}{n} + \frac{(x_p - \bar{X})^2}{\sum x^2 - n * \bar{X}^2}} \qquad \textbf{(6.45)}$$

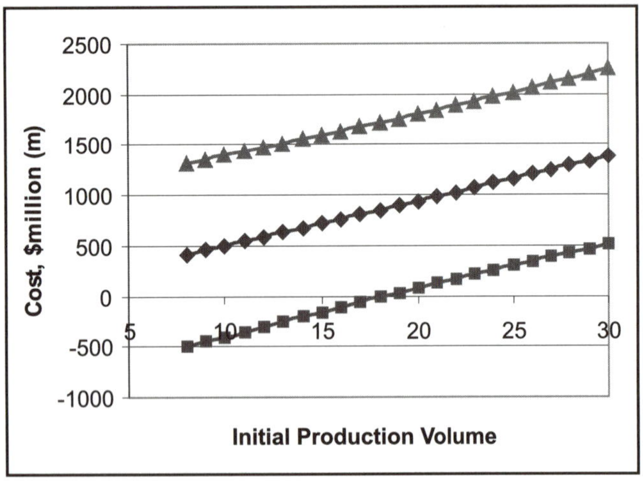

Figure 6.26 Prediction interval for forecast

A variety of methods, including Equation 6.45, exists for including increasing uncertainty as the model deviates from the sample. The fundamental idea is to achieve a relationship like Figure 6.26. The centerline is the predicted value for cost based on varying production rate values. The upper and lower lines reflect the 95% prediction interval for each independent value. Comparing the high and low lines against the actual estimates produces reasonable results only for the upper values, but not for the lower lines. For X values between 8 and about 17, the lower line shows negative costs – highly unlikely. This demonstrates the problem with using any equation without understanding the implications.

Figure 6.26, along with the R^2 and other metrics indicates that efforts to explain investment cost should be expanded to include other possible causes, like type of facility, location, composition of production, etc. Such analysis is absolutely essential for aninvestor trying to make accurate investment decisions.

Words of Caution

When applying the equations for inferential statistics, several mistakes tend to recur. Among these is the over reliance on R^2 to determine the best fit. Large correlations can always be obtained: the question is the relevance of the model to reality. Because the purpose is to predict relationships, the estimating equation must be consistent with the underlying physical and economic system. An R^2 of 65% may be preferred to an R^2 of 95% if it is matches theory better.

It is easy to revert to the trite phrase, "Figures lie, and liars figure." Books exist that portray the abuse of statistics, from the high correlation showing the relationship between births and the number of storks (Norway in the early 1900's) to the sperm whale catch and stock prices in the City of London. The notion of being able to get any desired value is true. Does this mean statistics are meaningless? Absolutely not, because the same argument holds for all analytical procedures. Any person abusing statistics will abuse their geoscience, engineering, business, etc. data. Data abuse or misuse exists in all disciplines, not just statistics.

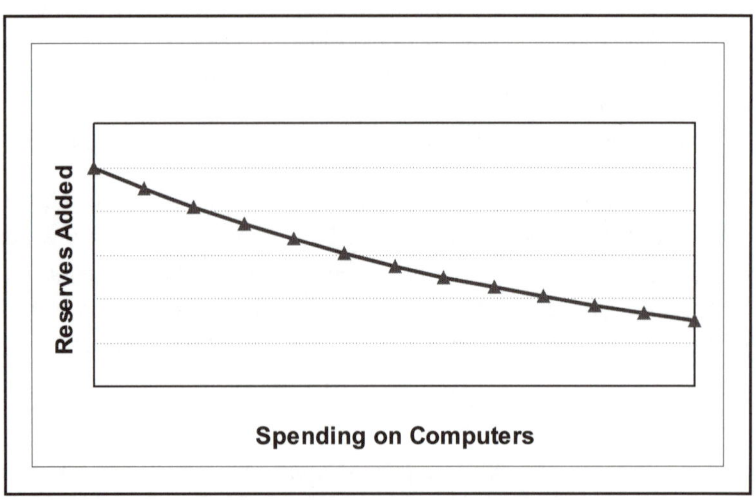

Figure 6.27 Spurious relationships

Figure 6.27 shows one example of a spurious relationship, relating spending on computers with mineral reserves added. The implication seems to be that purchasing faster, more expensive computers reduces reserves. Yet, mineral reserves were declining anyway, totally ignoring computer expense.

Conscious abuse of statistics is less common than unknowing misapplication of principles. An example of the misapplication of statistics can be seen in the estimated equation for predicting reserves in water drive reservoirs.(6.23) Equation 6.46 shows the basic relationship. The R^2 of 0.96 is unusually high for data without any time trend. Closer inspection shows why: by including both S_w and $1 - S_w$ the model explains 100% of the reservoir volume. This duplication is how to lie with statistics.

$$RO = 4259\left[\frac{\phi(1-S_w)}{B_{oi}}\right]^{1.312}\left[\frac{k}{\mu_{oi}}\right]^{0.0816}(S_w)^{0.463}\left[\frac{P_b}{P_a}\right]^{0.249}, \quad R^2 = 0.96 \qquad \textbf{(6.46)}$$

These words of caution lead to several fundamental rules for formulating and studying data variability. The rules include three golden rules, as follows:

Golden Rule 1. Use several types of estimation procedures as a check on the reasonableness of the statistical approach.

Golden Rule 2. Match the time and monetary cost of collecting and analyzing statistical values with the likely benefits of producing better evaluations; building expensive data bases and performing detailed statistical analysis is worthwhile only when it adds value.

Golden Rule 3. Relationships established from models are not a substitute for judgment; they complement judgment. This is the art and science of every evaluation.

Golden rule 3 is the simple, most important element in producing better evaluations. Relationships obtained from any and all models should never be worshipped. For instance, some of the basic correlations used to size separators originated in work done in the early 50's using limited data and data specific to Oklahoma. Forecasts based solely on judgment or personal opinion may also be fraught with danger. Both approaches have produced horrendous mistakes, ranging from the Edsel to Mukluk. But, together the judgment and science enhance the chance of investing wisely.

SUMMARY

Understanding and modeling variability allows formal recognition of risk, the initial step in managing risk. Every estimate, in every investment decision contains errors. The real question is "How bad are the errors?, "What is the impact of those errors?", and "Can the project survive these forecasting errors?" The statistical techniques outlined in this chapter merely formalize and organize the informal analytical procedures operating under the twin labels: experience and judgment. No methodology is perfect now nor ever will be. In fact, if a perfect, easily understood methodology ever did exist, the need for professionals would drop significantly.

The merits of every analytical tool depend largely on the judgment of the professionals involved. Inputting bad values or misinterpreting the results defeats the fundamental objectives of investment analysis, and, ultimately, may destroy the core assets of the business. Variability is the key feature of each investment decision. Without understanding variability, good decisions are tough, if not impossible to achieve. With a foundation of for understanding variability, the next chapters begin to apply the concepts.

REFERENCES

6.1 Kuhn, T., *The Structure of Scientific Revolutions.*

6.2 Bernstein, P., *Against the Gods*, John Wiley (1996).

6.3 Newendorp, P., and J. Campbell, "Decision Methods for Petroleum Investments," John M. Campbell & Co. (1968).

6.4 Campbell, J., "Statistics and Professional Applications," *The American Statistician* (Feb. 1995).

6.5 Campbell, J. M., *Oil Property Evaluation*, Prentice Hall (1959).

6.6 Roundtable discussion, *OGJ* (Oct. 2000).

6.7 Webster, A., *Applied Statistics for Business and Economics*, Irwin (1992).

6.8 *ibid.*

6.9 Beyer, H., *Standard Probability and Statistics*, CRC Press (1991).

6.10 Excel 2000 helpscreen, Microsoft (1994).

6.11 @Risk Users Manual, Palisade Corp (2000).

6.12 Pearson, K., "On a Method of Determining Whether a Sample of Size n Supposed to Have Been Drawn From a Parent Population Having a Known Probability Integral Has Probably Been Drawn at Random," *Biometrica*, 25, 379-410.

6.13 Cooper, D. and L. Davidson, *CEP* (Nov 1976), p.173.

6.14 Whitson, C. H., "Characterizing Hydrocarbon Plus Fractions," European Offshore Petroleum Conference (1980).

6.15 Brule, M, "Characterization Methods Improve Phase-Behavior Predictions," *OGJ* (Feb 1985), p. 87.

6.16 BestFit Users Manual, Palisades Corp. (1994).

6.17 Startzman, R. A. and R. A. Wattenbarger, "An Improved Computation Procedure for Risk Analysis Problems With Unusual Probability Functions," *SPE* Paper No. 13772 (Mar. 1985), pp. 123-127.

6.18 Iman, R. L., Davenport, J. M., and D. K. Ziegler, D. K. "Latin Hypercube Sampling (A Program Users Guide)," Technical Report Sand79-1473, Sandia Labs (1980).

6.19 Spearman, C., "The Proof and Measurement of Association Between Two Things," *American Journal of Psychology*, Vol. 15 (1904), pp. 72-101.

6.20 Taro Yamane, *Statistics: An Introductory Analysis*, Harper & Rowe, Inc. (1967).

6.21 Christ, Carl, "Econometric Models and Methods," John Wiley and Sons (1966).

6.22 Amemiya, Takeshi, *Advanced Econometrics*, Harvard University Press (1985).

6.23 API, *Statistical Analysis of Crude Oil Recovery and Recovery Efficiency*, Bulletin, D14 (Oct. 1967).

OTHER ARTICLES ON STATISTICS

Stanley, L. T., *Practical Decisions for Petroleum Engineers*, Petroleum Publishing Co. (1973).

Spiegel, M. R., *Statistics*, McGraw Hill Book Co. (1961).

Kaufman, G. M., *Statistical Decision and Related Methods in Oil and Gas Exploration*, PrenticeHall Inc. (1964).

Schlaifer, R., *Probability and Statistics for Business Decisions*, McGraw Hill Book Inc. (1959).

Miller, I. and J. E. Freund, *Probability and Statistics for Engineers*, Prentice-Hall Inc. (1965).

Grayson, C. J., *Decisions Under Uncertainty*, Harvard Business School (1960).

Lipschutz, S., *Probability*, McGraw-Hill Book Co. (1965).

Chierici, G. L, *JPT* (Feb. 1967), p. 237.

Smith, P. J. and J. W. Buckee, *SPE* paper 13776 (Mar. 1985), pp. 165-174.

Dedorey, G. J., "Estimating methods for proved recoverable reserves of oil and gas," 10th World Petroleum Congress, (1979).

Cain, W. O., *OGJ* (17 Nov., 1980).

Lohrenz, J., *OGJ* (10 Mar., 1986), pp. 72-79.

Sears, G. and N. Philips, "Fractured reservoir evaluation using monte carlo techniques," *SPE* 13797 (Mar. 1988), pp. 183-188.

Caldwell, R., *JPT* (Apr. 1986), pp. 447-452.

Keating, J., *JPT* (Apr. 1986), pp. 443-446.

Martin, B., *JPT* (Oct. 1988), p. 1383.

Garb, F., *JPT* (June 1988), pp. 765-778.

Genrich, J. and F. Summer, *JPT* (Sept. 1989), pp. 930-932 and 983-985.

Walls, M., *OGJ* (22 Jan. 1990), pp. 61-67.

Murtha, J., *JPT* (1994).

Sarshar, M. M., *et. al.*, *JPT* (March 1992), pp. 332-340.

Schuyler, J., *OGJ* (25 Dec., 1989), pp.139-142.

Schuyler, J., *OGJ* (8 Jan., 1990), p. 80.

Hallmark, T. L., "Detecting country risks to oil companies in lesser-developed and newly industrialized countries." SPE 19860 (Mar. 1989), pp.735-739.

Grassick, D., *et. al.*, *JPT* (Nov. 1990), pp.1374

Clapp, R. and R. Stibolt, *JPT* (Oct. 1991), pp.1252-1257.

Damsleth, E., *JPT* (Apr. 1992), pp. 402-408.

Bradley, M. and A. Wood, *JPT* (Nov. 1994), pp. 965-971.

NOTES:

CHAPTER 7

TIME SERIES VARIABILITY

Every investment analysis requires forecasts about technical and economic performance. Achieving the desired investment objectives depends critically on the ability to forecast future events, or, realizing that exact predictions are impossible, understanding the variability of those future events and selecting investments that avoid bankruptcy in bad times, and create opportunities in the good times. This is nothing more than the old phrase "buy low, and sell high." This section addresses time, for time is the basis of all risk. Bernstein argues that "time and risk are the opposite sides of the same coin, for if there were no tomorrow, there would be no risk."[(7.1)]

Each component of NCF and WACC face the risks associated with time: production, price, Opex, Capex, inflation, taxes, interest rates, etc. The best investors never try to measure these values exactly, because that is impossible. A favorite phrase in our consulting and teaching relates to the notion that, if we could predict "any" single variable exactly, we would be playing the future or options market from an exotic resort location, rather than teaching or consulting. Understanding the variation in each element, and then using that knowledge to control the investment risk accordingly, is the purpose of forecasting. Efforts to mitigate unknown or little understood risks are doomed to failure.

This chapter seeks to provide enough information about forecasting to encourage professionals to face the risks of time, rather than ignoring or burying it. The tornado diagrams, presented in Chapters 2 and 8, show the direct relationship between the performance metrics and time series inputs, like price and exchange rates. Every investment analysis, ever performed that allowed prices to vary, finds that cash flow and profitability depend on price as one of the most important variables. The importance of inflation and exchange rates reflect country specific issues, as they vary over time, but each impacts project performance. What is less evident is the dependence of other measures on these projections, like the fact that the inflation rate forms the foundation of the discount rate (Chapter 3) and escalation rates. Moreover, many multinationals believe inflation rates are the biggest influence on exchange rates. Even more troublesome, commodity prices alter the inflation rate.

Crystal balls that make perfect predictions of the future do not exist. Horace commented centuries ago "Many shall be restored that now are fallen, and many shall fall that now are in honor." Too many investors, recognizing the inherent inaccuracies in predicting the future, choose to either ignore it or simplify it by using one number. These investors then argue that using a single price forecast allows them to rank the investment opportunities. This and later chapters demonstrate why this argument misdirects decision-making, and leads to inferior investment performance.

The history (interpreted as failure) of forecasting has probably generated more ridicule of technical professionals, planners and economists than any other subject. Many of the jokes about economists (our favorite being "economists exist to make weather forecaster appear accurate") arose from silly forecasts. Classic examples of forecasting mistakes include the pronouncement by the famous economist Irving Fisher that the high price of stocks should not be a cause for alarm about 3 days before the stock market crash in 1929. Or, the pronouncements by the Nobel price winners in economics that their risk management company, Long Term Capital Management, was solvent, days before announcing the loss of billions of dollars. The ability to cite examples of forecast mistakes abounds, but finding mistakes in previous forecasts helps very little in making profitable investment decisions. Before beginning the discussion of forecasting, understand that anyone who makes forecasts will err; the real question is whether their mistakes cause irreparable damage or merely inconvenience the performance metrics.

The chapter begins with an overview of forecasting, tying the forecasting process to strategic planning (Chapter 1) and NCF derivation (Chapter 2). The concepts and ideas are applied to four common time series variables:

- Production forecasts
- Commodity price forecasts
- Inflation forecasts
- Exchange rate forecasts

These topics are covered with the intent to inform readers about the process and issues, not to create recognized experts in the field. Every investment decision includes forecasts about these variables, either directly or hidden in the black box called software. All subsequent technical and investment decisions ultimately flow from these inputs.

FORECASTING: ART AND SCIENCE

Everyone is a forecaster, making short-run forecasts in their personal lives: is it going to rain today or will I have a good day? Forecasts like this are more art than a science, since the actual forecast is quite subjective with little reliance on the scientific approach or detailed investigation of available data. Some investors certainly use the subjective approach, with some success, when financial markets rise beyond all reason. The evidence also suggests that the subjective approach destroys those gains when financial markets correct themselves.

Successful investors normally adopt a more scientific approach, usually at a greater cost, but not always improving accuracy. The drive for greater science results from the interaction of many forces acting in combination – greater government intervention, global warming, internationalization of the economies, and, lastly, volatility in commodity prices. Growth in the sciences contributing to forecasting has brought with it good and bad features. On the positive side, forecasters are equipped with a stable of methodologies, which allows anyone to attack the problem of predicting the future with a logic and set of assumptions that can be conveyed to interested parties. Well specified approaches to forecasts permits decision makers to appraise the reasonableness of the assumptions, methodology, and, hence, the conclusions.

The negatives side ensues when sophistication overshadows the quality of the input information and the decision makers understanding of assumptions and methodologies. Managers make investment decisions on poorly understood or possibly ignorance about the basis of the forecasts. To overcome this deficiency, five questions must be addressed by management. They are:[7.2]

1. For what purpose are the forecasts to be used: i.e., what decisions will be made on the basis of the forecasts?
2. Who will use the forecasts and how much must the user know about the premises to use the forecasts effectively?
3. What is the conceptual model used to generate the forecasts? In particular, which variables influence the forecast variable(s) and how, in a qualitative sense, are they expected to influence the variables being forecast?

4. What data is needed to develop the conceptual model, and, more importantly, what data is actually available?
5. How often are the forecasts to be produced? (Every hour, day, week, month, etc.).

The author of these suggestions, Gwellyn Jenkins, one of the world's foremost experts on forecasting, goes further by stating:

> *"Forecasting systems frequently go wrong not only because of poor technical quality of the forecasts, but also because insufficient attention has been paid to the relationship between forecasting and decision-making. Even where forecasting is done well, if insufficient attention is paid to the use of the forecasts by decision-makers, then the forecasts may be rendered useless, because they are ignored or manipulated by an organization's power structure."*(7.3)

Items 1 and 2 are essential to the process of understanding time-induced variability. Forecasts are generated for different purposes, from strategic planning to project valuation, each seeking to achieve different objectives. Long-range forecasts produced to analyze strategic plans seldom filter down to the operational, project valuation levels. Budgeting, then utilizes a different set of forecasts entirely. Operations oftentimes receive just one set of forecast values to determine investment metrics.

Items 3 through 5 require management attention. Forecasts can only be analyzed once the conceptual needs and data requirements are determined. When conflicting forecasts emerge, some frame of reference must exist to address the conflict. Quite often, a preconceived, biased option clouds the judgment of the decision-maker, since we are "all prisoners of our own experience." More importantly, the logical, orderly process allows management to trace the causes back to the initial assumptions, and correct any distortions.

Figure 7.1 shows the process suggested by Jenkins for integrating management decisions into the forecasting process. The benefits from implementing his system arise from the following results.

1. It distinguishes between policy variables, which are under control of the organization, and environmental variables, which fall outside the organization's control. (Review Chapter 1)
2. The scenario approach can be integrated by forecasting the environmental variables, like pessimistic, most likely, and optimistic, since forecasts without some measure of uncertainty are of limited value.
3. It generates different, but consistent forecasts needed by different levels of users.
4. It emphasizes the necessity of combining quantitative forecasts with subjective or judgmental forecasts.

Management review and approval of forecasts must recognize that few models are rich enough to "cope with the complexity of real life." The key driver in successful forecasting is the continual challenging of the forecasting process. Saying that a single forecast value deviated from the actual value contributes nothing to the discussion. That was known with certainty when the forecast was made. Questions that are more relevant concern whether the forecast approximated the variability in the forecast value, and did the investor employ that information properly and wisely?

Methods for forecasting are as varied and only as good as the person(s) generating the forecast and using the information, just like every other discipline. Matching the right tools with the investors forecasting needs is the challenge. Forecasting methods fall under three general headings: subjective, deterministic, and statistical. Subjective captures the feel, experience, or often times, just wishful thinking of the forecaster when they say, "I believe." The technically trained tend to dismiss this approach as being unscientific, but evidence suggests that some investors are quite successful using the subjective approach, although very few forecasters are consistently successful using the subjective approach.

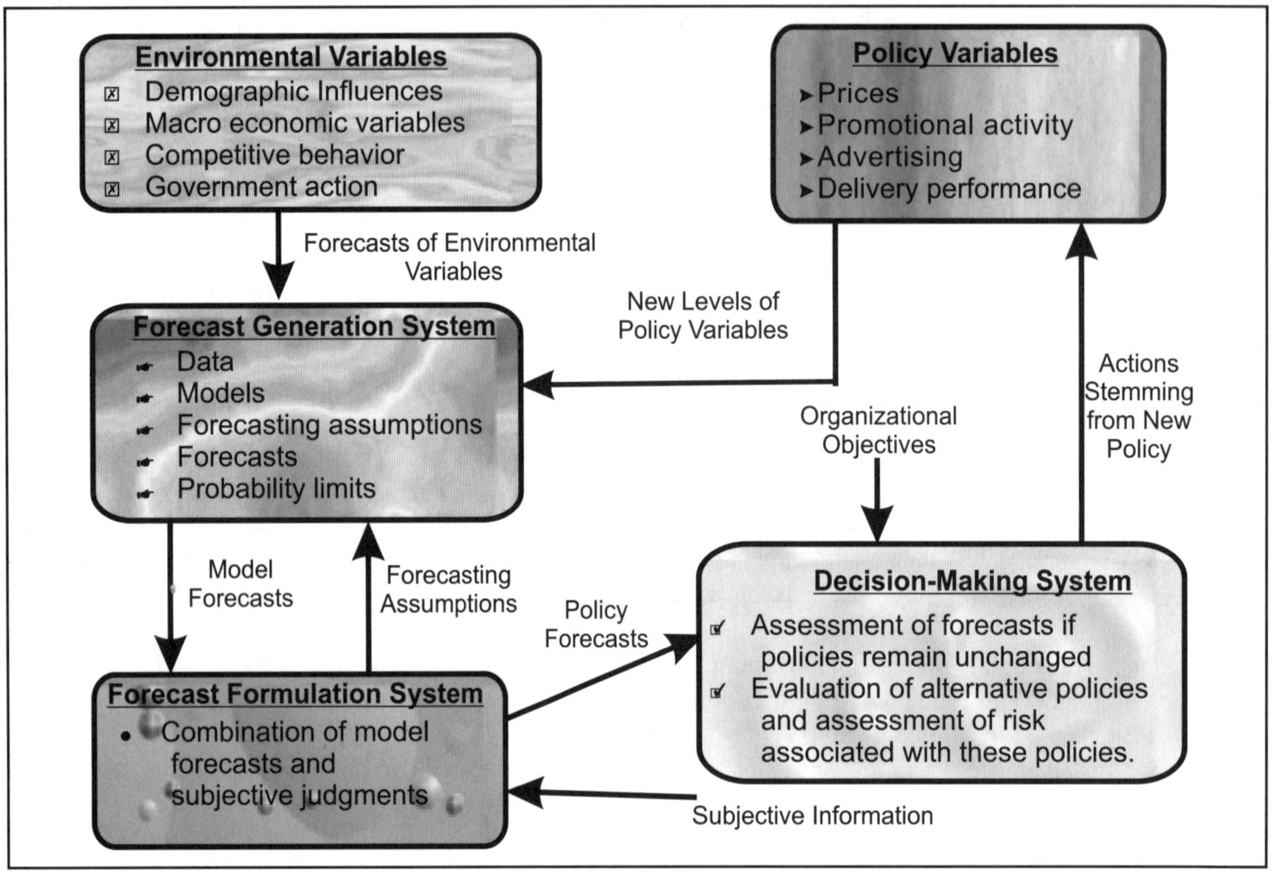

Figure 7.1 A forecasting system and its links with the decision-making system

CHAPTER 7

This chapter focuses on the statistical applications and models necessary to generate forecasts of the variability of various time series variables. Note that understanding variability is the objective, not providing just one value. Four separate topics cover the basic process: production volume, commodity prices, inflation, and exchange rates. Most of the attention is given to production volume and commodity prices, with inflation and exchange rates being of secondary importance.

FORECASTING PRODUCTION VOLUMES

Classical investment valuation assumed that future production volumes could be accurately characterized by single values over any time dimension – a week, month, or year. The choice of time frame varies across industries, depending on the nature of the product and the characteristics of the market place. Day traders in financial markets obviously work on hourly or daily units. Other products, like toys, worry about the Christmas season, because they make over half their profits in December. Most industries combine short-term and long-term forecasts, depending on the assignment of the respective departments.

A classical example of using historical information comes from the petroleum industry, where each well starts production at a particular rate and then declines over time. The main environmental driver here is the non-renewability of asset. The typical analysis begins by collecting historical production data, either on a monthly or daily basis, and plotting it relative to time, like Figure 7.2.

Actual production data exists for 48 months, or four years of production. The solid line running through the actual production represents the trend line for the data, which is then extrapolated for another four years. The most notable result of this process is the reduction of a highly variable data stream into a single line. The future production estimates are presented as if they were known with certainty, which is

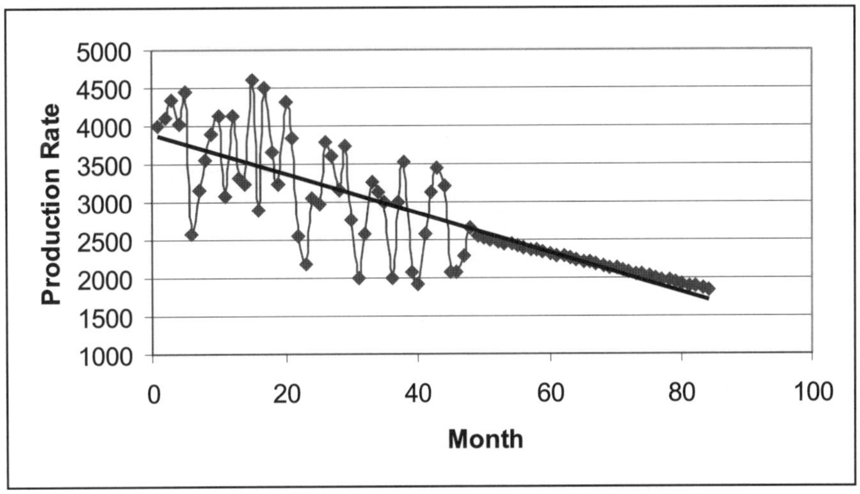

Figure 7.2 Predicted future production volumes

blatantly false. So, the question becomes how to characterize future variability in production volumes, instead of ignoring it.

Several approaches exist to measure and incorporate the risk into the analysis. Following the regression format outlined in the last chapter, a regression was run on the production data.

$$\begin{aligned} \text{Production}_t &= a_0 + a_1 * \text{Month } (1, 2, \ldots, 48) \pm e_t \\ &= \underset{(23.5)}{4051} - \underset{(5.49)}{33.61} * \text{Month} \end{aligned} \qquad \textbf{(7.1)}$$

where: production comes from historical production, month is integer values from 1 to 48, and α_0 and α_1 are the intercept and slope parameters, respectfully.

The intercept is 4,051 with production 33.61 units each month. The values in parenthesis are the t-statistics, which must be compared to the t-table in the back of the book. Since each value is greater than the test statistic of roughly 2.0, both parameters are statistically different from zero.

The statistical results are summarized in Example 7.1. The R^2 value of 0.396 indicates that time (the independent variable) explains less than 16% (= 0.396 * 0.396) of the variation in production. The adjusted R^2 lowers the 0.396 to reflect the small sample size, while the standard error of the regression (SE) measures the variability in the residual term, e, above. The F-statistic, which determines the significance of the entire equation, of 30.12 indicates that the R^2 value differs significantly from zero, or is more than just a spurious relationship.

Example 7.1: Results for Equation 7.1.

Statistics:
R-squared: 0.396
Adjusted R-squared: 0.3833
SE: 574.5
F Statistic: 30.213

The result indicates that much of the variation in monthly production depends on factors other than time. Moreover, the overall accuracy of the line, called a decline curve, is quite low. Investors make this calculation millions of times every year as part of their year-end reserve reporting and to predict future cash flows. Fitting a straight line to the actual data obviously misses the really important drivers behind production volatility. Extrapolating that line into the future discards any formal recognition of risk.

The P_{10} and P_{90} lines around the forecast line, as shown in Figure 7.3, indicate the potential deviation in actual production, which increases over time. One interesting point is the lower confidence interval

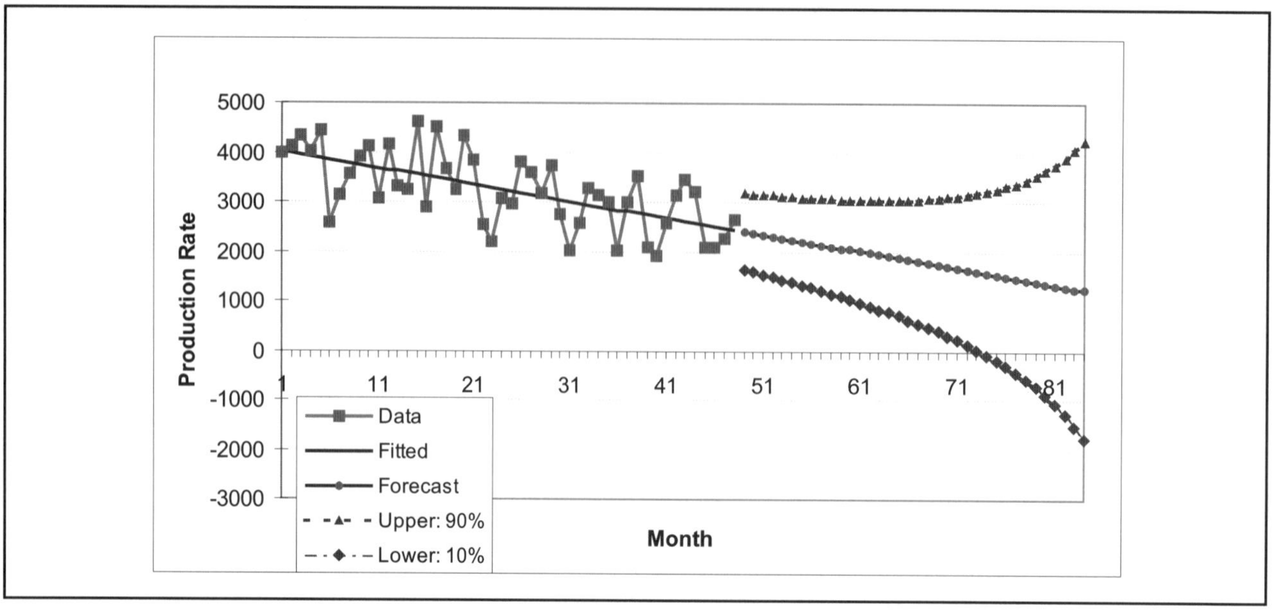

Figure 7.3 Historical data with variability in predicted values

that goes negative just past month 71. Since negative production makes no sense, the model must add a conditional statement indicating that negative values result in abandoning the well, causing the entire project to terminate at that point. This is an example of *options modeling*.

The easiest way to incorporate information about variability utilizes the previous information in Equation 7.2

$$\text{Production}_t = 4051 - 33.61 * \text{Month}_t \pm \text{Normal}\ (0,\ 574.5) \tag{7.2}$$

where the variables are defined before and Normal represents a normal distribution with a mean of zero and standard deviation of 574.5. When Gauss developed the regression equations, he specified that the equation for the line should be drawn such that the residual mean was zero, and the distribution of the error terms followed a normal curve.

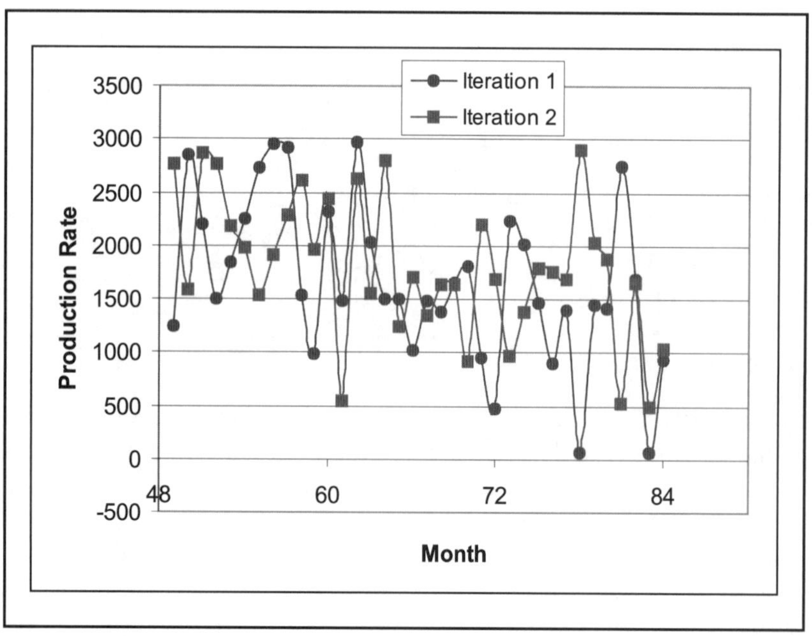

Figure 7.4 Production estimates for two iterations in simulation

When Equation 7.2 is inserted into a simulation model, each iteration results in production forecasts, like those shown in Figure 7.4. Each simulation iteration follows an entirely different pattern over the forecast period of 48 months. The variation in production, when multiplied by price, impacts the revenues received from the project. Iteration 1 shows several production values approaching zero starting about month 80. Depending on the investor's financial condition and needs, these months represent potentially worrisome periods. The prospect of deteriorating economics should warn the investor to begin to plan for ways to handle this situation, when and if it occurs. Relative to Figure 7.1, the investor needs to determine their options and choose the proper decision variables.

Computing the expected value after running several thousand simulations will yield the same straight line shown in Figure 7.3, but Figure 7.4 identifies the variation in production, allowing the investor to evaluate the consequences on their profitability or other investment objectives. By directly analyzing risk, the investor can determine the likelihood of bad (or good) outcomes, and the magnitude of those consequences.

This example demonstrates the simplest form of trend analysis; where the dependent variable rises or falls a certain amount each time-period. Another important element of production forecasting concerns seasonal variations in the product. Each product line may face very different seasonal variations. For instance, retailers receive as much as 20% of their gross sales in the 7 days after Christmas, as shoppers hunt for bargains. Combined with the pre-Christmas sales, the Christmas season may account for over 50% of yearly sales. Likewise, automobile sales are the highest at the end of the month and when the new product lines come out; whereas other products, like home heating depend on weather conditions.

Rather than begin a new example to illustrate seasonal effects, Equation 7.1 can be extended to include the effects of weather or other forces. Equation 7.3 shows two different possibilities: the first adds an independent variable to capture weather, and the second adds a component for changing demand for gasoline.

$$\text{Production}_t = \alpha_0 - \alpha_1 * \text{Month}_t + \alpha_2 * \text{Temp}_t * \text{Humidity}_t + \alpha_3 * \text{Miles Driven}_t \pm \varepsilon_t \qquad \textbf{(7.3)}$$

where: Temp = average or extreme temperature during the month,
Humidity = average or extreme humidity during the month (the product approximates wind chill),
Miles Driven = total automobile miles driven during the month.

The overall trend of a producing well or field may be downward, but the producer can expand or contract production depending on demand for their product. Cold winters or hot summers raise prices with the increasing demand. Likewise, summer time driving also increases demand and price, usually leading to higher prices; hence, greater profits to the producer. Every energy provider builds similar models. Generating the α coefficients merely requires collecting data on the identified variables and repeating the regression analysis discussed earlier.

The important lesson here concerns the utilization of the information obtained to understand and mitigate the risks, not to discard it. Under the classical system, the investor would insert the expected future values for temperature, humidity and miles driven into the equation to compute expected future production. Since the expected value of the error term is zero, the classical system reduces a stochastic, highly variable process to a simple, deterministic equation, like Figure 7.2, plus maybe some sensitivities or rudimentary scenario analysis. With the current toolkit, the investor can formally address variation by modifying Equation 7.3 as shown in Equation 7.5.

$$\begin{aligned} \text{Production}_t = \alpha_0 - \alpha_1 * \text{Month}_t + \alpha_2 * \text{Normal}\,(\overline{\text{Temp}_t}, 25\%) * \text{Triangular}\,(90\%, \overline{\text{Humidity}_t}, 120\%) \\ + \alpha_2 * \text{NLogNormal}\,(\overline{\text{Miles Driven}_t}, 20\%) \pm \text{Normal}\,(0, \text{SE}) \end{aligned} \qquad \textbf{(7.4)}$$

Where: all the variable names are as before, with the bar indicating mean or expected values for each variable, the % numbers indicating deviations from the mean for each distribution. The distributions and the respective parameters are for illustration of the concepts only.

Equation 7.4 reflects the classical mixed model, where some variables are known with certainty (Month), and others vary over time. Plugging Equation 7.4 into the economic model allows the investor to determine the variability of revenues, taxes, costs, NCF, and then their profit metrics. The investor will never know ahead of time the actual temperature, humidity or miles driven in a particular month, but historical data approximates the variability quite well.

Knowing the variability in production provides an estimate of risk, but the question of what to do with the information may still elude some. The decision variables (Figure 7.1) depend on the specific requirements of the investor. Suppose the production is used to generate electricity for the residential market. As production varies, the ability to supply the volume specified in a contract will also vary. If the contract contains a penalty (as they normally do) for failing to deliver the specified volumes, the investor must make some decisions about alternative supplies, and weigh the relative costs of those alternatives. And, the relative attractiveness of the alternatives will be influenced by the likelihood of occurrence, as established by Equation 7.4. Understanding risk forces the investor to formally consider their options ahead of time, as opposed to the all too often practice of scrambling to meet demand when these "surprises" crop up.

All industries face similar problems, where demand varies over time depending on product specific drivers, forcing suppliers to design and construct new plants to satisfy these changing demands. If they construct the facilities too early, excess idle capacity costs reduces profits, but, if the facilities are constructed too late, a competitor may preempt them and increase their market share, at your expense. A classical example of risk mitigation comes from electrical generation, where they must mix base, intermediate, and peaking electrical generation to supply their customers. By understanding the variability in the trend and seasonality, the chances of making the best decision increases exponentially. Methods for handling issues like these are covered in Chapter 10.

FORECASTING PRICES

Understanding price forecasts probably presents more problems and sources of errors in valuations than any other single component. Part of the complexity stems from the myriad of forces that interact to determine the price for any commodity or service, some tangible and others very intangible. Probably the toughest intangible component arises from the globalization of the world economy. With instant communication and sophisticated markets for options and futures, perceptions about the future may be more important than the real intrinsic values in the market place, be it the stock market, telecommunications, etc. Many lament the failure of the markets to reflect their perception of intrinsic value, without fully understanding that traditional value metrics, like stock price/earnings ratio, merely reflect the underlying dynamics of a national or international economy. All such metrics are fluid, not forever constant, and the successful investor adjusts to those underlying changes, not relying on rote, unrelenting application of old ideas.

Being critical of many investment applications still faces the reality that no one can predict the future with certainty. The best that can be hoped for is an understanding of the underlying drivers of price changes, understanding the variability in prices, and planning to mitigate the undesirable consequences of price declines, while taking of advantage of increases. This section explores the basic approach for predicting price variability, avoiding the notion that prices are ever perfectly predictable.

Remembering the imperfection in price forecasting is essential to avoiding historical investment failures. It would be very satisfying if everyone would remember and practice the basic tenets of investing: avoid excess optimism, never follow the pack, and take your profits when you can. But that expects too much, primarily because defining excess optimism, when you are in the pack, and the right time to take profits is never possible with certainty. Therefore, the analysis reverts to understanding the uncertainties.

One consequence of investment failure is certain, however. Everyone who has forecast prices ultimately admits their failure, as demonstrated later. The reaction to those failures is to ignore variability and assume price will be some value, x per unit, forever. Investors justify this simplification by arguing that prices can't be predicted anyway, so the purpose of the valuation is just ranking alternative investments.

Later chapters demonstrate why ranking under simplistic assumptions destroys value, because the investor never appreciates the potential profits accruing from variability.

The General Pricing Model

The supply and demand issues raised in the previous section combine to generate prices based on the concept of equilibrium. Many disciplines utilize equilibrium as a concept, but equilibrium is just a concept created by humankind to make calculations. Most disciplines talk about supply and demand, but price forecasting views the situation differently.

The basic equation assumes that suppliers maximize shareholder value by implementing the following equation:

$$\text{Profit (NCF)} = P * Q - r * K - w * L \quad \textbf{(7.5)}$$

where:

- Q = quantity of the product supplied
- P = the price of the product
- r = the cost of capital (WACC)
- K = the amount of capital used in production
- w = the cost of labor
- L = amount of labor used to produce the product

Supply describes the change in production (Q) as price (P) and costs (rK, wL) change. Supply curves are generated by holding costs constant, and varying prices, as Figure 7.5 shows. At a price of $2.50 per unit, 10 units of the product are supplied. When gas prices rise to $3.00 and $3.50 per unit, suppliers increase production to 15 and 20 units, respectively. When supply reaches the capacity limits, the curve becomes vertical.

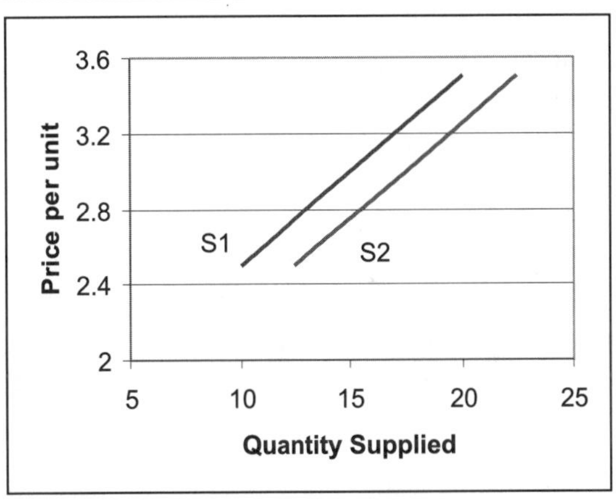

Figure 7.5 Example supply curve

Curve S_1 assumes that the other forces impacting supply, like cost, environmental regulations, etc. are held constant. Changing the cost of labor (Opex) or capital (Capex) shifts the curve in the opposite direction. Increasing Capex reduces the volume supplied at the same price. Curve S_2 demonstrates the increase in supply resulting from a reduction in Capex. At the same price, producers are willing to supply more of the product.

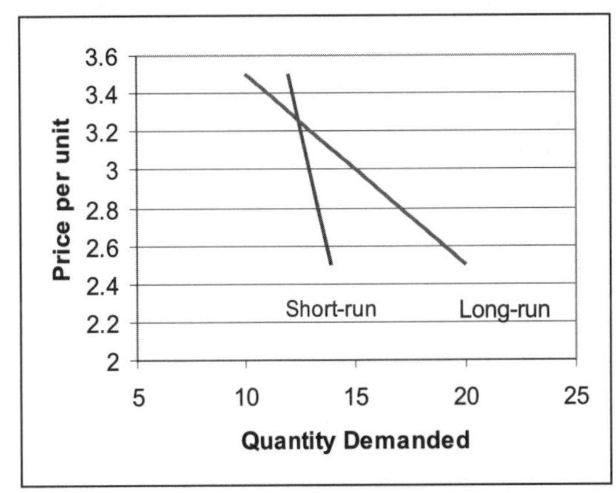

Figure 7.6 Example demand curve

Demand, like supply, responds to several economic forces, including price, income, price of substitute products, taste or preferences of consumers, and so on. Demand curves are normally generated by correlating historical demand levels with price, income, alternative costs, etc. By holding income and other variables constant, demand curves have a negative sloped relationship with price, as shown in Figure 7.6. The negative slope comes from a simple budget constraint: with the same income and an increase in product price, the consumer has to curtail consumption (demand) to stay within their budget. Two demand curves, a short-run and long-run, are shown to demonstrate changes in the curve over time.

Economists use the term – *price elasticity* – to describe the relationship between price and demand. Equation 7.6 defines elasticity using the information in Figure 7.6.

$$E_d = \frac{\%\text{ increase in demand (Q)}}{\%\text{ decrease in price (P)}} = \frac{\Delta Q \Big/ (Q_1 + Q_2)}{\Delta P \Big/ (P_1 + P_2)} \qquad (7.6)$$

$$= \frac{\dfrac{10-15}{(10+15)/2}}{\dfrac{3.5-3.0}{(3.5+3.0)/2}} = \frac{\dfrac{-5}{12.5}}{\dfrac{0.5}{3.25}} = -2.6$$

Where: Q represents the quantity demanded and P the price of the item, and the numerical values come from Figure 7.6 using the long-run curve.

The value of -2.6 indicates that demand declines 2.6% for every 1% increase in price. This is termed elastic demand. Computing the same value for the short-run curve yields a value of -0.48, or a 1% increase in price reduces demand by about a half a percent. This illustrates a product with inelastic demand. When $E_d = 1$, the term unitary elasticity is used.

Most products display similar demand elasticities, because economics never defines short versus long-run as a fixed unit of time; rather, the long-run varies according to the length of time required to replace the capital stocks associated with the commodity. The summer of 2000 demonstrates a good example. The price of gasoline more than doubled in a few days, yet, demand reduction for gasoline was insignificant, indicating a price elasticity of about .02. Why, because the stock of automobiles can't be adjusted very quickly, so the only way to reduce consumption was by limiting miles traveled. That option is limited due to vacation and job commitments, so most consumers just complained instead. The long-term option involves purchasing more fuel-efficient vehicles, which takes time. An old estimate is that it takes 12 years to improve fuel efficiency significantly. That 12-year number then becomes the time required to move from the short to the long-run.

Price forecasting begins by combining the supply and demand curves into one graph, like Figure 7.7. The intersection of the two graphs defines the price where supply and demand are in equilibrium, or Point A. At equilibrium, the price consumers are willing to pay for the commodity equals the price suppliers want to provide that quantity. The equilibrium price is $3 per unit and the quantity traded is 15 units.

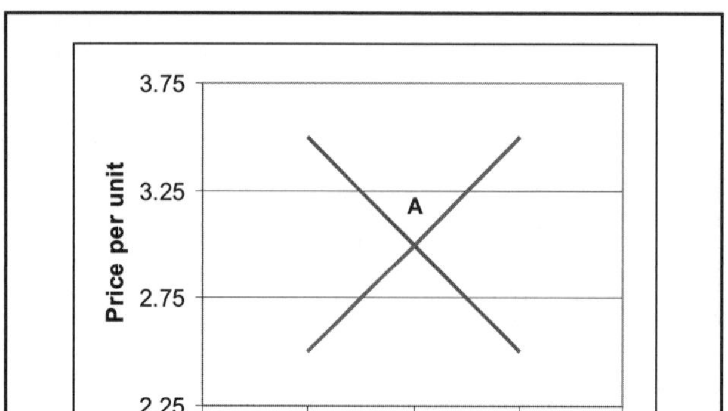

Figure 7.7 Equilibrium in supply and demand

The actual forecasting process applies this graphical process by building numerical relationships, like Equation 7.7. Three equations comprise almost every price forecasting model: a demand equation, a supply equation, and an identity equating demand and supply. The identity, which originates in the assumption of equilibrium, is the crucial element in the forecasting process. Actual data in the real world only reports the quantity exchanged between buyer and seller, not the quantity supplied or demanded. If the market is in disequilibrium, that data only represents the amount demanded or the amount supplied. Without an extensive data collection process, the forecaster never knows if the data represents demand or supply, making forecasting all but impossible. Dr. Campbell Sr. has noted in his engineering lectures, "equilibrium is just a convenient assumption to allow us to make calculations."(7.4)

$$\begin{aligned} Q_d &= \alpha_0 - \alpha_1 * P + \alpha_2 * Y + \alpha_3 * P_s \\ Q_s &= \beta_0 - \beta_1 * P + \beta_2 * W + \beta_3 * K \\ Q_d &= Q_s \end{aligned} \qquad \textbf{(7.7)}$$

Where: P is the price of the item, Y is income of the purchasers, P_s is the price of substitute or competing goods, and W and K are wages and capital as before. By assuming equilibrium, the first two equations can be set equal to each other and then solved for P, as shown in Equation 7.8.

$$\alpha_0 - \alpha_1 * P + \alpha_2 * Y + \alpha_3 * P_s = \beta_0 + \beta_1 * P - \beta_2 * W - \beta_3 * K \qquad \textbf{(7.8)}$$

Which reduces to:

$$P = \frac{\alpha_0 - b_0}{\alpha_1 + \beta_1} + \frac{\alpha_2}{\alpha_1 + \beta_1} * Y + \frac{\alpha_3}{\alpha_1 + \beta_1} * P_s + \frac{\beta_2}{\alpha_1 + \beta_1} * W + \frac{\beta_3}{\alpha_1 + \beta_1} * K$$

The simplified equation now exists in the same format as the production forecasts, where the slope and intercept parameters can be estimated using historical data. Then, once forecasts of the independent variables are obtained, future prices can be generated.

Example of Classical Application: Oil Price Forecasting

The general format outlined above becomes even more complicated when the details of specific commodities are incorporated into the analysis. Dozens of firms, worldwide, sell consulting services and actual forecasts on virtually every commodity known to humankind. If the forecast does not exist, it can be generated, for a fee.

The necessary ingredient for good forecasting involves understanding the nature of the market place (the sufficient conditions come later). Oil is traded worldwide, primarily in U. S. dollars, with the dominant suppliers located in the Middle East. In fact, they supply between 20-25% of world daily demand and are the low cost producers. The world price ultimately depends on the actions of the dominant low cost producers, called an *oligopoly.* These conditions and the assumption that the market is in equilibrium leads to the concept of *net back pricing*, which holds that the sales price at any point must be equivalent to the selling price of the low cost producer at a designated point. The low cost producer is typically taken to be Saudi Arabia, and the two main selling points are Houston and Rotterdam. These two locations are the primary inlet points of oil supplies to the U.S. and Europe, the major consumers of oil. Figure 7.8 illustrates the basic concept.

The example assumes Aramco sells the oil for $16 in Saudi Arabia, and then sells it in Houston for $18.75. The $18.75 represents the benchmark price that competing crudes selling in Houston have to compete against (ignoring any quality or energy differentials). If the crude tries to sell for more than $18.75, buyers will opt for the Saudi crude, and selling for less than $18.75 makes no sense economically.

With the price fixed by the low cost producer in Houston, the model can net back the price crude oil can sell for in Prudhoe Bay, Alaska to compete with Saudi crude in Houston. Assuming tariffs of $5.00 from Houston, across the Panama Canal and up to Valdez, AK, plus the pipeline tariff of $2.50, the maximum price at the inlet to the pipeline is $11.25, or the Houston price net back to the custody transfer point. European investors perform the same calculation for sales in Rotterdam.

Forecasting prices, therefore, requires understanding the forces that determine the $16 price in Saudi Arabia, and the transportation and processing fees throughout the world. The $16 price reflects supply and demand conditions worldwide, as do the expected tariffs. Once the model predicts the $16 price

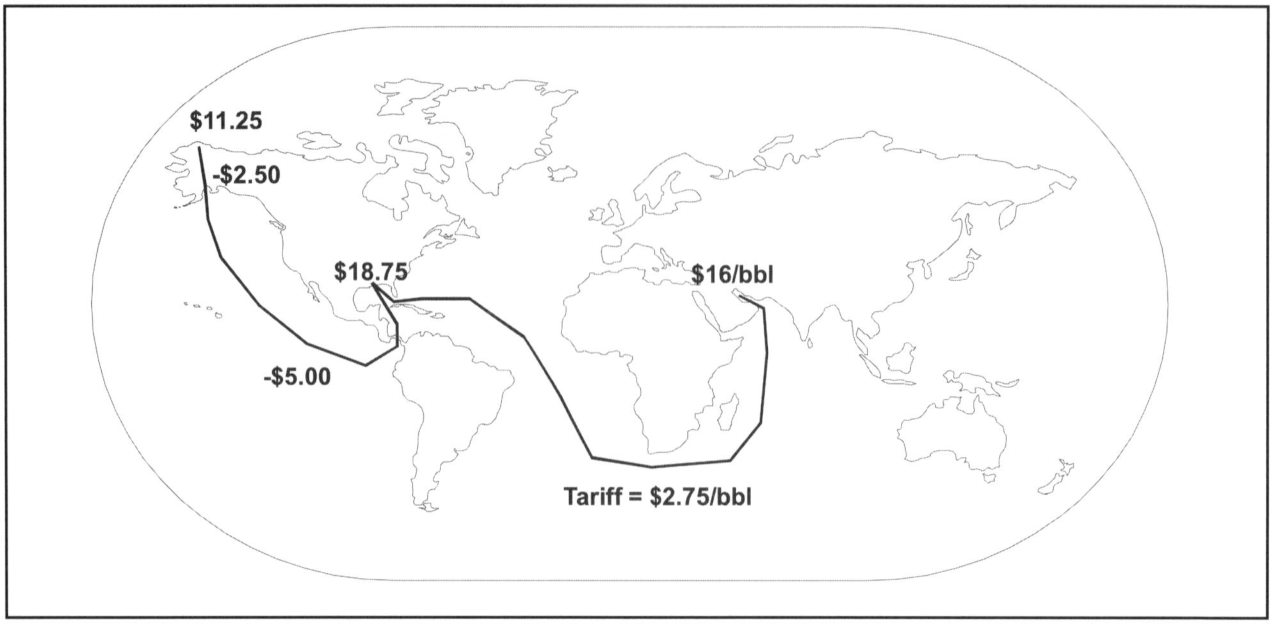

Figure 7.8 Example of net back pricing

using the equations described in the previous section, future prices can be obtained by predicting values for the independent variables, like income, labor cost, etc.

Most investors know that both the equations describing the model and forecasts of the independent variables are imprecise. To try to incorporate uncertainty, the most common practice is to perform *scenario analysis.* The scenario begins with the expected value predictions based on the netback pricing model, and then looks at the impact different worldwide conditions might have on the future values of the independent variables. For instance, a war in the Middle East could disrupt supply, changing the equilibrium position. Likewise, a major recession in consuming countries will reduce demand, again altering the equilibrium price. The output is a range of price forecasts. Figure 7.9 shows a simple format for scenario analysis.

Most investors work with more than the four scenarios shown here. Each set of scenario statements is converted into a specific value, which is then plugged into the forecasting model(s) discussed above for the specified number of years into the future. After having generated different forecasts, the results are merged into a base case, usually with specified sensitivities, often referred to as high and low

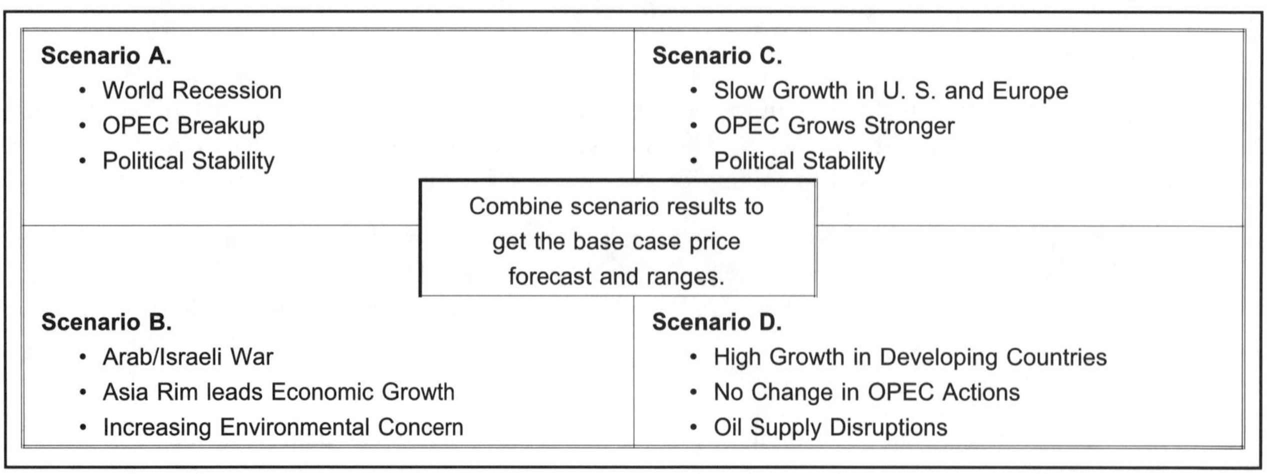

Figure 7.9 Example of scenario price forecasting

ranges. The price forecasts are rolled out to the professional staffs in a form similar to Figure 7.10. These typical straight line extrapolations probably provide the basis for the bulk of investment decisions.

The project metrics are normally reported using the base case price forecast, with the profit measures using the low and high forecasts presented as sensitivities. Before discussing the pitfalls in the implementation of this approach, it is important to realize that Figure 7.10 contains much of the information needed to conduct formal risk assessment, if only the information is used properly. Instead, most investment processes elected, usually unintentionally, to discard the salient risk information.

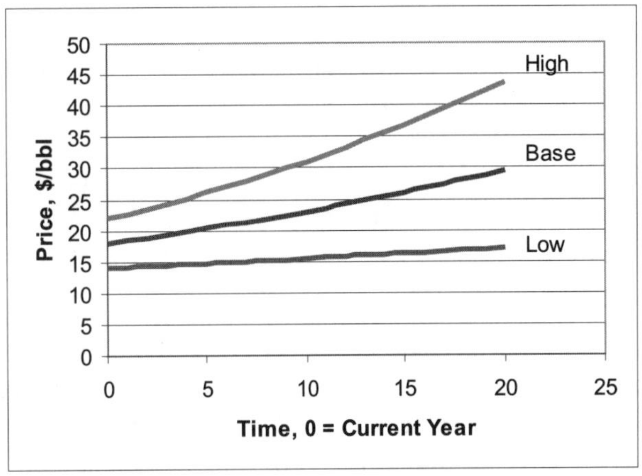

Figure 7.10 Common price forecasting format

The classical valuation process focuses on deterministic values, including price forecasts. One of the lessons learned from analyzing investment behavior is the tendency to give a greater weight to the latest information than justified, as explored in Chapter 8. Most investors tend to let current events dominate their thought process, including the formulation of scenarios. If the current hot topic addresses recession, then the scenarios tend to be weighted more with recession considerations. In financial markets, price changes for the last few days tend to carry a greater weight than price changes in ancient history, like 6 months ago. This problem plagues all price forecasting.

Figure 7.11 demonstrates the tendency to change the long-run oil price forecasts as current events varied, where the number by each line represents the year the forecast was used. David Anderson, an old friend and now investment banker dealing with the petroleum industry, claims that, after performing all the work described above, the industry just uses the *ruler method of forecasting*.[(7.5)] The ruler method follows a very exacting process – connect the last two data point with a ruler and then continue the line for as many years as the forecast requires.

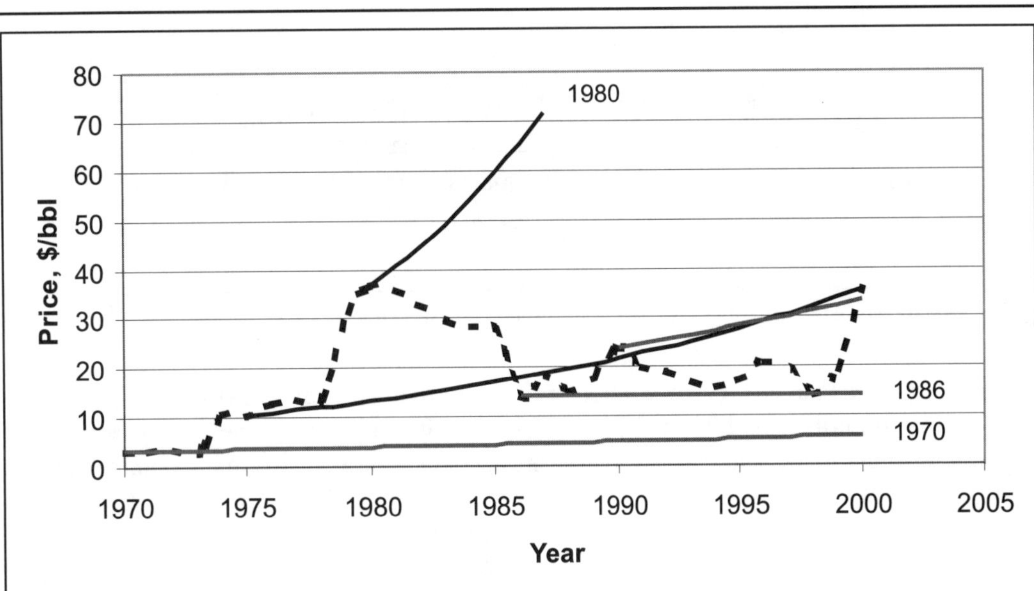

Figure 7.11 Changes in price forecasts for selected years

The price forecasts reflect actual values used by multinationals to compute project profitability. Each forecast follows the ruler method, almost exactly, in each instance. A figure presented later explains the lines in more detail. The crucial point here is that each of the forecasts in Figure 7.11 was generated by the process described so far. Even with detailed supply/demand, net back pricing, and scenario modeling, needlessly simplistic ruler method forecasts emerged, primarily because the investors tried to force price variability to fit their traditional, deterministic valuation process. Chapter 6 began the effort directed at understanding and incorporating risk, the next chapter utilizes the price, and production variability derived here to develop a process that properly values risky investments.

The drivers behind price volatility are shown in Figure 7.12, which shows the MOD and real or deflated price from 1860 to 2000. The highest real prices occurred in the first years, when the U. S. switched from whale oil to petroleum because the whaling vessels were committed to slaughtering humans. After that time, various peaks and troughs took place. Most of the peaks are associated with either technical change, like the industrial revolution, or wars, from WWI to the Iraq invasion of Iran. Most of the price downturns emanate from increased supplies, be they from Sumatra, Indonesia, or Saudi Arabia.

Figure 7.12 highlights a major problem when generating price forecasts: much of the variation originates with major structural changes (industrial revolution) or political events (wars). Neither of these environmental variables is forecastable with any degree of accuracy. The investor might know that these events have a reasonable chance of occurring, but predicting an exact year is beyond everyone's capability. These "shocks" to the system are the domain of *catastrophe theory,* because the discrete changes are catastrophic to continuous modelling.

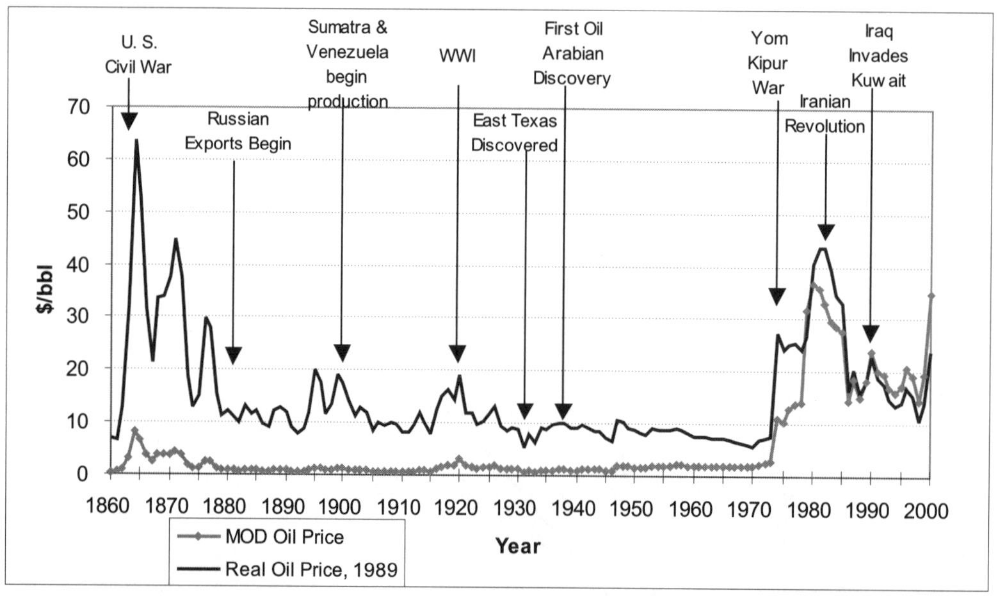

Figure 7.12 Timeline of historical MOD and real oil prices, 1987 is reference year

Catastrophic events have to be forecasted differently than regular, consistent changes in supply and demand. The format described in Figure 7.10 provides all the information needed to reflect risk in price forecasting, and the catastrophic events are covered next. The following example (Table 7.1) describes the *random walk* process, with and without drift (trend). Random walk is defined as any time series data where the yearly values are independent and identically distributed.

The basic random walk approach assumes a triangular distribution, with price ranging from \$14 to \$22 per barrel, to illustrate the concept. In year 0-1, each simulation selects an oil price. That oil price then carries into the next year, as the most likely or expected price, with the ranges specified as ± 20%.

TABLE 7.1

Random Walk Forecasting Specification

Random Walk without Drift	Random Walk with Drift
P_{0-1} = Triangular (10, 18, 30) P_{1-2} = Triangular [P_{0-1}*(1−0.2), P_{0-1}, P_{0-1}*(1+0.2)] P_{2-3} = Triangular [P_{1-2}*(1−0.2), P_{1-2}, P_{1-2}*(1+0.2)]	P_{0-1} = Triangular (10, 18, 30) P_{1-2} = Triangular [P_{0-1} *L, P_{0-1}*(1+d), P_{0-1} *U] P_{2-3} = Triangular [P_{1-2} *L, P_{1-2}*(1+d), P_{1-2} *U]

where: P = oil price in year 0-1, 1-2, or 2-3
(1 − 0.2) = L = the lower bound for oil price in a triangular distribution
(1 + 0.2) = H = upper bound for oil price in a triangular distribution
d = drift or trend in prices, may be plus or minus

After the simulation chooses a price in year 1-2, $P_{1\text{-}2}$ is carried forward into the next year to form the basis for the price selection.

The random walk with drift, allows a trend to exist in the pricing model, either up or down, as indicated by the 1+d amount. The equation only applies the 1+d to the middle component of the triangular curve. To be technically correct, the lower and upper values should also change by 1+d. The next effect of implementing either equation appears something like Figure 7.13. The price forecast line is one iteration in a simulation. Repeating the process for 2000 iterations leads to a price forecasting curve, much like Figure 7.10. If your organization provides low, base and high forecasts, the chances are quite good that these represent the P_{10}, mean price, and P_{90} forecasting intervals. Plugging those values into a triangular distribution (with the needed adjustment to convert the mean to a most likely value) one to generate a curve like Figure 7.13.

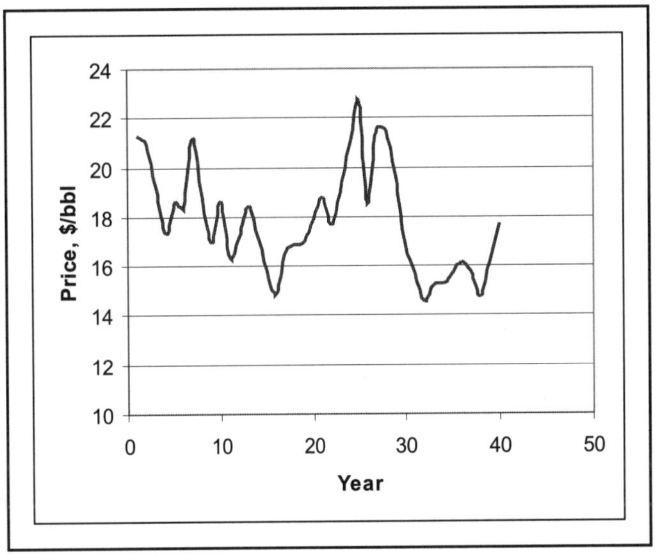

Figure 7.13 Price forecast with random walk

Implementing a price forecasting model using this process is more complicated than rotely applying the random walk equations. As specified above, they are unbounded, allowing prices to actually go negative. Making investment decisions is quite is easy if you have to pay the customer to take your product. Try building a similar model for any commodity price that interests you. When (if) unrealistic prices emerge, alter the basic model to incorporate the relevant constraints. If you have problems, please contact us at the email address located on the inside front cover.

We have encountered considerable reluctance to embrace the volatility concept. Many investors feel more comfortable computing profit metrics using one set of price data, then running a sensitivity using another price forecast. The repetitive, deterministic approach does provide insight about project robustness to changing prices. Figure 7.10 provides a classic illustration of three price forecasts used to generate three very different sets of project metrics. Chapter 2 highlights common errors in investment decisions, including price forecasts relying on the ruler method. Another error arises from the mistaken belief that prices will always increase over time. Figure 7.14 shows the price forecasts reported by the Society of Petroleum Evaluation Engineers, a group involved in buying and selling producing properties. SPEE conducts yearly surveys of the forecasts the members use to make their investment decisions. The average of the survey responses is then reported.

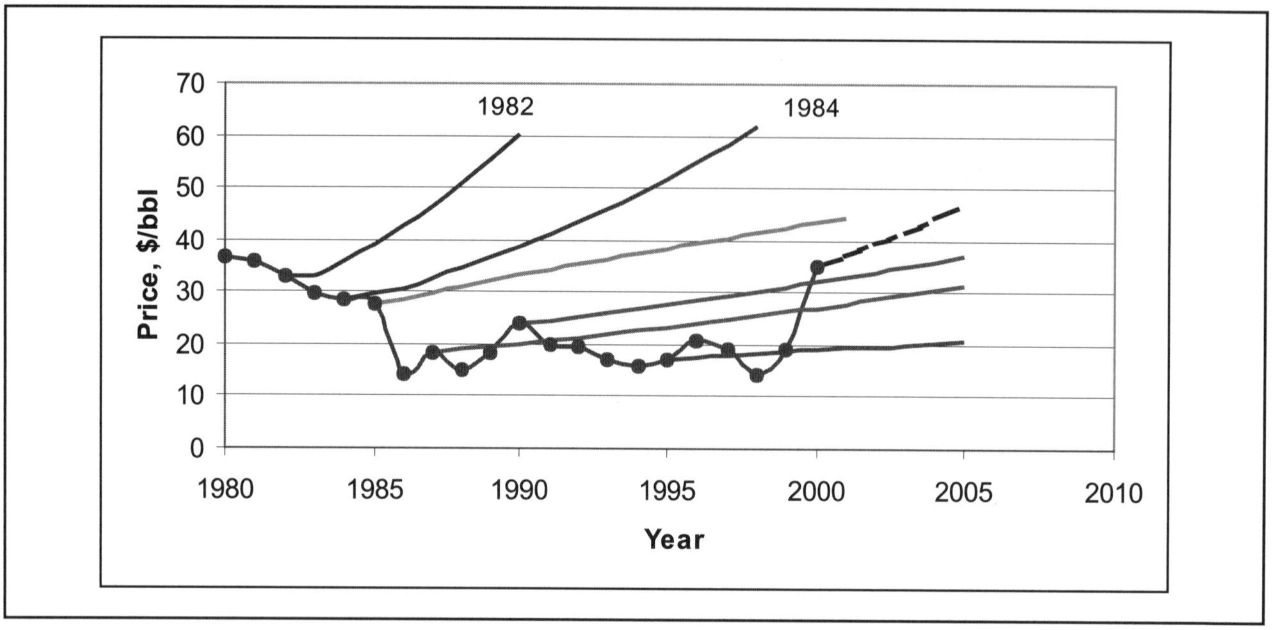

Figure 7.14 Price forecasts from SPEE

Figure 7.14 suggests a modified ruler method; namely, use the most recent data points when prices are increasing, and ignore current prices when they are declining. The two methods together imply that investors believe future prices will always be higher than prices right now. Criticism of this approach should be self-evident based on the graphs that summarize historical prices. Moreover, the same optimism exists in other financial areas, as witnessed by the shock of many investors when the telecommunication, technical stocks, and dot.com share prices plummeted recently. Many truly believed prices would never fall.

Some investors tried to counter the optimism ingrained in the ruler method and always increasing prices by adopting the *mean-reverting* price model. The mean-reverting approach extends the random walk by assuming that shocks occur that cause prices to move away from the mean, but natural market forces drive prices back to that mean. The mean-reverting model is derived from geometric Brownian motion (the foundation of thermodynamics),[7.6] which includes the random walk as a special case. Another name often referred to in the academic literature is the Ornstein-Uhlenbeck process. The best explanation and comparison of these concepts can be found in Investment Under Uncertainty by Dixit and Rubinfeld.[7.7]

Equation 7.9 defines the mean reverting process.

$$dP = \eta * (\bar{P} - P)dt + \rho dz \qquad \textbf{(7.9)}$$

where:

- P = the commodity price,
- η = the speed of reversion (like 1 to 4 years),
- ρ = the variability in P,
- $\bar{P}$ = the mean of price, and
- z = the mathematical formulation describing the change in a Wiener process over time.

Equation 7.9 says that the rate that the current price moves back to the mean or expected price varies according to the gap between the current price, P, and the mean value. Most practitioners prefer to estimate the relationship by running a regression on Equation 7.10,

$$P - P_{t-1} = a + b * P_{t-1} + \varepsilon_t \qquad \textbf{(7.10)}$$

and then calculating the following variables to input into Equation 7.9:

$$\bar{P} = \frac{-\hat{a}}{\hat{b}}, \qquad \hat{\eta} = -\log(1+\hat{b}), \qquad \hat{\rho} = \hat{\rho}_g \sqrt{\frac{\log(1+\hat{b})}{(1+\hat{b})^2 - 1}}$$

where all the variables were defined before and the ^ indicates estimated values.

Considerable debate has arisen over whether the commodity prices follow a random walk (geometric Brownian motion) or mean-reverting process. Dixit and Pindyck conclude that historical evidence is equally valid for both methods for oil and copper prices, but suggest that the mean reverting process is easier to work with when formally applying options analysis.[7.8] Other authors come to the same conclusion for other commodities.[7.9] One author, however, totally disagrees with the application of a mean-reverting process to non-renewable resources.[7.10]

Summary

Formal analysis of risk cannot create certainty where none exists, but it offers a vehicle for organizing ones thoughts, crystallizing investor prejudices about risk versus return, and highlights the type of information needed to improve investment performance. A variety of formats allow formal, direct modeling of the issues at hand. The graphs relating historical experience with oil price forecasting came from investors who conducted this detailed analysis, including information on variability or ignore it entirely. In every instance, they consciously elected to minimize the variability or ignore it entirely, because the tools for analyzing the variability were too restrictive, and most were unsure how to work with the output.

Later chapters discuss the tools and interpretation of these items in considerable detail, building on the variability in production and price discussed here, plus adding variability in Capex, Opex and scheduling. Even without formal toolkits, the variability in pricing helps understand the potential bottlenecks and opportunities that the project may face over time, called options thinking. The process is quite simple, start by building a model, like Figure 7.13. Then add that price forecast to your economic model, whatever forms it takes. If you don't have one, please contact us for a free spreadsheet.

Observe the yearly NCF values. In year 15 and between years 30-40 prices are quite low. Does your NCF suffer? If so, what are your options in your operating decision at those times to reduce or eliminate the problem? Conversely, Figure 7.13 shows prices rising significantly between year 15 and 30. Would you consider additional investments, selling the asset, etc.? The direct result of the analysis is to identify and appraise the options that arise from price variability. By repeating this process for multiple price forecasts, you will be amazed at the options that become obvious, that no one had considered before. This is a great tool for stimulating professional to achieve the challenge of "thinking out of the box."

Two quick summaries of the price forecasting section: first, the process described here just extends the traditional decision-making methods to accommodate the power of modern technology. Nothing in the decision-making process has changed. Second, no matter how many investors adopt similar forecasting formats, the variability in perceptions about the future, as shown in Figure 7.15, will continue.

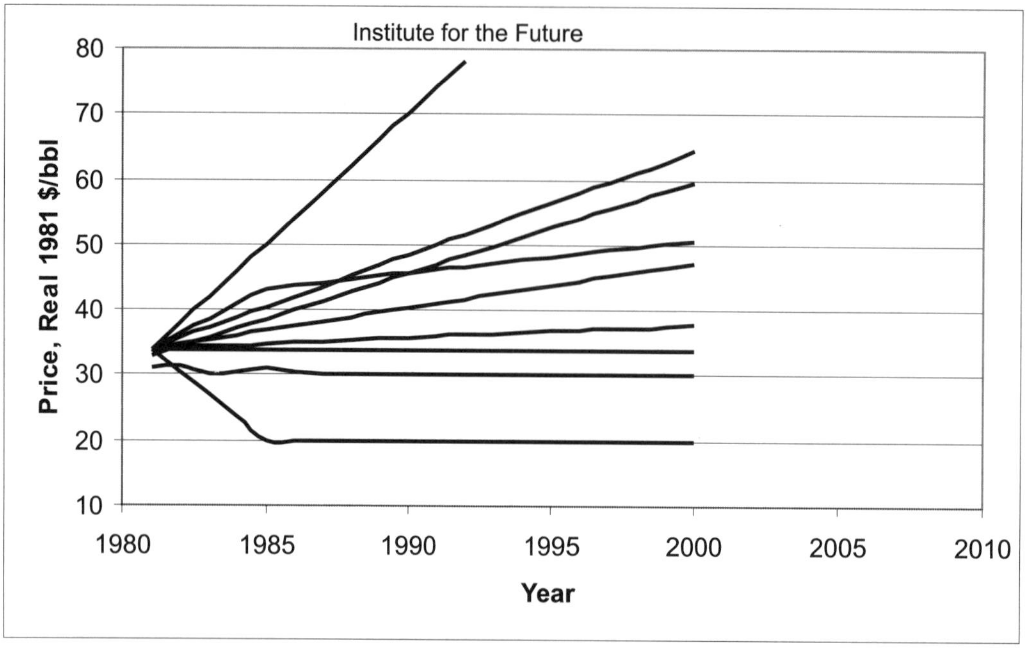

Figure 7.15 Example of price differences among investors and lenders

INFLATION FORECASTING

Perhaps more than any other input into the decision making process, inflation is used by everyone and understood by few. Most people hear monthly reports that inflation has risen by x%, and realize that the cost of living has increased by that amount. Yet, few know what the cost of living relates to and what causes the prices to change. Inflation measures the change in the general price level, or the prices included in each countries basket of goods and services. Only when many product prices increase together, to offset declining prices, does inflation exist. Annual rates of inflation have exceeded 15% in North America and Europe, and over 100% in other parts of the world.

Inflation reduces the volume consumers can purchase, which is one reason most governments try to control it. For example, a couple earning an income of $20,000 a year spends $2,000 on food and $5,000 on housing. At an inflation rate of 10%, the amount spent must rise by $700 (= 0.10 * 7,000) per year for the family to consume the same amount of food and housing. If income remains constant, the family must consume less food or less housing to stay within their budget.

Several measures of inflation exist, but all are weighted averages of specific products, based on *national income accounting.* All inflation measures distort the actual impact on the economy for several reasons. First, inflation reflects the weights of the goods and services in the basket. For example, averaging a food price increase of 5% and a housing cost increase of 15% gives an average inflation rate of 10% {(= 15 + 5)/2}. The consumer actually pays $850 (= 2000 * 0.05 + 5000 * 15) more, not the $700 indicated earlier. The underestimate occurs because housing, which has the higher inflation rate, also has a larger share of the budget.

Most countries use weighted inflation rates to correct for the problem above. In this simple example, each item is weighted by its relative importance in the budget 0.121 {(= 2000/7000)*0.05 + (5000/7000)*0.15) = 0.014 + 0.107}. The 12.1% inflation rate times 7000 equals the $850 amount computed above.

The weighted inflation rates impact consumers and investors in a multitude of ways. Some examples of ways inflation changes the economy include:

- Wages and benefits agreements between employees and employers.
- Pension payment to the retired
- Food programs for the poor,
- Medical benefits for the poor and retired, and
- Income tax brackets for personal and businesses.

Many consumers have their income or other benefits indexed to inflation. The indexing works well when a family consumes the items in the basket in the same percentage as the weighting scheme. A greatly simplified weighting scheme is summarized in Table 7.2, where the weights hopefully sum to 100%.

TABLE 7.2

Sample Product Weights for Measuring Inflation

Housing	40%
Clothing	15%
Food	20%
Medical	10%
Transportation	10%
Electronics	5%

This example assumes that the consumer pays a monthly amount for purchasing or renting their home. Many retired people, however, have paid off their homes, and don't have a housing payment. Any measure of inflation overstates their real cost of living, and any entitlement program confers extra benefits to them. Those same individuals may have much greater medical costs than the average consumer, however, which could understate their benefits. This problem reflects possible distributional biases arising from using averages. Some believe the elderly are discriminated against by the current weighting system.[7.11]

CHAPTER 7

A second problem emerges with changing technology, aging of populations and general shifts in consumption patterns. Inflation measures face considerable problems in adjusting for improvements in the quality of goods and services over time. Some increases measure improved quality in consumption patterns, like automobile safety, rather than general cost pressures. Countries, also, vary considerably in the frequency the weights are updated. Britain, for instance, updates its weights every year, but in the U. S., the weights change with the Census, or once every 10 years. Germany went 15 years before adjusting its weights. The net effect is to exaggerate price rises, by failing to incorporate consumer shifts away from higher price good to cheaper alternatives. This problem manifests itself in several ways, but one is in generating exchange rate forecasts for investment decision-making, as discussed in the next section.

Most nations employ different measures of inflation to serve different purposes, usually to reflect their national income accounting process. Some common inflation measures include:

1. Consumer or retail price index (CPI or RPI).
2. Wholesale price index (WPI)
3. Implicit GNP or GDP deflator (IPD)
4. Special drawing rights index
5. Trade weighted index.

Each element follows the national income and product accounts format, as shown in Figure 7.16, where: GNP, the far left column, is defined as follows in the Keynesian system:

$$GNP = C + I + G + (X - Im) = 727 + 178 + 256 + 5 = \$1,166 \quad \textbf{(7.11)}$$

where:

C = consumption expenditures,
I = Investment,
G = government expenditures,
X = exports, and
Im imports

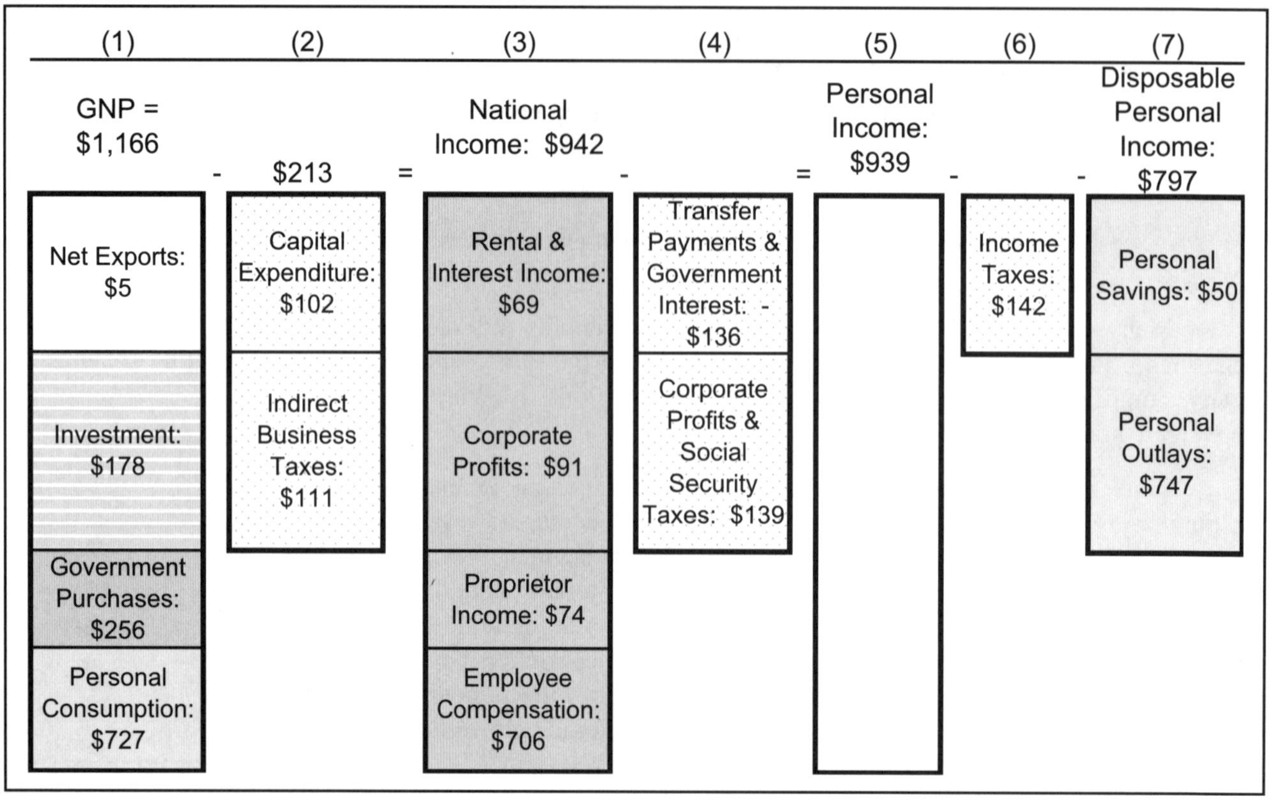

Figure 7.16 National income accounting example (All values in billion $)

The GNP column is based on the flow-of-product approach, while the columns to the right, which break the aggregate GNP values into their constituents, uses the earnings and cost approach. Figure 1.3 provided a diagram for this numerical system. Please make note that this approach is merely double entry bookkeeping applied to national accounts. A common variant of GNP is *Gross Domestic Product (GDP),* which values only goods and services produced domestically, not income arising from investments or operations abroad.

Before discussing inflation derivation from this format, it is important for everyone to realize that GNP or GDP reflect the quality of the data used, just like all technical measurements. Two problems challenge users of this information. One is that the data only reflects "reported" costs and profits. Many countries, especially those with very high taxes, have significant black markets, where people never report these values to avoid taxes, understating the value of a countries GNP. Secondly, as economies reduce traditional manufacturing in favor of services, serious concerns have arisen as to the accuracy of the accounts, especially when comparing current periods to historical ones.

Inflation estimates are computed by measuring the changes in these values. For example, assume GNP, in the following year, produced the following GNP in year t+1:

$$GNP_{t+1} = 727*(1.04) + 178*(1.06) + 256*(1.08) + 5*(1.02) = \$1{,}226.34$$

Inflation for the year is then:

$$\text{GNP deflator} = \frac{1226.34}{1166} = 1.05175 \quad or \quad 5.2\%$$

The implicit GNP deflator actually combines the inflation rates for the sub-section of the economy: consumption (CPI or RPI) relative to the other components. This aggregation captures value changes in every component of the economy.

Having illustrated the derivation of inflation, forecasting future inflation, which impacts future prices, costs, and the WACC, in investment valuations requires understanding competing views of the sources or causes of price changes. During the 1990's, most of the developed world experienced relatively minor inflation rates, often in the 2-3% ranges. This substantial drop in inflation from the last few decades led many to believe that the new, service oriented economies had eliminated inflation and unemployment as problems. The first few years in the 21st century destroyed this dream.

Historical inflation rates are analyzed from several perspectives. Figure 7.17a-c show the consumer prices for several different time frames and countries to illustrate how inflation patterns vary.

Figure 7.17a shows the long-term view with the U. S. CPI from 1913 to 2000. The early part of the 20th century showed widely varying patterns, ranging from highs in the upper teens to large negative values in just a few years. The introduction of formal economic training in treasury departments after the Great Depression has reduced the volatility in inflation rates, though some periods, like just after WWII and the OPEC price increases in the 70's sent inflation soaring. The pattern shows a dampening of the inflation rates relative to the early part of the century.

The inter country comparison, in Figure 7.17b, shows a similar pattern of declining volatility and convergence across countries in the 1970-2000 time frame. Several factors are credited for reducing the volatility. One is the formal management of the economy that was popularized with the advent of the Keynesian Revolution after WWII. Countries recognized the ability and opportunity to stabilize the gyrations in economic measures that took place, historically. The other motivating force is attributed to the globalization of the world economy, which has been taking place (at different speeds in each country) since WWII. Globalization includes increased trading among countries, but also includes the internationalization of communication, capital markets, and risk management. Investors can virtually analyze and consummate transactions in London, Buenos Aires, Hong Kong, and New York in fractions of

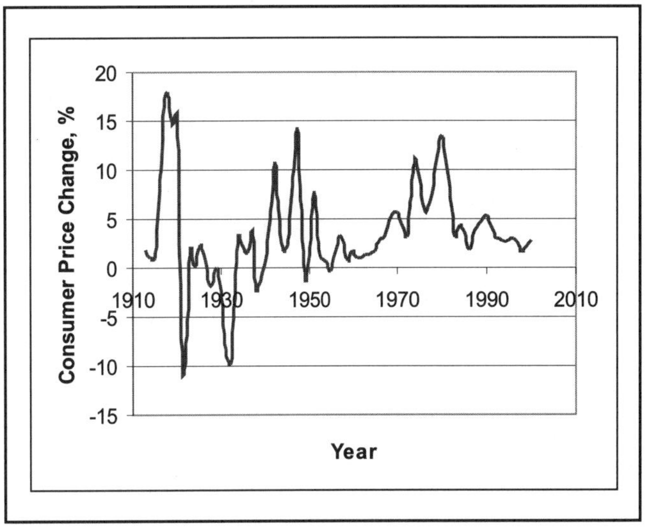

Figure 7.17a U. S. CPI from 1913 to 2000

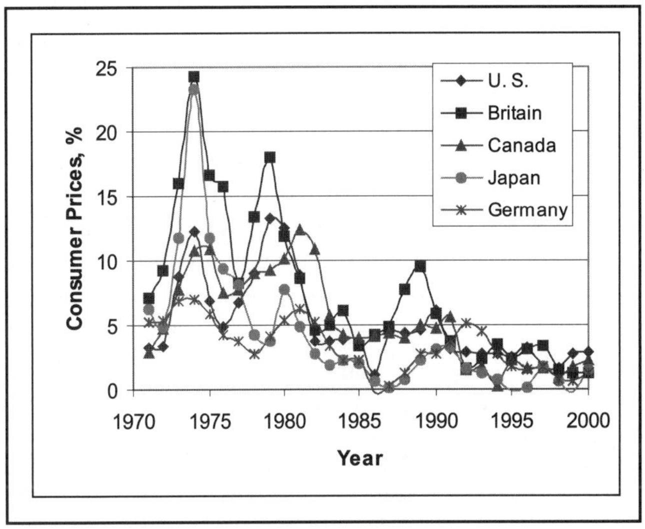

Figure 7.17b CPI's for selected countries, 1971-2000

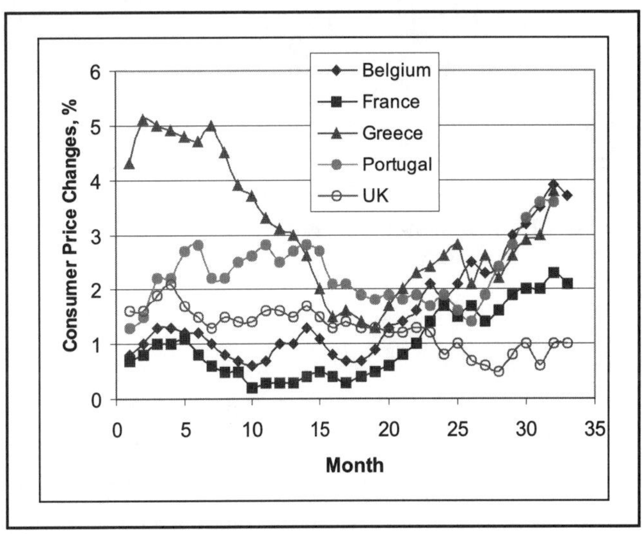

Figure 7.17c Consumer prices for monthly data from 1998 through 2000

a second. The swiftness with which money can move across international boundaries forces politicians to consider more than just local issues when making important political and economic decisions.

Similar volatility can be seen across countries using monthly data between 1998 and 2000 for selected EU countries. The countries included in the graph were selected because they demonstrate broad range of monthly inflation rates across political entities. The purpose is to demonstrate that volatility still exists, and can be significantly different within a relatively homogeneous area. Across the globe, the variation becomes even more important, and understanding that variation is critical for successful investing.

With some framework for understanding the pattern of changing inflation, the task turns to the battle of forecasting and controlling inflation, for both issues must be treated together, not separately. Two groups, the *Keynesians* and the *monetarists*, continually clash over the causes and cures for inflation. While most professional have no control over either group, the different philosophies do impact your estimates for the cost-of-capital and escalation forecasts for prices and costs.

Both groups admit that the other theory impacts inflation. Each believes their approach solves the problems easier and more efficiently, however. The reader should realize that many governments apply both approaches simultaneously in practice. One difficulty in applying either approach concerns the political, often emotionally charged environments, which surrounds the application of the concepts. The politically expedient approach often dominates sound economic cures.

Monetary Inflation

Nobel prize winning economist, Milton Friedman, resurrected the notion from classical monetary analysis that mismanagement of the money supply by central banks, and governments printing money to pay bills causes inflation. Through relationships between money supply and inflation, like those in Figure 7.18, some association between money supply and consumer prices appears to exist. The Keynesians retort that the correlations merely reflect the impact of other variables that they prefer to emphasize.

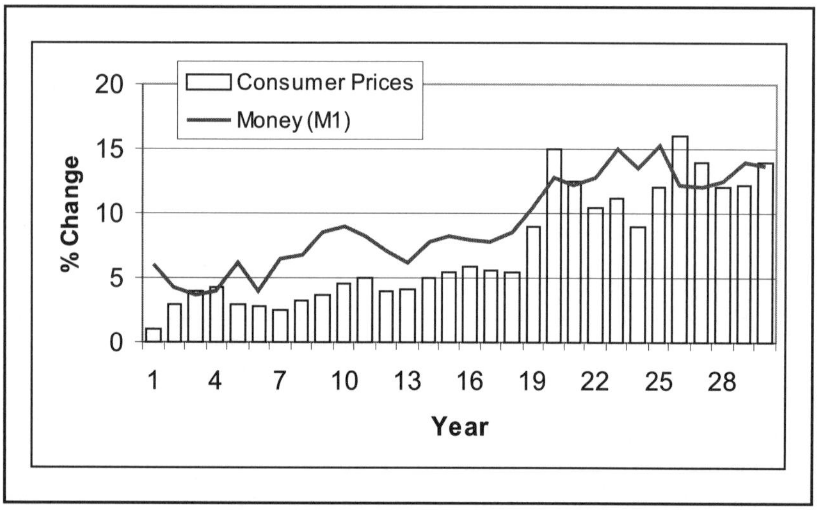

Figure 7.18 Money supply and inflation in IMF countries over specific years

The inflation and money supply amounts used in Figure 7.18 are trade-weighted averages of IMF member countries. The high inflation rate countries in the database, like Brazil and Mexico, financed large debt volumes by increasing the money supply.

Monetarist reduce the relationship in Figure 7.18 to the basic equation:

$$M * V = P * Y \tag{7.12}$$

where:

- M = the money supply,
- V = the velocity of money,
- P = the index used to measure inflation,
- Y = national income measured in constant currency amounts.

Money supply can be measured in a myriad of ways, with the designation following a format like M_1, M_2, M_3, etc. M_1 defines money as the total sum of currency and coins outside of banks plus checking accounts. M_2 adds time and savings deposit accounts to M_1; whereas, M_3 adds very large deposits by trust and firms to M_2. Some countries, like Britain, add categories, such as PSL2, which adds the money in building societies to M_3.

Velocity of money defines the number of times money changes hands each year. If the money supply is 300 and income is 900, each unit of money must change hands 3 times (=900/300). Most monetarists believe that the velocity of money remains constant over time, though recent evidence challenges this notion.

Monetarists dictate that money supply, which is the only controllable variable in Equation 7.12, be used to control inflation. If the following values are observed,

M = 300 billion P = 1.00 V = 4 Y = 1200 billion

Then, the equation 300*4 = 1.00*1,200 holds by definition. Supposing that real income is expected to rise to 1,500 billion next year due to improved productivity and the objective is zero inflation, the government must increase the money supply to:

$$M = \frac{1}{4} * P * Y = \frac{1}{4} * 1.0 * 1{,}500 = 375 \text{ billion}$$

or, should the government set the target inflation rate to be 4%, the money supply should increase by:

$$M = \frac{1}{4} * 1.04 * 1{,}500 = 397 \text{ billion}$$

Turning the equation around, suppose the central bank, bowing to political pressure, increases the money supply to 420 billion, causing prices to rise by:

$$P = \frac{M * V}{Y} = \frac{420 * 4}{1{,}500} = 1.12 \quad \textit{or} \quad 12\% \text{ inflation}$$

Inflation is controlled by matching the money supply with income; the problem being the anticipation of future income.

Keynesian Inflation

The competing view holds that inflation exists primarily due to excess demand for goods and services, and unemployment occurs when demand is insufficient. Figure 7.19 presents a simple case. As demand rises from 400 billion to 1,800 billion, holding money supply constant, the average price level goes from 8% to 15%. Supply curves are normally drawn as linear or straight lines in textbooks, but are really curvilinear. The aggregate supply curve follows a fairly flat relationship until quantity reaches about $100 billion, at which time the slope increases dramatically. The slope increase arises primarily from bottlenecks in the supply of labor or capital. Manufacturing plants have capacity limits, for example, and a fixed number of workers are available at any given point in time. When suppliers begin to reach these constraints, prices tend to rise.

The curve also illustrates the commonly observed situation, where quantities increase dramatically with no impact on price, but then a very small increase in supply and demand leads to a significant price increase. The quantity increase from $50 to $100 changed prices very little, but going to $120 billion increases price almost 50%.

Keynesians evaluate this situation by sub-dividing demand into the three components of GNP: consumption, investment, and government spending, as shown with the national income accounts.

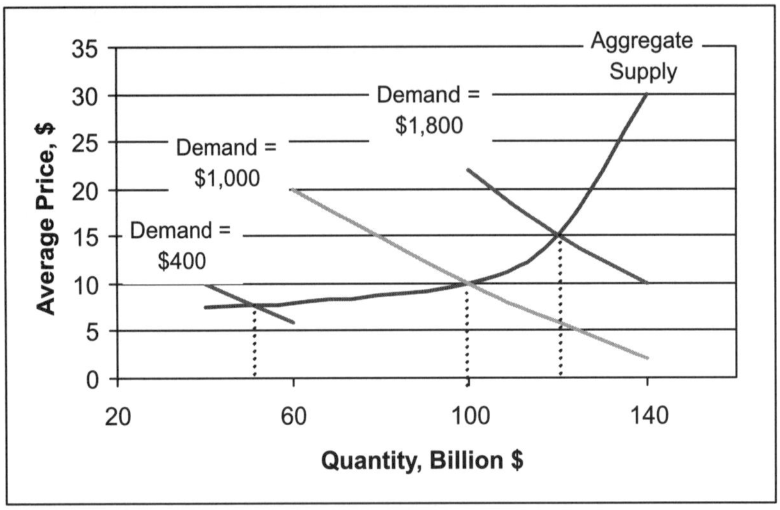

Figure 7.19 Keynesian inflation

Equilibrium in supply and demand in the economy occurs when the sum of consumption -C, investment -I, and government spending – G equally aggregate income. The 45° line in Figure 7.20 represents equilibrium at any given income and expenditure level. Initially, equilibrium exists at $400 billion. If expenditures rise to $1,800 billion, income must increase by the same amount to balance income and spending.

The figures are related because price time quantity sold equals income. If total income equals $1,000 billion (Figure 7.20), then price of $10 time a quantity of $100 billion (Figure 7.19) yield the same value. The important recognition in the Keynesian system was the role of the government as a purchaser of goods and services. This seems pretty basic today, but, prior to Keynes, governmental policy never recognized the role it played in influencing the economy. Keynes realized that governments can influence the economy by changing their level of demand; hence, shifting the curve along the supply line in these figures. When consumption and investment fail to employ the desired number of workers, government can increase employment by purchasing more goods and services. When private consumption rises too quickly, the government reduces demand to prevent price increases.

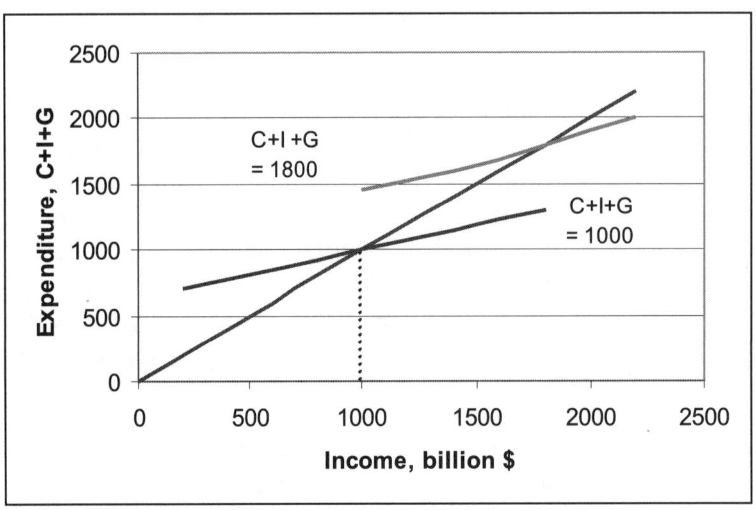

Figure 7.20 Keynesian inflation (continued)

The concept was for governments to overspend their budgets, creating deficits, to stimulate demand, and then repay that debt when the economy is running well. Governments essentially act as swing consumers. Over one or more business cycles, government borrowings and repayments should balance, leaving the government with no debt. Lessons from all countries suggest that political motivations make it easier to borrow than to repay debt. The cause is irrelevant, the consequences of excess borrowing without prudent management limits the growth of many countries, with the worst damage being in those that can least afford it.

Much of the world battles daily over the proper level of debt financing, to cut taxes or reduce debt, ways to spend borrowed monies, etc. These subjects are highly charged political events. In fact, outsiders observing the economic knowledge base at work express amazement at the concepts. Yet, few appreciate the constraints placed on economic application by the political system. Sound economics usually loses to politically motivated events, like re-electing the head of state.

Forecasting

Even with this simplified background of inflation, the problem of incorporating inflation forecasts into the valuation process requires some work. If you desire a forecast that reflects either the Keynesian, monetarist, or combination of each, many services provide forecasts for GNP, CPI or RPI, etc., by country and sub-region in a country, or combination of countries or regions, for a fee. The problem in all such forecasts is anticipating future growth in consumption, investment, or government spending (Keynesian), or anticipating government actions regarding the money supply (monetarists). Even if the forecasters know the relationship between these items and inflation, knowledge of future policy decisions is imprecise (See Chapter 1 again).

Some investors react to this imprecision by using the inflation in rate in their home country, arguing that it cannot be forecasted anyway. What jumps out from Figure 7.17, however, is the volatility in inflation rates across time and countries. Once the objective of understanding risk and trying to manage came to the fore, the variability in country inflation rates dominates the valuation process. The best approach, in our opinion, follows the logic used for commodity price forecasting, as shown in Table 7.3.

TABLE 7.3

Inflation Forecasting

Random Walk without Drift	Random Walk with Drift
I_{0-1} = Triangular (0.01, 0.03, 0.06) I_{1-2} = Triangular $[P_{0-1}*(1-0.2), P_{0-1}, P_{0-1}*(1+0.2)]$ I_{2-3} = Triangular $[P_{1-2}*(1-0.2), P_{1-2}, P_{1-2}*(1+0.2)]$	I_{0-1} = Triangular (0.01, 0.03, 0.06) I_{1-2} = Triangular $[P_{0-1}*L, P_{0-1}, P_{0-1}*(1+d), P_{0-1}*U)]$ I_{2-3} = Triangular $[P_{1-2}*H, P_{1-2}, P_{1-2}*(1+d), P_{1-2}*U)]$

where:

I = the consumer or retail price in year 0-1, 1-2, or 2-3

(1 – 0.2) = L = the lower bound for oil price in a triangular distribution

(1 + 0.2) = H = upper bound for oil price in a triangular distribution

d = drift or trend in prices, may be plus or minus

Because the inflation forecasts in a simulation follow a pattern similar to the one used to describe price forecasting, an example graph is omitted. Allowing for this type of forecast is crucial for the proper assessment of relative risk across countries. The format in Table 7.3 allows investors to differentiate between those countries that still experience swings in inflation, like that shown in Figure 7.17a for the U. S. in the early part of the 20th Century or the wide swings exhibited by the countries in the 1970's in Figure 7.17b, and countries with more stable, less fluctuating inflation rates.

High inflation countries present significant problems for investors. A recently completed analysis of a project in a country, currently facing inflation of 2% per month, indicated that total project costs could vary from $7.5 billion to $17 billion, with the bulk of the variation attributable to inflation. If this kind of variability in a cost estimate concerns you, consider trying the process outlined in Table 7.3.

EXCHANGE RATE FORECASTING

The last time series data stream that impacts investment valuation and risk assessment deals with movements of currency across countries. Some commodities, like crude oil, are bought and sold in U. S. dollars, regardless of the local currency. Most other commodities are exchanged using the local country currency, however. Since investment decisions ultimately involve comparing projects located around the world, most investors elect to use one reference point, usually the country and currency the headquarters are located – dollars for American companies, Sterling for British companies, and Yen for Japanese companies.

Exchange variation impacts valuations in two ways. First, accounting for profits and costs rise or fall with the exchange rate. Manager that set goals and establish incentive systems in terms of local accounting values encounter severe problems as exchange rates vary. Table 7.4 demonstrates the sensitivity in project valuation to changing exchange rates.

TABLE 7.4

Exchange Rate Impact on Profit Metrics

Metrics	Exchange Rates 1/1	1.75/1	1.25/1
NPV_0	28.2	21.2	35.3
NPV_5	19.1	14.4	23.9
NPV_{10}	11.6	8.7	14.5
NPV_{15}	5.3	4.0	6.6
OANPV	50.8	34.4	67.1
SIV	15.4	11.6	19.3

The project valuations, with the currencies at parity, change significantly when the local currency drops or rises relative to the home currency. Metrics that allow the impact of discounting to change over time, like OANVP and SIV, experience even greater changes than the classical NPV metric. This explains the common occurrence of an investment meeting all return criteria in the local currency, but being elevated or downgraded when compared to other countries.

The lesson of Table 7.4 echoes the, previously discussed, importance of non-technical elements to investors. Chapter 2 demonstrated via the decision hierarchy diagram that investors worry, as much if not more, about exchange rates, political events, and other non-technical elements as they do about the technical. In fact, most senior management "assumes" the technical elements have been done properly, thus, allowing them to direct their attention to other issues, like exchange rates.

Background of International Trade

Like the previous section, the fundamentals of international trade and exchange rates are covered first, before jumping into the details of forecasting. The entire issue of international trade, with the corresponding impact on exchange rates, elicits more emotional response today than perhaps ever before. Some believe that international trade is driving the continual improvement in the world's economy; others see the destruction of entire cultures, to the detriment of all. Recent attempts to disrupt World Trade Organization (WTO), International Monetary Fund (IMF), and other global organization meetings in the last few years attest to the deep conviction of the latter view.

To tie these emotions to the theme of this book, the difference between the two groups goes back to the use of averages versus measuring variability. The evidence clearly supports the notion that globalization improves the overall well being of humanity, <u>on average</u>. Even the most ardent traders recognize the unequal distribution of these benefits, however, which is the major battleground over globalization. Understanding the variability in benefits and costs, if these can even be measured and developing programs to mitigate the risks is equally as valid here as in making investment decisions.

Regardless of ones view, Figure 7.21 describes the basic process relating international trade and exchange rates. The variables driving the flow of money worldwide, as shown in the middle box, include relative prices between trading countries, relative incomes, relative interest rates, government spending, and, hence, the amount of government debt. These variables influence each other, as well. Government deficits depend on spending levels, for example.

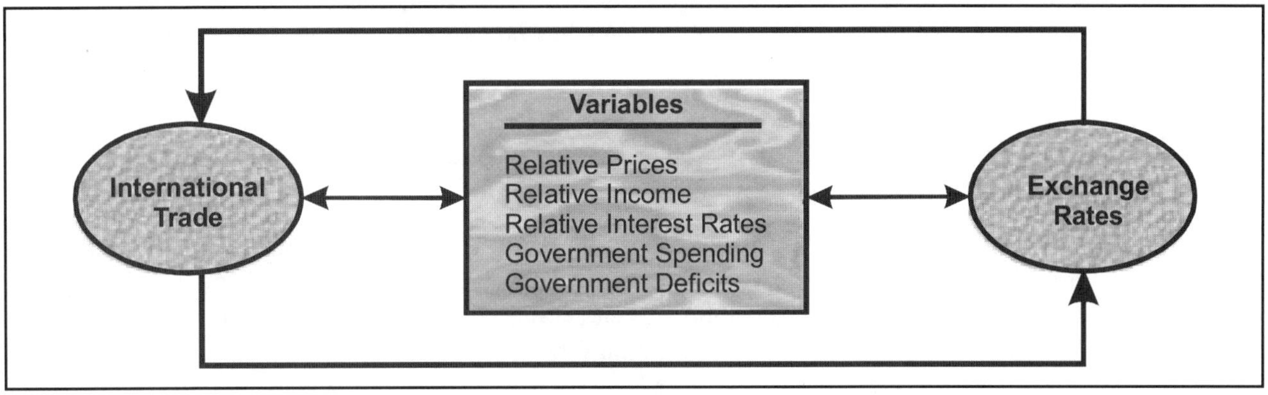

Figure 7.21 International trade and exchange rate relationship

Trying to balance the relative importance of the variables that determine supply and demand (exports and imports) in international trade and the prices that balance these elements (exchange rates) has perplexed scholars for generations. While accurate models of international trade still elude us, the importance of international trade is clear. Figure 7.22 graphs the relationship between international trade and the growth in GDP since 1950.(7.12) World trade, as measured by exports, has fed most of the growth in GDP over the reported time frame. The World Trade Organization (WTO), the international organization charged with promoting international trade and resolving disputes among trading partners, reckons that trade has driven most of the growth in the world in the last few decades. Certainly, increasing ease of communication (the Internet and B2B), markets for hedging price and inflation risk, etc., contributed greatly to the improvements, but serious obstacles remain in the quest for creating a truly global economy.

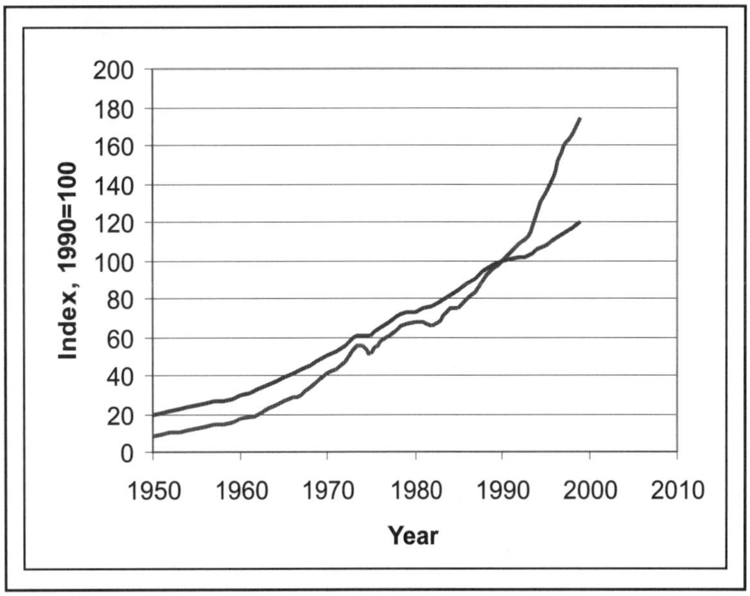

Figure 7.22 International trade and income

Facilitating trade requires destroying or minimizing the barriers to trade, primarily in the form of tariffs to imports, licensing restrictions to buy and sell in a country, and tax subsidies that give certain producers an advantage. Some common examples include:

- the Economic Union (EU) protecting banana shipments from former French colonies against competition,
- the U. S. subsidizing airlines producers, like Boeing, via military contracts,
- China imposing high tariffs under the guise of allowing industries to develop the skills to compete against foreigners (called the "infant industry argument"),

- Japan restricting competition by controlling domestic distribution systems, and
- the EU continuing the common agricultural policy (CAP) which protects some of the worlds most inefficient farmers from competition.

Every country, even those claiming to be in favor of trade, subsidize and shelter domestic producers, which reduces the wealth of their country and world simultaneously. The supposed champion of free trade, the U. S., subsidizes growing rice in the desert of California and sugar cane in Florida, both at 3-6 times above the going market price.

The reason protection destroys value comes from two basic notions. The first, "trade or perish," reflects the inability of some countries to sustain themselves. The food famines and medical crises in many countries can only be minimized by international trade.

The real essence of Figure 7.22 arises from the notion of "trade or be poorer." Without international trade, most consumers would forego the basic comforts everyone takes for granted: coffee, tea, chocolate, and tropical fruits. Even sugar would be scarce and costly. Users of depleting resources, like iron, coal, and petroleum, ultimately come to depend on others. Trading benefits everyone via the *Law of Comparative Advantage.*

This basic principle recognizes that consumers benefit by trading for goods and services that they could produce themselves depending on relative costs and production skills. Specialization (committing resources) lowers the cost of purchasing goods and services, as Table 7.5 demonstrates. Comparative advantage allows each country to specialize in the activities they perform the best. The first section shows Belgium producing and consuming 10 tens of each product before trade, and different values for Vietnam. Belgium exchanges rice for steel on a 1 to 1 ratio, while Vietnam trades slightly more than 3 tons of rice for one ton of steel.

TABLE 7.5

Benefits of International Trade

All values in million tons	Belgium		Vietnam	
	Steel	**Rice**	**Steel**	**Rice**
Before Trade:				
Production	10	10	6.66	20
Consumption	10	10	6.66	20
After Trade:				
Production	20		–	30
Consumption	12	10	8	20
Exports	8		–	20
Imports		10	8	

Since Belgium has a comparative advantage in steel (the rice to steel ratio is less than Vietnam, 1/1 compared to 1/3), international trade allows Belgium to produce steel and Vietnam to concentrate on rice. If the two countries agree on an exchange rate of 1.25 tons of rice per ton of steel, Belgium consumes 12 tons of steel, leaving 8 tons for export. At an exchange rate of 1.25 to 1, Belgium receives 10 tons of rice in exchange for 8 tons of steel. Vietnam consumes the same amount of rice, but receives more steel as the result of trading. Both parties consume more of either wheat or steel. An exchange benefits each country if the exchange rate (1.25/1) is better than the internal rate.

Figure 7.23 displays the improved consumption because of the trading relationship. What draws the ire of anti-traders is the disruption to the farmers in Belgium and steel workers in Vietnam. Specialization forces the farmers to move into steel making or some other line of work; thereby, disrupting their

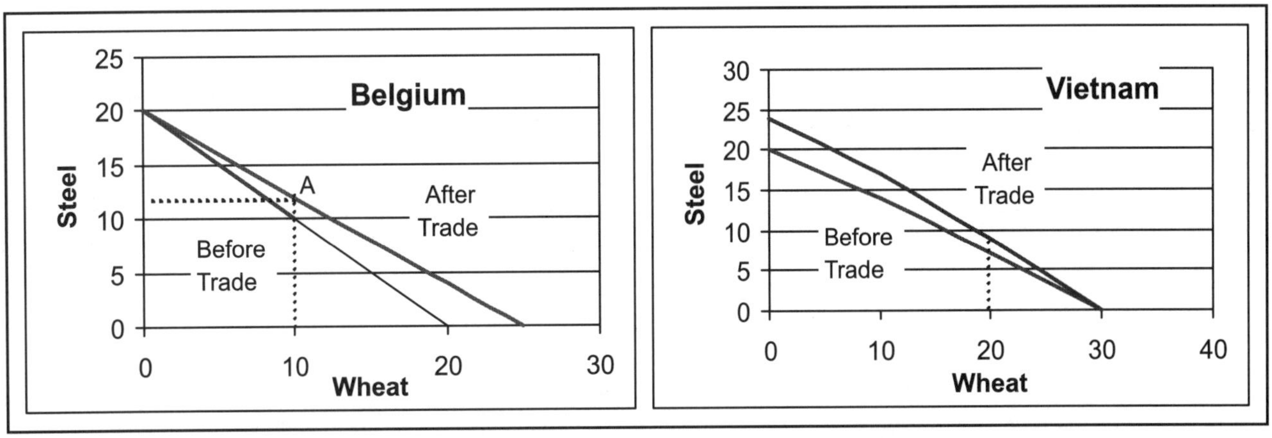

Figure 7.23 Comparative advantage

lifestyle. Each country must balance the benefits of increased consumption, usually at lower cost, versus subsidizing relatively inefficient workers lifestyles. Reaching decisions on these matters is both complex and emotional.

Accounting for International Trade

To resolve the questions of benefits, cheating, subsidies, worker dislocation, etc. requires a detailed set of accounts. The international trade accounts measure a subset of the national accounts associated with the movement of goods and services across national boundaries. Sample accounts for any country are normally available from the respective websites, or collections of countries can be obtained from several international agencies.[7.13]

The general term is *balance of international payments,* which values the flow of goods and services during the year. The basic format follows the double-entry bookkeeping discussed at several places in this book. Like most accounting processes, the developers elected to break the information into finer components to help them understand the international trading process. The three main categories are: current account, capital movement, and gold and reserve assets. The sum of these items equals balance of international payments, as shown in Table 7.6.

The current account records the trade in goods and services, and the exchange of gifts between countries. The term, *trade balance,* refers to just exports and imports, which is a net of $1,000 in the example. The current account captures the flow of merchandise and money, while the capital account records the international movement of funds reflected in financial assets and liabilities. The classifications within the category are based on the terms to maturity of the asset and the involvement of the owner in the daily activities of the asset; hence, the reference to long-term for assets held longer than one year. Direct investment versus portfolio management indicates the degree of management involvement in the asset. A company building a subsidiary in another country, which they controlled, is classified as a direct investment. When an investor buys shares or bond in another country, without exercising any control, it falls into the portfolio account.

Observe that the total balance of payments equals the official reserve accounts, a result required by the use of double entry bookkeeping. Gold is self-evident, but foreign exchange represents the currencies of other countries held by the example country that can be freely exchanged for their own currency. These numbers are readily available for any country.

TABLE 7.6

Balance of Payments for Example Country

Sources of Funds, + and Uses of Funds, –			
I. Current Account			**Net**
TRADE ACCOUNT			
Exports	5,000		
Imports	4,000		
Balance of Trade			1,000
SERVICE ACCOUNT			
Receipts for interest, dividends, travel & financial charges	2,500		
Payments for interest, dividends, travel & financial charges	-1,500		
Balance of Services (Invisibles)			1,300
UNILATERAL TRANSFERS			
Gifts received from abroad	500		
Grants to foreign countries, including military equipment sales	-1,000		
Balance of Services (Invisibles)			-500
Current Account Balance			1,800
II. Capital Account (Long-term Capital Flow)			
DIRECT INVESTMENT			
Sale of Financial Assets	2,000		
Purchase of Financial Assets	-4,000	-2,500	
PORTFOLIO INVESTMENT			
Sale of Financial Assets	5,000		
Purchase of Financial Assets	-3,000	2,000	
Balance of Long-term Capital			-500
Basic Balance			1,300
PRIVATE SHORT-TERM CAPITAL FLOWS			
Sale of Financial Assets	8,000		
Purchase of Financial Assets	-2,000		
Balance on Short-term Capital			6,000
Total Balance of Payments			7,300
III. Official Reserves Account			
Gold exports less imports			-5,000
Decrease or increase (-) in foreign exchange			-2,300

Like all knowledge systems, understanding the limitations of the numbers is also important. Four main problems limit the use of balance of payment figures. They are:

1. Effect of controls,
2. Lack of detail,
3. Balance of international indebtedness, and
4. Exchange rate movements (the critical bit for investment decision-making)

The numbers indicate monthly, quarterly, or yearly changes, but never indicate how the country achieved their results. Many countries, especially those fearful of competition, impose strict restriction on imports or heavily subsidize exports. Both situations indicate frictions in the system, either retarding growth or hiding potentially catastrophic financial events, like the huge bailouts required for Mexico, Brazil and some Asian countries. The World Trade Organization tries to monitor these possible problems and offer incentives to correct them. For financially strapped countries, the International Monetary Fund (IMF) seeks to bridge these barriers before loaning the country money.

To really understand changing finances, most analyst's focus on accounts that are more detailed, like agriculture, manufacturing, energy, services, etc. Trying to understand the sources in balance of payment movements is just as important as seeing the overall trend. Large groups of professionals spend their entire careers studying these accounts.

Exchange Rate Systems

The preceding accounting system provides the data needed to analyze trade movements, and, ultimately, to determine shifts in exchange rates. Before addressing the details of exchange rate forecasting, one additional component that impacts exchange rate needs to be understood: the type of exchange rate system. The nature and type of exchange rate system influences the risk associated with trading internationally. Exporters, as they sell products abroad, acquire claims in foreign currencies. Since they pay their wages and other bills in their home country, the conversion process, ease, and cost affects profitability.

Several, competing exchange rate systems exist currently, and several others have been tried over time. The principal criterion for evaluating exchange rate systems, includes:

- The degree of stability in the exchange rates,
- The extent to which market forces are allowed to operate, and
- The balance of payment adjustment mechanism.

Each system brings real benefits to the system, but also restricts international trade in other ways.

Pure Gold Standard

This exchange rate system answers the three questions by maintaining a stable exchange rate, with market operations free from direct controls, and adjusts via price and income changes. Exchange rate are based on the gold held by the country, so, comparing exchange rates really becomes a comparison of respective gold volumes. A major characteristic requires the country to redeem their currency at a specified rate. In the 1930's, when Britain and the U. S. were on the gold standard, sterling equaled 113 grains of fine gold and the dollar was traded for 23.3 grains of fine gold. The exchange rate was \$4.86/£ (= 113/23.3).

Countries faced serious adjustment problems under the gold standard, because every country held limited quantities of gold. It was quite common for a country to hold less than 10% of its currency value in gold, putting debtors (holders of that currency) at considerable risk of devaluation. Debtor nations frequently devalued their currencies to repay their debts.

Having a fixed standard, where traders believed that the currency was guaranteed by a fixed, valuable asset, promoted the growth in international trade for most of the 19th century and the first half of the 20th century. A fundamental tenet of the gold standard, namely, the subordination of the national economy to world stability, is unacceptable to many countries. Disequilibrium in international trade can only be corrected by altering national income or prices, which is abhorrent to many politicians. Some blame the Great Depression on the political shift to national, at the expense of international, issues. In essence, gold standard only works successfully when the countries are willing to accept internal disorder, like unemployment and inflation, to balance foreign trade. Most countries aren't.

Freely Fluctuating Exchange Rates

When Richard Nixon dropped the gold standard for the U. S. in 1971, many experts diagnosed the world's problem as inflexible exchange rates, and suggested the opposite: exchange rates that varied freely. This allowed countries to carry on a domestic policy of full employment and price stability, while balancing trade simultaneously. The risk shifts from the politicians to those engaged in international trade. Market forces of supply and demand determine the exchange rate, rather than gold holdings.

The volatile exchange rates that emerged created considerable concerns for traders. They might make a very attractive transaction, only to have their profits wiped out by exchange rate changes. These uncertainties led to considerable speculation. In politically and economic stable nations, speculation helps maintain the stability in the exchange rate over time. Once faith in the local governments vanished, the same speculation led to wild swings in exchange rates, magnifying the problems facing the country.

A true freely fluctuating system has never been implemented.

Exchange Controls

Governments, primarily in developing countries, often use controls to attack balance of payments problems and to promote industrial growth internally. Rather than solving the cause of the problem, they restrict economic and financial transactions by requiring approval of a control board. Foreign exchange sales must also be funneled through the control board. Usually, the control board exchange rates are set at fixed levels that often vary significantly from free market prices, creating a black market.

Various devices keep the balance of payment system under control, with the systems heart being power over international transactions. Probably the most commonly used system imposes multiple exchange rates on traders, where luxury good might have a 10/1 exchange rate, while food and medicine use a 5/1 exchange rate.

Exchange controls cause serious distortions in domestic economies when left in place very long. They tend to perpetuate the economic conditions that caused the problem in the first place. They also require a control board to make accurate decisions about thousands of products, with little success historically. India is a good example where the economic well being dropped significantly under exchange controls over the last 50 years. Efforts in the last few years to free up the system have increased economic growth exponentially. In spite of these problems, countries adopted exchange controls when faced with depressions, political instability, and economic failures. Generally, exchange controls can only be justified when it solves the problem with less suffering than other methods.

Flexible Exchange Systems

In an attempt to combine the advantages of the gold standard with freely fluctuating exchange rates, theoreticians created the flexible exchange system. Here, exchange rates are neither fixed at a predetermined level nor allowed to fluctuate freely. Instead, the local government, via designated agencies, like the Bank of England, the Federal Reserve Bank (US), or the Bundesbank (Germany) intervenes to buy and sell currency on the open market to keep the exchange within a specified range.

This system, in several variants, dominates the world trading system today. The IMF and other international organizations specify ranges for exchange rates. Within those bounds, no action is required. When the market exchange rate falls outside those bounds, the government intervenes to buy or sell the designated currency. A good example of this notion was the creation of an artificial "basket" currency, which is a combination of other currencies by the Economics Union. The *European Currency Unit (ECU)* combines member country currencies in the proportions shown in Table 7.7.[7.14]

The allowed bands of fluctuation are characterized by a set of adjustable bilateral central parities, and margins that defined the bandwidth of permissible fluctuation. The set of parities defined all possible combinations of EU constituent currencies. The borders are defined by the upper intervention point and the lower intervention point, which are currently about 15% on either side of the parity. When the market exchange rate reached either of these intervention points, the central banks are compelled to support the weak currency through open market operations (buying the weak currency and selling the strong one).

TABLE 7.7
ECU Basket Composition, January 2000

Currency	Value	Weight (%)
Belgian Francs	3.301	8.183
German Marks	0.6242	31.913
Danish Krones	0.1976	2.653
Spanish Peseta	6.885	4.138
French Francs	1.332	20.306
British Pounds	0.08784	12.452
Greek Drachmas	1.44	0.437
Irish Punts	0.008552	1.086
Italian Lira	151.8	7.840
Luxembourg Francs	0.13	0.322
Dutch Guilders	0.2198	9.87
Portuguese Escudos	1.393	0.695

Predicting Exchange Rates

Explaining exchange rate movements has always been difficult, and remains so now and in the future. Few even claim to understand why exchange rates change on a daily, weekly or monthly basis, much less trying to predict them over the life of a 30 to 50 year investment. To illustrate the variability, Figure 7.24 shows the nominal exchange rate for several countries against the U. S.$. Italy and Japan are separated because of the scale of their exchange rates relative to the other countries. There is no significance to the selection of the countries; these were readily obtainable from the WTO website.

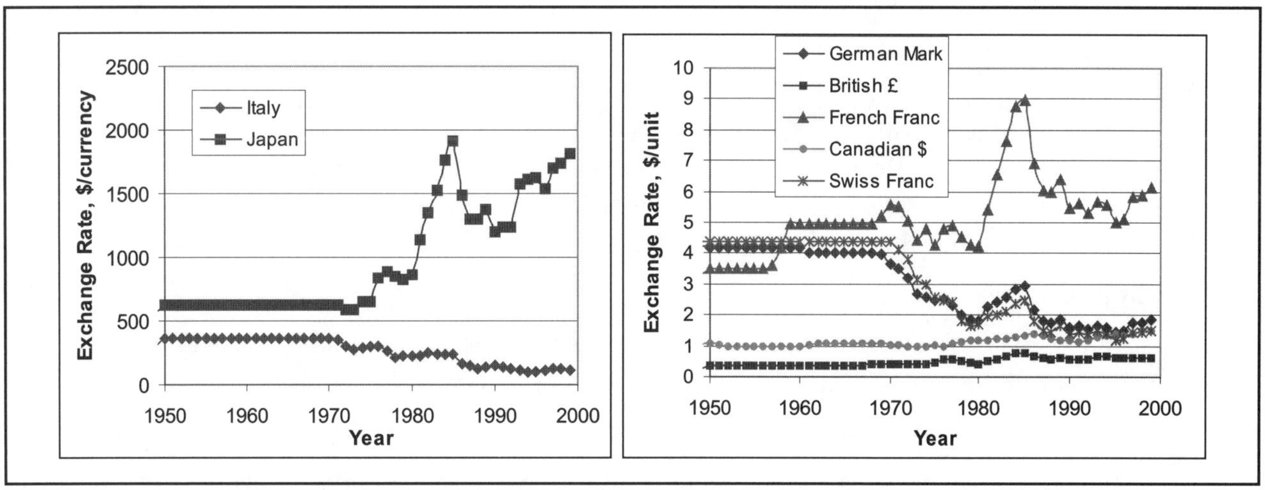

Figure 7.24 Nominal exchange rate variation for selected countries, 1950-2000

Several of the nominal exchange rates were almost flat until 1971, when the U. S. dropped the gold standard, allowing for most of the variation to take place after that point. Trying to explain exchange rate movements perplexes almost everyone, especially politicians trying to take credit for favorable movements, and then disbursing blame for perceived failures. Competing theories exist to explain the variability exhibited here, but, at the end of the day, each fails the acid test of providing good answers, most of the time.

The competing explanations for exchange rates include:

- Purchasing power parity (PPP),
- Cost changes,
- Portfolio Balance (PB),
- Fundamental equilibrium exchange rate (FEER), and
- Uncovered interest parity (UIP), and
- Intermediate-term model-based equilibrium exchange rate (ITMEER).

PPP believes exchange rates move toward the point at which inflation adjusted international purchasing power between countries is equal. Since inflation erodes purchasing power, the difference between the inflation rates in two countries determines the relative exchange rates. Example 7.2 provides a simple illustration of PPP.

Example 7.2: Malaysian ringitts are exchanged for the U. S. $ at a rate of 2.5/1. Starting with equal inflation rates in year 1, assume inflation is 10% in the U. S. in year 2. In year 3, assume the U. S. experiences a 5% inflation and Malaysia a 15% inflation.

	Year 1	Year 2	Year 3
U. S. Inflation	0%	10%	5%
Malaysian Inflation	0%	0%	15%
Exchange Rate	$\frac{2.5}{1}$	$\frac{2.5}{\left(1/1.10\right)} = 2.75$	$\frac{\left(2.5/1.15\right)}{\left(0.909/1.05\right)} = 2.51$

Inflation in year 2 increases the exchange rate to 2.75, indicating that more Ringitts are required to purchase the same amount of merchandise in the U. S. The higher Malaysian inflation rate in year 3 returns the PPP exchange rate back to about 2.5/1.

PPP follows from the "law of one price," which argues that, in the absence of transportation and other transaction costs, competitive markets will equalize the price of a good via the process of *arbitrage.* Suppose a medical drug sells for US$10 in New York and CDN$15 in Toronto. At an exchange rate of 1.5/1, the market is in equilibrium. Later the drug drops to CDN$10.0, which motivates consumers to buy more of the medicine in Toronto until the price is bid back up to CDN$15.0.

This process has three caveats:

1. transportation costs, barriers to trade, and other transactions costs are insignificant,
2. competitive markets for the product must exist in both countries, and
3. the law of one price only applies to tradable goods, not immobile items, like housing

Economists use two versions of Purchasing Power Parity: absolute PPP and relative PPP. Absolute PPP refers to the equalization of price levels across countries. Put formally, the exchange rate between Canada and the United States, $E_{CDN/USD}$, is equal to the price level in Canada P_{CDN} divided by the price level in the United States P_{USA}, or

$$\text{Exchange Rate}_{\frac{CDN}{U.S.}} = \frac{\text{Price}_{CDN}}{\text{Price}_{U.S.}} \tag{7.13}$$

Relative PPP refers to rates of changes of price levels, that is, inflation rates. This proposition states that the rate of appreciation of a currency is equal to the difference in inflation rates between the foreign and the home country. For example, if Canada has an inflation rate of 1% and the US has an inflation rate of 3%, the US Dollar will depreciate against the Canadian Dollar by 2% per year. This proposition holds well empirically especially when the inflation differences are large. Example 7.2 illustrated this situation for the U. S. and Malaysia.

A common misconception concerns the relationship between PPP and exchange rates in the short-run. Most analysts now believe that short-term exchange rate movements are news-driven. Announcements about interest rate changes, changes in perception of the growth path of economies and the like are all factors that drive exchange rates in the short run. PPP, by comparison, describes the long run behaviour of exchange rates. The economic forces behind PPP will eventually equalize the purchasing power of currencies; unfortunately, the equilibrating process may take more than 10 years, with 4 years being a minimum amount of time, assuming that you, the reader, accept the caveats mentioned above.

Probably the most often cited and lighthearted PPP measure is the Big Mac Index published by The Economist. Table 7.8 illustrates data included in one publication.(7.15) This "Burgernomics" approach to PPP suggests that in the long-run (4-10 years) the exchange rate should move to toward the rate that equalizes the prices.

TABLE 7.8

The Golden Arches PPP Standard

	Big Mac Price				
Country	**Local Currency**	**U.S. $**	**Implied PPP of the $**	**Actual $ Exchange Rate, 25 Apr., 2000**	**Under (-) or Over (+) Valuation**
Argentina	Peso 2.5	2.5	1.00	1.00	0
Australia	A$ 2.59*	1.54	1.03	1.68	-38
Brazil	Real 2.95	1.65	1.18	1.79	-34
Britain	£1.90	3.00	1.32	1.58	-20
Canada	C$ 2.85	1.94	1.14	1.47	-23
France	FFr 18.50	2.62	7.37	7.07	+4
Germany	DM 4.99	2.37	1.99	2.11	-6
Indonesia	Rupiah 14,500	1.83	5,777	7,945	-27
Japan	Yen 294	2.78	117	106	+11
South Africa	Rand 9.00	1.34	3.59	6.72	-47
Sweden	SKr 24.00	2.71	9.56	8.84	+8
Switzerland	SFr 5.90	3.48	2.35	1.70	-39
Taiwan	NT$ 70.00	2.29	27.9	30.6	-9

Figure 7.25 shows the common format for displaying either PPP or the Big Mac Index. Sweden, Japan, and France are overvalued, while the remaining countries are under valued by these measures. If you are reading this book several years after these dates, compare the actual exchange rate changes to these predictions.

The historical accuracy of PPP has been disappointing. Figure 7.26 shows the PPP movements for selected countries for the last 30 years. First, observe that the U. S. has a constant value of 1.0 over the 30 year period, because the y-axis measures PPP changes relative to the U. S. This is the format provided when logging onto the OECD website, as shown in footnote 13. Other countries, besides those shown in Figure 7.26 are available, but the sample illustrates the variability in PPP over 30 years. Other countries, like Italy, Japan, and Korea, also provide interesting patterns, but their scales disguised the volatility of interest here.

If PPP were the only cause of exchange rate variability, the line for each country would be horizontal to the x-axis. Any deviation from a horizontal line means that other forces influence exchange rate patterns over time. That is the essence of the ongoing debate about exchange rate forecasting. Several re-

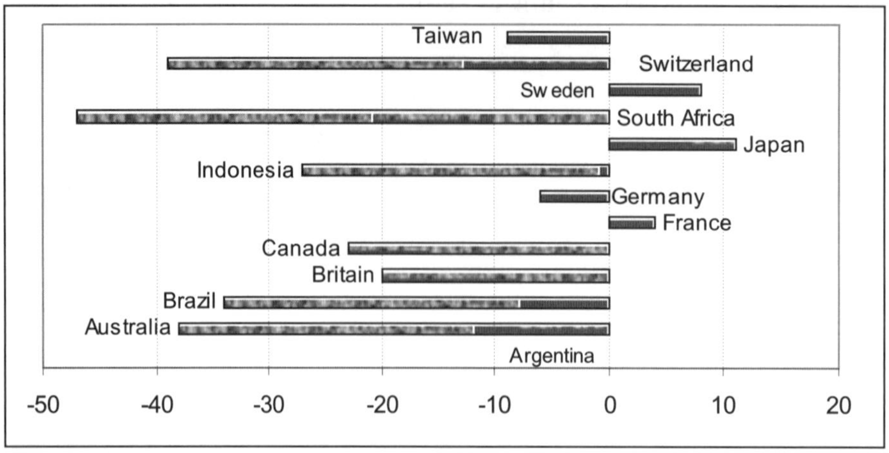

Figure 7.25 Big Mac PPP for selected countries

viewers reacted to this point by questioning the emphasis on PPP. The reason for allocating several pages on PPP results from its popularity with multinational investors. Rather than trying to predict exchange rates, they assume the exchange rates vary with relative prices, eliminating any need to predict exchange rates. That is the importance of the straight-line concept. Any country deviating from the PPP implied straight-line will have serious exchange rate changes that must be addressed directly; otherwise, major investment failures will continue to occur unless exchange rate variations are handled properly. This should be obvious since the last section explained where the price measure originated and their deficiencies.

Other theories are also offered to explain exchange rates. The *cost change* approach flows from the Keynesian notion that sellers set the price for products by figuring the cost of production and then adding a mark-up for profit. When exogenous shocks – political uncertainty, wars, technology changes, etc. – push the exchange rate off its equilibrium PPP; a number of years are required to re-establish equilibrium. The chances are very good that equilibrium may be nothing more than an artifact that allows professionals to make calculations, and never a reality.

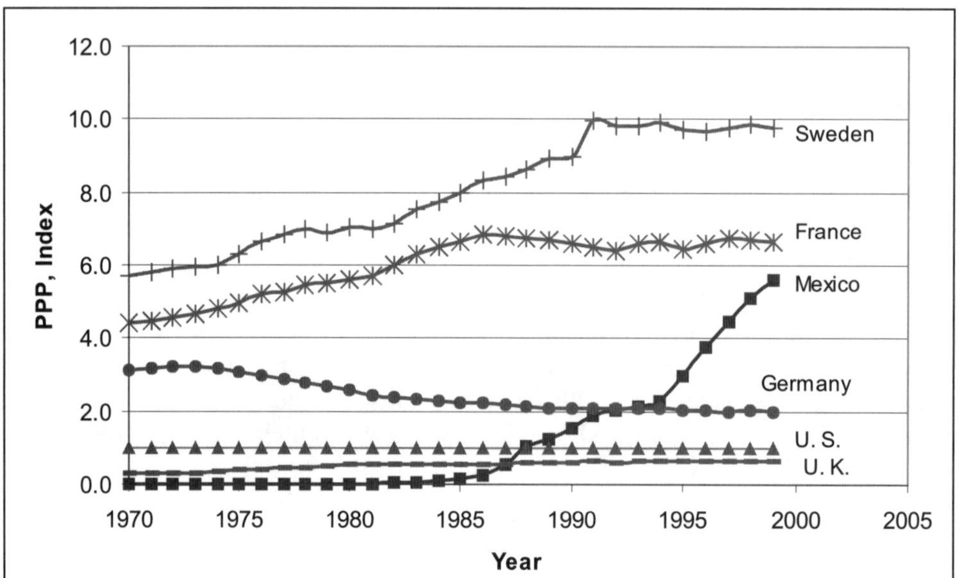

Figure 7.26 PPP over time for selected OECD countries

Traditional wisdom suggests that currencies with high inflation rates and large (and growing) current account deficits should fall. Unfortunately, the evidence fails to support traditional wisdom. The *fundamental equilibrium exchange rate (FEER)* defines the exchange rate as the one that produces a "sustainable" current account balance. Defining sustainable is crucial and this approach has difficulty in explaining actual exchange rate movements. It worked better when the world's governments controlled capital flows tightly. With the internationalization of the capital markets, only 1% of all world exchange is trade-related, the remainder involving the flow of money across international boundaries.

The *portfolio balance* (PB) method achieved popularity in the 1980's, due to the increase in cash in the capital accounts of international finance. Note that PPP and cost change focus on the current account only. The PB continues the logic of modern finance, and concentrates on how investors hold their financial wealth, including cash, checking accounts, and bonds domestically, but extended to include foreign currency and bonds here, especially equity exchanges. The pundits explain the continued rise in the U.S. stock exchange during the 1990's and first part of this century as the inflow of capital from investors looking for safer, higher return stocks. Two variables – interest rates and exchange rates – interact to explain the supply and demand. Figure 7.27 illustrates the relationship.

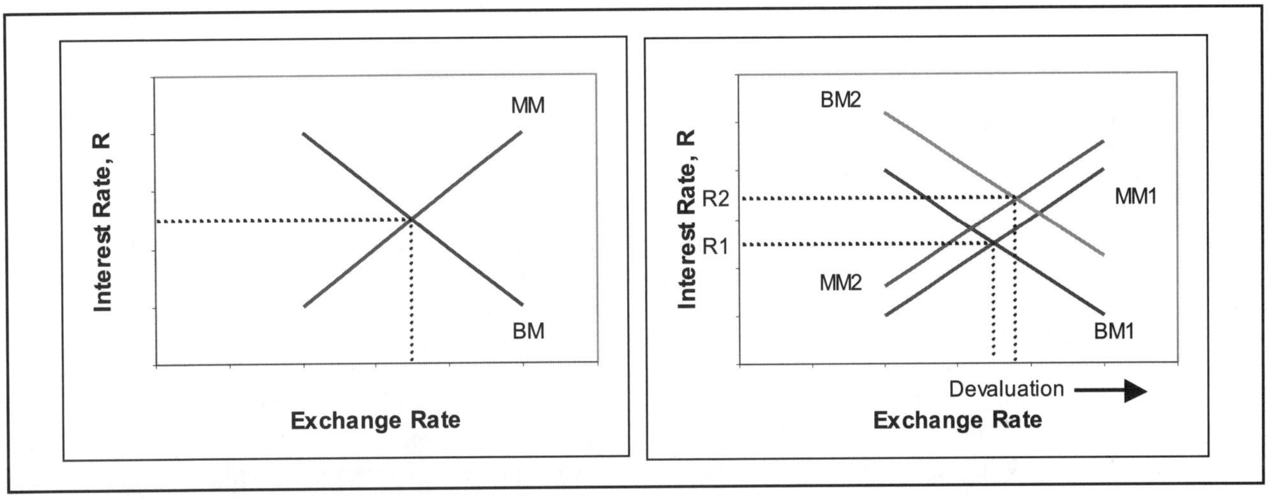

Figure 7.27 Portfolio balance and the effect of deficit spending

MM stands for the domestic money market, BM the domestic bond market, and R for interest rate. Exchange rate movements to the right signify devaluation.

The first graph shows a positively slope MM. When interest rates rise, investors reduce their money holdings, but, since the money supply (presumably) is held constant, the exchange rate falls. BM, the negative slope, indicates that higher interest rates in a country attract capital, domestically and internationally. Since the supply of these bonds are fixed (again by assumption), the only way investors will be satisfied with their existing portfolio happens when the domestic currency value of their foreign bond holdings falls. This happens when exchange rates rise.

The second figure applies the same concept to a country engaged in deficit spending, which is financed by issuing government bonds. Curve BM2 shifts to the right, because the residents need higher interest rates in order to motivate them to hold more bonds. Through wealth effects, the bond purchasers feel richer, increasing the demand for money – shifting MM1 to MM2. The combined effect shifts interest rates from R1 to R2. The exchange rate impact depends on the relative magnitude of the shift in each line. This example shows a devaluation in exchange rates even though interest rates rise.

While the graph helps explain the concept, serious difficulties arise in determining the location and shape of the curves, and when trying to quantify the shifts when interest and exchange rates occur. Even if that were possible, anticipating future changes in interest rates challenges all investors.

A slightly different approach, *uncovered interest parity (UIP),* starts with the notion that financial markets are efficient, incorporating the risk and return notions first presented in the WACC discussion in Chapter 4. If a risk-free dollar denominated bond pays 4% a year, and an equally risk-free £ denominated bond pays 7%, UIP follows the arbitrage notion that capital would flow into the higher interest rate bond, unless investors thought that exchange rate fluctuations would wipe out the differential. Assuming equilibrium, UIP suggests that the market expects the dollar to appreciate against sterling at 3% per year, which equalizes the returns from both assets. While conceptually intriguing, it's forecasting performance gives new meaning to the term – dismal science.

The method attempting to integrate the previous formats is the *intermediate-term model-based equilibrium exchange rate (ITMEER).*[7.16] The approach says exchange rates move to reflect interest rate differentials, plus a risk premium, which, in turn, varies with current account deficits, differences in asset yields, and overall domestic issues, like unemployment. Early evidence suggests that the approach predicts exchange rate movements better than any other method, though the evidence requires more work.

The upshot of all the work is that the value of a currency depends on three basic elements:

- Medium-term sustainable exchange rate: depends on the size of the current account deficit and the level of foreign debt that has to be serviced,
- Real interest-rate differential: with the real adjusting for price changes, and
- Risk premium.

Forecasting

None of the methods discussed above for explaining exchange rates provides and easily understood and applicable model for forecasting exchange rates for investment decision-making. If the investor desires to understand the variability in the exchange rates, the random walk or random walk with drift approaches described in Table 7.3 will work. Be advised though that the actual forecast will be quite bad.

If exchange rate risk poses a major problem to the investment, and the investor accepts the imperfect forecasting approaches, the best solution involves the use of hedging. The next section discusses the basic concepts of hedging, along with some examples of applications. Even better, hedging works for all the time series variables discussed in the Chapter.

HEDGING

Globalization of capital markets has stimulated excellent vehicles for minimizing, and, in some cases, eliminating the risks of future changes in commodity prices, inflation, and exchange rates. The previous sections demonstrated one approach, which tries to understand the volatility in each market separately. The hedging approach, the process of taking offsetting risks, tackles the risks of the future by using well-defined markets, most operating internationally. Acquiring offsetting risks in the market place, rather than trying to predict future market conditions, eliminates the risks that may damage investment performance.

Because many investors read about the colossal failures in hedging, like Barings Bank, Sumitomo Corp., Procter and Gamble, Daiwa Bank, Long-Term Capital Management, and Metalgesellschaft, management often treats hedging skeptically. The basic principle is that any hedging contract, which is based on assets that you hold now or will have, is essentially risk free. To make this market work, speculators or gamblers must exist to take the opposite position. This is no different in gambling on sports or any other activity. The critical difference is that the speculator absorbs the risk in exchange for huge upside benefits. The exception arises when the buyer and seller of a hedge both trade in that commodity or asset.

A variety of terms is used to describe the hedging process: *futures contracts, forward contracts, options, swaps, etc.* This section defines each first, and then illustrates how to use them to eliminate future price risks. Each of the items listed in the first sentence falls under the heading of a *derivative.* Each instrument (contract) provides a payoff that depends on the value of another underlying commodity (wheat, copper, oil) or financial asset (bond, currency of another country). Because the payoff derives its value from the prices of other assets, they are called *derivative instruments or derivatives.*

The major markets for financial and agricultural futures and options are the Chicago Board of Trade (CBOT) and Chicago Mercantile Exchange (CME). Over 50 exchanges perform the same function, with London offering the most extensive. Energy contracts are traded primarily on the New York Mercantile Exchange (NYMEX), and the International Petroleum Exchange (IPE) in London. The number of contracts signed each day is in the hundreds of millions, with values in the billions

Futures and Forward Markets

A futures contract requires the parties to buy or sell the commodity at a fixed price at contract maturity. Futures contracts were developed in the 1800's to allow farmers to manage their risks, and evolved into other industrial commodities, like gold, copper, oil, natural gas, etc., financial assets, like inflation and exchange rates, in the 1970's. The list of tradable commodities expands every time someone needs to hedge their risks. For energy, the list includes heating oil, leaded and unleaded gasoline, propane and natural gas. One book provides an excellent discussion of the application of futures and options to the petroleum markets.[7.17]

Though the futures contract specifies delivery of the product at a specific point, less than 2% of the contracts involve actual exchanges. The contract specifies quantity, 5,000 bushels of wheat, 100 ounces of gold, or 62,500 British pounds. The price for the contracts is determined by the interaction of buyers and sellers in very competitive markets. The futures market neutralizes all price risk, even those beneficial to the hedger. We know of one senior executive who bought futures contracts on petroleum when the market price was $22 per barrel, believing that oil prices were more likely to fall than rise. Less than a month later, Iraq invaded Kuwait, driving the price to over $30 at the contract maturity. Stories abound about how the executive lost over $300 million. In reality, the investment earned $300 million less than without the futures contract, which is different from losing $300 million.

Example 7.3 illustrates the process for implementing a futures contract. Ignoring, for the moment, some other important elements of the futures market, the seller has locked in a price for the next 5 years. Futures contracts are virtually risk free, because the contracts are highly standardized and the exchange guarantees that the transaction will take place, or, the exchange becomes an insurance agent. To make the insurance worthwhile, the exchange charges an insurance premium, called a margin payment. The margin differs significantly from a margin account in the stock market, which is essentially a down payment for the purchase of a stock.

Costs of participating in the futures market come in three forms: an *initial margin*, a *variation margin*, and *market to market* charges. The initial margin is an initial outlay in either cash or securities to the exchange that demonstrates each party's willingness and ability to consummate the transaction. For energy, the margin requirement falls between 5 and 10% of the contract amount. Most exchanges and brokerage houses also have a margin maintenance account, which is 60-85% of the initial margin, and varies with fluctuations in the price. As actual prices change relative to the contract, one of the contractors will receive a margin call to top up, or bring their margin back in line with original margin requirements. This changing "insurance premium" is what guarantees the integrity of the exchange.

In the marked to market transaction, the brokerage house calculates the profits and losses on every single account, and then bills or credits the gains or losses to each party. Suppose that on the very next day after the contract is executed, the price of the December 2001 contract goes to $24.78, or a $0.05 increase. The seller loses $5,000 (= 100,000*0.05). This amount is billed to the seller of the crude oil, while the buyer's account increases by the same amount.

Example 7.3: A producer plans on selling 100,000 barrels of light crude oil, each year for 5 years. The volatility in prices makes it difficult to plan their capital expenditures over the same time frame. Decide if the futures market can help?

Contract	Last	Open	High	Low	Most Recent Settle	Chg	Open Interest	Previous Days Total Volume	Last Updated
FEB 2001	29.48	29.35	29.90	28.98	29.41	-0.07	86100	93000	1/11/01 15:38:53
MAR 2001	28.10	28.15	28.47	27.70	28.22	0.01	91584	71062	1/11/01 15:38:53
NOV 2001	24.75	24.60	24.75	24.60	24.97	-0.02	14389	56	1/11/01 15:38:57
DEC 2001	24.52	24.50	24.52	24.15	24.73	-0.01	29622	2577	1/11/01 15:38:51
JAN 2002	N/A	23.95	23.95	23.90	24.51	0.88	12318	885	1/11/01 07:54:48
FEB 2002	N/A	23.65	23.65	23.65	24.29	0.85	7028	165	1/11/01 07:54:51
JUN 2002	23.10	23.10	23.10	23.10	23.47	-0.01	18339	1700	1/11/01 15:38:57
JUL 2002	N/A	22.83	22.83	22.83	23.31	0.76	2078	13	1/11/01 07:55:05
AUG 2002	N/A	24.14	24.14	24.14	23.16*	-0.93	815	0	1/11/01 07:55:14
SEP 2002	N/A	22.45	22.45	22.45	23.02*	0.72	5523	0	1/11/01 07:55:14
DEC 2002	N/A	22.10	22.10	22.10	22.63	0.74	18589	383	1/11/01 07:55:22
DEC 2003	21.66	21.66	21.66	21.66	21.71	0.05	11197	203	1/11/01 15:38:51
DEC 2004	N/A	20.87	20.87	20.87	21.41	0.74	5470	3	1/11/01 07:55:24
DEC 2005	N/A	20.15	20.15	20.15	21.16	1.24	4084	0	1/11/01 07:55:24
DEC 2006	N/A	21.50	21.50	21.50	20.91	-0.85	177	0	1/11/01 07:55:24

The first step requires information about the futures contracts. The table duplicates information available on the NYMEX exchange, with several months in 2001 and 2002 removed to save space. The table goes out to 2008, or for the 7-year life of futures trading. Most contracts go 30 consecutive months from the current month, and then in yearly increments of 36, 48, 60, 72, and 84 months prior to delivery.

Assuming a December sales date, the following transactions take place. Estimate the margin requirement assuming a 5% fee.

Date	Contract Size, bbls	# of Contracts Purchases	Price $/bbl	Revenue $m	Margin Requirement $m
+ 12 months	1,000	100	24.73	2.473	0.123
+ 24 months	1,000	100	22.63	2.263	0.113
+ 36 months	1,000	100	21.71	2.171	0.108
+ 48 months	1,000	100	21.41	2.141	0.107
+ 60 months	1,000	100	21.16	2.116	0.105

The last column summarizes the revenue to be received with certainty, before recognizing the costs associated with the transaction.

The brokerage house and exchange, again, change the values of the account so that the parties in the contract gain or lose. Futures markets are zero sum games as shown in Table 7.9, where someone always loses or gains, except the broker and exchange. These *market makers* make money at every step. Computing the margins and marked to market costs seems time consuming and tedious, but is really quite simple with computing power. Most players in the futures market have multiple contracts at any one time, and these costs are computed for all accounts. If the accounts are properly balanced, the additional costs may not be too great. Most participants, also, deposit treasury bills rather than cash to satisfy their margin requirements, which minimizes the impact of time value of money.

The short and long positions balance out, with the long position making the profit in this example, because prices increased relative to the original contract price. Had prices declined by the same amount the results would have changed. The party selling the contract sought to eliminate the risk of price movement. Engaging in the futures market did that, but imposed certain costs, including the margin requirements. The futures market allows sellers and buyers to eliminate most of the risk in a transaction, including commodity prices, inflation, and exchange rates. The question always ends up with the trade-off in the value of risk reduction relative to the cost. The benefit to the marketplace comes from the ability of the risk averse investor to transfer that risk to the risk takers, at a cost.

Table 7.9 assumes that the producer actually delivers the product to the designated point. As indicated earlier, that only occurs about 2% of the time. Rather than take delivery, the traders take an *offset position*; e.g., they purchase a contract opposite of the original. A buyer of a contract sells a contract of equal volume, and their profit is calculated as above. Some exchange, like IPE, in London allow the traders to settle with cash based on published prices on the last day of the contract.

TABLE 7.9

Example of Zero Sum Game in Futures Market for 1-Year Contract

	Short-Position	Result of Transaction	Long Position
Now	Sell contract for 100,000 barrels for $24.73		Buy contract for 100,000 barrels for $24.73
Dec 2001	Deliver barrels and receive $24.73	Actual Market Price = $25.00	Receive delivery of barrels and sell on spot market for $25 per barrel
Gain or Loss	+$2.473	-$27,000	+$27,000 = (25 – 24.73)*100,000

A forward contract extends the futures concept when the traders want to deviate from the standardized products dictated in the futures market. Each forward contract is written for and negotiated between a buyer and seller; whereas, the futures market contract is between each party and the exchange and broker. The forward contracts are not standardized and cannot be exchanged without agreement from the other party. The concept of default risk plays a much bigger role in this instance. The calculations follow the same format as the forward market.

Hedging exchange rates follows the same process. Example 7.4 is taken from Brealey, *et. al.*[(7.18)]

Example 7.4: Enterprise Oil bought $440 million of producing properties from a Texas company. At the current exchange rate of $1.743/£ Enterprise budgets £252 million. Enterprise was concerned that the $ would appreciate against sterling in the next two months when the transaction would be consummated. Assuming a 2-month forward rate of $1.730/£, determine the cash flow associated with hedging.

	Cash Flow, Millions	
	£	$
Now: Buy $440 m forward at $1.73/£	0	0
Month 2		
Pay for $	-254.3	+440
Pay for oil properties		-440
NCF, Month 2	-254.3	0

The slightly lower exchange rate of $1.73/£ available on the forward market increases the cost to £254.3. The actual rate went to $1.65/£, which would have cost Enterprise £266.67 million. Hedging in the exchange forward market saved £12.3 (= £266.67 – £254.3). See the source for other options.

Options Market

The options market builds on the concept of the futures market, but increases the flexibility of the traders. In the futures market, the traders had to buy or sell at the specified time. The options market gives the traders the right to consummate the deal at a specified time, but not the obligation. This increased flexibility, as you might guess, costs.

An option is the right to buy (*call option*) or sell (*put option*) an item in the future. The first example below demonstrates call options, then a put option example to contrast the futures market example is given

Two parties are involved in the options market, those seeking to hedge or secure their position and speculators. The difference is whether one owns an asset or is just speculating on price changes. Speculation plays a prominent role in market efficiency, and is effectively legalized gambling. Like most gambling, options should only be played with great care by those willing to live with the consequences of failure. Barings Bank, Long Term Capital Management and other companies have gone bankrupt or lost considerable sums of money by speculating.

Suppose a stock is selling for $100 right now. You believe that the price will rise in the future, but you do not have $100. The stock is selling for a premium (options contract price) of $10, and has an *exercise price* of $110 in three months time. By buying the option for $10, you get the right to buy the stock for $100 at the end of the option. If the stock price exceeds $110, it is termed as being *in the money.* If the price is below $110, the stock is *out of the money.* Financial options expire out of the money about 75% of the time.

Figure 7.28 illustrates the gains and loss to the investor. At a price below $110, the investor loses the $10 option premium. At $110, the investor exercises the option to buy the stock for $100 plus the option cost of $10 exactly offsets the gain of selling the stock for $110. If the stock rises to $120, the $120 raised by selling the stock yields a $10 gain (=120 – 110).

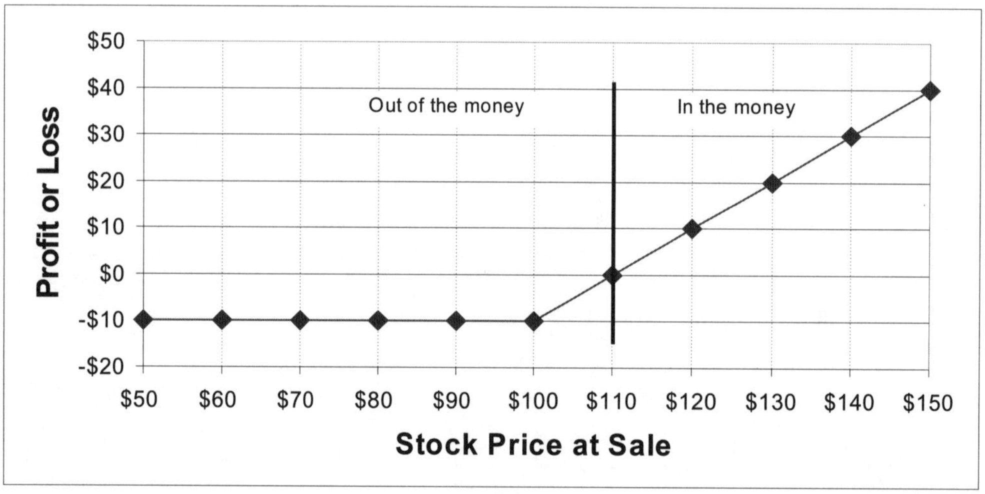

Figure 7.28 Example of financial options

The put option reverses the example. A seller of crude oil wants to receive the benefits of higher prices, but forego the financial losses associated with declining prices. Since options cover specific time periods, the first task is to assess the costs and benefit of entering into an options contract. The cost of purchasing a put option for light crude futures was taken from , and summarized in Table 7.10. The listed call and put options are shown in $0.50 increments. Combining the put costs with the same price data used to evaluate futures price, permits the investor to compare the costs and benefits of a put option.

TABLE 7.10
Put Prices for Selected Results in 24 months

Exercise Price, cents per bbl	Options Price, $/bbl
1800	1.43
1850	1.59
1900	0.90
2000	2.13
2100	2.54
2200	2.99
2300	3.34
2350	3.65
2400	3.98
2450	4.31
2500	4.62
2550	1.31
2600	5.27
2750	6.35
2800	0.96
3500	0.40

Example 7.5 illustrates the valuation process. Assume that management has performed sensitivities on the NCF's and realizes that the project destroys value when price falls below $20. The cost of the option, $2.13, falls between 5 and 10% of the value of the commodity, and that cost illustrates the impact on return of risk reducing behavior. The further spot prices fall below the $20, the greater the benefit to the party purchasing the option. Note, however, that if spot prices stay above $20, the options contract reduces value by $213,000. Reducing risk also lowers return, as expected, with the magnitude of the loss depending on actual spot price movements.

Example 7.5: Compute the NCF for the project assuming that a 2-year $20 put option can be purchased for $2.13. The sales volume was 100,000 barrels.

	Oil Price, $/bbl				
	14	16	18	20	22
Sales Revenue, $m	1.400	1.600	1.800	2.000	2.200
+ Payoff from Put Option, $m	0.6	0.4	0.2	0	0
Total Revenue, $m	2.000	2.000	2.000	2.000	2.200
- Cost of Put Option, $m	0.213	0.213	0.213	0.213	0.213
Net Revenue, $m	1.787	1.787	1.787	1.787	1.987
Benefit from Hedging, $m	0.387	0.187	-0.013	-0.213	-0.213

Swaps

Swaps tend to confuse many investors more than futures, forward or options markets, but really involve nothing more than two investors exchanging one stream of cash flows for another, contractually, rather than buying and selling assets. The swap format simplifies the process, allowing almost instantaneous movement of cash, without the legal, tax and time implications associated with acquisitions and dispositions of assets. Many wonder at the interest in swaps, but at the end of the year 2000, over $56 trillion in swap contracts were outstanding, compared with $5.4 trillion in the international bond market. See

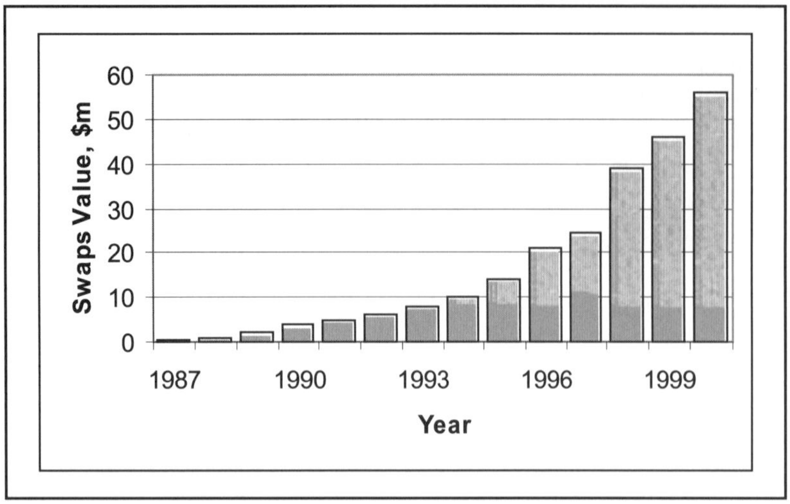

Figure 7.29 Growth in international swaps market

Figure 7.29 for a summary of the growth in the swaps market. In fact, some state, "swaps are the glue that binds together the world financial system."(7.19) Critics of globalization of markets should worry more about swaps than trade issues.

Swaps come in two forms: interest rate swaps and exchange rate swaps. Interest rate swaps dominate the market, especially in international banking, by allowing banks to balance assets and liabilities efficiently. A bank with an excess of short-term, floating interest rate savings accounts and few long-term, fixed rate assets can balance their portfolio by exchanging a swap with a bank in the opposite position. Combined with the ability to switch obligations and benefits between currencies, swaps permit considerable risk mitigating behavior, at a fairly low cost.

A classic example of an interest rate swap concerns a manufacturer that pays *LIBOR* (London Interbank Offer Rate). LIBOR refers to the interest rate that international banks lend to each other, rather than the more commonly heard phrase, prime rate, which captures the rate lenders give to the most credit worthy borrowers. The prime rate builds in a 1-3% premium above inflation, while LIBOR tracks expected inflation without the premium

Suppose the manufacturer borrows $500m at LIBOR for a new investment in another country. One concern in valuing the investment concerns changing inflation rates that could impact the interest burdens to the firm. Example 7.6 illustrates the benefits and costs associated with the manufacturer entering into a swap arrangement to fix the interest rate.

Example 7.6: The manufacturer issues $500m in floating rate bonds, and that LIBOR currently offers a 7% rate.

Process	Interest Rate		
	6%	**7%**	**8%**
Annual Interest paid on floating rate bond, $m= LIBOR*$500m	30	35	40
– Cash payment on swap (0.07 – LIBOR)*500m	05		-5
Total Payment, $m	35	35	35

The first row shows the actual interest payments for varying changes in LIBOR. A 1% drop in interest rates lowers the interest burden by $5m to the manufacturer, and the converse holds for an increase in interest. Faced with volatile interest rates, which management believes, has a better chance of increasing than decreasing, the firm enters into a swap agreement to pay 7% on the principal amount to a swap dealer (the opposite side of the market as in the forward and options market), and receive LIBOR times the principal. If interest rates rise to 8%, the manufacturer receives a $5m payment from the dealer, which offsets the increased cost on the bonds. Should inflation fall to 6%, the manufacturer pays the dealer $5m, again bringing their total cost to $35m.

Readers familiar with traditional financial markets probably realize that the classical approach to guaranteeing a fixed rate would be to repurchase the floating rate bonds and issue fixed rate bonds. The cost of repurchasing and then issuing the new bonds involves considerable transaction costs, both in the actual outlay of funds to bond holders, investment bankers, and time required to complete all transactions. The swaps market often provides a quicker, lower cost alternative.

The swap transaction has converted an actual, legally binding contract to pay a floating interest rate on bonds into a synthetic fixed rate to the manufacturer. This complexity creates considerable problems for the financial reporting process, and analyzing financial statements. Financial reporting currently requires the investor to report the terms under which the bonds were issued. By undertaking the swap, the investor has significantly altered their risk profile, and that change goes unreported in some countries, and those countries requiring detailed reporting, the analyst must dig deeply into the footnotes to glean the relevant information.

The second element of the investment concerned the investment in another country. The preceding example dealt with just borrowing the money in \$'s, and ignored the exchange rate issue of building the facility in another currency, raising the question of the best location to borrow money. Since interest charged on borrowings reflect the lenders perspective of a borrowers credit worthiness, borrowing money in \$'s may be cheaper than borrowing in another currency, say £. Example 7.7 shows one form the currency swap might take.

Example 7.7: Assuming the investor can borrow money at 6% in \$'s and 7% in £'s (assuming a 1.5\$/£ exchange rate) for a 4 year loan, determine the cash flow pattern.

	Year 1		Year 1-3		Year 4	
	\$	£	\$	£	\$	£
Issue dollar loan, \$m	500		-30		530	
Arrange currency swap						
Investor receives \$m	-500		30		-530	
Investor pays £m		333.3		-23.3		356.7
BT Cash Flow, m	0	333.3	0	-23.3		356.7

The effect of the exchange rate swap converts a 6% loan of \$500m to a 7% loan in £.

The process begins with the investor negotiating a deal with a bank (assumed to be British here), where the bank agrees to pay the investor enough money to service the interest on its dollar loan. The borrower takes the \$500m from the American bank and deposits it in the British bank for £333.3m (collateral). For the next 3 years, the British bank pays the investor \$30m, which is used to pay the American bank the equivalent amount. The firm must still pay interest on the principal at 7%, however, or the £23.3m. In Year 4, the last year of the loan, the British bank pays the investor \$530m, which pays off the American bank.

The real benefit to the swap arises from the reduced cost of borrowing to the lender, primarily by shifting the risk between the banks. The American bank knows the borrower to be a low risk firm, while the British bank may have never dealt with them. By depositing the \$500m in the British bank, the default risk to the British bank drops significantly, allowing them to offer lower interest rates. In this example, the British bank may have to charge 8-10% to the same investor for the same project.

SUMMARY

Forecasting the components of NCF over time involves considerable uncertainty that must be faced, not ignored, to invest successfully. The methods for forecasting are as diverse as the disciplines contributing their knowledge to investment process. This chapter outlines various approaches for recognizing the risks and mitigating the risks. Selecting the appropriate format depends entirely on the business environment each investor operates in. No one approach satisfies everyone's needs. The ideas contained in this chapter should provide some ideas and alternatives for consideration in trying to enhance ones investment performance.

The hedging concepts introduced in the last part of the chapter to mitigate price, inflation, and exchange rate risk are useful additions to the toolkit, though each form of hedging incurs costs as the price for reducing risk. While the concepts presented here introduce the basics, be careful when trying to implement them. Each approach involves the complex interaction of markets, which can destroy value if used improperly. There is a huge difference between hedging when buying and selling assets, be it commodities, interest rates, or exchange rates, and speculating. Speculators, like most gamblers, play by a different set of rules and motivations than the investor trying to maximize value. Our only advice is to avoid speculation unless you truly understand the rules of the game.

REFERENCES

7.1 Bernstein, P., *Against the Gods*, John Wiley and Sons (1997).

7.2 Jenkins, G., "Some Practical Aspects of Forecasting in Organizations," *Journal of Forecasting* (1982), pp. 3-21.

7.3 Jenkins, *ibid.*

7.4 Campbell, J., personal communication.

7.5 Anderson, D., personal communication.

7.6 In 1827, Scottish botanist, Robert Brown, described the motion of particles suspended in a liquid, which he attributed to the continuous impact with neighboring particles.

7.7 Dixit, A. and R. Pindyck, *Investment Under Uncertainty*, Princeton University Press (1994).

7.8 Dixit, A. and R. Pindyck, *ibid.*

7.9 Laughton, D., "Modern Asset Valuation and Project Pricing in the Energy Industry," *Journal of Energy* (2000).

7.10 Lund, D., "With Timing Options and Heterogeneous Costs, The Lognormal Diffusion is Hardly an Equilibrium Price Process for Exhaustible Resources," Unpublished manuscript, University of Oslo (1991).

7.11 *The Economist* (23 Dec., 2000).

7.12 World Trade Organization statistical summary (2001).

7.13 See WWW.OECD.ORG or WWW.WTO.ORG for sample accounts over time.

7.14 Pacific Exchange Rate Service, WWW.PACIFIC.COM.

7.15 *The Economist* (27 Apr., 2000). Updates can be found at WWW.ECONOMIST.COM.

7.16 Wadhwani, S., WWW.BANKOFENGLAND.CO.UK/SPEECHES/SPEECH53.PDF.

7.17 Errera, S. and S. Brown, *Fundamental of Trading Energy Futures and Options*, Pennwell (1999).

7.18 Brealey, R., Myers, S., and A. Marcus, *Fundamentals of Corporate Finance*, 3rd Edition, McGraw-Hill Irwin (2001).

7.19 *The Economist*, "Danger Signs" (10 June, 2000).

CHAPTER 8

ASSESSING AND VALUING RISK

The increasing emphasis on *risk assessment* and *risk management* impresses many as a relatively new phenomenon. This is a false impression, created by limitations in the tools available for measuring and quantifying risk. Mankind, probably from its inception, struggled with ways to handle the risks of living. Recent books, such as "Against the Gods,"[8.1] describe risk methods as a tool for demystifying religion and providing the knowledge base and thought process responsible for much of the progress that has transpired over the last few centuries.

This chapter outlines risk assessment methods, while Chapter 10 looks at risk management techniques. Risk was historically addressed using highly simplified and approximate procedures. These methods included increasing the discount rate, arbitrarily reducing sales volume or price, and applying basic sensitivity analysis. Such procedures originally reflected the limited calculation tools of the day. As computing power expands, more direct and accurate methods for addressing risk should replace the traditional, limited approaches.

Chapter 6 introduced the basic concepts of risk. Defining risk in an investment context continues to be an elusive concept, however. Though various definitions exist, we prefer the business definition; namely, risk is the chance of losing money or foregoing attractive investment opportunities, because this matches the goal of sound investment analysis; namely, to maximize shareholder value. Definitions focusing on project failure or the potential loss of money restrict the range of issues to be addressed too narrowly.

Risk assessment, at its simplest, is composed of two basic steps: specifying the likelihood of an event occurring (probability) and then quantifying the consequences of that event, using NPV or any other measure desired by the investor. Assessing risk involves addressing highly complicated and often interdependent issues. This complexity presents challenges, but provides a very real opportunity for excellence. To say that rigorous risk assessment is too complicated ignores the purpose professionals are hired by organizations and the tools available today. Chapters 1 and 2 defined professionals as any group building models to describe the real world. These models include the following various sources of risk:

- incomplete data,
- limited models,
- forecasts of the future,
- philosophical differences, and
- changing knowledge overtime.

Risk assessment involves trying to quantify the impacts of these elements on the important components of the valuation process. This process might also be called *error management,* since errors creep into all the values used to make investment decisions.

Investment analysis combines complex variables across different technical disciplines into a common denominator – money adjusted for taxes and then reduced to one value – NPV, BDR, NPV/INV, etc. Understanding the mechanics and interaction of the valuation process has a major bearing on organizations success or failure. Unfortunately, the only known constant in every valuation is that each input contains some error. The real question is how much error and the consequence of that error on the investment decision.

Figure 8.1 illustrates the basic process. All inputs regarding volumes, pricing, timing costs, and taxes vary. With varying inputs, selected outputs, like NPV in this example, also vary. This variability forms the foundation of risk assessment, or error measurement.

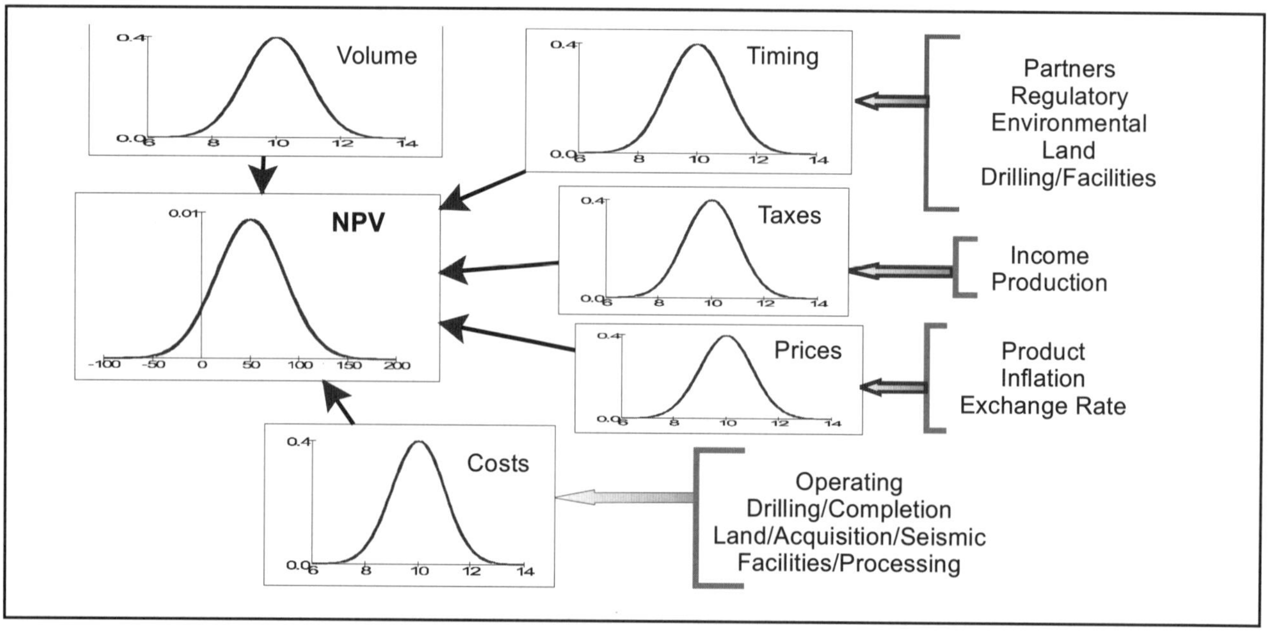

Figure 8.1 One example of risk assessment in investment valuation

Figure 8.1 stimulates an immediate question; namely, when is it appropriate to use formal risk assessment methods? The answer, like always, depends on the purpose of the analysis. Quick, simple, low costs, and high volume cases, like a workover in a field with hundreds of wells, only need the deterministic analysis outlined in Chapters 3 and 5. As cost and complexity increase, more formal methods are required. The transition point depends ones attitude toward risk, or utility, as explained later.

Building models involving the complex interaction of hundreds, if not thousands of variables challenge even the most experienced people. Most professionals recoil at the complexity of risk assessment at first encounter. The prospects of adding a distribution for any one variable, say price, over the life of the analysis can be intimidating. This first impression is typically overcome with experience, training and practice.

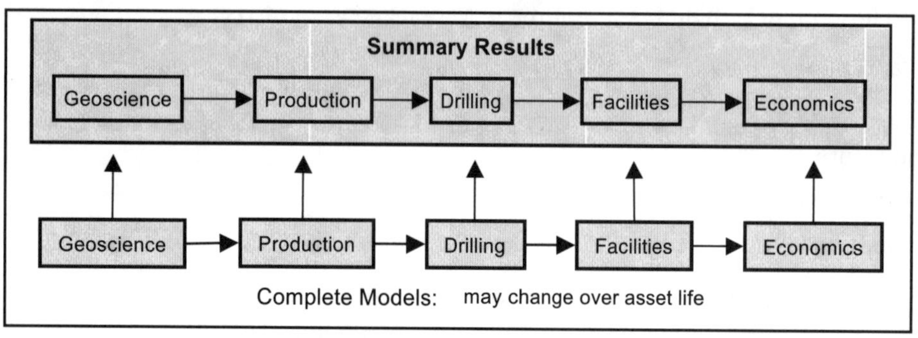

Figure 8.2 Simplified model analysis

One technique for facilitating the successful implementation of risk assessment methods is to remember the sequential nature of investment decision-making. Most projects involve detailed study by the respective specialty areas. Figure 8.2

highlights typical information flows. The complete models capture the detailed analysis in the respective disciplines. Information obtained in each discipline, however, is filtered when passed along to subsequent disciplines. The same process holds in risk assessment: only the relevant outputs of the discipline analysis need to be passed along or summarized.

Figure 8.3 expands on the elements that go into the detailed analysis at the discipline level. Observe that the three disciplines illustrated – geoscience, reservoir, and facilities – spend considerable time analyzing the details specific to their discipline. At the end, however, only specific pieces of information flow to the next phase. This reduced information flow hinders formal risk assessment because of the difficulty in tracking variables across disciplines without direct access to the analytical methods and software used to generate the information. Figures 8.2 and 8.3 have been adapted from the SIAM approach advocated by Dr. Steve Begg.

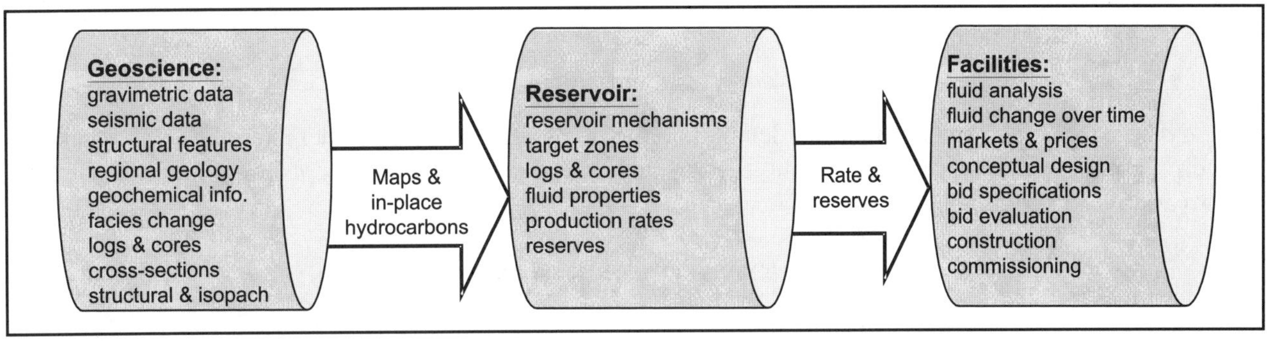

Figure 8.3 Example of detailed information flow

Formal risk assessment conveys more information or variability analyzed at each stage than the traditional deterministic point estimates. Providing distributions of reserves and production rates communicates opinions about the variability or risk in the numbers generated by each discipline to subsequent disciplines using that data, not just a single value.

Chapters 1-7 outline the process for building the investment decision-making model. Even if the process is understood and followed perfectly, data quality ultimately determines the results. One characterization of the data elements comes from Bernstein, where he cites an anonymous author as:(8.2)

The information you have is not the information you want.

The information you want is not the information you need.

The information you need is not the information you can obtain.

The information you can obtain cost more than you want to pay.

The most common approach is to identify the variables influencing the investment decision by following the sequence outlined in Chapters 1-7. Then, insert an arbitrary set of values to check the logic of the model, with the objective of refining the values later. The reasoning is that more precise numbers will be obtained once the relative importance of each variable is determined. *Anchoring,* the process of fixating on the first values used, often prevents the improvement in these values, as highlighted in Figure 8.4.

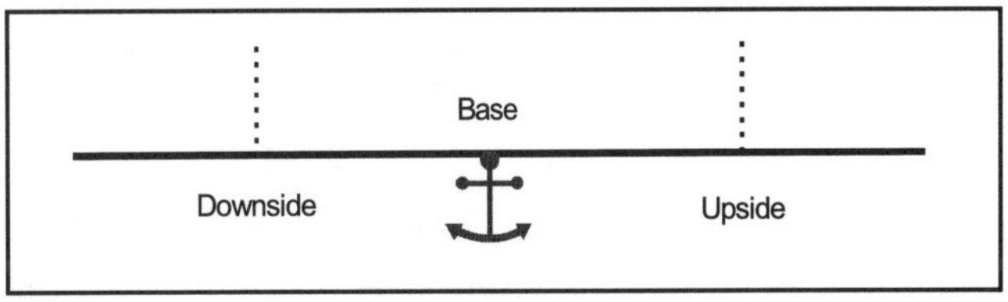

Figure 8.4 Illustration of anchoring

Anchoring arises for many reasons, but political and emotional motivations dominate. When a project first receives attention from peers and management, all data is subject to scrutiny. With each presentation and every modification of the model, that data becomes vested in the process unless continuously challenged. Altering any data or variable after several presentations involves change, and change disturbs most human beings.

No matter how well the risk investment process is applied, anchoring on poor or bad data can undermine the entire process. We recommend creating a data flow sheet that highlights the variables in the model and tracks the data values over the course of the project. This is much like project scheduling with the focus on data.

The basic concepts covered in this chapter include:

- Sensitivity analysis
- Decision trees
- Simulation
- Utility, and
- Measuring value when risk and utility are included

These concepts are outlined in detail in other texts, so we review them quickly. Emphasis is placed on applying the concepts in simple, easy to understand ways. The concepts are applied in Chapter 9 to a variety of examples

SENSITIVITY ANALYSIS

The simplest form of risk assessment observes the change in one or more measures of profitability with a variation in an input variable. This is the basic what if question which is so frequently touted in advertising for programs, like Lotus 1-2-3, Excel, What If, Toprank, etc. Computers have certainly facilitated answering *what if* questions. Unfortunately, it also generates more output than can be analyzed easily. Trying to present all combinations of what if results, simply and quickly, is a nightmare.

The sensitivity process entails deciding on the important output variables, like NPV first, then changing the inputs that impact NPV. Each iteration records the findings. Knowing when to stop the what if questioning and presenting the findings complicates the process. Even simple projects have thousands of combinations of what if questions.

A common outline for addressing data uncertainties, or what if questions, is outlined in Table 8.1. The variables considered here include 3 elements: the base case or initial guess, an upside and downside or low side. Again, remember that the base case is often subject to the anchoring problem. The upside and low side values reflect subjective opinions of staff at some point during the project life. As data becomes available or understood better, the sensitivity approach merges into the simulation method, described later in the chapter.

TABLE 8.1

Example of Project Sensitivity Analysis

Variable	Base Case	Upside	Lowside
Production Volume (units)	1,000	1,400	800%
Sales Price ($/unit)	17	19	14%
Exchange Rate ($/?)	1.60	19	1.2
Sales Delay (months)	0	-20	+30
Investment Delay (months)	0	-10	+24
Opex ($ million year)	5	4.9	5.5
Capex ($ million)	25	24%	33
Taxes (x.xx)	0.35	0.33	0.40

The list illustrates the type of uncertainties that are often considered. The base case and range values depend on the opinions of the professionals and should change over time as more, and better information becomes available. Sensitivity analysis enhances project analysis in two ways:

1. It helps identify the critical variables that determine project profitability and risk, and
2. It is easy to perform on the modern computer.

The ability to perform sensitivities also complicates the process. Managers know that the tool kit allows measurement of any *what if* question that can be thought of. This opportunity creates the following disadvantages:

- The number of solutions becomes cumbersome when too many what if questions are asked.
- There is no indication of the likelihood of a given what if case occurring.
- It does not take into account the dependency among the input variables.

The number of sensitivities on any project could run into the millions in even relatively simple projects. Even in Table 8.1, there are 30,240 permutations and 252 combinations for 10 variables taken 5 at a time (See Chapter 5). Obviously, this is more information than anyone can process effectively and efficiently.

More often than not, someone asks a what *if* question which has little or no chance of occurring. Such sensitivities just generate numbers that misdirect decision-making. Some also ask questions, like production volumes, without considering the corresponding impact on facilities design and operating cost. This dependence between components is significant, and must be recognized to generate meaningful sensitivities.

The main disadvantage of sensitivities, however, is that it produces more information than is possible to convey effectively. We know of people running hundreds of sensitivities in anticipation of manager's questions. When done, they had forgotten what they had run, and were unable to convey the results effectively. Too much information may be just as bad as too little in such cases.

The exercise of sound professional judgment, particularly with an effective team approach, can reduce the number of computer runs (suitable for decision purposes). Knowledgeable professionals usually can "bracket" the range of uncertain numbers in their specialty area. The result is an organized, logical approach toward uncertainty as opposed to the "mindless calculation orgy" that some purport to call risk analysis.

Recognizing the dependencies between variables, like production volume and Capex/Opex, increases the required number of sensitivities substantially. Even more critical than the cost of the computer and lost staff productivity is the handling of the information generated. This may be the information age, but that means the capability to generate information is greater than ever before, not that people know how to present and interpret the information. Most investors can assimilate only 10-15 cases effectively. Relationships become confused after this point and just interfere with decision-making.

Given that the ability to generate numbers exceeds the capacity to manage them, a more general format is helpful. Figure 8.5 shows a typical *spider diagrams* for displaying the impact of changing inputs on the desired output, NPV in the example. All lines on the graph go through the origin at 0% change on the x-axis and a $0 change in NPV. This format allows direct measurement of the typical question, "How does NPV change if Capex rises 25% or prices fall 25%?" Read from the selected value on the x-axis up to the desired line. For a 30% decline in price, observe the line intersecting at the star on the price and production line. NPV declines by roughly $60 million when price falls 30%.

The horizontal line, labeled breakeven, reflects the original NPV of the project. The project base case NPV is $43.3 million. By reading where this line intersects the selected variable line, the maximum change required to make NPV = 0 is found. Should revenue (either because of price or production) decline

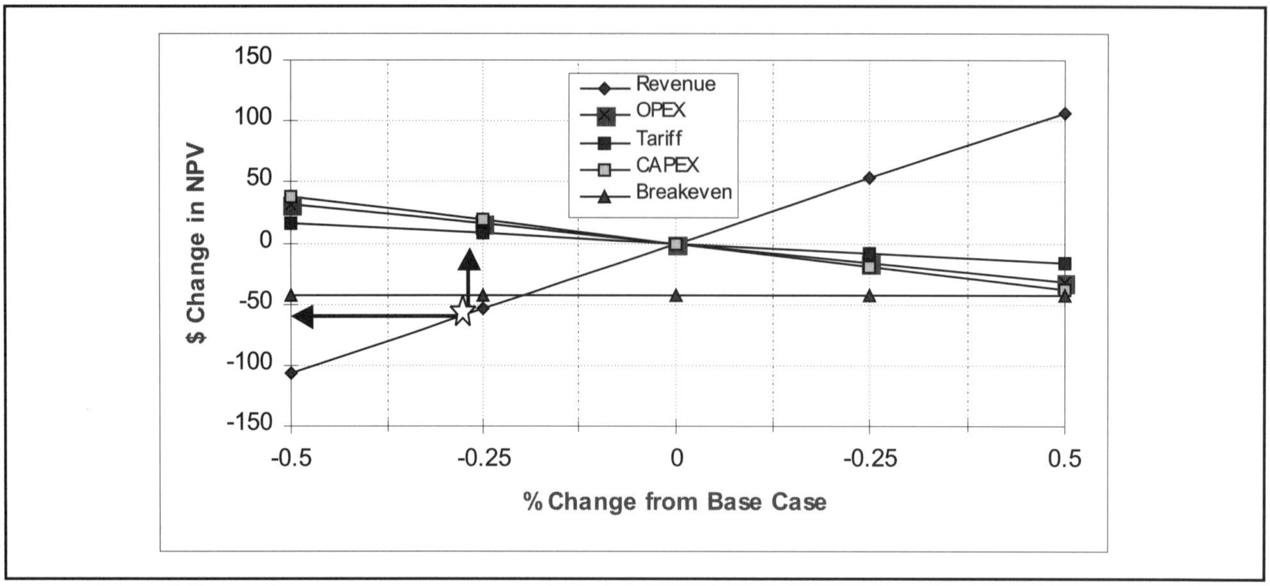

Figure 8.5 Spider diagram for sensitivity analysis

by about 20%, the project breaks even (NPV = 0). Similarly, Capex must increase by more than 50% before NPV reaches zero. Knowing the threshold for each variable reduces the need for extra sensitivities.

Multiple sensitivities may be accommodated, as well. If a question like "what is the impact of a 10% revenue drop and a 25 % increase in Capex on NPV" is asked, combine the calculations, as follows:

43.3 (original NPV) – 21 (revenue drop) – 19 (Capex rise) = $3.3 NPV

This example subtracts the two sensitivities from the original NPV. Project NPV falls to $3.3 million when the specified changes in price and Capex are recognized. Even more sensitivities can be included, if desired. Note that one graph captures a vast range of alternatives.

The slope of the lines identifies the most sensitive variables in the project. A major concern in risk assessment is the variables impacting the project the most. Here, the revenue line is the steepest, indicating that price and production volumes dominate NPV. The Capex line has the second steepest slope followed by Opex and then the tariff line. Given limited time and resources, more effort should be allocated to fine tuning price and production, and Capex, with less emphasis on Opex and tariff.

Spider diagrams, though helpful, become cumbersome as projects increase in complexity. For example, instead of worrying about just revenue, the focus shifts to the detailed engineering input. As the details increase, the graph becomes harder to read. One program, which tries to reflect the contribution of every input, is Toprank® from the Palisades. In this program, the output variable, like NPV, is selected. The program then searches the spreadsheet for every variable which influences that value, either directly or indirectly. These inputs are then changed by a specified amount, like +50% and –30%, as the user chooses. The results are then summarized in a tornado diagram.

Figure 8.6 shows the tornado diagram from the same example used to illustrate spider diagrams. Toprank uses the precedent feature in Excel to determine the cells that impact the selected output, NPV. In this example, Toprank found 2,959 cells that impacted NPV. Imagine the time required performing sensitivities on this number of cells. Included in the precedents are formulas and functions in the spreadsheet.

The program automatically selects all input variables influencing the output. The user can override the computer if desired to vary only the desired inputs. Of interest here, however, are the variables having the biggest influence – discount rate, production tax, and escalation rate. These variables are normally treated as constants, having been provided by corporate groups or local taxing authorities. This situation

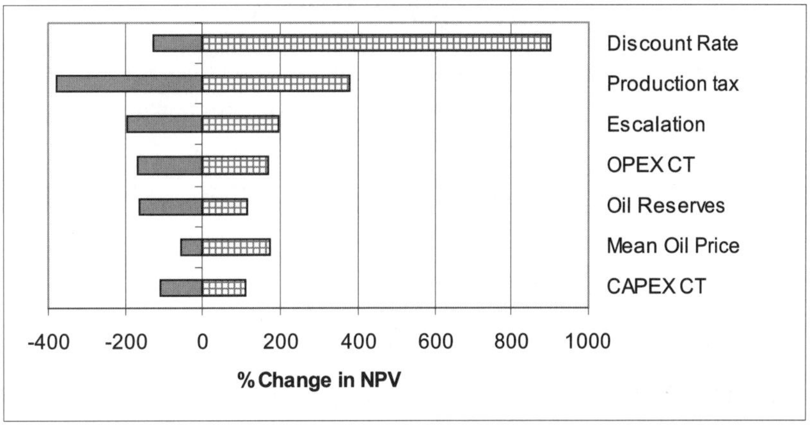

Figure 8.6 Example of tornado diagram

reemphasizes the old notion that people make the calculations they know how and like to make. Some people would focus their attention on the oil reserve number, and ignore all the other values in the list. Yet, as the tornado diagram shows, the investment results are quite sensitive to these other, ignored variables.

Many observe that Figure 8.5 and 8.6 reflect changes in one variable only. Toprank allows the user to specify multi What if questions. For instance, if volume increased, a corresponding increase in Capex or Opex might occur. Handling such interactions between variables is the professional's responsibility, but often is ignored in actual practice. Most canned programs don't allow the user to build in these interactions either.

Traditional sensitivity analysis generates information on the consequences on changes in variables, but ignores the likelihood of change. For instance, assuming that the cost-of-capital is correctly estimated, the discount rate may have a huge impact on NPV, but has little chance of changing. So, the tornado and spider diagrams may misdirect attention unless the likelihood of change is recognized.

Limitations of Sensitivity Graphs

The summary graphs of sensitivities are linear in each of the examples cited above. This holds as long as each input value is changed by the same amount, like a 10% increase in investment and so on. When data are changed for one or more years by a rate, which differs from the other years (a 10% rise for 3 years, then a 5% rise thereafter), the linearity condition is lost because of the time value of money calculation. You must rerun the computer program to compute these sensitivities.

Another exception arises in countries where tax is a function of another input. Canada, for example, makes royalty a function of production, Norway computed Statoils working interest and royalty based on production, and Alaska bases severance tax on production. The net effect is minimal in many cases, however.

More serious too most users are the standard rate and reserve sensitivities. As long as you change rate and reserves by the same amount, no problem arises. If just rate or reserves vary, then the timing of the project life changes, and this alters the NPV estimate in a non-linear manner. A separate run is needed for each rate or reserve sensitivity.

DECISION TREES

Variation in outcome and likelihood of change are captured in decision trees. The decision tree concept emanates from the gambling literature, where the quest was the search for a fair bet. The simplest decision tree merely represents Equation 8.1 in a graphical format.

$$\text{Expected Value} = (P_S)*(\text{Success Outcome}) + (1 - P_S)*(-\text{Failure Outcome}) \quad \textbf{(8.1)}$$

where: P_S = the chance or probability of success, and failure and success outcomes are captured in monetary terms

Some replace P_s with the term chance of success, COS.

The classical betting game flips a fair coin of head or tails. If it comes up heads, you receive \$5, but if tails occur, you pay \$1. Is this a fair bet? According to the expected value, you will receive on average \$2.00 (= 0.5*5 – 0.5*1). If you play the game a hundred times, you come out ahead; hence, this is a fair bet for you. Note that this equation assumes repetition. Playing the game only once results in either a \$5 gain or \$1 loss.

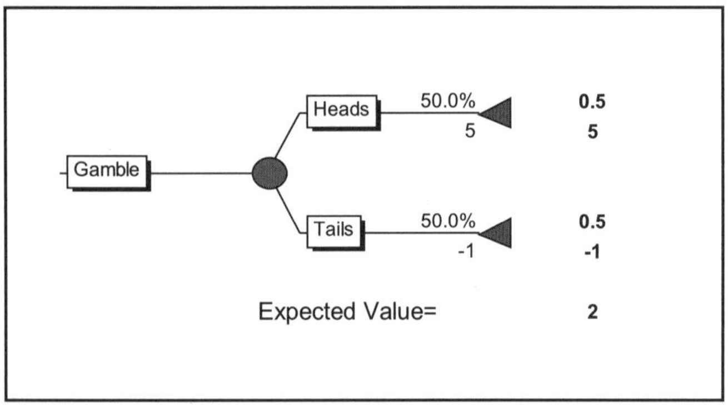

Figure 8.7 Decision tree for gaming example

Figure 8.7 shows the graphical representation of the expected value game. The circle captures a *chance node*, which reflects alternative outcomes. The triangle is an *outcome node.* The third element of decision trees is the *decision node,* as shown later. The user inputs the 50% probabilities and the consequence – win \$5 or lose \$1, and the computer generates the column of values. Like Equation 8.1, the expected value is \$2. If more than one chance node is included, the far right column sums the combined probabilities and outcomes.

Drawing decision trees was a pain until computer software became available. There are over a dozen programs, which draw decision trees, to our knowledge. Each program performs essentially the same tasks, so the choice of software is up to the user.

The gambling example illustrates the concept and is fine for gamblers where the odds of an outcome are well defined. For making investment decisions, however, the problem is more complicated because P_s or COS is unknown and must be estimated. A classic example is the weather forecast. Saying that tomorrow has a 20% chance of rain is an estimate based on meteorological interpretation, and is itself subject to error or uncertainty.

Risk Weighting and Expected Monetary Value

Analysis of uncertainties in the probability estimates is called *risk weighting (RW)* or *expected monetary value (EMV).* Equation 8.1 is the simplest format for computing such values. The primary difference is that P_S is estimated rather than being known in advance, or a priori. Estimates for P_S may be subjective or calculated based on available data.

EMV is the weighted average of the gain relative to the cost of failure. For instance, a friend offers to pay you \$100 if your team wins the league championship, but you pay them \$200 if someone else wins. The attractiveness of this bet depends upon your estimate of P_S. If you felt that P_S was expected to be 0.7, then the EMV of the bet is \$10 [= 0.7(100) – 0.3(200)]. In a gambling casino, you would make money by playing the game long enough for the averages to work in your favor.

CHAPTER 8

Probably the most common application of EMV is to discrete events, like win or lose, and success or failure. Among explorationists, the discrete event is the existence of a mineral deposit. In the petroleum industry, for example, P_s is the product other geological parameters, like the probability of a source of hydrocarbons (P_{soure}), the probability of a trapping mechanism (P_t), and the probability that the reservoir exists (P_r). Equation 8.2 expresses this simple geological relationship (P_{gs}).

$$P_{gs} = P_r * P_t * P_{source} \qquad \textbf{(8.2)}$$

P_{gs} measures whether a reservoir exists, but says nothing about the volume of reserves. Considerable effort has gone into building worldwide data bases to assess the accuracy of these numbers. In the absence of a good database system, subjective judgment and analogs usually dominate.

Other disciplines use the P_s concept as well. Equipment is either running or down, so the probability of having a generator supplying power to run electrical system is important. In research, the likelihood that the effort will lead to a marketable product is also a P_s. The legal system uses probability of success to determine the strategy most likely to win a case.

Faced with uncertain P_s values, graphing the entire set of outcomes conveys information about the consequences of varying P_s. Because Equation 8.1 is linear, Figure 8.8 can be drawn with just two points. On the left axis is the failure cost and the success NPV is plotted on the right hand vertical axis. The x-axis reflects values of P_s between 0 and 1. The straight line yields the EMV of a project for any given value of success. The success NPV is \$43 million. Failure reflects the after-tax cost of expenditures before giving up on the prospect or project. That value is \$21 million for the example.

Figure 8.8 shows EMV for any value P_s, or a complete range of sensitivities for the EMV values. The vertical dotted line represents the breakeven P_s. Equation 8.3 shows how the value is derived.

$$\text{Breakeven } P_s = 0 = P_s * \text{NPV of Success} - (1 - P_s) * (\text{NPV Failure}) \qquad \textbf{(8.3)}$$

or

$$\text{Breakeven } P_s = \frac{|\text{NPV Failure}|}{|\text{NPV Failure}| + \text{NPV Success}}$$

$$= \frac{21}{21+43} = 0.328 \quad \textit{or} \quad 33\%$$

At a 33% chance of success, the project will breakeven, or EMV = 0. At a P_s greater than 33%, the investment becomes a fair bet, and a loser at a P_s value less than 33%

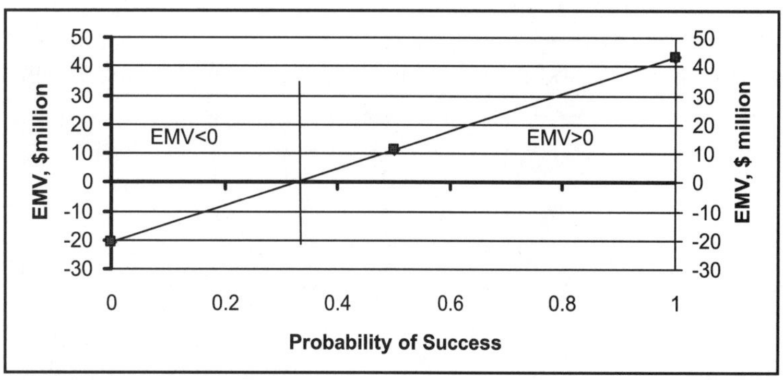

Figure 8.8 EMV example

Some have correctly noted that discrete events either occur or don't occur, and are never 33% successful. This is the problem with averages with discrete or integer data. If you stand with one foot in a bucket of boiling water and one foot in a bucket of frozen water, on average you are just right; yet, the pain would be excruciating. The correct way to react to P_s is to treat it as a strategy, just like going to a gambling casino. In most games of chance, you win or lose based on your decision. Gambling strategy forces the gambler to make decisions where the odds are in their favor after repeated throws of the dice or cards. Most investors invest in 10, 20, 30, or hundreds of projects and can therefore apply the same logic. Had the company invested in 100 projects like this one and 33 been successful, the EMV would equal zero.

Investors use EMV as one primary tool for ranking projects. Any project with EMV>0 is acceptable and the highest EMV projects are preferred. Lower down in the ranking are projects with negative EMV's, but positive NPV's. Investors often accept projects with negative EMV's when non-quantifiable (strategic) benefits exist. Common examples include investments required as part of the concession agreement, safety, and those, which might yield information about a basin or trend, or research. An exploratory well might provide markers with which to interpret seismic, for instance.

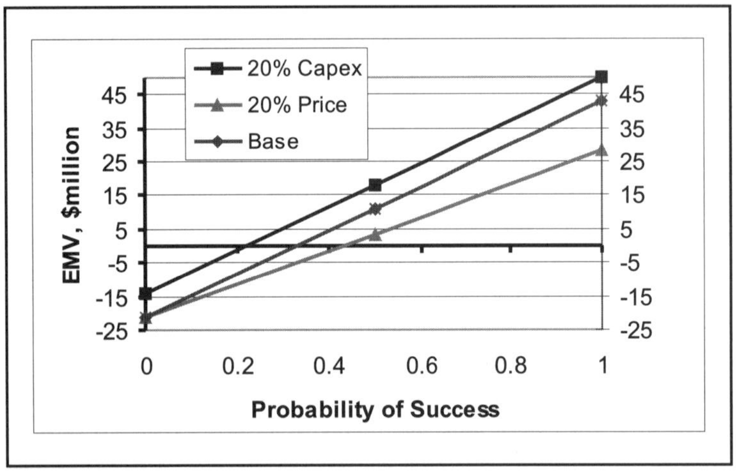

Figure 8.9 P_S vs. base case sensitivities

Formats, like Figure 8.9, prove useful in illustrating the dependency between P_s and sensitivities in the original inputs. The figure shows the change in EMV as the result of a 20% price reduction and a 20% reduction in Capex.

A 20% price reduction impacts the breakeven P_s much more than the same percentage change in Capex cost. The breakeven P_s rises to 45% for the price decline, and falls to about 22% for a Capex reduction. Project profitability relative to success vs failure risk is can be visualized much easier with such a graph.

Another variant of the same graph is used to contrast the economics of investment alternatives. A classic example compares using the company treasury to pay for the project (base case), or letting another party earn an interest in the project by paying all or part of the investment costs. This is called a *farmout.* When the other party pays the investment cost, the failure case falls to zero. On the other hand, they receive some of the rewards for successful projects, reducing our share of the profits by the same amount.

Figure 8.10 highlight the trade-off between using the treasuries money versus others money. The base line duplicates the values from the last graphs. The farmout line has an EMV of zero at a 0% P_S, rising to slightly less than $20 million at complete success. Since capital exposure is zero, the farmout option makes money at any non-zero P_S. At about 50% the two lines intersect, identifying the P_s at which investors would be indifferent between spending their own money or someone else's money. To the left of the line, the farmout EMV exceeds the other line, so the farmout adds more value. To the right of the line, using the treasuries money adds the most value. The conclusion should be easy to understand: spend your money for the good projects, and someone else's money for the high-risk projects.

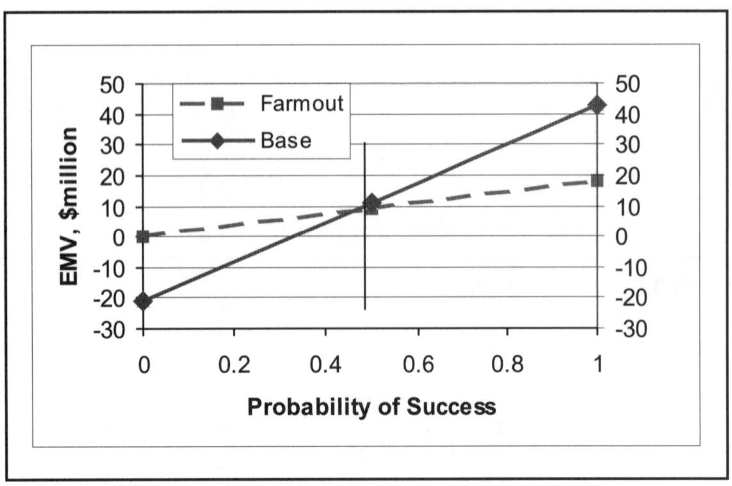

Figure 8.10 Trade-off between financing option and risk

The results of simulations can also be displayed in decision-tree form. Just split the continuous curves, like those shown in Chapter 6 and in the next section, into the desired number of sections, and then integrate the results. Figure 8.11 shows a simple distribution with three vertical lines. The low production case occurs 26% of the time, high volumes about 10% of the time and the base case occurs the remaining 64%.

CHAPTER 8

A decision tree helps organize and present information. We have seen projects rejected initially by management, accepted after the professionals organized the information using the tree approach. It is nothing more than a pictorial summary of a series of events. A summary increases in importance as projects increase in complexity. *The fundamental rule of every evaluation is that, investors reject what they do not understand.*

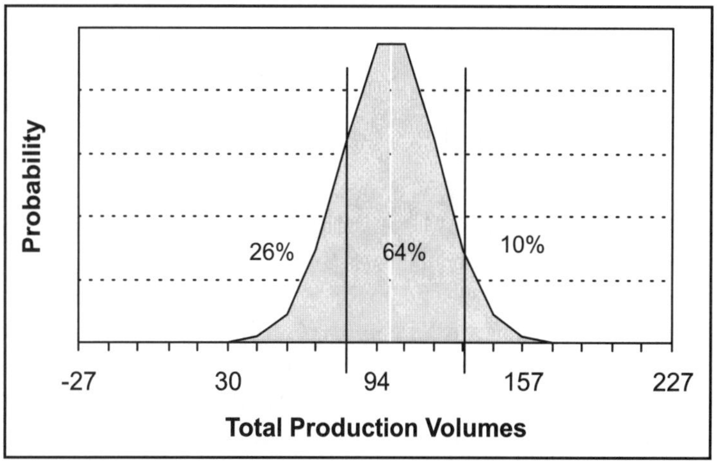

Figure 8.11 Converting continuous distributions to discrete probabilities

Figure 8.12 summarizes the three volume sensitivities along with the chance of getting any production at all. The first branch node identifies the success or failure with the specified probabilities. The second section lists the three volume alternatives from Figure 8.11. The probabilities at the far right are the product of the success probability times the volume probability.

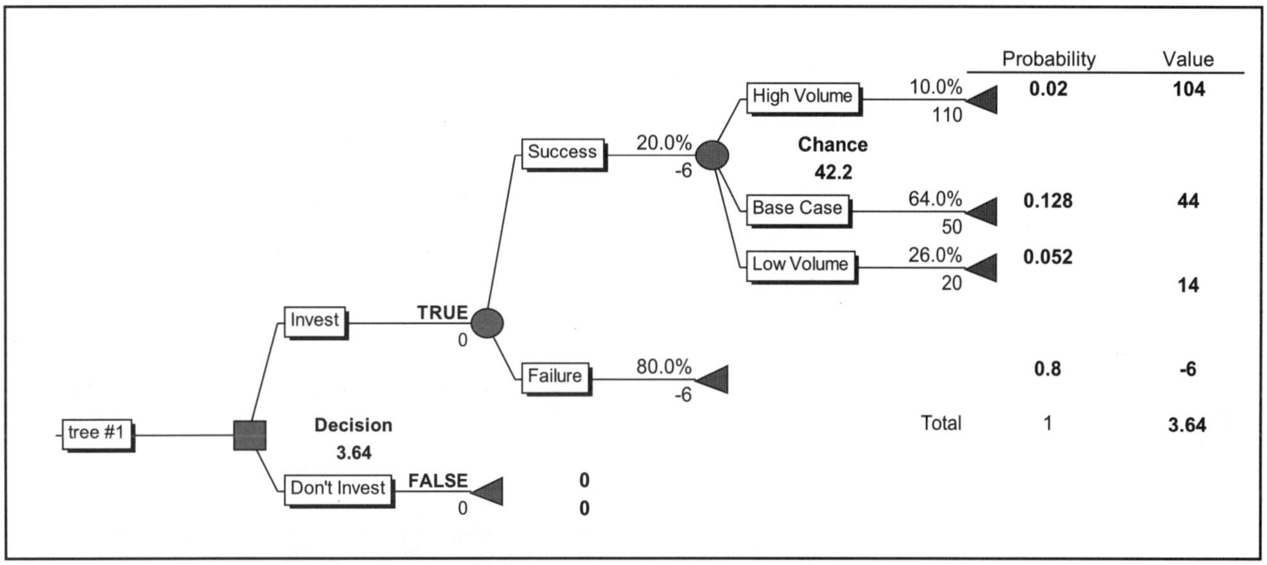

Figure 8.12 Tree for investing with success and volume risk

The tree builds from the left by first recognizing that two choices exist: invest or not. If no investment occurs, the tree ends. If the investment is made, two uncertainties – success risk and volume risk are recognized. The investment costs \$6 million with a 20% chance of success. If the \$6 million fails, then the project loses the entire \$6 million. The NPV's for the volume alternatives are summarized on the line next to the label, and then summarized in the last column. The final value for the high volume case is 104 (= 110 – 6). The probability column is the product of the success probability and the probability of high volume, 2% (= 20%*10%).

The expected value of the project is \$3.64 million, implying that the project adds value. An alternative question, however, concerns the risk. There is an 80% chance of losing \$6 million. Is the upside profit of \$3.64 million worth the gamble of losing 6 million? The answer depends on the investor's financial condition and attitude toward risk.

The software used here, Precision Tree, includes an algorithm that finds the best route through the tree. Next to the Invest box is the word true. This means that the computer checked all paths and found that the invest decision maximized the project expected value. Likewise, the false next to the Don't Invest box signifies that this path has a smaller value. The expected values within each chance node are computed as well. The chance heading of 42.2 is the average value for the three volumes multiplied by their respective probabilities.

Figure 8.13 extends the same project by recognizing the impact of a delay in bringing the project on line. Delays are quite common due to permitting and environmental restrictions, as well as political controversy. Branches 1-3 are the same as before. Delaying reduces the project NPV due to loss in the time value of money. The cost of delay may be entered next to the 2-year delay box, under the 50% value, or by rerunning all the cases after shifting values back 2 years. This second choice is the most common and accurate. The expected value of the project falls to $0.76 million when the delay is included. The project is still acceptable by most criterions, but would probably not be funded if budget constraints exist.

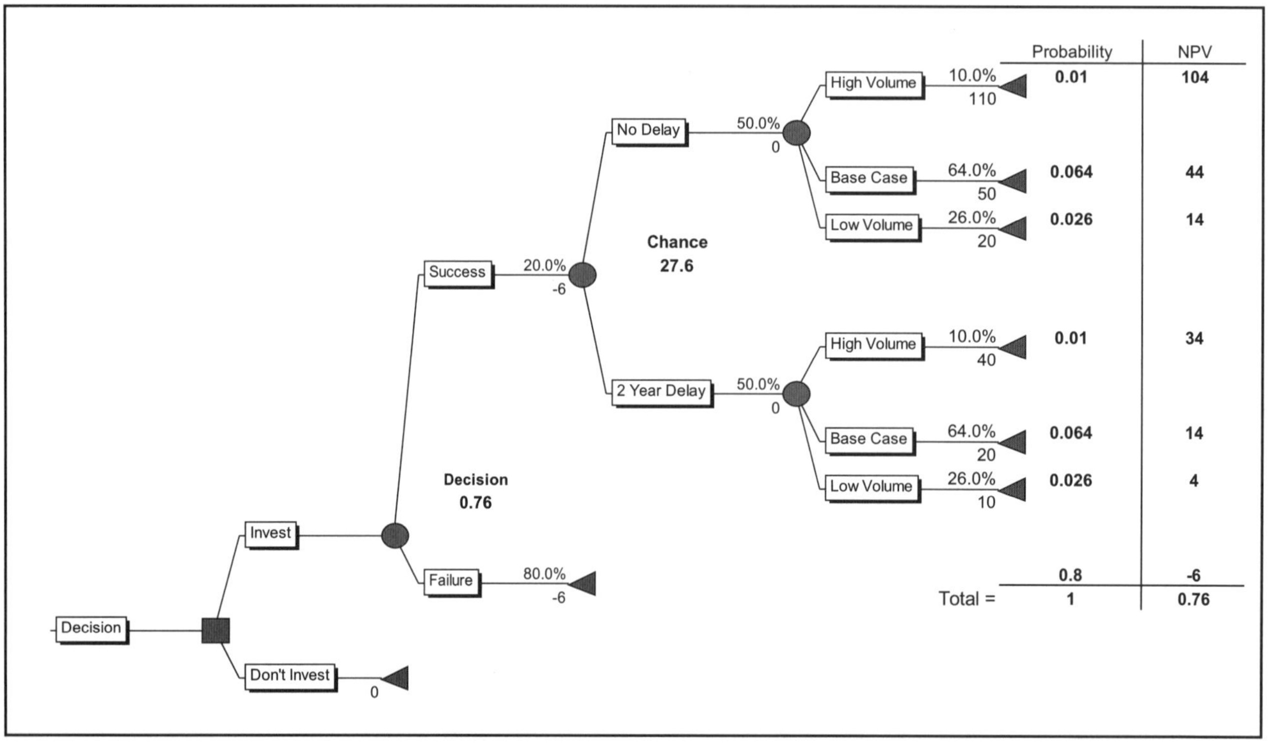

Figure 8.13 Tree with project delays added

NPV falls because the 2-year delay case destroys value due the time value of money. Observe that the NPV for the high volume case is $110 million if the project is completed on schedule. The NPV declines to $40 million under the 2-year delay case. The other values fall in a similar fashion. This finding suggests that the cause of the delay should be fleshed out, and methods to ameliorate the problem identified. Such marginal projects are often left unfunded when all projects are considered. Note that the project is still acceptable at certainty, with a $27.6 million NPV.

Figure 8.14 extends the delay case by recognizing that there is always the chance of farming the project out, as explained in Chapter 9. To keep the graph size manageable for the book, the entire tree in Figure 8.13 along the success path is reduced to on line in Figure 8.14. Before discussing the values, this situation occurs quite often. The number of variables becomes so large, the graphs become quite difficult to display to others. In a project with 10 variables, each with three outcome ranges, the resultant graph can only be displayed with high tech plotting capability.

Moving along the Invest and Success line, a 20% chance of receiving $27.6 million exists; likewise, failure has an 80% chance of losing $6 million. The combination yields expected economics of

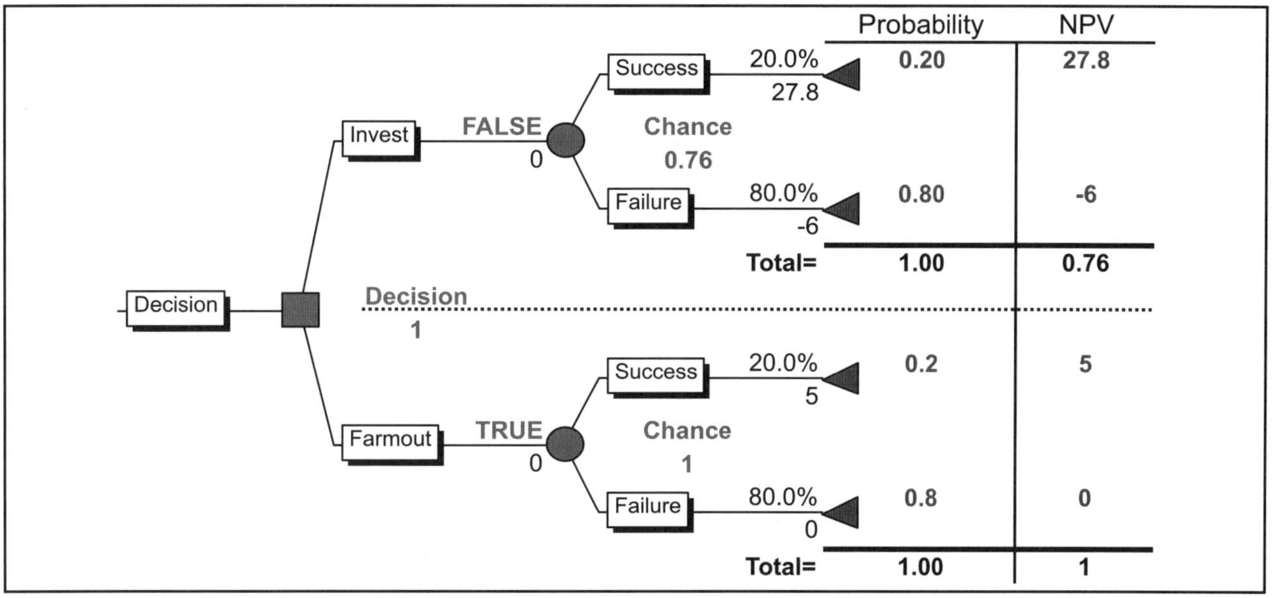

Figure 8.14 Invest vs. farmout example

$0.76 million, the same as Figure 8.13. Farm-out economics are presented below the dotted line. By farming out, the expected value falls to $1.00 million, consisting of $5 million if successful and $0 if failure. Offsetting the fall in expected value is the reduction in risk. Note that we cannot lose money by farming out, while there is an 80% chance of losing $6.00 million by taking 100% of the prospect. Refer to the EMV graphs, because this just compares the failure result.

Which is the better choice? On a straight EMV standard, the farmout NPV of $1 million exceeds the $0.76 million from investing. Some professionals insist that *optimism is essential to successful investing*. This is true. Business case histories identify successful investors that took huge risks and made money; on the other hand, more histories of business failures and lost jobs, assets, and prestige as a result of excess optimism exist. Striking the proper balance between the expected return and risk is the essence of risk management. The fundamental question is "Can I survive the loss?"

Surviving failure is called *gamblers ruin*. Though most references to gamblers ruin arise in the petroleum industry, it occurred in the late 1990's to a group led by two Nobel price winners in economics. The company, called Long Term Capital Management, Inc., estimated and managed risk in financial markets so that, on average, they made money. What they forgot is that a low probability of occurrence failure could be so severe that their capital was wiped out. Their situation demonstrates again that both the probability of occurrence and the value of the outcome is important

Figure 8.15 shifts the focus to manufacturing and process investments, where scheduling is an important issue. The plant being constructed goes through several stages, including 3 years of planning and permitting. At the end of 3 years, the project will be cancelled at a cost of $31 million, or a test module costing $113 million built. At the end of six years, the results of the decision to build the first complete plant are made. Then, a decision to expand the plant is delayed to year 10. The NPV's and probabilities at each stage are included.

The expected value of the project is $145.5 million, indicating an acceptable project, on average. The worst possible outcome is a loss of $113 million after the test module is constructed. The total probability of losing money is 28%.

One of the major factors impacting a process/manufacturing decision is the sale price over the life of the project. Most products experience wide fluctuations, or cycles over time, as shown in Chapter 7. Figure 8.16 summarizes two pricing alternatives for such projects: one, sell on the open market and take

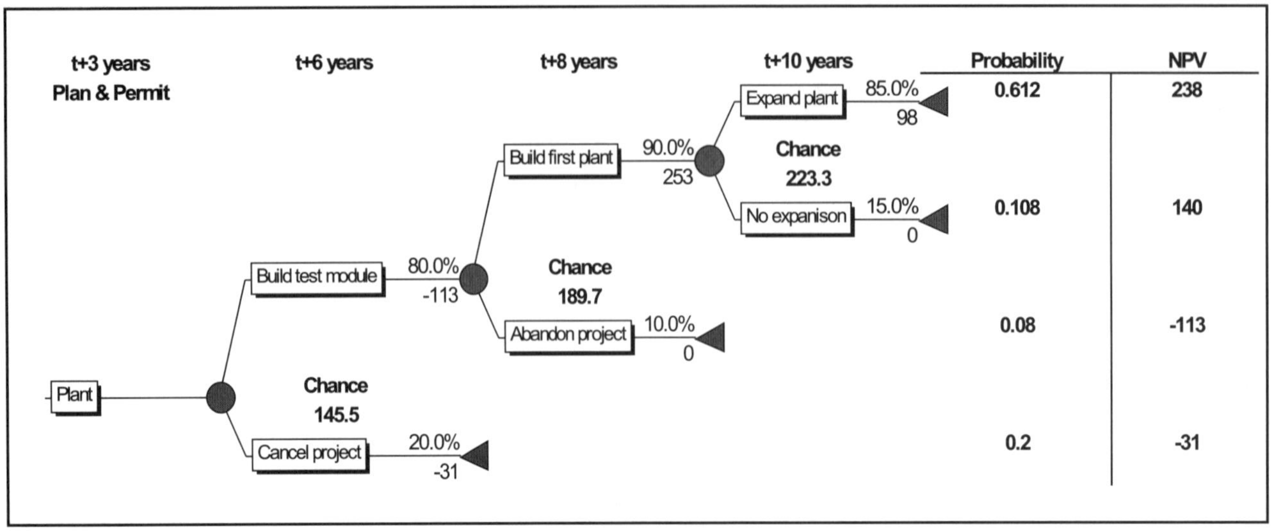

Figure 8.15 Planning, construction, and expansion project

what the market offers (called price taking), or two, negotiate a contract with fixed prices. The expected market price shows the variation common to most products. With a low price prevailing, the plant loses money, but makes money at the high and most likely price. The overall value of accepting market pricing is a $90 million NPV.

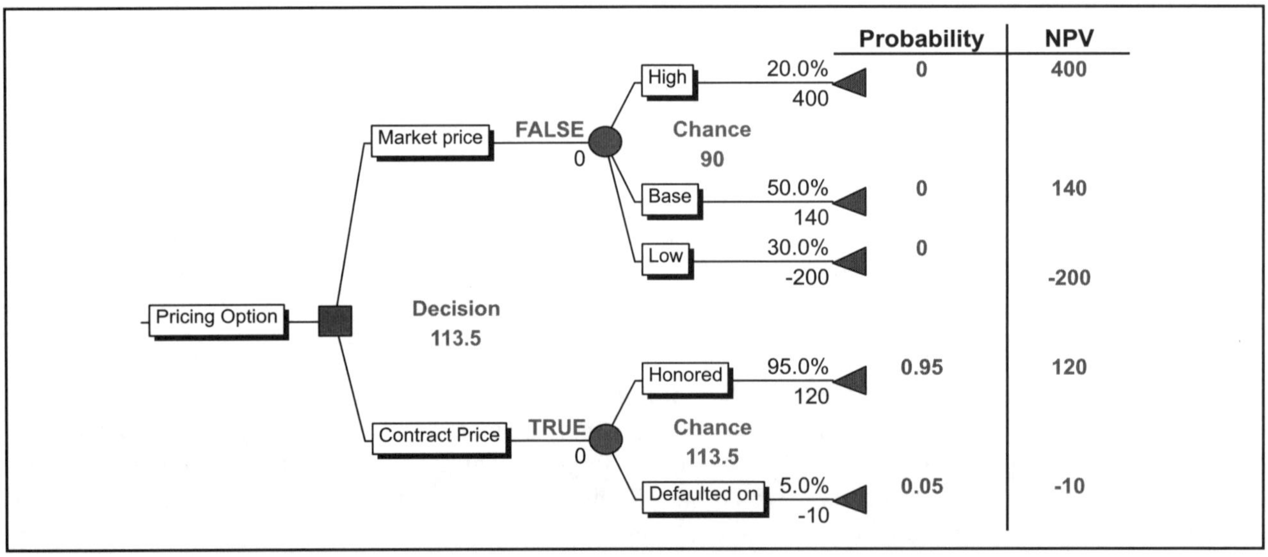

Figure 8.16 Comparison of pricing options

The contract price recognizes that the guarantor of the price may default on the contract, though the odds are quite low. The contract price is lower than the base case market price, hence the NPV of $113.5 million. Should the purchaser forfeit on the contract; the process loses $10 million with a chance of 5%. Still, even with default risk, the expected value of the contract exceeds the expected value of living by the whims of the market.

Which is the best choice? The decision-makers must trade-off the value of a relatively certain contract against the possible upside gains and downside losses of the market. The decision depends on risk tolerance, which in itself reflects the business environment and financial condition of the investor. Later sections in this chapter and Chapter 10 explore risk tolerance and ways to measure it.

Summary of Decision Trees

Graphical summaries of projects, with or without probabilities, are easy to formulate. One of the major obstacles to their use is the difficulty many have in interpreting them and feeling the information helps make decisions. We had one case where a professional responded to the discussion by saying that they had tried using such a format, and their boss (who was also present), rejected it. After talking about the problem and discussing the merits, the boss publicly apologized to the professional.

The lesson for professionals presenting decision trees or any other unfamiliar tool to an unreceptive audience is that it is like advice from your parents: *if it is unsolicited, it is usually rejected.* Sticking to your principles and continuing to provide such information usually leads to some degree of acceptance over time, but that acceptance must be cultivated, not imposed. The lesson for the manager is that they should encourage their staff to explore new ways of analyzing investments, and presenting the results, not just computing numbers the way the manager is familiar with.

SIMULATION TECHNIQUES

Decision trees and sensitivities generate useful information about investment risks. The major limitation emerges because the sources of risk seldom fall neatly into discrete outcomes, characterized by three or four branches. Recognizing that risks are continuous fits many investment situations better. The simulation process introduced in Chapter 6 often appears complicated; yet is quite simple. It merely condenses a large set of input combinations into a more readily interpretable information system.

Common responses to simulations include, "It is nothing but a giant game," or, "All you're doing is deluding yourself that you're being sophisticated." Since simulations just combines sensitivities, in a weighted, orderly, logical manner, these statements imply that sensitivity analysis is also useless. Once the investor even asks a sensitivity question, the simulation process has begun. The only real difference is whether all the questions are asked, or just the questions one thinks of. This problem accounts for the omission problems outlined in Chapter 2.

Simulation benefits decision-making by defining the distribution of profitability, however measured, and any other metric, like cash flow, ROCE, etc. Simulation generates a more complete set of risk and return measures that can be analyzed individually or incorporated into formalized portfolio management.

For readers unfamiliar with the output from a project analysis simulation, Example 8.1 displays a simplified approach to simulation, along with a comparison of older risk approximation methods. The first table shows the low, ML and high values for common components in the profit metrics. The second two columns compute the mean and standard deviation for a triangular distribution. Before the advent of modern computing power, people used to simplify the process by assuming the NPV metric was a normal or lognormal distribution, called the *parameter method.*[8.3] If that was true, using the formulas for the normal distribution could approximate the range of outcomes. Some still use this approach though methods that are more accurate exist. The simplification is not wrong; it just assumes conditions that may not exist for individual investment opportunities.

Example 8.1 conveys several interesting points for those unfamiliar with simulations. First, many believe just looking at the minimum and maximum sensitivities highlights the variability or risk in the project. In the first table, NPV ranges from -\$12 to \$34 million. The simulation shows a minimum of \$-42 and a maximum of \$66 million, which differ significantly from the sensitivity values. The gap occurs because the sensitivity approach falsely assumes that all values are low or high at the same time, which has almost a 0% chance of occurring. In actuality, the minimums occur when the project experiences low revenues and high costs. Some then argue for subtracting the high costs from the low revenue, yielding a minimum value of -\$72 (100-40-90-30-12). The net effect is that sensitivities understate project variability.

Example 8.1: Using the following information, compute the mean, P_{10} and P_{90} values using the parameter method and compare to a simulation of 1,500 iterations assuming a triangular distribution.

Variable	Low	ML	High	Mean Value	Standard Deviation
Revenue	100	120	160	126.67	12.47
Opex	10	18.6	30	19.53	4.10
Capex	35	57.4	90	60.80	11.29
Intangibles	15	21.2	40	25.40	5.31
Land Acquisition	6	8.4	12	8.80	1.23
Project NPV	34	14.4	-12	12.13	18.15

The low, most likely, and high values are given in the first 3 columns, and the last 2 columns use the triangular distribution mean and standard deviation equations in Chapter 6. Assuming a normal distribution, the P_{10} and P_{90} values are the mean ± 1.64 ∗ standard deviation, or 12.13 ± 1.64 ∗ 18.15. P_{10} = -17.6 and P_{90} = 41.9.

Parameter	1500
Minimum =	-41.78
Maximum =	66.22
Mean =	12.13
Std Deviation =	18.35
Skewness =	0.06
Kurtosis =	2.86
Mode =	16.34
10% Perc =	-11.14
50% Perc =	11.70
90% Perc =	35.77

Figure 8.17 summarizes a simulation result using the same data and 1500 iterations. A solid line is drawn vertically from 0.0, indicating the break-even point. The shape of the curve indicates why the parameter method and simulation always produce divergent results. The curve does not fit a normal distribution exactly, a key assumption of the parameter method. The mean values from the simulation and the approximation equal \$12.13 million. Variability differs significantly, however. The P_{10} value is -\$17.6 for the parameter method, while the full simulation only goes to -\$11.1, though the P_{90} values are much closer. The cause of the difference is explained by the kurtosis estimate of 2.86, indicating a symmetric, but taller, thinner distribution relative to a normal curve.

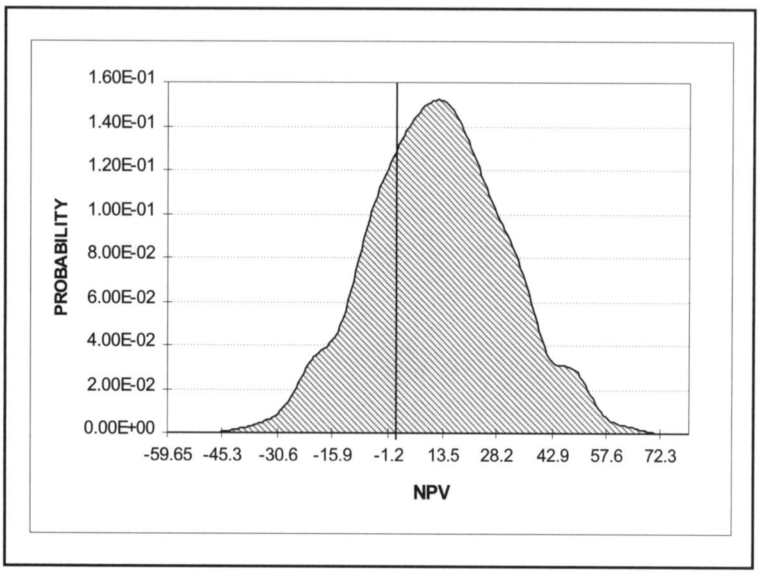

Figure 8.17 Simulation results of NPV

The standard deviation is roughly \$18 million and the other values are explained in Chapter 6. Though interesting, the important information regarding risk assessment comes from the graph. The area to the left of the line is the chance the project will fail to meet the NPV standard, about 21% here. The project has a 21% chance of losing money, or, conversely, a 79% chance of making money.

In a world full of risk, investors need accurate estimates of risk and return. An investor faces considerable risk in this project, and the level or risk is distorted by sensitivities, decision tree, and the parameter method.

Do we accept the project? It depends on ones financial position and attitude toward risk. Reading the probability of making money off the graph is difficult. A commonly used substitute for Figure 8.17 is the cumulative probability in Figure 8.18. This figure indicates the probability of making money (about 79%), which emphasizes the benefits of the project instead of focusing on the negative impact of losing money (21%).

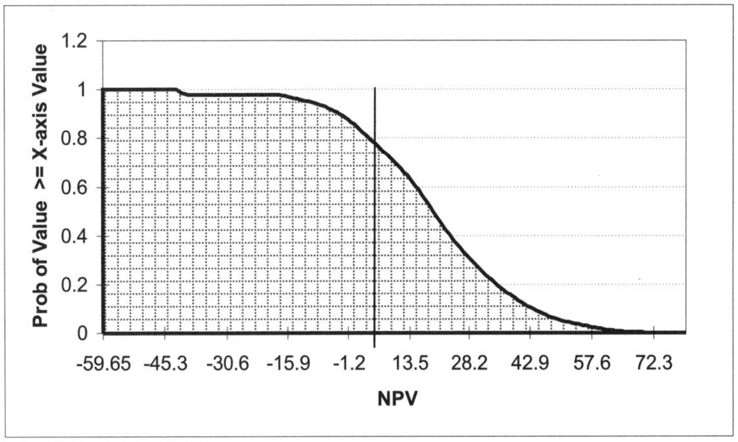

Figure 8.18 The cumulative probability of NPV > 0

The output of simulations generates information on the measures of value (Chapter 5), and indicators of risk (standard deviation and probability of losing or making money). Running simulations involves tackling several basic questions. These include:

- How many iterations to run?
- Do dependencies or interrelationships matter?
- How complicated should the model be?

Each of these topics is addressed separately.

Number of Iterations

Statements about the proper number of iterations face the prospect of oversimplifying the problem. For most simulations, the objective is to select the number of iterations until the output metrics, like mean and s_d, recur in every run, or, at least, change very little. Consistency or stability is necessary to avoid the embarrassment of having to explain totally different values to management every time a new run is made.

The problem of iterations hinges on the complexity of the model and the shape of the distributions. Very complex models and odd shaped (multimodel or highly skewed) input distributions require more iterations to achieve the desired stability. Most simulation software includes the option to run thousands of iterations and have the computer determine when stability is reached. The software usually defines stability relative to percentage changes in the mean, standard deviation, and values like P_{10} and P_{90}. If the specified values change by less than a user-defined percentage, say 1%, the computer assumes that stability exists.

Example 8.2 illustrates the variation in the NPV model used in Example 8.1 for 6 different simulations of 1500 iterations, using different seed values. Observe that the mean value is $12.13 million in all 6 simulations, but that the P_{50}, mode and standard deviation vary considerably, with the mode being wildly erratic, varying from about $4 to $29 million. The mode is almost always the last parameter to stabilize, because most software uses the peak of the bar chart to compute it. As the number of iterations changes, the bar chart takes on a very different look.

The other parameters vary, but it is hard to say if it is too much. The common risk measure, standard deviation, has a low value of $17.87m and a high value of $18.79m, or about a $1 million swing.

Example 8.2: Compute the measures of value, standard deviation and other measures for 6 separate simulations, and then compare the output for stability.

	Simulation #						
Variable	**1**	**2**	**3**	**4**	**5**	**6**	**Average**
Minimum =	-34.55	-50.08	-41.46	-33.39	-39.71	-38.19	-39.56
Maximum =	63.12	56.80	62.77	66.38	61.18	61.97	62.04
Mean =	12.13	12.13	12.13	12.13	12.13	12.13	12.13
Std Deviation =	18.79	18.10	18.32	17.91	17.84	17.87	18.14
Skewness =	0.16	-0.07	-0.06	0.15	0.02	0.07	0.04
Kurtosis =	2.62	2.83	2.62	2.79	2.78	2.91	2.76
Mode =	13.04	10.64	12.93	17.27	28.71	4.06	14.44
10% Perc =	-12.44	-10.30	-12.82	-11.09	-11.44	-10.19	-11.38
50% Perc =	11.64	11.23	12.81	10.81	12.02	12.13	11.77
90% Perc =	37.90	37.00	36.07	35.47	35.22	35.07	36.12

With an average of about $18 million, the percentage change is roughly 5%. Is this too much? The answer is definitely yes for this simple model, because rerunning it at 3000 iterations takes only a few seconds. Resolving the stability issue is a practical one: if time permits, run as many iterations as needed to stabilize the results. Without showing the results, running 6 iterations at 3000 produces less than a 1% change in the standard deviation.

For the mode value, stability (defined as less than a 1% change from high to low value with 6 simulations) only emerges when 8000 iterations are run. The decision on stability depends on the parameters used to make the investment decisions. If the mean parameter is used, less than 1000 iterations are needed in most projects. For the standard deviation and percentiles (P_{10}, P_{50}, and P_{90}), the old adage of 300 to 500 iterations for each independent variable still holds. For the mode value, run as many iterations as time allows, but be aware that the mode will always fluctuate more than the other parameters.

Example 8.3 demonstrates how the parameters change as the number of trials or iterations increases. Each run uses a different seed value. As the model increases in complexity, the requisite time will expand. The complexity versus accuracy issue is addressed later in this section.

Example 8.3: Compare the output parameters for each run of the simulation using different number of iterations.

	Trials						
Parameter	**1,500**	**5,000**	**7,500**	**10,000**	**15,000**	**20,000**	**30,000**
Minimum =	-41.78	-46.57	-43.05	-51.34	-50.59	-46.74	-50.68
Maximum =	66.22	70.01	68.74	73.91	75.29	76.72	76.62
Mean =	12.13	12.13	12.13	12.13	12.13	12.13	12.13
Std Deviation =	18.35	18.13	17.96	18.20	18.13	18.12	18.23
Skewness =	0.06	0.07	0.04	0.06	0.04	0.06	0.04
Kurtosis =	2.86	2.77	2.73	2.81	2.78	2.78	2.75
Mode =	16.34	32.52	10.29	17.59	25.30	16.25	16.15
10% Perc =	-11.14	-6.89	-11.22	-11.19	-11.00	-11.17	-11.42
50% Perc =	11.70	11.59	11.98	11.92	11.89	11.84	12.02
90% Perc =	35.77	35.86	35.59	36.08	35.89	36.08	36.00

Dependencies: Do they matter?

The simplest answer to this question is yes. Dependencies impact every decision metric and the estimated variability, usually quite significantly, and, since risk assessment is concerned with measuring variability, ignoring dependency distorts the output and understates the value of conducting formal risk assessment. The most common way to incorporate dependency is with the correlation coefficient, as explained in Chapter 6. The basic lesson to be observed here is that the importance of modeling dependencies is a function of how interdependent the variables are. Low correlations can effectively be ignored, but as the correlation increases, recognizing dependencies begins to matter. Example 8.1 assumed *independence* between the variables used to derive NPV.

Example 8.4 compares the impact on the output distribution for different levels of correlation. The first matrix assumes that all the variables are correlated with each other at a 75% rate. Land acquisition cost is assumed to have zero correlation with any other input. This example seeks only to illustrate the impact of correlations on the output parameters, not to depict actual modeling behavior. For example, it is likely that revenue correlates with the size of the production systems: larger facilities produce more higher volumes. In addition, at higher production volumes, total operating costs probably will increase, though per unit Opex might fall.

Comparing the results across the three cases produces startling differences, except for the mean value, which matches perfectly. The equivalence of the mean values stems from the symmetry in most of the input distributions, and seldom occurs in actual practice. To make sense of this result, remember that the NPV equation is revenue less costs. With high correlations, high revenues are associated high costs, reducing the chance of high revenue combined with low costs; hence, NPV will never be as high or as low as the zero correlation case. The P_{10} and P_{90} show the same pattern for the same reason.

Example 8.4: Compare the output parameters from a simulation of 5000 iterations and constant seed value using different assumptions about the correlation between variables. Use the following correlation matrix for the high correlation case and then convert the values to 0.25 for the low correlation. Re-run the no correlation case with the same seed value.

	Revenue	Opex	Capex	Intangibles	Land Acquisition
Revenue	1	0.75	0.75	0.75	0
Opex	0.75	1	0.75	0.75	0
Capex	0.75	0.75	1	0.75	0
Intangibles	0.75	0.75	0.75	1	0
Land Acquisition	0	0	0	0	1

	Correlation		
Parameter	High (0.75)	Low (0.25)	None (0)
Minimum =	-24.56	-47.53	-48.76
Maximum =	51.50	67.93	71.28
Mean =	12.13	12.13	12.13
Std Deviation =	11.62	16.36	18.07
Skewness =	-0.13	0.03	0.06
Kurtosis =	2.72	2.84	2.76
Mode =	11.39	7.03	8.86
10% Perc =	-3.44	-9.27	-11.32
50% Perc =	12.45	12.21	11.99
90% Perc =	27.09	36.27	35.17

The low correlation case falls between the high and no correlation case. An old rule-of-thumb held that correlation could be ignored when the correlation is less than 0.5. This rule originated when computational tools were much more primitive. Generally, we recommend building the model to reflect the correlations that impact the project. If the difference between the low correlation case and the no correlation case is trivial, then drop the correlation values from the analysis. Better investment decisions emerge when all potentially relevant information is incorporated, then deleted as importance is established. Omitting forces in the name of simplicity is a contributing factor in almost all failed investments, however defined and measured.

Simplicity versus Complexity: The Trade-Offs

Adding dependencies is often viewed as increasing complexity into the investment decision process, unnecessarily. Most investment models, especially deterministic ones, ignore the major cause of poor investments: the omission of important variables altogether or the interaction among variables. Risk assessment as it is practiced today continues this flaw. The general view is that a simple risk model is better than the best deterministic model. Though this may be true, just because of the recognition of variability, it has yet to be demonstrated that better investment decisions result, to our knowledge. Establishing the right balance between simplicity and complexity, adjusted for variable investment objectives will provide an interesting challenge in the coming years.

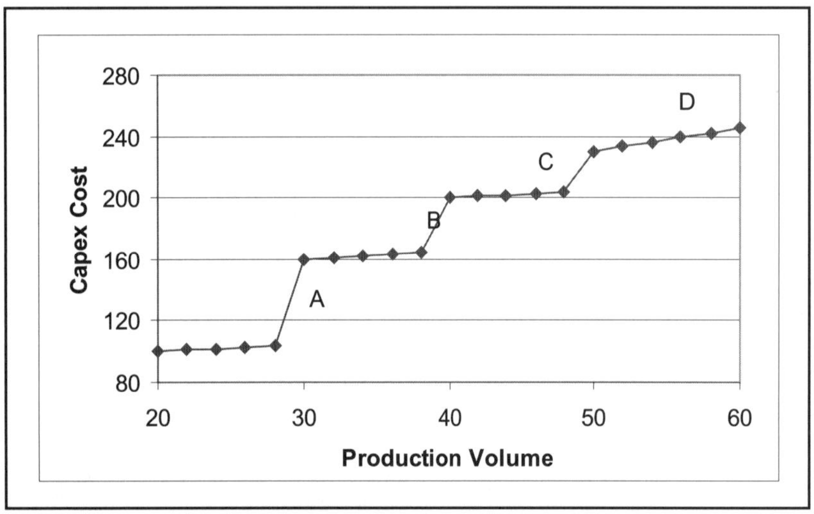

Figure 8.19 Sample relationship between volume and cost

Good models integrate the interrelationships into the calculations. A common example is given in Figure 8.19. Production volumes are associated with the size of the production facility, and size impacts Opex and Capex in the investment model. The step function indicates that the scale of the facility varies as the desired production volume changes. Option A might be a facility that works best for low volume production, while B through D indicate different engineering efficiencies. The relationship is presented as a deterministic curve, but each facility segment could be computed with a distribution, if desired. The graph indicates that many investments have interrelationships, which are not always statistical, but reflect design options. Note also that this idea continues on to Opex, taxes and the other elements of the investment model.

Most traditional, commercially available software ignores the ability to incorporate such relationships directly into the model. Newer programs, designed to handle risk and optimization, do have the ability to model the relationships, but have faced considerable reluctance to replace the older approach. The tide is beginning to turn in the favor of the newer software, because users recognize the need to consider dependencies.

Adding detail takes time and that increases cost, while simplicity achieves answers faster and at lower cost. Our recommendation is to build the most sophisticated model that time allows. The key word here is time allows, especially as new types of investments, i.e., those investments, which are totally new, or no experience exists, are encountered. Also to be factored into the decision is the cost of a mistake. Simple models are fine for small, inexpensive investments. As costs and risks rise, the complexity needs to increase as well.

The tendency is to build a simple model with the idea of expanding it later as new information becomes available. Unfortunately, the pressure arising from problems of the day often prevent the commitment of resources to conduct the expansion. What begins, as a good intention never comes to fruition?

Even deterministic analysis suffers from the omission problem. How often does someone perform a sensitivity on production volume without changing Opex or Capex, change product price without measuring the corresponding impact on sales volume.

This simplicity versus complexity debate exists even among people who know better. Simplicity in risk assessment has its origin in two factors: limitations of the tools available to analyze risk and organizational structures that separate the sources of data in the investment model. The first element results from slow computers with limited capacity. So, early practitioners designed ways to simplify the models to achieve the objectives of their specific group. These designers knew they were sacrificing the details of risk assessment. Current users of the classical system have forgotten this limitation, even as technology has resolved most of the problems.

Organizational restrictions provide a major impediment to proper risk assessment. The petroleum industry provides a classical example of how separation of function distorts the process. Exploration is responsible for identifying prospects for drilling, then that prospect is passed along to reservoir engineers, drilling engineers, design and cost engineers, and finally to commercial analysts. Figures 8.1-8.3 highlight this process. Often these people are located in different departments located around the world. Each group works on their part, separately, in the sequential process. The net effect is that relationships, like Figure 8.19, often get lost in the complex interactions among the groups.

Following the exploration example cited above, detailed simulations on the probability of success, P_S, and reserves are quite common. Figure 8.20 displays one reserve simulation result. Given the reserve distribution, the analyst passes along either one number, like the mean reserve number or P_{50} reserve, or the entire distribution to engineers who design and cost the production system. With the values generated, the minimum reserve number needed to generate a positive NPV or other value measure is computed. The analysis ignores the dependency between the production system and production volume.

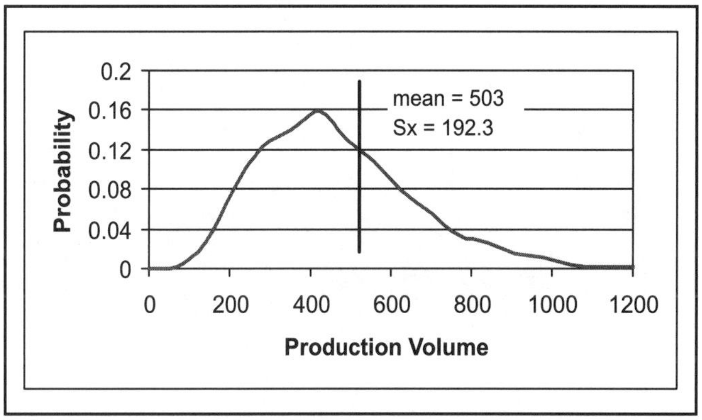

Figure 8.20 Reserve distribution with deterministic inputs

The second approach uses the SRA system. SRA stands for simplified risk assessment. Though an improvement, it still may seriously distort the risk assessment, usually underestimating risk. Refer to Figures 8.1-8.3, which assume that the distributions from each element can be combined without capturing the interrelationship between the variables.

Figure 8.21 highlights a simple dependency that has nothing to do with statistics, but reflects good model building. The graph shows that at medium production the floating production and offshore loading system (*FPSO*) would be used. At the high reserve value, a *spar* is selected, and at the low volume, a *tension leg platform* (*TLP*).

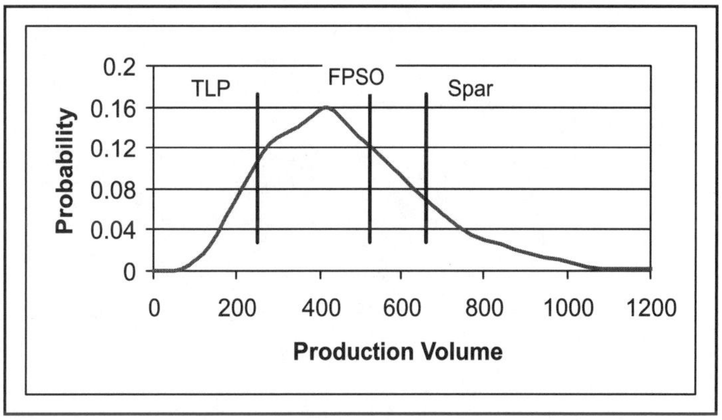

Figure 8.21 Example of dependence in modeling

For those unfamiliar with the petroleum industry, these options reflect alternative development options, and the choices are for purposes of illustration only.

Figure 8.21 captures an essential feature of options thinking. Certain events or actions are conditional upon other events, production volume in this case. Other mitigating events that might alter the choice of production system include the price of the produced product and the geographical environment (country, weather, and terrain, etc.). As the mitigating factors change over time, the investment options change dramatically

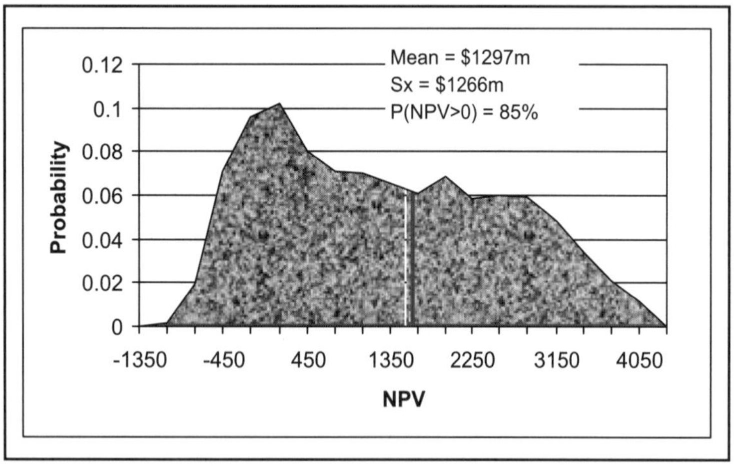

Figure 8.22a Simplified model of offshore development

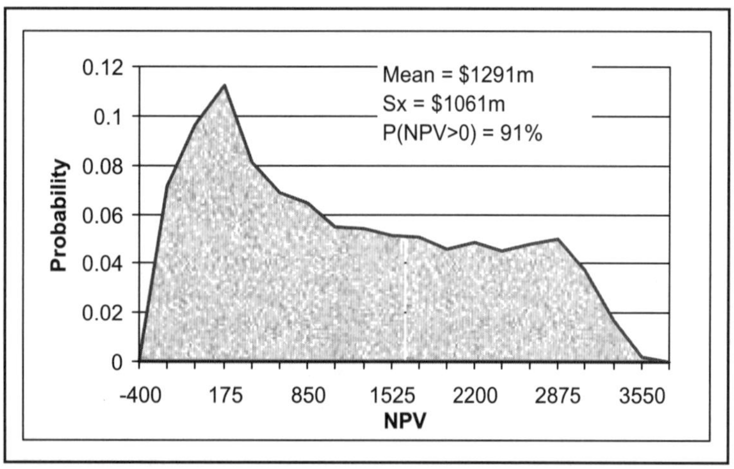

Figure 8.22b SRA model of offshore development

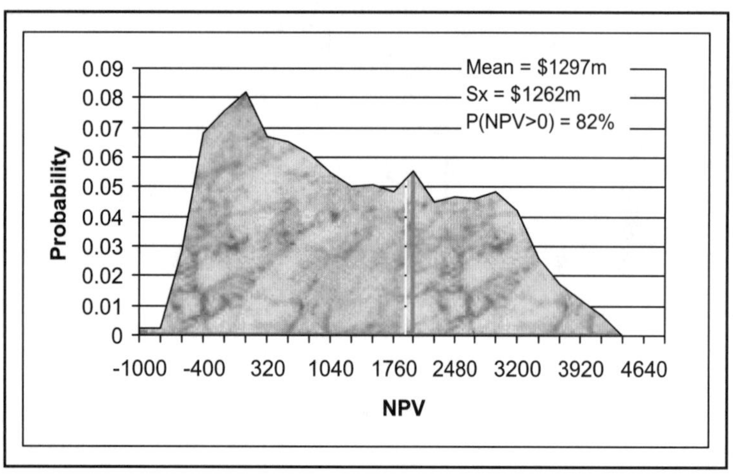

Figure 8.22c Detailed model of offshore development

Figure 8.22a-c demonstrates the extreme differences between the two most common, simplified approaches and a more complex, representative model. The first figure highlights the volume simulation with certainty engineering and economics. Figure 8.22b follows the SRA approach, where distributions are generated by the respective disciplines and integrated at the economic stage. Figure 8.22c uses Figure 8.21 to capture the changes in design and costing for varying volume estimates. Model three changes the type and size of facility, number of wells drilled, pipeline size and layout, etc. as reservoir characteristics and price vary over time. This is the type of complex, interdependent model seldom developed, but is much closer to real events.

The simplified model, Figure 8.22a has a higher mean NPV ($1507 million) and lower standard deviation ($540 million) than the other two models. Because only reservoir size varies, the standard deviation ignores the impacts of costs, scheduling, production timing, prices, etc. Generally, the simpler models understate the overall project riskiness. Even though we use the term simple here, a fairer description would be narrowly focused model, or a model focused on specific components of the problem. There is nothing wrong in concentrating on reserve variability at some stage in investment decision-making. But, cavalierly simplifying the other components to obtain an approximation of value (NPV here), clearly distorts the perception of both value and risk.

One argument presented to justify using Figure 8.22a is that the results are used for ranking alternatives and don't measure value directly. This logic defeats the purpose of undertaking the risk assessment and valuation, and only works if the combined effects of the ignored components have the same variability. This condition seldom occurs. Moreover, investment decision-making seeks to maximize value at any given level of risk. With poor or inaccurate measures of risk and value, the chances of satisfying these objectives are quite small.

The SRA model has a lower NPV ($1291 million) and higher standard deviation ($1266 million), because Capex and Opex vary with production. Cases of lower reserves and higher costs than the deterministic case reduce overall profitability and more than doubles variability. The SRA approach gives a much more realistic estimate of value and variability than the simple, or narrow model.

The complex model produces virtually the same NPV ($1291 million) and P_{50} value as the SRA approach (not shown). What differs is the risk estimate ($1061 million), or about 20% less than the risk measure from SRA, but still about double the simple approach. The smaller risk emerges because the model assumes that lower volumes lead to different, usually more flexible, production facilities. The direct, more complicated linkage of the components of the NPV or *discounted cash flow model* (DCF) always has a significant impact on the risk measures.

Whether the differences in the risk measures influences investment decisions hinges on how the outputs are used, as discussed in the next two chapters

Before turning to ways to use this information, another troublesome issue in risk assessment bears a brief discussion. Some organizations still perform detailed risk assessment on the components of the DCF model, except for one variable: sales price. The argument is that assuming a constant price, like a mid cycle or low cycle value, ignores variability, but we're just ranking the projects anyway. This ignores the importance of price as a variable component, and as a driver for future options in design and operation. First, on the matter of whether price volatility matters, Figure 8.23 reran Figure 8.22c with the same seed value and 5000 iterations, assuming prices vary rather than being constant. The model assumes a mean reverting process, as explained in Chapter 7, with random fluctuations.

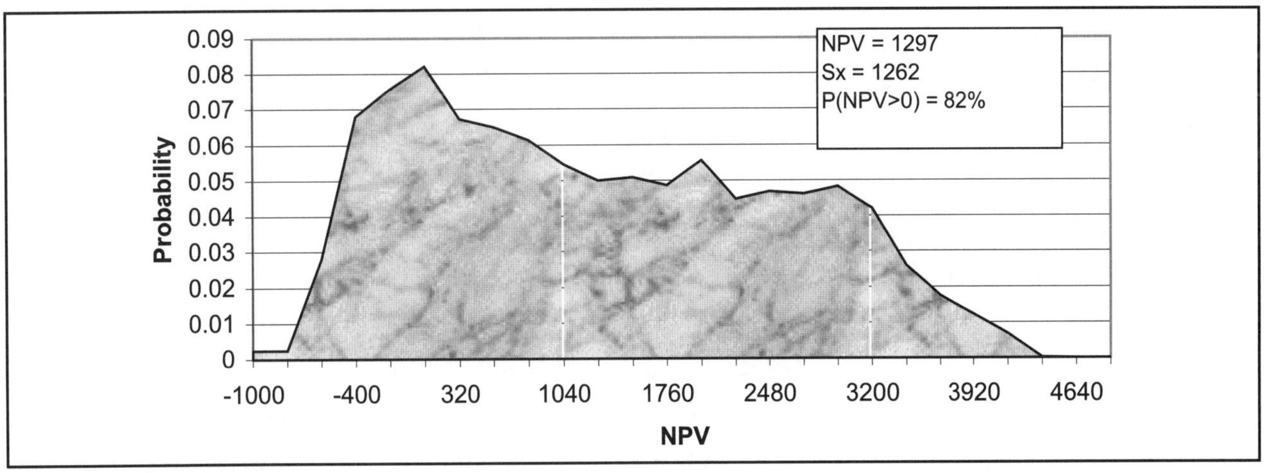

Figure 8.23 Complex offshore model with price volatility

Observe that the mean value is about the same as before, but that the standard deviation and probability of making money change considerably. The deterministic price approach had the project with a 91% chance of making money; whereas the chance falls to 82% when prices are allowed to vary.

Returning to the ranking argument used before, ignoring price variability is "less bad" when only one internationally marketed commodity is considered – like crude oil. Once, other commodities, which may be sold in local markets (gas) or totally different products like chemicals, jet fuels, coal, copper, are considered, the ranking argument is specious (apparently sound and reasonable, but fallacious).

Probably the single, most important source of investment risk comes from price volatility. Ignoring price volatility means that the resulting outputs distort the real risks, often catastrophically. Technical professionals dislike having to address price risk, primarily because it lies outside their knowledge domain. Even if prices cannot be predicted, understanding the development and operating options open to the investor as prices vary can only enhance the chance of a successful investment.

Limitations of Simulations

Simulation results provide additional information for investment decisions. The simulation process, like every other tool used by professionals, has shortcomings, however, which must be recognized.

One problem arises from the nature of the simulation process itself. In order to keep the simulations from repeating itself, the starting point for selecting the random numbers must vary with each run. This re-seeding has become easier in the last few years with software improvements. Older programs, which have not been updated, still start the simulation at the same point, and, thus, always give the same answer. This erroneously implies that simulations always give the same answer. Actually, the simulation results should change every time you make a run, because a different combination of values is selected.

Second, building sound risk analytical models requires labor, time and willingness. These components are all in short supply in many organizations.

VALUING RISK

Current investment practice splits risk assessment into three main components:

- project risk,
- corporation risk, and
- market risk.

The last section addressed the project risk phase, but ignored the latter two. Corporate risk is really about portfolio management. A project with a very high standard deviation, and, hence, high risk, may actually lower corporate risk, if it is negatively correlated with other projects. Vertical integration, where the organization controls the production, shipping, marketing, manufacturing, and retailing of a product, is a classic example. John D. Rockefeller started the notion that, if he sold his crude oil to his refinery, and the processed gasoline to his station, he made money on the gasoline when crude oil prices were low, and made money on the crude when those prices were high. The key was to balance all levels to maximize shareholder value.

The last risk component, market risk, is captured in the discount rate, as illustrated in Chapter 4 and applied in Chapter 5. Adding risk to the discussion forces a serious need to revisit to this issue, which is handled below.

Traditional discussions of risk valuation begin with a discussion of *utility theory*, or the more commonly used phrase today, *preference theory*. Stated simply, utility theory recognizes that the satisfaction from having an item determines its attractiveness. In case you wonder about this, watch the advertising on television as a vehicle for increasing our desire (or utility). Though a very simplified statement about utility, it raises the notion that satisfaction plays an important role in decision-making, especially in the reaction to risk.

Prior to the last 30 years, most scholars assumed that investors, both individual and organizations, were rational. Recent research suggests that investors are rational, on average, but specific investment decisions may be irrational. In fact, the rational model is correct in principle, it just simplifies behavior too much.

This section outlines the basic principles of risk valuation. Once the underlying concepts are presented, the task turns to formulating risk, value and utility into measures that can be used to compare risk and return on investment alternatives.

Utility and Valuation

Terms applied to recognize utility include: *risk averse, risk neutral, and risk taker.* The best way to illustrate these concepts is with an example. Given a choice of a sure $50,000 return or an opportunity that has a 50% chance of paying $100,000 and zero if a failure, what would you do? Risk neutral investors are indifferent between the two options; risk averse people take the sure $50,000 and those taking the gamble are classified as risk takers.

The above example has been used to define risk aversion for decades. Recent work has turned this example around to illustrate some problems in the definition. Consider the mirror image of the problem, where now you face a sure loss of $50,000 or a 50% chance of losing $100,000. The great bulk of the people studied would take the gamble, indicating risk taking; yet, they were risk averse when faced with the above gain. Does this mean investors are irrational?

Students of the psychology of decision-making have modified the term risk averse to state that most people are *loss avoiders*.[8.4] Without going into great detail, Figure 8.24 modifies traditional utility theory to fit the current perception of investment behavior. The most important element of the figure is the asymmetry in the curve. The steepest portion of the curve is near the origin, indicating that investors are most sensitive to the first money gained or lost. For instance, the first $1000 gained or lost impacts value more than $1000 gained or lost after, say, $100,000. This is nothing more than the *marginal utility* concept.

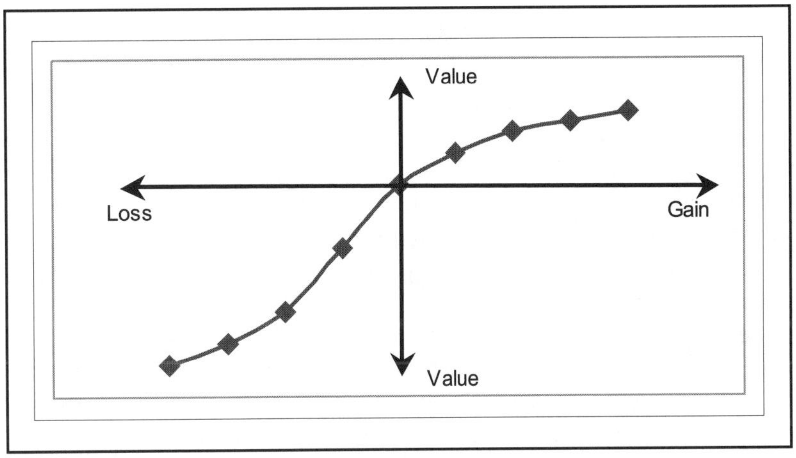

Figure 8.24 Example of the psychology of value

The asymmetry in the curve, with the portion of the curve on the loss side impacting value more than the gain, has been labeled, *inconsistency*. Whether this is the appropriate term is unclear to us, but it does capture the tendency among investors to imagine things could be slightly better, but infinitely worse. Some label this pessimistic, but this inconsistency rears its ugly head in almost every study ever done. Our favorite is a famous study asking respondents to rank the risks they fear most. Table 8.2 highlights the responses relative to the actual risks.

This inconsistency arises because the major, catastrophic loss overwhelms the everyday incidents. Also, a second cause is *overconfidence* in decision-making. Events dealt with on a regular basis or more familiar are treated with greater certainty than events we have no control over or experience with.

TABLE 8.2

Perception of Risk versus Actual Risk

Perceived Risk	Actual Risk
1. Nuclear accident	1. Home accident
2. Plane crash	2. Car accident near home
3. Car accident while traveling	3. .
4. .	4. .
5. .	5. .
6. .	6. .
7. .	7. .
8. Car accident near home	8. Plane crash
9. Home accident	9. Nuclear accident

Ongoing research into behavioral psychology suggests that inconsistency occurs because of three factors. These are:

- Mental accounting,
- Overconfidence, and
- Risk attitudes.

Risk attitudes are just Figure 8.24. Mental accounting introduces the notion that people's preferences depend on their reference points: a person investing their life savings of $100 views risk differently than billionaires like Bill Gates or Gordon Getty. The classic example of mental accounting has been demonstrated by simple investment examples. Suppose you make $100 in the morning and then lose $100 on another investment in the afternoon. You breakeven for the day, but most surveys indicate that people feel like failures at the end of the day. The contradiction arises because of the loss function and most decision-makers tend to view the investments as separate events, not as a combined portfolio. Also, time matters. If the loss occurs in the morning and the gain in the afternoon, the investor ends the day on a positive note.

Overconfidence plagues most investors. Some call it optimism; others associate it with the human model. Basically, most investors acquire too much information from the available data (or more than is warranted) and believe they are right more than they really are. A classic example is from the medical profession. A study of doctors diagnosing pneumonia showed they believed they were right 90% of the time. In reality, they were right 50% of the time. Another group people love to chide, stockbrokers, were asked to give the 90% confidence interval for a select group of stocks. If correct, the actual stock price should have fallen outside the range 10% of the time. Actual stock prices fell outside the range over 35% of the time.

Before mocking these groups, several engineering and economic studies perform the same analysis. Capen surveyed several thousand engineers, asking each respondent to give a specified range, like the 80%, confidence interval on 10 questions. Comparison of the right answers to the estimated range found almost exactly the same result as the doctors and brokers.[8.5] With an 80% confidence interval, the exactly right person would miss 2 questions, or have the right answer fall outside their ranges two times. In every location, the average number of misses averaged about 5 wrong answers. We conducted the same quiz at a forum of risk experts, including those advocating using 80% confidence intervals, and replicated the results almost exactly.[8.6]

An interesting question addresses whether the knowledge of formal risk methods reduces such overconfidence. We have duplicated Capen's questionnaire for over 20 years, with thousands of respondents, and find less than 1 in 50 people with 1-3 misses and most in the 4-7 miss category. A 1990 study in the Harvard Business Review[8.7] performed the same quiz on over 1,000 business executives around the world. They cite that executives at IBM and Royal Dutch Shell averaged 5 misses, while investment bankers and brokers averaged 6 misses. Overconfidence seems to plague all disciplines, regardless of locations, and has failed to improve over time, even when with given to a group of risk experts.

Before moving on to quantifying loss avoidance or risk aversion, think about the implications of these ideas for the risk assessment methods discussed so far. The studies indicate that variability or ranges are understated, which implies the measures of variability produced from any method are also underestimated. This consistent underestimate becomes critical when trying to formally address risk mitigation strategies, because, again, investors can't solve problems they are unaware of.

Tversky and Kahneman estimate that investors making decisions with uncertainty weigh prospective losses twice as heavily as prospective gains.[8.8] To illustrate this notion, Equation 8.4 adjusts the risk weighting or EMV method by doubling the failure component.

$$RW = P_s * NPV_{success} - 2 * (1 - P_s) * NPV_{failure} \tag{8.4}$$

Loss avoidance partially explains the tendency of investors to believe that they are prudent, give greater weight to recent data (at the expense of long-run averages or statistical odds), and crowd together to follow the trends in investment patterns. While many professionals immediately observe that these characteristics fit their organization's management, be careful about the glass house you may live in. The same authors find that management is less risk averse than professionals, whose loss avoidance weight is about 3, not 2. Example 8.5 shows the impact of applying the risk aversion.

Example 8.5: Compare the risk weighted values using the Tversky approach to the common risk neutral results from Equation 8.3.

$$\text{Breakeven } P_s = \frac{|\text{NPV Failure}|}{|\text{NPV Failure}| + \text{NPV Success}} = \frac{21}{21+43} = 0.328$$

$$\text{Breakeven } P_s = \frac{|\text{NPV Failure}|}{|\text{NPV Failure}| + \text{NPV Success}} = \frac{2*21}{2*21+43} = 0.494$$

$$\text{Breakeven } P_s = \frac{|\text{NPV Failure}|}{|\text{NPV Failure}| + \text{NPV Success}} = \frac{3*21}{3*21+43} = 0.594$$

The effect of emphasizing losses by weighting them by 2 raises the breakeven P_s to almost 50%, up from the risk neutral P_s of 33%. At a weight of 3, the value rises to almost 60%!

Two methods are used to measure the loss avoidance preferences of investors: *certainty equivalence* and *risk-adjusted discount rates*. Each is addressed in turn.

Certainty Equivalence

The actual definition of certainty equivalence is the return on a risk-free investment that needs to be offered to make the investor indifferent between it and a risky portfolio. In one industrial application, certainty equivalent is defined as "the no-risk, certain amount of cash the investor requires in order to be willing to exchange, or sell their rights to gamble."[8.9] This statement is prophetic, because a hot topic today is *options theory*, which is covered at the end of the chapter. Notice that certainty equivalence assumes that an option exists to take the risky or risk free investment.

Certainty equivalence seeks to trade-off the relative importance of the two elements of risk discussed earlier: chance of success/failure and magnitude of success/failure. A simple example will clarify the concept. Suppose two investment alternatives exist. Investment A has a 50/50 chance of being successful, with success earning \$100 million (m) and failure costing \$40 million (m). Investment B has 20%

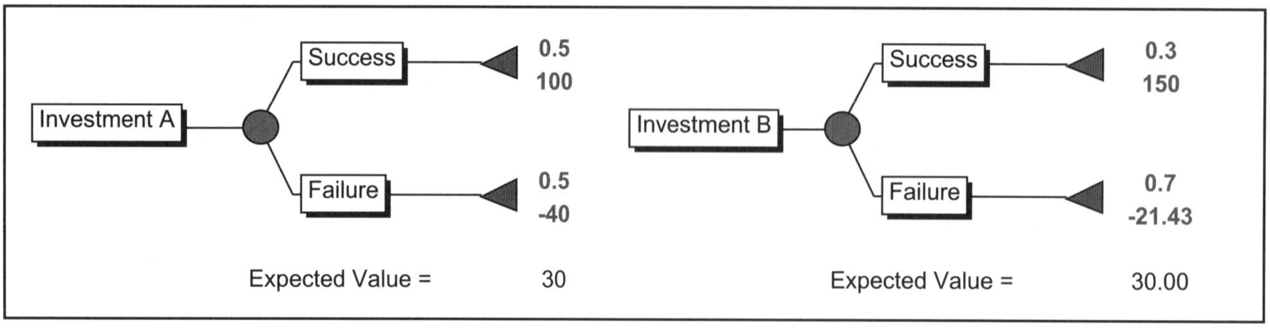

Figure 8.25 Trade-off between two investments

chance of earning \$150 million and an 80% chance of losing \$21.4 million. Figure 8.25 shows the simple alternatives.

Both investments have the same expected return of \$30 million, but investment A has the larger loss potential of \$40 million. Risk averse investors recognize the larger loss and might rank B, even though A has a higher chance of success, because of the potential for a greater loss.

Figure 8.26 displays certainty equivalence graphically. The figure plots risk versus return as shown in several chapters. A higher return with increasing risk should be fairly obvious. Three lines are shown – for two risk averse investor of α=4 and α=2, and a risk neutral or α=0 investor. The intersection of the line with the intercept measures the certainty equivalence. This is the risk free, expected return, which gives the same utility as any point along the respective line.

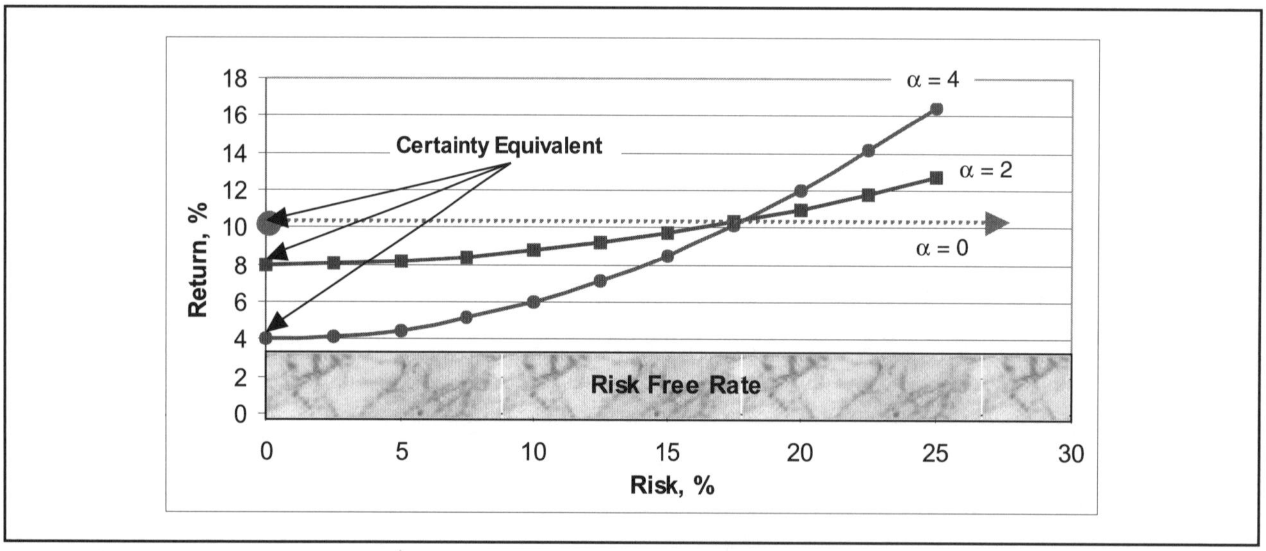

Figure 8.26 Certainty equivalence for three different investors

In comparing stock market returns, which is the source of Figure 8.26, risk and return are measured in %. As explained earlier, the basic relationship in selecting the discount rate from Chapter 4 is:

$$\text{Required Return} = \text{Risk Free Rate} + \text{Risk Premium} \tag{8.5}$$

The risk free rate shown in Figure 8.26 is essentially treasury bills for investors buying stocks or shares. The risk free rate, or certainty equivalent, of the individual investments may be higher due to their specific risk characteristics of the project or the investor.

The figure contrasts the certainty equivalent for three different investor risk tolerances. The risk neutral investor has a required return equal to the certainty equivalent. The less risk averse investor, α=2, has the higher certainty equivalent, while the more risk averse investor has the lower certainty equivalent. Assume 3 different investors agreed on the risk and return values for an investment (where the lines cross). The risk neutral investor would value the investment at 10%, and the most risk averse investor would appraise it at 4%.

Equation 8.5 is modified for most investments, as follows:

$$RAV = C_X = E(r) = \text{Certainty Equivalence (CE)} \qquad \textbf{(8.6)}$$

where: RAV or C_X = risk adjusted value
E(r) = expected return of profit measure, like average NPV

The C_X is referred to in the literature as the certainty equivalent value. We use RAV because more authors use RAV than C_X. It should be real obvious that the critical element in the analysis is the measurement of CE, which requires some idea of risk tolerance, α, in order to obtain RAV. Much of the initial work in risk tolerance was based on the notion of discrete probabilities, and then extended to continuous probabilities. The alternatives are addressed in turn

Discrete Certainty Equivalence

People have been measuring discrete risk tolerance since the 50's, with considerable success.[(8.10)] Newendorp first applied the concepts to the petroleum industry in the late 60's, as a student of Dr. J. Campbell Sr.[(8.11)] His book in 1975 plots risk aversion based on his surveys of industry executives.[(8.12)]

More recently, M. Walls has written extensively about measuring risk tolerance (RT) successful in industrial applications. The process works by first giving the participants an RT worksheet, like that shown in Table 8.3.[(8.13)]

TABLE 8.3

Risk Tolerance (RT) Worksheet

Project	Outcome	Value	Probability	Circle the desired participation level (%)					
1	Success	35	0.5	100	75	50	25	12.5	0
	Failure	-15	0.5						
2	Success	45	0.15	100	75	50	25	12.5	0
	Failure	-3	0.85						
3	Success	22	-0.30	100	75	50	25	12.5	0
	Failure	-4	0.70						
4	Success	14	0.80	100	75	50	25	12.5	0
	Failure	-9.5	0.20						
5	Success	16	0.20	100	75	50	25	12.5	0
	Failure	-1.4	0.80						

Since investors never measure their risk tolerance directly, the analysis must infer or reveal the investor's preference or tolerance indirectly. The investor circles the desired choice of participation in each of the 5 projects, ranging from 100% to 0%. As the probabilities and gains/losses vary, the selection reveals the investors attitudes toward risk.

The equation for integrating the information in the table is shown in Equation 8.7.(8.14)

$$C_x = -\frac{1}{r} * \ln\left[\sum_{i=1}^{n} p_i * e^{-r*x_i}\right] \tag{8.7}$$

where:

p_i = the probability of the *ith* outcome occurring
x_i = the value of the *ith* outcome,
r = risk tolerance value
e = natural log

The investor never sees basic relationship provided by Equation 8.7. Figure 8.27 shows the underlying relationship for several working interest options for a hypothetical project. Since r is unknown, the graph plots values for C_x on the y-axis and r on the x-axis by solving Equation 8.7 for different values of r to generate these lines.

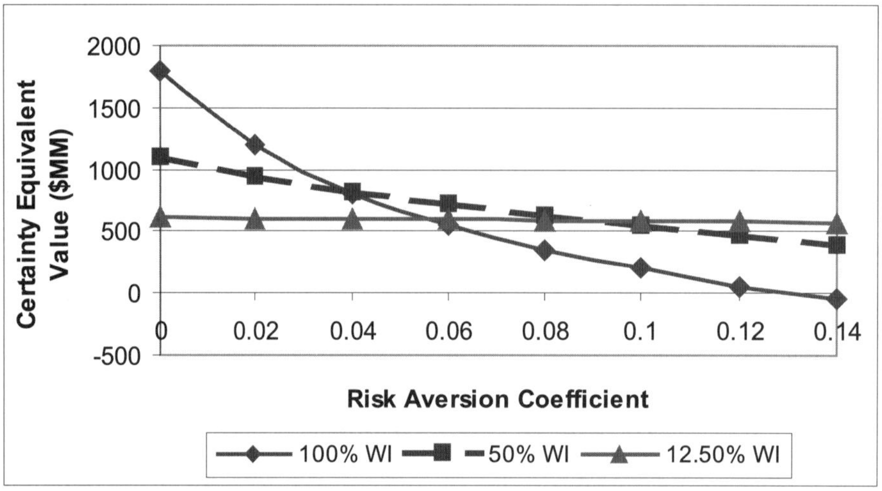

Figure 8.27 Example of inferring the risk tolerance value

The task is to select the WI option that maximizes the C_x value. Since the investor chooses a WI value in the questionnaire, the analysis deduces the risk aversion coefficient. When the investor chooses the 100% WI position, the lines indicate that the risk tolerance is less than 0.04 because the 100% WI line has the largest value. It should make sense that investors prefer to invest more in low risk projects. At a zero risk coefficient, the investor is risk neutral. As risk increases, the preferred or maximum C_x option changes. Between risk values of roughly .04 and .09, the 50% choice has the highest value. As risk increases even more, the highest value occurs with the 12.5% working interest.

Suppose that the respondent circled the 50% working interest. Assuming that the investor seeks to maximize their utility, this implies that the risk aversion or tolerance is between the .04 and .09 range. Repeating this same process for a number of investments estimates the overall risk tolerance for the investor. For a company, the decision-makers arrive at the portfolio of projects and the group risk tolerance can be derived. The results provide the equivalent of an expected or average risk tolerance, without understanding the variability in risk tolerance across project types.

The practitioners in risk tolerance or utility recognize that the exponential utility function might be more appropriate. An entire body of literature has been developed that expands the functional forms of utility. The loss avoidance function in Figure 8.24 is actually an extension of this example. Since this text seeks only to introduce these topics, the extensions are left to the reader.

Continuous Certainty Equivalence

Discrete examples are very useful for illustrating the concepts. But, most analysis of investments deals with continuous distributions, like the early parts of this chapter. Extending the utility concept to continuous investments follows basic statistical theory. The discrete cases assumed two outcomes: success or failure, which is just a binomial distribution. Statistics has long showed that a normal approximation exists for the binomial distribution.

Researchers have applied the normal approximation to generate Equation 8.8.[8.15]

$$RAV = C_x = \bar{X} - \frac{1}{2} * r * s_x^2 \quad \textbf{(8.8)}$$

where all the values are defined as before.

Observe that the equation has come full circle to the utility concept of certainty equivalence. If the investor were risk neutral, just the mean value for X would be used to make decisions. The product of the three terms following the minus sign generates equivalent values to those shown in Figure 8.27.

Applying the Concepts

Traditional risk assessment methods avoided the need to measure loss avoidance by assuming that the standard deviation captured the essence of risk. This simpler approach is expressed in Equation 8.9.

$$\text{Coefficient of Variation} = \frac{S_x}{\bar{X}} \quad \textbf{(8.9)}$$

where: S_x = standard deviation of desired measure, like NPV

$\bar{X}$ = mean value of desired measure, like NPV

The variability index gives a dimensionless number that is much like the efficiency ratios discussed in Chapter 7. RAV stands for risk-adjusted value and is based on utility.[8.16] Example 8.6 applies the risk-adjusted approaches using the simulation outputs from Figures 8.22 and 8.23.

Example 8.6: Compute the Coefficient of Variation and RAV for the following 6 projects using NPV and standard deviation. Assume *r = 0.05.*

Project	1	2	3	4	5	6
Mean NPV	21.3	9	12.3	14.1	9.3	12.8
Standard Dev. of NPV	25.28	19.12	8.8	20.48	4.6	22.56
NPV/RiskCapital	0.87	1.00	1.37	1.08	2.02	2.00
Coefficient of Variation	1.19	2.12	0.72	1.45	0.49	1.76
RAV	5.32	-0.14	10.36	3.61	8.77	0.08

The first two rows are determined from simulations of the projects. The third is the standard efficiency measure, as discussed in Chapter 5. One can back calculate the investment capital using the mean and the NPV/RiskCapital row. The variability index suggests that project 5 varies less per value received, while project 2 varies the most per received value. Some users of this approach place the mean NPV in the numerator for convenience.

RAV reduces the mean value to correct for risk aversion and changes the relative ranking of the projects. Project 3 becomes the highest ranked project with RAV, even though it was about in the middle using traditional measures. Project 2 actually goes negative while Project 6 is almost zero. In the real world management authorized all of the projects. Is there an inconsistency? Is management really risk averse? What is happening?

The answer lies with the loss avoidance notion. Standard deviation measures variability around the mean, including the upside as well as the downside. Loss avoidance and the asymmetry of investing places greater weight on the downside, but traditional standard deviations give equal weight to each, a classic example of the model being too simple to capture the important impacts.

One correction to model loss avoidance directly uses the concept called: *semi-variance.* Semi-variance focuses on a subset of the overall project standard deviation. Equation 8.10 defines the concept,

$$S_x^{<T} = \sqrt{\frac{1}{n}\sum_{t=1}^{T}(x_d - x_t)^2} \qquad \textbf{(8.10)}$$

where:

x_d = the value of any number below the specified target number,
x_t = the specified target number,
n = the number of values below the target number, and
T = the number of values less than the target number.

The traditional symbol for the calculated standard deviation, S_x, now includes the superscript, $<T$ to indicate that the standard deviation concept still applies, but restricted to certain values in the data set.

Setting the target value is quite easy for most investors if the concept of pure loss avoidance is accepted. The target value is zero. Investors faced other objectives, like an ROCE greater than 15%, could modify the target value to be any desired value as a result of these constraints.

Example 8.7: Compute the standard deviation and semi-variance from the following simulations for a project risk assessment. Assume the target value is NPV = 0.

Run	1	2	3	4	5	6	7	8	9	10
NPV	-12	25	18	-5	-7	25	-11	16	29	40

The standard deviation, S_x, is 18.91. The semi-variance number, based on the 4 negative numbers, is 9.21.

$$\sqrt{\frac{1}{4} * \left\{(-12-0)^2 + (-5-0)^2 + (-7-0)^2 + (-11-0)^2\right\}} = 9.21$$

Loss avoidance worries only about the downside, and this appears to match many investors perspective, only variation in the degree of avoidance. Redoing the numbers in Example 8.6 yields positive RAV's. Though the management looking at these projects was unaware of the RAV concept when making the decisions, their subjective decision-making process matched this simple loss avoidance approach almost exactly.

The semi-variance approach assumes that investors are indifferent to volatility above the target mean. Many investors reject the semi-variance notion out of hand, arguing that they focus on the upside, not the downside. The utility function can be expanded to consider multiple risk parameters. One expression, which combines the semi-variance approach and the overall variability notion, is given in Equation 8.11.

$$RAV_{combined} = \overline{NPV} - r_T * S_x^2 - r_{sv} * (S_x^{<T})^2 \qquad \textbf{(8.11)}$$

where:

r_T = aversion to variability in total returns
S_x^2 = variability in total value measures
r_{sv} = aversion to downside risk or semi-variance
$S_x^{<T}$ = variance of returns below target value, from Equation 8.11

CHAPTER 8

Example 8.9: Compute the $RAV_{combined}$ using the following data, and assuming r_T = 0.01 and r_{sv} = 0.015.

Project	1	2	3	4	5	6
Mean NPV	21.30	9.00	12.30	14.10	9.30	12.8
Variance of NPV	25.28	19.12	8.80	20.48	4.60	22.56
Semi-Var. of NPV	12.25	6.22	3.14	7.22	2.00	7.55
RAVcombined	12.66	4.76	11.38	9.12	9.03	6.86
RAV	5.32	-0.14	10.36	3.61	8.77	0.08

where: $12.66 = 21.30 - 0.01 * 25.28^2 - 0.015 * 12.25^2$

This broader definition of RAV yields a very different ranking than the RAV from Example 8.6. The variance values are duplicated from that example, and only the semi-variance numbers are new. The other change is the preference for risk. In Example 8.6, the risk preference, r, was set to 0.025. The combined values for risk preference in this example still equal 0.025, but with a greater weight on the downside. All project RAV's are positive, though project 2 is only barely so. Even with the greater weight attached to loss avoidance; the projects add value to the treasury.

The general reaction to loss avoidance is recognition that actual investment decisions vary with individual and group preferences, but dismay over the ability to generate the values used to make the equations work, e.g., the respective values for r. One solution provides an approximation, like using the value of 2 obtained from the work of Tversky, or another alternative. Bourdaire, *et. al.* assume that the risk preference depends on the wealth of the investor.*(8.17)* Since wealth cannot be observed directly, the authors assume that the budget level of the investor acts as a proxy for wealth. The approach converts the previous equations by assuming that:

$$r = \frac{1}{2*B} \tag{8.12}$$

so, the RAV equation becomes:

$$RAV = \overline{NPV} - \left[\frac{S_x^2}{2*B}\right] \tag{8.13}$$

Chapter 10 gives an example of ranking projects using RAV versus other, more traditional value metrics. The RAV for the previous example at different budget levels is shown in Example 8.9.

Note that RAV falls as the budget decreases, implying that risk tolerance decreases at smaller wealth positions. This is one reason smaller organizations are perceived to be more risk averse than large

Example 8.9: Compute the RAV_{budget} for the following budget amounts.

	Project	1	2	3	4	5	6
	Mean NPV	21.3	9	12.3	14.1	9.3	12.8
	S_x of NPV	25.28	19.12	8.8	20.48	4.6	22.56
Budget							
80	RAV	17.31	6.72	11.82	11.48	9.17	9.62
60	RAV	15.97	5.95	11.65	10.60	9.12	8.56
40	RAV	13.31	4.43	11.33	8.86	9.04	6.44
20	RAV	5.32	-0.14	10.36	3.61	8.77	0.08

CHAPTER 8

ones. Also, Bill Gates, Gordon Getty, and other billionaires invest in riskier projects than the less affluent. A second interesting observation is that the budget line of 20 yields the same RAV as Example 8.6. A budget of 20 when multiplied by 2, and the product divided into 1 gives the same 0.025 risk measure. Perhaps, risk aversion may also be revealed by the authorized budgets.

Some readers perceive utility to be an academic exercise, with little, or no practical value. Whatever ones view, loss avoidance, risk tolerance, or whatever name is used, is a hot topic in investments. When measuring risk was virtually impossible, the question of risk tolerance was moot. Now that the tools for quantifying risk are at everyone's fingertips, risk tolerance becomes a provocative question. Our hope is that future work will refine the notion of preference by realizing that it is more complicated than just a value for r, and can be analyzed in far greater detail, with the benefit of including it in formal risk assessment and valuation metrics.

RISK ADJUSTED DISCOUNT RATE

The alternative approach to the direct estimation of risk tolerance comes in the form of adjusting the discount rate. Most practitioners prefer this method for incorporating risk, because of the inherent problems in trying to classify investor(s) risk tolerance or utility. Generally, most management, especially senior management detests having their investment habits classified.[8.18, 8.19] Even more important, most investors believe they understand discounting; though Chapter 5 questions this position.

Chapter 4 derived the discount rate in two ways: as the weighted cost-of-capital and as the sum of the risk free rate plus a risk premium, and Chapter 5 illustrated the application of the competing methods. The risk premium adjusted the valuation process to reflect each projects, or component of NCF, contribution to organizational risk. Historically, most organizations applied an average risk premium to every project, regardless of the real risk. This simplified approach seriously distorts portfolio management by ignoring the real options to the investor, leading to investment patterns which conflict with investment objectives.[8.20]

One simple approach utilizes the coefficient of variation, as defined in Equation 8.9. Moyers, *et. al.* suggest adjusting the risk premium.[8.21] Their objective approach is to compute:

$$k_A^* = r_f + \alpha_A \qquad \textbf{(8.14)}$$

where:

r_f = the risk free rate, like 3%,
k_A^* = the project risk adjusted discount rate,
α_A = $(v_A/v_T) * \alpha$,
a = risk premium for the firm or organization, as defined in Chapter 3, (like 7-10%),
v_A = coefficient of variation for the project, and
v_T = coefficient of variation for the entire organization.

Equation 8.14 adjusts the average risk premium by the ratio α_A. The riskier projects have the premium increased, while the safer projects are evaluated using smaller discount rates.

The measures of risk assessment and valuation discussed so far deal with the overall project. Chapter 5 introduced the concept of *modern investment valuation (MIV),* which demonstrated that the elements comprising NCF (price, production, Capex, Opex, and taxes) face substantially different risks, with those risks varying over time, without explaining how to quantify these issues. The next section addresses methods for quantifying risk at the individual component level.

Example 8.10: Derive the risk adjusted discount rates for the previous examples using Equation 8.14, assuming the risk free rate is 3% and the risk premium is 8%.

Project	1	2	3	4	5	6	Average
Mean NPV =	21.3	9	12.3	14.1	9.3	12.8	13.13
S_x of NPV =	25.28	19.12	8.8	20.48	4.6	22.56	18.40
k_x^* =	6.8%	12.1%	4.1%	8.3%	2.8%	10.1%	7.4%

Where: 0.068 or 6.8% = (25.28/21.3)/(18.4/13.13) * 0.08

Note that the average of the standard deviations is the square root of the summation of variances, not the standard deviation (about 16.4). This is the reason that the average of the adjusted discount rates is 7.4%, not 8%.

MIV, AND FINANCIAL AND REAL OPTIONS THEORY

MIV and options theory is a subset of a discipline, called *contingent claims analysis*. These methods emphasize that valuing investments is contingent on other conditions. The simulation examples demonstrated the importance of the linkage or dependency between input variables. Options attacks the same problem, but from a different perspective. Rather than simulating the variability, it searches for an analog or a direct measure in the market. Product prices for agriculture and energy have futures and options markets that provide information about the markets expectations for future pricing. Traders in these markets claim that they can guarantee prices for up to 10 years by creating derivatives of these contracts.

The best analogy regarding MIV and its special case, real options, compares the classical process and MIV to blackjack and poker.[8.22] In blackjack, the gambler places their bet and waits for the outcome, while poker permits the gambler to put a small amount down and then keep increasing the bet, contingent on each round of cards. Classical investment decision-making assumes the investor is playing blackjack, while the modern approach follows the poker analogy. Does the opportunity to change the bet (or investment) over time convey any benefit by altering risk or improving profitability?

Options analysis began with the opening of the futures market on the Chicago Board of Trade in the early 70's. By now, most professionals have heard of futures and options for petroleum, agricultural, interest and exchange rate, etc. These are traded virtually worldwide on exchanges in New York, London, etc. Options differ from futures in several ways, but both look at prices for commodities or assets, months or years into the future.

Options analysis originated in financial markets, and has since moved into analysis of real or tangible assets. A considerable body of knowledge has accumulated in both areas. This section summarizes the financial markets first, and then applies the concepts to real assets, or traditional investment theory. While the underlying ideas are fairly simple, the application is fraught with considerable risk.

Financial Options

An option is the right to buy (*call option*) or sell (*put option*) an item in the future. The examples used here will highlight call options, because that is closer to traditional investment decision-making.

Two parties are involved in the options market, those seeking to hedge or secure their position and speculators. The difference is whether one owns an asset or is just speculating on price changes. This discussion focuses on asset owners, not speculators. Speculation plays a prominent role in market efficiency, and is effectively legalized gambling. And, like most gambling, should only be practiced with great care by those willing to live with the consequences of failure. Barings Bank, Long Term Capital Management, and other companies have gone bankrupt or lost considerable sums of money by speculating.

Suppose a stock is selling for \$100 right now. You believe that the price will rise in the future, but you don't have \$100. The stock is selling for a premium (options contract price) of \$10, and has an *exercise price* of \$110 in three months time. By buying the option for \$10, you get the right to buy the stock for \$100 at the end of the option. If the stock price exceeds \$110, it is termed as being *in the money.* If the price is below \$110, the stock is *out of the money.* Financial options expire out of the money about 75% of the time.

Figure 8.28 illustrates the gains and loss to the investor. At a price below \$110, the investor loses the \$10 option premium. At \$110, the investor exercises the option to buy the stock for \$100 plus the option cost of \$10 exactly offsets the gain of selling the stock for \$110. If the stock rises to \$120, the \$120 raised by selling the stock yields a \$10 gain (=120 – 110).

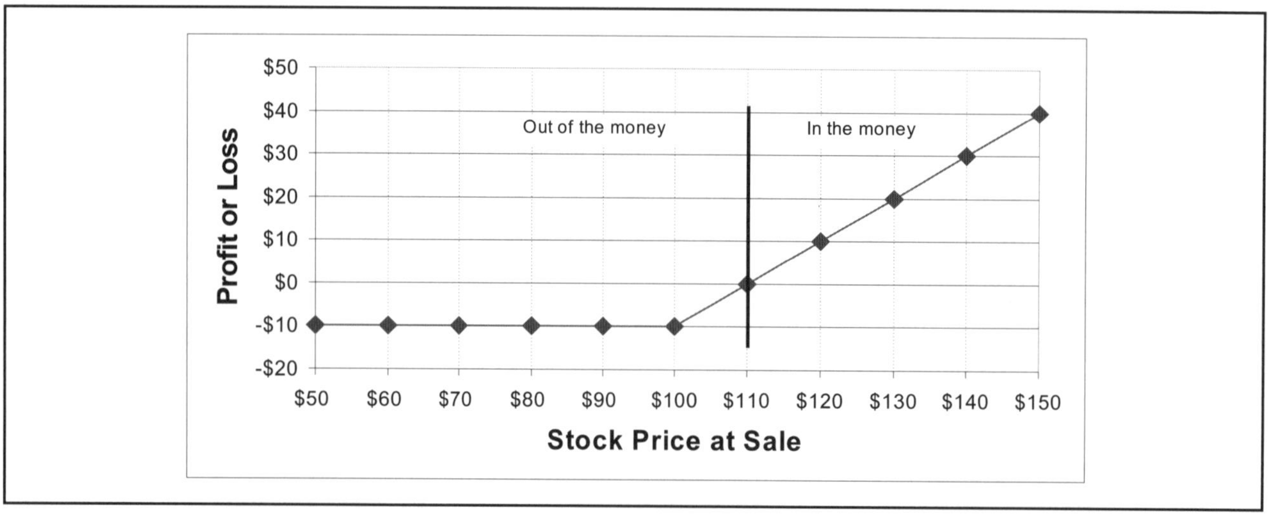

Figure 8.28 Example of financial options

Though a simple example, this is the essence of the options market. The difficult part of the options market is the determination of the options premium or the options value. Two distinct methods exist for determining the option value: the binomial method and the Black-Scholes (B-S) method. The binomial approach is discussed later because it dominates the approach used in valuing real assets.

The Black and Scholes model is summarized in Equation 8.15:

$$C_o = S_o * N(d_1) + X * e^{-r*T} * N(d_2) \tag{8.15}$$

where:

S_o = the current price of the stock
X = the exercise price of the option
T = the time period of the contract
e = 2.71828, the base of the natural log function
r = the risk-free interest rate
$N(d)$ = the probability that a random draw from a standard normal distribution will be less than d. (See Chapter 5 or use the spreadsheet function for a normal distribution)

$$d_1 = \frac{\ln(S_o/X) + (r + \sigma_X^2/2) * T}{\sigma_X * \sqrt{T}}$$

$$d_2 = d_1 - \sigma_X * \sqrt{T}$$

σ_X = standard deviation of stock price changes

The model is simpler than it appears, being much like the risk weighting or EMV computation by balancing the gains and losses of money by the likelihood of the event occurring. The examples even define a breakeven chance of success. B-S computes the options price that makes the investment a fair bet, or, given the chance of being in or out of the money, what price allows the investment to break-even, on average.

Example 8.11 demonstrates the application of the B-S model, assuming a $100 price, and an exercise price of $108. Plugging these values, along with the other required information given in the example, the options value comes out as $2.412. At an exercise price of $108 and the purchase price of the contract of $2.412, the stock price must climb above $10.412 for the contract to fall in the money.

Example 8.11: Compute the OANPV of the call option, assuming a current price of $100, exercise price of $108, a standard deviation of price of 7%, a risk free rate of 4%, and a 3 month duration for the contract, so T = 3/12 or 0.25.

$$C_o = 100*0.0290 + 108*e^{-0.04*0.25}*0.0267 = \$2.412$$

$$N\left(\frac{\ln\left(\frac{100}{108}\right) + \left(0.04 + \frac{0.07^2}{2}\right)*0.25}{0.07*\sqrt{0.25}}\right) = 0.0290$$

$$\text{where } N\left(0.0290 - 0.07*\sqrt{0.25}\right) = 0.0267$$

The d_1 and d_2 coefficients are risk-adjusted probabilities that the call option will expire in the money, while S and X are the benefits and costs of the option. If the N(d) terms are close to one, the option is the stock price less the NPV of the exercise price. When the N(d)'s are close to zero, Equation 8.18 must be close to zero. The value of a bet is worthless when it has little chance of making money.

The real driving force behind options theory is the counterintuitive notion that value increases as variability increases. The more volatility in the stock price, the greater the chance that the stock will be in the money. Take the extreme case where a stock value never changes, or $s_x = 0$. No one would ever buy an option because the stock price can't change. But, as the s_x increases, the option takes on a larger value, since the chances of being *in the money* rises.

This has been a very simple illustration of the financial options market. Probably the best text on this subject is by S. Errera and S. Brown.[(8.23)]

Real Options

Options theory provides the foundation for questioning investment decisions using classical discounted cash flow (DCF) analysis. The MIV approach explicitly recognizes the ability to change the investment magnitude and pattern as new events occur, rather than being irreversible; e.g. once investors approve a project, it goes forward with no review of economic conditions or changes ever being made. The MIV literature explicitly recognizes that decisions can be altered over time, contingent on new, unexpected conditions in the economy, be it price, market, new technology, etc. changes.

A commonly cited list of options available is given in Table 8.4, reflecting the typical textbook approach to the problem. Some of the categories overlap, but convey some interesting ideas of how the investment process changes over time.

TABLE 8.4

Example of Options Investment Applications(8.24)

Category	Description	Important In:
Option to defer	Management holds a lease on some land. It can wait x years to see if output prices justify construction.	All natural resource extraction industries, real estate development, farming, and paper products
Time-to-build analysis	Staging investments as a series of outlays creates the option to cancel the enterprise in mid-stream if new information is unavailable. Each stage can be viewed as an option on the next stage.	All R&D industries, especially pharmaceuticals, and electricity generation, and startup ventures.
Option to alter scale	If market conditions vary, the scale of the operation can be adjusted accordingly.	Natural resource industries; chemicals and other cyclical industries; fashion apparel; and real estate.
Option to abandon	If market conditions deteriorate rapidly, management can abandon current operations and sell capital equipment and other assets.	Capital-intensive industries, financial services, new products.
Option to switch	If prices or demand changes, management can change the product mix of the facility. Alternatively, the same output can be produced with different inputs.	Output shifts: electronics, toys, specialty paper, autos.Input shifts: feedstock dependent facilities electric power, chemicals.
Growth options	An early investment (R&D, lease, strategic acquisition) is a prerequisite or link in a chain of interrelated projects opening up future growth opportunities (new products or new markets).	All infrastructure-based industries, esp. high tech, R&D, multiple products, multinationals, and strategic acquisitions.
Multiple interacting options	Real life projects often involve a collection of various option. The combined effect may be different than the sum of their separate values.	Almost every real life project.

CHAPTER 8

Black & Scholes Real Options Valuation

The options literature developed the concept of options analysis net present value (OANPV), as specified in Equation 8.16.

$$OANPV = NPV + C_0 \tag{8.16}$$

where NPV is the project net present value and C_0 is the result of the B&S equation given in equation 8.15.

The initial options literature just copied the B-S format and applied it to real investments. The only change is in the definition of the components of the B-S equation. For real investments, the exercise price, X, is the discounted value of the AT investment (the cost of option). The current price, S_0, is the NPV of the project, excluding the AT NPV of the investment (Instead of Revenue – Capex – Opex, just use Revenue – Opex).

The logic of the movement to real investment is the analogy that the share price, in an efficient market, is just the present value of future cash flows, which is the NPV notion in project investing. The cost to acquire the right to have the option is the investment. The big issue, as we shall see, is defining the investment properly.

Example 8.12 highlights the OANPV for one project. Note that the traditional NPV of the project is \$70.8 million (\$110.8 – \$40). The options literature calls this the *biased NPV.* The OANPV is much larger because the project is almost guaranteed to be in the money. Hence, the value to the treasury is \$142.4 million, not the \$70.8 given by the traditional NPV.

Example 8.12: Compute the OANPV for a project with an NPV excluding the investment or option of \$110.8 million, and NPV of investment of \$40 million, a 25% standard deviation, a 2% risk free rate, and a 1 year maturity period. Also, verify which assumptions the OANPV is most sensitive to.

$$\text{OANPV} = 110.8 - 40.0 + 71.6 = \$142.4 \text{ million}$$

$$71.6 = 110.8 * N(d_1) - 40 * N(d_2) = 110.8 * 0.999 - 40 * 0.999$$

where: $$N(d_1) = 0.999 = N\left(\frac{\ln\left(110/40\right) + \left(0.02 + 0.25^2/1\right) * T}{0.25 * \sqrt{1}}\right)$$

The critical driver in the B-S model are the ratio, ln(110/40) and the standard deviation. As the standard deviation increases, the greater the chance the project will be in the money. Note that in OANPV, greater variability improves project profitability, while classical risk assessment assumes the goal is to minimize variability. This conflict is the major, unresolved issue in investments today.

As the exercise price (\$40 in the example) increases relative to the price (\$110), the value of the option decreases, simply because the chance of being in the money decreases.

Figure 8.29 compares the biased NPV and OANPV for a hypothetical project. The two lines overlap until the risk-free discount rate, when the OANPV increases for every discount rate after that point. The gap between static NPV and OANPV represents the value of the right to delay a project, or react to contingencies. The two lines diverge at the point OAIRR, which reflects the risk free rate.(8.25)

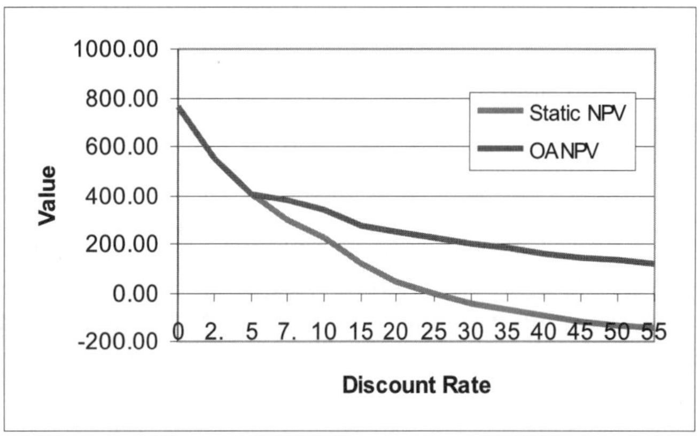

Figure 8.29 Comparison of biased NPV and OANPV

This figure highlights several interesting aspects about OANPV. First, observe that classical DCF indicates the project turns negative between a discount rate of 20 and 25%. At those same rates, OANPV indicates a positive value. Many projects that have negative NPV's become positive with OANPV, reflecting the ability to respond to changing business conditions over time. The OANPV may also lie below the NPV line when the cost of the option is much greater than the price, S_0.

Table 8.5 repeats the alternative value measures for the projects used at the end of Chapter 5, with the addition of the OANPV. The risk premium in the second row reflects the adjustments described earlier using the square root of N, or years in the project. The other values are used as before, except for SIV (strategic investment value) and VCV (venture capitalist value), which are described in Chapter 5 and other publications.(8.26) NPV/Inv is just the traditional profitability index, with investment being the maximum exposure or most negative cumulative cash flow.

The purpose here is to compare the biased NPV with the OANPV. The workover and single economics have positive NPV's, but negative OANPV, indicating that the short payout time and quick returns eliminate the possibility of being in the money, or the opportunity to respond to changing business environments. The rate acceleration and multi-well gas field development show the OANPV doubling and quadrupling the NPV values, respectively. Even more interesting is the contrast between the offshore

TABLE 8.5

Comparison of Profitability for Selected Projects (all money values in $million)

					Offshore Development Options		
	Workover	Single Well	Rate Acceleration	Multi-Well Gas Development	Fixed Platform	FPSO	Subsea with Tieback to Existing Platform
Years in project	10	15	30	36	50	50	50
Risk Premium	.034	.027	.018	0.018	0.015	0.15	0.15
NPV_5	2.41	2.4	-17.98	65.92	474.0	384.7	339.6
NPV_{10}	2.11	1.57	6.52	29.2	57.1	92.64	137.1
NPV_{15}	1.88	0.97	12.27	12.01	-156.6	-56.3	27.9
IRR (BDR)	None	27.4	7.9%	23.2%	11.05%	12.7	16.9
SDV	2.5	2.29	-61.8	99.5	289.1	415.8	427.2
$OANPV_{10}$	-13.51	-8.68	14.5	89.8	1017.4	627.5	579.3
VCV_{10}	2.1	0.86	-110.2	113.5	520.4	746.6	543.3
DPO_{10} (yrs)	<1 year	3.89	2.8	10.3	15.8	13.0	9.5
EPI	4.42	0.48	0.43	1.71	0.13	0.21	0.44
Project Investment ($mm)	0.5	6.0	27.7	124.9	2208.0	980.2	666.0

development options. Note that the NPV_{10} ranks the Subsea tieback option as the best, and the fixed platform as the lowest. OANPV reverses the ranking, because owning the platform provides a multitude of options, like charging a processing and transportation fee, like those identified in Table 8.4.

Before moving into the binomial options approach, one extension of the B-S model is called the *European options model.* In the European model, no money changes hands between the time the contract is issued and the contract maturation. In the financial markets, the owner of a share often receives dividends during the contract period, called the *American options model.* Receiving money during the contract period alters the risk/return relationship.

The extension of the B-S model to allow for dividend payments (dividend is just the financial terminology for any flow of money between the contract initiation and maturation) is the Merton model.

$$OANPV = e^{(\delta)(t)} * S_o * N(d_1) - X * e^{-r(t)} * N(d_2) \tag{8.17}$$

where all the values are the same as the B&S model, except for δ, which is the payout rate.

The payout rate represents the difference between the investors required rate-of-return and the rate of price appreciation earned on the asset. If the asset is a petroleum reservoir, for example, as the project goes through the stages of exploration and development, the option holder gets a price appreciation (the reservoir is known to exist), but no direct payout until development occurs. Until development does occur, the shortfall or payout rate measures the opportunity cost of keeping the option alive.

Like most concepts, the equation is much simpler than coming up with the input values. Users of the Merton model derive the value for δ from the futures market. It is essentially the risk free rate less the cost of holding an asset. Since the risk free rate is normally 3-5% and holding cost is 1-2%, deriving δ is quite simple. It also has little impact in most analysis.

Binomial Options

Introducing real options followed the analogy to financial options. Most applications of options, especially in the mineral industry, use the binomial options method, because it resembles decision trees. Figure 8.30 shows the basic tree approach. It is called the binomial model, because only two outcomes are allowed, usually a high or low value. The simple example includes price, production, and cost, but ignores time. Even with two outcomes and three variables, the number of combinations increases quite rapidly. The example also follows the format from the decision-tree section presented earlier in the chapter.

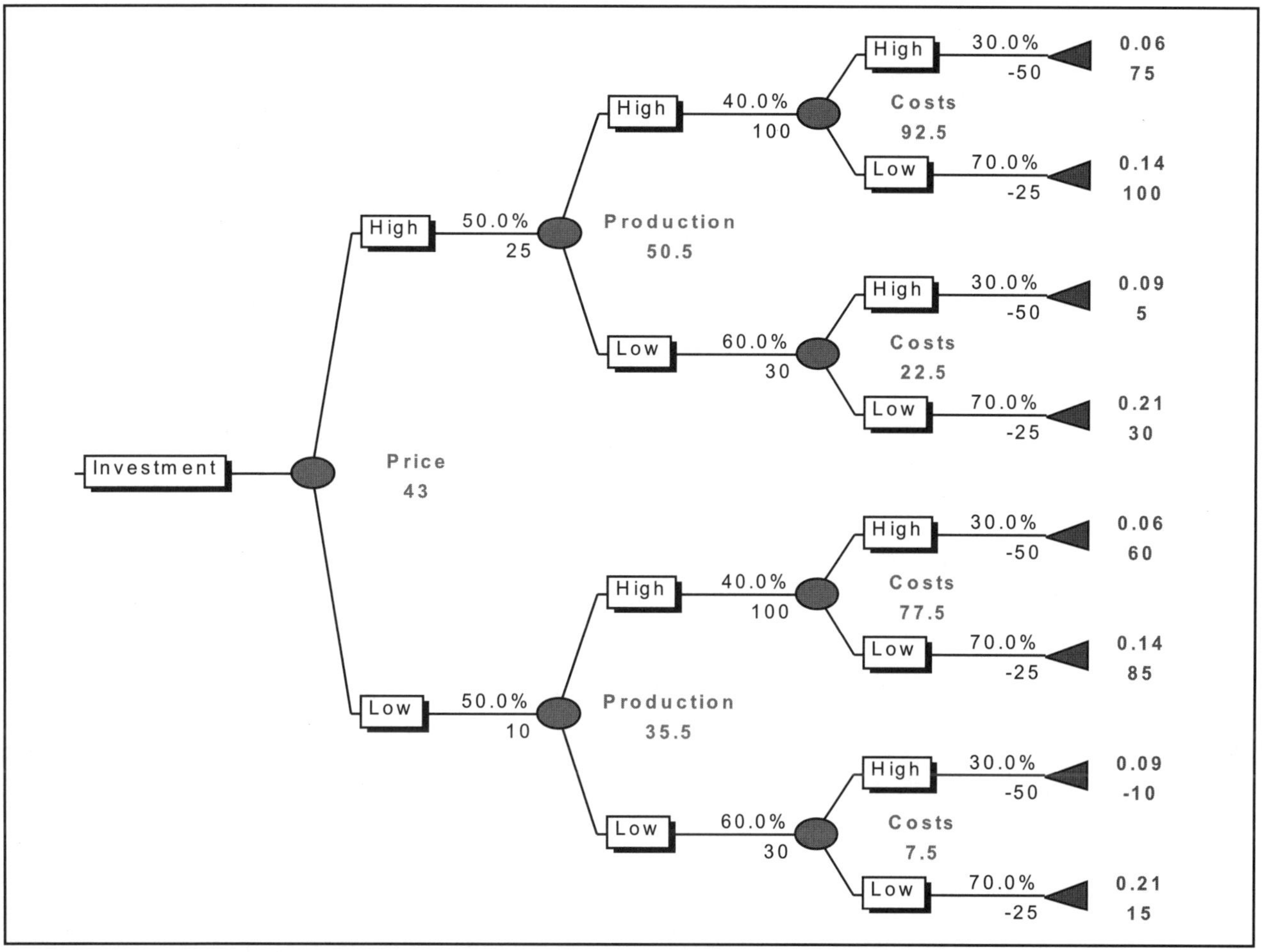

Figure 8.30 Simple example of binomial process without options

The classical or static decision tree ignores several important elements. One is time, and the other is the interrelationship among the investment variables, though time and dependencies are related. The simple format assumes the investor makes a decision now and follows the course of action through, without ever responding to changing business conditions. Relative to the simple tree, the low price, low production and high cost line generates a $-10 NPV. Faced with that situation, the rational investor would seek ways to collect more information as a means to reduce the chance of losing money, via market surveys, R&D, contracts, etc., which is ignored in this framework. All the decision trees shown so far only indicate possible alternatives that could occur, the probability of occurrence, and the valuation of the consequence.

The classical format ignores the connection between actual decision opportunities (options) and changes in business conditions as they vary over time. Not only can the investor change the investment pattern at any given point in time, the nature of the investment options varies dramatically over time. Falling prices lead to curtailing production or stopping production altogether, as chemical plants do during periods of low prices. This example applies to the case where the production system already exists, and can only be changed with a major capital expenditure (called the clay stage). Before the production system is designed and constructed, the investor can change the size, type, location, etc. (the putty stage) in response to new and changing information.

The modern approach now recognizes that investment move through various stages over their life. Each phase is characterized by different concerns and options. Identifying the relevant issues at each stage and the key drivers in each stage guides the decision-making process. To be fair, good investors have always tried to link the decision framework with these timing and dependency (option) issues, though the limited toolkit strained the abilities of all but the very best investors. The current toolkit allows anyone interested in applying the process to handle these complex interaction of forces, as they vary over time. The early chapters began with the notion that the modern era merely builds better and more complete models for exactly this reason.

Figure 8.31 demonstrates that decisions occur throughout the investment process. The example ignores the probabilities and values to focus on the basic concept. As events unfold, the investor can alter the way they respond from that point forward. Many options arise at every step along the way, like quitting or trying to sell the asset, take on partners, etc. Others, like running seismic, ultimately lead to the same option, just deferred until after the information is collected.

Observe how complicated the tree is. When other important issues are included, like price variability and time, the process becomes even more unwieldy. Figure 8.32 defines as much of the problem as possible in limited space. It extends Figure 8.31 by analyzing development options over time, with different pricing scenarios. We let you explore the options yourself without discussion here.

Under the binomial and multinomial format, the best alternative is computed in several ways, but the most common is called *dynamic programming.* The dynamic programming process begins at the far right of the tree and works its way to the left, much like the previous examples did. More details about the algorithms for doing this can be found in other sources.[(8.27, 8.28)] Even without going through the details for finding the best path through the maze, the complexity of the problem should be clear.

The options thinking expressed in the trees still requires valuation. The basic process is similar to the one outlined for the Black and Scholes model, requiring much more detail than possible in this book. Instead, the following two sections demonstrate the applications of options thinking and valuation.

Before illustrating two options applications, some authors believe that MIV and options process differs from the simulation procedures outlined above.[(8.29)] The authors accept that the flexibility issues could be included to obtain expected values and distributions, but don't believe obtaining information about the optimal policy to be too complicated. We disagree. In the example used by the authors to illustrate options flexibility, over 52,000 nodes on the tree existed, even when only 5 years of options were considered. Imagine what the number of nodes when 30-50 year project lives exist. A real opportunity exists for combining the MIV process with the lessons from simulation.

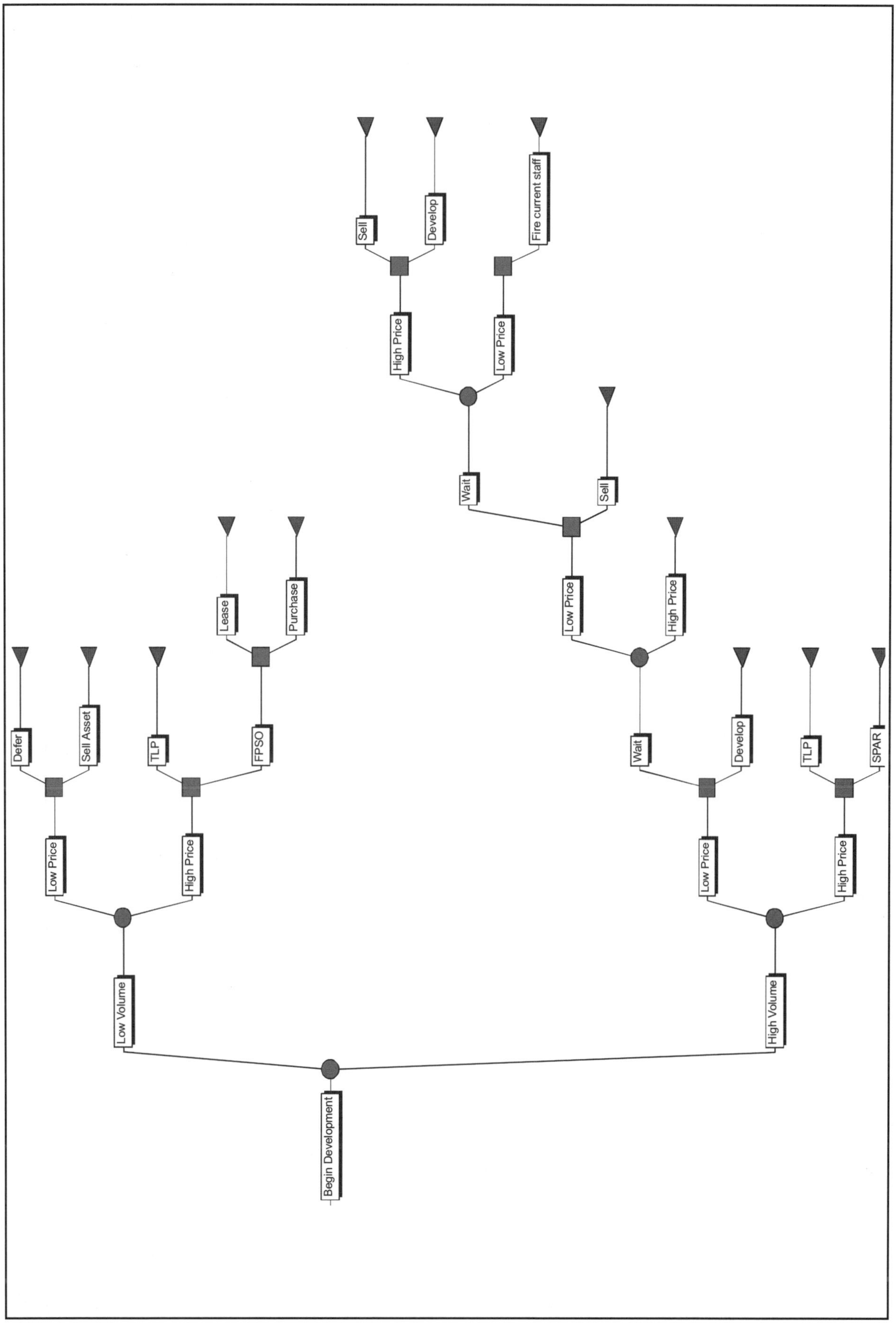

Figure 8.31 Options thinking with contingencies

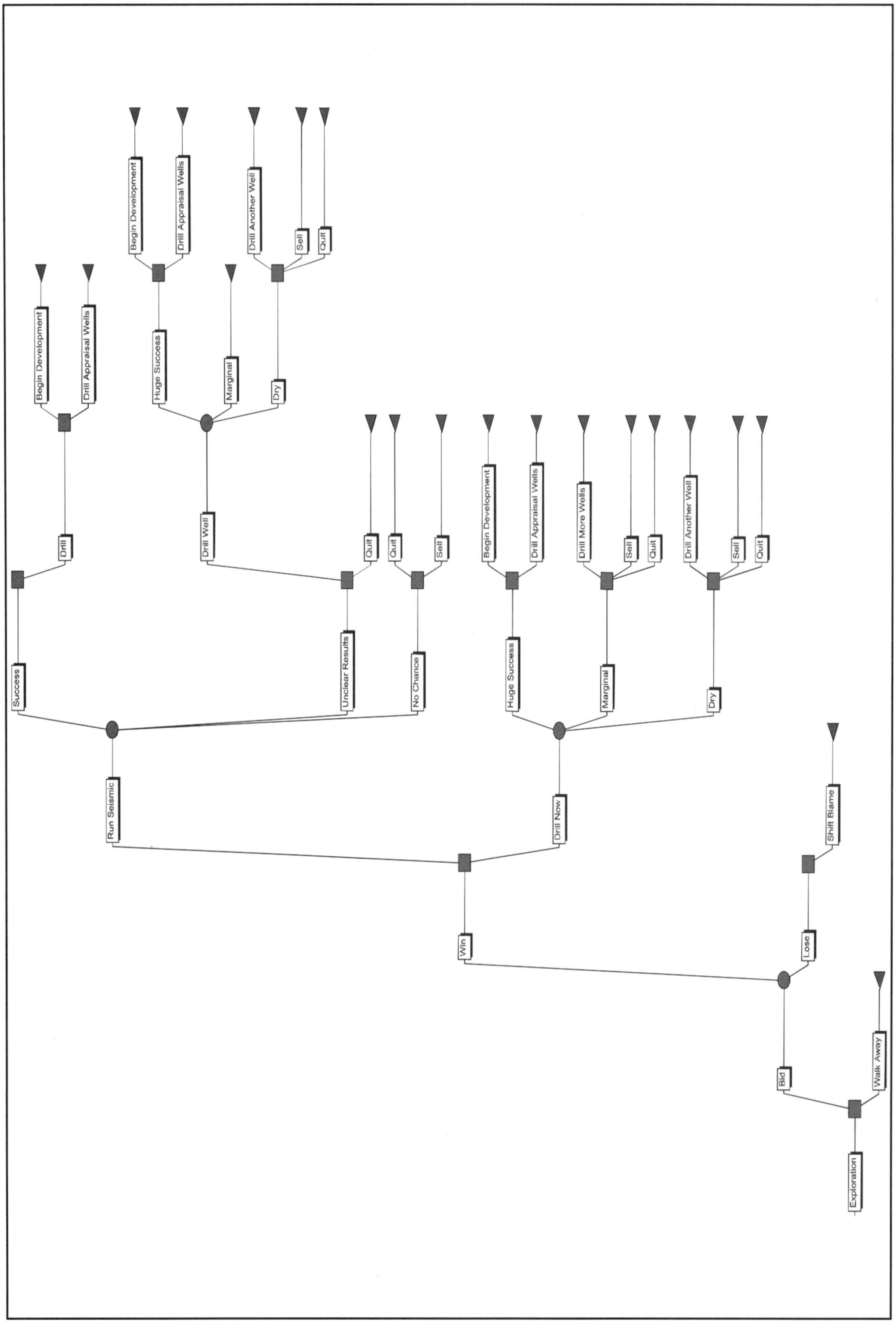

Figure 8.32 Options thinking with price variability and contingencies

Phased Development Scheme

An investor has the option to develop a field in three phases. Phase I is considered the most lucrative. The preferred course of action is to develop Phase I, and wait to gather information before committing to Phases II and III. Experience gathered in Phase I would help refine the costs and benefits from the later phases. Classical DCF prepares the following estimates of value for the three phases.

TABLE 8.6

Traditional Valuation of Phases

(all values in $MM)	NPV	Discounted AT Capex
Phase I	67.0	384.0
Phase II	22.4	210.0
Phase III	-1.3	81.0
Total	87.8	675.0

The values reported in Table 8.6 assume each phase is independent of each other and will proceed at a fixed time during the live of the concession. Management, in other words, ignores the flexibility opportunities, accepts the investment now, and then never looks at it again. Of course, this scenario ignores the reality that management will review the particulars of each phase with every price change and new set of information. Yet, the traditional approach ignores the value of the ability to alter each phase. The benefit of recognizing the options value in each phase is shown in Example 8.13.

Example 8.13: Based on the following information about Capex, volatility, etc., use the Merton model to estimate the options value of each phase and compare the results to traditional DCF.

Inputs	Phase I	Phase II	Phase III	Total
Project NPV, S	67	22.4	-1.3	87.8
Capex NPV, X	384	210.0	81.0	675.0
Time to maturity, T	2	16	13	
Oil price volatility, σ	18%	18%	18%	
Risk free rate, r	6.22%	7.18%	7.07%	
Payout rate, d	8.98%	9.94%	9.83%	
Option Value	3.83	11.75	8.3	23.63
Total OANPV	70.83	33.9	9.6	114.33
Years to exercise price	1.23	8.59	11.31	

The biased project NPV, from the last column in the first row, is $87.8 million, while the total options NPV is $114.33, for an improvement of $23.63 million. Observe that Phase III improves from a negative NPV to almost $10 million because of the opportunity to take advantage of higher prices.

The option value for Phase I is low, even with higher values for the project, because the time to maturity is 2 years. The 2-year horizon leaves little time to be in the money. The higher options value in Phase II results from the combination of a 16-year maturity period and large NPV's. Phase III benefits from the 13-year horizon, which allows enough time to take advantage of any upward price volatility.

The last column, years to exercise price, gives the length of time required before the volatility in price moves the project to being in the money. Though measured in time, it reflects the binomial probability distribution. Based on the input values, the computer generates the binomial figure as shown earlier. Then the computer asks how long it will take before there is a reasonable chance the project will be in the money.

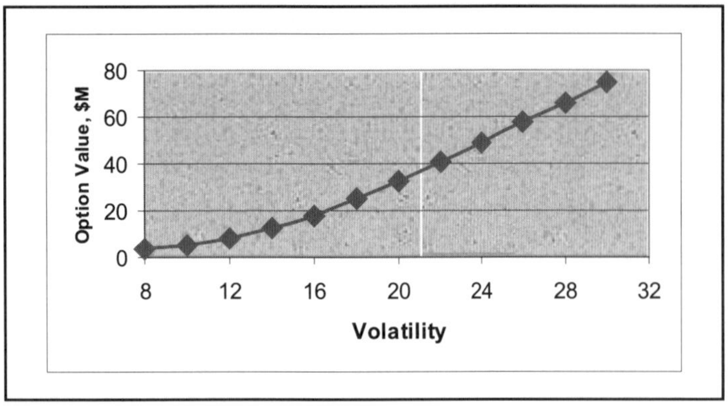

Figure 8.33 Relationship between volatility and option value

The critical inputs in options analysis are the NPV of the investment, NPV of the project, and the volatility measure. Saying that, the NPV of the project relative to the investment is an extension of classical DCF. Volatility, however, presents a relationship that is counterintuitive at first glance. Figure 8.33 shows the relationship between volatility and option value for the phased development. The options value increases as volatility increases because the chance of being in the money rises.

Petroleum Exploration Scheme

Petroleum projects follow a normal pattern of leasing, seismic, exploration drilling, delineation and finally the staged development, like the previous example. Traditional NPV values the series as if they were one project starting today. Each element is really an option that can be rejected, delayed or modified depending on conditions at the time the decision must be made.

Consider the following stages of a petroleum project in South America. The basic format, with probabilities, is provided in the decision tree in Figure 8.34.

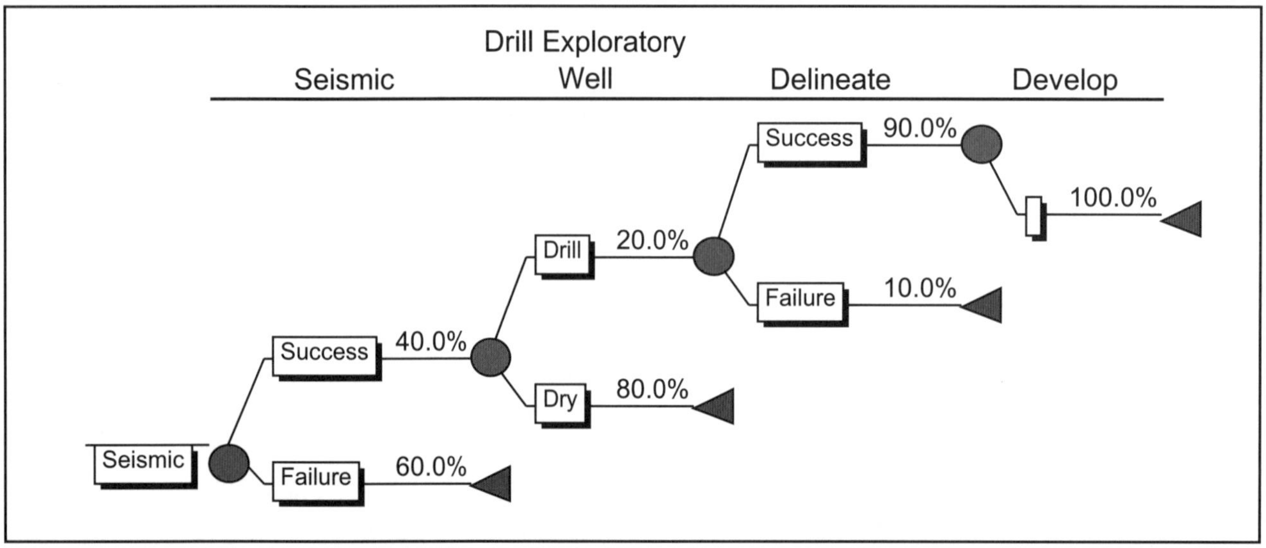

Figure 8.34 Decision tree of exploration alternatives

Example 8.14 summarizes the traditional and options analysis for the project. Note that the economics for the project are negative using the traditional NPV approach. The NPV at the exploration, delineation and development stages are all negative. With the options value, the negative NPV becomes a positive OANPV, implying that the project is worthwhile to undertake. Again, the conservatism inherent in classical NPV rears its ugly head.

Example 8.14: Based on the following information compute the options value and compare the results to the traditional NPV values.

	Exploration	Delineation	Develop	Total
Project NPV, $m	-13	2	8	-3
Capex NPV, $m	26	45	97	168
Time to maturity, T	3	4	15	
Standard deviation, σ	27%	27%	27%	
Risk free rate, r	6.35%	6.44%	6.70%	
Payout rate,	9.11%	9.20%	9.46%	
Options Value, $m	0.167	7.79	14	21.957
OANPV, $m	-12.833	9.79	22	18.957

Real Options Summary

The real options literature provides a considerable number of examples about the benefits to the formal recognition of flexibility or options in projects. Though the examples are useful, options methods, like all other tools, have limitations. First and foremost, is the selection of the volatility or standard deviation. Real options began as a reaction to simplified price forecasts, like a flat price, either escalated or non-escalated. These organizations often argue that the real purpose of the analysis is ranking, not value measurement. Our disagreement with this argument has been identified in several places in this book.

Simple straight-line extrapolations fail to capture the flexibility and alternative decisions made when prices vary. If the model reflects only price volatility, the standard deviation is just the volatility in the respective product price. Companies using one, restrictive price forecast will forego many excellent investment opportunities. Real options help measure the value from variability, rather than ignoring it.

If detailed project risk assessment is the objective, then meaningful volatility measures can only be achieved by running a complete simulation. Once the effort to construct the simulation approach is made, the need for real options analysis may be unnecessary. Some people see real options theory as just an approximation to the results of simulation.

Another element is that real options only changes the accept or reject decision. Faced with limited budgets, ranking using real options analysis may be very close to traditional NPV rankings. We have never seen a comparison of real options ranking or portfolio management applications and compared to traditional measures. Considerable work needs to be done to understand the trade-offs here.

SUMMARY

This chapter outlines the basic knowledge associated with risk assessment and management practice. While each methodology improves classical DCF metrics, often significantly, which have essentially remained static since the early 1900's, serious questions remain. Fundamental to these questions is the basic issue of whether better investment decisions actually emerge. Right now, most people believe they will. No organization has adopted the ideas and concepts, and implemented them in a rational, orderly process long enough to answer the question to provide hard evidence. Some have worked with bits and pieces and realized the deficiencies of the existing methods. But, no organizations, to our knowledge, can show, in a scientifically accepted manner, that the newer methods improve investment decision-making with absolute certainty.

The advocates of one or more of these methods argue that decisions must be improved. But, that isn't a convincing argument, especially to those who want proof. The only way to obtain the necessary proof is to try the newer methods, which many organizations are now beginning to dabble with. What remains to be seen is which methods will dominate and, which will go by the wayside. Like most technical knowledge bases, we have our biases and like placing bets with colleagues. But, if the lessons of this chapter hold true, the volatility in knowledge will surprise us all, and make for a very interesting business climate in the next several decades for those who embrace, rather than hide from, formal risk assessment and management.

REFERENCES

8.1 Bernstein, Peter, *Against the Gods*, John Wiley and Sons (1996).

8.2 Bernstein, Peter, *Ibid.*, p. 202.

8.3 Davidson, Lynn and Dale Cooper, "A Simple Way of Developing Probability Distribution of Present Value," *Journal of Petroleum Technology* (Sept. 1976), pp. 1069-1078.

8.4 Tversky, Amos and D. Khaneman, "Rational Choice and the Framing of Decisions," *Journal of Business* (Oct. 1986), S251-78.

8.5 Capen, Ed, "The Difficulty of Assessing Uncertainty," *JPT* (Aug, 1976), pp. 7-14.

8.6 SPE Forum on "Risk, Options and Portfolio Management," Breckinridge, CO (2000).

8.7 Russo, Edward and P. Schoemaker, "The Overconfidence Quiz," Harvard Business Review (Sept.-Oct. 1990), p. 236.

8.8 Tversky, *ibid.*

8.9 Newendorp, Paul, *Decision Analysis for Petroleum Exploration*, Petroleum Publishing Co. (1975), p. 187.

8.10 Neuman, John Von and O. Morgenstern, *Theory of Games and Economic Behavior*, Princeton University Press (1953).

8.11 Newendorp, Paul, *Application of Utility Theory to Drilling Investment Decisions*, Doctoral dissertation, University of Oklahoma (1967).

8.12 Newendorp, Paul, *Decision Methods for Petroleum Exploration*, *ibid.*, p. 158.

8.13 Walls, M., "Corporate Risk Tolerance and Capital Allocation: A Practical Approach to Implementing an Exploration Risk Policy," *JPT* (Apr. 1995), pp. 307-311.

8.14 Cozzolino, J., "A Simplified Utility Framework for the Analysis of Financial Risk," Economics and Evaluation Symposium of SPE (1977).

8.15 Raiffa, H., "Decision Analysis: Introductory Lectures on Choices Under Uncertainty," Addison-Wesley (1968).

8.16 Bodie, Zvi, *et. al.*, *Investments*, Irwin McGraw-Hill (1999), p. 151.

8.17 Jean Marie Bourdaire, *et. al.*, "Reserve Assessment Under Uncertainty – A New Approach." OGJ (10 June 1985), pp. 135-140.

8.18 Walls, M., *et. al.*, "Integrating Business Strategy and Capital Allocation: An Application of Multi-Objective Decision Making," *Engineering Economist* (Spring 1995), pp. 247-266.

8.19 Walls, M. and James Dyer, "Risk Propensity and Firm Performance: A Study of the Petroleum Exploration Industry," *Management Science* (1995).

8.20 Campbell, J., *et. al.*, "Measuring Strategic Investment Value," SPE paper 56453 (Fall 1999).

8.21 Moyer, R., *et. al.*, *Contemporary Financial Management*, West Publishing (1981), pp. 258-259.

8.22 Rowe, Richard, personal communication.

8.23 Errera, S. and S. Brown, *Fundamentals of Trading Energy Futures and Options*, PennWell Press (1999).

8.24 Trigeoris, L., "Real Options: An Overview," in *Real Options in Capital Investment*.

8.25 Ross, Stephen, "Uses, Abuses and Alternatives to the Net-Present-Value Rule," *Financial Management*, vol 24, No. 3, Autumn 1995, p. 96-102.

8.26 Campbell, J., *ibid.*

8.27 Clemen, R., *Making Hard Decisions*, Duxbury Press (1996).

8.28 Luenberger, D., *Investment Science*, Oxford Press (1998).

8.29 Smith, J. and K. McCardle, "Options in the Real World: Lessons Learned in Evaluating Oil and Gas Investments," Operations Research (Jan.-Feb. 1999), pp: 1-15.

OTHER ARTICLES OF INTEREST

Campbell, J., *et. al.*, *Mineral Property Economics*, Vol. I., Campbell Petroleum Series (1977).

Davidson, L. B. and D. Cooper, *JPT* (Sept. 1976), pp. 1069-1079.

Sears, G. F. and N. Phillips, SPE 13777 (Mar. 1985), pp. 183-187.

Cooper, D. and L. Davidson, *CEP* (Nov. 1976), pp. 173-179.

Bourdaire, J. M. *et. al.*, *OGJ* (10 June, 1985), pp. 135-140.

Ricks, R., *OGJ* (30 Sept., 1985), pp. 68-72.

Smith, P. and J. Burkee, SPE 13776 (Mar. 1985), pp. 165-180.

Startzman, R. and R. Wattenbarger, SPE 137172 (Mar. 1985), pp. 123-130.

Buckley, J., "Stochastic Dominance: An Approach to Decision Making Under Risk," *Risk Analysis*, Vol. 6, No. 1 (1986).

Genrich, J. and F. Sommer, *JPT* (Sept. 1989), pp. 930-995.

Schulyer, J., *OGJ* (11 Dec. 1989), pp. 87-90.

Schulyer, J., *OGJ* (25 Dec. 1989), pp. 140-142.

Schulyer, J., *OGJ* (8 Jan. 1990), pp. 78-80.

Lohrenz, J., *OGJ* (10 Mar. 1986), pp. 72-74.

Kinchen, A., *JPT* (Apr. 1986), pp. 461-467.

Caldwell, R., *JPT* (Apr. 1986), pp. 447-452.

Keating, J., *JPT* (Apr. 1986), pp. 443-446.

Garb, F., *JPT* (June 1988), pp. 765-778.

Martin, B., *JPT* (Oct. 1988), p. 1383.

Caldwell, R. and Johnston, D., *OGJ* (30 Dec. 1985), pp. 136-144.

Hallmark, T., *SPE* (Oct. 1989), pp. 735-739.

Walls, M., *OGJ* (22 Jan. 1990), pp. 61-64.

Grassick, P., *et. al.*, *JPT* (Nov. 1990), pp. 1374-1419.

Higgins, J., *JPT* (Sept. 1990), pp. 1102-1104.

Hightower, L. and A. David, SPE 22016 (Mar. 1991), pp.53-64.

NOTES:

CHAPTER 9

INVESTMENT APPLICATIONS

This chapter applies problem formulation and risk assessment methods to common investment situations. Emphasis is placed on identifying the main issue(s) in the investment, presenting the results, and comparing classical performance metrics relative to modern, risk adjusted measures. Discussion of the intermediate steps – collecting data, developing NCF's, and performing sensitivities, are minimized, as other chapters covered the basic processes, though some of these elements are dealt with. Each topic discussed focuses on the benefits from expanding the traditional investment options list, and the extra information gleaned by analyzing the elements of risk directly, rather than embedding risk in the more limited deterministic format.

The first quest goes to the heart of Figure 2.10, where the first step was to Formulate Question(s). This process goes by the name of *Open Framing* in modern decision analysis.[9.1] Chapter 2 illustrated that professionals analyze the questions they address fairly well; it is the questions ignored, omitted, or not asked that destroys value. Poorly defined questions and issues restrict risk analysis and risk mitigation efforts to such an extent that the odds of investment failure increase significantly. Identifying the important components of an investment reduces wasted time, and highlights the major issues deserving investor attention.

A clear, concise summary of the analysis helps management understand the important issues better during their review of the recommendation. Even the simplest project often appears complex, when organized and presented poorly. Simplicity and logical structure illuminate the merits of a project, emphasizing that the professional understands, clearly and concisely, the issues and solutions in the investment. This allows the professional to market the technical quality of their work, as well as demonstrate their business acumen.

Most presenters try to convey everything they know about a subject, as quickly as possible, assuming, often erroneously, the listener knows or cares about that subject as much as they do. This includes authors of books like this, who must constantly battle to convey the essence of the ideas and concepts, without preaching. The tendency is to try to impress everyone with how much we know, at the expense of communicating the message effectively. The same holds true in reporting the results of an investment review; yet, over-detailed, long-winded discussions produce the same result as they do in writing a book: boredom and disinterest.

The book "Successful Communication: Strategies and Practices," a companion book in the Campbell Petroleum Series Inc. (CPSI), provides valuable techniques for improving the effectiveness of presentations.

Each investment opportunity is analyzed here in two ways. First, the questions to be addressed and quantified are discussed using the CIV process. Next, the risks are analyzed formally, leading to a comparison of the alternative valuation methods. The examples assume the reader has read and understood the material in Chapters 1-8.

Topics covered include:

- Least Cost Analysis: Capital versus operating cost, and reliability issues,
- Property sales and acquisitions,
- Lease versus purchase
- Project Scheduling
- Cost Estimation
- Production payment financing
- Farm-out or farm-in, and Non-Consent or Sole Risking
- Process versus by-pass
- Lease bid evaluations
- Value of Information
- Value Chain Analysis
- Point Forward or Yet-to-Spend Analysis versus Full Cycle

LEAST COST ANALYSIS

Virtually every project faces the difficult task of selecting the optimal combination labor and capital. Even though projects evolve differently, they usually become more capital intensive and automated over time. The increasing reliance on capital stems partially from rising labor costs, which typically cause the project to reach its economic limit faster. Replacing Opex with a capital intensive process prolongs the economic life of the asset and increases ultimate production.

Another way of formulating the question is: "Should capital be spent now in order to reduce labor costs in the future?" This entails installing facilities for producing, storing, monitoring, and shipping products by remote control, rather than manually. This situation characterizes the least cost problem "Is it cheaper to produce with capital or labor?" Lowering production costs often means greater profitability, given the same production level. The application of robots in production systems to reduce labor costs has received considerable attention for just this reason.

A second question concerns whether installing a higher capital cost system improves the reliability of the production system. Reliability addresses several questions. Will the system operate longer before failing (production ceases)? Will the production system yield fewer defects? Once broken, can it be fixed faster? These and other questions go to the heart of many investment decisions. Jack Welch, the CEO of General Electric, and considered by many to be the best manager of the last 20 years, adopted the 6σ rule. He wanted the production system to produce parts where defects occurred less than 1 time in 1,000,000 parts.

On the issue of time it takes to restart the system, our favorite experience is a single malt distillery manager in Scotland, who had a fully automated system to mix water at the right temperature with the grain located right next to a manual system operated by a person using a joystick. The manager was using the manual alternative, with the lights to the automated system in stand by mode, because the automation system required a Ph.D. to operate it. The manual system worked well with anyone they could find from the local labor pool (the bar).

Spending money now yields two potential benefits: reduced future labor costs and, hopefully, increased production due to improved operating time and fewer defective products. The main sources of risk and uncertainty arise in the estimate of labor savings and improvements in reliability. For labor savings, there are two questions: "What is the cost per hour of labor and how many hours are truly saved?" Don't even begin the analysis until everyone agrees on the cost of labor, by category, per relevant unit (hour, month, or year). We have seen projects where estimated labor costs range from $50/hour to $250/hour, totally confusing the decision-making.

The main characteristic of least cost analysis is the absence of production. Most investment decisions derive their main benefit from producing and selling some commodity. Here, the analysis assumes that the investment is profitable; the real question is selecting the most efficient production system. Lowering the cost of an already profitable investment obviously adds value.

Deterministic Analysis

Several, equally acceptable methods for comparing the Capex vs. Opex trade-off exist. The most time consuming approach runs the entire project twice: once with the Opex option and once with the Capex option costs, each with the same production volume. This approach chooses the option with the best value measure, say NPV. This approach follows the classical DCF approach outlined earlier and requires no modification of existing software. Since these least cost decisions normally arise in the operating environment, information about production volumes, prices, etc. may not be available to the analyst or require considerable effort to acquire. A common compromise recognizes that the benefit of Capex vs. Opex is the increment between the two runs. In taking the increment, however, all the elements common to both files, like production, cancel out, leaving just the Capex and Opex values. Example 9.1 shows the basic process.

Example 9.1: A production system has experienced a dramatic rise in operating costs. By spending $25 million now to automate the production system, engineering estimates that it can save $5 million in Opex. This Opex is currently expected to rise at 5% per annum. Assuming a 35% tax rate and an 8-year project life, recommend the Opex or Capex option. Use a 10% discount rate and mid-year discounting.

	Opex								
Year	0-1	1-2	2-3	3-4	4-5	5-6	6-7	7-8	Total
BT Opex	5.00	5.25	5.51	5.79	6.08	6.38	6.70	7.04	47.75
– Tax Relief	1.75	1.84	1.93	2.03	2.13	2.23	2.35	2.46	16.71
= AT Opex	3.25	3.41	3.58	3.76	3.95	4.15	4.36	4.57	31.03
NPV10	3.10	2.96	2.82	2.70	2.57	2.46	2.34	2.24	21.19

	Capex								
Year	0-1	1-2	2-3	3-4	4-5	5-6	6-7	7-8	Total
BT Capex	25.00	0	0	0	0	0	0	0	25.00
Depreciation	3.58	6.13	4.38	3.13	2.23	2.23	2.23	1.13	25.00
– Tax Relief	1.25	2.14	1.53	1.09	0.78	0.78	0.78	0.39	8.75
= AT Capex	23.75	2.14	-1.53	-1.09	-0.78	-0.78	-0.78	-0.39	16.25
NPV_{10}	22.64	-1.86	-1.21	-0.78	-0.51	-0.46	-0.42	-0.19	17.22

The AT Opex options costs slightly more than $21 million over 8 years, while the AT Capex costs $17.22 million. By spending $17.22 the project saves $21.19 in Opex, or enhances the treasury by the difference of $3.97 million (= 21.19 – 17.22).

Example 9.1 (cont'd.) demonstrates a quicker way to generate the same answer, with one computer run rather than two. Dealing with incremental cash flows directly reduces the time spent playing with the computer and yields the same conclusion.

Faced with uncertainties in the cost of the Capex and the Opex savings, Figure 9.1 shows the spider diagram for both components. The breakeven line corresponds to the NPV of the project of $3.97.

Example 9.1: (Cont'd.) Incremental analysis.

Incremental Capex vs. Opex									
Year	**0-1**	**1-2**	**2-3**	**3-4**	**4-5**	**5-6**	**6-7**	**7-8**	**Total**
– AT Opex	-3.25	-3.41	-3.58	-3.76	-3.95	-4.15	-4.36	-4.57	-31.03
– AT Capex	23.75	-2.14	-1.53	-1.09	-0.78	-0.78	-0.78	-0.39	16.25
= NCF	-20.50	5.56	5.11	4.86	4.73	4.93	5.13	4.97	14.78
NPV_{10}	-19.54	4.82	4.03	3.48	3.08	2.92	2.76	2.43	3.97

The intersection of the Capex and Opex lines with the breakeven line identifies the percentage change in the initial input values before the project breaks even. Capex must increase by about 23% and Opex must fall by roughly 25%. Since project economics are additive, an increase of roughly 12.5% for each element will also produce a zero NPV.

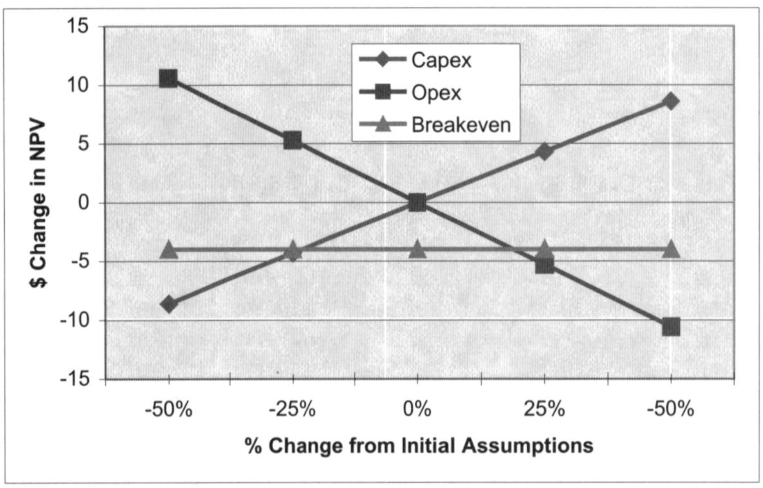

Figure 9.1 Spider diagram for least cost analysis

If one is confident of the initial input assumptions, this appears to be a good project, so far. Other components of least cost problems include salvage value, redundancy in equipment and lost or deferred production.

Salvage Value

Installing the equipment leads to the possibility that it can be sold at the end of the project: *salvage value.* Selling the equipment for a profit creates a positive cash flow to the project. The tax consequence from the sale is easy to compute. Generating a reasonable estimate of the salvage value is the most complicated aspect of the analysis. This task faces considerable uncertainty, and most analysis conveniently elects to ignore salvage value, because of that uncertainty. This is an excellent example where formal risk assessment helps capture important information.

The tax calculation follows normal convention in computing the tax obligation based on the profit from the sale. Equation 9.1 shows the calculation process.

$$\text{Tax} = \text{TR} * (\text{Sales Price} - \text{Tax Basis}) \qquad \textbf{(9.1)}$$
$$\text{NCF} = \text{Sales Price} - \text{Tax}$$

where: TR = the appropriate tax rate, and
Tax Basis = the original purchase price less cumulative depreciation

Example 9.2: Compute the NCF contribution of a $10 million sale in year 7-8 of the equipment from the previous example, assuming a tax rate of 20% and a zero tax basis.

$$Tax = 0.2*(10.0-0.0) = 2.0$$

$$NCF = 10.0 - 2.0 = 8.00$$

If the $8 million is discounted at 10%, then 8*0.4892 = $3.91 can be added to the original NPV of $3.97, which almost doubles the value of selecting Capex option.

The tax basis is zero in the example, because the disposition of the asset occurred after complete depreciation occurred. Had the project been terminated at the end of year 3-4, the tax basis would be $7.8 million (= 25 – 17.20), where 17.20 is the cumulative depreciation through the first four years. The profit is reduced to $2.2 million (= 10 – 7.8). Some refer to the $2.2 million as recapture of depreciation.

This example assumes a 20% tax rate, which is called the *capital gains rate* in countries that use it. The rate used here is the capital gains rate in the U.S. at the present time. Capital gains tax rates are sometimes lower than ordinary income tax rates to encourage investors to buy and then hold investments for extended periods. Investments held for less than a certain time period (usually a year) are taxed at the ordinary income tax rates, which may be anywhere from 30-60% depending on the country. Profits on investments held longer than the specified time are taxed at the lower capital gains rate. In the U.S. an investor reduces the effective tax rate from as much as 40% to 20% by holding the asset for longer than 18 months.

Reliability (Redundancy)

Mechanical equipment possesses the nagging habit of failing, usually at the most inopportune times. Failure may include ceasing to operate or performing at less than design capacity. When equipment fails, the entire system is impacted, usually by reducing the production flow. Producing less means selling less, and that reduces revenues. A common question encountered when people tour production system is "Why is that equipment idle?" Quite often, that equipment is used to backup other equipment. If operating in an area with unstable electricity supplies, producers often install their own generating capacity.

The costs incurred to invest in back-up equipment depend mainly on revenue losses during downtime, and the cost of restoring producing systems to normal operating conditions. Generating estimates for both numbers require detailed information of the production system and markets, and are subject to considerable risk.

Examples of investment decisions involving reliability include:

- Sizing equipment, i.e. pumps, compressors, turbines, assembly lines, etc.
- Surplus capacity for storage, and
- Inventory of spare parts.

Production lost, foregone or deferred reduces NCF by the number of days or hours the system is expected to be down multiplied by the value of the sales during the time period. A system down 3 days, which produces 2,000 units, requires inputting the product of these numbers and sales price as a reduction in NCF. Some products are more complicated, however. Perrier lost over half of its future sales because of a scare about quality, and customers realized that other bottled waters were just as good. If the downtime, for whatever reason, causes the buyer to switch brand loyalties, estimating the impact becomes quite difficult.

The optimal least cost alternative obviously depends on the estimate of lost production. Example 9.3 demonstrates a simple application of production losses using the binomial distribution from Chapter 4

Example 9.3: Given the reliability estimates for the three electricity-generating options from the binomial example in Chapter 6, determine the least cost choice based on the following information. The system needs 10,000 kW to operate at design capacity.

Alternatives	Probability of Uptime, %	Cost, $million	Excess Capacity, kW	Cost/KW of Excess Capacity, $/kW
2 - 5000	0.9500	30	0	0.0
3 - 5000	0.9963	45	5000	15.0
3 - 4000	0.9685	39	2000	6.5

The best approach is to input the values into the proper computer program and select the best alternative. The quicker solution converts the excess capacity costs into annualized values. The appendix to Chapter 5 gives formulas with examples for annualizing costs. Using the annualizing equations gives:

$$3-5000\ \text{Cost} = 15 * \left[\frac{0.10(1.10)^8}{1.10^8 - 1}\right] = 2.81 \qquad 3-4000\ \text{Cost} = 6.5 * \left[\frac{0.10(1.10)^8}{1.10^8 - 1}\right] = 1.22$$

The annual cost of excess capacity is $2.81 million for the 3-5000 kW option, $1.22m for the 3-4000 kW option, and, obviously, $0 for the no excess option. The second issue is the amount and value of lost production. Assuming 5,000 units are lost per day of downtime, at a value of $20/unit, the summary looks like the following.

Reliability	Annual Days Lost	(1) $ Loss/Year	(2) $ Cost/Year	(3) = (1) + (2) Total
0.9500	18.25	1.82	0.00	1.82
0.9963	1.35	0.14	2.81	2.95
0.9685	11.50	1.15	1.22	2.37

The least cost alternative chooses the 2-5000 kW units, even though it incurs a higher revenue loss. The value of the production fails to offset the higher installation cost in this example.

for three electricity-generating options. At 5000 units, the 2-5000 units have the lowest cost, at $1.82 million per day.

Finding in favor of the 2-5000 units depends on several assumptions; one being the number of units lost. Figure 9.2 compares the least cost values relative to changes in the magnitude of lost production. The conclusions appear to be quite sensitive to the assumptions about the production losses. When the production volume reaches around 9000 units, the 3-5000 option has the lowest cost. The 3-4000 option is actually the least cost between about 8500 and 9000 production units, though it is hard to see from the graph.

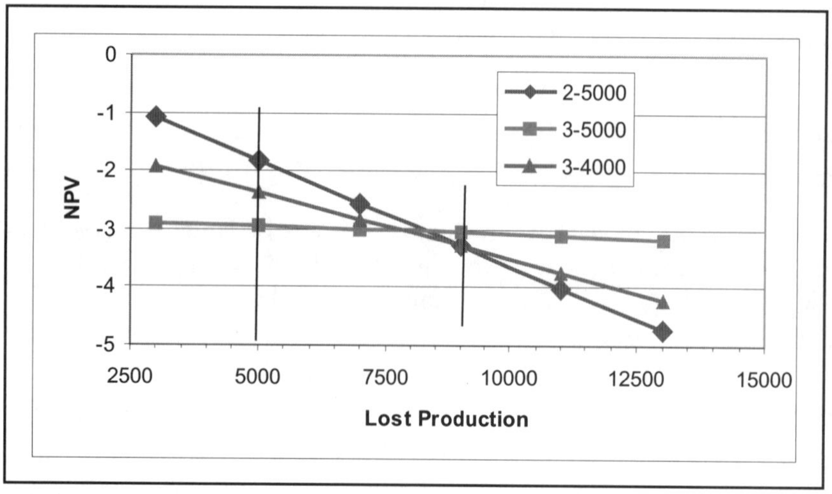

Figure 9.2 Sensitivity to production volume

Actual problems would also address other issues, like annual operating and maintenance costs. Other sensitivities, like price, could also be performed. Making a decision faced with the uncertainties in the inputs is still difficult, even with this information. Knowing that one option is cheaper at a certain production loss, which may have no chance of occurring, confuses, more than aids, decision-making. This problem expands when other sensitivities are added. It should make sense that extra capacity is justified mainly when the cost of downtime is high. If there is no cost to the system being down, backup or redundancy makes little sense.

Stochastic Analysis

The basic approach described in the deterministic section probably accounts for the huge majority of incremental, least-cost decisions in the operating environment. While the deterministic approach adequately captures the essence of the issue, it is like the old joke about bikinis; namely, "What a bikini reveals is interesting, but what it hides is even more interesting (individual preferences play a role here)."

Part of the problem arises from the very nature of incremental approaches. The project this example was taken from was budgeted for more than $1 billion. The addition of $15 million for extra reliability has little impact on total cost, and is often perceived as being quite trivial. In reality, however, every group working on the project, often as many as 10-20 independent ones, might consider adding an incremental $15 million. The combined additions could result in a major project cost over-run. Preventing small, insignificant increments from accumulating is a major challenge for project management.

The conflict between the objectives in the design stage and operations comes to the forefront of investment analysis. On a pure profit basis, adding redundancy to the system cannot be justified. But, that decision will probably be overturned in the operating phase. Stochastic analysis of the same numbers shows why, as Example 9.4 illustrates

Example 9.4: Decide which option to recommend based on the following distributions.

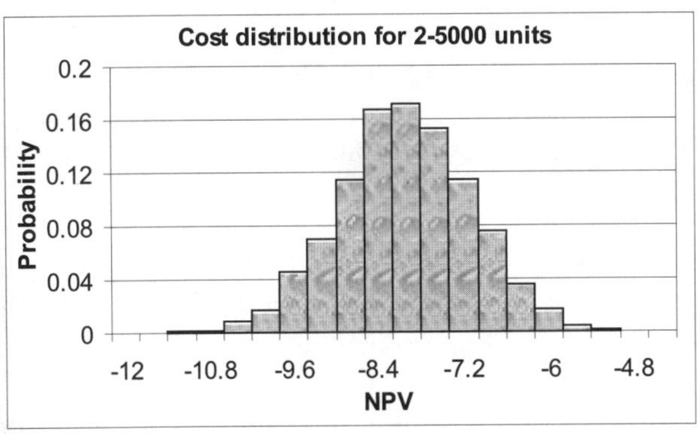

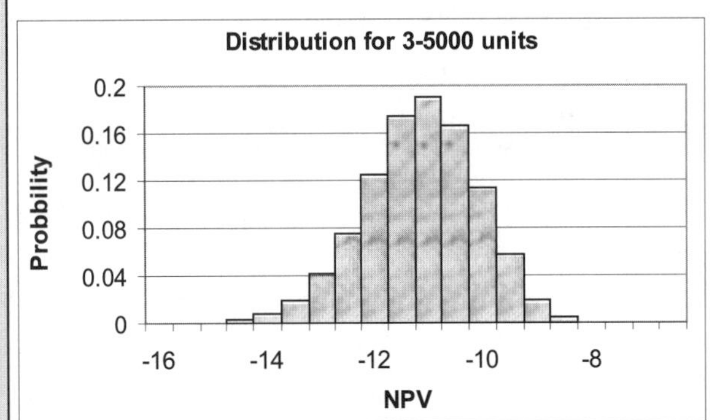

The same problem was run on the incremental inputs, using a stochastic approach. The basic input distributions are input as follows.

- Product price: triangular(14, 23.25, 25) = mean price of $20
- Inflation: triangular(2%, 5.9%, 7%) = mean inflation of 5%
- Failure rate: binomial(365, .05) ⇒ number of days system fails
- Production: triangular(4500, 4800, 5700) = mean production of 5,000 units.
- Capex for 3-5000 units: lognormal(15, 1.5)
- Capex for 3-4000 units: lognormal(6.5, 0.65)

The underlined numbers are the values used in the previous examples. Note that the triangular distribution numbers don't use the same values. One of the biggest mistakes in practice arises from taking mean value estimates and inserting them into a triangular distribution asking for the most likely estimate. The impact is often significant, so beware.

Example 9.4: *(Cont'd.)*

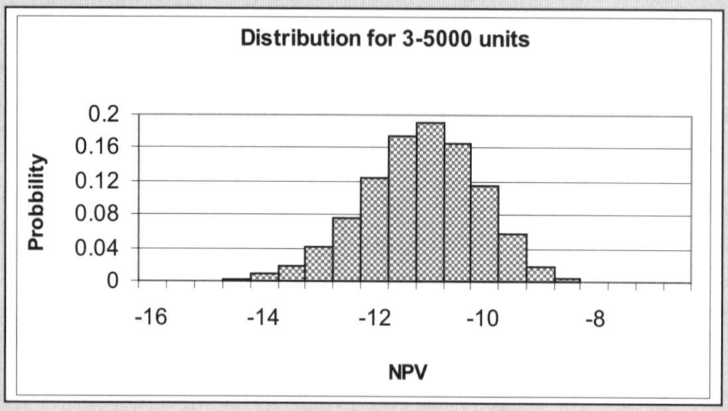

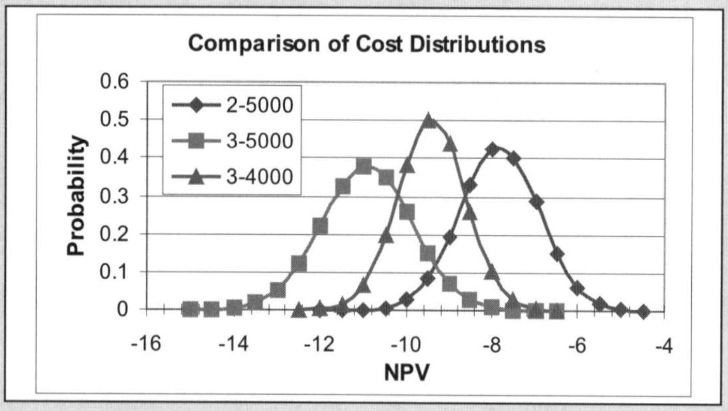

The distributions display similar patterns relative to the deterministic valuation; whereby, the 2-5000 units have the lowest average cost of \$6.81 million. The 3-4000 option has a mean value of \$9.4 million, and the most reliable system rises to \$10.9 million. Simple cost minimizing objectives would favor an operation with no redundancy.

What the deterministic valuation misses is the variability in these options. The last figure conveys the three options on the same graph to highlight the overlap among the alternatives. Based on just the average or most likely values, the 2-5000 option seems the best choice.

Most design decisions would recommend ignoring the extra capacity. This conclusion ignores other, equally important issues. First, the 2-5000 cases is not the low cost option 100% of the time. There a considerable number of cases where the other options have lower costs. This raises the notion of risk aversion in the organization.

A second, more important issue concerns the timing of the costs. The traditional valuation process assumes time is fully addressed in the discounting process; yet, today most management emphasizes the importance of cash flow, both in their decision-making and setting of performance contracts with operating units.

The cash flow aspects of the problem are illustrated in the continuation of Example 9.4. The same simulations recorded information about the NCF patterns over the 8-year project horizon. The first graph highlights the NCF pattern for the 2-5000 option. Observe how the pattern expands each year as inflation, price and production volatility expand. Conversely, the 3-5000 case reverses the NCF pattern such that the later years show almost no volatility. In fact, on the scale used here, it almost appears to be a single line. The line is slightly positive after year two, because the tax relief from the depreciation schedule offsets the sales loss from a power outage.

On a pure profit based motive, the 2-5000 option has the lowest NPV_{10}. At a lower discount rate, the higher costs of the 2-5000 NCF in future years are weighted more heavily, shifting the preferred choice. For the sake of this example, assume 10% is absolutely right. Are their trade-offs between the choices? Absolutely. The 3-5000 option spends more money up front, but effectively stabilizes the NCF in future years to almost certainty. The 2-5000 option defers expenditure now, but incurs costs, which may be quite significant, over the course of the project life. When investors face multiple objectives, like stability, as well as profitability, the choice between the options becomes less obvious.

Example 9.4: *(Cont'd.)*

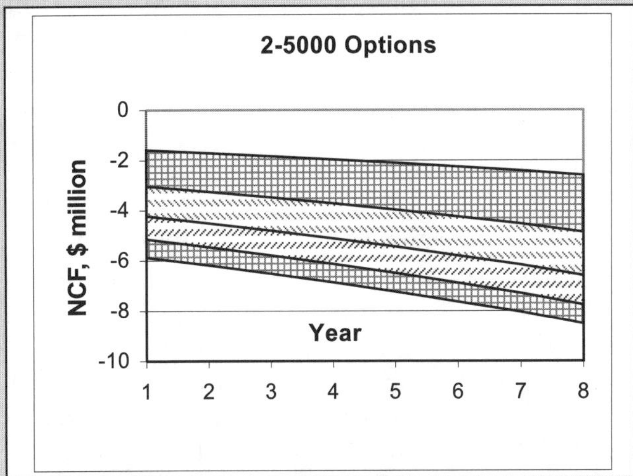

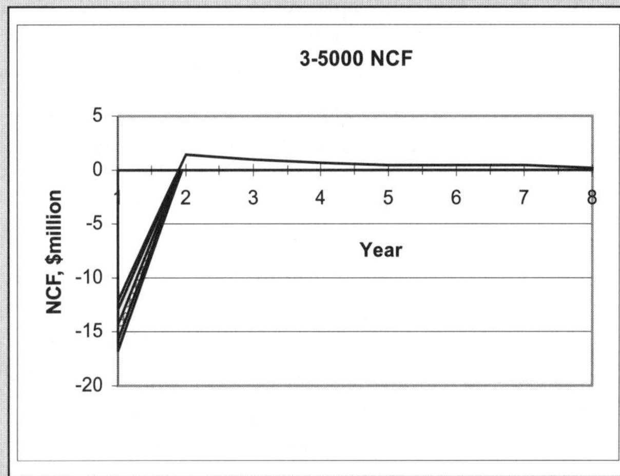

In actual investment situations, the design team typically elects to forego the extra capacity to bring the project in under budget. Once operations commence, the yearly costs become a higher priority, so operations installs the extra capacity and explain it as design error.

ASSET SALES AND ACQUISITIONS

The majority of investment decisions involve new projects or expansion of existing ones. As combinations of forces, like strategies and market conditions, change, buying or selling existing assets may provide superior performance. Asset owners sell for many reasons: their scale is too small in a market to satisfy profit objectives, they divest entire lines of business to focus on core or better understood businesses, the entire business line is seen as being unprofitable, etc. Whatever the reason, asset owners commonly sell or divest existing properties. For the opposite reasons, someone usually is willing to buy the assets, especially if the cost of acquiring is significantly less than construction. Classic examples include real estate and chemicals, where periods of optimism and consequent overbuilding are followed by bankruptcies and sales. Buying an asset for 10% of the original value lowers costs, giving the owner considerable pricing flexibility.

Whatever the motive, assets are constantly bought and sold. Even governments now realize the benefits to selling their telecoms, travel, water, and electrical generation industries. Buying or selling existing assets follows the same analytical process outlined earlier, though the critical risk components change with market conditions for the product, logistics, Opex, and market share dominating the formal risk assessment. These elements are highlighted first in a traditional deterministic example, and then expanded to reflect stochastic issues.

Approval for the sale/purchase of assets follows the NCF derivation process. The complicating factor in some countries arises from the computation of taxes on both sides. Two taxes – capital gain or loss, and ordinary income – are involved. The following example shows the economics of a sale using U. S. taxes. A purchase just reverses the process.

The following steps establish the minimum sales price.

1. Compute the NPV from continued operation.
2. Compute the capital gains and ordinary income tax on a sale.
3. Sell the asset only when the offer price exceeds the minimum price.

The minimum price is the sum of the NPV from continued operations and the tax from the sale of the property. Computing the taxes on the sale (Step 2), first requires splitting the NPV generated in step 1 into two categories: equipment value and then the goodwill or residual value. Purchased assets normally have existing buildings, production equipment, etc. Equipment has a book value (original cost less cumulative tax depreciation), which, when deducted from the NPV computed in Step 1 leaves the value associated with future production. Goodwill typifies most businesses, especially technology, like software houses, where the .com businesses sell for far more than their equipment value, even when losing money. Goodwill in the mineral industry is called leasehold value.

The gain or loss on the equipment is taxed at the ordinary income tax rate, and goodwill gain and losses are taxed at the capital gains rate. Those locales without a capital gains tax usually tax the entire sales at the ordinary income tax rate. Just substitute the appropriate income tax rate for the capital gains tax rate in the following examples.

Example 9.5: Your organization wants to sell an asset with an estimated NPV of $3.1 million (m), and equipment value appraised at $1m. With this equipment value, the goodwill or leasehold value is $2.1m. Assuming $0.8m in accumulated depreciation, ordinary income tax of 35%, and a capital gains rate of 20%, compute the tax burden from selling the asset.

	Goodwill/Leasehold	Equipment
Sales Price	$2.10	$1.00
– Tax Basis	0.00	0.80
= Taxable Gain	2.10	0.20
* Tax Rate	0.20	0.35
= Taxes Owed	$0.42	$0.07
Total Tax = 0.42 + 0.07 = 0.49		

Adding the total tax of $0.49m to the producing present value yields $3.59 (= 3.1 + 0.49). An initial response is that $3.59m is the minimum sales price (MSP). This is incorrect. Taxes depend on the total sales price, creating a dependency in the calculation. Most software wastes a considerable amount of time iterating to find the MSP. A shorter, quicker approach solves the following equation.

$$\begin{aligned} MSP &= \frac{NPV + |CGT - IT| * EPP - IT * ETB - CGT * LTB}{1 - CGT} \\ &= \frac{3.1 + |0.20 - 0.35| * 1.0 - 0.35 * 0.80 - 0.20 * 0}{1 - 0.20} \\ &= \frac{2.97}{1 - 0.2} = 3.71 \end{aligned} \tag{9.2}$$

where:
MSP = minimum sales price,
NPV = present value of ongoing operations,
CGT = capital gains tax rate,
IT = ordinary income tax rate,
ETB = equipment tax basis,
LTB = goodwill or leasehold tax basis, and
EPP = equipment purchase price.

Selling the property for $3.71m generates the same value as continuing to operate the property, after-taxes. Reject all offers less than $3.71m, and accept offers exceeding this amount. Work through the previous example using $3.71m to verify that this sales price equals the continued production NPV.

Property purchases reverse the process. The cost of the property is split between goodwill and equipment. Equipment is depreciated using the appropriate depreciation schedule and leasehold is depleted using either straight-line or percentage depletion. This follows the format for the standard analysis.

The deterministic valuation process misses the critical aspects of making buy and sell decisions for existing assets. As Chapter 8 demonstrated, the classical DCF process fails to properly account for the options available to the owners of assets. The following example highlights the problems by valuing an asset deterministically and stochastically.

The NPV_{10} from continued production is \$323m, while the IRR and PI can't be computed because there is no investment. SIV is constant regardless of discount rate for the same reason. SIV treats the cash flows like a government Treasury Bill. The MSP was computed, as in the previous example, assuming 30% of the value was equipment, and the equipment was fully depreciated. At a 10% return standard, the MSP is \$423m, or \$100m more than NPV_{10}.

Asset transactions are a constant source of entertainment as buyers and sellers jockey to achieve the best results. This is an excellent reminder that value depends on the perspective of the participants, and not an immutable law. The continuation of the example displays the distribution of the MSP and the maximum purchase price (MPP) based on the NPV distribution. MSP is computed as before and MPP splits the purchase price into equipment and goodwill/leasehold and then computes the tax relief using the proper capital recovery schedule for the U. S.

Example 9.6: Determine the value of holding an asset producing at a rate of lognormal(5000. 500) units per day, a price per unit that is triangular(14, 23.25, 25), and Opex per unit that is lognormal(5, 0.75).

	5%	10%	15%
NPV	640.7	323.8	196.6
SIV	548.5	548.5	548.5
IRR	None	None	None
NPV/Inv	None	None	None
MSP	836.9	423.0	256.8
MPP	823.5	388.1	227.4

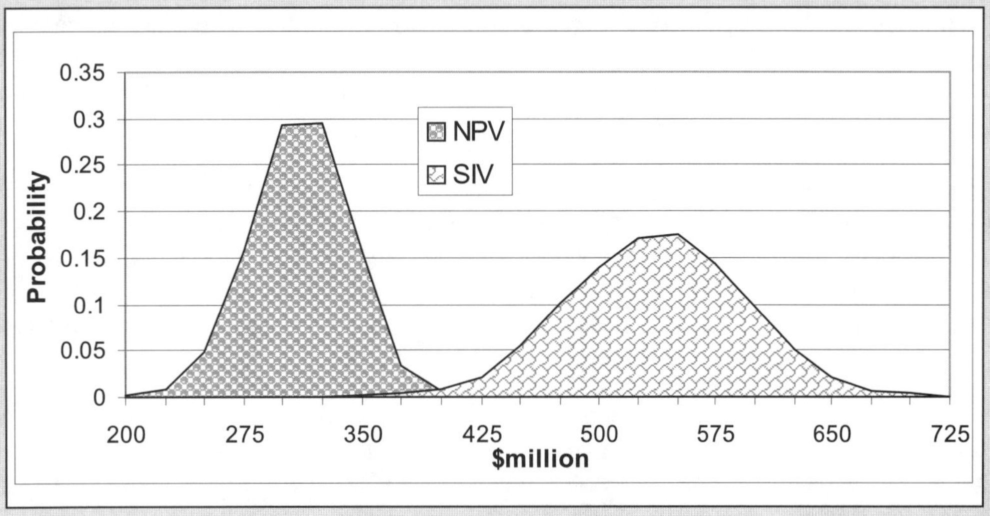

The tabular data for the two variables are:

	P_{10}	P_{50}	Mean	P_{90}	s_x
NPV_{10}	282.7	324.4	324.0	363.1	31.1
SIV_{10}	476.5	549.6	548.5	620.6	56.3

CHAPTER 9

Using the same discount rate, prices, production, etc. in the continuation of Example 9.6, observe how the MPP is lower than the MSP, though the two distributions show considerable overlap. Without the visual display of the ranges, the expected value of the MSP is about \$423m and the MPP is around \$388m. The same company couldn't transfer a property among its own divisions, just because of tax considerations.

Example 9.6:
(Cont'd.)

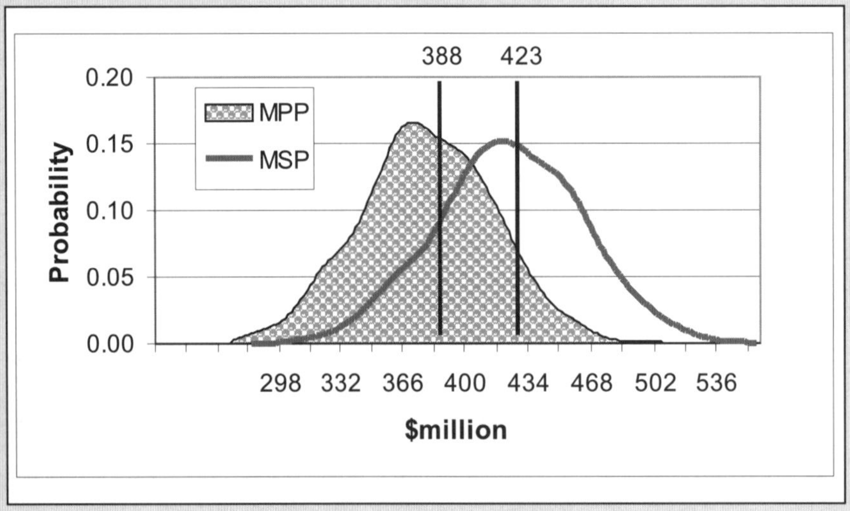

The situation is far more complicated when simple DCF rules dominated. Sellers often valued the asset by lowering the discount rate to arrive at the MSP. So, even though they might use 10% to value new investments, a 5% or 8% discount rate might be used for an asset disposition. Lowering the discount rate increases the MSP (\$423 vs. \$836 in the example). This captures the traditional attempt at options thinking. The lower discount is justified by the concept that we operate the asset and have detailed knowledge of the operating characteristics; hence, lower risk.

The same organization trying to purchase an asset normally raises the discount rate to accommodate the extra risk, often to 15-25%. Yet, the same information exists in both cases. Ownership of the asset is the only real difference. The primary investment rule, "Buy low and sell high," dominates the property sales/acquisitions process, and these criteria satisfy the basic rule.

A better way to value asset transfers is to ask, "What price captures the most value from the asset?" The MSP P_{10} and P_{90} values are \$369m and \$474m, respectively. The \$474m produces about the same value achieved by lowering the discount rate to 7%, which reflects a typical reduction from 10%. Artificially reducing the discount rate attempts to enhance the gain from asset disposition. The formalized risk approach, however, provides much better insight and perspective than the simple reduction in the discount rate.

With the gap between purchasing and buying, it amazes some that any transactions occur at all. Most asset transfers take place as the result of different strategies, business environments, economies of scale, etc. As investors regained their focus on their core properties in the late stages of the 20th century, multinationals sold peripheral assets, either in business lines or geographically, to those with niches in that market; likewise, some assets were simply shut down or sold for scrap as over supply in industries, like steel and automobiles, became apparent. Also, vertical integration, such as electricity generation buying gas supplies, allowed for more favorable pricing.

Difficulties in establishing fair market value retard the rate of property transfers. Who can argue with the concept of fair value; yet, defining such values accurately remains elusive. Our favorite definition says, "Fair is a value higher than the purchaser wants to pay and lower than the seller desires, but close enough that each party agrees to the transaction." It is important to reiterate that asset transfers occur because investors view the world differently; hence, use considerably different inputs for sales, prices, taxes, discount rates, etc. to reflect the differences that drive the market place.

LEASE VERSUS PURCHASE

An alternative to the outright purchase of equipment is leasing, which assumes that the profitability of the project has already been established. Leasing has always been an option in investment decision-making. Until the early 1990's, however, leasing was perceived to be a higher cost method for acquiring assets. Individuals jumped on the leasing bandwagon primarily for automobiles, because the lease payments are treated as Opex, and deductible from income tax. It was also especially attractive to small businesses that were cash flow constrained: they didn't have the money to purchase the needed or desired equipment outright. This led to the odd situation where old manufacturing organizations that were worshipped as the epitome of well managed organization, like General Electric, were making more money by loaning money via leasing than manufacturing products in their traditional lines of business.

Large organizations generally lease when cash flow limits their ability to acquire needed equipment immediately, or when rapid technological changes may obsolete equipment in the near term (like computers). Most equipment is leased for the first reason. Equipment needed for only a short time span, typically less than two years, is usually cheaper to lease than buy, especially if the company cannot use the equipment after that time, or it is a very specialized piece of equipment.

Another, more onerous reason for leasing is the desire to circumvent several constraints. Capital budget restrictions benefit leasing because it comes out of the operating budget, not the capital budget. By carefully structuring the lease terms, the manager may stay within their authorization level, eliminating the necessity of reporting the transaction to higher levels.

Lease/buy evaluations encompass two steps. First, the justification for the entire project follows classical DCF process: revenues must exceed costs, after adjusting for taxes and the time value of money. Second, the choice of financing entails acquiring the equipment at the least cost. Minimizing the costs of acquiring maximizes profit, since the same revenue stream is involved in each funding option.

The attractiveness of leasing depends on the terms offered by the lender, which absorbs the risk of obsolescence and idle equipment, and embeds this risk in the lease cost. The primary advantage of leasing – the lease payment is a tax deduction and not a tangible expenditure – is offset when the leasing company charges high interest rates.

Higher lease costs arise from more than just the risk. Leasing companies acquire equipment with borrowed funds, just like everyone else, and their cost of borrowing is often greater than the cost of money to multinationals, which have a better credit rating. This is not always true for smaller companies, however. Lease rentals must recover the lessor's interest payments, as well as repaying the principal on the loan. These payments increase when the risk of obsolescence, and unrented time rises. Lessees should realize that these and other costs (like the profit and overhead of the leasing company) are built into the lease payment.

Several methods for evaluating leases exist, some quite esoteric. The following classical DCF approach matches the format used to date by selecting leasing or buying based on the smallest NPV, though investors differ significantly in the selection of an appropriate discount rate. Some opt to use the normal return standard, while others lower the value to reflect that the costs – the lease rental or purchase fee – are known with certainty. Others argue that the after-tax cost of debt is best, since leasing is just a form of borrowing. Choice of the discount rate impacts the decision process greatly.

The basic NCF pattern is easily determined from the leasing agreement and purchase quotations. Leasing shows a lower initial cost and higher cash outflow over the life of the project. Purchasing has a higher initial cost, since the product is bought now, but has a positive cash flow after the first year from the depreciation and other tax savings. The question is which stream of cash flows adds more value.

Example 9.7 displays the basic lease/purchase NCF derivation. The choice again is quite simple: Do we spend money now or over the life of the project. At a zero discount rate, leasing is more expensive because of the high cost of the rentals over a five-year period. As the discount rate rises, the cost of leasing declines, reflecting that most of the cost occurs in the future. The cost of purchasing declines very slightly, because the bulk of the costs fall in the first year, diminishing future tax savings.

Example 9.7: Choose between buying a compressor that costs $800 thousand (k) plus another $200k to install, versus leasing for $400k per year. The compressor will cost $50k per year to maintain for each option. An 8% sales tax is charged on all expenditures. Develop the NCF alternatives and then value each option. Use 8 year SL depreciation.

Compressor Leasing Cost, $ Thousands

	Year						
	0	**0-1**	**1-2**	**2-3**	**3-4**	**4-5**	**Total**
Rental	0.0	-400.0	-400.0	-400.0	-400.0	-400.0	-2000.0
+ Installation	-200.0	0.0	0.0	0.0	0.0	0.0	-200.0
+ Sales Tax	-16.0	-32.0	-32.0	-32.0	-32.0	-32.0	-176.0
+ Maintenance	0.0	-50.0	-50.0	-50.0	-50.0	-50.0	-250.0
= Total Cost	-216.0	-482.0	-482.0	-482.0	-482.0	-482.0	-2626.0
– Tax Relief	-75.6	-168.7	-168.7	-168.7	-168.7	-168.7	-919.1
= AT Cost	-140.4	-313.3	-313.3	-313.3	-313.3	-313.3	-1706.9

Compressor Purchasing Cost, $ Thousands

	Year						
	0	**0-1**	**1-2**	**2-3**	**3-4**	**4-5**	**Total**
Purchase Price	-800.0	0.0	0.0	0.0	0.0	0.0	-800.0
+ Installation	-200.0	0.0	0.0	0.0	0.0	0.0	-200.0
+ Sales Tax	-80.0	0.0	0.0	0.0	0.0	0.0	-80.0
+ Maintenance	0.0	-50.0	-50.0	-50.0	-50.0	-50.0	-250.0
– Salvage Value	0.0	0.0	0.0	0.0	0.0	300.0	300.0
+ Abandonment	0.0	0.0	0.0	0.0	0.0	-20.0	-20.0
Total Cost	-1080.0	-50.0	-50.0	-50.0	-50.0	230.0	-1050.0
Depreciation	0	-125.0	-125.0	-125.0	-125.0	-125.0	-625.0
Other tax relief	-80.0	-50.0	-50.0	-50.0	-50.0	-70.0	-350.0
– Total Tax Relief	-28.0	-61.3	-61.3	-61.3	-61.3	-68.3	-341.3
= AT Cost	-1052.0	11.3	11.3	11.3	11.3	-298.3	-708.8

The cost of purchasing is almost half the cost of leasing, but the popularity of leasing suggests either gross financial ignorance, or other forces at work. Certainly financial ignorance plays a role. The NPV profile of the two options is graphed in the continuation of Example 9.7. The breakeven discount rate of the project is defined at the vertical line, which is very close to 30%. At discount rates below 30%, purchasing is the lower cost. Leasing is preferred at higher discount rates since the future lease costs are treated as being almost meaningless.

The lease versus buy decision favors buying on a pure economic basis, usually. Purchasing dominates leasing primarily when the purchaser has access to a lower cost of funds. Almost everyone, except those with a poor credit history, can borrow money cheaper than the rate offered by leasing firms. Many leasing companies build an interest charge of 18-25% into the lease rental, often with *points* of 5-25%

Example 9.7: *(Cont'd.)* Construct the NPV profiles for leasing and purchasing using the NPV function in your spreadsheet.

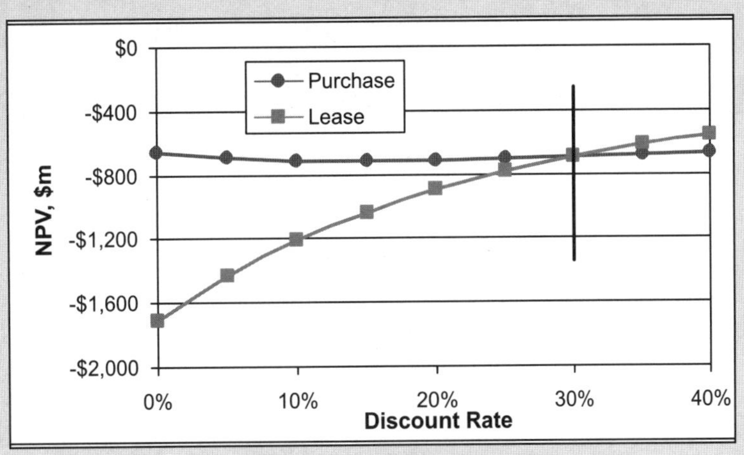

percent included in the costs. Points are a fee for handling the loan transaction. If you borrow $1000 with a five-point charge, you receive only $950, but repay the full $1000.

Faced with a purchasing cost advantage, the question is: why lease? Borrowers prefer leasing when budget constraints exist, the equipment is only needed for a short period, or the risk of technological obsolescence is high. Budget constraints are perhaps the most common explanation for leasing. An unacceptable reason for leasing is to circumvent company authorization levels. By leasing, funds from the capital budget are not required; thereby, foregoing the need to obtain authorization from higher levels. This practice is often justified on the basis of expediting acquisition of the equipment, but usually leads to higher costs and, thus, lower profits.

The leasing companies effective interest charge in the previous example may be computed by solving the equation for i:

$$\text{NPV} = I_n\left[\sum \frac{1}{(1+i)^t}\right] \tag{9.3}$$

$$800 = 400\left[\sum \frac{1}{(1+i)^t}\right] \quad \text{becomes} \quad \left[\sum \frac{1}{(1+i)^t}\right] = \frac{800}{400} = 2$$

where NPV ($800k) is the cost of the equipment, and I_n ($400k) is the annual cost of the lease. The equation solves for the value of i that yields a value of 2, which is slightly more than 40% before-tax. This implies an after-tax return in the 20+% range, which far exceeds the cost of borrowing money. The value was found by solving the summation in brackets for the value of i that equals 2 over a 5-year period using "goal seek" in our spreadsheet.

Paying the rather exorbitant rates to the leasing firm may be justified depending on the useful life of the asset. The continuation of Example 9.7 illustrates the effect of project life on the leasing decision. The figure is based on the incremental NCF between leasing and buying, and is generated by using the typical IRR function in a spreadsheet. The line represents the equilibrium point between leasing vs. buying, modified for the length of the lease.

Assuming a 10% discount rate, leasing dominates when the useful life of the equipment is less than 3.5 years. For any asset with a longer life, purchasing is the lower cost option. This highlights the potential for leasing to bridge the financing gap when temporarily short of money. The key word here is temporary, however.

Example 9.7: *(Cont'd.)* Use the incremental NCF for leasing vs. purchase to compute the IRR assuming a 3, 4, and 5-year asset life.

	0	0-1	1-2	2-3	3-4	4-5	Total
ΔNCF	-911.6	324.6	324.6	324.6	324.6	611.6	998.2

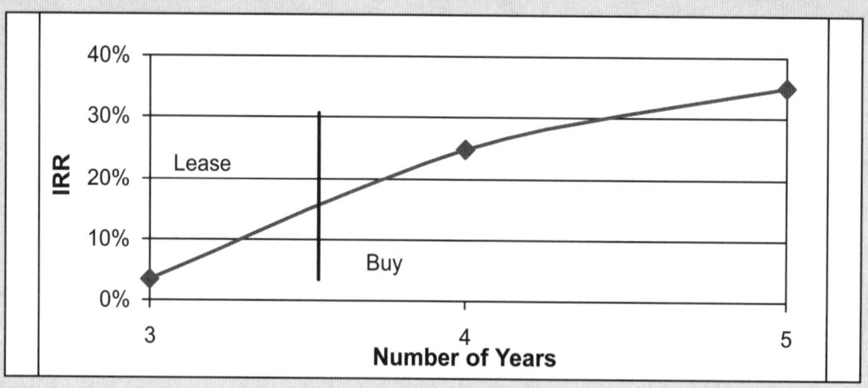

Expanding this analysis to include risk raises the usual interesting questions about what is really at risk in the analysis. Most lease payments are fixed by contract, tax relief via depreciation impacts the analysis very little, and the purchase price is fixed. The maintenance costs may differ, but that impacts both alternatives equally. Only the salvage value is really unknown as the analysis is presently defined.

A significant benefit of formal risk analysis emanates from the necessity to rethink the analysis. Some readers may have observed that the graph of IRR vs. Years assumes salvage occurs at the end of year 5, even if it was a 3-year lease. Salvage value normally varies with project life. If the project lasts 3 years, the compressor would probably be worth more than after being used for 5 years. The following example highlights the impact on the previous NPV profile graph when the lease period is allowed to vary between 3 and 5 years. Now the intersection of the lease NPV line intersects in the range from 25-35%, not the single intersection point observed earlier. This highlights the impact of variability of the assumptions on the decision. Fortunately, at a 10% rate, the variability still has no impact on the final decision.

Example 9.7: *(Cont'd.)*

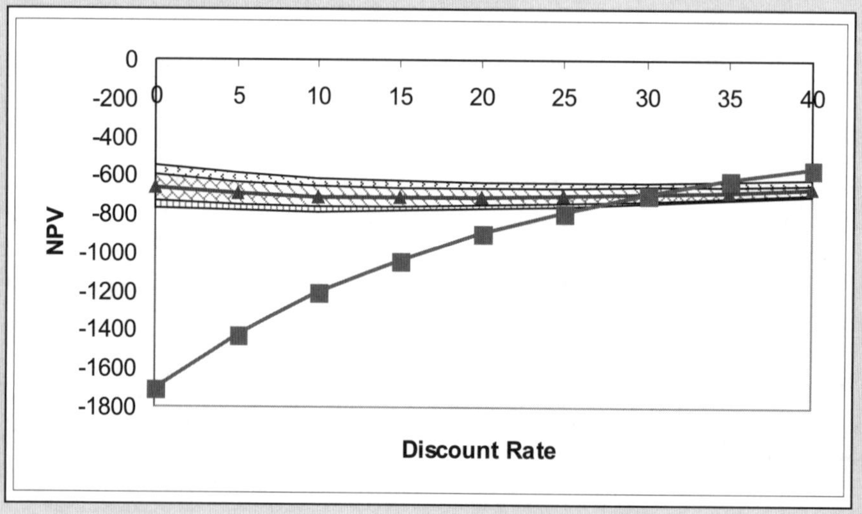

PROJECT FINANCING

Project financing continues the previous examples attempt to explore the best options for funding projects. Rather than using investor funds to finance the investment, lenders, like banks, World Bank, Asian Development Bank, etc., offer to finance the development. Most third world projects are financed in such ways. Projects in Europe and North America use bank lending when it provides a lower cost source of financing via favorable interest rates. With the surplus of available lending capital during the last part of the 20th century, the offered interest rates compared very favorably to internal financing.

The borrower realizes the following benefits from external borrowing:

- The production payments bear a variable rate, which is retired once long-term rates become attractive.
- It is a lower cost source of funds than equity financing.
- The loans are stated as non-recourse.

Variable interest rates are attractive when interest rates are high or are expected to fall in the future. Lenders also reduce the offered rate when they acquire collateral to a secured asset, especially one located in a politically stable location. *Non-recourse* means that the lenders only have the investment asset as collateral, not the assets of the entire organization.

The terms of project financing develop through negotiation. Lending managers typically challenge every step, from asset selection through documentation. Components of the analysis entail more inputs than the standard corporate evaluation; in particular, the bank takes a totally different perspective than the company. The negative side of financing is the time and cost to acquire the funds. Internal company approval processes are simple, quick and efficient relative to the process associated with acquiring external financing.

The basic negotiation process includes the following steps:

1. An economic and production analysis of on each asset, including the interest payment.
2. Interested banks return a term sheet, summarizing the most important items and the amount they will loan.
3. The company tax and legal counsel review drafts of the term sheets.
4. Bank engineers review asset and production estimates once both parties accept the term sheet, and revise loan amount based on their findings.
5. Bank and company staffs negotiate a final term sheet.
6. Bank legal counsel drafts all documents, including conveyance, mortgage, and credit agreement.
7. The company and legal departments review these drafts for comments.
8. All parties negotiate the final terms.

Finalizing the terms depends on the number of parties involved in the process. More time is required when the financing is syndicated (more than one lender is involved). An extra two to four weeks may be added to the process for each extra lender involved.

Inputs into the negotiation process are summarized in the following pages. All financing differs to some degree, so the professional must be prepared to negotiate in a flexible way. The following outlines situations common to most production payments.

Project financing occurs on assets owned by the company, held by an affiliate, or in the possession of a third party. Multinationals often create a separate company to address legal liability issues, usually in the most tax and legally favorable country. This affiliated company often exists only on paper; using the operating staff of the parent company (Holland is a current favorite). This enhances the non-recourse provision, preserves the legal lending limits of the bank, and simplifies transactions when syndicates are involved.

Three documents exist in all production payments:

- The credit agreement,
- Conveyance of production payment, and
- The mortgage.

The credit agreement specifies the loan amount, the interest rate used (prime rate, Certificate of deposit, or LIBOR), and the duration of the interest rate before a change is made (1, 3, or 6 month intervals).

The conveyance details the amount of the production payment and its disposition. The conveyance typically dedicates all of the lease revenues to the production payment until the loan is repaid. Most agreements allow the borrower to pay off the loan balance at any time without penalty.

The mortgage assigns all proceeds as security for payment of the note, interest, and terms of default. Most mortgages limit the banks rights to the production payment only. Banks take the subject properties in the event of a default. Defaults typically include material misrepresentation, bankruptcy, or breach of covenants.

Failure to repay the loan according to the amortization schedule, due to production or price deficiencies, does not lead to a default, as long as the other covenants have not been breached.

Technical Contributions

Like the lease/buy decision, the primary task revolves around establishing the investment merits of the investment, rejecting bad ones and accepting the attractive opportunities. Unattractive investments, using normal profit metrics, cannot be made better by project financing. Funding the property through a production comes only after development is justified. Project financing, like leasing, is a least cost decision.

Assets with the following characteristics make the best candidates for project funding.

1. High and stable production rates,
2. Slow or no decline in producing rates,
3. Stable production history,
4. Simple legal environment,
5. Well established markets for product,
6. Low risk political environment or guarantees by international organizations like the World Bank,
7. Unencumbered production,
8. Low operating and transportation costs, and
9. Majority ownership and operation by a respected organization.

These conditions, taken together, mean that banks seek low risk projects. Lenders lower the loan amount and/or raise the interest rate as their perception of project risk changes. It is useful to note that the lenders perception of risk almost always exceeds the borrowers. The fundamental issue to lender concerns the size of the loan and the corresponding interest rate. Each lender uses different tests to determine the size of the loan. Some examples include:

- One-half of the before-tax project NPV,
- The before-tax NPV of half the average producing rate,
- A-ten year payback test,

- ➢ The 2 to 1 before-tax NPV of outstanding loan balance.
- ➢ Two-thirds of the sum of after-tax NPV plus depreciation and depletion, and
- ➢ A 1.25 to 1 debt coverage ratio (See Chapter 3).

Several major differences arise here. Measures of NPV vary by lender according to their expectations of medium term interest rates and the current market lending rates. Lenders also seldom escalate product prices, preferring to use constant prices or prices that are capped at a certain level. Even though the term NPV exists in many lending decisions, the NPV estimate often falls well below the borrowers perception of value.

Example 9.8: Determine the value of the following project NCF using the standard measures of value. Assume an 8-year SL depreciation, depreciation begins when the tangible Capex is spent, and a 35% income tax rate. All $ values in millions.

Years	Net Revenue	Opex	Tangible Capex	Expensed Capex	Interest	Principal	IT	MOD NCF
0-1	0.00	0.00	10.80	21.60	0.00	0.00	-8.03	-24.37
1-2	0.00	0.00	38.34	89.46	0.00	0.00	-33.46	-94.34
2-3	0.00	0.00	38.70	90.00	0.00	0.00	-35.34	-93.36
3-4	80.99	17.80	24.03	57.14	0.00	0.00	-2.78	-15.20
4-5	170.34	35.65	0.00	0.00	0.00	0.00	42.25	92.44
5-6	173.07	34.50	0.00	0.00	0.00	0.00	43.61	94.96
6-7	165.25	30.50	0.00	0.00	0.00	0.00	42.27	92.48
7-8	134.00	22.90	0.00	0.00	0.00	0.00	33.99	77.11
8-9	99.54	15.75	0.00	0.00	0.00	0.00	24.90	58.89
9-10	74.73	10.95	0.00	0.00	0.00	0.00	19.58	44.20
10-11	54.90	7.45	0.00	0.00	0.00	0.00	15.56	31.89
11-12	25.07	3.15	0.00	0.00	0.00	0.00	7.67	14.25
Total	977.89	178.65	111.87	258.20	0.00	0.00	150.21	278.95
NPV_5	693.48	128.48	98.26	226.47	0.00	0.00	89.31	150.96
NPV_{10}	504.35	94.62	86.99	200.22	0.00	0.00	50.99	71.52
NPV_{15}	375.00	71.14	77.57	178.27	0.00	0.00	26.44	21.57

Payout	DPO	IRR	NPV/INV	SIV
6.43	7.61	18%	0.37	122.45

Most lenders use ½ the BT NPV as the base standard. All of the methods are, in our opinion, simplistic and arbitrary. Each approach implicitly admits that the lenders do not know enough to analyze the risks formally. The approximations are surrogates for formal risk assessment and management, and applications of such approximations go a long way toward explaining the recurring need to bailout lenders on a regular basis.

Classical DCF investment approaches favor project financing, unless some important alterations are understood. Total NCF equals $278.95m undiscounted. Discounting generates an NPV_{10} of $71.52m. The project satisfies most profit metrics at certainty. Simple sensitivities indicate that revenue would have to fall about 14% before NPV becomes zero, at the desired 10% discount rate. The NPV/INV value is 0.37, which is quite reasonable for larger, multinational projects. The SIV rises to over $122.45m, and the IRR is 18%. Both values are common, though not quite as robust as some investors would like, creating the opportunity for outside lenders to provide the requisite capital.

Example 9.8, cont'd recomputes the NCF and profitability estimates assuming that project Capex are financed at an 11% interest rate. The principal values are negative in early years, followed by positive

Example 9.8: *(Cont'd.)* Recompute the value of the project assuming that all the Capex is financed at a 11% interest rate. Use the same IT rate as before.

Years	Net Revenue	Opex	Tangible Capex	Expensed Capex	Interest	Principal	IT	MOD NCF
0-1	0.00	0.00	10.80	21.60	3.56	-32.40	-9.28	5.72
1-2	0.00	0.00	38.34	89.46	17.62	-127.80	-39.63	22.01
2-3	0.00	0.00	38.70	90.00	31.78	-128.70	-46.47	14.69
3-4	80.99	17.80	24.03	57.14	40.71	-81.17	-17.02	39.51
4-5	170.34	35.65	0.00	0.00	32.57	74.02	30.85	-2.74
5-6	173.07	34.50	0.00	0.00	24.42	74.02	35.06	5.07
6-7	165.25	30.50	0.00	0.00	16.28	74.02	36.57	7.88
7-8	134.00	22.90	0.00	0.00	8.14	74.02	31.14	-2.20
8-9	99.54	15.75	0.00	0.00	4.07	74.02	23.48	-17.78
9-10	74.73	10.95	0.00	0.00	0.00	0.00	19.58	44.20
10-11	54.90	7.45	0.00	0.00	0.00	0.00	15.56	31.89
11-12	25.07	3.15	0.00	0.00	0.00	0.00	7.67	14.25
Total	977.89	178.65	111.87	258.20	179.16	0.00	87.50	162.50
NPV_5	693.48	128.48	98.26	226.47	143.77	-61.10	38.99	118.61
NPV_{10}	504.35	94.62	86.99	200.22	117.37	-95.57	9.91	90.81
NPV_{15}	375.00	71.14	77.57	178.27	97.28	-113.98	-7.61	72.32

SIV = $125.8m and NPV/INV is 0.46.

values starting in year 4-5. Negative values represent cash inflows to the company, since NCF is computed as revenue minus all other categories. The cash inflows reflect the receipt of money from the bank, less the interest payment until year 3-4. In year 4-5, the project starts repaying the loan and accumulated interest. Details of the interest are omitted because of space limitations.

The project profitability jumps to $90.81m as the result of the financing. The difference between the internal financing NPV of $71.52m and financing of $90.81 measures the value added by using the lenders money instead of higher cost equity capital. Simple project risk measures decline significantly: minimum revenues decline to 17.8%, up from the 14% for the internal fund valuation. PF appears superior to the option using internal funds in this example (and most of the actual cases we have seen.)

The improved valuation metrics from PF results from the classical DCF simplifications. PF's superiority emanates from the cash flow pattern in the principal and interest payment columns in Example 9.8. Interest payments, before-tax write-offs, total $179.16m over the life of the project. Principal sums to zero, because the amount received from the lender are paid back on an undiscounted basis. On a discounted basis, the borrower appears to be ahead by $95.57m (remember the negative is a positive gain to the borrower), more than offsetting the interest payments.

Example 9.8: *(Cont'd.)* Graph the alternative NCF for each option.

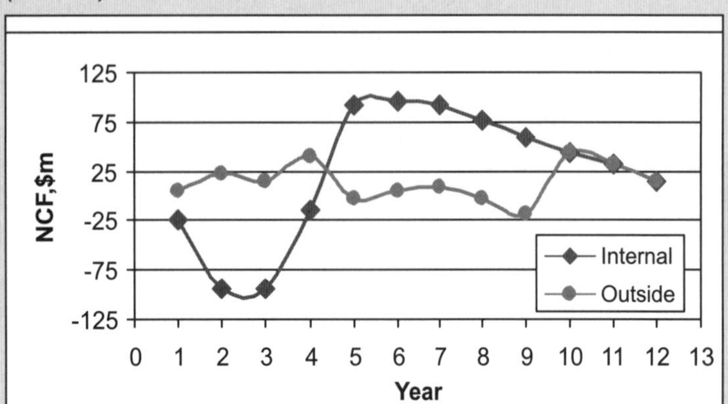

The graphical expression of the difference between internal vs. project financing is shown in the continuation of Example 9.8. The internal financing option shows the usual negative NCF in the early years followed by positive NCF in the last years. Outside financing realizes its benefits by having positive NCF in almost every year, except in the few years when the interest payments cause slightly negative values. This stability shows up in the NPV computation.

The contradiction becomes even more apparent when the undiscounted cash flows are evaluated. The project actually reduces the flow of money to the treasury with PF (from \$278.95m to \$162.50m. Financing reduces the value of the project by \$116.46 (= 278.96 –162.50). This amount arises from the after-tax cost of interest payments (= 179.16 ∗ (1 –0.35).

The breakeven discount rate on the difference between the two sets of NCF is about 7.8%. At discount rates below 7.8%, the internal funding option comes top, while above that value, use someone else's money. Think about whether this makes sense?

PF dramatically impacts the risk profile of the project, which cannot be observed in a deterministic framework. The following example displays the distribution of the NPV_{10} for internal and external financing, as well as the distribution of the NCF for each alternative.

The risk distributions are generated using the NCF values at the first part of the example. The revenue stream assumes a Normal distribution with the deterministic values taken as the mean, and the standard deviation computed as 10% of the mean. Opex and Capex assume a lognormal distribution with the mean and the standard deviation determined in the same manner. The risk assumptions are simplified to highlight the hidden assumptions in PF.

Both funding alternatives satisfy the positive NPV requirement by adding value to the treasury. As the deterministic results confirmed, PF has a higher NPV, but considerable overlap in the two distributions exists. Comparing the NCF distributions highlights why PF has a higher NPV. PF shifts the NCF burden from the initial cash outlay to the middle periods of the project when the loan is being repaid. Risk, defined here as a negative cash flow, occurs in the first 4 to 5 years. With PF, the potential for negative values occurs in years 5 to 9. Also, internal financing is guaranteed to have negative cash flows, while the PF NCF may be positive.

Example 9.8: *(Cont'd.)* Assess the risk of the internal vs. external financing options

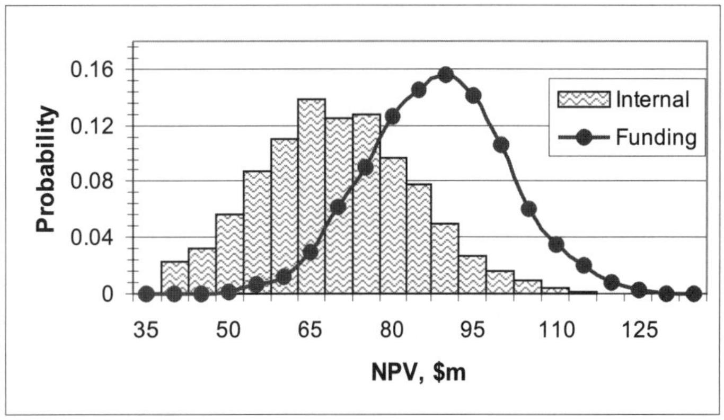

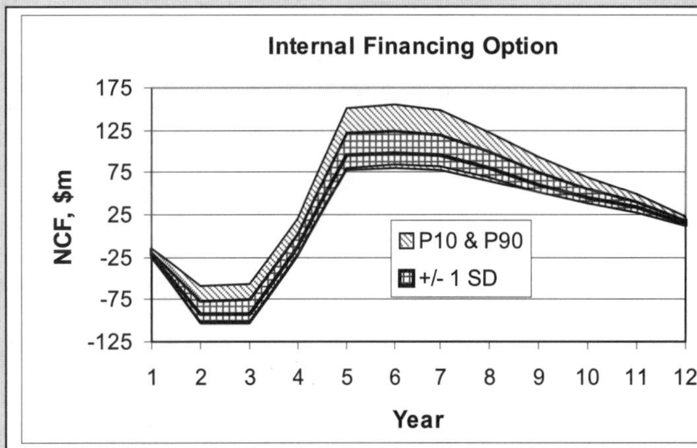

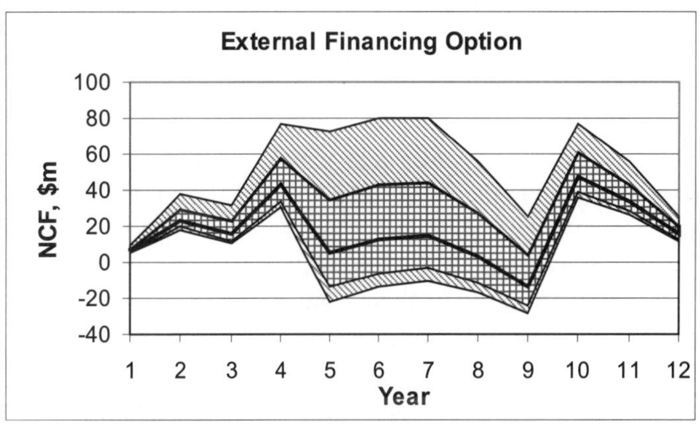

PF appears preferable only because it is intuitively better to finance at 7% after-tax (11% BT) than to use the investors discount rate of 10-15%. The implicit assumption is the cost-of-capital remains unchanged when the PF is used. In other words, the shareholders and lenders are content to supply funds to the corporation at pre-PF interest rates, even though assets are mortgaged to the non-recourse PF lenders. This is doubtful. Riskiness of the cash flows to these internal lenders increases dramatically with leverage. The benefits of leverage only accrue to the firm when it minimizes corporate cost-of-capital, not project cost-of capital.

PF creates the illusion of separating corporate and project financing, and some multinationals even establish subsidiaries to handle PF. The evaluation process assumes that negative cash flows offset taxes from other profitable projects. This is a valid assumption when the project ties directly to the corporation, but does it apply when the project is handled as a separate entity? What is the value of an interest payment when production falls so far that production cannot meet the interest and principal payment? Does the tax write-off accrue to the corporation or the subsidiary? If it goes to the corporation, does the standard return standard apply?

These questions illustrate the specter of applying one model of profitability to another situation that deviates significantly from the basic analytical process. Recognition of these limitations is the necessary first step in using PF correctly. Assuming the organization was already at the minimum cost-of-capital, PF alters future capital costs by raising the debt level.

To properly assess the impact of PF, the cost of moving away from the minimum cost-of-capital (discount rate) for all remaining projects must be factored in. The basic equation is:

$$\begin{aligned} \text{NPV} = {} & \text{NPV of internal financing} \\ & + \text{NPV of financing arrangement} \\ & - \text{NPV of the increased cost on future projects} \end{aligned} \quad \textbf{(9.4)}$$

Equation 9.4 is just the NPV of PF less the cost of other projects. Table 9.1 displays the type of relationship for different budget sizes. Assuming a capital budget of \$1 billion and a 3% change in the cost of capital the NPV_{10} of PF becomes \$15.81m (= 90.81 – 75).

TABLE 9.1

NPV Cost of Changing Capital Structure ($M)

Annual Capital Budget ($m)	Change in Cost-of-Capital (%)				
	1	2	3	4	5
50	1.32	2.57	3.75	4.87	5.92
100	2.64	5.14	7.50	9.73	11.80
500	13.20	25.70	37.50	48.70	59.20
1,000	26.40	51.40	75.00	97.30	118.40
5,000	132.00	257.00	375.00	487.00	592.00
10,000	264.00	514.00	750.00	973.00	1,184.00

Table 9.1 suggests that small firms should use PF more than larger firms, because of the lower cost. When a smaller firm uses PF to finance a major project, it leverages itself more than larger firms. This raises the risk premium. For example, when a corporation with annual capital expenditures of \$5.0 billion undertakes a \$300 million PF project, it shifts it cost of money by less than 1/2%, whereas, a firm with a budget of \$500 million increases its cost by 4-5%. Smaller firms use PF in spite of Table 9.1 to enter into a new country, tax avoidance, etc.

While the basic approach shown in Equation 9.4 is the theoretically correct method for handling PF, most investors prefer the quick and easy route of changing the hurdle rate. Instead of using the 10%

rate in the examples, they employ the AT cost-of-debt. Since the IRR of the project was slightly more than 7%, the AT debt cost would suggest that internal financing is the cheaper alternative. PF is just debt financing disguised under a different name.

The example used in this section covers common characteristics of PF. When the lending source is a private bank, PF fails the economic test in the majority of cases. When the lender is an international organization, like the World Bank or Asian Development Bank, who guarantees the loan, PF makes much more economic sense. Such guarantees lower the cost of borrowing and avoid the recourse issue. Exploring the PF option makes perfect sense for large, risky investments, especially in these countries perceived to be risky and have the backing of international lenders.

FARM-OUT & NON-CONSENT AGREEMENTS

Farm-outs and standouts continue the discussion of alternative funding methods. These methods originated in the petroleum industry, but similar formats exist in chemicals, manufacturing, pharmaceuticals, etc., just the names differ. Farm-outs and non-consent decisions arise when one party has the right to participate in a project or is already participating in a project, and decides to alter their ownership interest. The investment opportunity conveys the obligation to invest money, and the project may be wholly owned or have partners. These provisions apply when one or more parties declines to participate in the project, for whatever reason.

The investment situation follows a common scenario. An investor acquires an asset from the original owner: for the petroleum industry, this means acquiring the mineral rights for a lease or tract. Then, for some reason – budget restriction, risk concerns, change in core strategy, etc., the investor elects to discontinue entirely or alter their funding commitment. One option, of course, is selling the asset or the rights. When considerable upside potential exists or no one can be found to buy the investment rights, the middle ground lets a third party fund the investment in exchange for some of the benefits, if any ever accrue.

Farm-outs or farm-ins, and non-consent (or sole risking and stand-out) offer methods for this partial sale of an investment opportunity. Farm-outs (selling part of ones interest) normally take place in mature areas between multinational companies and independents. Independents historically initiated farm-outs, seeking access to acreage held by companies with large land holdings. Since companies with large exploration plays tend to acquire more acreage than they have funds to explore and develop internally, farm-outs accelerate the rate of exploration and development. In periods of tight budgets, farm-outs allow the acreage holder to drill wells, as leases are about to expire, or to avoid revenue loss due to drainage in competitive reservoirs.

Standouts or non-consent terms exist in most operating and partnership agreements. Whether partners enter into an agreement through forced pooling or voluntarily, disagreements often come up over the best course of action to take; whether sizing production facilities, scheduling, technology type, product disposition, and so on. In order to avoid long delays over such arguments, one or more partners may standout or go non-consent when declining to invest in all or part of the project. This expedites negotiations and minimizes conflicts among the partners.

Like most legal provisions, a unique terminology has grown up for each option. One commonly hears that an investor farmed-out with a 12.5% *overriding roya*lty (ORRI or ORI) and a 30% *back-in working interest* (BIWI). An ORI is similar to the royalty paid to the original mineral owner, except it is paid to the party farming the lease out. If I get a lease from the government, I pay them a royalty (say 12.5%). Then, if I farm-out, the party farming-in also pays me a royalty as well (12.5%). The royalty typically means that I pay no Capex or Opex costs, or am *carried* by the party farming in. This becomes expensive to the party farming-in, because the government and I receive 25% of the revenue, leaving the farm-in party to pay all costs from 75% of the revenue. This is not as bad as it appears, because the farm-in party had no exploration costs.

Many farm-in agreements switch from the ORI to the BIWI at a reversion point. BIWI means the farm-out party converts their royalty to a WI (or comes back in as a WI owner, paying their WI share of Opex and Capex) at the reversion. Reversion most commonly occurs when the farm-in party recovers all investment costs (payback), but can be negotiated on anything, like production volume, length of time, etc. The chance of achieving payback is critical in deciding to negotiate a BIWI provision.

Non-consent (NC) differs from farm outs in several important ways. First, NC comes about with existing partners in a project. Most partnerships recognize that partners will disagree on one or more aspects of the investment. To avoid the time and cost of litigation, NC provisions are written into the operating agreement (partnership terms). This allows the partners to go ahead with the investment, without agreement from the dissenting partners; hence, the term non-consent.

Second, the terms of compensation change. The partners that sole risks or implement the NC provision effectively fund the other partners WI. If we own 75% of an asset and impose NC on the other partners, we pay 100% of all the Capex and Opex, though the other partners still own 25% of the asset. To compensate us for the additional risk, the term, *penalty*, is used. We receive enough money to recover the 25% investment cost, plus a penalty, usually expressed as 200% to10,000% penalty. The partner standing-in at a 500% penalty recovers the initial cost plus a penalty of 5 times that amount. So, if a project costs \$100m, we might fund \$25m for the other partners and then recover that \$25m plus another \$\$125m. The unit or partnership agreement defines the penalty. Standard agreements exist for international projects.*(9.2)*

Penalties may be paid from production of the project (but this can be a contentious issue) or by writing a check for the entire amount. The penalty also varies by location. As costs and risk increase, the penalty rises to discourage partners from avoiding their cost burden. A favorite memory of ours is the time one firm sole-risked another on a North Sea exploratory well, paying \$5m for another party at a 5,000% penalty. Watching that party trying to negotiate their way out writing a \$250m check was interesting.

Simplified Evaluations

Farm-outs could never be justified if projects were risk free or budget limitations never led to lease expirations. The value of farm-outs on an NPV basis is always less than the 100% working-interest economics at certainty (except for the shady investment companies who use other peoples money to complete noncommercial wells). Farm-outs do warrant consideration when risk is recognized and budgets are limited.

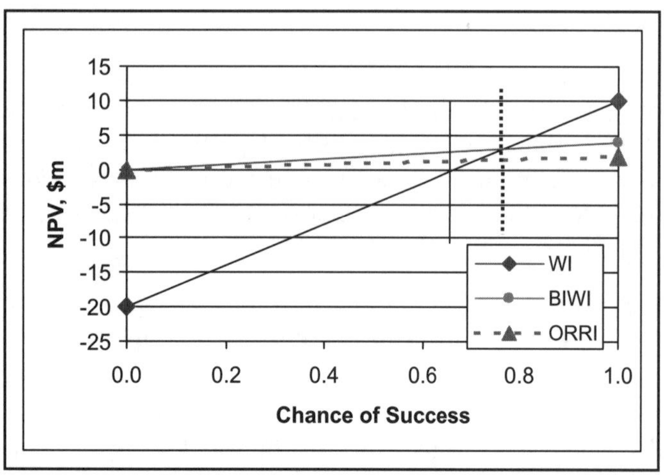

Figure 9.3 NPV vs. P_s for various drilling options

Figures 9.3 and 9.4 depict two typical situations. The first shows a project with an estimated NPV_{10} of \$10 million at certainty, and an NPV_{10} of \$20m for the failure file. The 100% working interest (WI) case has a minimum probability of success of about 67%, meaning that, if 67% of the projects achieve the certainty result (\$10m) and 35% are fail, the project will just break even. The project would normally be approved if past decisions had successes in excess of 67%, as indicated by the solid vertical line. Also shown are the alternatives of a straight 1/8 override (ORI), and a 1/16 ORT with a 40% back-in working interest (BIWI).

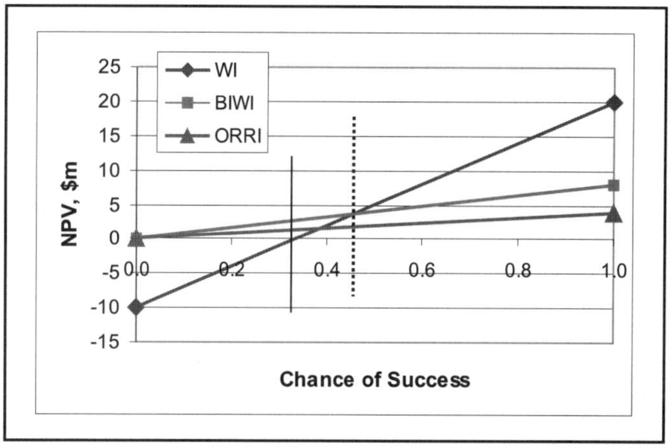

Figure 9.4 NPV vs. P_s for different risk/return combination

The best alternative depends on risk. The farm-out NPV_{10} exceeds the drill economics for any P_s less than 78%, as indicated by the dotted vertical line. The override is greater than the NPV_{10} of the drill case around 72%. Override economics are typically less than the farm-out case when dealing with deterministic economics, though this conclusion changes when more detailed risk assessment occurs. These findings should be self-evident: use your money to invest in the least risky ventures and someone else's for high-risk projects.

Figure 9.4 relates risk and return with a lower failure NPV_{10} and a higher certainty NPV_{10}. The minimum P_s drops to about 33% for the WI alternative. The BIWI has a higher NPV_{10} when P_s is around 50%. This situation is much more likely to engender the use of our money because of the lower risk.

The relationship between the working-interest, back-in, and override alternatives is the same in both figures. As the risk increases, the best strategy shifts to reducing front-end investments as much as possible. Farming-out is preferred when the evaluation indicates limited upside potential and high front-end costs. As either the dry hole costs fall or the potential increases, the decision shifts to drilling the well.

Straight overrides produce lower cash flows than back-in working interests, except in marginal wells. Acreage, which produces low success prospects, or low production often produces more revenue with straight overrides than with the BIWI option. Investors seldom choose straight overrides, because of the fear of missing a highly profitable investment. Reviews of past farm-outs show that a strategy of taking overrides on a prospect with little payout potential would have created more wealth than adoption of a typical back-in strategy. This conclusion cannot be observed here, because the figures ignore the chance of payback.

NC examples follow are very similar profile. Figure 9.5 shows the same P_s graph for the WI case versus the NC with penalties of 300% and 500%. The WI economics are the same as Figure 9.4. The NC economics are similar to a farm-out: the NC party avoids the front-end investment and foregoes some revenue in exchange. The cost of foregone revenue may not impact the decision as much as the cost of failure depending on budget conditions and risk tolerances.

The WI case is preferable relative to the 300% option when the P_s is greater than around 75%. As the penalty increases, however, the minimum P_s declines, as shown with the 500% case. As the penalty becomes higher, the NC option is effectively eliminated from an economic perspective.

This classical, simplified risk format for farm-out and NC highlights the basic risk vs. return trade-off again. Similar analysis provides the supporting foundation for billions of dollars in investments. Though better than a deterministic analysis, several serious limitations exist.

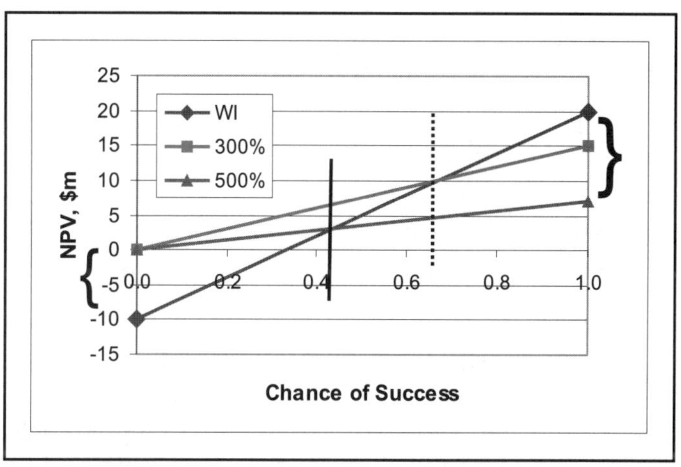

Figure 9.5 NC vs. WI at different penalties

First, discrete events like success or failure require care when being used in a statistical format. This situation is covered in a separate section of this chapter. Second, this analysis ignores the variability in production, prices, costs, etc. Since the choice between a straight ORRI and BIWI, for example, depends on the chance of obtaining payback, which depends further on investment, price and production, the wrong investment option may result with a partial or incomplete risk assessment, and often does.

Risk Analysis

The following example provides one, common application of risk weighting or EMV calculations to investments. It gives the EMV distribution for a project for three cases: WI, farm-out and non-consent.

Example 9.9: Derive the distributions for a project with three choices: WI, farm-out with a 12.5% royalty and 30% BIWI, and non-consent with a 300% penalty.

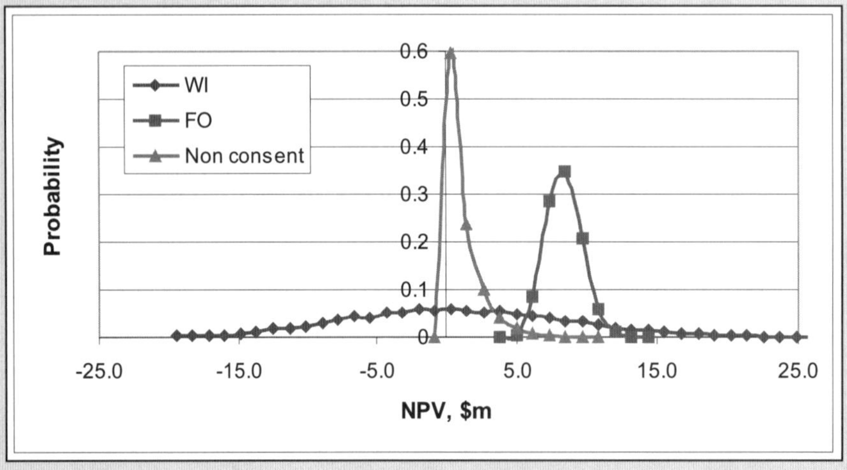

Option	EMV	P_{10}	P_{50}	Mean	P_{90}	SD
WI	1.43	-8.82	0.97	1.16	11.20	7.95
FO	8.96	7.39	8.91	8.95	10.54	1.57
NC	0.14	0	0.11	0.70	2.16	1.18

The P_s values are assumed to be about 25% for the EMV calculations. Observe from Example 9.9 that the EMV for the FO option is the highest at 25%, as verified earlier. The NC distribution appears to intersect the x-axis less than zero, because of Excel graphing characteristics. No NC actually fall below zero.

CHAPTER 9

Technical and Non-technical Issues

The FO option appears to be the best choice based on both the traditional EMV or distribution results. One non-technical issue is important to remember when considering the options. Only use the NC option in exceptional cases. The business world in any industry is smaller than people realize. Good faith partnerships are critical for success: now and in the future. By electing NC and FO, this faith is often shattered beyond repair. Part of the analysis must consider the damage to ones business relationships.

Several technical issues rear their ugly heads in this example. First, EMV combines two different discrete states – success and failure – together to arrive at a mean value. Example 9.9 disguises the nature of these states. Example 9.9 continued demonstrates the complexity that arises from the bimodal distribution. This result is bimodal, because there are two outcomes. If we had three states, the distribution is trimodal, etc. The vertical, dotted line is the mean of the two discrete states. Stop and think about what the mean or risk weighted value (EMV) means to you in this situation?

This example is like tossing a coin. With a 50/50 chance of a heads or tails, each outcome is a discrete event: a head or tail. The average combines the two events. This dichotomy has been obvious for years.(9.3) Decision-makers accepted the simple EMV for comparing projects, and now use the distributions of EMV. This simplification falls apart, however, when multiple risky investments combine as part of portfolio management, as shown in Chapter 10, because of the distortion in the relative attractiveness of the alternatives, when various risk and return weights are allowed for.

Example 9.9: *(Cont'd.)*

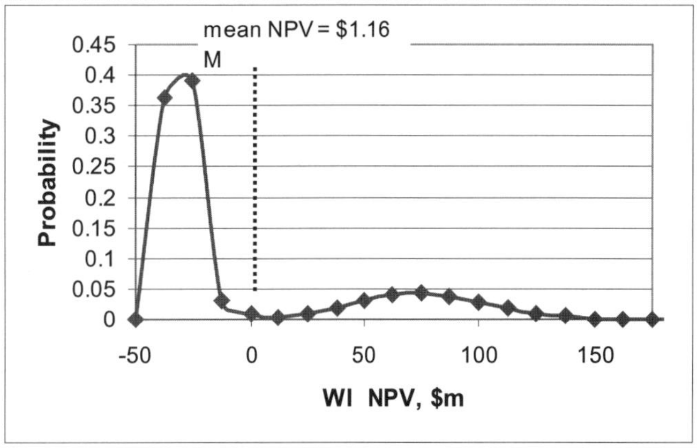

SCALING & LINKING PROJECTS

Deterministic investment analysis has considerable difficulty answering some of the most important questions facing the decision-maker; namely, how large to make the production system and linking the project to other investments to reduce risk. Traditional approaches answer these questions by performing sensitivities on production system, and select the one with the largest profit metric. This approach fails to capture the corresponding impacts of changes in price, cost, and sales volatility. Second, the output of one project becomes the input to downstream projects. Chemical plants need feedstock, refineries require crude oil, processing plants need gas feedstock, automobile manufacturing requires steel, computers need chips, etc. The common practice is to treat each component separately, and then add the separate profit metrics to obtain the corporate valuation.

The classical system works fine when the valuation treats the inputs deterministically; again, because it only deals with the expected value. When trying to assess project riskiness, the traditional approach grossly distorts risk. The scaling and linking of multiple projects profoundly impacts the performance metrics and decision-making process, almost totally annihilating the classical investment approach.

This section illustrates one approach, but you should appreciate that the impact of scaling and linking varies considerably across industries. Wal-Mart believes buying items from independent suppliers optimizes performance. Some dislike the high-pressure tactics Wal-Mart uses to lower supply price, but that is the nature of the business. Sears, on the other hand, elected to buy the Kenmore name of white goods to obtain control of the production system. In automotive, General Motors tried to own most of the suppliers that contributed parts to their cars, but the business-to-business Internet made this a high cost, inefficient structure.

Other examples include electrical generation, which began to purchase natural gas production as a convenient means of guaranteeing supply to power peaking units. When gas producers realized that cheap turbine driven electricity generation provided a secure, stable demand for gas supplies, they invested in electrical generation to provide an outlet for their gas production. Virtually every industry has the opportunity to participate in supplying its needs or shipping, distributing, selling its output.

In this section, the example of gas processing is used to illustrate the scalability and linkages between projects. Processing facilities liquefy gas, because gas demand may be limited and/or liquids are more profitable. The basic plant decision follows the same format as the other evaluations discussed to date. Several considerations exist in all plant evaluations that complicate the decision process. Probably the most significant is deciding which liquids to recover. One can recover almost all of the liquids, if willing to invest the money in capital and operating cost. The real question, as always, is can enough money be made from the production of the liquids to make a profit on the capital and operating cost.

Scalability

Like most technical areas, the term scalability conveys an illusion of precision. Figure 9.6 shows the simplest relationship between production volume and plant size. Observe that a step function indicates that most production systems require scaling up the production components at some volume levels. This form exists when one basic, production system exists. Distinct breaks occur at well-defined production volumes. In this example, increasing production volumes also cause the slope of the cost line to change, indicating rising costs with higher production rates.

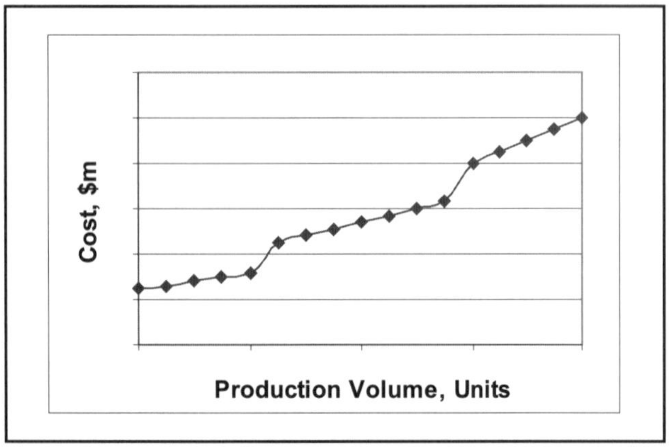

Figure 9.6 Scaling one production system

Though Figure 9.6 assumes that just one type of production system is considered, which is merely scaled up to achieve higher production volumes. This ignores or omits the likelihood that other production systems also exist. Expanding the modeling process to recognize risk leads to formal consideration of alternative production systems directly, rather than indirectly. In fact, this section illustrates why classical investment methods seldom reach the best decisions. Before moving into the formal analysis, the simplified system is shown in Figure 9.6a.

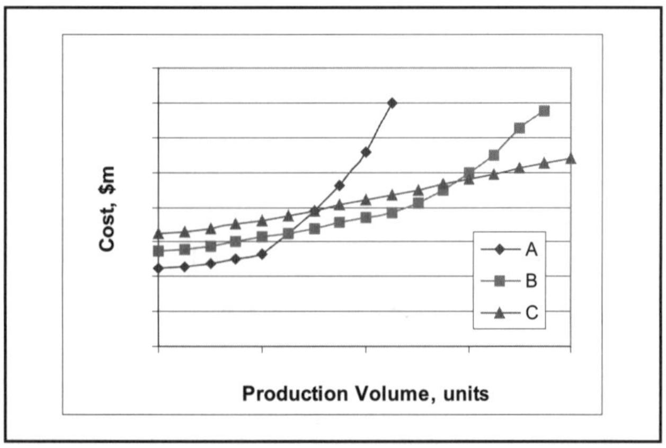

Figure 9.6a Scaling with alternative production systems

The gas-processing example used here employs the situation in Figure 9.6a. Three alternative production systems are considered: a *turboexpander* plant, a *mechanical refrigeration* system, and a *short-cycle* unit. Expanders recover up to 99% of the propanes and between 50-90% of the ethane, depending on the gas composition and economics. If ethane is recovered, capital costs are required to add a demethanizer to remove any methane condensing across the expander (at –150°F). Mechanical refrigeration, which dominated prior to the introduction of expanders, recovers between 30 and 50% of the propanes and 80-90% of the butanes at -20°F. Refrigeration systems can operate at temperatures below this level, but capital costs rise due to changes in metallurgy. The simpler short-cycle system, recovers roughly 20% of the butanes and 80% of the gasolines. It is used mainly for lean gas streams, especially where low production volumes and limited gas markets exist.

For those unfamiliar with the gas liquids market, the basic features of *natural gas liquids (NGL's),* and the sub-units, *liquefied petroleum gases (LPG's)* are shown in Table 9.2. Gas not converted to liquids is called residual gas, and is sold at a price commensurate with its energy content, normally measured in British Thermal Units (1 BTU = amount of heat needed to raise 1 pound of water 1°F). The table shows the basic components, its chemical name, and the major end uses of the product.

The price of NGL's is more volatile than crude oil or natural gas, reflecting the demand changes for end use products, like gasoline. The typical deterministic analysis would estimate production of the

TABLE 9.2

Summary of Basic Features of Natural Gas Liquids (NGL)

Component	Formula	End Uses
Ethane	C_2H_6	Petrochemical feedstock for manufacture of light olefins and ethylene. Not other significant commercial uses.
Propane	C_3H_8	Petrochemical feedstock for manufacture of light olefins and propylene. Commercial and residential fuel, grain drying and transportation
Iso-butane	iC_4H_{10}	Primary use as feedstock for alkylation unit in refinery. Petrochemical feedstock, commercial and residential fuel.
Normal-butane	$C4H_{10}$	Primary use as gasoline fuel blending component in refinery. Petrochemical feedstock, commercial and residential fuel,
Natural Gasoline	$C_5\,H_{12}$ - $C_{10}H_{22}$	Refinery feedstock (often blended with crude oil). Petrochemical feedstock.
The butanes are sold as a mix when used in fuel. They are often mixed with propane in a fuel mix called LPG.		

natural gas feed stream, the resultant liquid output stream, sales prices for each product, Opex and Capex, etc. and then generate Table 9.3.

TABLE 9.3

Deterministic Economics of Alternative Processing Options

	NPV, $m	NPV/INV	IRR, %	SIV, $m
Turboexpander	275	0.85	24	425.1
Refrigeration	180.4	0.80	31	390.1
Short-Cycle	90.4	1.21	35	275.2

The expander option adds more value (NPV), because of the higher value of the liquid streams, primarily ethane and propane. The efficiency ratios are lower than the other alternatives due to the larger investment outlay, and the IRR is also less, because of the initial capital expenditure. Most investors would opt for the expander option based on these numbers, which they did in great numbers in the last several decades.

Do the findings change when risk is formally considered? Figure 9.7 shows the NPV distribution when sales volume, price, and cost risks are introduced.

The turboexpander still has the largest expected value, but also has more risk associated with it. The short-cycle (SS) earns the least, but has almost no risk of losing money. The mechanical refrigeration unit falls between these two results. Moreover, the expander is skewed to the left, while the other options are more symmetrical.

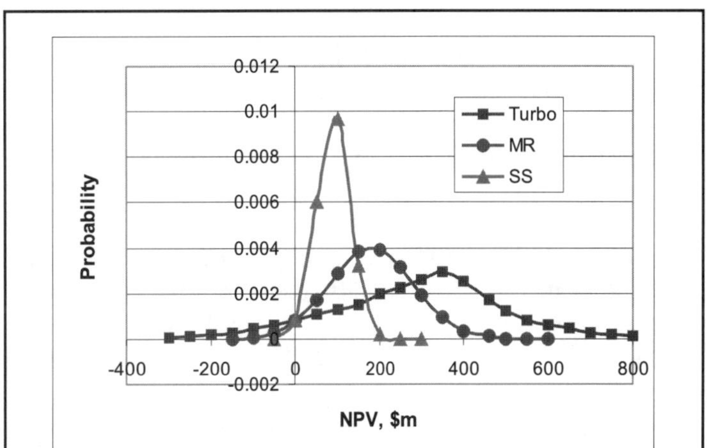

Figure 9.7 Value distributions for processing alternatives

This type of analysis dominates most applications today, and is quite misleading. The primary benefit of risk analysis is the understanding of the elements of a project causing the risk, hopefully, leading to amelioration of the problems. This example merely adds risk on top of a misleading deterministic framework, and though better, misses several critical points.

Review of the simulations leading to the negative NPV's (always recommended) shows that the worst results arise when the plant sells ethane and propane at a market price below the cost of recovering the liquids. Does this make sense? Of course not, since the expander permits rejection of the ethane and propane (selling the gas) when prices are too low. This *options* thinking requires modifying the analysis to require rejecting ethane when prices fail to cover Opex (which most software makes quite difficult).

When the model includes the ability to reject ethane, the expander NPV distribution looks like Figure 9.7a. The distribution from the simulation was drawn as a normal distribution, though it is still slightly skewed to the right. Note that only the expander has the flexibility to process part of the gas stream; the other choices produce all or none of the liquids. Observe that the risk falls quite dramatically relative to the previous graph.

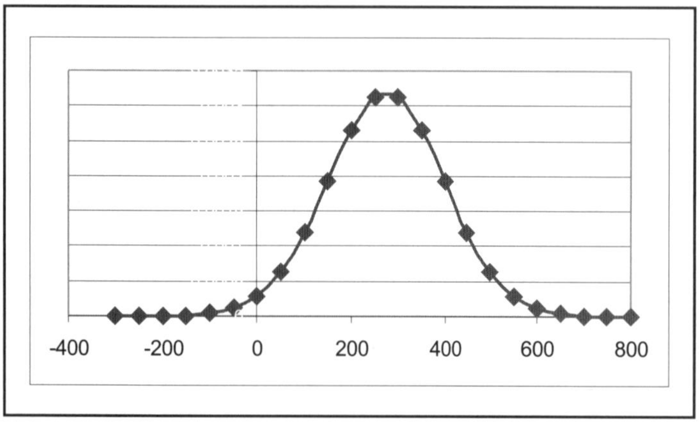

Figure 9.7a Expander distribution with option to reject

Risk analysis is very insightful in its own right. An additional benefit arises from the ability to demonstrate the incomplete modeling that often takes place. Many investors argue that they can handle risk subjectively as well as this formal analysis. In fact, the subtle art of decision-making actually applies this process informally. The main lesson to be learned from this example is that risk analysis is more than just the application of statistics; it also demands good modeling of the *options* available at each stage in the project life. This element requires as much effort as the risk analysis segment, and is just as important.

Linking Projects

In the process example shown above, the metrics support accepting the project. While even the project metrics appear fine, the real risk and return trade-off still eludes us. The analysis to this point assumes that this is a stand-alone or independent project. Suppose this is part of a portfolio of projects, which may be tied together. The issues becomes whether the linking or tying projects together impacts the value and risk metrics.

Linking projects takes many forms, but goes back to the vertical integration concept. If one owns the production, processing/manufacturing, distribution, and retail stages, volatility in profitability in one stage may be offset with changing results in other segments. This reduces volatility as projects are linked or aggregated, and some call this risk reduction. This is the essential task of *portfolio optimization.*

Deterministic analysis ignores the portfolio problem by implicitly assuming independence among the projects. Merely, adding the expected value metrics produces the gain to the treasury. Trying to measure risk destroys this simplicity, because the risk measures are directly tied to each other. The processing example was feasible only because a supply of gas was available. The portfolio question is whether the investor should own the gas supply, the process plant, or both (or parts of both to really complicate the question). The actual answer depends on the objectives and business environment of the firm, but the impact on risk can easily be demonstrated. Figure 9.8 shows the NPV distribution from adding the gas supply project (which hasn't been discussed so far) and the process facility (the turboexpander option), assuming independent project cash flows. The second distribution shows the corresponding risk analysis when the two project NCF's are linked.

The graphs are drawn using the mean and standard deviation from the simulation, assuming a normal distribution for simplicity. The curves are slightly skewed to the left for the process facility and skewed to the right for the gas field.

Several interesting point arise. First, the combined distribution assuming independent projects has only a slightly higher chance of the project losing money than the process facility alone. This is because the two are totally independent: a loss in one project may be offset by a gain in the other.

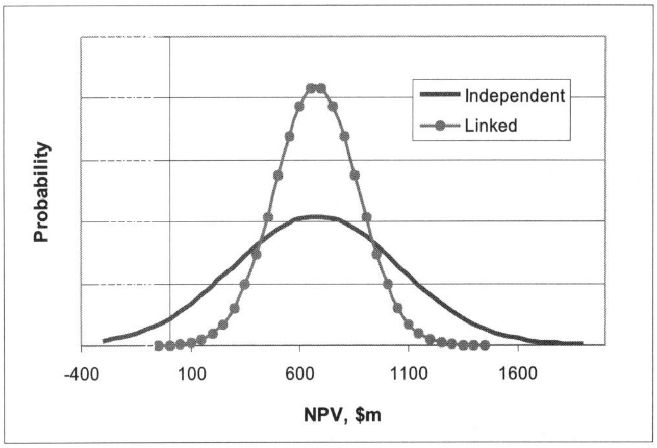

Figure 9.8 Comparison between linked and independent project risk analysis

The linkage occurs because one of the most important risks is the gas sales price. In stand-alone or independent analysis, a low gas price might lead to a negative NPV. By linking the low gas price to the process facility, the lower cost of feedstock raises the profit margin at the plant, making the total profitability profitable. Note that the chance of losing money from both projects is almost nil. When gas prices are high in the field, the profit margin at the plant is squeezed.

Many seek some general guidelines for knowing when combining projects is desirable. The complicating problems in this quest include: different magnitudes of investments, varying tax regimes, volatility in prices for the inputs and outputs, etc. The net effect is that every combination of projects differs, and we have never observed any general rules-of-thumb that apply in one industry, much less across industries.

One lesson is clear, however. Careful analysis of risk metrics, not just profit metrics, provides unique insights about the interrelationship between profitability and risk, and actions that can be taken to manage risk. Without the information garnered from Figure 9.8, making sound investment decisions is very difficult. One rule-of-thumb is applicable here. In fast growing, new industries (telecommunications and Internet come to mind), formal risk analysis may not be as critical, because the field is growing so fast, any product makes money. But, the computer hardware and software industries thought double-digit growth would go on forever in the 1980's. They too are now worried about risk mitigation, as much as traditional mining, manufacturing, transportation, etc.

Chapter 10 continues this line of thought by showing how to determine the best choices of linked or interconnected projects using the *optimization* software available today.

PROJECT MANAGEMENT, COSTING, AND SCHEDULING

In generating the examples used so far, estimates of Capex and Opex have been assumed. This section explores methods for generating these estimates and the importance of risking. Professionals charged with generating cost estimates willingly adopt the concepts of risk analysis, because they know that single, point estimate values distort and mislead investment decision-making. Conveying ranges of possible and likely values communicates the inherent volatility in the values. The main bottleneck in the implementation of risk lies with the end user. We had a situation where an engineer prepared a detailed risk analysis of the cost of drilling a well. In presenting the findings to the end user of the numbers, management uttered the classical refrain "just give me the right number to use in the economic assessment."

Earlier in our careers, this attitude disturbed us immensely, leading almost to the same attitudes conveyed in "Zen and the Art of Motorcycle Maintenance."[(9.4)] Aging helped us understand that the real cause is the confusion and discomfort caused by trying to integrate the complex data emanating from the specialist disciplines. The preparer of the cost estimate is paid to analyze the inherent intricacies in the data, but the user must integrate that detail from multiple disciplines into an organized, intelligible process. In doing this, it is easier to "keep it simple," unless tools are available to communicate and analyze the relevant details. These tools are now available.

Since the majority of books readers have never managed a complete project over its life cycle, this section begins with a brief overview of the process, and then illustrates the application of the basic principles in three separate stages: detailed cost estimation, scheduling and project management. Each topic deserves a separate book to really grasp all the relevant details, and those books exist.

The basic format for sound project management follows Figure 9.9. The example is based on an organization entering a country to take advantage of a business opportunity.

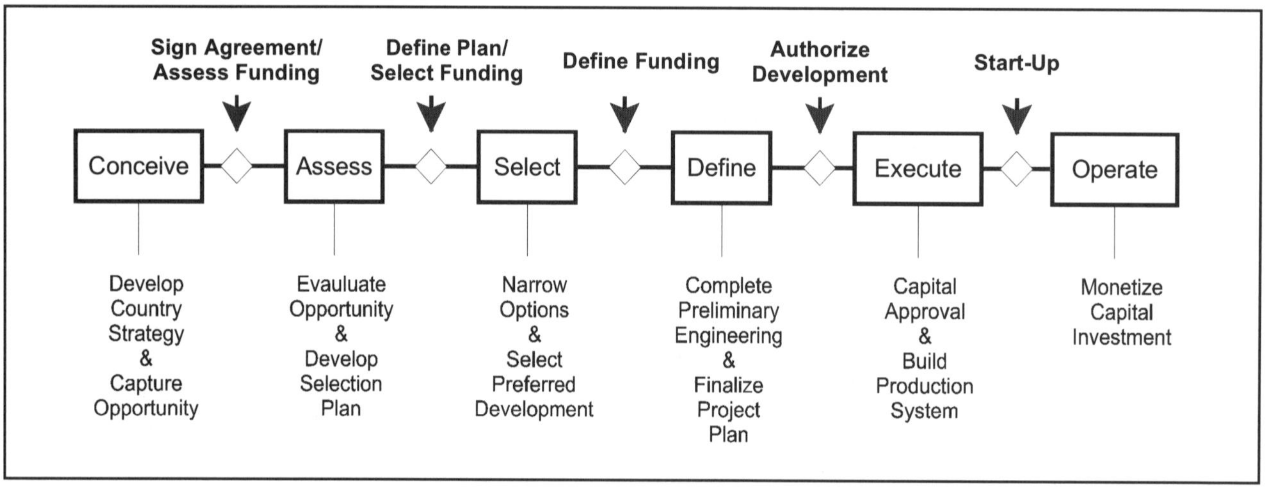

Figure 9.9 Stages of project management

The boxes indicate the process followed at each stage. The Conceive stage, for instance, reflects the formulation of the country strategy and the opportunities to be captured. The Assess stage scopes out the options available for meeting the strategy and establishment of the criterion for making a decision. In the Select stage, the options are narrowed down to the most viable, maybe two or three, and the preferred method chosen. The Define stage completes the detailed engineering and scheduling of the project construction. The Execution stage actually builds the production system, while the last stage deals with operating the facility.

The diamonds between the gates indicate what some call the "gates" of project management. Gates show the decisions that have to be made at the end of each stage. For instance, the first gate requires establishing the necessary funding levels and contracts needed to operate in the local country. These gates are much like a decision node in a decision tree. At each gate, the process of making the decision may force the project management to move back to a previous stage, because of uncertainties or new information. Even though the diagram implies a flow from left to right, moving backwards also occurs.

Applying such diagrams encourages the application of consistent processes in managing projects within organizations. This corrects the tendency of a program manager to treat each project as a unique event, rather than a process that can be followed to minimize bad decisions. Even novices to the subject realize quite quickly how complicated building a production facility in a new country might be, requiring contributions from all engineering, geoscience, accounting, legal, commercial, etc. disciplines. Without some structure, egregious errors often result.

In the early stages, estimates of cost or value vary considerably. Good project management yields cost and value estimates that follow the pattern in Figure 9.10. Moving through the project over time should cause the gap in estimates to close, until, at the very end, the estimates bracket tightly the actual outcome, as indicated by the happy face.

Unfortunately, poor project management typically leads to cost estimates like the star, and value estimates like the crossed circle. Chapter 2 outlined several examples and causes for these distortions.

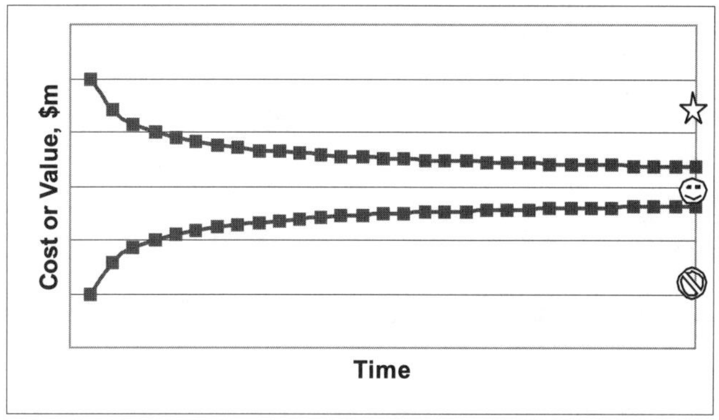

Figure 9.10 Objective of project management

The format shown in Figure 9.10 has been summarized more precisely in the cost estimate classification matrix for processing industries, as shown in Table 9.4. The accuracy range, purpose of estimate, preparation effort, etc. is clearly outlined. The originating source of the table is an excellent document for those who want to explore cost estimation more.(9.5)

TABLE 9.4

Cost Classification System

	Project Characteristics	**Secondary Characteristics**			
Estimate Class	**Level of Project Definition:** Expressed as % of complete definition	**End Usage** Typical purpose of estimate	**Methodology:** Typical estimating method	**Expected Accuracy Range:** Typical variation in low and highs	**Preparation Effort:**[a]
Class 5	0% to 2%	Concept screening	Capacity Factored, Parametric Models, Judgment or Analogy	L: -20% to -50% H: +30% to +100%	1
Class 4	1% to 15%	Study or Feasibility	Primarily Stochastic	L: -15% to -30% H: +20% to +50%	2 to 4
Class 3	10% to 40%	Budget, Authorization, or Control	Mixed, but Primarily Stochastic	L: -10% to -20% H: +10% to +30%	3 to 10
Class 2	30% to 70%	Control or Bid Tender	Primarily Deterministic	L: -5% to -15% H: +5% to +20%	4 to 20
Class 1	50% to 100%	Check Estimate or Bid Tender	Deterministic	L: -3% to -10% H: +3% t +15%	5 to 100

Note (a): The range index of 1 equals .005% of project costs, so 100 equals .5% of project costs

Simple Cost Estimation

Traditional cost estimating provides the CAPEX estimates used in project valuation. In the deterministic framework, one number is generated, often with a contingency element to account for "risk." Example 9.10 shows a very simplified construction cost estimate, the way they are often summarized for management. These are the estimated costs at the completion of the project.

The major dilemma facing project managers is the accuracy of these values. Do they reflect unbiased estimates or are the costs under estimated to justify the project? More importantly, there is no way to tell if the results are going to be a happy face or star, like shown above.

Example 9.10: Simple construction cost estimate.

Cost Estimates for One Project	
Category	**Cost, $million**
Design	10,250
Equipment	25,000
Support Structure	17,100
Electrical, plumbing, etc.	11,350
Labor	17,600
Indirects	26,111
Total	107,411

Faced with large cost estimates, sound management practice demands more information about which components are most sensitive to change, and are the most critical to project success. Knowing which risks can be managed and which are totally beyond ones control is also important.

The simplest and easiest way to introduce risk is to gather the cost estimators into a room and ask them to put ranges on these values. For simplicity, just ask for the low, most likely and high values for each cost category. The first problem that arises concerns the relationship between the cost in Example 9.10 and the most likely. The odds are quite high that the cost estimate in Example 9.10 differs significantly from the most likely value. It may be the first set of numbers are an expected value, a P_{50}, or just the number that allows the project to satisfy the investment objectives of the organization. (Review anchoring at the beginning of Chapter 8). Having said this, we will assume that the costs are truly the most likely value.

Example 9.10a adds the high and low estimates for the cost categories based on the advise of the experts. The last column computes the average for the cost estimate assuming a triangular distribution for the values. (Note: a triangular function is assumed for simplicity.)

Example 9.10a: Cost estimates with ranges. All costs in $million.

Category	ML	Low	High	Average
Design	10,250	9,225	12,300	10,592
Equipment	25,000	23,750	27,500	25,417
Support Structure	17,100	16,245	18,810	17,385
Electrical, plumbing, etc.	11,350	10,215	12,485	11,350
Labor	17,600	16,720	19,360	17,893
Indirects	26,111	24,805	39,167	30,028
Total	107,411	100,960	129,622	112,664

The original, most likely cost of $107m rises to an average cost of over $112m, with an extreme low of about $100m , rising to a high of around $130m. Chapter 8 pointed that that the odds of experiencing the low or high total is almost zero, and these totals are often omitted from reports to highlight the minimal chance of occurrence. The simulation results reported in Figure 9.11, based on 5,000 iterations, demonstrates this.

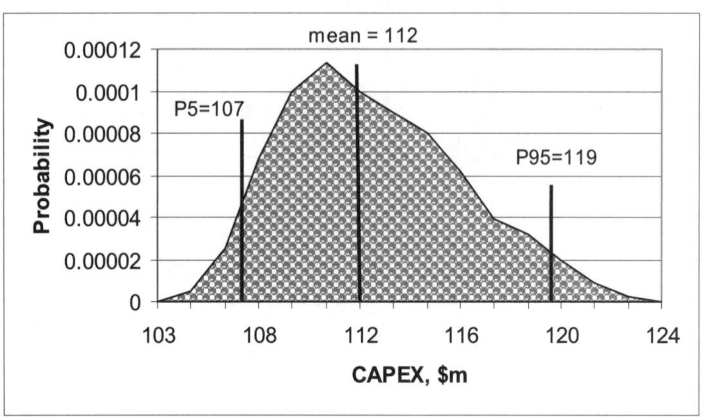

Figure 9.11 Simple cost estimation

The mean cost value is still $112m as before. The minimum value in the 5000 iterations is $103m and the largest is $124m. Both values differ from the total in the low and high columns above, supporting the notion that the common practice of combining the low and high values overstates the range of outcomes.

With a range from $103m to $124m, which value should be used in analyzing the project? The answer is all of them. The mean value is useful when working at operating company or corporate level for portfolio decisions, along with the standard deviation. The most likely value has the highest chance of occurring for a single project. However, when dealing with partners where authorizations are required, probably the P_{95} or P_{90} value should be used.

A more important issue relates back to dependencies between cost inputs. A simple, highly effective format for introducing dependencies is the correlation matrix. We recommend using the correlation matrix only in the early stages of the project management for reasons explained later in the scheduling section.

Example 9.10b adds correlations between the various components of the cost estimation. These data are usually generated subjectively by experienced staff, or by using data from similar projects. Either way, as Chapters 6 and 8 indicate, the correlation values themselves are subject to some uncertainties. Example 9.10b extends the same example by adding a correlation matrix for the interaction among the variables.

Example 9.10b: Correlation among inputs.

	Design	Equipment	Support Structure	Electrical, Plumbing, etc.	Labor	Indirects
Design	1	0.65	0.37	0.87	0.44	0.95
Equipment		1	0.25	0.42	0.35	0.56
Support Structure			1	0.24	0	0.6
Electrical				1	0.25	0.87
Labor					1	0.5
Indirects						1

Most simulation software allows the user to input these correlations. Unfortunately, older software never tested to see if the inputs complied with the basic properties of matrices. Without going into the details of matrix algebra, the basic rule is that the matrix cannot have negative determinants. This means that the correlations actually imply that there is more causation in the model than can possibly take; effectively the correlations explain more than 100% of the variation. Sportscasters are fond of saying that an athlete gave 110%, but matrix algebra won't allow it.

Example 9.10c: Modify correlation based on *eigenvalues.*

	Design	Equipment	Support Structure	Electrical, Plumbing, etc.	Labor	Indirects
Design	1	0.63	0.36	0.85	0.43	0.93
Equipment		1	0.24	0.41	0.34	0.55
Support Structure			1	0.23	0	0.59
Electrical				1	0.24	0.85
Labor					1	0.49
Indirects						1

When the software computed the determinant for the "symmetric, idempotent" matrix, it found a negative determinant and then used the eigenvalues to modify the input correlations. The initial correlations were modified as shown in the following example. In general, the changes are minor and actually have minimal impact on the results unless the correlations are highly exaggerated.

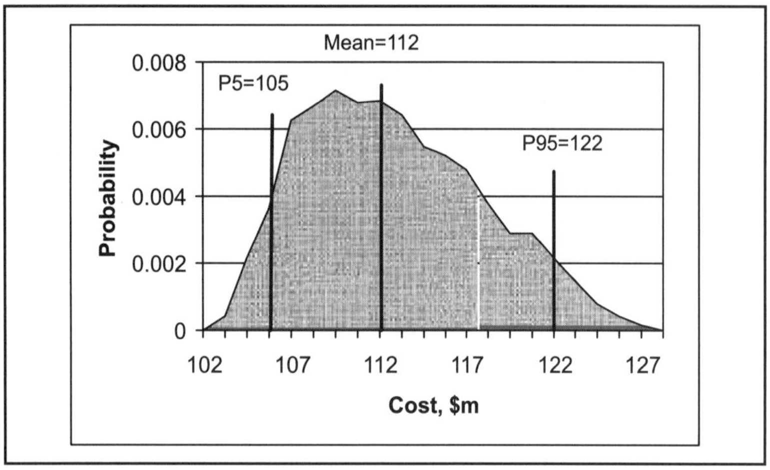

Figure 9.12 Cost distribution with dependency

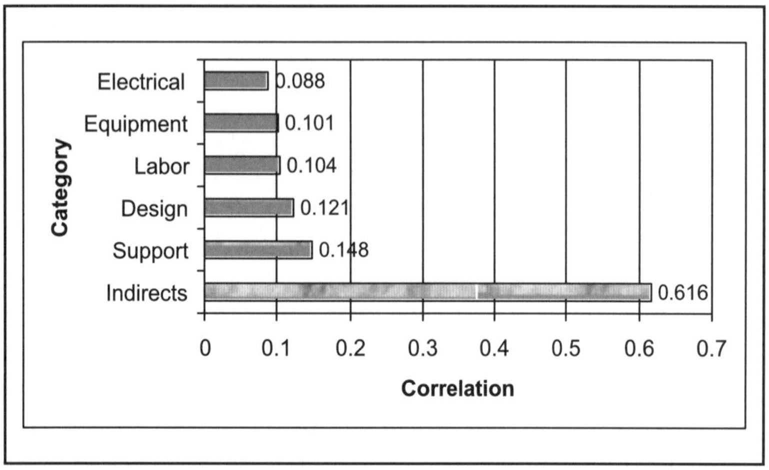

Figure 9.13 Tornado diagram for simple cost estimate

The impact of the positive correlations is at the edges of the distribution, as seen in Figure 9.12. The mean still equals \$112 million, but the P_{95} rises to \$122 from \$119, while the low value falls to \$105 from the uncorrelated value of \$107.

This difference is trivial, especially in the early, conceptual stages of a project. What is important here, besides the variability, are the sources of that variability? Project management is about understanding the sources of risk and seeking to correct or minimize the problem. Tornado diagrams provide the best source of information about where to look for risk mitigation. Figure 9.13 shows the tornado diagrams for the cost estimation example.

The tornado diagram for the cost estimates is given in Figure 9.13. The indirect category dominates the variability in project cost, with a correlation over 61%. None of the other variables contributes more than 15% to the variability in the cost estimates. This conclusion should be self-evident based on the initial ML costs and the distributions assigned to the project. In the presentation of the original data in Example 9.10a, the indirect and equipment were about the same magnitude, but the equipment category had very little variation in the estimate. Indirect costs varied almost 50%, however. This variation dominates the generation of the tornado graph.

The next question is "So what?" The benefit of the tornado diagram arises from the ability to select the critical inputs for detailed analysis. The tornado diagram directs attention to the sources of the indirect cost, and says lets minimize effort put into the electrical, etc. and equipment cost right now. By the time the detailed phase is reached, more attention may be required, but not now.

Contingency Analysis

A common practice in the cost estimation is to include a category called: *contingency costs.* Some common definitions of contingency can be found in an article by Lorance and Wending.[(9.6)] The cited definitions include the following:

- An assessment made by a team of professionals, of the amount of funds which, when added to the line item estimate will reflect an equal chance of under run or overrun given relative stability of the scope and assumptions upon which the estimate is based.
- An amount added to an estimate to allow for changes that experience shows will likely be required. May be derived either through statistical analysis of past projects or by applying

experience from similar projects. Usually includes changes in scope or unforeseeable major events such as strikes, earthquakes, etc.[9.7]

- A contingency reserve is a separately planned quantity used to allow for future situations, which may be planned for only in part (sometimes called "known unknowns"). For example, rework is certain, the amount of rework is not. Contingency may involve cost, schedule, or both. Contingency reserves are intended to reduce the impact of missing cost or schedule objectives. Contingency is normally included in the project cost and schedule baseline.[9.8]
- The amount budgeted to cover costs that may result from incomplete design, unforeseen or unpredictable conditions, or uncertainties. The amount of the contingency depends on the status of the design, procurement, and construction and complexity and uncertainty of the component parts of the project. Contingency is not to be used to avoid making an accurate assessment of expected costs.

Taken together these definitions seem to mean that contingency is anything you want it to be. In reality, most investors define contingency as a percentage of the mean or P_{50} cost estimate. The selection of the range is computed from the cost estimate percentiles. Example 9.10d gives the percentiles and the contingency computed assuming an 80% confidence interval.

Example 9.10d: Derive the contingency cost if the investor wants to be at or less than the designated cost 90% of the time.

		Contingency	
Percentiles	**Cost $M**	**Amount**	**%**
10%	106.2		
20%	107.8		
30%	109.2		
40%	110.6		
50%	112.0	8.4	7.5
60%	113.6		
70%	115.4		
80%	117.5		
90%	120.4		

The 90% confidence value is $120.4 million, so if we use the P_{50} value of $112 as the base case the project needs to add $8.4 (120.4 – 112.0) to be 90% sure that they will fall below the cost estimate. The same logic can be applied to other categories, if needed. Should the investor decide to use the expected value, and that value differs from the P_{50}, a little more work is required, but the process is the same as that illustrated here.

While contingency is a very important concept in cost estimation, the approach used to generate the cost estimates to this point misses the main objectives of project analysis. First, working on summary cost estimates ignores the critical aspect of scheduling and timing. Historically, summary costs were easier to generate because of the limited analytical tools. Building detailed schedules with specific costs takes far less time with current software. Project analysis requires the time specific cost estimates, not summary costs presented here.

Second, the correlation method for addressing dependencies at a summary level fails to capture the significant relationships between variables, over time or in the aggregate. Building detailed schedules, including interactions across inputs, whenever possible enhances the understanding of all these issues. The next section addresses deterministic and stochastic project scheduling

Scheduling and Management

Part of successful project management depends on the understanding of how the components change over time and interrelate with each other. A multitude of software packages allow detailed scheduling of projects, in the form of Pert or Gantt charts. An Internet search using Gantt, Pert, or project management produces multiple sites with applicable software that can be downloaded for free or at low cost. These are useful for the beginner to develop a feel for the process.

The fundamental question posed by many is, "Why bother with the extra work?" The answer is multifaceted, but boils down to "improving your cost estimation" and project management. The critical importance of cost and revenue timing on performance metrics, because of the time value of money, makes detailed understanding of schedule a critical element in risk assessment and management. In fact, failure to understand the importance of scheduling means the investment is probably sub-optimized. Moreover, though the correlations used above improve cost estimation, they seldom capture the interrelationship among the cost components adequately.

Figure 9.14 displays a basic Gantt chart using the same cost categories from the previous examples. The example assumes 14 time periods, without defining the units (months, quarters, years, etc.). Assuming consistent analysis, the total cost in the last column should equal the previously used costs. The basic process multiplies the time required for each task by the appropriate period rate. Moreover, each category can be subdivided into finer grids depending on the level of detail desired.

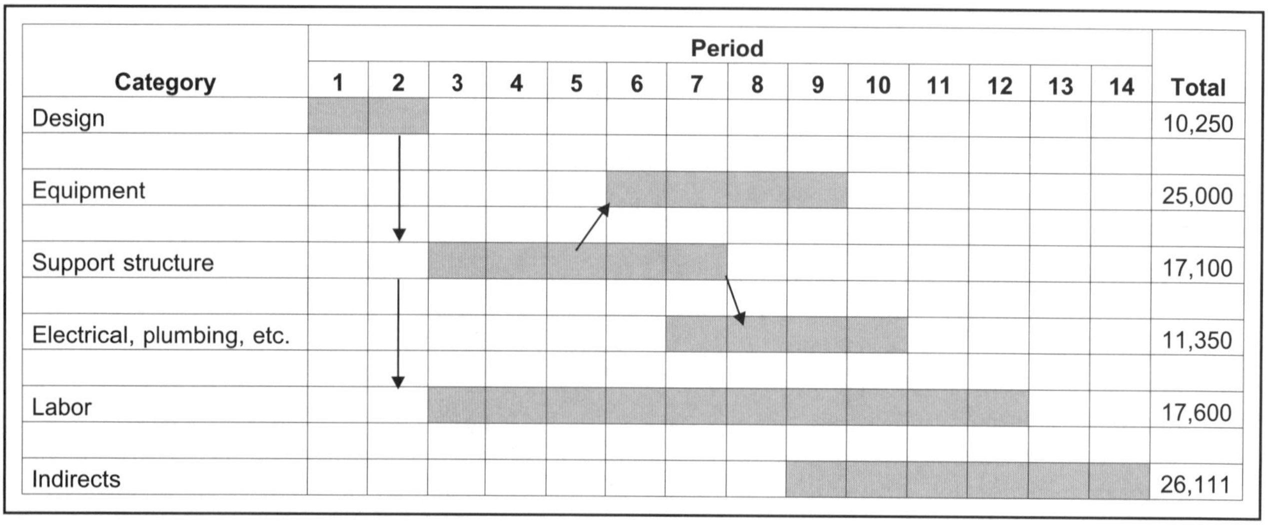

Figure 9.14 Example of Gantt scheduling diagram

Such formats are ideal for incorporating a major component of risk'; namely, the time required to complete a task. The plan may call for 5 periods to complete the support structure, but bad weather, strikes, and delays in the delivery of construction materials may cause significant delays in the timing. Even worse, later stages, like equipment installation and the associated electrical, plumbing, etc. depend on the support structure before they can start. Delays in one-component force modifications in other components. Depending on the actual contract provisions, the effects compound as the project progresses. Statistically, this is a case with significant dependence between the components.

Previous students have often asked about the source of the correlation cited earlier. Figure 9.14 indicates the primary cause of the correlation. A few arrows are included in the figure to show that one component begins at a specific time relative to another component. For instance, beginning the support structure before completing the design makes little sense. Likewise, installing the equipment requires the support structure to be at a certain stage.

Though very simple, the figure highlights the major dependencies between the project components. Figure 9.15 expands the Gantt chart to include delays at each stage. The cross hatched lines indicate a delay in the design stage that delays the onset of the other components. The checkerboard boxes reflect variation in the timing of each component, independent of the other stages.

Those familiar with Gantt charts realize the simplicity of the example. The real world can be far, far more complicated. However, the objective here is to illustrate the impact of detailed versus simpler risk assessment, not to explain detailed project management and scheduling.

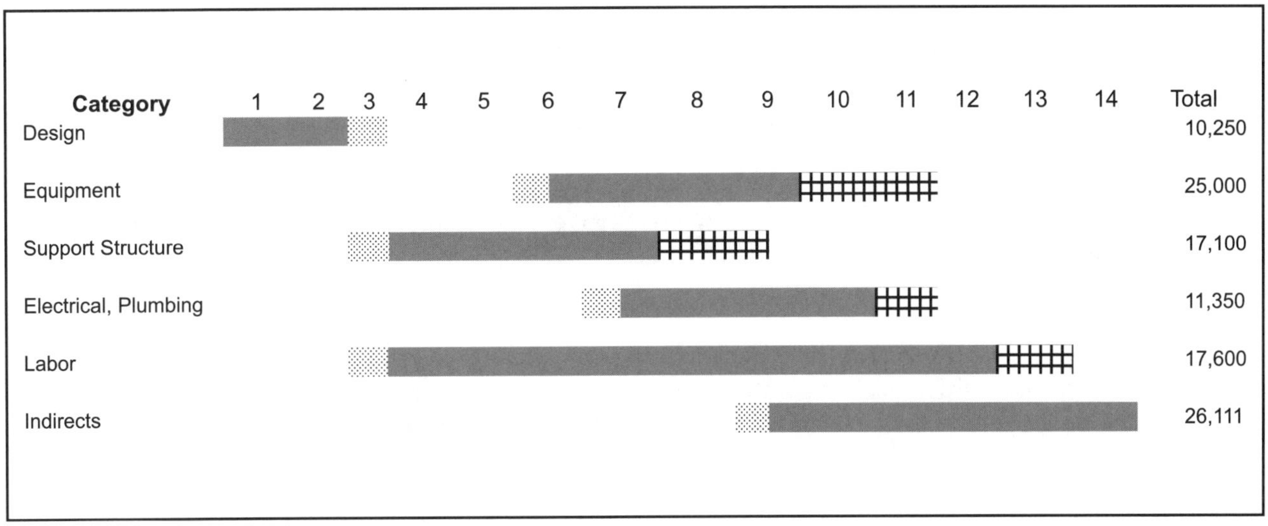

Figure 9.15 Gantt chart with time risk

The impact of linking schedules, as opposed to using correlations among categories, is clearly defined in Figure 9.16. The detailed scheduling displays an entirely different risk pattern from the simple correlation. The difference is caused by the perfect dependence between the cost categories when detailed scheduling occurs. Correlations, even with large numbers, fail to accurately capture the sequential nature of the project components.

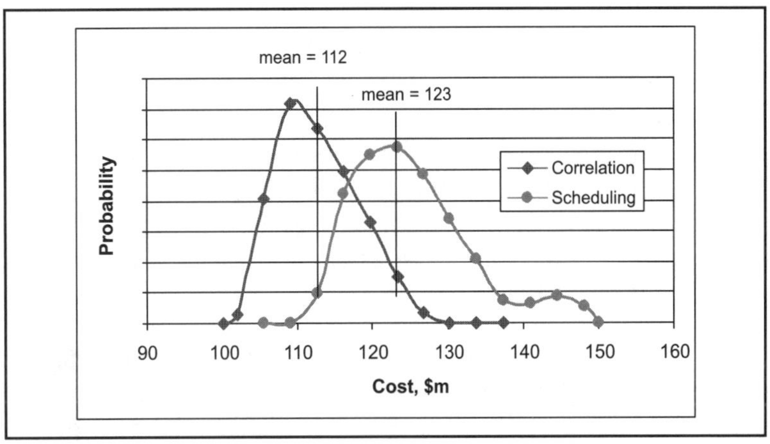

Figure 9.16 Comparison of risk with detailed scheduling vs. correlations

Not only are the means quite different, the entire nature of the curve varies. The correlation approach misses the higher costs, and the relative likelihood of significant cost overruns. The bi-modal cost curves shown in the scheduling option dramatically impacts investment decision-making and risk perception.

The scheduling curve more accurately depicts the likely cost variation and pattern owing to its formal recognition of the sequential aspects of design and construction. Cost estimation models that ignore the sequential scheduling of events will usually misrepresent possible outcomes. It is possible that the correlation approach could approximate the scheduling result. To be sure that the cost estimates represent future events fairly, those correlations must be established very carefully and with some rigor.

Judgment obtained from experienced personnel helps immensely in generating such correlations. For younger staff, however, nothing beats developing formal project schedules and then following the progress. The lessons learned from this approach ultimately define "experience." As an anecdote, I had a long chat with a construction engineer while waiting for the weather to clear enough for our plane to take off. He stated that he could estimate construction costs and timing within 10% of actual (for a multinational fast food chain), with very little effort. Assuming this was true, I asked him how long he had worked before he could do this. Without hesitation, he said, "20 years and the mistakes I made probably outweigh the savings I generate now."

BIDDING & ASSET ACQUISITION

Acquiring the ownership of any asset, be it minerals, a McDonalds chain, a cellular phone franchise, etc. at a price that allows the investor to make money, dominates the factors that determine the ultimate success or failure of an investment. Two forces contribute to most to investment success: amount paid for the asset, and adequate financing until the asset begins to produce revenues. This section addresses determination of a fair bid for any type of asset. While the process is the same across industries, the specific tax recovery schemes will differ.

Bidding schemes come in a variety of formats, but all involve money flowing from the bidder to the seller. The primary differences entail the guarantees related to the money flows, and, hence, the relative risk to the buyer and the seller. Some common bidding formats include:

- Cash payment up front
- Royalty bid
- Profit sharing
- Working interest
- Work program
- Cash and WI combination
- Capital recovery profit sharing

The up-front cash payment probably covers more than 90% of the asset exchanges, because it is easy and simple. Royalty bid are typified by franchisees, especially restaurants, where a specified percentage of every dollar received goes to the owner. This may be up to 15%. Under profit sharing, the investor pays all costs, but disburses a fixed percentage of the profits (after cost recovery) to the original owner. Under the WI format, the seller will pay directly some costs. Under the work program, the buyer acquires the right to the asset by spending money directly on the asset, instead of giving it to the seller. This is quite common with fixed aging assets, like a building, and mineral acquisition, where the work program runs seismic and drills well.

The actual mechanism for transferring ownership depends on the relative needs and objectives of the buyer and seller, and is limited only by their creativity and the willingness to work together. This section illustrates the cash payment or bonus system because of its dominance. The same issues apply to the other formats, but the relative risk and return trade-off differs.

CHAPTER 9

Deterministic Approach

The classical approach to asset valuation follows the format outlined in Example 9.11. The AT NPV of the asset is the estimated revenue less the relevant cost estimates. The simple process in the example has an NPV of $30m, found by inputting the cost and revenues into the appropriate software.

The process appears quite simple and it really is. What concerns the parties involved is "Am I paying too much," or "Am I selling too low." The answer, of course, depends on ones views about the future, and that is the source of contention in asset exchanges. The seller sees the upside potential and the buyer weights the risks more.

Example 9.11: Determine the NPV of the asset being acquired. All values in $m.

After-tax NPV_{10} of:				
(1) NCF	= (2) Revenue	– (3) Opex	– (4) Capex	– (5) Bid
30	100	15	45	10

Ignoring input risk, asset valuation follows a logical process that begins with formulating the problem as shown in Equation 9.5. This would be the case of a franchisee looking to become a restaurant or auto supply dealer. In addition, mineral companies compete in the same manner.

$$\text{NPV} = \text{AT Revenue} * (1 - \text{R}) - \text{AT Opex} - \text{AT Capex} - \text{X} * \text{B} \qquad \textbf{(9.5)}$$

where: R is royalty rate, X is the after-tax impact of the bonus, and B is the bonus or sale price.

Because most asset transfers involve competition against unseen and often unknown competition, establishing the maximum payment that will achieve the specified objectives under alternative conditions first. In the example, a \$15 M BT bonus generated a \$10 M AT bonus, so X = 0.667 (= 10/15). The Chapter 8 appendix describes how to establish X if you don't have access to the right software. If R = 0, then the maximum bonus payment is:

$$0 = 100 * (1 - 0) - 45 - 15 - \text{B} * 0.667, \quad \textit{or}$$

$$\text{B} = 40/0.667 = \$59.97 \text{ million}$$

The maximum bonus payment exceeds the project NPV owing to the tax-relief. In countries where bonus payments are excluded from tax computations, the maximum bonus equals the project NPV.

Solving for the maximum royalty follows the same process.

$$0 = 100 * (1 - \text{R}) - 45 - 15 - 0, \text{ or}$$

$$\text{R} = 40/100 = 0.40 \text{ or } 40\%$$

Since successful bids combine royalty and bonus, Figure 9.17 combines the two options into one graph. The negatively sloped curve intersects the respective axis at the maximum royalty and bonus. Below the line and toward the origin, NPV increases. NPV reaches its maximum at the origin: no royalty or bonus. Bonus and royalty combinations above and to the right of the line yield a negative NPV.

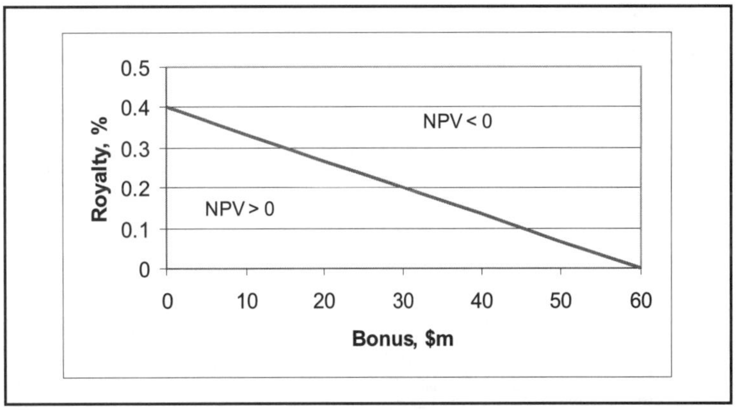

Figure 9.17 Bonus and royalty trade-off

In formal bid evaluations, investors observe how the line changes with different assumptions, like prices, volumes, Capex, etc. Figure 9.18 extends the last graph to include an 80% reduction in volume and a 90% Capex sensitivity. The NPV at the 80% volume level is 10 = 100 ∗ 0.8 – 45 – 15 – 10. The maximum royalty equals 0.25 = (30 – 10)/80 and the maximum bonus is \$30m = 20/0.667.

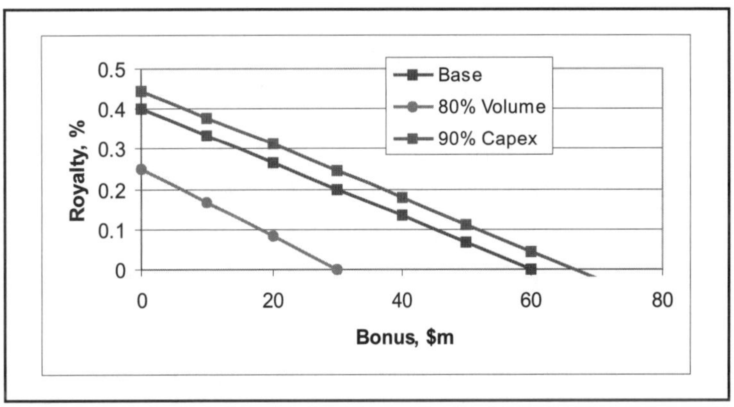

Figure 9.18 Sensitivities on maximum royalty and bonus

The maximum combination of royalty and bonus changes dramatically as the inputs vary, though volume has a greater impact than Capex. This simple analysis emphasizes the importance of the analysis assumptions on the value estimates. As price, cost, discount rate, overhead charges, etc. vary between buyer and seller, and across competitors, estimated value can adjust dramatically.

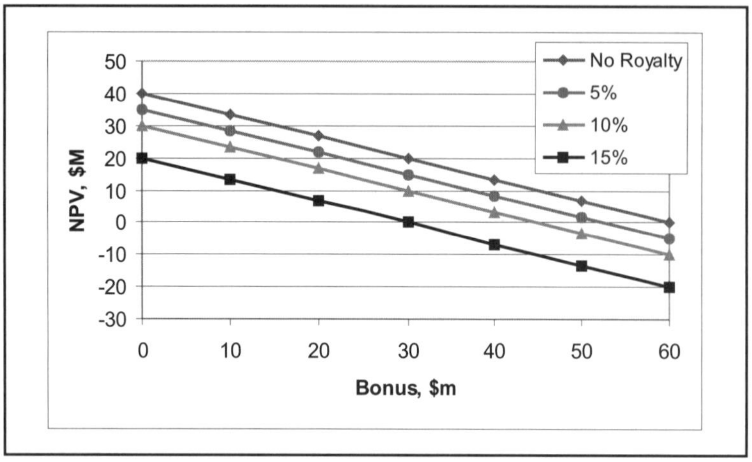

Figure 9.19 Maximum bonus at various royalty rates

The last two graphs convey information about NPV relative to the breakeven point (NPV = 0). Though useful for determining maximum bids, making a bid decision requires direct information on the NPV for different bid amounts. To read NPV for alternative bid amounts requires manipulating the basic equation slightly. Figure 9.19 displays a separate line for different royalty rates. The x-axis gives the pre-tax bonus bid, and the y-axis now measures the project NPV for the specified royalty and bid amounts.

At a 10% royalty rate, a BT bonus of $30 million generates a positive NPV of $10 million. Decision makers can easily determine the combination of royalty and bonus to achieve the desired return.

Such formats work quite well when the asset exists with certainty. In those instances, where reserves may not exist, that uncertainty must be recognized. The *EMV* (Chapter 8) includes the chance that the asset exists (or doesn't exist). The basic equation again is:

$$\text{EMV} = P_S * \text{NPV of Success} - (1 - P_S) * \text{NPV of Failure} \quad \textbf{(9.6)}$$

where: P_s = chance of minerals existing, and the other variables are defined as before.

Equation 9.6 can be modified to define failure as the sum of the bonus cost plus any expenditure needed to establish the existence of the minerals, usually one or more wells plus maybe some seismic. Assuming that the well cost (AT) is $5 million, the equation becomes:

$$\text{EMV} = P_S * \text{NPV}_S - (1 - P_S) * (\text{NPV}_F + X * B)$$

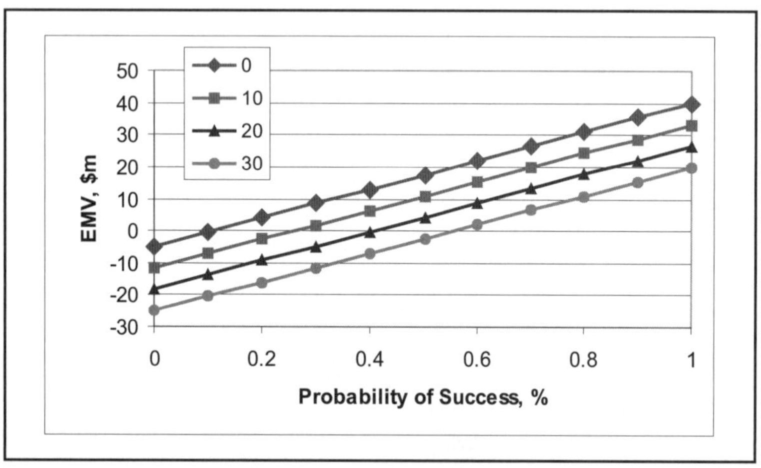

Figure 9.20 Maximum bonus at various royalty rates

Because two variables are uncertain here, P_s and B, the graphs normally include a range of bonus lines based on previous graphs. Figures 9.19-9.20 provides guidance on the maximum bids that can be made. Investors seldom bid the maximum, so they establish guidelines, like 50% of the maximum bid. The rule changes depending on the competitive interest in an investment opportunity. Analysts construct graphs like Figure 9.20.

The project EMV varies with the chance of success and the bonus bid. One important piece of information is the breakeven P_s for each bid curve. For no bonus bid, the line crosses the x-axis at around 10%. The breakeven point shifts to 25%, 40%, and about 55% as the bid amount goes to 10, 20, and 30 million, respectfully.

The information contained in these graphs, though commonly used and informative, still fails to indicate what bid will enhance our chances of winning. All the graphs establish boundary conditions, but never suggest the best strategy. This approach merely conveys information about bid guidelines based on our assumptions. No information exists about risk in the valuation or the any consideration of competitors. Competitor issues are addressed in *game theory,* which this book doesn't cover.

The psychological and emotional objectives of bidders equal the importance of the technical elements in the valuation metrics, and may actually be more important. Like many forms of gambling (which some characterize investing as a legal equivalent to investing), the most optimistic bidder wins the asset, only to lose the war if they bid too much. In fact, the surest way to maximize the sale of your assets is to hold a public auction. Just the process of holding a competitive bid tends to escalate the winning price, as the competitive juices of the bidders takes hold, as EBAY.com demonstrates daily..

Besides the differences in assumptions that influence bids, other elements play a significant role. We have seen instances where people bid more than $400 million more than the expected value because they had been told they would have to leave one office location (San Francisco) and move to another (Houston) if they were unsuccessful. The bid was justified by inflating production volume and success values. Others acquired assets, for office locations in the mountains, seashore, or overseas, by being optimistic. Such situations occur a small percentage of the time, but happen enough to make the post evaluation of bids very entertaining.

Formal Risk Analysis

The accelerating movement toward direct risk assessment significantly alters the thought process in formulating bids. The classical format permits direct comparison of only 2 to 3 variables at a time, when reality dictates that many more variables interact to determine ultimate success or failure. The acquisition analysis outside the mineral industry carefully integrates the multitude of forces determining value, not just one element. Most mineral companies are just now beginning to move beyond their historical sub-surface focus.

The limited perspective was certainly understandable when deterministic methods ruled. In addition, the sub-surface professionals were the first to embrace stochastic methods. Mineral industry professionals perceive that a unique set of conditions applies to them: they can't touch or feel their manufacturing system, the mineral deposit. Though true, all industries engaged in research and development or developing a new product with unknown demand face similar failure risk. This section begins with the classic mineral limited format, which focusses on just the sub-surface, and then proceeds to the more detailed approach.

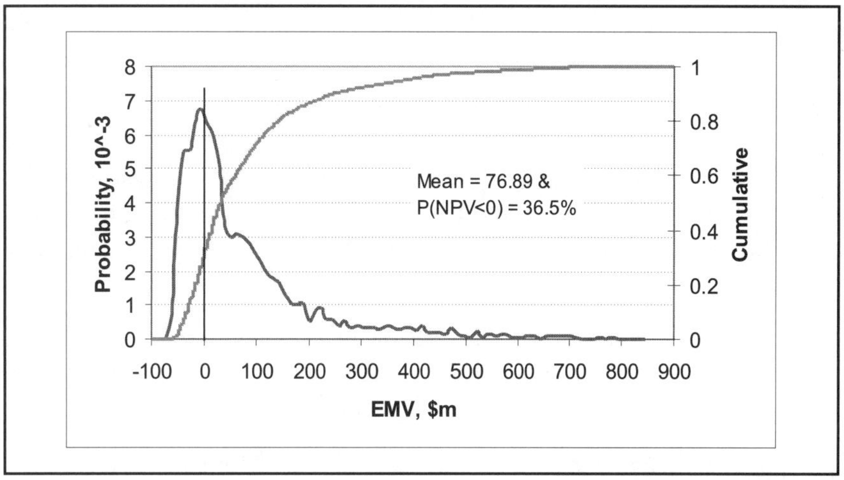

Figure 9.21 Relative and cumulative EMV for subsurface bid analysis

Traditional mineral analysis assumes that only three variables vary: reserves, probability of success, and cost of failure. The actual distributions are unimportant, but can be obtained by contacting the authors. The mean EMV is $76.89 million, based on a P_s that ranges from 10% to 25%. Observe that the investment loses money, over 36% of the time. The number reflects the combination of P_s and the occasions when the project loses money, because the reserve volume is too low to recover the investment cost. The median or P_{50}, as read from the cumulative values on the right y-axis, is slightly more than $80 million.

CHAPTER 9

As an aside, a continual debate rages over the benefits of presenting a relative curve (left y-axis) or a cumulative curve (right y-axis). No simple answer exists; it depends upon the users comfort and experience. Our belief is that both graphs together add more value than a single graph. The cumulative graph disguises the irregular outcomes, but communicates directly the P_{50} and chance of losing money. Computing and graphing such curves is so easy, we prefer to see both.

Figure 9.18 showed the EMV based on volume and cost risks. The important question is still "what do I offer for the asset?" Without knowing the specific circumstances of the competitive bid, the sources of money, etc., easy answers are elusive. One useful approach modifies the EMV computation, as shown in Equation 9.7. The equation seeks to find the bid that yields a \$0 EMV.

$$0 = P_s*(NPV - B*X_1) - (1 - P_s)(W + B*X_2) \quad \textbf{(9.7)}$$

where: B is the bonus payment, X_1 is the AT, discounted impact from a commercial success, W is the cost of failure (\$M), and X_2 is the AT discounted impact of a bid that wins the asset, but loses money. The element of interest is B. To find the value that sets the equation equal to zero, inserting the equation into MathCAD™ gives the following result.

$$B = \left[\frac{-(P_s*NPV - W + P_s*W)}{(-P_s*X_1 - X_2 + P_s*X_2)}\right] \quad \textbf{(9.8)}$$

For any combination of the inputs, the equation computes the maximum bonus. The distribution for maximum bonus, based on the previous graph, is shown in Figure 9.22.

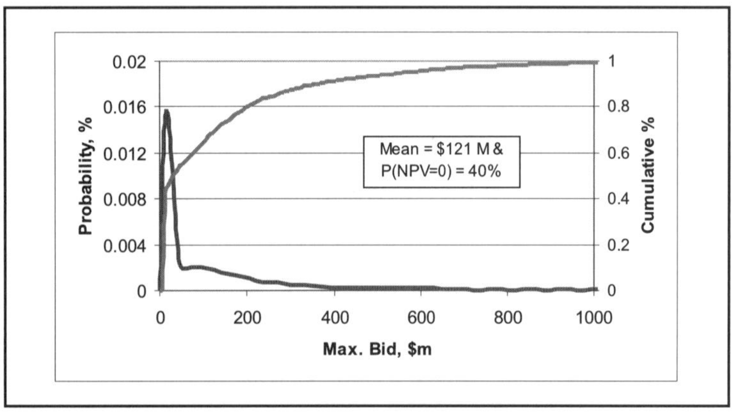

Figure 9.22 Maximum bonus for subsurface bid analysis

The mean or average bonus bid that sets EMV equal to zero is \$121 million. This value exceeds the EMV, excluding bonus by the effective tax relief from expensing failed investments, or using the appropriate capital recovery process when successful. The example follows the US convention by depleting the bonus using units-of-production.

The example seeks the maximum bonus that will generate a \$0 EMV for the project. Since sales volume may be inadequate, the chance of success is too low, or a combination of both, the simulation suggests that no bid would be the best outcome in 40% of the cases. This is slightly higher owing to the impact of the bonus.

The unresolved question still concerns the bonus to bid. Analysis by Ed Capen, John Lohrenz and others in the petroleum industry suggests that, historically, a mean value bid yields about a \$0 EMV, as expected, or \$121 million in this case. This suggests that the analytical process is correct.

The difference between the analysis of historical performance and future decisions is crucial. The historical perspective reflects actual variation among the inputs – prices, Opex, Capex, inflation, etc, not estimates. The crucial question turns to the sensitivity of the models used to approximate such variables. Previous chapters addressed the failures in the individual variable estimates; while, the combined impact of the variability among the inputs attracts our attention.

Figure 9.23 highlights the difference between the subsurface approach and a more complete approach, where all variables, including price, inflation, Opex, etc. are allowed to change. The analysis uses 5000 iterations and the same seed values, as outlined in Chapters 6 and 8.

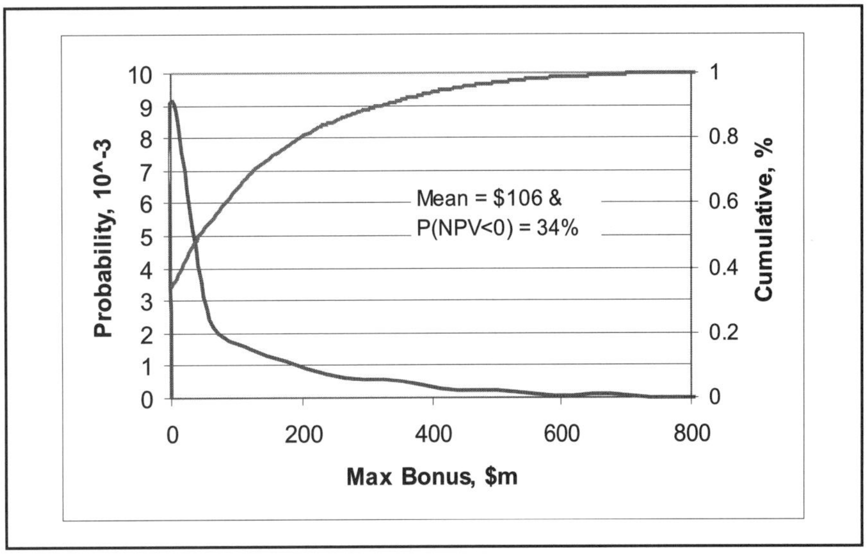

Figure 9.23 Maximum bonus for detailed bid analysis

Several important elements differ between the two models. First, the mean bonus bid falls to $106 million, down from $121m. The roughly 12% lower value indicates that the simpler models overstate the bid price. Still on the negative side of changes, observe that the scale stops at $800m for the detailed model, while the subsurface model goes to almost a billion. Clearly, the simpler models place a greater weight on upside potential, even though the chances are quite small,

The detailed model improves the perception of risk, as well. The lowered probability that the value falls below zero (34% instead of 40%) suggests that the subsurface model overstates risk (by this measure). The discrepancy arises from the simplifying assumption that volume changes don't impact costs in the subsurface model. Recognizing that volume leads to different production decisions mirrors reality, and that reality reduces risk. Some call this options thinking, meaning the investor has the option to alter the production system later on.

Determining the best bid still eludes us. Part of the problem stems from the vast differences in the objectives of the bidders: some view the process as a competition, where beating the opposition dominates, others seek to add value to the treasury. The two positions often conflict with each other and lead to some very odd results in the real world. Credible evidence comparing the "right bid" to the actual bid has never been presented, primarily because of the problem in quantifying "right." Without detailed knowledge of bidder objectives, establishing "right" is difficult.

Historical studies attempt to quantify bid value relative to true value, but lacking information on discount rate, pricing, strategic issues, the analysis can only address pure profit objectives. Though making a profit dominates investment decision-making, other, equally important issues impact bid decisions.

The previous figures graphically represent a common format for bid analysis, based on EMV. The entire process understates the real economic variability. Figure 9.24 shows why.

Failure costs vary from roughly negative $10 to $30 million, and the success case ranges from negative $100 million to over $3,500 million. EMV produces an average amount of $72 million, which appears to be very different from the two curves separately.

This format captures a major complaint of risk assessment methods; namely, the formal assessment of risk encourages risk aversion. Those organizations that have successfully implemented risk methods receive considerable criticism from technical professionals. These professionals argue that the methodology stifles creativity and risk taking. They are right about the consequences, but forget the motivation. EMV originated from the gambling industry, and perhaps the best way to understand the contradiction is to return to the gambling analogy.

EMV measures a fair bet, but gambling establishments, worldwide, guarantee that the bettor usually has less than a 50/50 chance of winning, with a $1 bet winning a $1. Lotteries offer even worse odds. Why then do people buy lottery tickets with less than 1 in 10 million chance of winning, or sit for hours playing blackjack, keno, or other games where the EMV is negative. Chapter 8 discusses some of the

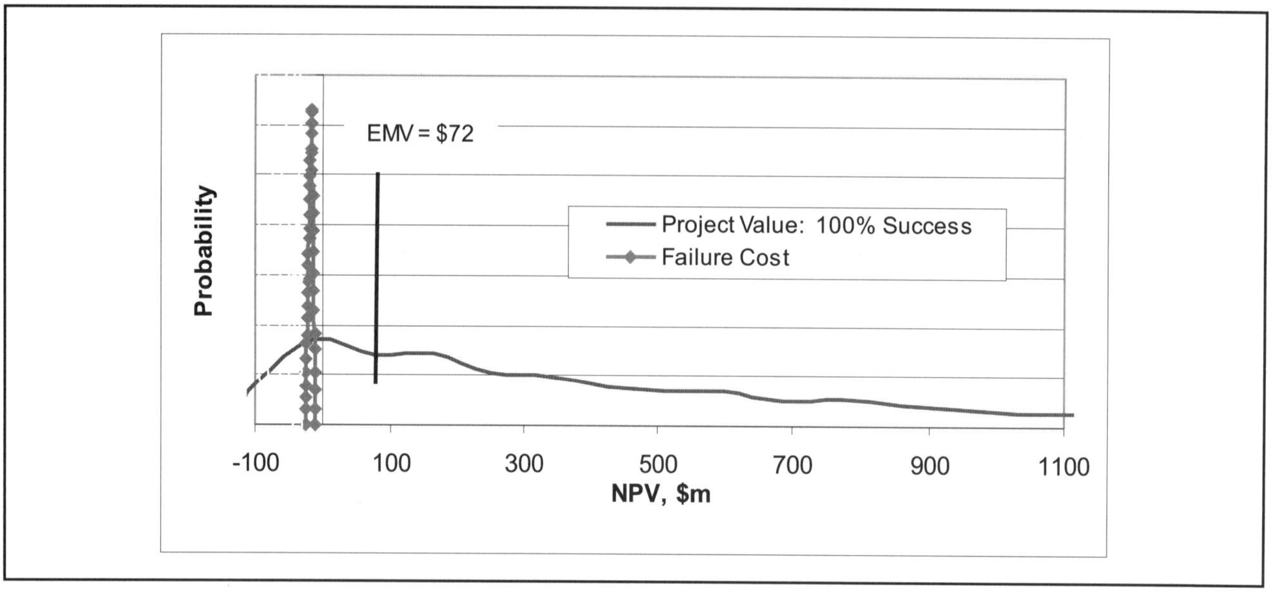

Figure 9.24 Combination of distributions to generate EMV

utility reasons, but we believe people see the upside, like that in Figure 9.23, and decide to go for it, especially if they believe in their science. Risking \$10 million to win \$1,000 million represents favorable odds to many technical professionals.

Is such an approach reasonable? Careers have been made on winning the lottery. EMV, being a discrete combination of two very different distributions, understates the upside, especially to a gambler, and, therefore does encourage risk aversion. The risk assessment critics are correct in this case. Does this mean risk assessment wastes time and resources? No, it means EMV tells only part of the story, not that risk assessment fails. EMV conveys very useful information about part of the risk story, but the successful investor will establish additional metrics as well.

VALUE OF INFORMATION

Most investment decisions are made when one or more important pieces of information face considerable uncertainty. This may include the existence of the supply, market demand, cost of raw materials, transportation network, safety or effectiveness of the product, etc. Investors seek to reduce the risk from these issues by engaging in research and development, clinical trials, market surveys, test marketing, and any other vehicle that collects information. Collecting information costs money and the balance between the cost of collection and improved investment performance challenges all investors.

This section outlines two, distinct methods for measuring the trade-off. One follows the classical *Bayesian statistics* approach, and the other continues the risk oriented methods used in the last section on bid analysis. In both instances, the question becomes "How much should be spent to optimize the risk & return trade-off of an investment opportunity." Many authors address the information valuation process.[9.9,9.10] Spending money to collect information must reduce risk, increase profit, or change the risk/return trade-off to enhance the treasury.

Bayesian Approach

Bayesian statistics originated with the works of Thomas Bayes (1701-1761), an English clergyman and philosopher. He was seeking tools for helping him in his study of the theory of logic and inductive reasoning. In the pursuit of improved decision-making, he developed Equation 9.9.

$$P(E_i|B) = \frac{P(B|E_i)*P(E_i)}{\sum_{i=1}^{n}[P(B|E_i)*P(E_i)]} \quad \textbf{(9.9)}$$

where E is an event that is captured in a set of N mutually exclusive and exhaustive events, and B is another non-zero event.

Many students have studied Bayes theorem and concluded that they would rather study thermodynamics. After rereading several statistical texts in writing this section, this notion has merit. In reality, however, Bayesian statistics formally addresses one of the major problems or worries plaguing risk based investment analysis: the source and quality of the probabilities. Rather than discuss the details of the equation, just accept that Bayes extends the decision tree concept discussed in Chapter 8 for the moment.

Bayes expanded classical statistics, which builds its foundation on actual occurrences of events or on a likelihood function, like saying volume follows a lognormal distribution. Both approaches produce a set of probabilities. However, Bayes believed that the future differs from the past, or new technology might alter the relevance of historical information. He sought a vehicle for adjusting historical or classical probabilities as new information, feelings, or opinions arose. A rational, orderly adjustment process of classical probabilities is the main purpose of Equation 9.9. In Bayes time, they referred to the new information as *subjective probabilities,* but the new information could also be quantitative.[9.11]

Figure 9.25 highlights the adjustment process. The first starts with the *prior distribution*, which is merely classical probability. The second box collects additional information, from a survey, subjective judgment, or research. This sample probability modifies the historical probability by first creating a *joint probability,* which is the product of the first two sets of information. After adjusting the product to normalize the probabilities, the result is a *posterior probability.*

Prior Probability	* Sample Probability	= Joint Probability	Posterior Probability
P (E)	P (B|E)	P (B, E)	P (E|B)

Figure 9.25 Simple illustration of Bayes theorem

Many believe the Bayesian system fails to capture reality, and, therefore, try to ignore it. The process addresses the problem of finding a mechanism for updating historical values, as new information becomes available. A current application of Bayesian analysis includes the clinical trials for establishing the merits of new drugs. The old approach split the test subjects into two groups: one receiving the new drug, and the other receiving a placebo. The relative differences between the two groups at the end of the study are attributed to the new drug. In life threatening illnesses, that meant the placebo group died at a higher rate. Bayesian statistics allows the researchers to update the control group and adjust the probabilities as the study goes along, reducing unnecessary deaths. A more common application exists in Microsoft Windows. The Office Assistant, which responds to help requests, modifies your typed in question based on recent keystrokes and activities to determine the list of responses to give you. That's why some of the responses seem so strange on occasion.

Example 9.12 begins with the basic decision tree and then expands the analysis to include imperfection. To use the Bayesian terminology, the probabilities are prior probabilities. Based on the

Example 9.12: Based on the following information for The Little or No Chance Prospect, make a recommendation to gather additional information.

1. Probability of Success: Trap ∗ (Reservoir, Source, etc.) = Total

   0.30 ∗ 0.6 = 0.18

2. Economics (NPV): Dry Hole = –$6.0 million

   Success = $21.0 million

3. Seismic research (NPV): $0.96 million if successful, and $0.72 if the prospect is dry. The BT cost of seismic is $1.2 million.

In a world with perfect research, the decision tree appears as follows:

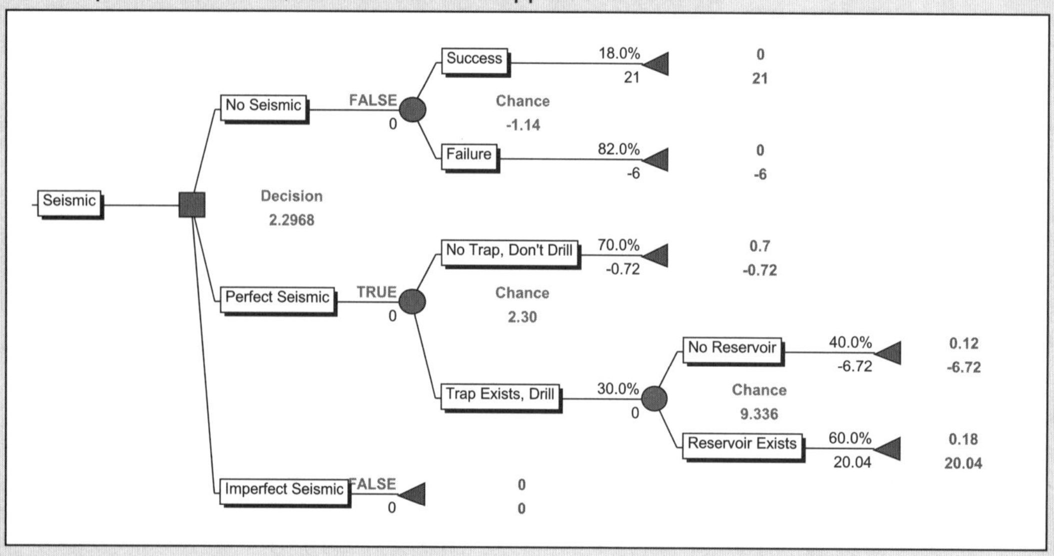

information in the tree, the value maximizing choice is to run the seismic, assuming the seismic is perfect, or 100% reliable.

Research or data collection seldom enhance value directly; they change the odds of events occurring. Running 3D seismic increases understanding about the subsurface environment and greatly improves the estimated probabilities. The process of collecting information is imperfect, however. The last line in the tree, called imperfect seismic, contains no information, because the Bayesian probabilities haven't been developed yet.

When talking about perfection or imperfection, perfect seismic means that when a trap does exist, seismic identifies it 100% of the time. This does not mean that if seismic identifies a trap, one exists 100% of the time. This allows the seismic to indicate a trap, even though none exists (a Type II error of accepting the null hypothesis when it is false). This benefits the analysis, because the probability of a trap goes to 1.0, from the 0.3 in the example, so the overall P_s becomes 0.6 instead of 0.18.

To obtain the Bayesian revised probabilities; assume that the seismic is 85% reliable for the moment. The complicating factor is the dependence between the P_{Trap} and the seismic reliability. The re-weighting of the joint probability is illustrated in the extension of the example.

Each column in the two tables sums to one, as statistics requires. If $1.2 million is spent on seismic, the odds of correctly identifying a trap rise to 70.8%, from the original 30% value. Similarly, the second table show that the chance of believing a trap exists, when none really exists, falls to 7%. Observe

Example 9.12: *(Cont'd.)*

Conditional Probabilities when Seismic Indicates a Trap				
State of Nature	**Original Value**	**Seismic Reliability**	**Joint Probability**	**Revised Probability**
Trap	0.30	0.85	0.255	0.255/0.36 = 0.708
No Trap	0.70	0.15	0.105	0.105/0.36 = 0.292
Total	1.00	1.00	0.360	1.00

Conditional Probabilities when Seismic Indicates No Trap				
State of Nature	**Original Value**	**Seismic Reliability**	**Joint Probability**	**Revised Probability**
Trap	0.30	0.15	0.045	0.045/0.64 = 0.070
No Trap	0.70	0.85	0.595	0.595/0.64 = 0.936
Total	1.00	1.00	0.640	1.00

that the summation of the joint probabilities is also 1.0 (= 0.36 + 0.64). The probability of success increases to 36% from the original 18% by running seismic with 85% reliability.

The outcomes are threefold: 1) don't drill when the seismic indicates no trap (64% chance); 2) a successful well occurs (0.425 = 0.6∗0.708); and 3) a dry hole occurs when seismic indicates a trap (0.575 = 1 – 0.425). These probabilities are taken from the last example and combined with the 60% chance of a reservoir existing.

Example 9.12 (Cont'd.), combines the revised probabilities with the cost and value estimates to compute the benefits of running the uncertain seismic.

Example 9.12: *(Cont'd.)*

	(1)	**(2)**	**(3)**	**(4)=(3)∗(2)**	**(5)=(1)∗4)**
Event	**NPV**	**Probability**	**Chances**	**Total**	**Revised Probability**
Success	20.04	0.425	0.36	0.153	3.066
Dry Hole	-6.72	0.575	0.36	0.207	-1.391
Do not Drill	-0.72		0.64	0.640	-0.461
Total		1.00			1.214

Running imperfect seismic enhances value by $1.214 million. The graphic exposition of the numbers is:

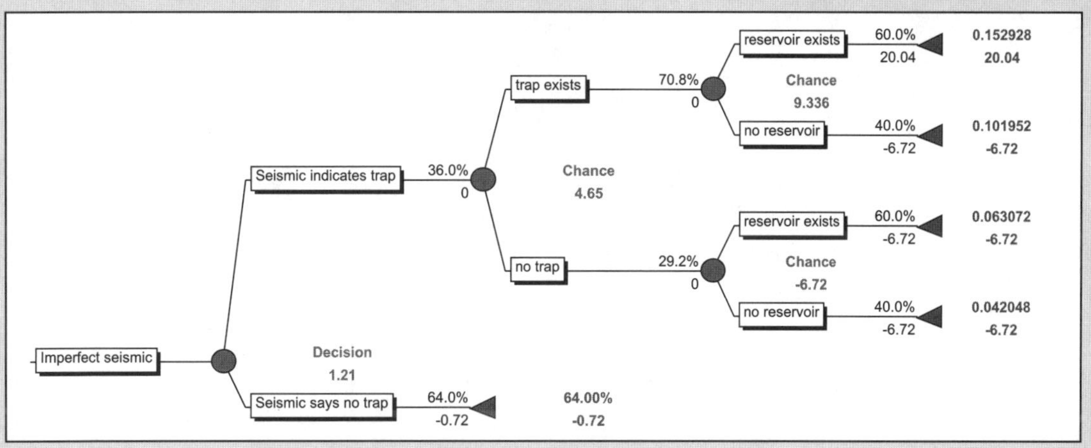

In previous editions of the book, we suggested that you trace the values back to previous examples. With the advent of good graphics software, a simpler approach is to show the information as a decision tree. The main difference between the graph and table is that the graph expands the dry hole row in the table to the three causes of failure. The sum of 0.1019, 0.063, and 0.042 in the tree equals the 0.207 in the dry hole and column 4 cell.

While the Bayesian analysis illustrates the basic concept for valuing imperfect information, several key areas are ignored; namely, seismic cost variation and uncertainty over the degree of imperfection in the seismic. Since reliability and cost both vary, it is sometimes useful to determine the combination of reliability and cost that generates a breakeven NPV (= 0). The Bayesian format can be extended to show the trade-off in cost and reliability, as shown in Equation 9.10

$$\text{Break even SC} = \frac{P_s * NPV_{success} - P_f * NPV_{DH}}{\left\{(1-P_T)*\frac{NPV_{AT\,SC\,DH}}{SC_{BT}} + P_s*\frac{NPV_{AT\,SC\,Success}}{SC_{BT}} + P_f*\frac{NPV_{AT\,SC\,DH}}{SC_{BT}}\right\}} \quad \textbf{(9.10)}$$

where:

P_s = the probability of success when both trap and reserves exist, for any given reliability (0.18)

P_f = probability of dry hole when seismic indicates a trap is present, (0.12).

P_T = probability of a trap, (0.3)

$NPV_{Success}$ = NPV of a successful well ($21.0)

NPV_{DH} = NPV of dry hole ($6.0)

$NPV_{AT\ SC\ Success}$ = AT NPV of seismic cost when well is successful, (= 0.96)

SC_{BT} = BT undiscounted cost of seismic (= 1.2)

$NPV_{AT\ SC\ DH}$ = AT NPV of seismic cost when well is a failure, (= 0.72)

The values in parenthesis are from the previous examples to help explain the terms. The probabilities differ slightly, because the focus is on the reliability question. The new terms, $NPV_{AT\ SC\ Success}$ and $NPV_{AT\ SC\ DH}$, when divided by SC_{BT}, convert the units for the problem to a per dollar unit. The 0.72/1.2 (= 0.6) value means that every dollar of seismic cost for a dry hole costs the investor $0.60. All the units in the denominator are on a per dollar basis, and gross up the monetary units in the numerator to before-tax amounts.

Example 9.13 illustrates the computation of the breakeven value at 100% and 85% reliability. As reliability decreases, the amount that can be spent also declines.

Example 9.13: Derive the breakeven seismic cost for 100% and 85% reliability, and then graph the findings.

100% Reliability

$$\text{Max SC} = \frac{0.18*21.0-0.12*6.0}{(1-0.30)*\frac{0.72}{1.20}+0.18*\frac{0.96}{1.20}+0.12*\frac{0.72}{1.20}}$$

$$= \frac{3.78-0.72}{0.42+0.144+0.072} = \frac{3.06}{0.636} = \$4.81 \text{ million}$$

Inserting the value of 4.81m into the basic equation confirms that this is the breakeven amount.

$$NPV = 0.7*(-4.81)*\frac{0.72}{1.20} + \left[21.0-4.81*\frac{0.96}{1.20}\right]*0.18 + \left[-6.0-4.81*\frac{0.72}{1.20}\right]$$

$$= -2.02 + 3.087 - 1.066 = \$0.0$$

Example 9.13: (Cont'd.)

85% Reliability

$$\text{Max SC} = \frac{0.153*21.0 - 0.207*6.0}{(0.64)*\frac{0.72}{1.20} + 0.153*\frac{0.96}{1.20} + 0.207*\frac{0.72}{1.20}}$$

$$= \frac{3.21 - 1.24}{0.384 + 0.122 + 0.124} = \frac{1.97}{0.636} = \$3.12 \text{ million}$$

The difference between the two cases is the result of the changing probabilities (0.7 to 0.57, 0.18 to 0.153, and 0.12 to 0.207). This illustrates the updating of classical probabilities as new information emerges.

A better format for presenting reliability issues is shown in Figure 9.26, where the solid line captures the breakeven combination of BT seismic cost and reliability, for the current data. NPV exceeds zero to the right of the line, thereby adding value, and destroys value to the left of the line. The dotted line shows the line for the same information when all inputs vary within a simulation context. At all reliabilities, the simulation shows a considerably lower breakeven or maximum seismic cost. This again illustrates the distortions that arise when the complexity of investment decisions are ignored.

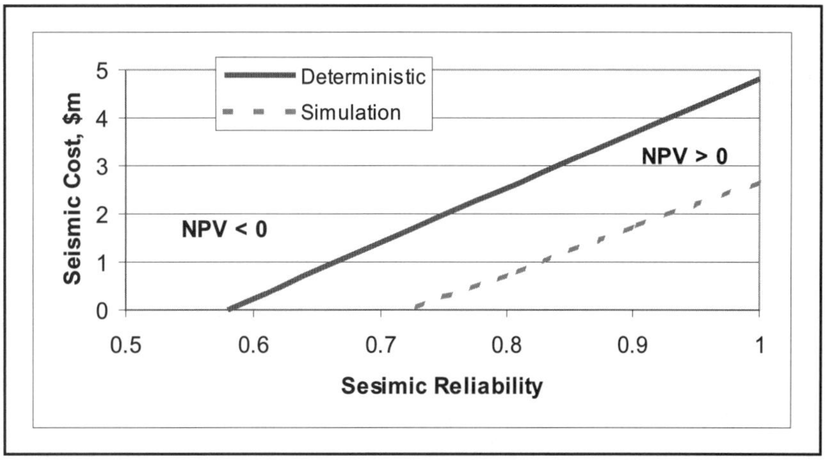

Figure 9.26 Sensitivity of breakeven line

Simulation Approach

Though Figure 9.26 derived the appropriate amount to spend on seismic with different degrees of seismic reliability, another format integrates the elements of the dotted line. Using the seismic information to alter risk or return profiles must still be portrayed to the investor. Figure 9.27 displays the overall impact of running the seismic.

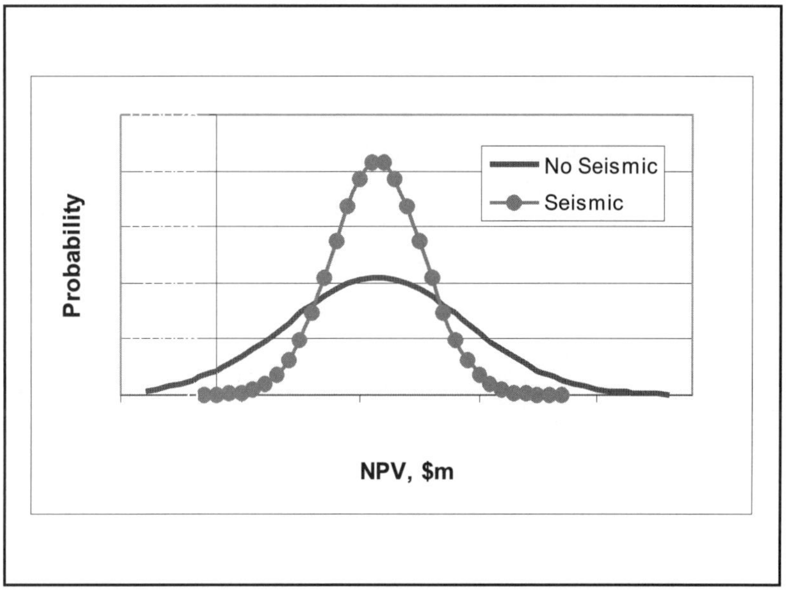

Figure 9.27 Economic benefit from running seismic

The actual distributions were simplified to fit a normal distribution, even though they were slightly skewed. The simplification illustrates that the overall mean of the two options was about the same. The

CHAPTER 9

benefit arises from reducing the volatility. The seismic option almost eliminates the probability of losing money; whereas, drilling without seismic overlapped into the negative quadrant.

The standard deviation is also smaller, which given the same mean NPV implies that seismic improved any of the risk adjusted value metrics discussed in Chapter 8. Even the simple ratio of risk to return favors running seismic.

Do not be misled by the analysis to date. All the examples demonstrate situations where the additional expenditure reduced risk or added value. Many cases have existed and will occur in the future, where the additional expenditure conveys no value at all, either in improving return or in reducing risk. Research and development fails sometimes, for a wide variety of reasons. Those failures lead to increased costs and no additional benefits, essentially making the No Seismic line broader, rather than narrower.

VALUE CHAIN ANALYSIS

One of the most difficult investment decisions centers on the need to model the interaction between different business entities, each with unique working interests, taxes, cost structures, etc. Modeling interactions improperly means that investors undervalue the real contribution of an asset to the treasury, ultimately leading to the misallocation of capital, and is crucial for investors truly serious about maximizing shareholder value. Multinational investors are composed of geographically and vertically related business entities, which sometimes interact with each other and other times deal with third parties.

Most valuation, whether risk or return, treats each business entity as a separate unit. The classical vertically integrated firm might separate their organization along business lines, like exploration or R&D, production, pipelines and transportation, processing, and retail sales. Exploration or R&D finds new commodities to sell. Production then decides the best way to bring it to market. Then, transportation conveys the product for processing, which then ships the final product to the retailer. Typically, each individual business entity performs a valuation from their perspective, where they buy materials from the previous unit in the chain and receive revenue from selling the output to the next link in the chain. When value is positive at every step along the chain, value presumably increases for the entire organization.

The word presumably was used in the last sentence, because just obtaining positive performance metrics may not actually maximize shareholder value. These suboptimal solutions occur quite frequently owing to the complexity in formulating value chains in traditional software. This chapter introduces one example for analyzing risk assessment, and then Chapter 10 considers optimization issues. Figure 9.28 shows a common value chain where three separate producing fields flow into a central platform, the Glenfiddich Platform, where the gas and liquids are processed and shipped to different onshore site locations. The investor has a WI in one satellite field, the Laphroaig Field, and the central processing unit, but no WI in two other fields, which pay a processing fee to Glenfiddich. The output from Glenfiddich then flows into two separate pipelines to onshore processing facilities. The investor has a different WI in Laphroaig, Glenfiddich, and the pipeline system.

Treating Laphroaig as a separate business entity means that the valuation deducts the cost of processing and transportation throughout the entire chain. These cost deductions reflect the Laphroaig treasury, not the investor treasury, because the investor receives revenues at Glenfiddich and the pipeline. Since the tax regimes often differ between the Laphroaig, Glenfiddich, and the pipeline system, maximizing value at each stage, treating each independently, often destroys investor value.

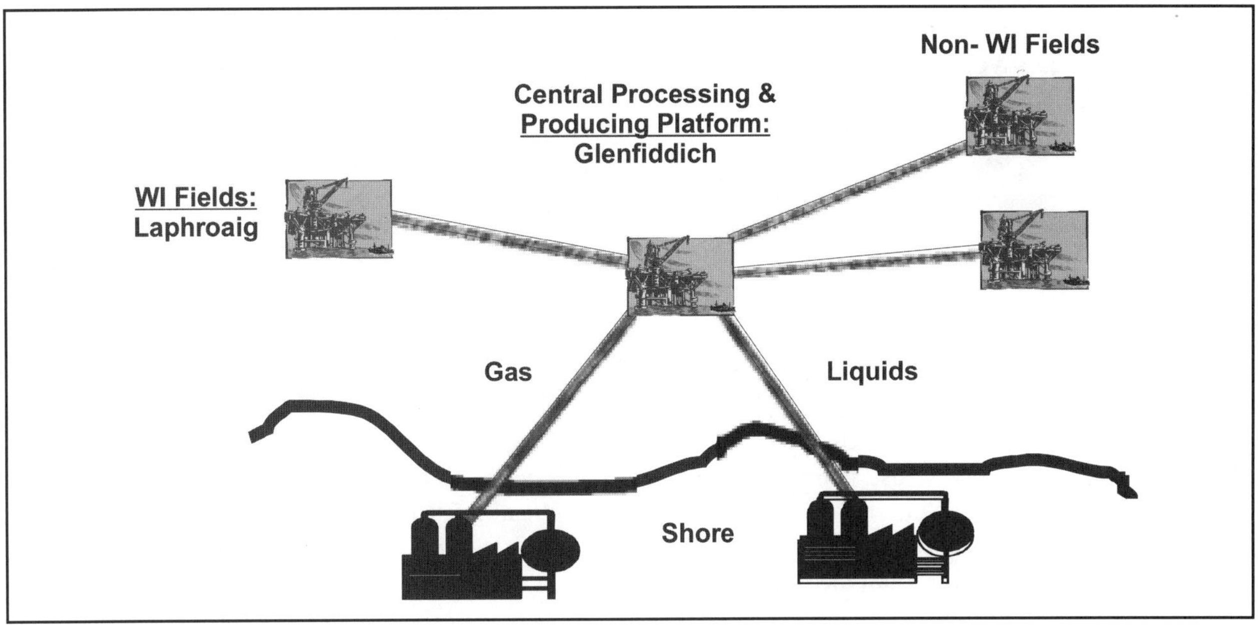

Figure 9.28 Value chain analysis

Deterministic Approach

The interaction across the segments can be analyzed in several ways. The one fitting most current software the best creates a variable category called downstream benefits. Suppose Laphroaig deducts a \$0.10 per Mcf processing fee, and a \$0.25 per Mcf pipeline tariff when performing economic valuations. The true value of producing an additional Mcf is understated in the traditional format, because the \$0.10 and \$0.25 are revenues to Glenfiddich and the pipeline, which contribute to the treasury. For Laphroaig to value any investment properly, it must properly recognize the value of that production received downstream of the Laphroaig facility.

Because most investors already have separate models of each unit, the easiest approach adds an incremental Mcf to Glenfiddich and observes the increase in the value metric, say NPV. If it increases by \$0.01 per Mcf, then each additional unit increase adds \$0.01 to the treasury. Likewise, a value of \$0.06 for the pipeline means that every unit increase in Laphroaig production adds \$0.07 in value. When performing Laphroaig economics, the \$0.07 times the unit volume increase can be added directly to the existing NPV (since these values are already presumably discounted, AT numbers).

The downstream benefit approach works quite well under linear tax regimes, but falls apart when a regime introduces rates, which vary with production volumes, investment, etc. The more complete approach consolidates all the segments into one model, where production from Laphroaig generates revenue for Glenfiddich and the pipeline. The model then sums the value from all the segments.

A common result finds that the optimal decision charges Laphroaig a high tariff and processing fee, because more value might be added from the tariffs than producing. This situation has existed for centuries. Faced with different ownership terms, price structures, tax rates, tariffs, adding value means taking ones profits in the most beneficial stage of the value chain.

The example in Figure 9.28 actually understates the complexity in the real world. Quite often, several pipeline alternatives may exist, and more than two different non-WI fields may come into the processing system. Moreover, when the pipeline and processing system is free from regulation, they can charge any rate they can negotiate, and that rate may vary for each field. In a deregulated processing and tariff arrangement environment, which is most of the world, understanding the value chain for negotiating these rates becomes critical.

The deterministic values for the value chain analysis are summarized in Example 9.14. The details are omitted here to save space. The Excel spreadsheet used to generate the values can be obtained by contacting us on the email address in the front cover.

Example 9.14: Determine investor value for Laphroaig, Glenfiddich and the pipeline. All $ values in millions (m).

Value Metric	Laphroaig	Glenfiddich	Pipeline	Separate Total	Value Chain
NPV	9.43	28.76	32.24	72.47	72.47
SIV	34.19	137.64	250.36	422.19	279.41
OANPV	33.86	231.61	177.79	443.25	468.53

NPV produces the same value, $72.47m for both the sum of the three units and for the value chain. The SIV value declines, because combining the investment costs from all the projects delays discounted payout. OANPV yields an increasing value, apparently indicating that options exist within each project and across projects. This seems more intuitively plausible to us. Note again that the classical value metric, NPV, is significantly less than the other project measures.

Understanding value differences helps prioritize technical efforts, but understanding the relative contribution of the contributors to these values facilitates understanding the sources of value. Example 9.15 outlines the contributions of individual elements in the valuation process. This approach replicates the sensitivity approach first shown in Chapter 8.

Example 9.15: Determine the sources of value for the respective projects.

	1 BCF per year for 10 years for Glenfiddich			1 BCF per year for 10 years for Laphroaig			1 BCF per year for 10 years for Non-WI		
Unit	NPV	SIV	OANPV	NPV	SIV	OANPV	NPV	SIV	OANPV
Glenfiddich	0.229	0.913	0.464	0.006	0.024	0.012	0.006	0.023	0.011
Laphroaig	0.000	0.000	0.000	0.053	0.151	0.101	0.000	0.000	0.000
Pipeline	0.026	0.102	0.053	0.026	0.102	0.053	0.041	0.157	0.082
Total	0.256	1.015	0.517	0.086	0.277	0.166	0.046	0.180	0.093
Value Chain		1.125	0.520			0.174		0.196	0.094

	10% Increase in Gas Tariff			10% Increase in Condensate Tariff			10% Increase in Other Field Tariff		
Unit	NPV	SIV	OANPV	NPV	SIV	OANPV	NPV	SIV	OANPV
Glenfiddich	-0.088	-0.045	-0.022	-0.039	0.001	-0.010	0.000	0.000	0.000
Laphroaig	-0.044	-0.035	-0.023	-0.015	-0.012	-0.008	0.000	0.000	0.000
Pipeline	0.320	0.195	0.124	0.182	0.110	0.070	0.206	0.128	0.080
Total	0.113	0.100	0.037	0.070	0.065	0.023	0.099	0.076	0.032
Value Chain		0.087	0.035		0.055	0.022		0.077	0.031

The first table in the example values additional production from the three producing sources, divided by total production to give a per BCF value addition. The Glenfiddich and Laphroaig measures add more value than the non-WI, because the latter only contributes tariff and processing revenue. Though observe that the Non-WI production increase contributes more to the pipeline metrics than either of the two WI fields, due to the higher tariff charges.

The second table highlights the give and take in a system when tariffs change. The percentage change in NPV, SIV and OANPV for a 10% increase in the respective tariffs produces the conflicts between the respective business entities. For the gas tariff, all metrics decline for the producing fields, but increase for the pipeline, as profits are shifted to the pipeline. The relative change varies with the respective ownership provisions, tax rates, cost structures, etc. A 10% increase improves the overall value to the treasury by 11.3%. The improvement stems from the model assumptions that the pipeline operated at a lower effective tax rate than the producing fields (25% versus 35%).

The value contribution also varies by metric, with NPV showing a much greater increase when tariffs rise, but lower values when production increases. OANPV and SIV yield smaller increases for the tariff change, because of their formal consideration of the respective risk measures, discounted payout (SIV) and volatility (OANPV), remain constant, thereby, minimizing the impact of the tariff increase. Increasing production lowers the risk amounts by reducing discounted payout (SIV), and increasing the ratio of discounted value to discounted investment (OANPV).

The traditional deterministic analysis in value chains can be extended to include the classical tornado diagram or spider diagram. Figure 9.29 shows the tornado diagram, and Figure 9.30 is the spider diagram, using NPV for the output metric. These diagrams were generated using the TopRank software from Palisades.[9.12] A similar analysis was performed on OANPV and SIV, yielding exactly the same rankings, with only the magnitude of the values changing.

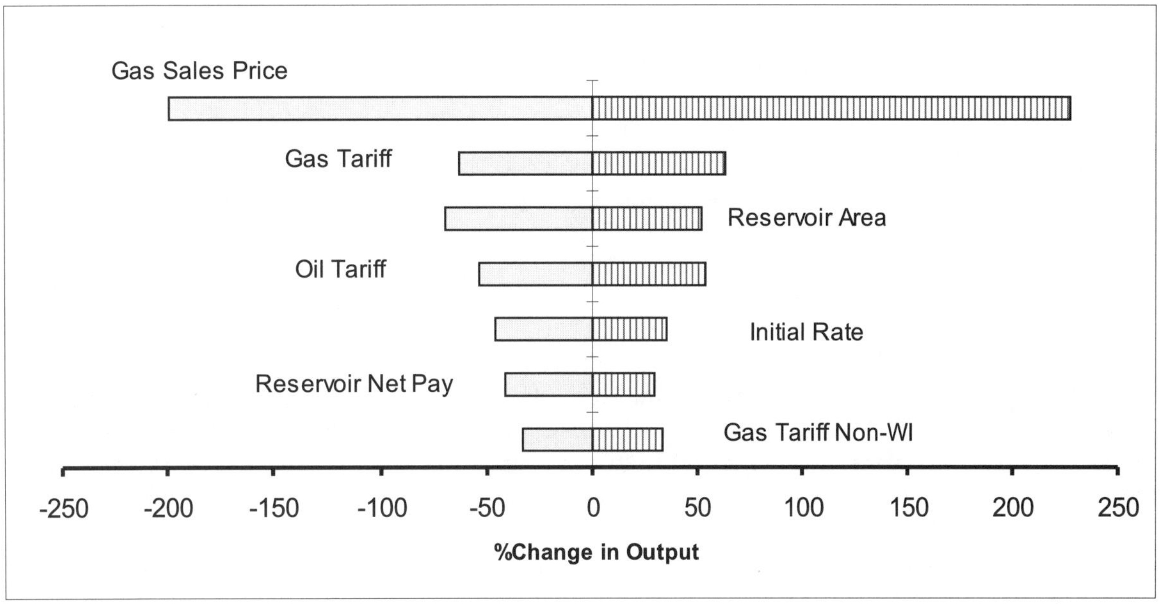

Figure 9.29 Tornado diagram for value chain analysis

Gas sales price dominates both diagrams, as is usually the case. The tornado diagram also emphasizes the importance of the tariffs, which reflects the value chain format. Stand-alone valuations would never show tariffs as being important. In addition, the reservoir characteristics, areal extent, initial rate, and net pay, impact the value metric considerably. The tornado diagram and several variants comprise much of the reporting process currently, but the spider diagram actually communicates more information in about the same space.

One added benefit gleaned from a spider diagram is the relationship between the inputs and outputs. A straight line indicates a linear relationship, while a curved line indicates a non-linear relationship. Second, the length of the lines indicates the likelihood of possible change in each variable built into the model. For instance, the Non-WI gas tariff varies from ±100%, while reservoir area only varies by ±30%, but influences the profit metric considerably more than the non-WI tariff. The spider diagram conveys both the likely range of values and corresponding impact on the chosen metric. Finally, the slope of the spider diagram communicates the differential impact of each variable.

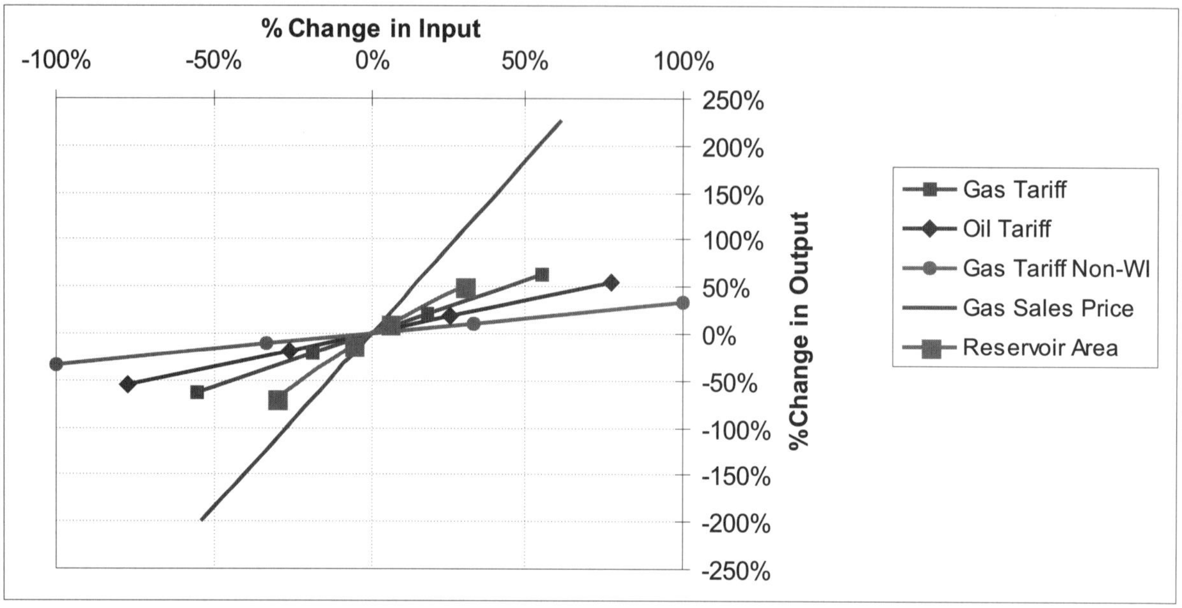

Figure 9.30 Tornado diagram for value chain analysis

The importance of the differential impact is highlighted by the exclusion of net pay and initial rate in the spider diagram. The spider diagram ranks condensate prices for 6 years ahead of these two variables, because even though a 10% change in each alters the metrics, the chance of that chance occurring was perceived to be quite small in this example.

Stochastic Analysis

The simulation results, based on 5000 iterations, are given in Example 9.16 for NPV, SIV, and OANPV, along with a table summarizing the outputs. The software produces the usual histograms, but they have been converted to lines using a spline function to convey the distribution overlap. The classical

Example 9.16: Perform a simulation on value chain using 5000 iterations. Values in $ million = m.

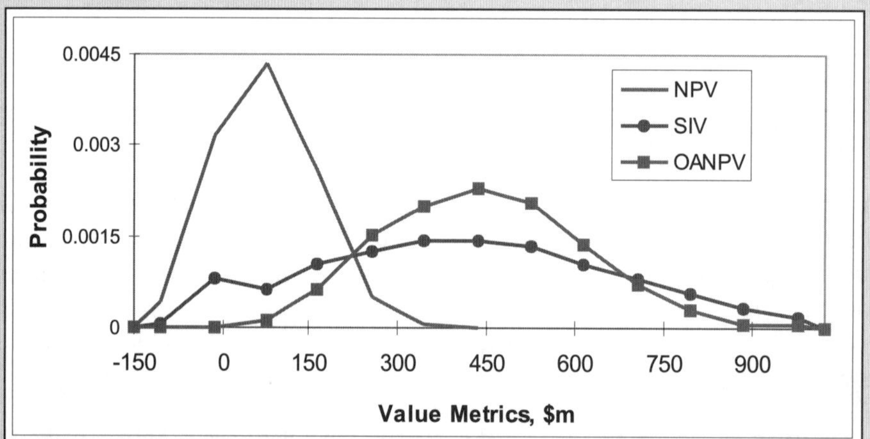

Metric	Mean	S_x	P_{10}	P_{50}	P_{90}	Mode	P(<0)
NPV	73.9	82.1	-29.0	70.6	181.5	94.53	20%
SIV	420.6	262.0	70.8	409.0	770.0	511.1	6%
OANPV	446.7	164.5	239.8	439.8	662.5	447.6	0%

performance measures, grossly understates the mean return and overstates the standard deviation relative to the modern metrics that recognize time diversification and options opportunities. Moreover, the NPV indicates about a 20% chance of losing money, while SIV is about 6% and OANPV suggests the chain has almost no chance of losing money.

This set of values reinforces several comments made earlier. First, MIV criticizes the classical process for understating future options that have value. Just comparing the means, the alternative measures exceed classical NPV by roughly 6 times, and, second, the ratio of the standard deviation to the mean is considerably higher with NPV. Both indicate that NPV might value the chain less than it is really worth, or, conversely, overstate the real risk. This goes to the heart of a phrase heard too often, "risk assessment discourages investment." Looking at these results suggests just the opposite.

Another relevant criticism of CIV concerns the limited ability to differentiate between the sum of the parts and the entire system. NPV assumes that summing the individual components reflects the total value of the chain to the treasury. OANPV and SIV suggest otherwise, because of the interactions between the respective components. The system distribution of NPV looks exactly like the NPV distribution in the previous example. SIV and OANPV suggest something entirely different, as Figure 9.31 demonstrates.

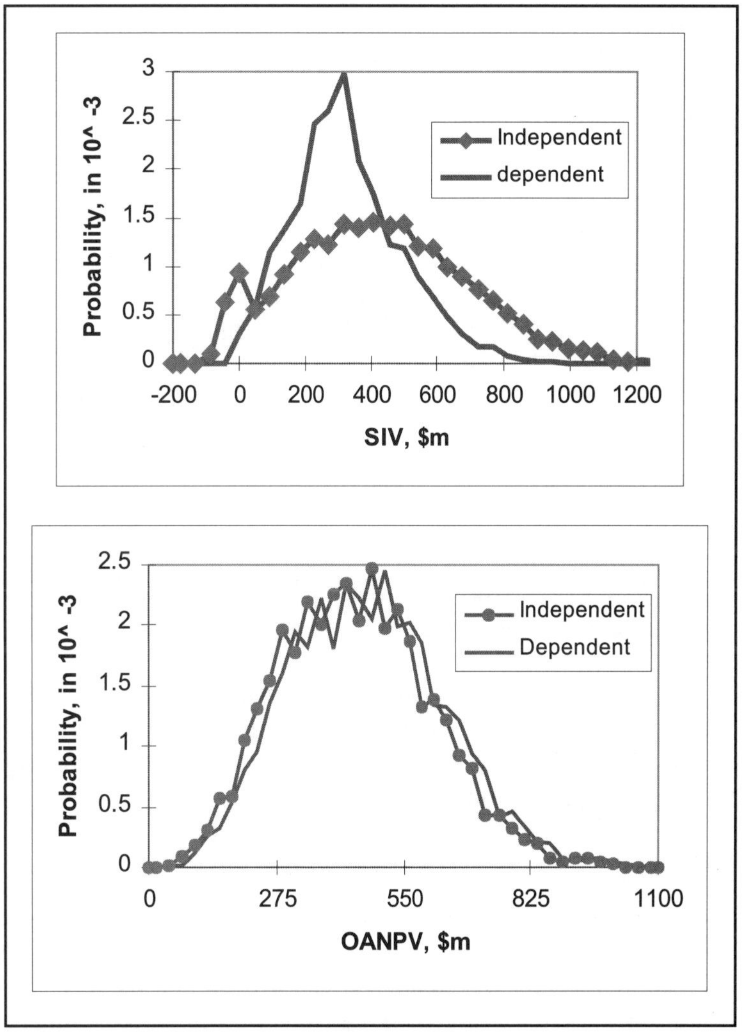

Figure 9.31 Comparison of distributions from individual summation versus total project

Recognizing dependencies reduces the mean from about $420m to roughly $300m for SIV, a significant decline. The standard deviation also diminishes, from $262m to $164m. The impact of the dependency across the projects is a reduced return, along with lowered risk. This format corrects the tendency among many investors to treat the returns from the projects independently, but to simultaneously argue that the linkage reduces risk. Risk certainly does fall, but so does the return.

OANPV increases risk and return metrics when the dependencies are recognized, though the changes are slight. The mean NPV goes to $471m from $446m, and the standard deviation increases by $2m from the original value of $164m. Presumably, the options benefits were already included in the independent values, so formally recognizing the dependencies adds little additional information.

Another aspect of performing value chains concerns the knowledge gained relative to the cost of performing the analysis. Building these models involves considerable time and effort. To build the model used here properly required over three days time, and that was from an experienced person who knows both value chain logic and the project intimately. Those seeking to duplicate the same analysis should allow at least two weeks to have the first working module. Then, the real work begins.

The benefit of the effort to understand the value chain comes partly from the previous discussion, but really shows up when trying to understand cash flow patterns. Many senior managers now recognize that the performance metrics disguise much of the useful information sought from the investment analysis, especially from a portfolio perspective. A commonly heard phrase in senior circles is "we are a cash flow company," which highlights the importance of understanding the timing of cash receipts and disbursements. Profit metrics hide important timing differentials across projects. These investors elect to analyze potential cash flow variations, rather than infer them from classical profit metrics (which is tenuous even by the very best investors).

Figure 9.32 compares the positive cash flow patterns for the value chain, first assuming independence of the project cash flows, and then adding dependencies. The value chain format was converted back to an independent format, where the NCF for the pipeline, Glenfiddich, and Laphroaig were computed independently, except that gas sales price for Glenfiddich and Laphroaig was the same. Figure 9.32 shows only one profile because the results between the two runs are statistically and visually insignificant. Should this be a surprise? No, because the major driver behind the value chain metrics is gas sales price. Holding the single, most significant input constant effectively prevents significant differences from emerging.

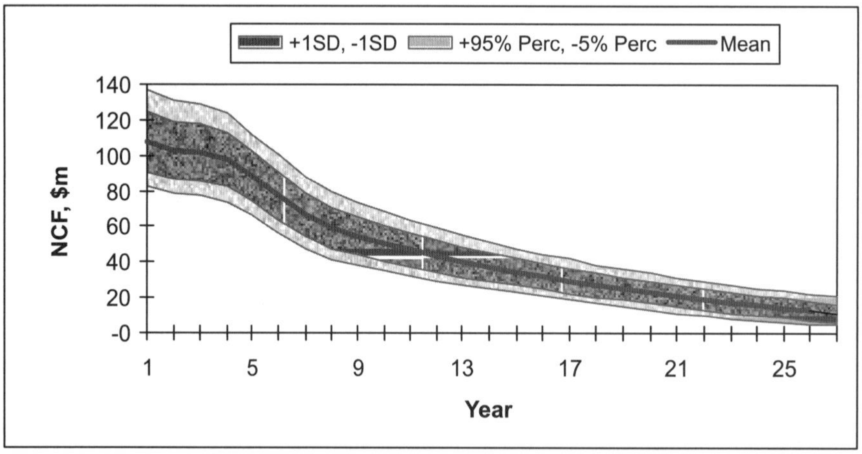

Figure 9.32 Comparison of independent and dependent cash flows

The profit metric distributions differ slightly, with the independent metrics showing less volatility. The probably of NPV < 0 for the independent case falls to 14%, while the dependent NPV fell below 0 about 20% of the time. In the independent simulation, the high and low inputs offset set each other, rather than working in unison. No graph is shown for space reasons.

Summary

Building value chains requires considerable time and energy. Adding value demands considerable attention to framing the questions that need to be answered. In this example, the question revolved around the contribution of WI production relative to non-WI production, given a specified interest in the pipeline. More intriguing questions emerge when negotiations begin about actually setting the tariff rates and choosing the pipeline WI that achieves all the investor's objectives. The next chapter covers these optimization and negotiation issues

POINT FORWARD VS. FULL CYCLE VALUATION

The last, of many possible topics addressed here compares an age-old problem with the proper risk perspective: defining the proper time perspective for analyzing the investment. One group likes to look at all the information from the start, which is normally historical, and combine that with future expectations, called the full cycle approach. Any historical events fall under the heading of *sunk costs.* Investment texts recommend basing all decisions on incremental cash flows, or, just the cash flows occurring from this *point forward* or *time forward.*(9.13, 9.14) Most multinational investors stipulate that decisions be based on incremental evaluations, or the point forward approach. The different time perspectives impact investment decisions dramatically, and this section demonstrates why each contributes to the valuation process, just in different ways.

Example 9.17 demonstrates a simplified contrast between point forward and full cycle cash flows. Project expenditures began 3 years ago, amounting an MOD amount of $55m. The investor has to make a decision at time zero (now) to invest an additional $50.78m to generate cash flows for four additional periods. The first column, labeled full cycle at time -3, computes the NPV of the total project to be -$41.65. NPV was computed using the Excel function with no modification. Certainly, this investment destroys value on a full cycle basis, and future proposals for similar investment require careful scrutiny.

Example 9.17: Given the full cycle and point forward costs, make a recommendation about investing in the project. All values in $million (=m).

Time Period	Full Cycle NCF @ time –3	Full Cycle @ Time 0	Point Forward NCF	Abandon
-3	-50.00	0.00		
-2	-5.00	0.00		
-1	0.00	0.00		
0	-50.78	-124.38	-50.78	-72.6
1	20.00	20.00	20.00	
2	20.00	20.00	20.00	
3	20.00	20.00	20.00	
4	20.00	20.00	20.00	
NPV_{10}	-41.65	-60.98	10.56	-72.6

The current issue concerns, not the historical merits of the project, but whether the investor should commit an additional $50.78 this year to the project. Incremental or point forward argues that only current and future cash flows should be included, not sunk costs, as shown in the last column. The point forward analysis suggests that the project adds $10.56 million value to the treasury.

The sunk cost or full cycle devotees argue that the middle column reflects the true situation better. The -$124 million is found by compounding the historical costs to time zero at the specified 10% discount rate in order have the same reference point as the point forward valuation. Full cycle economics suggests a loss of $60.98 million. Which is right? Both solutions are correct, but answer different questions.

Full cycle correctly identifies that the investment reduced value over the entire time frame. This indicates that future investments in similar projects should be avoided unless the causes identified, and the relevant corrective decisions formulated. This is like an investor in the stock market asking themself why they bought a particular stock at all. Once the stock is bought, the issue becomes how to achieve their objectives from this point forward, which sometimes means engaging in "loss minimizing" behavior rather than profit maximization.

Incremental analysis leads to the correct decision by recognizing that the investor has two choices at time zero: abandon the project then and lose an NPV_{10} of -$72.6 million (the 50 and 5 million in years –3 and –2 compounded to year 0), or make the investment and lose "only" about $62 million (=72.6 – 10.56). Hardly an attractive choice, but every investor faces the prospect of having to spend additional money to "cut their losses".

As the other topics covered in this chapter, formally recognizing risk helps understand the greater complexities in the decision process. The full cycle advocates recommend against the incremental approach, because of their experiences in, what they consider, the abuses of the approach. We have had similar encounters. The problem, however, arises from the failure to recognize changes in risk, not any defects in incremental valuation.

Our experiences with the distortions come from well drilling investments. The investment begins with a project cost and profit estimates, concluding that the investment is attractive. Then, part way into the project, problems occur during drilling, either totally losing the hole or having to redirect the drilling program. Faced with this decision, incremental analysis includes only costs from that point forward (ignoring all costs to that point), but still includes all future revenues. With lower cost and the same future values, project valuations actually improve. A common result: a well initially estimated to cost \$15m might end up costing \$50m that still never reaches the target reservoir. Why, because incremental valuations suggested that continued drilling made money.

Blaming incremental valuations misses the target. The real culprit actually belongs with failing to address risk correctly. Figure 9.33 displays the process from initiation. Once the investor decides to drill, three outcomes can emerge: dry hole (30%), no problems with drilling leading to a success of \$25m (50%), or drilling problems can crop up (20%). Drilling leads to the largest expected value of \$5m, hence the true next to the drill decision. The example suggests that sidetracking makes sense if a problem exists, even though the incremental or additional cost of \$5 million cuts the expected value of that option to \$2.5 million. Observe that the total success probability after the sidetrack decision equals 70%, which is the same value as the sum of the no problem and problem probability. In other words, the existence of a problem, at any point, has no impact on the risk of subsequent events.

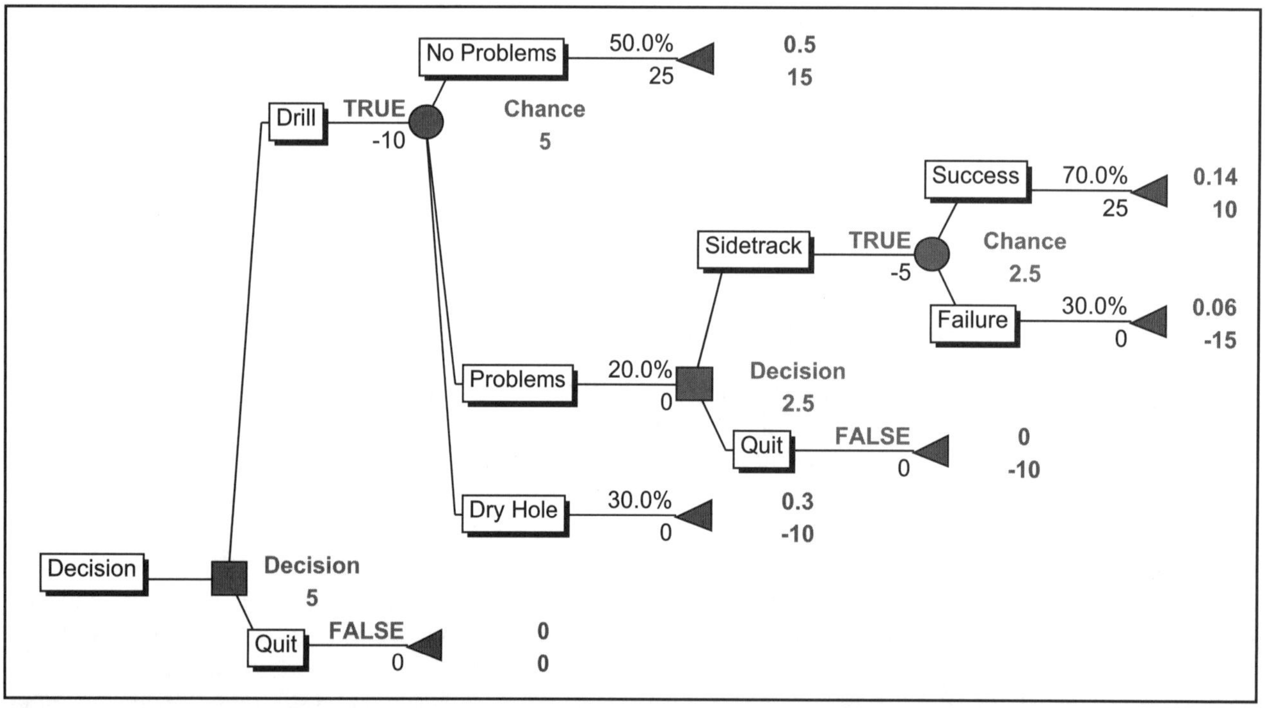

Figure 9.33 Example drilling decision

This analysis fails to capture the increasing risk as the project proceeds. The first sidetrack indicated that our knowledge of the situation was imperfect, suggesting that further problems may arise later on. In fact, as Dick Westney explains in his project management course, once problems begin, the chances of future problems increase.[(9.15)] Some even advocate that the risk increases exponentially.

Figure 9.34 demonstrates the impact of the probability changes on the decision structure at various stages during the project. To save space, the tree begins with the problem outcome in Figure 9.33 and follows the path along several different lines of outcomes. The success probability falls to 30%, and the chance of more problems rising to 70%. If problems arise a second time, the decision to quit or sidetrack more requires and additional \$5m outlay, which if successful, leads to a \$15m NPV, which appears quite good. Look at the decision outcome after the second problem, which is -\$7.5m, indicating that the expected value from that point forward is negative, because the probabilities of success are changing, rather than remaining constant as they were before. The last sidetrack only has a 10% chance of success and 90% failure chance.

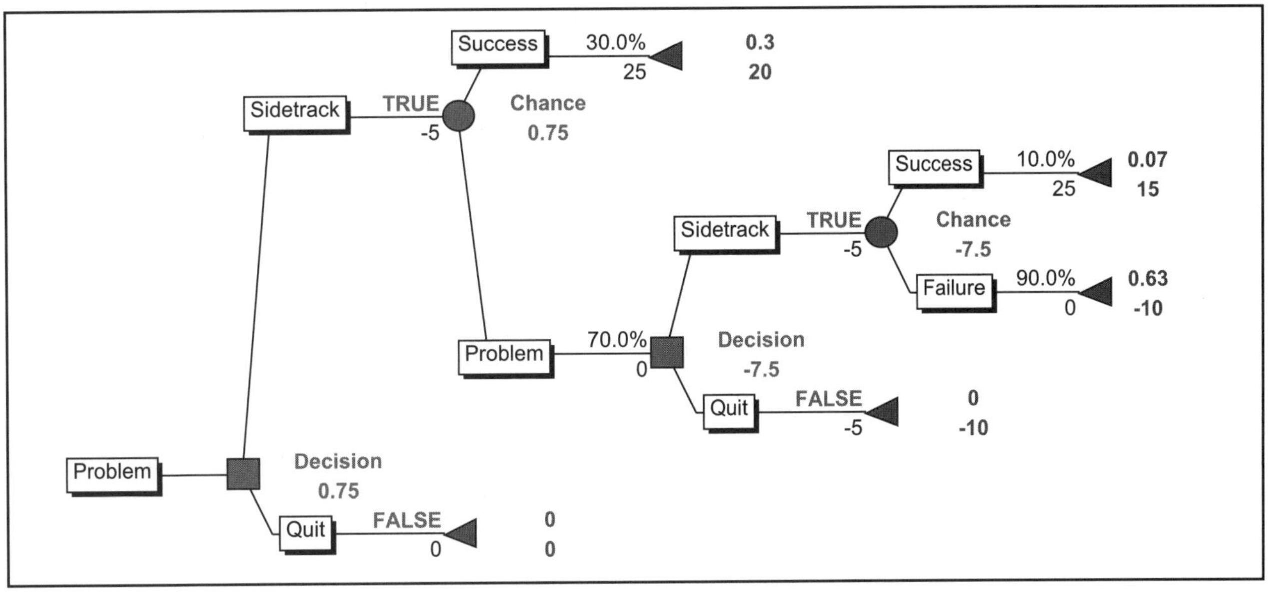

Figure 9.34 Incremental analysis with changing risk

The problem with classical incremental analysis was the focus on certain paths through the tree. After the first problem, certainty economics would look at the \$20 million outcome and indicate sidetracking looked good. After the second problem, the \$15m NPV indicates a good decision as well.[(9.16)] Adding probabilities and costs of failure contradicts the deterministic results, indicating again that deterministic analysis misleads, as much as it may help, investors to achieve their desired objectives.

As an extension of the analysis, Chapter 8 spent some time discussing risk aversion and ways to measure risk tolerance. The tree discussion in this chapter assumes that the investor is risk neutral, or a dollar lost affects utility equal to a dollar gained. Since all the evidence suggests that investors are risk averse, Figure 9.35 duplicates Figure 9.33 assuming a risk tolerance of 2. The entire project comes very close to just breaking even, without worrying about potential problems.

SUMMARY

This chapter presented common investment decisions from the perspective the classical deterministic and newer risk assessment approaches, alongside valuation methods emanating from modern asset valuation. The ease and usefulness of the deterministic process should be readily apparent, especially to those just being introduced to the subjects. The benefits of formally recognizing risk should also be obvious. Formal risk assessment and valuation provides insights that were impossible to glean from deterministic analysis, even with sensitivities, and spider or tornado diagrams. Most of the sections also tried to identify actions available to investors to mitigate recognized risks.

The next chapter takes the identified risks and seeks to find the optimum or best choices available to the investor. The principles are applied at both the project and portfolio levels. For those interested in

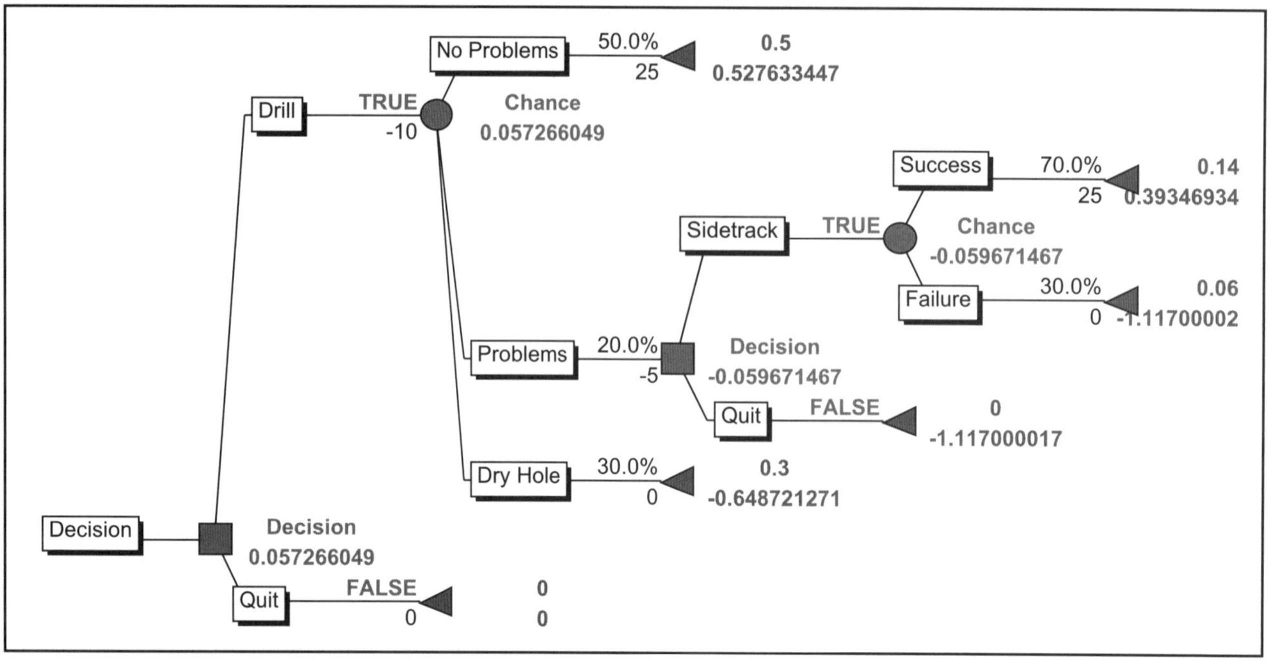

Figure 9.35 Incremental decision tree with risk tolerance

detail or additional subjects, please email us. We are very interested in expanding our database of investment applications beyond the usual risk manual. All industry applications are desired. The email address is: Risky Biker@Cs.Com. If this gives you some idea of our recreational endeavors, you are a prime candidate for risk assessment.

REFERENCES

9.1 Coopersmith, Ellen, "Decision-Making is Human," Oil and Gas Executive, Vol. 3, No. 4 (2000).

9.2 "Model Form of International Operating Agreement," Barrows Company, New York, NY.

9.3 Newendorp, P., *Decision Analysis for Petroleum Exploration*, Petroleum Publishing Co. (1975).

9.4 Pirsig, Robert, *Zen and the Art of Motorcycle Maintenance*, Quill Publishing (1974).

9.5 American Association of Cost Engineers (1997), *Recommended practice no. 18R-97, Cost Estimate Classification System – As Applied in Engineering, Procurement, and Construction for Process Industries*, Morgantown, WV, AACE.

9.6 Randal Lorance and Robert Wendling, "Basic Techniques for Analyzing and Presentation of Cost Risk Analysis," http://www.cbpro.com/support/whitepaper/lorance.html.

9.7 American Association of Cost Engineers, *Standard Cost Engineering Terminology, Cost Engineers Notebook*, Morgantown, WV (1990).

9.8 Project Management Institute, *Project Management Body of Knowledge (PMBOK)*, Upper Darby, PA. (1996).

9.9 Uhler, R. S. and Bradley, P., "A Stochastic Model for Determining the Economic Prospects of Petroleum Exploration over Large Regions." Journal of the American Statistical Association, June 1970.

9.10 Newendorp, P., *ibid.*

9.11 Paffenbarger, R. and J. Patterson, *Statistical Methods*, Irwin (1977).

9.12 "TopRank," Palisades Corp. (1995).

9.13 Brealy, R. and S. Myers, *Principles of Corporate Finance*, McGraw-Hill (1996).

9.14 Francis, J., "Investments: Analysis and Management," McGraw-Hill (1980).

9.15 Westney, D., personal communication.

9.16 Note that this is not true incremental decision-making. Most tree software works on cumulative costs, so the graph only reports a $15m NPV because it deducts the first sidetrack cost as well. To be a true incremental representation, the value should only reflect the current sidetrack cost of $5m. Most good tree software allows the user to override this situation.

CHAPTER 10

OPTIMIZATION OF PORTFOLIOS AND PROJECTS

Methods for optimizing investments have been discussed for decades; yet, few professionals have ever applied formal optimization procedures to actual project or portfolio analysis. Some areas have been far more aggressive about applying optimization procedures: refineries and assembly lines may re-optimize every hour or two. Refineries use various optimization procedures to determine output based on refinery capabilities, characteristics of petroleum stocks, and output price and demand. The processing industry uses optimization for selecting product mixes, investment mix, and logistical problems.[(10.1)]

Most professionals understand optimization, in its simplest form, easier than statistics. Maximizing profits or minimizing costs are perceived as being good activities, if not the cornerstone of sound investment decisions; yet, experience demonstrates that few investors achieve these objectives, except by accident. Traditional sensitivity or what if approaches reflect a brute force approximation of the optimization question. After building a *base case,* numerous iterations or scenarios are performed to determine a better combination of inputs. Selecting input combinations and the number of iterations to perform depend on the time available, and the interests of the person(s) performing the calculation. Usually investors repeat the iterative process until the time for the final presentation arrives. This approach makes perfect sense when dealing with low cost, familiar investments. Complex, high-risk investments limit the ability to vary more than a few variables at a time; thus, reducing the likelihood that the final answer truly achieves or even approximates the optimum, however defined.

Even as the tools for optimization become readily available, the task becomes harder, not easier. With limited tools, optimum was treated as maximizing NPV or some other classical profit metric, like IRR. With the expansion of the toolkit, defining optimum correctly challenges all investors. Does the optimum occur at the engineering level, from the shareholder perspective, to the senior executive, to the staff, or others? Do these optimums conflict with each other? And, do mechanisms exist to reconcile the likely contradictions. Improved ease of optimization raises critically important questions that have been historically subsumed, because they couldn't be answered, except subjectively by those responsible for making the investment decisions.[(10.2)]

The improved toolkit for assessing and managing risk encourages the continued changes in organizational structure that improves the cooperation and communication among disciplines (knowledge). Achieving optimality, however defined, requires the close interaction of every discipline involved in the investment process. The sequential relationship between geoscience, the engineering disciplines, economics, legal and management necessitates that each fully communicates the range of uncertainties and alternative outcomes to others; otherwise, opportunities are missed, making optimization impossible. Communication of reasonable outcomes is the critical phase in addressing the full range of available options. Investors cannot optimize what they fail to consider.

Applying optimization methods historically require detailed understandings of the underlying mathematical procedures, be they differential calculus or nonlinear optimization techniques. Acquiring the relevant knowledge, then programming, these techniques required more skill and time than normally available to professionals. Improved software and hardware permit investors to ask and answer optimization questions using spreadsheets as is, or with low cost add-ins, or purchasing commercial software specifically designed for the task. Users need to know what questions to ask, how to tell the computer to solve the question, and then understand the output. The underlying math matters less than asking the right question(s) and building the model to answer those questions.

Optimization methods are as much about understanding the patterns of knowledge that exist between geoscience, engineering, political, and economic variables, than pure math. The real benefit stems from the knowledge that comes from understanding these interactions, and employing that knowledge to make better investment decisions. The methods of optimization are obviously discussed, but, more important, are the issues of how and what questions to ask. Most investors already ask the basic questions, without following up with the appropriate analysis.

Planning, strategic thinking, budgeting and analyzing investments are natural applications for optimization. Mao indicates that picking among competing projects by ranking according to some criterion, then selecting them in order until the budget is exhausted often misleads decision makers. Simplified ranking by some arbitrary measure, like NPV or NPV/INV, only works when, each project is small relative to the total capital budget (less than 5%), each project contributes little to overall corporate risk, and the concept of an optimum is associated with just one variable. If these assumptions are correct, ranking in the traditional manner yields portfolios near the optimal combination. When projects are large, optimal portfolios may not result, because of project indivisibilities. The ranking must be applied to all possible combination of projects, not just each individually. As the number of projects increases, the number of possible combinations rises quite quickly.[10.3]

Commercially available computer software is used to illustrate applications of optimization. Various software packages, including Solver that comes with Excel and Lotus, Solver Premium from Frontline Systems, OptQuest from Decisioneering, and Evolver and RiskOptimizer from Palisades Corp, are used to illustrate the concepts without endorsement or criticism. Solver screens are used to illustrate input and output because spreadsheet owners already have access to Solver at no additional cost. We find all software systems to be quite useful and recommend interested parties to try these packages or commercial software specifically tailored to attack these problems.

OPTIMIZATION: A REVIEW OF THE BASICS

Most people were introduced to optimization with differential equations, which, like statistics books, were usually sold back to the bookstore immediately after the final exam. From a practical viewpoint, the concept of optimization dominates most business behavior. The common, but often detested, phrase, *maximizing shareholder wealth,* reflects the fundamental optimization question. Elements of wealth maximization include cost minimization in development and operations, maximizing production, and so on. Faced with a multitude of variables, each impacting profitability and risk differently, achieving an optimum is highly unlikely without a logical, orderly process, except by accident.

This section minimizes the mathematics of optimization in favor of geometry to facilitate understanding of the basic concepts. Graphical formats direct attention to the fundamental questions, not at the solution methodology. Besides, most people don't remember much of their calculus training anyway. Purists cringe, but, very simply, reduced manning levels don't permit such time allocations nor justified with the computer software available today.

These shapes reflect the basic concept of optimization, like maximizing profits or minimizing costs. Any reference to maximization or minimization becomes a subset of optimization. The typical graph looks something like Figure 10.1. The x-axis is usually the decision variable, like number of wells to drill, size of facilities, production volume, etc. The y-axis reflects the calculated variable: the cost of operations or construction, economic measures like NPV, NPV/INV, SIV, and so on. The peak point, A, tells the decision maker what x-axis value achieves the desired optimum. In Figure 10.1, the maximum value of y, defined as profitability for this example, occurs along Point A. The x-axis refers to the number of wells in a proposed field development. Drilling about 10 wells maximizes profit. Profitability isn't defined, but could be measured by NPV, PV/INV, SIV, OANPV, etc., or any other desired metric.

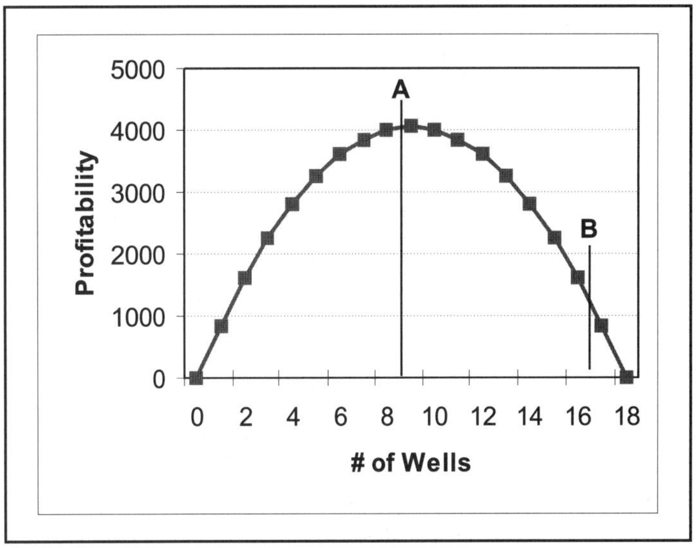

Figure 10.1 Example of a simple optimization

Situations, like Figure 10.1, occur frequently, primarily because the technical staff chooses the number of wells to maximize production, not profitability. About 17 wells, line B, were drilled, because the controlling discipline chose to maximize production. Yet, the optimization process shows that drilling fewer wells (9), and reducing production, investment profitability, hence shareholder wealth, increases.

This illustrates the problem of defining the optimization point: at each step along the project path, like sizing and facilities and transportation systems, selecting the right inventory level, and so on, or some profit metric. The investment, demonstrated by Figure 10.1, sought to maximize ultimate production, not profitability. As simple as idea is, defining the point of the optimization matters. Traditionally, each discipline optimizes the decisions in their area of knowledge. This process almost never achieves the optimum for the entire project. Many investments, which have been declared uneconomic, could be economical by sub-optimizing at the individual technical stages. Understanding when this counter intuitive result matters should be one objective of the optimization process. This requires understanding the complete system involved in the successful construction and operation of the investment.

Minimization, like the cost containment programs, whether on capital or operating costs, have become increasingly popular. Most developments can trade-off capital and operating costs, as illustrated in Chapter 9. Increasing Capex, like with automation systems or use of stainless steels, reduces operating costs. Another common example relates cost to production volumes. As production volumes increase, the cost per unit of Opex often falls, while Capex rises.

A good example of cost minimization concerns offshore platform operations during inclimate weather. As storms approach, the operating manager must decide when to shut the platform down to prepare for the storm. Premature shutdown of the platform reduces production and revenue. Delaying shutdown increases the risk of storm damage to the platform or support vessels. Figure 10.2 shows the variation in costs relative to shut down time prior to the arrival of bad weather. The cost and likelihood will depend on platform type, location, weather, etc., but the basic relationship described in Figure 10.2 occurs quite often.[(10.4)]

The cost minimum occurs along line A, which is about 15 hours. At less than 10 hours, the damage to the platform dominates the cost function, while after 15 hours, lost revenue governs the cost function. The graph just illustrates common sense: Preparing for bad weather makes perfect sense, but not so early that lost production and revenue destroys value.

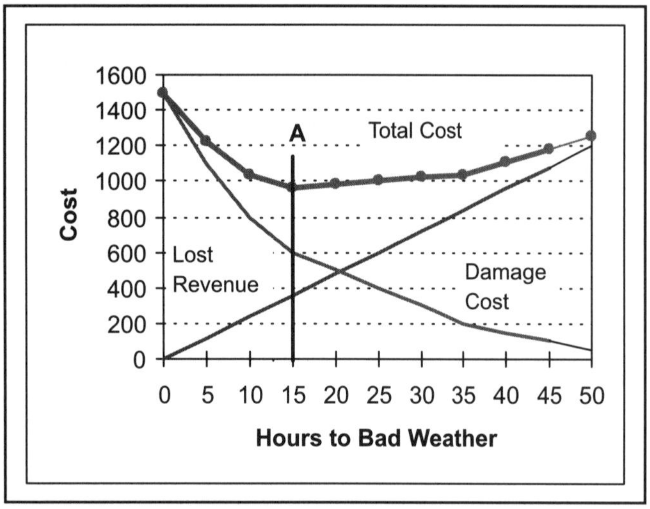

Figure 10.2 Handling bad weather

The two examples of optimization – project maximization and cost minimization – illustrate simple optimization principles. Other, more complex, optimization applications exist. The real world confronts us with additional problems, which greatly increases the complexity of the calculation. Other major obstacles include lack of resources, like budgets, limited markets for products, or physical constraints, which prevent obtaining a minimum or maximum. The constrained optimization situation was solved for the simplest of cases by Lagrange in calculus classes. The basic problem is first defined as an equation to maximize or minimize. The next equation(s), which extends the examples in Figures 10.1 and 10.2, defines the constraints on the optimization.

Rather than repeat the differential calculus of constrained optimization that most have successfully forgotten, a simple example will suffice. Suppose that the budget for wells in Figure 10.1 permits drilling a maximum of 5 wells. Drilling 5 wells reduces project profitability below the maximum and recovers even less of the reserves than is technically feasible. An option of course is to drill less than 5 wells, but differential equations really aren't needed to tell us that 7 wells maximizes profits subject to the budget constraint. Figure 10.3 adds line C, which reflects the budget constraint. By limiting the budget, the project profitability is suboptimal, as is recovered reserves.

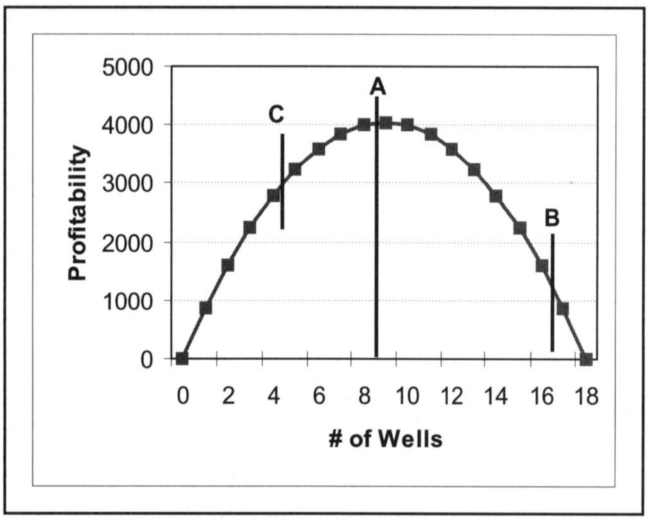

Figure 10.3 Example of constrained optimization

Historically the issues outlined in these figures were addressed by Lagrangian calculus or optimization tools, like linear programming (LP). Most spreadsheets solve simple, one-constraint problems, like these; by using the *goal seek* option. After inputting the equations, goal seek changes the number of wells (Figure 10.1 and 10.3) or shut down time (Figure 10.2) to achieve the maximum or minimum cost. Unfortunately, goal seek can only change one variable at a time. Investment planning usually involves simultaneous alteration of multiple components.

As the complexity of problem increases, either by increasing the number of constraints or by including more variables to evaluate, neither graphical nor traditional calculus yields easy or quick solutions. Before the advent of better software, most professionals avoided trying optimization techniques for two reasons: one, projects were seldom simple enough to fit the graphical or Lagrange multiplier method, and, two, few had the computer expertise to work with the programs available. Now that optimization tools are available with the purchase of most spreadsheets or as a separate add-in's, ignoring the potential applications reduces productivity, if for no other reason than time is limited for running sensitivities. In addition, simple solutions fail when faced with multiple objectives, like reducing operating costs, adding value, etc. Being able to assess, understand, and trade-off conflicting objectives and constraints influences the ultimate success or failure of an investment.

THE MODEL FORMULATION PROCESS

Formulating optimization models is an art, bordering on a science. It is an art, because it always involves approximation of the real world. The artistic ability required to develop simple models, which are nevertheless good approximations to reality, equates to painting a Mona Lisa.

Five major steps dominate good modeling, as outlined in Chapter 1. They are:

1. Formulate the problem: understand the real issues, not just the stated ones.
2. Plan the analysis: designating the steps in solving the model
3. Examine the data and premises: gathering and generating the input data for the problem;
4. Perform analysis: solving or running the model,
5. Report results: implementing the solution."

This process is iterative. Upon reaching step 4 and 5, the modeler realizes that something has been left out or omitted from the analysis. New data becomes available or the logic may be wrong. Several iterations are required in the process to achieve stated objectives, e.g., one seldom develops the most appropriate model the first time through. Of these steps, the easiest is Step 4, because the computer does the work.

Steps 1, 3, and 5 are, if not the most difficult, at least consume the most time. Success with steps 1, 3, and 5 depends on being very familiar with the underlying processes being studied. Step 2 on the other hand requires the most skill.

All companies and industries have historically failed to perform step 1 very well. Keith Milheim, during his tenure as editor of the JPT, constantly preached the need to understand the new paradigm. He correctly points out that many of our mistakes originate in the misspecification of the problem, or simplifying the problem to do the calculations we know how to make and like to make. Mr. Milheim's traditional example of misspecification has always been the question to water flood a field or use existing production methods, when the real question was the best utilization of a producing field, including selling it. Optimization forces the user to develop a flow sheet of issues and consequences. Just the process of defining the problem helps focus attention on the right issue(s).

Step 2 is the most difficult for most people, including us. Experience with modeling, like spreadsheets, builds expertise, and an understanding of the importance of constructing a logical flow. Unfortunately, that flow often fails to coincide with the needs of mathematical optimization. Constructing optimization models after building traditional deterministic spreadsheets often yields multiple error messages on the first few runs, with each error message suggesting gross incompetence, or so it seems. Further review proved the error messages correct. It wasn't an error in the logic; it was an error in formulating the problem such that the algorithm could successfully solve it. Everyone working with stochastic or optimization methods learns to build valuation models that capture the essence of the problem better than the traditional deterministic approach. Learning the lessons of Chapters 8-10 will change the way you view investment modelling, forever.

The third step reflects failure to collect and analyze much of the available data. Engineering generates considerable information about costs, uptime, performance, etc., but seldom collects and stores that data in an easily analyzable format. Geoscientists like to refer to their disciplines as not being as data constrained as engineering, but, in truth, that is not always the case. Engineering does generate more data, but the data seldom exists in a readily available format.

The common practice of sequentially analyzing each project, where disciplines perform computations in isolation from each other, compounds the problem. Information is passed on in sequence, culminating in the project economics. This stand alone, isolationist approach often produces *satisficing* results. This is a modified economics term to reflect that the process is designed to exceed a hurdle imposed by management, not generate an optimal result. The movement to discipline teams helps reduce this organizational defect, but still avoids several critical issues.

Optimization, however, requires formally recognizing the relationship between production rates, Capex, Opex, scheduling, etc. Regardless of whether the relationship is linear or nonlinear, such information is absolutely essential to sound investment planning. Most evaluations are based on a single, desired production number, where engineers then manually develop a production scheme using experience and judgment. They seldom expand this to develop equations regarding cost of facilities, Opex, process type, and building the relationships amongst the variables. Several efforts are underway today to overcome this limitation. By building cost and process, relationships, available to all at the touch of a button, improved risk assessment, management and optimization emerges.

With extensive databases and the ability to construct empirical relationships, optimization becomes much easier. Now, answers about the optimum development schemes, instead of satisficing, as before, surface. We have done this for multiple projects worldwide, with excellent results; primarily, management and technical professionals understand the real tradeoffs in the design and operation of the projects.

Model Formulation: An Example

Step 4 requires solving the basic model. The general format works with conceptual methods or templates. Most industries, unfortunately, have few or no templates to work with, requiring every analysis to start from scratch or re-invent the wheel.

Most optimization problems reflect two main elements: specification of the goal(s) of the analysis, called the *objective function*; and the *constraints* in the system. Limited resources like capital, flow rates, fluid composition, operating costs, geology, illustrate common constraints.

The basic profit maximization model looks something like Equation 10.1.

Maximize:

$$\text{Profit} = P_{oil} * \text{Oil} + P_{gas} * \text{Gas} + P_{cond} * \text{Cond} + P_{NGL} * \text{NGL} \tag{10.1}$$

Subject To:

$$\begin{aligned} \text{Capex}_{oil} + \text{Capex}_{gas} + \text{Capex}_{cond} + \text{Capex}_{NGL} &= \$X \\ \text{Opex}_{oil} + \text{Opex}_{gas} + \text{Opex}_{cond} + \text{Opex}_{NGL} &= \$Y \\ (\text{Oil} + \text{Gas} + \text{Cond} + \text{NGL}) * \text{Reserves} &= \text{Z BOE's} \\ \text{Annual Cash Flow} &= \$W \end{aligned}$$

where:

P_{oil} = price of oil,
P_{gas} = price of gas,
P_{cond} = price of condensate,
P_{NGL} = NGL price, and
the other values relate to Capex or Opex costs, reserves and cash flows.

Estimates for production, prices, Capex and Opex costs, cash flows, etc., need to be provided, as well as specific values for W, X, Y, and Z. Constraints capturing other investment issues could be added, as well.

TYPES OF OPTIMIZATION MODELS

This section introduces optimization methods with two project examples, one technical and one economic. To implement these ideas, access to a basic spreadsheet program, like Excel or Lotus, plus the willingness to ask the right questions are the only requirements. Each section outlines an optimization procedure and then illustrates the concept with an application. The chapter concludes with an application to a multifield development plan, including transportation.

Different optimization techniques solve various types of questions, each with different functional forms. The simple examples, discussed above, dealt with linear systems, but other, more complicated functional forms exist. Most real world problems cannot be solved by linear systems of equations without significant modifications in the model format. In fact, virtually every equation, be it geophysical, engineering, or economic, is nonlinear. With limited computing power, converting non-linear systems to linear ones produced major time saving in the computations. Reducing complex systems to linear approximations required time and a good understanding of the solution techniques, unfortunately. The need to convert to linear systems diminishes as computer-processing power increases, and new computational processes are developed.

The major programming techniques used in industry, and readily available now are outlined here. The review and examples are, by no means, exhaustive. Introducing the basic concepts and illustrating the improvement in investment planning from the adoption of optimization techniques are the goals of the following sections. Even simpler, we hope to wet your appetite for optimization. With core fundamentals established, moving to books devoted entirely to optimization principles and applications should be easier and less time consuming. Like other chapters, entire books are reduced to a few pages herein.

Optimization techniques include *linear programming* (LP), *integer programming* (IP), *quadratic programming* (QP), *stochastic programming* (SP), *dynamic programming* (DP), *nonlinear programming* (NLP), *genetic algorithms (GA)*, etc. The basic LP format is covered first, and then later sections extend the framework. The LP technique is outlined first for several reasons. First, many professionals studied LP in school and just need a refresher. Second, the LP format provides the foundation for most other optimization methods. Also, LP is simpler to describe graphically and to formulate sample models.

Linear Programming (LP)

Linear programming derives its name from extending equations, like Equation 10.1. In the form of equation 10.1, special solution methods are unnecessary. Lagrangian calculus could solve for as many objectives and constraints as desired, limited only by the time needed to reach an answer. The LP format covers more complicated situations, primarily because investment planning seldom encounters constraints, which require a particular value to occur exactly. Opex and Capex objectives generally must be less than specified value, while production or profit constraints are usually specified to be greater than some target value.

The basic LP solution technique, called the simplex methods, was developed by George Dantzig in the early 50's to handle allocation problems.[(10.5)] It is now recognized that Kantorovich, the Russian mathematician, developed a similar method as early as 1939, but was unknown in the west until 1960.[(10.6)]

To illustrate the basic formulation, Equation 10.1 is simplified for a processing facility, with the option of selling gas or converting some gas to NGL's. Equation 10.2 summarizes the basic alternatives. The profit maximization indicates that gas sells for $2.0 per mcf and NGL for $15.0 per barrel.

Maximize:

$$\text{Profit} = 2.0 * \text{Gas} + 15.0 * \text{NGL} \tag{10.2}$$

Subject To:

$$0.25 * \text{Gas} + 3.5 * \text{NGL} = 20 \ \$K$$
$$\text{Gas} = \$100 \text{ MMcf}$$
$$\text{NGL} = 1{,}000 \text{ bbls}$$

Three constraints are imposed on the system. The first requires operating cost to equal $20,000 per month. The second and third require gas to be less than 100 MMcf per month and NGL's to equal 1,000 barrels.

This problem appears simple, but suppose management requires the plant to reduce operating costs below the specified level. Equation 10.2 could be solved using formal calculus. Linear programming extends this framework to allow inequalities to be expressed in the relationship. Producing exactly 100 MMcf or 1000 barrels or spending exactly $20,000 often proves to be quite difficult. The constraints reflect the most that can be produced or spent. Reality dictates that lesser volumes or costs might be better. LP extends Equation 10.2 by substituting inequalities for the equalities in the subject to section. Equation 10.3 illustrates the changes. The inequalities force the model to consider ranges of solutions, rather than single point estimates. NGL recovery must also be less than 15.5 barrels per Mcf.

Maximize:

$$\text{Profit} = 2.0*\text{Gas} + 15.0*\text{NGL} \tag{10.3}$$

Subject To:

$$0.25*\text{Gas} + 3.5*\text{NGL} \leq \$20{,}000$$
$$\text{Gas} \leq \$100 \text{ MMcf}$$
$$\text{NGL Recovery} * \text{Gas} \leq 1{,}000 \text{ bbls}$$
$$0 \leq \text{NGL Recovery} \leq 15.5$$

The following graphical framework depicts the underlying framework for solving LP questions. We forego describing the basic simplex method and other LP solution techniques, as other sources are designed to document the details of these methods.[10.7-10.9] The focus here is on setting up the problem and interpreting the output, not the mechanics of solving the problem. The computer will do the basic work. Once the professional understands the importance and flexibility of optimization, you can always acquire more information about the solution mechanics.

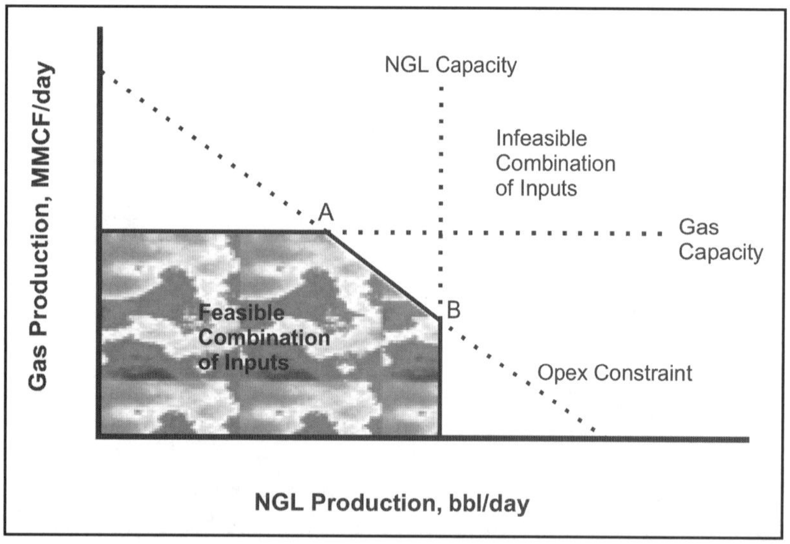

Figure 10.4 Gas and NGL constraints

Step 1 in the solution mechanics begins by graphing the constraints depicted in Figure 10.4. The gas and NGL production volumes are listed as the x and y-axis, respectively. The vertical line reflects maximum NGL production, while the horizontal line signifies gas production capacity. The downward sloping line captures the operating cost constraint. *(Please note that x and y scales have been adjusted to fit the space for this figure.)*

Each constraint is a combination of a dotted and solid line. The solid line defines the area termed the *feasible region*. The intersection of the three lines occurs at Points A and B. Any movement from the solid lines toward the origin reflects a feasible combination of gas and NGL production, and Opex cost. The solid line specifies a production combination, which satisfies all constraints; hence the term feasible region. Outside the solid lines, one or more constraints is exceeded. The non-shaded area is called the *infeasible region*

LP determines the optimum production volume by adding a series of lines to the graph based on the profit equation (10.3). The profit equation is linear. By trying different combinations of gas and NGL's, the optimum is determined. Figure 10.5 adds three profit curves, labeled Revenue 1, 2 and 3. The axes are, again, daily NGL and gas production. With specified prices, revenue is the sum of the products.

Revenue curve 1 indicates a starting point. The intersection of Revenue 1 with the solid line occurs in the vertical stage of the NGL capacity line. Increasing the volume of gas and NGL's shifts the revenue curve upwards to point B. Since Revenue 2 exceeds Revenue 1, the combination of gas and NGL production at Point B is preferable. Further increasing revenue to Revenue 3 intersects the constraints at Point A, again a better result. Note that if the revenue lines had been parallel to the AB segment, several combinations of gas and NGL production would yield the maximum profit.

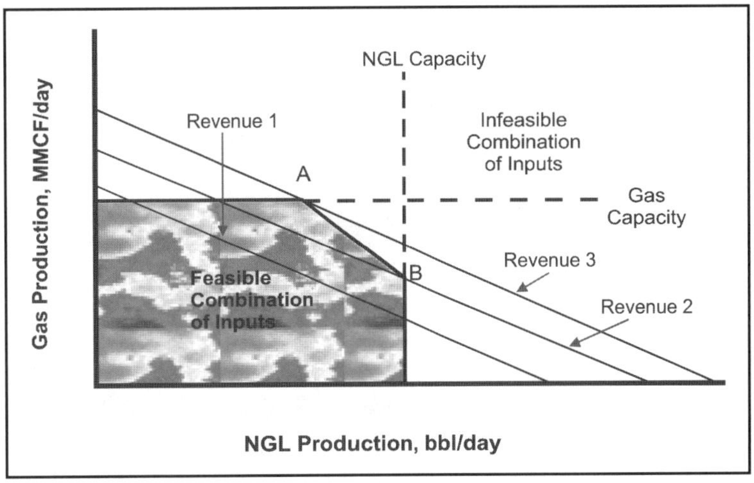

Figure 10.5 Optimal production leel to maximize profit

Example 10.1 converts the values and relationships formulated in Equation 10.3 into a spreadsheet format. The first column defines the decision variables to be changed in the model: gas and NGL production. The second column specifies production volume, followed by the price and cost per unit of volume produced. The last column multiplies price times production, then sums the total value. Total revenue is the sum of the revenue components; total cost is derived similarly. Total profit, in the last row, is the difference between revenue and cost.

Example 10.1: LP formulation for Gas vs. NGL plant split.

	Volume	Price Per Unit	Revenue
Gas, MMcf	66	2.00	132.00
NGL, bbls	1,000	15.00	15.00
		Total	147.00
	Production	**Cost Per Unit**	**Cost $m**
Gas, MMcf	66	0.25	16.50
NGL, bbls	1,000	3.50	3.50
			20.00
		Total Profit	127.00

If this was a traditional deterministic analysis, the results in the example would be followed with the typical what if analysis, requiring changes in the production combinations and recording the results. The fundamental question always becomes when to stop the What If process. Optimization formally defines the stopping point as the production volume that maximizes profit and satisfies all constraints. The What If process usually takes some time, although it is fairly easy in this simplified model. As the models become increasingly complex, the number of trials increases exponentially.

The actual event, which forms the basis of this example, arose because the plant was given a fixed objective for operating costs for the fiscal year. The first reaction of the engineer was to maximize NGL production, since NGL's are worth more than gas in the market place (on a BTU equivalent basis). The key point is that the outcome was preconceived based on the relative value of gas versus NGL's. The recommended solution: produce 1000 barrels of NGL and then enough gas to stay within the operating budget and production constraints. This is the situation illustrated in Example 10.1. Total profit is $127,000 when NGL recovery is maximized. But, does this method maximize value?

Setting up the spreadsheet for optimization requires three main components: defining the cell to be maximized (total profit), the changing cells (gas and NGL production), and the constraints. The name convention in Excel is used, so that the cell with total profit of $127,000 has been named Total_Profit. The production cells were named in the same manner.

Manual solutions fail to consider other alternatives, and may be suboptimal. To illustrate this point, total profit is optimized using Premium Solver. Access the Solver option on your specific

SCREEN 10.1 Optimization of Production

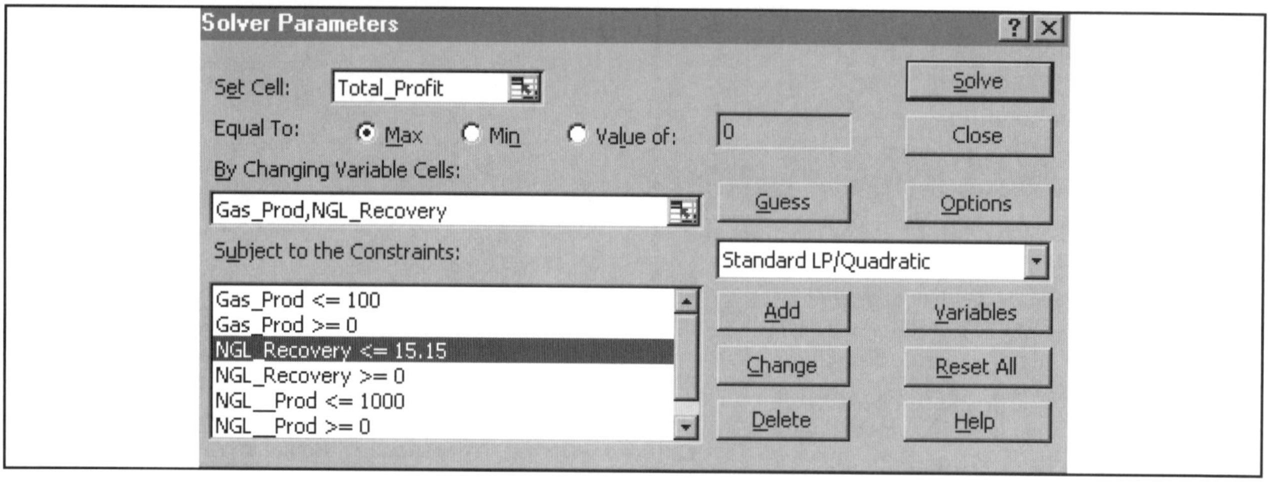

spreadsheet under the Tools menu. If solver fails to show up, click on the Add-Ins and click on Solver. If the Solver option isn't available, you will need to access the Excel disk and load it. The resulting input panel looks like the input panel in Screen 10.1. The basic format should be clear by now. First, the inputs ask which cell is being optimized – Total_Profit. Then tell the software to search for a maximum, a minimum, or set a specific value. Considerable flexibility is conferred with this option. Next, tell Solver to find a solution by changing cells Gas_Prod and NGL_Prod. Note, by changing the production streams, the following revenue, cost, and profit cells change. The spreadsheet formulation must connect the changing cells to the Set Cell and Constraints; otherwise, no changes occur in the computation. This is sometimes hard to remember and implement.

The buttons, like options, guess, add, change, reset all, delete, etc., are explained quite well in the associated manuals and help screens. The box labeled Standard LP or Quadratic specifies the solution methodology to be used. The choices are LP or nonlinear. This box comes with Solver Premium and is purchased separately. We recommend purchasing the enhanced version of Solver or Whats Best if you are going to use optimization tools often or for complicated projects. The versions that come with Excel limit the analysis to like 200 constraints, which is easily exceeded as the user develops familiarity with the process.

With the information contained in the input boxes, the optimal combination of gas and NGL production can be determined. An additional constraint restricting the budget to less than \$20 thousand (k) is hidden below the scroll bar in the Subject to the Constraints: section.

Before illustrating the solution, a common mistake is in specifying the constraints. The computer solves equations much faster than manual computations, but does not understand limits on values. Saying that Gas_Prod $\leq$ 100 MMcf seems obvious. Forgetting to tell the computer that Gas_Prod must also be greater than 0 occurs quite often when first learning to use optimization techniques. Without the greater than 0 constraint, the computer will search from 100 MMcf to $-\infty$. This is bad enough with costs, but negative production, and other impossible physical values distort the results beyond recognition. Trying to explain negative production or other physically impossible results usually proves to be quite embarrassing.

Clicking on the solve button required less than 5 seconds on a 450 Mhz PC. The solution in Premium Solver alters the original spreadsheet to show the answer. In What's Best, a separate spreadsheet is generated with the answer, but both programs reach the same solution. The solution is summarized in Example 10.2. Bypassing all of the NGL's, at a cost of \$3.50 per unit, and producing only gas increases total profit to \$140,000, a \$13,000 increase over the maximize NGL option. This is called a *bounded solution*, because the optimal point occurs at the boundary of one of the xy lines.

Example 10.2: Solution to Gas vs. NGL optimization.

	Production	Price Per Unit	Revenue
Gas, MMcf	88	2	160.00
NGL, bbls	0	15	0
		Total	160.00
	Production	**Cost Per Unit**	**Cost $M**
Gas, MMcf	80	0.25	20.00
NGL, bbls	0	3.5	0
			20.00
		Total Profit	140.00

Finding that the intuitive solution differs from the LP solution offers the best example of how LP aids investment planning. The intuitive solution, based on the correct impression that NGL's are worth more than gas, ignored the binding constraint of costs. Profits are a function of value relative to cost, not just sales price. The inability to look at the system of equations together, rather than one at a time, prevented a system assessment. If operating costs were not a constraint, the plant should produce NGL's first, and then gas. Operating costs were a stated objective here, and should be formally recognized.

LP improves the investment decision, because it compares the objectives and constraints simultaneously. It also helps those setting objectives understand the likely consequences of specific goals. Whether the objectives are profit, reserves, Opex, etc., understanding the impact of how setting goals impacts decision making always improves the outcome. The movement toward business units or assets teams certainly corrects deficiencies in the traditional organization. But, the key element is setting objectives properly. Our experience suggests that objective setting, could be benefit from a more focused, organized systems approach, rather than the often arbitrary, in appearance and fact, objectives. Budgeting and strategic planning will be discussed later to illustrate other optimization procedures.

Faced with the result shown earlier, an argument can be made to relax the operating cost constraint. Evaluating a higher Opex is easily evaluated because the example is so simple. Just keep adding NGL production and keep track of profit and cost. This trial and error approach follows traditional practice. LP provides output, which describes the relationship between increasing Opex and profit. Of course to understand the output of such tables, one has to know the meaning of a unique set of terms.

Example 10.2a shows two tables. The first describes the answer report. The columns describe the cell reference, cell name, cell value (for the final solution), the original formula, the status of the constraint (was the cell limit reached) and, finally, a variable called the *slack variable*. All but the last cell are repeats of the input information. The slack cell is computed from the third and fourth columns. If the solution value equals the maximum value, the cell is considered binding and there is no slack, meaning it can't be changed. Opex, for example, was $20,000 with a maximum of $20,000; thus, there is no slack or room for change in Opex. Zero slack means a binding constraint exits.

The sensitivity report generates more confusion than the answer report, primarily because different terms are used for linear versus nonlinear models. Whatever the term used, they reflect common sensitivity analysis. Everyone has changed one or more spreadsheet values, then hit the recalc key. The sensitivity report summarizes the impact of changes in values used to compute the objective function, and the right hand side of the constraints, like 100 barrels per day.

The first three columns in the Changing Cells section repeat information from the spreadsheet. The last column, the *reduced gradient* column, is also called the *slack variable* or the *dual value*. Reduced gradient normally signifies a nonlinear problem, while slack and dual reflect linear formulations. Both capture the impact on the objective function (profit) by altering the changing cell by one unit. The Changing Cells section measures the impact of altering the nonbinding variables only. Please make note of this.

The reduced gradient value deviates from zero only when a constraint is binding. The negative 13 indicates that adding one barrel of NGL production would reduce profit by $13. The units of the dual or

Example 10.2a: The answer and sensitivity reports for gas vs. NGL optimization.

Constraints					
Cell	**Name**	**Cell Value**	**Formula**	**Status**	**Slack**
$C$4	NGL__Prod	0.0	$C$4<=1000	Not Binding	1000
$C$4	NGL__Prod	0.0	$C$4>=0	Binding	0
$E$10	Total_Cost	20,000.0	$E$10<=20000	Binding	-
$C$3	Gas_Prod	80.0	$C$3<=100	Not Binding	20
$C$3	Gas_Prod	80.0	$C$3>=0	Not Binding	80
$C$13	NGL_Recovery	0.0	$C$13>=0	Binding	0
$C$13	NGL_Recovery	0.0	$C$13<=15.15	Not Binding	15.15

Sensitivity Report

Changing Cells			
Cell	**Name**	**Final Value**	**Reduced Gradient**
	Gas_Prod	80	0
	NGL_Recovery	0	0
Constraints			
Cell	**Name**	**Final Value**	**Lagrange Multiplier**
$C$4	NGL__Prod	0	0
$C$4	NGL__Prod	0	-13
$E$10	Total_Cost	20,000.00	7.00

reduced gradient follow the units of the objective function (profit or $'s here). Because LP deals with simultaneous equations, adding 1 barrel of NGL production would increase cost and the Opex constraint is still $20,000 per day. Since 1 barrel of NGL adds $3.50 in cost, gas production at $0.25 must be lowered by enough Mcf to reduce Opex by the same $3.50. Making the appropriate changes in the Exhibit 10.1 spreadsheet gives a new profit value of $139,987, or a value $13 less than the optimum profit.

Observe that the reduced gradient or dual value is a sophisticated sensitivity. It assumes that the rest of the system must change when other variables change. LP thus formally recognizes the interrelationships in the system, which the user is forced to perform manually in most sensitivities.

Another, often asked sensitivity concerns the benefit of relaxing constraint values, like $20,000 per day. Had management been somewhat arbitrary in selecting a $20,000 per day Opex, knowing the benefit of increasing or decreasing the budget constraint would be useful. The Constraint section of Example 10.2 repeats the spreadsheet values again in the first three columns. The last column, Lagrange Multiplier, refers to the added profit realized from increasing the constraints. Only the $20,000 Opex constraint was critical in this simple example, so only one of the constraints is listed. For every dollar added to the Opex constraint profits would increase by $7. This result is easily computed from the raw data: gas sells for $2.0 and costs $0.25, for a net of $1.75. If the Opex constraint increases by $1.00, 4 extra Mcf can be sold for a net gain of $7.00 (= 4 × $1.75). A Lagrange multiplier is given for every binding constraint in more complicated example, eliminating the need for repetitive sensitivities.

As the terms dual and reduced gradient are used to differentiate between linear and nonlinear optimization, shadow prices are substituted for Lagrange multipliers to designate a linear relationship, while Lagrange signifies nonlinear constraints. Output from most spreadsheets uses the nonlinear labels as a general convention. These columns also apply to linear formulations as well.

The issue of linearity also impacts interpretation of the gradient and Lagrange columns. If the system of equations is linear, then extrapolating the results beyond the current values is accurate. For nonlinear equations the values are accurate only around the solution value. When working with nonlinear systems, always be careful to actually check the sensitivity values by changing values in the spreadsheet before quoting the results to someone else or using them to make decisions.

The terms linear and nonlinear are used throughout the chapter. LP methods require really three conditions to hold for a linear system to exist. These include:

- Changing a single variable causes a proportional change in other variables,
- The variable interactions are additive (no multiplication or division), and
- All variables are real numbers.

These conditions hold for the direct solution of problems. Virtually every problem, even if it deviates from these conditions can be modified to satisfy the three constraints. In the early mainframe days, LP users spent as much time linearizing their non-linear models as formulating the problem. As computer hardware and software improved, this requirement diminished, though it is still useful in certain cases.

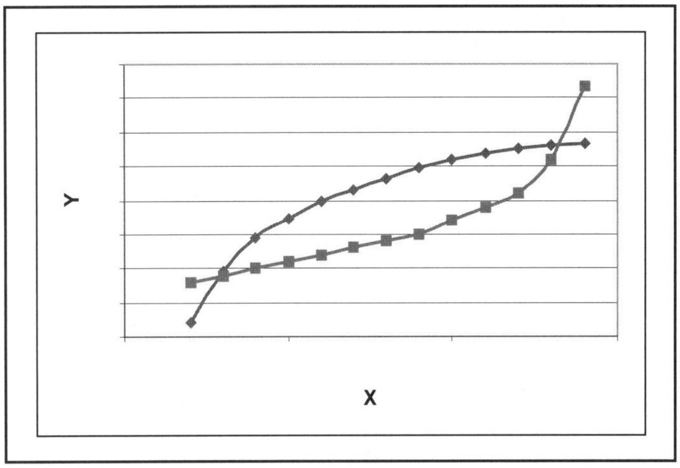

Figure 10.6 Nonlinear optimization

Current technology allows the user to solve non-LP problems without manipulating the model formulation. We include all of these methods under the heading of non-LP methods. The use of the term non-linear as applied here deviates from normal practice, but does indicate the processes involved. Figure 10.6 demonstrates a simple nonlinear relationship to evaluate.

Non-LP Programming

Non-LP programming methods deviate from the simplex method, which relies on matrix algebra to simplify the computation. Some, like integer programming, begin with the simplex method and then switch to other algorithms. These methods have become so easy and cheap, one economist, Herbert Scarf, has made the statement, "For studying large firms, pack up your derivative in mothballs."[(10.10)] The same holds true for much of the engineering rules of thumb developed during the slide rule era and now programmed into most software. The precise outline for non-LP solutions depends on the professional usually. More importantly, most real world problems mix elements of each programming technique. Any attempt to describe actual practice with one method normally involves excessive distortions. The categories described here generally fit the label being discussed, but could and often do include elements of other methods.

Integer Programming (IP)

Many real world events preclude the use of real numbers; for example, companies normally build facilities using integer units (1 or 2 plants, not 1.5 plants). A common and famous denigration of statistics asks how a family can have 2.3 children. Budgeting reflects the most common application of IP in our experience. Shifting from a system, like LP, which allows real numbers to IP, which allows only integers, reverses the way math is normally taught. Normally, teachers begin with integer values and then go to real numbers. It is fairly common for professionals to assume that IP is simpler than LP for this reason. Nothing is further from the truth.

Integers increase the computational complexity, because computers use floating point arithmetic, where the value of 1 is characterized as 0.99999999 or 1.00000001. All values are computed to 8, 10, 12, 16, etc. decimal places depending on the precision being used. When integer values are reported, they represent a rounding process. For this reason, IP takes as much or more time to solve as many other optimization procedures. The typical process involves solving the problem first using the simplex method. Then, the program changes the LP solution in small increments until the changing cells satisfy the integer constraint. This procedure is called *branch-and-bound optimization.* Stripped of jargon, this means that the computer conducts sophisticated sensitivities until the constraint is satisfied.

The problem with iterative methods, such as *branch-and-bound*, is the extra time required to achieve a solution. The few seconds to find the LP solution often increases several orders of magnitude to find an IP solution. The length of time depends on the version of the software being used, machine speed, and the specification of the problem tolerance and precision. Solver and What's Best offer industrial or faster solution versions. The industrial versions are faster, on any machine, and more robust. As regards computing time, the faster the machine, the better.

IP is illustrated using a simple budgeting situation faced by every investor. With a limited budget, the combination of projects, which satisfies stated objectives, has to be selected. In an idealized world, omnipotent executives assess the relative merits of each project, and then seek the combination that achieves corporate objective(s), be it maximizing shareholder value, employment, stability, or individual bonuses. The classical decision system attempted to achieve the specified objective(s) by integrating various measures, like WACC, and then computing NPV or NPV/INV. The process then ranks the acceptable projects according to these measures until the budget is exhausted.

Various articles have even been written suggesting that ranking projects by NPV/INV is the only measure needed.[10.11] This is naive at best, and dangerous in reality. Such advice worked very well in the 50's and 60's, but once firms moved into larger, higher cost investments, the premise behind the exclusive use of NPV/INV evaporated. With billions of dollars being committed to single projects, the risks and possible returns totally destroy the premises that made NPV/INV viable as the only decision rule, if it ever was. The problem with relying on NPV/INV exclusively or in combination with other measures of value arises from evaluating the measures independently. Simply ranking projects from best to worst discards huge volumes of information, and ignores the interrelationship amongst the projects. Worse, NPV/INV assumes a large number of project to choose from, a low cost of identifying and investing, and that no project could jeopardize corporate financial security.

Previous chapters also demonstrate that the classical profit metrics ignore other, equally as important, elements in the valuation process. Risk, however specified, or risk tolerance can now be defined and measured much better than possible under the classical system. Good investment planning seeks to include these measures into the decision-making process. A commonly used term is *portfolio management*, which is defined as choosing the combination of projects that achieves the investors desired trade-off in risk and return. This trade-off can be defined over one time-period (a year) or multi-periods. The term used to define the risk and return trade-off is the *efficient frontier*, as shown in Figure 10.7.

The efficient frontier describes the maximum return from a portfolio of projects for any given unit of risk. Figure 10.7 measures risk and return on a percentage basic to normalize the values for the size of the portfolio, allowing small and large investors to use the concept. For internal usage, the x-axis could be the standard deviation of the return (in \$'s or any other desired currency), and the y-axis measured by NPV or other metric. The efficient investor selects a portfolio along the line. An investor with a portfolio measured by the diamonds earns a smaller return for the same level of risk. The line is sometimes referred to

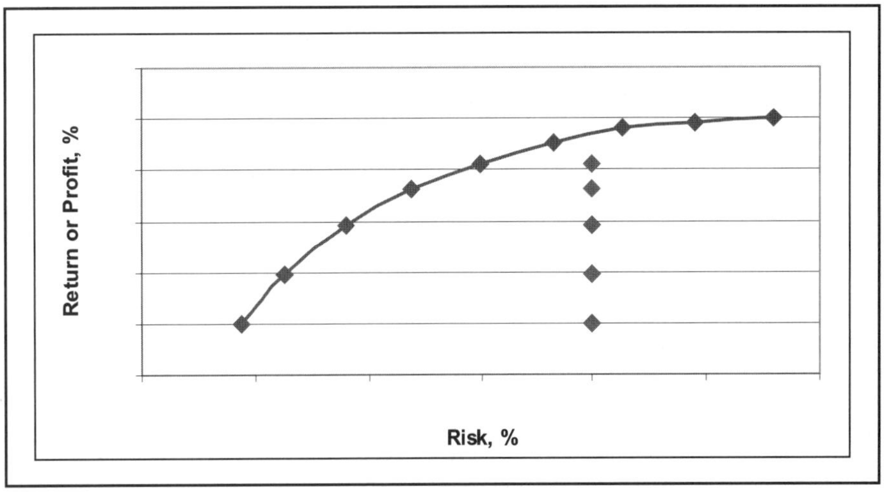

Figure 10.7 The efficient frontier of a portofolio of projects

as a fully diversified portfolio. Sometimes the graph is presented with the axis switched, so the graph reflects risk per unit of return. The concept is the same as Figure 10.7, with exactly the same interpretation.

As nicely, as the efficient frontier concept describes the trade-off, it ignores the additional aspect of project selection that creates even more problems for the decision-maker – the multiple goals and objectives that conflict with each other. Every investor must address more than just the objective of maximizing shareholder wealth, including: production replacement, Opex reduction, strategic issues, Capex limitations, and financial constraints like *ROCE* (See Chapter 4). Other objectives are piled on top of these. Simplified ranking methods never test to see if better combinations of projects exist. They normally reflect only one feasible solution, not necessarily the optimal solution. To properly evaluate the combined impact of including or excluding projects, more detailed analysis is necessary.

The easiest way to illustrate the search for the optimal portfolio begins with the standard spreadsheet approach. Here projects are listed on a spreadsheet along with whatever measures of value are desired. Example 10.3 shows one such list of projects. The first column provides the project number, followed in order by NPV, NPV/INV, reserves added, P_s, expected monetary value, and standard deviation. This is a highly simplified list, but adding additional columns of other summary variables just requires extra columns.

Example 10.3: Measures of value for 16 different projects. All values in $m (million).

Project #	NPV	NPV/INV x.xx	Mean Reserves MMBOE	Project Cost	P_s	EMV	NPV Stand. Dev.
1	21.3	1.70	7.2	12.50	50%	4.40	31.60
2	9.0	2.00	6.4	4.50	60%	3.60	23.90
3	12.3	3.08	12.0	4.00	24%	-0.09	11.00
4	14.1	1.88	7.8	7.50	22%	-2.75	25.60
5	9.3	2.16	6.4	4.30	20%	-1.58	24.50
6	12.8	2.98	4.5	4.30	22%	-0.54	28.20
7	13.2	2.75	7.3	4.80	22%	-0.84	24.90
8	9.5	1.79	4.7	5.30	75%	5.80	14.90
9	9.5	1.07	4.4	8.90	85%	6.74	12.20
10	14.2	3.80	8.6	3.74	32%	2.00	15.70
11	14.9	0.81	6.3	18.50	80%	8.22	29.50
12	11.4	4.56	8.8	2.50	22%	0.56	26.30
13	15.5	1.20	14.8	12.90	90%	12.66	17.40
14	14.9	1.57	7.9	9.50	85%	11.24	25.30
15	10.6	2.47	6.1	4.30	45%	2.41	25.80
16	14.8	1.64	5.6	9.00	53%	3.61	29.50
Total =	207.30	1.78	118.80	116.54		55.44	366.30

The values follow standard project measure. Those maximizing shareholder wealth would rank according to NPV in column 2 until the budget is exhausted. The absence of a discount rate in the NPV column indicates that any discount rate could be used. Those favoring capital efficiency would use the NPV/INV column. Others might opt for emphasizing the organic growth aspects association with increased production. Project cost could reflect a single or multiple year estimates, depending on the orientation and practices of the company. The Ps signifies the project chance of success. The higher risk projects are associated with exploration, while the higher Ps's capture more typical development options. EMV measures the weighting of P_s and NPV's, further adjusted for dry hole or failure costs (See Chapter 8 for detail discussion). The standard deviation measures the variability of project NPV's obtained from a Monte Carlo simulation, and will be used later to formally include risk.

Faced with the 16 projects outlined in Example 10.3, the most commonly used approach is to sort the values from best to worst based on a criterion like NPV/INV which produces the ranking in Example 10.3a. Project 12 has the highest NPV/INV of 4.56, project 10 the next highest and so on. Note also that NPV/INV tends to be inversely related to project cost – the lower the cost, the higher the NPV/INV (See Chapter 5).

Example 10.3a: Ranking results using NPV/INV. All values in $m, except as noted.

Project #	NPV	NPV/INV X.XX	Mean Reserves MMBOE	Project Cost	P_s	EMV	NPV Stand. Dev.
12	11.40	4.56	8.80	2.50	0.22	0.56	26.30
10	14.20	3.80	8.60	3.74	0.32	2.00	15.70
3	12.30	3.08	12.00	4.00	0.24	-0.09	11.00
6	12.80	2.98	2.20	4.30	0.22	-0.54	28.20
7	13.20	2.75	3.30	4.80	0.22	-0.84	24.90
15	10.60	2.47	12.30	4.30	0.45	2.41	25.80
5	9.30	2.16	2.10	4.30	0.20	-1.58	24.50
2	9.00	2.00	6.40	4.50	0.60	3.60	23.90
4	14.10	1.88	7.80	7.50	0.22	-2.75	25.60
8	9.50	1.79	4.70	5.30	0.75	5.80	14.90
1	21.30	1.70	7.20	12.50	0.50	4.40	31.60
16	14.80	1.64	15.60	9.00	0.53	3.61	29.50
14	14.90	1.57	13.20	9.50	0.85	11.24	25.30
13	15.50	1.20	14.80	12.90	0.90	12.66	17.40
9	9.50	1.07	9.50	8.90	0.85	6.74	12.20
11	14.90	0.81	18.00	18.50	0.80	8.22	29.50
Total =	207.30	1.78	146.50	116.54		55.44	366.30

Adding a budget constraint of $40 million lets the investor determine the preferred projects. Summing the projects from the top until the threshold of $40 million is reached yields the following results:

Project #	12	10	3	6	7	15	5	2	Total
Cum Cost $m	2.50	6.24	10.24	14.54	19.34	23.64	27.94	32.44	39.94
Cum. NPV $m	11.4	25.6	37.9	50.7	63.9	74.5	83.8	92.8	106.9

The NPV/INV ratio selected eight projects with a total cost of $39.94 million and increased shareholder value by $106.90 million. This approach requires nothing more than the ability to use the sort feature in a spreadsheet.

The same solution can be obtained by formulating the problem in an optimization framework. Assuming the investor wants to optimize NPV, the spreadsheet has to be modified to allow the project parameters to vary as the combination of projects selected changes. Example 10.3b transforms Example 10.3b to illustrate the introduction of the integers that specify which projects are to be selected.

Example 10.3b: Basic format for optimizing project portfolio. All values in \$m, except as noted.

Weight	NPV	NPV/INV x.xx	Reserves MMBOE	EMV	RAV @\$40	Budget	Project#
1	21.3	1.7	7.2	4.4	8.8	12.5	1
1	9.0	2.0	6.4	3.6	1.9	4.5	2
1	12.3	3.1	12.0	-0.1	10.8	4.0	3
1	14.1	1.9	7.8	-2.7	5.9	7.5	4
1	9.3	2.2	2.1	-1.6	1.8	4.3	5
1	12.8	3.0	2.2	-0.5	2.9	4.3	6
1	13.2	2.8	3.3	-0.8	5.4	4.8	7
1	9.5	1.8	4.7	5.8	6.7	5.3	8
1	9.5	1.1	9.5	6.7	7.6	8.9	9
1	14.2	3.8	8.6	2.0	11.1	3.7	10
1	14.9	0.8	18.0	8.2	4.0	18.5	11
1	11.4	4.6	8.8	0.6	2.8	2.5	12
1	15.5	1.2	14.8	12.7	11.7	12.9	13
1	14.9	1.6	13.2	11.2	6.9	9.5	14
1	10.6	2.5	12.3	2.4	2.3	4.3	15
1	14.8	1.6	15.6	3.6	3.9	9.0	16
Total =	207.3	1.8	146.5	55.4	94.6	116.5	

The main difference between the two spreadsheets is the addition of the first column, labeled weight. Weight indicates the amount of each project to be included in the budget. If the number is one, the weight of one is multiplied by NPV, reserves, etc., and summed to determine total budget values. A zero weight means the project is excluded from the budget.

Screen 10.2 shows the input provided to Solver. Total_PV was selected for maximization, so the task is to find the combinations of projects, which maximize NPV. Total_NPV is the sum of the NPV column, or \$207.3 in Example 10.3b. The changing cells reflect the values of the weights for the 16 projects, as represented by the values in the Weight column. Three weight constraints are added: the weights have to be greater than 0, less than 1, and equal to an integer value. The combined effect of the three assumptions restricts the weights equal to either 0 or 1. The other two constraints: Total_Cost ≤ 40 is the budget constraint, while NPV/INV ≥ 2 is an additional constraint added to see

SCREEN 10.2 Solver Setup for Optimizing NPV

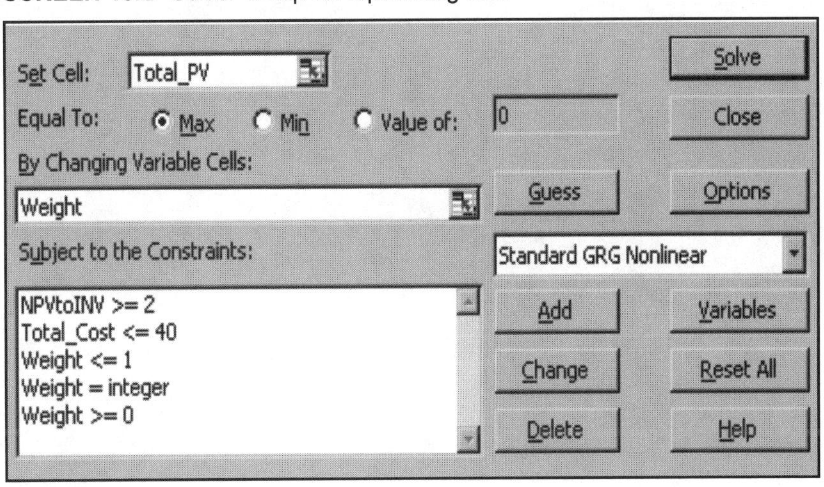

if the profit ratio is binding or not. The intent here is to show why and when NPV/INV meets the needs of the firm; conversely, cases where simple ranking fails to satisfy the overall objectives are illustrated.

The solver input is as basic as it appears. Clicking on the Solve button initiates the run. The branch and bound approach takes far longer than the LP solution method, lasting about 2 minutes on a 450 Mhz pentium with loose precision and tolerance specifications. The extra time is required to force the weights to either 0 or 1. The branch and bound method begins by solving an LP approach, and then iterating from the LP solution until all values in the weight column become 0 or 1. A rough estimate is that the algorithm converged after trying about 750 different combinations of branches and bounds.

After solving the problem, the basic solution looks like Exhibit 10.3c. The integer program obtained exactly the same values as the NPV/INV ranking, spent the same amount of money, and returned the same profit. The 0 and 1 values in the weight column indicate the final selections. This indicates that ranking using NPV/INV or any other criteria often produces the same results when only a few or simple constraints exist. This is the reason ranking with NPV/INV and other measures produced good results historically. Most projects were fairly small, the primary, if not only, objective was profit maximization, and secondary issues were ignored or minimized. When investors began to adopting multiple, often conflicting objectives, combined with incursions into higher cost, higher risk projects, and formal introduction of risk assessment and management, ranking becomes imprecise, often misleading producing misleading results.

Rather than incorporate significantly greater complexity into the analysis, the benefits of optimization can be illustrated by adding just one new constraint. A common goal is to increase ultimate production, or increase reserves in the mineral industry. Example 10.3c, the optimization with a budget constraint, showed that the projects selected increased reserves by 63.5 MMBOE. Adding the objective of increasing reserve additions by more than 70 MMBOE to the list of investment objectives complicates the ranking with any single measure. One approach recombines selected projects until the reserve objective is achieved. The number of combinations of 16 projects taken 8 projects at a time (the original number needed to consume the budget) is 12,870, the analyst would have to manually generate 12,870

Example 10.3c: Optimized rankings for projects. All values in $m, except as noted.

Weight	NPV	NPV/INV x.xx	Reserves MMBOE	EMV	RAV @$40	Budget	Project #
0	0.0	0.0	0.0	0.0	-12.5	0.0	1
1	9.0	2.0	6.4	3.6	1.9	4.5	2
1	12.3	3.1	12.0	-0.1	10.8	4.0	3
1	14.1	1.9	7.8	-2.7	5.9	7.5	4
1	9.3	2.2	2.1	-1.6	1.8	4.3	5
1	12.8	3.0	2.2	-0.5	2.9	4.3	6
1	13.2	2.8	3.3	-0.8	5.4	4.8	7
0	0.0	0.0	0.0	0.0	-2.8	0.0	8
0	0.0	0.0	0.0	0.0	-1.9	0.0	9
1	14.2	3.8	8.6	2.0	11.1	3.7	10
0	0.0	0.0	0.0	0.0	-10.9	0.0	11
1	11.4	4.6	8.8	0.6	2.8	2.5	12
0	0.0	0.0	0.0	0.0	-3.8	0.0	13
0	0.0	0.0	0.0	0.0	-8.0	0.0	14
1	10.6	2.5	12.3	2.4	2.3	4.3	15
0	0.0	0.0	0.0	0.0	-10.9	0.0	16
Total =	106.9	2.7	63.5	2.8	-5.8	39.9	

combinations to verify the same results. Ranking becomes very complex when even more objectives, like Opex reduction, financial objectives – like ROCE or Net Income, or cash flow, are added. Imagine how complicated this becomes for multinationals, with the additional stipulation that some monies must go to each geographical entity. Although overly simplistic, the optimization process is a vehicle for running these 12,870 iterations and then using the max function in the spreadsheet to select the best choice.

The easiest solution is to expand the constraints in the Solver setup to include a reserve objective. The change to the Solver input box is not shown, since just one line item is added to the constraints section. The solution to the IP is summarized in Exhibit 10.3d.

Example 10.3d: Optimized Ranking With Reserves > 70 MMBOE.

Weight	NPV	NPV/INV x.xx	Reserves MMBOE	EMV	RAV @$40	Budget	Project #
0	0.0	0.0	0.0	0.0	-12.5	0.0	1
1	9.0	2.0	6.4	3.6	1.9	4.5	2
1	12.3	3.1	12.0	-0.1	10.8	4.0	3
1	14.1	1.9	7.8	-2.7	5.9	7.5	4
0	0.0	0.0	0.0	0.0	-7.5	0.0	5
1	12.8	3.0	2.2	-0.5	2.9	4.3	6
0	0.0	0.0	0.0	0.0	-7.8	0.0	7
0	0.0	0.0	0.0	0.0	-2.8	0.0	8
0	0.0	0.0	0.0	0.0	-1.9	0.0	9
1	14.2	3.8	8.6	2.0	11.1	3.7	10
0	0.0	0.0	0.0	0.0	-10.9	0.0	11
1	11.4	4.6	8.8	0.6	2.8	2.5	12
0	0.0	0.0	0.0	0.0	-3.8	0.0	13
0	0.0	0.0	0.0	0.0	-8.0	0.0	14
1	10.6	2.5	12.3	2.4	2.3	4.3	15
1	14.8	1.6	15.6	3.6	3.9	9.0	16
Total =	99.2	2.5	73.7	8.8	-13.5	39.8	

Adding one constraint – reserves >70 MMBOE – reduces NPV by almost $10 million, while still spending the $40 million budget. Selected projects now include: 2 to 4, 6, 10, 12, 15, 16, which differs significantly from the earlier solution. Two companies, faced with the same investment prospects and investment criterion, select entirely different investment combinations, due to the way the objectives are specified.

The budget specification process oftentimes fails to adequately understand the influence objectives have on investment behavior. The often-cavalier attitude toward setting these objectives compounds the problem. Far too many investors set arbitrary objectives, without grasping the impact on the ultimate investment patterns. By analyzing the information in Example 10.3d, executives can begin to visualize how investment patterns vary as specific objectives are combined. Does adding a reserve objective, which leads to a reduction in NPV, increase value? The answer is perhaps. Every summary measure reflects different aspects of investing. NPV emphasizes the next ten years, while reserve additions focus on replacing assets, a longer term view. Seeking a balance between conflicting short and long-term objectives, however well the objectives have been formulated, is as complex as the most sophisticated engineering analysis. The various programming tools strive to understand the complex interactions between investment objectives.

Example 10.3 describes the basic, non-LP process. The process utilized here is actually a combination of *integer programming* and *goal programming*. IP should be self-evident at this point, while *goal programming* captures multiple objectives. Available software cannot optimize multiple objectives right now. To achieve multiple optimization include the other variables of interest as constraints.

Quadratic Programming (QP)

Example 10.3 optimized proposed investments using traditional categories by ignoring risk. The current focus on risk assessment can also be included in the investment decision process. The *portfolio* concept, described in Figure 10.7, creeps into almost every budgeting or strategic planning process. Project selected in Example 10.3 represent a portfolio, without ever incorporating risk formally into the decision-making. Quadratic programming is often used to meld common risk and return measures into the planning process. QP extends LP by adding the capability to square various terms.

Portfolio management began with the work of Markowitz,[10.12] and extended by Markowitz and others.[10.13] Hightower and David have applied the same principles to petroleum exploration.[10.14] Most texts describing quadratic optimization reverse the format used by Markowitz, as shown in Equation 10.4.

Minimize: $$\sum_{i=1}^{n}\sum_{j=1}^{m} x_i * x_j * s_{ij} \qquad (10.4)$$

Subject to: $$\sum_{i=1}^{n} x_i * r_j \geq 0.12 \qquad \sum_{i=1}^{n} x_i = 1$$

where: x = the percentage of the portfolio allocated to asset i or j.

The common set up asks the algorithm to minimize risk, while requiring return to exceed some value: 12% in the example. The format in Equation 10.4 differs from many applications, because it originated in the stock market. The x_i variable pertains to the percentage of the portfolio that each asset represents. The j's correspond to the relationship between one asset and another asset. The σ indicates the variance-covariance matrix. Variance is just standard deviation squared, and covariance measures the degree of relationship between assets. Covariance is correlation with values ranging from plus to minus infinity, instead of -1 to 1. These terms are covered in detail in Chapter 6.

Variances measure risk, rather than standard deviations, because classical statistics shows that when combining dispersion measures, one should always use variance to weight each value correctly. Since standard deviations are actually derived by first computing variances, then taking square roots, the variance more accurately measures relative dispersion than standard deviation. More importantly, it puts a greater weight on values further away from the mean, which reflects most peoples risk definition.

The constraint in Equation 10.4 measures the return objective. The product of x and r yields the average return from the portfolio. A return of 12% was assumed for illustration only. If there were three assets with expected returns of 10%, 12%, and 16%, the expected return, assuming equal splits of the three assets is, 0.33*10 + 0.33*12 + 0.33*16 = 12.54. Therefore, the constraint is a weighted average of the three assets returns.

While this specification occurs quite often, we prefer the original Markowitz idea for two reasons: First, Markowitz defined the problem the way most people actually make the decisions, and two, it incorporates risk in the way outlined in Chapter 8. Equation 10.5 shows the basic format used by Markowitz.

Maximize: $$\mu - A * \sigma^2 \qquad (10.5)$$

Subject to: $$\sum_{i=1}^{n} x_i = 1 \quad \text{and} \quad 0 \leq x_i \leq 1$$

The variables are the same as in Equation 10.1, with the addition of A and μ. The μ term is the average return of the portfolio (12% in the constraint above), whether measured as NPV, SIV, or some other parameter. The A measures attitude toward risk. As discussed in Chapter 8, many standard parameters assume a risk neutral attitude. Expected monetary value is a classic case. Equation 10.5 allows information about risk to be inserted directly, whereas Equation 10.4 requires additional work to incorporate risk tolerances.

The added benefit of Equation 10.5 is the ability to draw inferences about risk preferences, based on investment decisions. By giving managers carefully designed investment portfolio options, their selections reveal values for A. Understanding A is fairly simple. A value of 0 implies that decision makers are risk neutral. Observe that if A=0, the standard deviation doesn't matter and projects are ranked according to project NPV. Switching to a NPV/INV ranking still assumes A=0 and makes risk synonymous with capital expenditure, which ignores other, relevant risk components.

Management, in all industries, is commonly characterized, as being very risk averse and this perception is often associated with a derogatory sneer or statement. Recent analysis of risk attitudes suggests that management mirrors society if they truly are risk averse. A concept called *prospect theory,* asserts "people making decisions in uncertain conditions weigh prospective losses twice as heavily as putative gains." The authors also conclude that people "tend to pay too much attention to recent data and not enough to long-run averages or statistical odds. These biases, taken together, motivate people to crowd together and follow trends."*(10.15)*

The project rankings in previous budgeting examples can be extended to include risk by utilizing the standard deviation information in the last column of Example 10.3. Standard deviations for each project were obtained by applying Monte Carlo simulation techniques to each project (See Chapter 8). A direct approach used to incorporate risk aversion into project ranking was the risk-adjusted value (RAV), as introduced in Chapter 8. It should be obvious that the primary obstacle to implementing Equation 10.5 is choosing a value for A. RAV circumvents this problem by assuming that utility can be expressed exponentially relative to budget size. The basic equation is repeated in Equation 10.6.

$$RAV = \overline{X} - \left(\frac{\sigma^2}{2B}\right) \qquad \textbf{(10.6)}$$

Under RAV and the Markowitz formulation, projects with no standard deviation ($\sigma = 0$) rank on the value measure, NPV, SIV, etc. The portion of Equation 10.6 in parenthesis behaves like the $A*\sigma^2$ in the Markowitz specification. Risk consists of two components: variability in returns (σ^2) and attitude (A in Markowitz and 1/2B in RAV). In RAV the aversion level is approximated by the variance relative to the budget level. Higher variances relative to a given budget increase the value in parenthesis, thus, lowering the RAV.

Examples of RAV rankings are provided in Example 10.4 for three budget rankings: $10, $20, and $40 million. At $10 million the top ranked projects are 3, 9, 10, and 13. Increasing the budget another $10 million adds only project

Example 10.4: Example of RAV results with various budget sizes. Values in $m.

	RAV for Budget of:		
Project #	**10**	**20**	**40**
1	-28.63	-3.66	8.82
2	-19.56	-5.28	1.86
3	6.25	9.28	10.79
4	-18.67	-2.28	5.91
5	-20.71	-5.71	1.80
6	-26.96	-7.08	2.86
7	-17.80	-2.30	5.45
8	-1.60	3.95	6.72
9	2.06	5.78	7.64
10	1.88	8.04	11.12
11	-28.61	-6.86	4.02
12	-23.18	-5.89	2.75
13	0.36	7.93	11.72
14	-17.10	-1.10	6.90
15	-22.68	-6.04	2.28
16	-28.71	-6.96	3.92

8 to the approved list. Doubling the budget to $40 million makes all projects positive, with projects 3, 10, and 13 clearly better than the others, with RAV values exceeding 10. The remaining projects have RAV's less than 9, with most less than 5.

As the size of the budget increases, the RAV of all projects rises, although at different rates. More importantly, the relative ranking of projects differs with budget level. Project 1, for instance, is the worst project at a $10 million budget, but the fourth best at the $40 million budget level. Project 1 has a high NPV and the highest standard deviation, which hurts the project at low budgets. With higher budgets, the standard deviation decreases in importance, as it should for risk averse investors.

Table 10.1 compares the RAV ranking with the NPV/INV ranking, using a $40 million budget. Note that the RAV used 4 fewer projects to spend the budget, while producing a much lower NPV. Adding formal risk measures typically reduces value measures like this. Also notice that the RAV selected larger projects, which are often precluded using NPV/INV measures.

TABLE 10.1

Comparison of NPV/INV and RAV Rankings

NPV/INV Ranking									
Project #	**12**	**10**	**3**	**6**	**7**	**15**	**5**	**2**	**4**
Cum Cost $MM	2.5	6.24	10.24	14.54	19.34	23.64	27.94	32.44	39.94
Cum. NPV $MM	11.4	25.6	37.9	50.7	63.9	74.5	83.8	92.8	106.9
RAV Rankings									
Project #	**13**	**10**	**3**	**1**	**9**				
Cum Cost $MM	12.9	16.6	20.6	33.1	42.0				
Cum. NPV $MM	15.5	29.7	42	63	72.5				
RAV Optimization									
Project #	**13**	**10**	**3**	**8**	**7**	**4**			
Cum Cost $MM	12.9	16.6	20.6	25.9	30.7	38.2			
Cum. NPV $MM	15.5	29.7	42	51.5	64.7	78.8			

To correct the slight overrun in budget of $2 million using the sorted RAV rankings, Solver was used to optimize RAV, subject to the $40 million budget constraint. As explained earlier, optimization benefits arise when marginal projects have to be traded off. The bottom three rows reflect the optimization results. The last two projects, 1 and 9, fall out in favor of three projects: 8, 7 and 4; thereby, increasing NPV to $78.8 million.

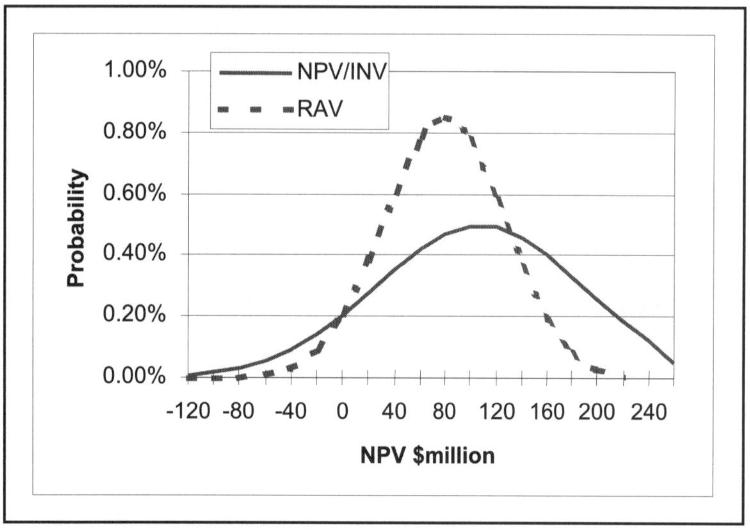

Figure 10.8 Distributions for two portfolios

What is the benefit of using RAV if NPV/INV yields a higher portfolio value? NPV/INV totally ignores variability. Choosing a portfolio based on NPV/INV yields σ = $80 million, while the optimized RAV has σ = $46.6, or about half. If we remember that RAV formally includes risk aversion, the objective should be to reduce variation in outcomes, which RAV achieved successfully.

Figure 10.8 draws the relative frequency distributions for the two portfolios assuming a normal distribution (probably unrealistic). The NPV/INV portfolio extends further to the right by a significant amount, and slightly more to the left. RAV approaches the x-axis or zero probability NPV outcome at about -60 on the low end and 200 at the upper end. The NPV/INV portfolio lies between about -120 and 270. Note that the results are consistent with the risk and return trade-off concept discussed throughout the book.

RAV optimization reduced portfolio variability. Some question whether σ truly measures the risk of the project. This line of reasoning holds that only the NPV's to the left of the mean or median indicate risk; others prefer to evaluate NPV's less than zero. The term, *semi-variance* (see Chapter 8), has been coined to capture such measures. To reflect these reduced variability measures, just compute variance if the value is less than the mean, zero or any other value you care are about. Another modern approach defines, *value at risk (VaR)*, which computes the maximum potential loss over a given time period and confidence level.[10.16] Others seek to go beyond some of the limitations of Var.[10.17]

Semi-variance measures help understand the impact of risk, at the cost of omitting the opportunities lost by focusing on avoiding losing money. Being too conservative harms shareholder value just as much as losing money. We have even seen a senior executive of a major company, himself accused of being highly risk averse, chastise the professional staffs for failing to offer investments with upside potential. Many professionals believe their management cares more about reducing risk than investing for the upside, except in a few, rare cases. Settling this issue is absolutely critical, especially if the refined procedures presented here are to be used effectively. Everyone has mission, vision, goal statements now, but few are confident that the values are measured properly.

The rankings using RAV could be expanded to reflect other, more complicated issues. But the main purpose, illustrating the difference in rankings when formally recognizing risk, has been served. To be fair, other profit metrics would yield partially or totally different rankings, as shown in Chapter 5. That differences arise with alternative ranking formats is unsurprising, the key issue is the basis and assumptions underlying the metrics chosen to make the investment decisions. The task of deciding measures trading off profit, variability and budget matches strategic objectives better than classical, one dimensional metrics. The next example highlights this difference.

Incorporating risk precisely requires knowledge of the covariance or correlation between assets. This input is often ignored in practice, implicitly assuming that individual project performances are independent. Newer simulation software allows direct evaluation of project correlations quite easily and we urge everyone to use this feature. In the absence of correlation information, Example 10.5 assumes zero correlation, which means Equation 10.4 minimizes the variances of the portfolio only.

Columns 1 and 2, labeled NPV/INV and RAV, repeat the results discussed earlier. Columns 3 thru 5 show the solutions for minimizing variance with three NPV constraints: > 50. > 75, and >100. Observe that NPV/INV has the highest NPV ($106.9) and the highest σ ($70.4). Moving to RAV lowers NPV ($74.2) and σ (40.7). Likewise, column 3 with the NPV requirement greater than 50 has a lower return and risk. As NPV constraint is relaxed, NPV and σ increase. In column 5, where NPV > 100, is allowed, the projects selected and values look remarkably like the NPV/INV results, differing only in the swapping of projects 4 and 5. Ranking by NPV/INV looks very much like a process for maximizing return, while maximizing risk, in this example.

The first reaction, to results like these, is often to ask what was really gained. We think at least two benefits accrue. One is a direct measure of risk and risk's impact on budget portfolios. More risk averse investors might prefer lower NPV's to keep risk down. Greater risk takers could opt for, perhaps, the portfolio described in column 4. Those virtually ignoring risk might select columns 1 or 5.

The second benefit originates in the opportunity to infer attitudes about risk. Presenting similar information to budget and strategic planning committees, and comparing the selected decisions with the values, provides insight about risk attitudes. People incorrectly assume, quite often, that risk attitudes cannot

Example 10.5: Portfolio selection and values using selected investment standards.

Projects Selected	Ranking Categories		Equation 10.4 with:		
	NPN/INV (1)	RAV (2)	NPV>50 (3)	NPV>75 (4)	NPV>100 (5)
	2	3	8	2	2
	3	7	9	3	3
	4	8	13	8	5
	6	9	14	10	6
	7	10		13	7
	8	13		14	8
	10				10
	12				12
	15				13
Value					
NPV	106.9	74.2	49.4	75.4	102.3
NPV/INV	2.5	1.87	1.35	1.9	2.7
Reserves	63.5	52.9	42.2	59.7	60.4
σ	70.4	40.7	36.2	45.8	67.3
RAV	44.7	53.4	32.9	49.1	45.6
Budget	39.9	39.6	36.4	39.9	37.7

be identified. While all risk estimates reflect the underlying attitudes imprecisely, careful analysis of selected decisions provides useful clues, insights, and potential biases that may be unconsciously lowering investment performance. Consultants are available who show organizations how to infer risk from investment decisions.[10.18]

NON-LINEAR OPTIMIZATION

The previous examples focus mainly on applying optimization methods to the portfolio selection process. Since most professionals spend their careers working on individual projects, examples, dealing with the process of modeling and choosing the optimal development scheme, are equally as appropriate. The reason for leaving these applications to the last is the result of the highly nonlinear computations associated with technical and economic optimization. The solution methods used so far – linear programming, integer programming, quadratic programming, etc. – deviated from textbook applications to illustrate the basic principles. This section extends the analysis to include individual project valuations, with highly nonlinear relationships.

Common examples where optimization helps aid investment decision-making, include:

- Number of and size of production units,
- Construction scheduling and project management,
- Capacity and timing of production facilities,
- Contractual terms, like processing fees and tariffs,
- Operating cost of alternative designs, and
- Reliability of alternative operating systems.

Optimizing these combinations in multinational organizations requires all the knowledge bases from Chapter 1, and person-years of time. Achieving the proper level of integration and communication across disciplines is quite difficult, even though considerable work force allocations and well-defined processes exist.

Restrictions on labor commitment, the rush to first production, etc. often forces the project team to limit their focus to 2-5 alternatives, and maybe only 1-2 evaluated fully. The option found with the highest profit metric used by the investor is then recommended for final approval. This solution is really the best among the options considered, not really the true optimum. This *second best* solution may be acceptable, but may not optimize shareholder value. The errors identified in the post appraisals, in Chapter 2, result directly from this second best problem,

Two different project examples demonstrate the value or benefits from employing optimization techniques. The first looks at a single field development, with the name withheld to protect the involved parties. It deals with large expenditures to increase gas-handling capacity in an oil field. Hydrocarbon reservoirs produce both oil and gas, with gas being, historically, valued less than oil. Gas, being harder to store and more costly to transport, added less value than liquid production. The mineral owner, typically the country, correctly seeks the most value from all natural resources. In remote or offshore locations, complying with these resource management regulations means re-injecting the gas back into the reservoir, as part of the reservoir management program. At some point in the reservoir life, the cycling of the gas may reduce ultimate oil production, and expenditures must be undertaken to remove the gas from the system. The need to optimize the gas and oil handling drives much of the engineering and business interest in liquefied natural gas (LNG) and gas-to-liquids technology (GTL).

The second example extends the evaluation to address the possibility of a conceptual design with a multifield, offshore development. Each field has it's own specific timing and size issues like the first example. In addition, however, a pipeline needs to be built to carry the fluids to the custody transfer point. An option to take different working interests in the pipeline complicates the decision. Here, the question becomes much more involved than in a single field, because pipeline tariffs are a major cost, which cannot be determined until ownership, scheduling and timing of the pipeline is settled. Pipeline issues cannot be resolved until the field development schemes, fluid types, and production rates are guessed. This simultaneity continues the value chain problem introduced in the previous chapter.

Normal practice calls for each separate component of the full field and pipeline development to guess the others costs using current rates in the area. In reality a simultaneous relationship exists, which cannot be adequately measured using traditional sequential analysis. Though complex, addressing the simultaneous interrelationship is absolutely critical with large cost, high risk projects.

Case 1: Single Field Expansion

An existing oil field has been reinjecting gas for pressure maintenance to comply with no flaring rules. Gas channels have been created (the gas flows from the injection point to the producing well,) after almost 20 years of operations. Limited gas-handling capacity is forcing the producer to reduce the production rates from all wells, as the result of rapidly rising GOR's. The investor must expand gas-handling capacity to maintain prudent production and recovery rates, or accept lower oil production rates. Management agrees to the fundamental need to expand gas handling, but asks the staff to determine the optimal expenditure pattern consistent with current corporate guidelines and strategies. Management, of course, would like to delay any spending until absolutely necessary. To play on a common phrase, this is "just-in-time" spending.

Ignoring cost and economic constraints, the reservoir group believes that an additional 350 million barrels (55.65 m^3 million) can be recovered by investing in new facilities, expanding existing facilities, and drilling new wells. Additional wells are needed to correct current channeling problems. The exact number and location of wells, of course, impacts the volume of recoverable reserves, and the willingness to spend facility capital to handle the extra production.

Finding the optimal expenditure and timing pattern complicates the evaluation. The number and timing of wells drilled depends on the desired level of reserves to recover, and profit metrics. Likewise, costs per barrel, both Opex and Capex, also depend on the additional reserve volume and timing of well production. Pipeline tariffs, for instance, often hinge on the flow volumes. More importantly, oil price might even impact the optimum level of expenditure and timing.

Providing answers to such investment decisions becomes complicated, so quickly, that most analysis focuses on three or four scenarios. The hope is that the solution approximates the best case, but, in reality, it is usually the first solution that satisfies current corporate objectives with some cushion built in for variation in inputs. Many advocate *scenario analysis,* but you will find that building the model for a true optimization will ultimately include all possible scenario cases, with little or no additional work.

Such problems can be solved using the optimization features within current spreadsheets. In some respects, the toughest part of non-linear optimization is the most critical anyway: defining the problem. To define the problem in a form understandable by the software, the professional must understand the interaction amongst the variables, and the fundamental question(s) being addressed. Failure to adequately address these issues is probably the main cause of investment failures anyway. The real benefit to utilizing optimization is often not the actual solution, but being forced to set up the problem in a logical, consistent, realistic manner. After setting the problem up, many solutions become self-evident. Review Chapter 2 if you have forgotten why this is important.

The basic problem formulation is presented in Example 10.6. The data input format comes from the spreadsheet used to illustrate basic and advance economic issues in our training courses. Most of the categories are self-evident. Working Interest, WI, is set to 1.0 for convenience. Escalation rate is the value used to estimate future values for price, Opex, and Capex (Chapter 3). The program assumes all values are input in real terms (See Chapters 3 and 4). Royalty, for each product, are stipulated at the bottom. Various prices, including Opex per barrel or other units, and Tariff, per relevant unit are computed as well. These values are escalated using the escalation rate value.

Example 10.6: Data input for field development optimization.

Project Start Date:	This year	**Name:**	HK Oil	
Discount Rate (.xx)	0.15	**Project:**	Oil Field Gas Handling Expansion	
Working Interest (.xx)	1.00	**Current Date:**		
Overhead Rate (.xx)	0.00	**File Name:**	Socially Irresponsible, UnLTD	
Corporate Tax Rate (.xx)	0.37			
Escalation Rate (.xx)	0.04	**Price For:**		
Failure Cost ($MM))	200	Oil-$/bbl	Gas-$/Mcf	Other
Prob. of Success (.xx)	0.70	17.00	1.50	14.00
Sensitivity Range +/-	50%			
Bonus & LH ($MM)	0.00	**Operating Cost, $Per:**		
Economic Limit	1	BBL	Mcf	Units
Decimal Value For:		3.28	0.00	0.00
	Royalty			
Oil	0.125	**Tariff- $ Per:**		
Gas	0.000	BBL	Mcf	Units
Other	0.000	3.00	0.00	0.00

The Opex and Tariff inputs depend on the production rate. Field operating expenditures are mixed between variable components, like fuel, electricity, etc., and fixed components. As production increases, the operating costs per barrel decline for the fixed component, although the variable component should stay roughly the same. Though the precise relationship is very field specific, evaluation of field performance led to the development of a three-tiered format for estimating Opex per barrel. Figure 10.9 summarizes the Opex curves as a function of production.

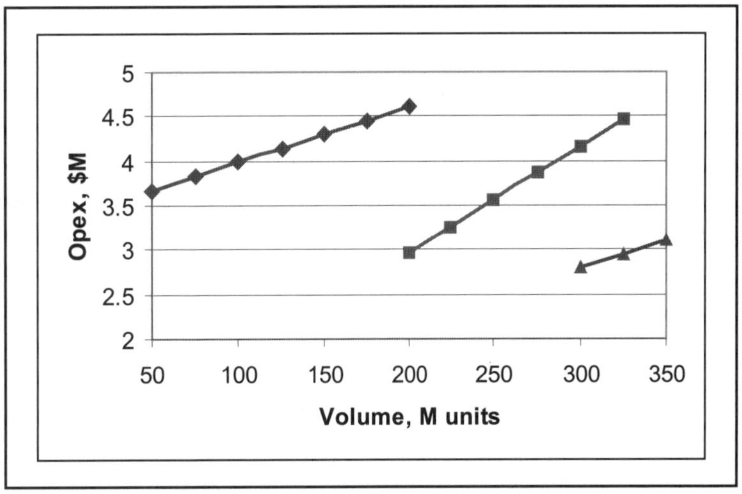

Figure 10.9 Opex input data

The Opex costs are split into three tiers. The first tier covers Opex from 50 million bbls to less than 200 million barrels. The upward sloping portion of the curve was based on the overall cost per barrel derived from engineering estimates. The upward sloping curves were justified on the basis that using operating equipment more intensely requires more power and maintenance. The middle line covers Opex from 200 to 300 million barrels, and the last curve reserves produced in excess of 300 million barrels. These formulas lie behind the Opex per barrel input sheet shown above.

Negatively sloped operating cost curves exist in other cases. This figure is field specific, and is not intended to reflect general situations. To obtain these relationships, field-operating performance should be collected by an engineer who understands the underlying premises in the data.

Figure 10.10 provides the same information for facility capital expenditures. The graphs are converted to spreadsheet notation using conditional, or If, statements. The impact of the discrete change makes it tougher to utilize standard calculus procedures. Scale changes occur at the 200 and 300 million barrel marks, marking shifts in facility design. The values and relationships embedded in the curves reflect engineering judgments about facility design schemes for this project, and, like in the Opex figure, will differ for other producing fields.

Well costs were fixed at $8 million per well. Well productivity varies, however, as the number of wells needed to drain the reservoir change with reserve volume. A parabolic shape is included in the spreadsheet allowing for the first few wells to produce quite prolifically, with the next wells producing less until a plateau is reached, when additional wells decline in productivity. By changing reserves, the number of wells needed to produce that volume of reserves also changes. This formally recognizes a common deficiency in current analysis: where maximum recoverable reserves are estimated, then well number is computed.

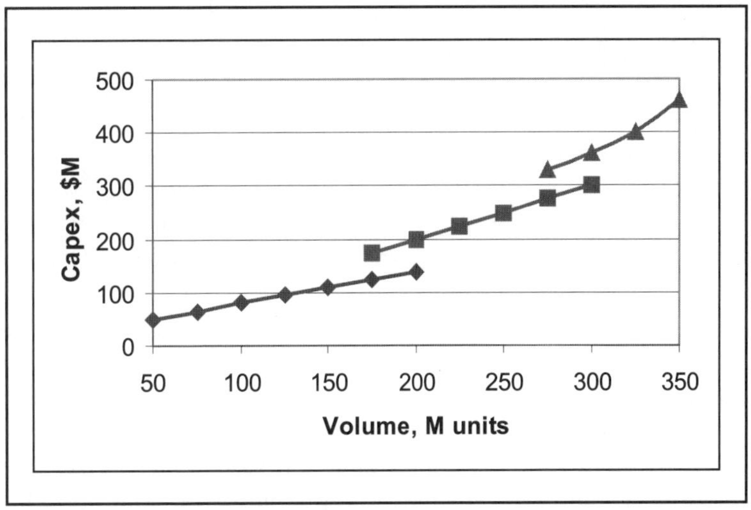

Figure 10.10 Capex input data

In addition, the formulation considers limitations in the drilling schedule. Most projects can drill only a certain number of wells each year. A constraint is added that limits the number of wells drilled each year to a maximum of eight. If, for example, twenty wells are needed, the constraint allows the program to schedule when the wells are drilled. Two forces are at work: first, drilling wells sooner adds production, and second, drilling wells later, delays costs.

The constraints are summarized in Example 10.7. The first four constraints limit the number of wells that can be brought on line each year. With gas handling facilities being installed over four years, fluid handling was believed to be limited to these volumes. Such production constraint also prevents the software from drilling all the wells in the first year to maximize NPV. The last two constraints in the first column specify reserve production between 50 and 350 million barrel, as per reservoir engineering recommendations. Drilling constraints are shown in the second column. Due to weather imposed drilling limitations, no more than eight wells can be drilled in a year; likewise, no more than 40 wells would be allowed.

Example 10.7: Constraints used in field development example.

Additional Production in Year 1 < 7.5 million bbls	0 ≤ Wells drilled in year 1 ≤ 8
Additional Production in Year 2 < 15 million bbls	0 ≤ Wells drilled in year 2 ≤ 8
Additional Production in Year 3 < 20 million bbls	0 ≤ Wells drilled in year 3 ≤ 8
Additional Production in Year 4 < 30 million bbls	0 ≤ Wells drilled in year 4 ≤ 8
50 ≤ Reserves produced < 350 million barrels	Total wells drilled ≤ 40

With these costs and the basic economic relationships outlined in Chapters 3 and 5, the software found an optimum when maximizing NPV_{15} by varying the number and timing of wells drilled. The results of the optimization are presented in Example 10.7a. The first set of rows summarizes the well completion schedule, by year and cumulative production from the project, (155 million barrels). The value of 4.677 in year 1 indicates that five wells were drilled, but after allowing for partial year production, the effective production rate was less than five wells for a full year. Summing the well completion schedule yields about 14.6 wells. This is an odd result, but indicates the impact of ignoring the option to set the total well count to an integer. Since integers prolong solution time significantly, we usually ignore the integer option while testing the model, and then turn it on for the final solution.

Example 10.7a: Output summary from single project.

	Year 1	Year 2	Year 3	Year 4
Well Schedule	4.68	5.40	4.53	0.00
Total Reserves = 155.5 million barrels				
Parameter:	**Discount Rate**			
	0%	**10%**	**15%**	**20%**
NPV, \$m	478.4	136.7	65.9	22.27
NPV/INV	2.66	0.91	0.48	0.17
SIV, \$m	456.4	336.6	289.5	214.7
DPO - years	8.3	6.2	6.9	8.6
Year	0-1	1-2	2-3	3-4
AT NCF	-30.8	-66.9	-82.1	74.7

The normal economic parameters are shown at four discount rates: 0%, 10%, 15%, and 20%. All values are computed using MOD units. The NPV_{15} of the project is about \$66 million. The profit ratio approaches 0.5. SIV is about four times larger than NPV, indicating again the added value from valuing cash flows after the debt has been repaid. Discounted payout shows that debt being repaid toward the end of year 6. For cash flow constrained investors, the last row summarizes the after tax (AT) net cash flow to the project. The project satisfies normal investment objectives.

The solution is interesting, but the fascinating aspect concerns the excluded alternatives. First, projects faced with the opportunity to add 350 million barrels (55.65 m^3) would be designed to recover this volume. Typically, design efforts start with the objective of maximizing recovery, and then alter this volume until current profit guidelines are met. Here, the optimal recovery is 155 million barrels, not 350, with the expected subsequent impact on costs and production volumes. As Figure 10.1 illustrated, designing the project to recover maximum reserve, 350 million barrels here, destroys value.

Second, the major constraint in the project was originally thought to be the capacity limitations in production, not the well drilling schedule. Virtually all of the values could be enhanced by increasing production capacity. In this example, the limitation is associated with both the well schedule and production limitations. Relaxing or eliminating the production constraints increases the rate of drilling and project economics. If this were a new project, the feasibility of increasing pipeline capacity would be an appropriate question to pursue. For existing projects, knowledge of the real constraints encourages professionals to address means of resolving the binding problems, not just the perceived problems.

The output reports provide clues to the important issues. Example 10.7b shows the answer report for the optimal solution. The Target Cell section reminds us that the process maximized NPV in cell $L$9, based on a starting value of $20.73 million, and the final value was $65.95 as reported in Example 10.7a. The increase occurred because the model allowed reserve volume to change with the production system, rather than specifying a reserve volume and then designing the system. The common, latter approach cost the treasury almost $45 million ($65-$20).

Example 10.7b: Optimization Answer Report.

Target Cells			
Cell	**Name**	**Original Value**	**Final Value**
$L$9	NPV15	20.73	65.95
Adjustable Cells			
Cell	**Name**	**Original Value**	**Final Value**
$CU$8	wells_year1	#N/A	4.68
$CU$9	wells_year2	#N/A	5.38
$CU$10	wells_year3	#N/A	4.53
$CU$11	wells_year4	#N/A	0.00
$CJ$8	well_count	#N/A	14.588

Constraints					
Cell	**Name**	**Cell Value**	**Formula**	**Status**	**Slack**
$CV$49	cumprod	155.46	$CV$49<=350	Not Binding	194.5
$CV$49	cumprod	155.46	$CV$49>=50	Not Binding	105.5
$CV$8	Prod_Limit_Year1	7.50	$CV$8<=$CY$8	Binding	0.00
$CV$9	Prod_Limit_Year2	14.99	$CV$9<=$CY$9	Binding	0.00
$CV$10	Prod_Limit_Year3	20.01	$CV$10<=$CY$10	Binding	0.00
$CV$11	Prod_Limit_Year4	17.00	$CV$11<=$CY$11	Not Binding	13.00
$CU$49	Total Wells	14.59	$CU$49=$CJ$8	Binding	0.0
$CU$10	wells_year3	4.53	$CU$10<=8	Not Binding	3.47
$CU$10	wells_year3	4.53	$CU$10>=0	Not Binding	4.53
$CU$11	wells_year4	0.00	$CU$11<=8	Not Binding	8.00
$CU$11	wells_year4	0.00	$CU$11>=0	Binding	0.00
$CU$12	wells_year5	0.00	$CU$12<=8	Not Binding	8.00
$CU$12	wells_year5	0.00	$CU$12>=0	Binding	0.00
$CJ$8	well_count	14.59	$CJ$8<=40	Not Binding	25.412
$CJ$8	well_count	14.59	$CJ$8>=3	Not Binding	11.588

The constraint section provides information about the relative importance of the input variables. Most constraints have two inputs: one for an upper bound and one for the lower bound. The first two rows, called cumprod, show that cumulative production was specified to fall between 50 and 350 million barrels. Since the final answer, in the cell value column, was 155.46, the Status column indicated that the constraints were nonbinding. The slack column measures the difference between the Cell Value and the Formula value, so 350 – 155.46 = 194.5. The slack variable is a sensitivity, quantifying the magnitude of change needed to reach the boundary or binding condition

The important binding constraints are Prod_Limit_Year 1-3. Notice that all three years are binding with zero slack. Increasing pipeline and facilities capacity faster than allowed with the capital expenditure schedule would improve the project metrics dramatically. The Sensitivity Report, as summarized in Example 10.7c, provides some clues to the possible magnitude of improvement.

Example 10.7c: Optimization reports for reduced gradients or sensitivities.

Changing Cells				Constraints			
Cell	Name	Final Value	Reduced Gradient	Cell	Name	Final Value	Lagrange Multiplier
$CU$8	wells_year1	4.68	0.00	$CV$49	cumprod	155.50	0.0
$CU$9	wells_year2	5.38	0.00	$CV$49	cumprod	155.50	0.0
$CU$10	wells_year3	4.53	0.00	$CV$8	Prod_Limit1	7.50	1.39
$CU$11	wells_year4	0.00	-0.47	$CV$9	Prod_Limit2	14.99	1.12
$CU$12	wells_year5	0.00	-1.78	$CV$10	Prod_Limit3	20.01	0.63
$CU$13	wells_year6	0.00	-2.96	$CV$11	Prod_Limit4	17.00	0.00
$CU$14	wells_year7	0.00	-4.01	$CU$49	Total Wells	14.6	1.8
$CU$15	wells_year8	0.00	-4.95	$CJ$8	well_count	14.59	0.00
$CU$16	wells_year9	0.00	-5.79				

The Cell and Name columns, in the Changing Cells category, are the same as before, and the Final Value column repeats the solution. The *reduced gradient* column measures the impact on the optimized value of adding one unit to the optimized variable (NPV_{15}), with a negative value indicating a reduction in NPV and positive values an increase. Adding one well in year 9, for instance, would lower project NPV by a value of -$5.79 million. The other *reduced gradient* values are interpreted similarly.

The Constraint section specifies the impact of relaxing the production capacity constraints. Please note that the names for Prod_Limit's have been shortened. The *Lagrange Multiplier* is another sensitivity, measuring the increase or decrease in the objective, NPV here, by relaxing the constraint. A value of 1.39 means that relaxing the binding constraint of 7.5 million by one unit (a million) adds $1.39 million to NPV.

Sensitivity values must be interpreted with care in nonlinear optimization. The estimates are usually fairly accurate around the final value. Adding or deleting one well or changing the production constraint one unit often provides good answers to the sensitivity. Extrapolating much beyond a one-unit change could often distort the interpretation, depending on the degree of nonlinearity in the problem. The more non-linear the constraint, be careful about using these values. Non-linearities are compounded by discontinuities in the formulas. If the final value occurs at the boundary of a discontinuity, a sensitivity involving the step function gives erroneous results.

An important consideration in interpreting optimizations requires determining if the solution achieved a local or global optimum. Most non-linear problems are very sensitive to the initial starting point.

Multimodal curves like Figure 10.11 exist quite often. The search for the investment that maximizes shareholder value implies finding the global optimum, not the local one. Applying optimization concepts to historical project decisions suggests that most project formulations and approvals never get past the first local optimum that meets specified investment guidelines.

The search routines used by Solver and What's Best require the user to specify a starting point. The various algorithms then decide which direction to go. These algorithms are referred to as hill climbing or gradient methods,. If the starting point was at x = 0, the methods would climb to the apex of the curve by changing the values in increments. Once the value being maximized or minimized began to decline, the negative slope suggests that the maximum had been passed, so the solution algorithm moves back to the original maximum. Determining if another, higher hill exists somewhere else has motivated considerable research in optimization discipline, as discussed in the next section.

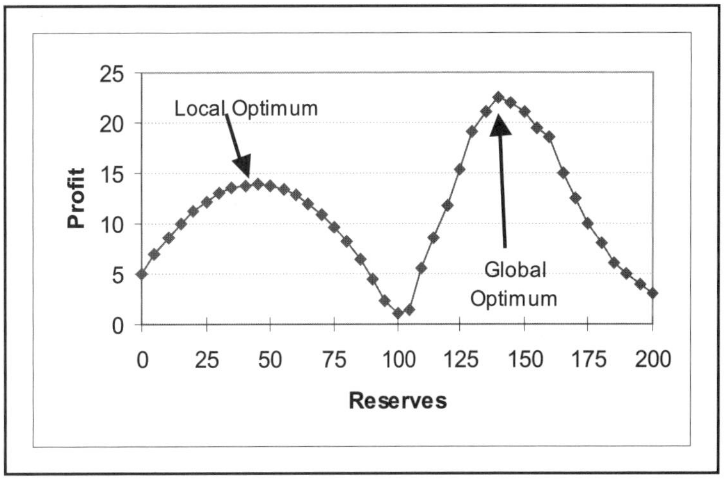

Figure 10.11 Local versus global optimum

Optimization software offers several solution techniques to handle non-linear formulations. Screen 10.3 shows the Solver options panel used to solve the gas-handling example. The bottom boxes are recommended for solving non-linear problems. Try different combinations from the Estimates, Derivatives, and Search options, and then solve the model again. For more information, see the help screen in your spreadsheet or the Optimization section in the spreadsheet manual.

SCREEN 10.3 Options for Nonlinear Optimization

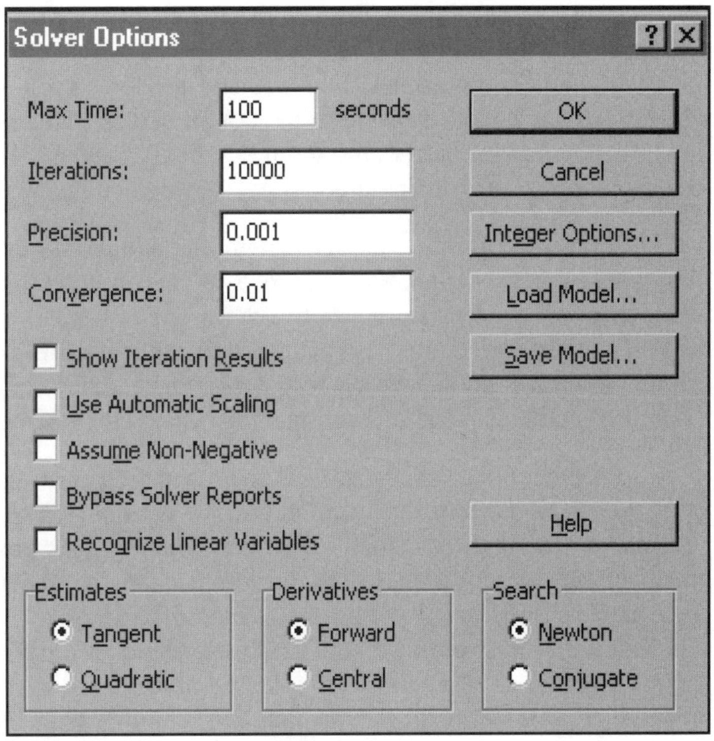

For those who are neither well versed or interested in a Ph.D. in optimization techniques, the easiest way to test for alternative solutions is to vary the starting point for the changing cells. The solution to the field development example tried 15 different values for well_count and four well schedule variants. When all of these "sensitivities" produced virtually the same solution, the confidence in having achieved a global optimum, instead of a local optimum, increases substantially. Changing the starting point and then re-computing the solution works well when the curve follows a smooth pattern, like Figure 10.11. When discontinuities or a lot of local minimums exist (called noise), the trial-and-error approach may fail to establish the true optimum, or require so many different runs that the process becomes overly tedious.

Several participants in our seminars have correctly pointed out that having to alter the starting conditions seems to offset the benefits of optimization. The point is well taken, partly. Fighting the battle of trying to achieve, even, a local optimum forces the professional to understand the system being modeled. Most spreadsheets are really nothing more than a series of equations, where varying one decision variable alters other variables, usually the profit metrics. In a relatively simple economic valuation, NPV was found to have over 7,000 precedents, or other cells that impacted the NPV value. The relationships between variables, especially the ones that reflect decisions, which can be changed, are needlessly neglected.

METAHEURISTIC OPTIMIZATION

Faced with the problem of having to linearize a non-linear system or repeat the calculations several times to test for the global optimum, several alternatives to the classical, calculus based optimization methods were developed. The ones discussed here fall into the category of metaheuristic methods, including *genetic algorithms (GA), simulation annealing (SA), scatter search, taboo*[(10.19)] and other search routines, because several software companies sell packages that perform these calculations, at very reasonable prices: Three software packages are used to illustrate the process – Evolver, Solver, and OptQuest, though other, good software exists. A simple review of the process follows next, and then the procedures are applied to a specific application to allow direct comparison of the results. Please interpret the findings as being specific to the example, and not a generalized result to all problems.

One dictionary defines heuristics as "an approximate and self-learning technique for improving solutions," while another describes it "as a teaching method which encourages the pupil to proceed by their own investigation." Meta just means "beyond the usual" or, in technical applications, the combining of more than one technology. Some of the heuristic methods add the concepts of *neural networks* to describe the learning process. Regardless of the search process being used, all solution methods use iterative approaches with the ability to escape local optimums; thereby, increasing the chances of finding the global optimum. Some approaches, like GA and scatter search, generate a set of solutions for each iteration, which is retained and compared to the next iteration. This permits the model to better estimate the population, and to adapt or learn as the set of solutions changes. The SA and tabu methods maintain only one solution at each iteration. Entire books exist, which compare and contrast the relative differences.

The GA algorithm, the first attempt at addressing these problems, embodies the principle of evolution, where the search process follows a random process by allowing the solution to mutate or crossover, rather than the rigid paths dictated in the calculus based methods. Genetic algorithms take samples from the dimensional space more thoroughly, thus, increasing the odds of finding the global optimum. For readers new to optimization, starting with a genetic search process is a good way to begin the path to improved modeling and investment decision-making, especially when dealing individual projects.

Metaheuristic optimization is like switching from deterministic analysis to stochastic analysis. It takes longer to perform the calculations, but it usually provides a better answer. For those familiar with classical optimization methods and local versus global problems, these procedures probably don't help much, because users are used to manually changing the initial conditions to sample the entire space; whereas, this software does the manipulation for you. The solution alternatives can be manipulated to achieve similar answers when the user understands the difference between each, and manually adjusts for those differences. The classical, calculus based non-linear methods normally converge faster when the problem is well defined, with continuous relationships. Discontinuous and combinatorial (sequencing) functions are solved best using the metaheuristic algorithms.

Another real, but often overlooked, benefit associated with the optimization process stems from the ability to validate the logic of the model being used to evaluate a problem. What oftentimes appears to be a well-validated spreadsheet unravels when exposed to the rigor of the optimization logic. Variable's impact outcomes when they should not, and important relationships are either omitted or misestimated. These problems exist even when the professionals have considerable experience with applying the concepts.

Plenty of opportunities exist for applying the concepts. The single field, gas handling expansion application explains the basic principles. Another common usage involves multi field developments, where the objective is to define a development scheme for several projects, with different components and timing, to maximize profit. The buzzword today for this task is *value chain.* The case 2 example continues the value chain problem introduced in Chapter 9.

Case 2: Value Chain

Young, rapidly growing industries seldom need to worry about planning the entire system. Rapid growth forgives lack of attention to details, as telecommunications is on the verge of discovering. As an industry matures, the projects become larger, more costly, and riskier, making understanding and planning for complex interactions far more important. With limited capital on higher cost and risk projects, modeling the interaction of the individual components becomes essential. Ignoring the interaction occurs quite often when the pressure to start production as soon as possible is severe.

Figure 10.12 duplicates the value chain example from the previous chapter. Two reservoirs, called the Laphroaig and Glenfiddich, were discovered several years ago. Both reservoirs contained gas with associated condensate. Several appraisal wells in each field established the commerciality and reservoir properties to the partner's satisfaction. The reservoirs are located in a different block, each with distinct fiscal regimes regarding royalty and production taxes.

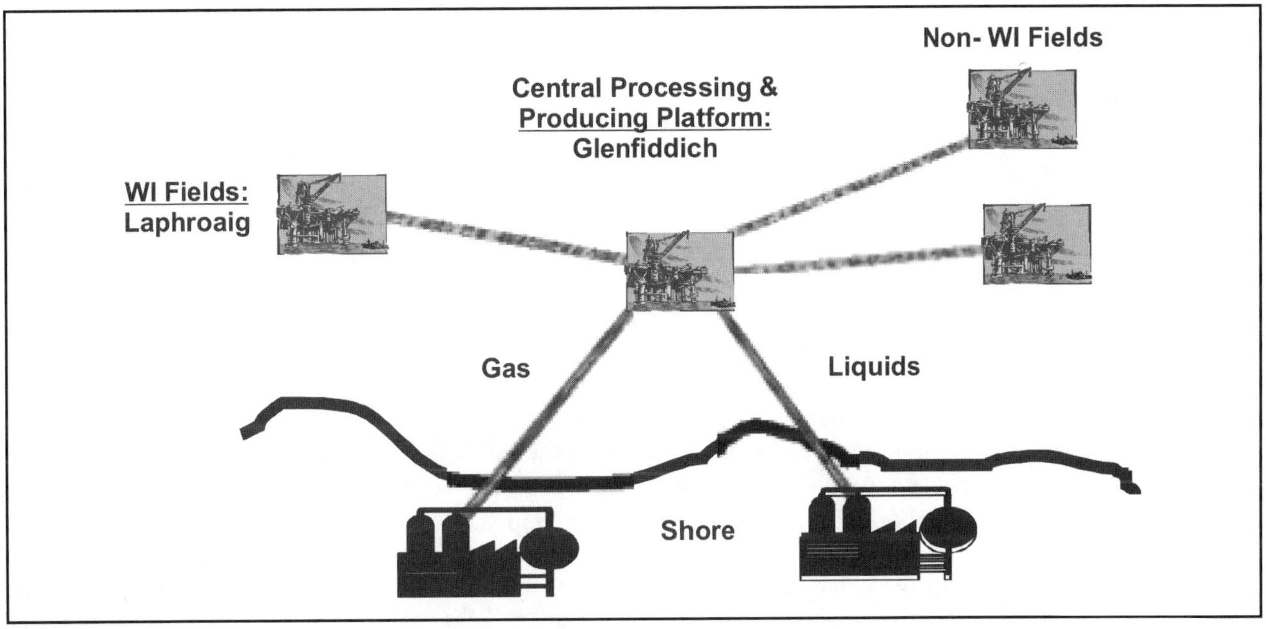

Figure 10.12 Value chain for an offshore project

The discussion in Chapter 9 formally analyzed the risks at each stage in the development, assuming a specific WI position in the pipeline and distributions around the pipeline tariffs. Since production has no value until sold at the onshore plants, some decision about the pipeline size and ownership must be made. Deciding on the optimal WI position in the pipeline hinges on the pipeline profitability, which depends, in turn, on the eventual tariff rates charged by the pipeline? Tariffs are determined by free market forces, and regulated by the government. Rates are determined based on what the market can bear. Gas pipeline tariffs fall between $0.15 and $0.65 per Mcf, depending on the area and availability of competing pipelines. Oil pipelines charge as much as $4.00 per barrel, but rates can be found as low $0.50 per barrel.

Agreement on ownership and tax conditions, though different for each field, has been reached, but the pipeline ownership remains unsettled. More importantly, most of the partners might opt out of the pipeline, if possible, because of budget constraints. The option of paying a higher than normal tariff appeals to several WI owners, as shown in Example 10.8. To complete the project, other WI owners must pick up the extra cost.

Example 10.8: Working Interest Positions in Multi-Field Development

Company	Glenfiddich (%)	Laphroaig (%)
Your Company	40.00	7.97
Fly By Night Drilling	25.00	0.00
Socially Irresponsible Inc.	22.22	0.00
Colombian Flower Growers	5.23	0.00
Teamsters Pension Fund	0.00	10.00
Mass Extinction Marine Devel.	0.00	35.50
SWAG Petroleum	0.00	25.28
RP^2, LTD.	7.55	21.25
Total	100.00	100.00

The choice of the best tariff rate becomes quite complicated, because the revenue to the pipeline company is a cost to the Glenfiddich and Laphroaig fields. Setting the tariff too high penalizes the fields, while low tariffs punish the pipeline owners. Finding the right balance between tariffs impacts the decision to participate in the pipeline and the choice of WI.

Similar situations exist worldwide. Most joint ventures, whether voluntary or forced upon the partners by the local government, involve trade-offs, and these tradeoffs involve solutions to simultaneous equations. Standard sensitivities fail to capture the full range of issues and options. Equally as important, each individual component must pass investment hurdles if the entire project is to go forward. Both fields must have positive profits to justify building the pipeline and onshore plants. The problem is one of allowing every each field and the pipeline a reasonable return, but not giving up too much.

Anyone who has been involved in joint ventures recognizes this dilemma. The investor needs the cooperation of others, but wants to capture as much of the profit share as possible. Finding the right balance between these conflicting objectives represents an excellent optimization problem. Complicating the decision for the investor, if it elects to participate in the pipeline, is the realization that a major cost to the field, the tariff, is a profit to the pipeline. What's best for our treasury may depend as much on differential WI's and taxes than any technical situation. Many tax regimes burden wellhead or field profits more than downstream profits.

Solving the simplified problem defined here involves non-linear programming techniques, but it also combines elements of *game theory.* Game theory seeks to define how competitors or partners respond to actions. The issues associated with game theory directly are omitted here for space reasons, but anytime an investors actions impact others, the tenets of game theory apply.

To analyze the problem, five sheets were constructed in Excel. Four sheets incorporated the development and tax information for Laphroaig, Glenfiddich, the non-WI fields, and the delivery oil and gas system pipeline, named the DOG system. Timing and investment magnitudes were assumed to be fairly certain. Since the last example dealt with modifying investment magnitude and timing, these elements are held constant here. Gas and condensate tariffs were included as a cost. The tariff of Laphroaig was set equal to the tariff of Glenfiddich to eliminate discrimination between fields.

The DOG worksheet summed production from the two WI fields and non-WI fields into it's volume column, which was then multiplied by the tariff rate for the respective fields to give total revenue, guaranteeing that changes in field costs were offset by revenues in DOG's revenues. DOG is allowed to charge different tariff rates to the non-WI fields. The value of pipeline revenues does not exactly offset the field tariff costs, because of tax differences. The assumptions for taxes and prices are summarized in Example 10.8a.

DOG's prices are the tariff to be determined by the program. Royalty and production rates vary depending on the tax regime in place when the acreage was assigned. DOG pays neither royalty or production taxes. Lastly, the CT rate varies between upstream and downstream, as is the practice in some countries. It should be noted that these rates emulate those found in several countries, not any single country.

A fifth worksheet totals the results of the two fields and pipeline. A separate worksheet is needed for two reasons. First, computing various profit measures like *discounted payout* and SIV requires the sum of the individual project net cash flows, unlike NPV, which can be summed directly from the individual projects. NPV/INV can be computed directly only when INV is defined as discounted investment. When INV equals maximum cash outlay, it is the max cash out of all the projects that matters.

The Excel spreadsheet used to generate this information is available from the authors by emailing Dr_Biker@Compuserve.Com

Example 10.8a: Prices, Costs, and Tax Rates for MultiField Development Optimization.

	Glenfiddich	Laphroaig	DOG
Prices			
Gas, $/Mcf	2.15	2.15	Tariff Rate
Oil, $/bbl	16.00	16.00	Tariff Rate
Opex			
Gas, $/Mcf	0.25	2.75	0.10
Oil, $/bbl	0.25	2.75	0.25
Royalty			
Gas, %	12.5	0.00	0.00
Oil, %l	12.5	0.00	0.00
Production Taxes			
Gas, %	3.00	0.00	0.00
Oil, %l	3.00	0.00	0.00
Corporate Tax Rates	0.35	0.35	0.25

The total sheet consolidates the decision variables with the output reports, allowing the user to view the consequences of changing a decision variable. This is good practice even if only scenarios or sensitivities are used to make decisions. Some software requires the decision variables to be on the same sheet as well. By placing all of the values in the total sheet, it is easier to view changes in the total profit measures when altering original input values. Rather than copy the Solver input box, which wouldn't allow us to see all of the constraints, Example 10.8b summarizes the inputs.

The Set Cell and Changing Cells have been discussed. The first two constraints force the computer to set the tariffs, which allows the producing fields to earn a return greater than $10 million for all the fields. The minimum values for development consent at the field levels were determined based on partner meetings, and imply an NPV/Inv requirement. Forcing the pipeline to earn a NPV between $10 and $350 million came from the range experienced in the area. The oil and gas tariffs specified in the second column also came from existing practice. The Cum Project NCF for two years reflects a company cash flow limitation dictated by management. The WI constraint recognizes operating limitations in the region.

Example 10.8b: Model formulation for Multi-Field Optimization.

Set Cell:	Maximize sum of NPV for Glenfiddich, Laphroaig, and Dog
Changing Cells:	Oil tariff, gas tariff, and WI share of pipeline project, oil and gas processing fees for Laphroaig and non-WI fields.
Constraints:	
NPV of Laphroaig > $10 million	Cum Project NCF, Year 1 ≤ $-150 million
NPV of Glenfiddich > $10 million	Cum Project NCF, Year 2-3 ≤ $-250 million
$10 million ≤ NPV of Dog ≤ $350 million	$0.10/Mcf ≤ Gas Line Tariff ≤ $0.50 per mcf
0 ≤ WI in DOG ≤ 0.5	$0.25/bbl ≤ Oil Line Tariff ≤ $4.00/bbl
$0.2 ≤ Laphroaig oil processing ≤ $0.6 / bbl	$0.4 ≤ non-WI oil processing ≤ $.8 / bbl
$0.02 ≤ Laphroaig gas processing ≤ $.06 / mcf	$0.04 ≤ non-WI gas processing ≤ $.08 / mcf

Deterministic Results

The initial Solver solution is shown in Example 10.8c for each of the projects and their sum. NPV of the project was maximized by opting for a 30.5% WI in the pipeline, and setting the gas tariff at $0.10 per Mcf and the oil tariff at $3.196 per barrel. This combination yields a total NPV_{10} of $176 million and an SIV of $563 million. OANPV is $681 million. The breakdown of the same information by project is also shown. The last two rows show that the NCF constraints are satisfied, and the contribution by project to total NCF. This combination satisfies all objectives and appears to provide a reasonable return to all partners.

Example 10.8c: Solution to Multi-Field Optimization. All $'s in millions.

Values	Total	Laphroaig	Glenfiddich	DOG
NPV @				
10%	176.25	10.09	59.58	106.58
15%	24.69	1.10	-6.82	30.43
SIV @ 10%	563.77	36.11	237.85	572.5
OANPV	681.37	35.11	294.01	325.12
DPO @ 10%, Years	10.73	10.27	11.71	9.9
Changing Cells				
DOG WI	0.305			
Gas Tariff	0.100			
Oil Tariff	3.196			
Non-WI gas tariff	0.650			
Gas Processing Fee	0.08			
Oil Processing Fee	0.80			
Constraints				
NCF Year 1-2	-150.0	-8.0	-84.4	-57.6
NCF Year 2-3	-213.3	-20.1	-124.6	-68.6

Pipeline ownership benefits arise from the transportation and processing of other field hydrocarbons, in this example. The processing fees of $0.08 per mcf and $0.8 per bbl, and the gas pipeline tariff of $0.65 represent the maximum allowed in the model. The model tells the owners to charge the maximum allowable rate to the non-WI fields. By owning and operating the downstream facilities, the investor creates an effective portfolio, where the tariffs balance or offset reduction in gas and liquid prices. Risks still exist, however, in that the development of other, non-WI fields is beyond control of the investor. Should the risks be deemed too high, the other extreme position is to stand out of the pipeline system altogether. Paying a tariff makes sense for small WI owners of the fields, especially if this is the only commitment in the area or if concerns about political stability dominate.

To test the sensitivity of the solution to the type of optimization process and starting condition, the model was re-run using four different software packages and four different starting conditions. The four software packages were Solver, Solver Evolver, Evolver, and OptQuest. Solver Evolver, Evolver, and OptQuest are metaheuristic approaches, while Solver uses traditional hill climbing approaches. Example 10.9 shows the initial starting conditions and the variability in the output, along with the time required to reach a solution. The objective is to test the trade-off between solution stability relative to time required to reach a solution. The other issue relates to the question of how, if at all, the initial starting point impacts the final answer.

The Solver hill climbing method solved the fastest and produced exactly the same results in all four cases, with only the solution time varying. The compatibility across the four alternatives occurs because the model contains continuous relationships, or, conversely, no discontinuous relationships that

Example 10.9: Given the following starting values for the decision variables, solve for the optimum results.

Decision Variables	Starting Values			
Starting Conditions	**1**	**2**	**3**	**4**
Pipeline Working Interest	0.200	0.450	0.050	0.550
Gas Tariff	0.500	0.150	0.450	0.330
Oil Tariff	2.000	0.500	0.950	1.850
Gas Tariff Other	0.400	0.300	0.150	0.600
Other Processing Fee - Gas	0.060	0.040	0.020	0.030
Other Processing Fee - Oil	0.400	0.400	2.000	5.000
Laphroaig Processing Fee - Gas	0.040	0.040	0.040	0.040
Laphroaig Processing Fee - Oil	0.250	0.250	0.250	0.250

Final Results	Solver				Solver Evolver			
	1	**2**	**3**	**4**	**1**	**2**	**3**	**4**
Pipeline WI	0.30	0.30	0.30	0.30	0.30	0.30	0.30	0.30
Gas Tariff	0.10	0.10	0.10	0.10	0.13	0.21	0.11	0.10
Oil Tariff	3.20	3.20	3.20	3.20	3.57	3.25	3.73	3.02
OF Gas Tariff	0.65	0.65	0.65	0.65	0.57	0.52	0.56	0.65
OF Gas Process Fee	0.08	0.08	0.08	0.08	0.08	0.08	0.08	0.07
OF Oil Process Fee	0.80	0.80	0.80	0.80	0.68	0.70	0.67	0.63
NPV for								
Glenfiddich	59.58	59.58	59.58	59.58	51.80	44.83	52.81	54.91
Laphroaig	10.09	10.09	10.09	10.09	9.41	8.10	9.66	10.42
Pipeline	106.58	106.58	106.58	106.58	104.52	99.23	102.29	101.02
Total NPV	176.25	176.25	176.25	176.25	165.73	152.17	164.77	166.35
Total OANPV	681.37	681.37	681.37	681.37	659.95	632.37	655.35	661.19
Solution Time: minutes	0.15	0.12	0.08	0.16	12	14	18	17

Final Results	Evolver				OptQuest			
	1	**2**	**3**	**4**	**1**	**2**	**3**	**4**
Pipeline WI	0.24	0.24	0.24	0.24	0.29	0.30	0.27	0.29
Gas Tariff	0.50	0.49	0.50	0.50	0.10	0.10	0.15	0.10
Oil Tariff	3.98	3.91	4.00	4.00	3.56	3.80	1.89	3.25
OF Gas Tariff	0.65	0.65	0.65	0.65	0.65	0.65	0.65	0.65
OF Gas Process Fee	0.08	0.08	0.08	0.08	0.05	0.06	0.08	0.04
OF Oil Process Fee	0.80	0.77	0.80	0.80	0.80	0.80	0.76	0.77
NPV for								
Glenfiddich	12.13	12.72	12.19	12.19	50.50	51.07	58.82	49.88
Laphroaig	2.23	2.44	2.21	2.21	10.41	10.12	10.07	10.65
Pipeline	160.33	157.58	161.14	161.14	111.73	123.81	69.21	102.17
Total NPV	174.69	172.74	175.54	175.54	172.65	185.01	138.11	162.71
Total OANPV	654.28	650.30	655.99	655.99	668.66	699.14	589.25	646.40
Solution Time: minutes	29	28	21	24	28	41	32	20

Where: OF refers to the non-WI fields

plague calculus based algorithms. Solver Evolver produced NPV's below the NPV's produced with Solver by roughly $10 million, and took considerably longer to reach a solution, for this sample problem, again indicating that the model is fairly smooth.

Evolver generated NPV's close to the values determined by Solver, but with very different combinations of decision variables. Pipeline WI falls to 24%, and the tariff charges to the WI fields rise dramatically, going from the minimum allowed value of $0.10 per mcf to $0.50 per mcf. Observe also that, even though the total NPV's are similar, the split between the two WI fields and the pipeline shift dramatically because of these changes.

The OptQuest results produced the most variability, yielding the highest total NPV of $185 million, about $10 million more than the next highest value, and the lowest NPV of $138 million; clearly indicating a sensitivity to the starting solution that requires additional solution time. The simulations were cut-off after 120 minutes. The variability in the outputs reflects the design of OptQuest to address more complicated issues than the one outlined to this point.

Several reviewers of this material asked what to make of these results. First, the results demonstrate the sensitivity of the optimization output to the starting conditions, and the type of search algorithm used by the software. Each software solution is designed for certain types of problems, and normally written quite well. However, for practical users, the issue always becomes matching the tool with the problem. Many user applications do not require the sophistication built into the metaheuristic approaches. For those just beginning to explore the applications of optimization, we recommend starting with simple models and using the already owned Solver program. If, and only if, you begin to add discontinuities into the model and combinatorial issues, like the project scheduling or the traveling salesmen problem, then investigate moving to the metaheuristic approaches.

Second, the process of varying the starting point works quite well when the model is devoid of *noise*. Noise represents a nice way of saying that the model follows a symmetrical or continuous form, like Figure 10.11. Figure 10.15, several pages forward from here, indicates a considerable number of peaks and valleys, even after smoothing the output distribution. The significant number of local optimums often overwhelms the process of trying different starting conditions.

Third, the variability in the solutions is a good, not a bad, result. The essence of this problem revolves around negotiating pipeline WI and tariff rates with partners and competitors. The different combinations indicate substantial opportunities to compromise on rates and WI, and still generate the same value to the investor, a win-win situation. Knowing the degree and type of flexibility allows the negotiating team to pursue a multitude of objectives, while appearing to be reasonable, and still achieving the desired performance metrics.

Stochastic Optimization

The previous example ignored information about variability in product prices, cost estimates, inflation, taxes, and all the other variables, which previous chapters spent considerable time estimating. The deterministic approach employed the expected value for each of these variable inputs in computing the optimum; yet, variations in production, prices, costs, etc. definitely influence the attractiveness of any decisions. More importantly, setting tariff rates needs to capture the volatility associated with production rates. Successfully negotiating a high tariff, on production that never occurs, destroys the best-laid investment strategy.

The process of integrating optimization with the stochastic valuation is called *stochastic optimization*. Once the stochastic model has been constructed, adding optimization allows investors to explore the strategy that reflects their risk perspective, not just optimizing expected values. Risk averse investors might ask for the combination of decisions that maximizes NPV or OANPV at a 95% certainty level, or the combination of decisions that has a 90% chance of generating positive cash flow for the next 10 years.

Case 2 built in a constraint that NCF in year 1-2 could never be larger than \$-150m, and the following year was constrained to \$-250m. Stochastic optimization allows the investor to select the decisions that have the best chance of actually realizing these constraints.

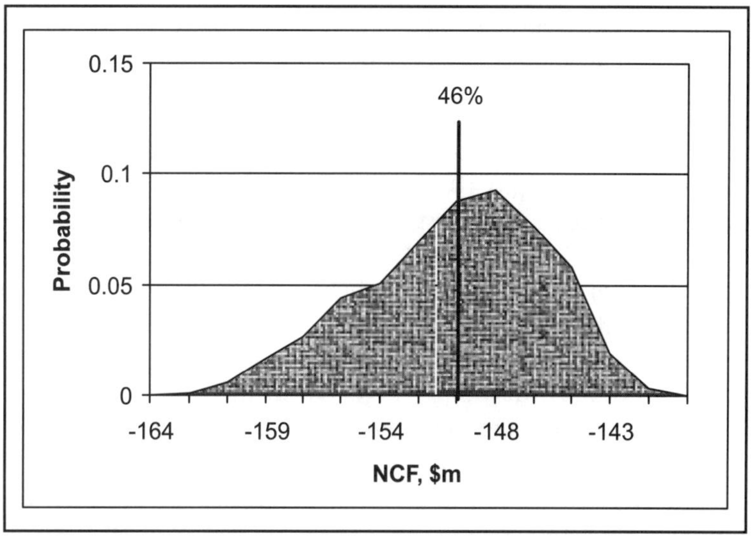

Figure 10.13 Variation in NCF for optimum decision variables

Figure 10.13 illustrates the problem with traditional methods. The problem specifies variability in development costs, including a restriction from management that $NCF_{1\text{-}2}$ cannot be more than -\$150 million. The deterministic optimization, following classical valuation procedures by using expected values, generated the solution to the decision variables. To test the consequences from applying the solution variables to the project valuation, the stochastic value chain risk model was re-run with the optimum decision variables. The project has a 46% chance of exceeding the budget constraint of \$-150 M, given the optimum decision variables. This worrisome outcome arises because the NCF constraint was a binding variable in the optimization, using averages or expected values. Allowing development costs to vary shows the enormous potential for a cost overrun. The failure to capture the linkage between variability and the best decision variables explains, partly, the historical investment performance outlined in Chapter 2.

Until recently, answering such question required running a simulation, optimizing the decision variables for that simulation, and then manually choosing the best solution from all the individual simulation optimums. Two software packages, OptQuest by Decisioneering and RiskOptimizer by Palisades, provide solutions to these questions currently. OptQuest is designed to solve these types of problems, not the deterministic computations described above. Using OptQuest for deterministic calculations is like using a cannon for bird hunting.

OptQuest describes the methodology as demonstrated in Figure 10.14.*(10.20)* The process splits the optimization part from the simulation model. The simulation establishes the typical distribution for inputs and outputs, then the optimization process determines the best combination of decision variables. The optimization results then flow back into the simulation model, allowing the analysis to repeat itself until the user-defined conditions for stopping are met. Both software packages approaches follow similar processes; though differ in several important ways. Comparing the alternative software is not the intent here; rather,

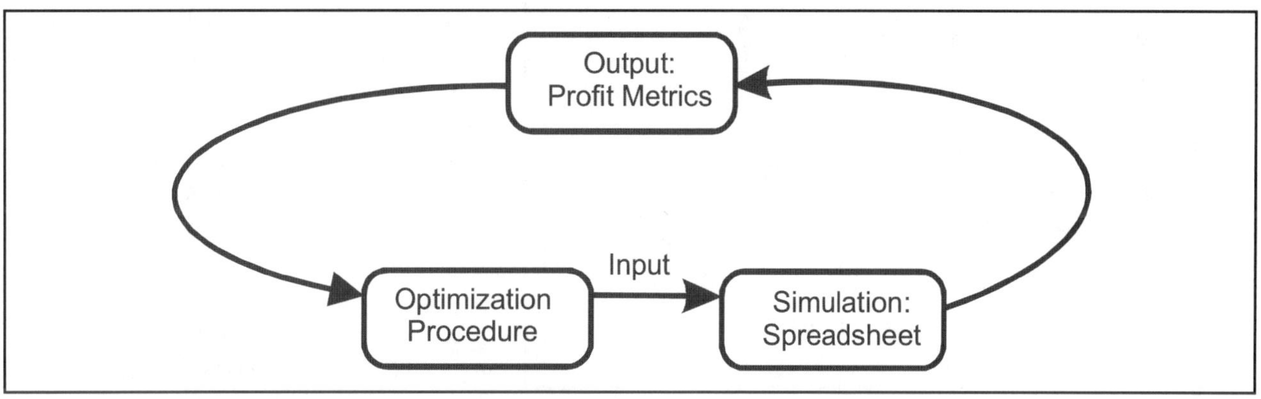

Figure 10.14 Solution approach for risk optimization

the discussion seeks to motivate you to explore the benefits of evaluating your investments more completely and accurately. Both approaches are better than basing individual investment decisions on expected values.

Combining the statistical elements of the Case 2 problem developed in Chapter 9 gives the following results. Example 10.10 summarizes the risk optimization for two different settings in RiskOptimizer and one setting in OptQuest. The constraint was added that the NCF had to have a 90% probability of being less than -$150. Two RiskOptimizer solutions are presented to illustrate the sensitivity to user-controlled settings. The column, labeled recipe, tells the software that the decision variables can be sampled independently, or treated independently. The total NPV of $118m drops significantly from the previous value of $176m, with the run lasting for more than an hour. The recipe solution builds a set of solutions, which allows low tariffs and high WI positions in the pipeline. Since the pipeline WI position depends on the tariffs charged, the independence creates a considerable number of infeasible solutions for the software to analyze. Of the 1000 simulations (with an optimum for each simulation), over 720 were infeasible.

Example 10.10: Summarize the findings for the risk optimization on the value chain problem.

	RiskOptimizer		
Decision Variables	**Recipe**	**Combine**	**OptQuest**
Pipeline WI	0.240	0.263	0.268
Gas Tariff	0.150	0.166	0.109
Oil Tariff	2.156	2.410	3.115
Non-WI Gas Tariff	0.639	0.65	0.624
Non-WI Gas Process Fee	0.057	0.08	0.071
Non-WI Oil Process Fee	0.386	0.8	0.663
NPV			
Glenfiddich	41.63	56.44	59.09
Laphroaig	10.69	9.27	10.27
Pipeline	65.87	83.13	88.36
Total NPV	118.18	148.86	154.37
Total OANPV	537.39	609.23	622.86
Solution Time - minutes	115	97	235

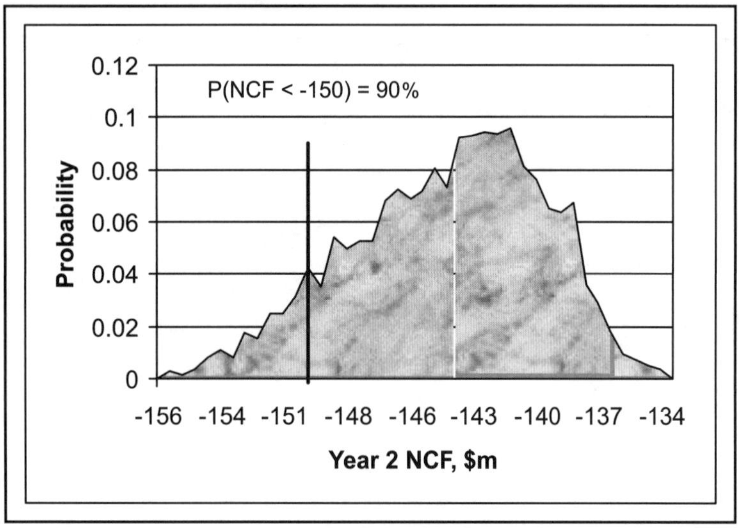

Figure 10.15 NCF distribution from RiskOptimizer

The "combine" column raises NPV to $148.86m, which is much better than the $118m result. Specifying the "combine" option asks the software to treat the decision variables as related events, allowing for a much faster solution time and better output. The combined variables included pipeline WI, gas tariff, oil tariff, and non-WI gas tariff, with the remaining processing tariff decision variables treated as recipes, or independent events.

The final output provides interesting, and logical results. Figure 10.15 shows the NCF distribution for year 2. The solution defines the decision variables that maximize NPV, within the specified boundaries of the decision variables, and has a 90% chance of keeping costs less than -$150m. Considerable portions of this book discuss the trade-off between risk and return. The unconstrained optimums in Example 10.9 earned an NPV around $176m, but with a 46% chance of overrunning the NCF constraint in Year 1-2. If a decision-maker elects to adhere to the NCF constraint, the project foregoes roughly $30m (= 178 – 148) in return to reduce risk.

The OptQuest solution took considerably longer, but yielded slightly better results, for all three fields and total NPV and OANPV. The OptQuest program was run several times, because several sets of initial conditions caused the software to spend considerable time on infeasible solutions. This situation may result from user error or inexperience. The problem of defining the problem to reach a solution occurred with RiskOptimizer as well

Both solutions allow for a good demonstration of the relative risk and return trade-offs. The cost overrun, from Figure 10.13, was a maximum of $14m (= -164 – 150). Reducing the chance of an overrun to 10%, from 46%, lowers the return to the investor by about $30 M. Is this reasonable? Does the trade-off capture strategic and current objectives? The answer depends on the level in the organization of the affected parties, the incentive system, current business and financial environment, etc. Chapter 1 raised these issues without describing methods for resolving the conflicting objectives.

Several interesting lessons usually emerge from performing such analysis. First, the analysis usually shatters the myth that one, and only one, way exists to go forward with a project. Each combination imposes unique risk and return. Investors can only make intelligent decisions on issues that have been addressed and communicated. This process certainly provokes understanding.

Second, the process of acquiring understanding involves frustration. The "right" answers do not appear magically with every run. A considerable learning curve exists with the process, both in understanding the underlying solution process and, more importantly, in learning to define the problem. So many investment analyses exist in a fuzzy, gray zone with regard to issues and decision variables. This process forces the professionals and decision-makers to agree on objectives and communicate with each other.

Third, understanding the complexity and learning to match the solution options with the nature of the problem was the hardest part of stochastic optimization. The metaheuristic approaches offer a wide range of options, and knowing when to use one option versus another still reflects more art than science. Employing trial-and-error methods is of minimal value when the solution time requires 6-8 hours. The user needs to carefully read the manual and experiment with the examples provided with the software when choosing among the available solution alternatives. This may take several days, and then, the real learning begins.

SUMMARY

Chapter 1 introduced the technology of business, including the knowledge assembled to achieve investor objectives. Current management emphasizes objectives, like optimization, maximization, excellence, socially responsibility, and environmental awareness. Almost every mission and vision statement places maximizing shareholder wealth at the pinnacle. Many of the modern catch phrases, like optimization and maximization, unfortunately, have become politically correct words, without anyone really understanding what the words mean or knowing how to achieve them. Defining strategies and then formulating objectives, goes well beyond this text, because the process varies so much across organizations, as it should. Even when well-defined strategies and objectives exist, matching knowledge garnered from the respective disciplines with available tools to achieve assess and mitigate risk seldom reaches the desired level, in practice.

Chapter 2 highlighted the basic investment process, including historical information about investment performance, along with some simple possible causes. Now that the text has addressed some of the modern advances in the decision-making process, we can return to that point. Trading-off the returns from an investment relative to the risks captures the essence of the problem. Measuring returns, however defined, was simplified to fit existing tools, usually limited to means or expected values of complex physical and economic systems (Chapters 3 – 5). In fact, the concept of equilibrium in most disciplines is just a convenient assumption to allow one to make calculations.[10.21]

Beginning with Chapter 6, formal risk assessment methods, readily available to everyone with a computer were introduced, along with software add-ins, and applied to a variety of investment opportunities: production, price, cost, scheduling, modeling independence and dependence, etc. Everyone hopefully followed the discussion in this text and can now apply the concepts to investment elements relevant to their knowledge base.

Being able to perform the task of formal risk management, versus being willing or appreciating the benefits are two distinct issues. A serious learning curve exists with all these topics. Every chapter in this book simplifies complex bodies of knowledge to demonstrate the benefits of learning the skills. One can earn a Ph.D. in areas reduced to a paragraph or sentence in this text, much less a chapter. We strongly suggest adopting the baby model: learn to crawl before trying to walk. Just as the neuro-muscular skills needed to crawl must be acquired before the walking, the knowledge base must be built up by working with simple problems. Our experience is that bright, experienced professionals try to "get it all" in one endeavor, and, when repulsed by failure, blame the messenger, not the message. Though a trite phrase, it explains some of the failure to get investors to adopt the message.

Start with simple spreadsheet problems and then introduce complexity as skills are mastered. This is akin to watching professional athletes, like Tiger Woods, and then deciding to be a golfer, without appreciating the learning process Mr. Woods went through to achieve that performance level. Time constraints from every direction limit ones ability to add new knowledge to their professional toolkit, but the successful are the ones who always find time to stay ahead of the competition. This material does that.

The challenges facing every investor require expanding their knowledge base. Milton Keynes once observed, "All agents suffer from deficient knowledge about the future, and adopt quasi-rational strategies to deal with it."[10.22] We hope that this text has stimulated your interest and motivation to at least explore the potential applications, and wish you well, as you embark on what will be a very interesting journey. During that journey of constant learning, remember: "Risk can be mitigated when assessed, understood, and communicated, but never eliminated."

REFERENCES

10.1 Shaw, G. C., "Tools for Better Decisions, *Hydrocarbon Processing* (Mar. 1987), pp. 51-54.

10.2 This paragraph was inserted because of the sage advice provided by John Howell III, who provides consulting advice to companies to answer these questions.

10.3 Mao, James T., *Quantitative Analysis of Financial Decisions*, The Macmillan Co. (1969).

10.4 Chen, Henry, "Computer program uses simulation to help manage weather sensitive projects," *OGJ* (24 June, 1985), pp. 80-86.

10.5 Dantzig, George, "Maximization of Linear Functions of Variables Subject to Linear Inequalities," in Koopmans (ed.), *Activity Analysis of Production and Allocation*, John Wiley and Sons (1951).

10.6 Kantorovich, "Mathematical Methods of Organizing and Planning Production," *Management Science* (July 1960), pp. 366-422.

10.7 Schrage, Linus, *LINDO: An Optimization Modeling System*, 4th Ed, San Francisco: The Scientific Press (1991).

10.8 Dantzig, George, *Linear Programming and Extensions*, Princeton: Princeton University Press (1960).

10.9 Mao, *ibid.*

10.10 Scarf, Herbert, "The Allocation of Resources in the Presence of Indivisibilities," *The Journal of Economic Perspectives* (Fall 1994), pp. 111-128.

10.11 Seba, R. D., "The Only Investment Criterion You Will Ever Need," SPE 16310 (Mar. 1987).

10.12 Markowitz, H. M., *Portfolio Selection, Efficient Diversification of Investments*, John Wiley and Sons (1959).

10.13 Markowitz, H. and A. Perold, "Portfolio Analysis with Scenarios and Factors," *Journal of Finance* (1981, Vol. 3), pp. 871-877.

10.14 Hightower, Lee and A. David, SPE 22016 (Mar. 1991), pp. 53-64.

10.15 Bernstein, P., *Against the Gods*, John Wiley and Sons (1997).

10.16 Butler, C., *Mastering Value at Risk*, Prentice-Hall (1996).

10.17 Dowd, K., *Beyond Value at Risk*, John Wiley and Sons (1998).

10.18 See M. Walls, Colorado School of Mines, (303) 273-3492.

10.19 Cvijovic, S. and J. Klinowski, "Taboo Search: An Approach to the Multiple Minima Problem," *Science* (3 Feb., 1995).

10.20 Glover, F., Kelley, J., and M. Laguna, "The OptQuest Approach to Crystal Ball Simulation," WWW.decisionseering.com.

10.21 Campbell Sr., J., address to the National Academy of Engineers (2000).

10.22 "Skidelsky on Keynes," *The Economist* (25 Nov., 2000).

OTHER ARTICLES OF INTEREST

"Rational Economic Man", *The Economist* (24 Dec., 1994), p. 91.

Lasdon, L. S., Warren, A., Jain, A., and M. Ratner, "Design and Testing of a Generalized Reduced Gradient Code for Nonlinear Programming," *ACM Transactions on Mathematical Software*, 4:1 (1978), pp. 34-50.

Lason, L. S., "Solving Sparse Nonlinear Programs Using GRG," *ORSA Journal on Computing*, 4:1 (1992), pp. 2-15.

Shogan, Andrews S., *Management Science*, Englewood Cliffs, NJ.: Prentice Hall, Inc. (1988.)

Winston, Wayne L., *Operations Research*, Boston, MA.: PWS-Kent (1992).

Williams, H. P., *Model Building in Mathematical Programming*, 3rd Ed., San Francisco: John Wiley and Sons (1990).

NOTES:

GLOSSARY OF TERMS

The following terms, particularly legal ones, might be defined in several ways.

Abandonment Value — The amount expected or actually received from the sale of property, plant or equipment before its economic life has been completed. Also called "salvage value."

Accelerated Depreciation — The process, as permitted by tax codes, of rapidly writing off the cost of an asset. Compared to normal (straight-line) depreciation, this technique reduces early life income tax payments by deferring tax payment until later periods.

Acceleration Investment — An investment, which increases present worth by causing investment, benefits to be received earlier. Total benefits on an undiscounted basis, however, may increase, decrease or remain unchanged.

Ad Valorem Tax — A tax on property that is levied as a proportion of the property's value or fixed assets. Paid to a sub-state or national government depending on the country.

Amortization — An accounting term referring to the process of writing off the cost or value of an asset over its expected service life. Intangible assets such as acquisition costs for non-producing properties, lease bonuses, title clearing expenditures, geological and geophysical cost are "written off" or "amortized" in amortization accounts. Tangible assets such as physical equipment or in-place reserves are written off through depreciation or depletion accounts.

Area of Mutual Interest (AMI) — Any area, which, by prior agreement, is the subject of mutual sharing of ownership of any leasing rights acquired.

Asset — An accounting term for an item owned by a company. An asset is typically classified as a fixed or tangible asset (e.g., petroleum reserves, land, equipment), an intangible asset (e.g., lease bonuses, patents, license agreements, trade marks), or a current asset (e.g., cash securities, notes, inventories, accounts receivable).

Assignment — An assignment is a legal document whereby one party transfers all or a portion of his interest to another, subject to specific considerations.

Assignee (Grantee) — The assignee is the party to whom an assignment is made.

Assignor (Grantor) — The assignor is the party who makes the assignment.

Authorization for Expenditure (AFE) — A request for approval of funds for a given project.

Barrel Royalty — This results from a royalty assignment wherein the grantee gets not a certain percentage but revenue equivalent to a certain number of barrels (or MMscf) per day.

Barrels of Oil Equivalent (BOE) — The quantity of NGL or natural gas necessary to equate on a Btu basis with a barrel of crude oil. For natural gas, 5.8×10^6 Btu equals one barrel of oil equivalent. For NGL, 1.455 barrels of NGL is equal to one barrel of oil equivalent.

Base Case — A reference case to be compared with alternative investment choices or outcomes.

Bond — A debt security (certificate of indebtedness) issued by a government, an agency of a government, or a private corporation.

Bonus — See *Lease Bonus*.

Book Value — The original cost of an asset minus total write-offs taken to date. This is the value reflected in a firm's financial statements.

Bottom-Hole Contribution — A form of test well contribution in which the contributor pays an agreed upon part of the test operator's cost, contingent upon the well successfully reaching target depth. In return, the contributor receives all geologic information, logs, etc., from the test.

Bottom-Hole Money — This is paid regardless of whether the well is dry or a producer. In all other respects it is similar to, and contributed for the same purpose as, dry hole money.

Break-Even Analysis — An analysis of the relationship between revenues and costs to determine the sales volume (called breakeven point) required to offset costs.

Capital Allowance (CA) — Term used in the U.K. to denote method of receiving tax relief for a capital expenditure. Calculated as 25% of the undepreciated value for most oil and gas capital expenditures in the U.K. See depreciation for further discussion.

Capital Assets (TCAP) — Capital assets are the dollar value of assets that are tangible and which may be appraised by inspection. This includes buildings, machinery and equipment of all types which depreciate in value with age and usage. Also included in this category are negotiable instruments such as stocks, bonds and any unencumbered cash.

Capital Expenditure (CAPEX) — An accounting term usually applied to expenditure on fixed assets – i.e. items that have a life beyond the current year. The value of such items is usually depreciated over a time period specified by the country tax authority. Other items with short life, and expenses such as operating costs, are treated as revenue items and are deducted in full immediately.

Capital Gain (or loss) — The excess (or deficit) of proceeds realized from the sale or exchange of a capital asset over (or under) its book value. Capital gain may create an income tax liability.

Carried Interest — A carried interest is an agreement between two or more partners in the working interest whereby one party (carried party) does not share in the working interest revenue until a certain amount of money has been recovered by the other party (carrying party). This type of arrangement may result when the carrying party advances all or part of the development costs of the carried party, or where land brokers use the device for a portion of their profits. It is also a provision in some farm-out agreements. Carried interest may apply to a single well or an entire lease.

Cash Flow (CF) — Annual (usually) payments and receipts for a particular project. It should be made clear when quoting CF`s whether they are ***real*** or ***MOD*** (money of the day). See NCF.

Cash Flow (Pre-Tax) — Cash revenues less cash operating expenses before deduction of taxes. In accounting terms, net income plus book write-offs.

Cash Flow Projection — The process of calculating and developing period-by-period estimates of future cash receipts and expenditures. Often called NCF

Cash Flow Timing — Either the time cash flows occur from one period to another (e.g., t, t + 1, t + 2), or the time cash flows occur within a single period (e.g., beginning, middle or end of year).

Constant Dollars (or Pounds) — A monetary unit for prices or costs in any given year from which the effects of inflation or deflation have been removed relative to a base year. Also called "real dollars."

Compounding — The arithmetic process of determining the final value of a payment when compound interest is applicable.

Concession Agreement — A form of allocating mineral resources where the owner transfers the rights to the minerals in exchange for a royalty and/or bonus. The contractor then pays income taxes to the local government. (See the U. S. or U. K. in Chapter 6)

Controllable Expense — An operating expense over which managers and supervisors are deemed to have a degree of control. For example, salaries, repairs, maintenance, materials supplies, rentals, contract services, freight, transportation and utility expenses.

Corporate Objectives — The goals toward which an organization's operating and development plans are directed.

Cost of Capital (CoC or WACC) — The payment (expressed as a percentage) which must be made to sources of capital for the use of their funds.

Cost of Finding — The amount of money spent per barrel of oil equivalent in locating reserves.

Current Dollars (or Pounds) — A monetary unit for prices or costs previously realized or which are projected to actually occur in any future year. Also called "nominal" or "money of the day."

Debt Financing — Funds obtained through borrowing, typically from the sale of bonds or commercial paper, or by directly borrowing from a bank or other creditor at a fixed rate of interest. A debt obligation does not involve any transfer of ownership in the company.

Debt to Equity Ratio — measures the proportion of fixed debt in the total capital structure. Computed as either debt divided by equity (D/E or gearing) or debt divided by debt plus equity [D/(D+E)]. The larger the ratio, the greater the risk, which increases the cost of borrowing money.

Decision Tree — A schematic technique for studying the joint impact that various uncertainties have upon investment return for alternate decision choices. See EMV.

Deferred Expense — An accounting term for an expense paid out for a benefit, which may not be received for one year or more. For example, an advance payment on a contract such as a premium on an insurance policy, or development costs for a new product. Also called a "deferred charge."

Deferred Investment — A budget term for a contractually binding agreement requiring fixed payments for more than one year in exchange for the use of an asset. For example, a long-term lease.

Deferred Taxes — Financial book charges based on the timing difference in write-offs for book and tax purposes. Not a real flow of money.

Deflation — Returning ***MOD cash flows*** or ***fund flow***s to ***real*** terms by dividing through by ***inflation*** factors. (See Inflation).

Dependent Investment — An investment whose cash flows are affected in some way by the acceptance or rejection of other investments.

Depletion — Depletion describes the production of a wasting asset, which, in turn, reduces in value as the supply decreases. This, then, is both *physical* and *economic* depletion. However, the tax aspects of depletion are those usually considered. For many tax purposes the minerals must not only be produced, but also sold, to be covered under depletion provisions.The word *depletion* is often used as an abbreviation for *depletion allowance*, i.e., that deduction which may be lawfully taken under provisions of the income tax statutes.

Depreciation — An accounting and tax term for allocating a portion of tangible asset cost to a time period. Property, plant and equipment (PP&E) are depreciated, as well as all the costs of developing producing wells and related facilities. Commonly used depreciation methods include straight-line and accelerated depreciation methods such as declining balance or sum-of-year's digits.

Development Well — A development well is one drilled on property that is considered proved. Consequently, this designation is arbitrary to the same degree as the property classification.

DD&A — stands for depreciation, depletion and amortization, as defined earlier. Fixed assets are depreciation, wasting assets like mineral production depleted and intangible assets amortized. DD&A generally relates to financial books and is based on the revenue matching principle, where deductions are matched to revenues.

Discounting — A procedure which restates (reduces) a future cash flow to an equivalently valued cash flow occurring today.

Discounted Cash Flow (DCF) — Cash flows are estimates of future payments and receipts – usually on an annual basis. These are generally calculated in MOD terms. The DCF method then takes account of the fact that we would prefer to have a "real" sum of money in our hands now rather than later, because if we did, it could be re-invested to make more money. Thus, it "costs" us something to receive it later (opportunity cost). The converse is true of capital costs (they cost less tomorrow than today because – inflation apart – the money can be kept in use in our financial system earning money). The purpose of DCF is to measure this time effect on value and cost, and it is a separate process from looking at inflation effects.

Discounting — is the exact mathematical inverse of compounding.

Discount Rate — The rate used to discount fund flows in the DCF method and evaluation (e.g., for a discount rate of 5%, year n fund flow is divided by 1.05 to the (n-1) power). It should be chosen to represent the real rate of return the business can expect to make and as such represents the rate that can be expected by investing in other (or opportunity) projects.

The following points need to be taken into account when choosing the discount rate:

- Historic company earnings rates are a guide, but future opportunities may differ.
- If most of a company's capital is borrowed, the rate should at least exceed the loan rate! Where a company's capital is from several sources sometimes an average cost of capital may be used to derive a minimum discount rate.
- The relative risk of one business to another.
- Future investment opportunities — limited, anticipated rate of return?

Dividends — Payments to stockholders as compensation for the use of their funds

Division Order — A division order is the instructions, signed by all interests, to the oil or gas purchaser showing how the purchase price is to be divided. Normally, all money due the working interest is paid to the operating interest who, in turn, apportions it in accordance with the interests held. All royalty is normally paid directly by the purchaser, although this is not always the case.

Downstream — The refining/marketing segment of the petroleum industry.

Drill Versus Drop — An incremental economic decision, which compares drilling a well with the alternative of not doing so.

Dry Hole — An unsuccessful well; a well drilled to a certain depth without finding commercial quantities of oil or gas.

Dry-Hole Contribution — A test well contribution payable only if the test turns out to be dry. Contrasts with bottom-hole contribution. This is one method of spreading the risk in developing wildcat acreage, since data from a well will serve to help correlate available information on offset acreage.

Economic Life — Economic life is the shortest period between investment start-up and (1) economic limit, (2) time at which salvage value exceeds NPV of future Real Cash Flow, or (3) time at which operations must cease due to contractual obligation.

Economic Limit — Generally refers to that production rate of an asset at which current cash expenditures start to exceed current cash receipts before income taxes. Thus, continued production at a rate below the economic limit would result in a net cash loss.

Efficiency Ratios — Measure the ratio of NPV to some definition of investment. The ratio reflects the efficiency of capital investment in a project (See Chapter 5).

Enhanced Oil Recovery (EOR) — Sophisticated recovery methods for crude oil, which go beyond the more conventional secondary recovery techniques of pressure maintenance and water flooding. EOR methods now being employed includes micellar-surfactant, steam drive, polymer, miscible hydrocarbon, CO_2 and steam soak. Some fields require one of these methods for even initial recovery.

Enhanced Recovery — Enhanced recovery is the recovery of oil and gas made possible by artificially supplying energy to the reservoir. This includes water and miscible flooding techniques, repressuring operations, gas drives, etc.

Environmental Investment — An investment required to comply with government regulations designed to provide ecological benefits.

Equity Financing — Funds obtained from retained earnings (internal financing) or from selling stock (external financing).

Escalation — The rise in price of a single commodity. Reflects combined effect of inflation and supply/demand changes.

Excise Tax — A general term applying to any tax levied internally upon some phase of the production or distribution of commodities.

Expansion Investment — An investment, which adds benefits by increasing the extent or the scope of a project. One type of incremental investment.

Expectation — Short for mathematical expectation, a statistical concept. The probability weighted average outcome of a chance process.

Expected Monetary Value (EMV) — In a prospect evaluation, given a risk of Ps (25%), a successful EPV (Expected Present Value) of S ($100) and a cost F ($20), then the following tree can be drawn.

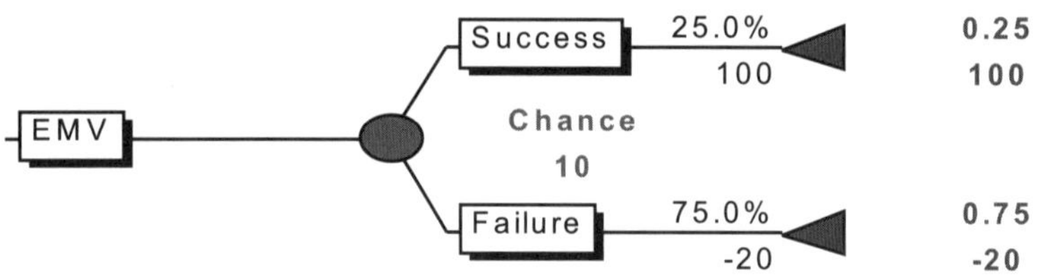

EMV of 10 in this simple example is the expected outcome. This assumes that worldwide all such prospects can be pooled and, of course, that the P_S values are correct!

Expected Present Value (EPV) — In prospect evaluations, a range of possible reserve sizes is usually given. Costs, etc. are then estimated for a single point in this range and from this an ***NPV (Net Present Value)*** calculated. If there is time, a number of estimates can be prepared for a number of different production volume and then the ***NPV's*** can be plotted against the probability of each case. From this plot the Expected Present Value can be derived, which is the weighted average ***NPV***.

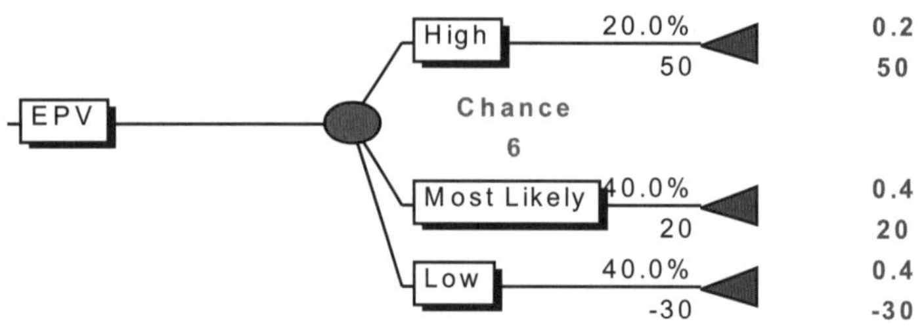

Expenditure — A cash disbursement of funds designated for investment.

Expense or Expensed — A disbursement or outlay, which is subtracted from current revenue. In book or taxable income computations, this may be either Opex (e.g., salaries and wages) or expensed investments. The entire amount receives tax relief in the year the cost is incurred.

Exponential Decline — A decline based on the logarithmic function. $f(t) = e^{-r*t}$, where r = rate, and t = time.

Farm-In Agreement — This most often occurs after commercial production is found. The finder needs more capital to develop the property than is available. One or more partners are found to develop the mineral property. As assignment of interest is made in consideration of specific services provided.

Farm-out Agreement — This is the name applied to a specific form of assignment wherein the lessee grants a conditional interest to a third party in consideration for the development of a prospect within a specified length of time on given acreage. It is usually undertaken where the lessee has leases on a relatively large block of acreage and does not wish to undertake the sole cost of developing it. In most instances this form of agreement is between a major company and the independent operator who cannot afford to acquire large acreage. Most farm-outs contain the following stipulations in oil and gas operations:

The grantee will drill a well in a diligent and workmanlike manner to a certain geological formation or to a specified depth, on a limited block of acreage, in a specified length of time.

Any geological or test information obtained from such drilling must be made available to the grantor.

If the well is a producer the grantee is assigned the well acreage subject to an overriding royalty to the grantor. After the return of a specified sum to the grantee, the override is usually discontinued and the grantor comes in for a share of the working interest. This last provision is sometimes optional to the grantor. On successful completion of the subject well the grantee is usually assigned all or a partial interest in certain undeveloped acreage in the vicinity of the well. Where the grantee is a drilling contractor, he is often given the contract to drill all future development wells on the given acreage under specified terms.

If the well is dry, the grantor retains all lease interest held prior to the agreement.

The grantor is free of all cost and liability incurred in drilling subject well.

This type of agreement is often an ideal solution to property development. It frees the independent of large and often prohibitive survey and leasing costs and, yet, permits use of his drilling equipment. On the other hand, it is a means of developing and proving acreage by the lessee at relatively small cost. It is, therefore, a form of agreement that is often advantageous to both parties in that it allows each to perform that portion of the development most compatible with his current situation. It is sometimes used to develop acreage, which the lessee cannot develop before expiration of the lease or where he feels that the chances of success are less favorable than elsewhere.

Fixed Expense — An operating expense, which does not change in relation to the volume of production or sales of merchandise or services. For example, rent, mortgage, insurance, property tax and equipment lease payments.

Forecast — The formulation of possible future events of economic conditions (e.g., evaluation premises) through a comprehensive study and analysis of available pertinent information.

Gas-Oil Ratio (GOR) — The number of a thousand standard cubic feet of natural gas produced with a barrel of oil (usual units are Mcf/bbl or m^3/m^3).

General and Administrative (G & A) Expense — A component of controllable expense for management or service departments involved in administration and not directly identified with a specific operating function. Also called "overhead."

Gross Domestic Product — Same as GNP, but limiting the valuation to goods and services produced domestically, disallowing income received from overseas operations.

Gross National Product (GNP) — Values goods and services in a country. Computed by summing personal consumption, government expenditures, investments, and exports and then subtracting imports.

Gross National Product (GNP) Deflator — Published monthly by government, this index is comprised of the aggregate market value of final goods and services produced by the entire nation. The GNP Deflator or equivalent is used for representing changes in the average level of all prices. Hence, percent changes in the GNP Deflator are indicative of general inflation.

Income — An imprecise term for the gain or benefit derived from an expenditure of capital or labor over a given time period. In financial statements, this is an accounting computation, broadly defined as revenues minus expenses.

Income Tax — A monetary assessment levied by a government, based upon taxable income.

Incremental Investment — An investment. which increases project benefits by enlarging its scale or reducing its costs. This includes expansion and maintenance investments.

Index — A numerical ratio constructed by dividing a series of values by a base value from the series.

Inflation — Change in the cost of goods and services over time.

Intangible Assets (ICAP) — Intangible assets are the class of assets that includes all types of minerals and research. No value may be established by direct inspection and the asset does not necessarily depreciate with time. It loses value only when produced and furthermore cannot be replaced.

The exact differentiation between a tangible (capital) asset and an intangible asset is somewhat arbitrary. From a practical standpoint, such differentiation depends on the current applicable tax provisions governing a specific type of property. Evaluations should not rely solely on past evaluations since the laws regarding intangible assets change.

Intangible Drilling and Development Cost (IDC) — A portion of the cost incurred in drilling a well which is expensed for tax purposes by capital and depreciated for book purposes. For example, well labor, fuel, hauling and supply expense.

Interest — A charge of a sum paid for the use of borrowed money or credit. Usually it is calculated as an annual percentage on outstanding principal.

Internal Rate of Return (IRR or DCF-ROR) — The discount rate, which sets the Present Value of a cash flow stream equal to zero.

Investment — An expenditure of funds to acquire physical or financial assets from which benefits are expected to occur for more than one year. (Capex)

Joint Venture — A project where the working interest is shared with one or more partners.

Lease — An oil lease is in reality not a lease in the general sense of the term. It is rather the delegation of exclusive rights to capture such minerals from the mineral owner (lessor) to a lessee. In return the lessee gets to keep and sell the greater part of these minerals as compensation for his efforts. The remainder, or royalty, belongs to the mineral owner – that portion to be recovered for him at no cost, by the lessee.

In other words, the lessee recovers the entire minerals, but a portion of the sale proceeds must be paid to the lessor without charge. In some instances the lease contract, however, does call for a small processing charge to be paid by lessor. For example, he might bear a portion of the cost of processing gas so that it can be sold.

Lease Bonus — A Lease bonus is a cash payment to the potential lessor by a potential lessee as an inducement to give a lease on a property. Where the bonus is large, it is sometimes paid over a period of years, in which case it is known as a deferred bonus. This payment is normally amortized over the life of the lease. This amortization is referred to as cost depletion.

Lease Delay Rental — This is an annual rental paid to the lessor by the lessee in lieu of production during the life of the lease. In some cases, such rentals are paid even after production is obtained.

Lease Financing — Obtaining the use of an asset (without obtaining title to it) by entering into a contractually binding agreement to make certain minimum payments over a fixed period of time exceeding one year.

Leaseback — The practice of selling an asset such as a plant, machine, computer or ship to an outside investor and then renting it back under a long-term lease.

Leverage, Financial — The use of funds obtained at a fixed cost in the hope of earning more on assets purchased with the funds than the fixed cost of their use, or equivalently, the act of controlling a certain amount of investment worth with a smaller amount of money. For example, the purchase of land with a 10 or 20% down payment in anticipation of price appreciation can be considered a use of financial leverage.

Liability — An accounting term for a claim against a company. A liability is typically classified as a fixed or long-term liability (e.g., mortgage bond, debenture, bank loan) or a current liability (e.g., account payable, accrued interest payable, accrued taxes payable).

Lien — A lien is a legal device used by creditors for the nonpayment of either labor or equipment. It prevents removal of equipment from a lease under court jurisdiction. In preparing a valuation the presence or absence of such liens must always be determined.

London Interbank Offer Rate (LIBOR) — The interest rate banks lend to each other on overnight borrowings. Large, risk free organizations borrow at LIBOR.

Maintenance Investment — An investment, which sustains benefits (i.e., by preventing revenue losses or losses of cost increases) or postpones asset replacement. One type of incremental investment.

Margin — A term with multiple meanings. "Margin" or "Operating Margin" generally refers to the result of operating revenues less operating expenses. "Margins" may also refer to a percentage value representing net income as a percent of revenues.

Marginal Tax Rate — The Corporate tax rate that is applicable to any change (increase or decrease) in taxable income. The tax rate used for investment evaluation should be a marginal tax rate.

Maximum Cash Exposure or Outlay (MCO) — Used as one definition in computing efficiency ratios, and defined as the most negative cumulative NCF, either undiscounted or discounted. (See Chapter 7)

Maximum Efficient Rate (MER) — An MER is a theoretical number that presumably will optimize ultimate recovery and/or economics. It is normally expressed as volume of production per day, per well or per lease (or field) unit. Such numbers possess some value for general guidance purposes. They are sometimes used (erroneously) as a standard by which the efficiency of a given operation is judged.

Mean Value — A statistical measure reflecting an arithmetic average or a probability weighted average of values.

Median — The 50/50 chance point in a statistical distribution. For a data set, it is a point such that half the cases lie below it and half above it.

Mineral Rights — Mineral ownership legally may be separate from surface ownership except where otherwise provided. The mineral owner therefore has the right to recover said minerals from the premises.

Minimum Return — The currently approved discount rate to be used in the present worth and present worth to investment ration computation. The minimum return establishes a threshold for investment acceptance based upon the cost of investment funds.

Minimum Royalty — This form occurs only where the rate paid depends on quality, quantity and price of oil. It is the minimum payment under such an agreement.

Model — A numerical or mathematical representation of a financial or economic situation. Accordingly, a "cash flow" or "investment" model is specifically designed to evaluate the effects of making an investment.

Money of the Day (MOD) — See ***Real***.

Monte Carlo Simulation — A technique for generating probability distributions of investment return when the probability distribution for each investment uncertainty is known or can be approximated.

Most Likely Outcome or Value (MODE) — That outcome or value with highest probability of occurrence.

Mutually Exclusive Investment (MEI) — An investment, which, if accepted, eliminates other comparable investments from consideration.

Net Cash Flow (NCF) — This term refers to the total or aggregate of all receipts and expenditures applicable to a particular investment (e.g., revenues less expenses, capital investment, changes in working capital and payment of taxes). Also see ***Cash Flow***.

Net Income — An accounting term for revenues less cash and non-cash or book expenses, which may be expressed before or after tax.

Net Present Value (NPV) — NPV of a Project is quoted at a particular ***discount rate*** and must state whether it is ***real*** or ***MOD***. It is arrived at by summing *NCF,* discounted at the given rate, over the life of the project. (See Chapter 5)

It is a measure of the incremental worth of going ahead with that project today, over and above the ***opportunity cost of capital***.

Net Profits Interest — An interest in a property, which entitles the owner to receive a stated percentage of the net profit as defined in the instrument creating the interests.

Net Revenue Interest (NRI) — Working interest (WI) ***less*** the Royalty interest (R) and, if applicable, any Overriding Royalty and Production payment interests. NRI = WI∗(1 – R).

Non-Cash — An accounting amount, which directly affects the computation of book income and net income but does not generate or require a cash outlay during the period. Book charges such as depreciation, depletion and amortization are examples.

Non-Controllable Expense — An expense item over which managers and supervisors are deemed to have no direct control. For example, federal, state, local taxes, property taxes, license fees, insurance and depreciation expenses.

Non-Operating Interest — Non-operating interest is the portion of the working interest not charged with operational responsibility on the lease.

Obligation Investment — An investment, which is undertaken to satisfy contractual commitments or other legal liabilities.

Off Book — See On Book.

Oil-Gas Ratio — Barrels of condensate per million cubic feet of gas produced (BPM).

Offset Royalty (Oil and Gas) — This is a misnomer and is really a payment from the lessee to the lessor in lieu of drilling an offset well. Said sum is theoretically equal to the revenue that would be received by the royalty owner from such an offset well if one is required in the lease agreement. It is in reality a form of compromise in those situations where the operator does not feel that said offset well would be profitable. Owing to its intangible nature the amount of such payment must be negotiated.

On Book — Liabilities reported on a balance sheet are defined as on book. Liabilities, which don't have to be reported in financial reports, are termed off book. Some feel keeping liabilities off book improves the debt/equity ratio and lowers the cost of borrowing money.

Operating Expense (Opex) — Generally, a cost of conducting business activities or, specifically, cost directly involved with production or services. All costs are deducted in the year incurred for both financial and tax books.

Operating Interest — The operating interest is that portion of the working interest charged with operational responsibility of the lease. This interest handles all accounting, charging or remitting to each interest its share of expenses and profits.

Operating Statement — A tabulation of data generally of a financial nature, such as revenues and expenses for a specific period, e.g., week, month, or year.

Opportunity Cost of Capital — This is the expected overall ***rate of return*** of a business. Usually only projects that equal or exceed this ***rate of return*** will be accepted, although there may be other reasons (political, strategic?) for making exceptions. One measure of the opportunity cost may be the return required in stock markets for shares in this business. The opportunity cost is usually used as the ***discount rate***. (See NPV).

Opportunity Cost — The highest valued opportunity necessarily foregone. This indirect cost is equal to the cash value of benefits from the best alternative not chosen.

Ordinary Income — Income from normal operations of a firm. Excludes income from sales of capital assets.

Overhead — A component of controllable expense for management or service departments involved in administration and not directly identifiable with a specific operating function. Also called "general and administrative expense."

Overriding Royalty (ORI or ORRI) — This is an additional royalty created out of the working interest and having the same term as this interest. It is said to be "carved out" if such royalty is assigned free of all operating and development expenses. It is said to be "reserved" if the lessee assigns the working interest and retains only a fractional share. The latter is the more common and usually results from the activities of a land broker who obtains leases for the sole purpose of ultimately assigning them to a third party for development purposes. This form of royalty may also become a part of a Farm-Out Agreement.

Ownership in Fee — An owner in fee owns both surface and minerals under the property covered by a lease.

Pipeline Proration — This is a limit on the amount of oil purchased by a line that results in oil production less than that available. It is usually a temporary measure brought on by temporary loss of refining capacity, storage problems or fluctuations in market. This is often a significant factor in past production history or future value of a lease and, as such, should always be investigated.

Payable — An accounting term for a cash payment to be made for goods or services received.

Payout — This is a somewhat ambiguous term that is used to denote the length of time necessary for recovery of the original investment. It may refer to the gross payout based only on gross revenue before operating costs and taxes, net revenue before taxes, or net revenue after taxes.

When net revenue is used in an agreement it is necessary to specify a means of allocating costs and the bookkeeping methods to be applied.

Play — An area of localized exploration activity based on a geological hypothesis regarding existence of conditions favorable for mineral occurrence.

Plug and Abandon (P&A) — To fill a well bore hole with cement or other impervious material, and discontinue all further drilling at that site.

Premise — A forecast of future conditions upon which a cash flow model is developed. Premises are prepared by operating groups and are negotiated with and approved by executive management.

Prepaid Expense — An accounting term for an expense paid out for goods or services not yet received, but which are to be received in less than one year.

Present Value (PV, PW, or NPV) — The value of a discrete or continuous cash flow stream discounted at some discount rate.

Price Earnings Ratio (P/E Ratio) — Defined as the market share price divided by the earnings per share, as specified in the income statement of the annual report or accounts. The larger the value, the greater the market values future activities. Some use the ratio of 1/(PE) as an indicator of the effective market discount rate. (See Chapter 4).

Primary Recovery — Refers to the production of oil and gas in which only natural processes are relied upon for the movement of fluids from the reservoir into the well bore. Measures total of reserves recoverable without additional expenditures. Contrast with secondary recovery.

Prime Rate — The rate offered to the most credit worthy borrowers, like New York prime. The rate usually includes a 1-2% premium for risk over LIBOR.

Prior Capital Employed — Specifies the amount of capital spent on a project previous to the reference year. Money spent in previous years is ignored in point forward analysis, but is included in full cycle analysis. See Sunk Cost.

Probabilistic Analysis — An analytic procedure that identifies which items of cash flow are uncertain and determines how this uncertainty affects the probability of achieving various levels of investment return. Includes a variety of techniques.

Probability Distribution — The definition of the mathematical behavior of a random variable by specifying its possible values together with their respective probabilities.

Probability of Success — The chance of a future event being a success. Given similar circumstances in the future, a past history of 80 out of 100 wells being productive would indicate an 80 probability of success. The probability of drilling a commercially productive well. See *EMV*.

Probability Tree — A visual display showing combinations of uncertainties, their probability of occurrence, and the probability of each combination. See Decision Tree and Chapter 8.

Production (Oil) Payment — A production payment entitles the owner of the payment to a specified portion of the production for a limited time, or until a specified amount of money has been received. It is almost like a royalty, except that it expires when a given amount of money has been received.

It usually arises as a means of paying back a loan from a bank or some other lending institution. It often calls for paying back the principal plus interest from a given percentage of production. This percentage will vary depending on the reserves, the credit rating of the borrower, and his efficiency of operation.

Production Sharing Contract (PSA or PSC) — A form of mineral contract where the local government maintains ownership of the minerals. The operator recovers their expenditures via cost oil. The remaining profit oils is split between the country and contractor, who then pays income tax on their share of the profit oil. (See Indonesia in Chapter 3 as an example)

Profit — An imprecise term generally perceived to reflect the financial return from an investment. Profit is commonly defined as the excess of revenues over all costs and is also considered to be equivalent to income.

Proration — This refers to the artificial control of producing rate imposed by regulatory bodies in an attempt to enforce good conservation practices and to hold production within the limits of the current market. The methods used vary, none of them being entirely satisfactory to all parties.

Under such a program the allowable production is controlled monthly, either on a per well or a per lease basis. One method is to limit production to a specified amount per day for the full month, whereas another is to let the well produce its tested potential for a given number of days per month.

With the first method; i.e., a per lease basis, it is theoretically possible for one well to produce the entire lease allowable. Where a per well allowable is used, it is difficult, if not impossible, to enforce the order where common tank batteries are used. This fact often makes it difficult to determine individual well production characteristics for evaluation purposes, in the absence of individual well tests.

The allowable is normally established on the basis of market demand, formation depth, specific producing formation, producing characteristics and any special field rules. For example, when oil production is accompanied by a high gas-oil ratio it may result in lowering the allowable if the ratio is above that established as desirable. The only exception is where such flare gas is properly utilized. Most states make periodic checks for this purpose.

Prospect — A target for exploratory drilling activity that consists of one or more specific geologic objectives.

Proved Property — A proved property is one probably containing commercial quantities of oil. Normally, a property is considered proved if all geological and geophysical information is positive, nearby wells are commercial and apparently on the same structure, and there are no negative values to be considered, except the usual error in the interpretations above. In general, a property must be at least partially developed before it is considered proved.

Rate of Return — An imprecise term used to refer to either IRR or accounting ROR.

Rateable Take — Rateable take refers to the orders sometimes issued by regulatory bodies requiring common carriers (usually pipelines) to take products from all customers in proportion to the number of wells served or the capacity of those wells. It is normally instituted where total well capacity exceeds pipeline capacity to insure that all sellers are able to market their fair share of the oil. It is at best a controversial issue between producers and marketers where used.

Real and Money of the Day — Costs are usually calculated in today's money – e.g. year t (2002 $'s). If these costs are applied to future dates they are said to be in ***real*** money terms. To convert to ***Money of the Day*** (MOD) they are inflated using the appropriate ***inflation*** factors. The MOD costs represent today's estimate of what we will actually pay in the future. Computer models usually use real costs as input, and then inflate and carry out calculations in MOD terms.

Why bother to ***inflate*** everything?

Depreciation. For tax calculations, past ***CAPEX*** may usually be deducted from income before calculating tax. The deduction is only allowed at actual cost. Since there is usually a time lag between ***capital expenditure*** and income receipt, this means that calculations ignoring ***inflation*** would undervalue the tax payment.

Cost Recovery. Similar arguments apply to those countries where costs are recovered out of production. In this case the profit oil will be incorrectly calculated if ***inflation*** is ignored.

Working Capital. In Exploration this is usually insignificant, but in other business streams it can be important. If working capital (the net sum of what you owe people and they owe you – ignoring long term loans) is assumed as equal to 10% of turnover, then even for a ***static*** business with no real increase in turnover there is a ***real*** requirement to fund working capital:

Real Dollars — Synonymous with constant dollars.

Real Rate of Return, RROR — The rate of return (ROR) or ***real*** rate of return (RROR) is the % rate which when used to ***discount*** a given ***NCF*** gives an ***NPV*** of zero. It is equivalent to the rate of interest or return that would need to be received from investing the CAPEX in a bank or other project.

Although a useful concept, two points should be noted:

- It takes no account of risk.
- It assumes that positive cash flows can immediately be reinvested at the same ***rate of return***.

(Also known as discounted rate of return, internal yield, IRR, DCF-ROR. See Chapter 5.)

Receivable — An accounting term for an amount of money to be received for goods shipped or services performed.

Recovery Factor — That portion of the total reserves in a reservoir, which it is believed, can be produced (expressed as a percentage of total reserves).

Replacement Investment — An investment in an asset, which replaces an existing asset. One type of mutually exclusive investment.

Return on Investment (ROI) — A form of efficiency ratio, usually measured on an undiscounted basis. (Chapter 5)

Reserves — Reserves are that quantity of oil or gas that should be produced by the methods outlined in the report under the conditions specified. For oil, the standard unit is either cubic meters or the API barrel (42 U. S. gallons) measured at atmospheric temperature and pressure. For gas the unit is either standard cubic feet or standard cubic meters, as measured at a given base temperature and pressure.

Revenue — The amount received for the sale of production of manufactured products. Generally, the mathematical product of unit price and volume. The chief source of value added in most investment evaluations.

Reversionary Interest — This is similar to a carried interest, differing only in the sense that the type of interest held by each party changes after a specified set of conditions has been met. A typical example might be found in a farm-out agreement. Lessee A retains a 1/16 or 7/8 overriding royalty until B recovers $300,000 from drilling a successful farm-out. After this recovery, the override reverts to a one-half working interest, the override becoming null and void. Therefore, A is said to have a reversionary one-half interest in the property.

Ring Fence — In very few countries, a company's income and costs may all be pooled together in calculating tax (this is broadly true in New Zealand). In many countries, however, certain "ring-fences" are applied which prevent companies from doing this. (The reasons for this broadly are to ensure the governments receive their anticipated share of the hydrocarbon resources irrespective of which company is involved). These ring-fences can be at a number of levels:

- Field
- Contract Area
- Business Company

i.e., for a Company Ring Fence all operations of one company may be allowed to be grouped together, while for a field ring fence, costs of developing an adjacent field will not be allowed to be offset against income of field's onstream.

Risk — Denotes the possibility of a monetary loss or an unachieved objective. Sometimes, a formal distinction is made between risk and uncertainty. Risk is associated with an objective probability distribution and uncertainty with no probability distribution (or a subjective probability distribution). See Chapters 6-10.

Risk-Adjusted Rate of Return — The rate of return which when used to ***discount NCF*** gives an ***EMV*** of zero – i.e., the rate at which the risked cost and ***EPV's*** are equal.

Risk-Adjusted Value (RAV) — The process of adjusting NPV for the utility associated with the gain or loss of money. See Chapter 8.

Royalty — Royalty is the interest of a party owning minerals in the ground where another party (the working interest) has gained the right to capture such minerals under a lease agreement. Such royalty interest is normally free of all costs of capture except for special treating costs that might be specified in the lease or assignment. This term is often used as an abbreviation for the term landowner's royalty. There are many specific forms of royalty.

Salvage — The amount expected or actually received from the sale of property, plant or equipment, before or after tax. Also called "capital recovery."

Secondary Recovery — Refers to various processes for increasing the ultimate recovery of oil and gas by supplementing the natural reservoir drive mechanism. Examples are waterfloods and pressure maintenance projects. Contrast with primary recovery.

Sensitivity Analysis — An analytic procedure, which quantifies the impact various items of cash flow have upon investment return.

Severance Tax — A tax levied upon the value of natural resources removed from the land. A production tax in the U. S. paid to the State government.

Sliding Scale Royalty — A royalty varying in accordance with the amount of production, e.g., a 1/8 royalty if the production is 100 barrels per day or less, and a 3/16 royalty if the production is greater than 100 barrels per day. Difficult problems of interpretation of the sliding scale royalty clause arise when governmental regulations on a unitization agreement limit production on the amount of oil allocated to a particular tract.

Success — The outcome of drilling a well from which a firm elects to produce hydrocarbons, i.e., the outcome of drilling in which a dry hole does not result.

Sunk Costs — Those costs which have already been incurred, and which therefore do not affect yet-to-spend economics for a given project except for their effect on subsequent taxes.

Surface Owner — Ownership of the surface rights does not necessarily give a party any interest in the minerals unless this is specified. In the absence of such mineral rights the surface owner is not a party to the lease agreement. However, he is seriously affected by it for a portion of the land has to be appropriated for access roads and drilling locations.

The lease specifically gives the lessee the right to build the facilities necessary for drilling and production, but furthermore requires payment of damages.

Surrender — To give up the economic interest in a mineral lease by discontinuing payment of agreed upon rentals or otherwise allowing the lease to expire.

Tangible — Refers to an asset having material substance, as for example, equipment. A property whose value can be determined by objective appraisal.

Taxable Income — The computation of income in accordance with tax codes so as to serve as the basis for computing income taxes. Generally differs from book income (as reported in financial statements) because of different depreciation and depletion accounting procedures.

Turnkey Well — A turnkey well is one in which the drilling contractor drills, completes, and equips a well under the same contract. This is opposed to the standard drilling contract, which usually calls for so much per foot and/or a daily fee, the operator assuming responsibility for completion and equipment.

Uncertainty — Refers to a lack of definite knowledge about an event or outcome. Also, an uncertain event or outcome.

Unitization — Unitization is the process whereby the owners of adjoining properties pool their reserves and form a single unit for the operation of the properties. The revenue from operation of this unit is then divided in accordance with the basis established in the unit agreement.

The purpose of such an agreement is to produce the reserves more efficiently and thus to increase the profit to every participant. It is particularly important where secondary recovery is anticipated.

Unproved Property — Unproved property is possibly productive but, as the name implies, not considered proved. Since there are usually no nearby wells, the only indications of possible oil or gas are taken from regional geological studies and/or general geophysical surveys.

Utility Theory — The branch of decision theory, which recognizes that investment gains and losses differs uniquely across individuals (See Chapter 8).

Value at Risk An attempt to identify the causes of risk and policies for reducing risk as historically applied to financial portfolios. It measures the worst expected loss that an investor can suffer for a given time interval *under normal market conditions* at a given confidence level.

Variable Expense — An expense, which varies with business or production volume.

Variance — A statistical measure of dispersion around a mean value. It is the probability weighted average of the square of differences between all values and the mean value.

Weighted Average Cost of Capital — see ***Cost of Capital***.

Wildcat Well — A wildcat well is one drilled on unproved property. A well is sometimes designated a semi-wildcat for those in between cases where property classification is uncertain.

Working Capital — The funds required for project startup or to support continued operations. In accounting terms, defined as current assets less current liabilities. (Chapter 4)

Working Interest — The working interest is the total interest minus the royalty. For all practical purposes it is an interest in the oil and gas in place that is liable for the cost of developing and operating a property. It is formed by the granting of a lease by the owner of the mineral rights.

Write-Down — To reduce the value of an asset on the financial books. The reduction in values is treated as an expense on the income statement. (Chapter 4).

Write-Off — An accounting term for a non-cash or book expense. It is the cost of a long-term asset allocated, period-by-period, over its deemed life. Also called an "Extinguishment." For example, depreciation, depletion and amortization expenses.

Write-Up — To increase the value of an asset with no corresponding disbursement of funds. This seldom happens in the real world as financial books are based on actual transactions. (Chapter 4).

Yet-to-Spend Economics — Measures of project performance that consider only the project expenditures and benefits that have not yet occurred. Tax effects of past expenditures which impact on future cash flows should be considered.

APPENDIX

VALUATION ABBREVIATIONS

AFE	Authorization for Expenditure	NPRI	Net Profits Royalty Interest
AMI	Area of Mutual Interest	NPV	Net present value, also PV or PW
APR	Annual Percentage Rate	NPV/INVT	Capital Efficiency
BOE	Barrels of Oil Equivalent	NRI	Net Revenue Interest
CAPEX	Capital Expenditures	OANPV	Options Analysis NPV
CAPM	Capital Asset Pricing Model	OGR	Oil-Gas-Ratio
CF	Compound Factor	OH	Overhead
CT	Corporate Income Tax	O & M	Operating and Maintenance Costs
DB or RD	Declining or Reducing Balance	OPEX	Same as O & M
DCF	Discounted Cash Flow	ORI	Overriding Royalty Interest
DD&A	Depreciation, Depletion, and Amortization	PCR	Post-Completion Review
DF	Discount Factor	P/E	Price Earnings Ratio
DPO	Discounted Payout	PI	Profitability Index, another term for NPV/Invt
D/E	Debt to Equity Ratio	PIA	Post Installation Appraisal
EOR	Enhanced Oil Recovery	PO	Payout
EMV	Expected Monetary Value	Ps or COS	Probability of Success
EPV	Expected Present Value	PSC	Production Sharing Contract
EV	Expected Value	PRT	Production Related Taxes or Petroleum Revenue Tax
FI	Farm-In	PV or NPV	Net Present Value
FO	Farm-Out	PW	PV or NPV
FV	Future Value	RAV	Risk Adjusted Value
G&G	Geological and Geophysical	RO or ROV	Real Options Valuation
GDP	Gross Domestic Product	ROACE	Return on Capital Employed
GNP	Gross National Product	ROA	Return on Assets
GOR	Gas-Oil Ratio	ROE	Return on Equity
ICAP	Intangible Capital	RNCF	Real Net Cash Flow
IDC	Intangible Drilling Costs	RROR	Real Rate of Return
INV or INVT	Investment	SL	Straight Line Depreciation
IT	Income Tax	SIV	Strategic Investment Value
IRR	Internal Rate of Return	SYD	Sum of Years Digits
LIBOR	London InterBank Offer Rate	SWOT	Strengths, Weaknesses, Opportunities, and Threats
M or k	Denotes Thousands	TCAP	Tangible Capital
MM or M	Denotes Millions	UOP	Units of Production
MOD	Money of the Day, or Current Dollars	VaR	Value at Risk
NCF	Net Cash Flow		
NI	Net Income	WI	Working Interest
NPI	Net Profits Interest	WACC	Weighted Average Cost-of-Capital, also CoC

STATISTICS AND DISCOUNTING TABLES

Student t Distribution Table						
= TINV (probability, degrees of freedom)						
	Critical Value for Error of α =					
df	0.25	0.1	0.05	0.025	0.01	0.005
1	1.000	3.078	6.314	12.706	31.821	63.656
2	0.816	1.886	2.920	4.303	6.965	9.925
3	0.765	1.638	2.353	3.182	4.541	5.841
4	0.741	1.533	2.132	2.776	3.747	4.604
5	0.727	1.476	2.015	2.571	3.365	4.032
6	0.718	1.440	1.943	2.447	3.143	3.707
7	0.711	1.415	1.895	2.365	2.998	3.499
8	0.706	1.397	1.860	2.306	2.896	3.355
9	0.703	1.383	1.833	2.262	2.821	3.250
10	0.700	1.372	1.812	2.228	2.764	3.169
11	0.697	1.363	1.796	2.201	2.718	3.106
12	0.695	1.356	1.782	2.179	2.681	3.055
13	0.694	1.350	1.771	2.160	2.650	3.012
14	0.692	1.345	1.761	2.145	2.624	2.977
15	0.691	1.341	1.753	2.131	2.602	2.947
16	0.690	1.337	1.746	2.120	2.583	2.921
17	0.689	1.333	1.740	2.110	2.567	2.898
18	0.688	1.330	1.734	2.101	2.552	2.878
19	0.688	1.328	1.729	2.093	2.539	2.861
20	0.687	1.325	1.725	2.086	2.528	2.845
21	0.686	1.323	1.721	2.080	2.518	2.831
22	0.686	1.321	1.717	2.074	2.508	2.819
23	0.685	1.319	1.714	2.069	2.500	2.807
24	0.685	1.318	1.711	2.064	2.492	2.797
25	0.684	1.316	1.708	2.060	2.485	2.787
26	0.684	1.315	1.706	2.056	2.479	2.779
27	0.684	1.314	1.703	2.052	2.473	2.771
28	0.683	1.313	1.701	2.048	2.467	2.763
29	0.683	1.311	1.699	2.045	2.462	2.756
30	0.683	1.310	1.697	2.042	2.457	2.750
60	0.679	1.296	1.671	2.000	2.390	2.660
120	0.677	1.289	1.658	1.980	2.358	2.617

When the computed t value exceeds the number from this table, accept the alternative hypothesis that the number is significantly different from zero.

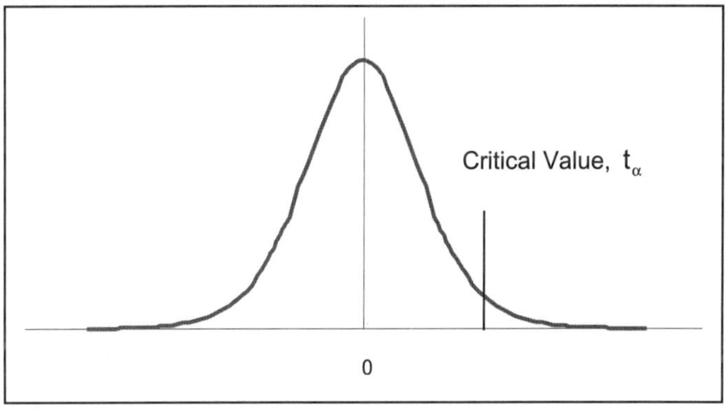

Chi-Square Distribution Table						
= CHIINV (probability, degrees of freedom)						
	Critical Value for Error of α =					
df	**0.2**	**0.1**	**0.05**	**0.02**	**0.01**	**0.001**
1	1.642	2.706	3.841	5.412	6.635	10.827
2	3.219	4.605	5.991	7.824	9.210	13.815
3	4.642	6.251	7.815	9.837	11.345	16.266
4	5.989	7.779	9.488	11.668	13.277	18.466
5	7.289	9.236	11.070	13.388	15.086	20.515
6	8.558	10.645	12.592	15.033	16.812	22.457
7	9.803	12.017	14.067	16.622	18.475	24.321
8	11.030	13.362	15.507	18.168	20.090	26.124
9	12.242	14.684	16.919	19.679	21.666	27.877
10	13.442	15.987	18.307	21.161	23.209	29.588
11	14.631	17.275	19.675	22.618	24.725	31.264
12	15.812	18.549	21.026	24.054	26.217	32.909
13	16.985	19.812	22.362	25.471	27.688	34.527
14	18.151	21.064	23.685	26.873	29.141	36.124
15	19.311	22.307	24.996	28.259	30.578	37.698
16	20.465	23.542	26.296	29.633	32.000	39.252
17	21.615	24.769	27.587	30.995	33.409	40.791
18	22.760	25.989	28.869	32.346	34.805	42.312
19	23.900	27.204	30.144	33.687	36.191	43.819
20	25.038	28.412	31.410	35.020	37.566	45.314
21	26.171	29.615	32.671	36.343	38.932	46.796
22	27.301	30.813	33.924	37.659	40.289	48.268
23	28.429	32.007	35.172	38.968	41.638	49.728
24	29.553	33.196	36.415	40.270	42.980	51.179
25	30.675	34.382	37.652	41.566	44.314	52.619
26	31.795	35.563	38.885	42.856	45.642	54.051
27	32.912	36.741	40.113	44.140	46.963	55.475
28	34.027	37.916	41.337	45.419	48.278	56.892
29	35.139	39.087	42.557	46.693	49.588	58.301
30	36.250	40.256	43.773	47.962	50.892	59.702

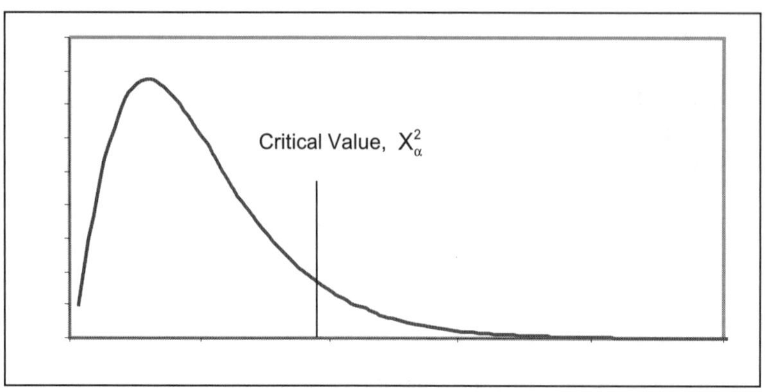

Mid-Year Cash Flow, Annual Interest from Equation 5.8

$$DF = \frac{1}{(1+i)^{t-0.5}}$$

Year	Discount Rate											
	5%	7%	8%	9%	10%	11%	12%	13%	15%	20%	25%	30%
1	0.9759	0.9667	0.9623	0.9578	0.9535	0.9492	0.9449	0.9407	0.9325	0.9129	0.8944	0.8771
2	0.9294	0.9035	0.8910	0.8787	0.8668	0.8551	0.8437	0.8325	0.8109	0.7607	0.7155	0.6747
3	0.8852	0.8444	0.8250	0.8062	0.7880	0.7704	0.7533	0.7367	0.7051	0.6339	0.5724	0.5190
4	0.8430	0.7891	0.7639	0.7396	0.7164	0.6940	0.6726	0.6520	0.6131	0.5283	0.4579	0.3992
5	0.8029	0.7375	0.7073	0.6785	0.6512	0.6252	0.6005	0.5770	0.5332	0.4402	0.3664	0.3071
6	0.7646	0.6893	0.6549	0.6225	0.5920	0.5633	0.5362	0.5106	0.4636	0.3669	0.2931	0.2362
7	0.7282	0.6442	0.6064	0.5711	0.5382	0.5075	0.4787	0.4518	0.4031	0.3057	0.2345	0.1817
8	0.6936	0.6020	0.5615	0.5240	0.4893	0.4572	0.4274	0.3999	0.3506	0.2548	0.1876	0.1398
9	0.6605	0.5626	0.5199	0.4807	0.4448	0.4119	0.3816	0.3539	0.3048	0.2123	0.1501	0.1075
10	0.6291	0.5258	0.4814	0.4410	0.4044	0.3710	0.3407	0.3132	0.2651	0.1769	0.1200	0.0827
11	0.5991	0.4914	0.4457	0.4046	0.3676	0.3343	0.3042	0.2771	0.2305	0.1474	0.0960	0.0636
12	0.5706	0.4593	0.4127	0.3712	0.3342	0.3012	0.2716	0.2452	0.2004	0.1229	0.0768	0.0489
13	0.5434	0.4292	0.3821	0.3405	0.3038	0.2713	0.2425	0.2170	0.1743	0.1024	0.0615	0.0376
14	0.5175	0.4012	0.3538	0.3124	0.2762	0.2444	0.2165	0.1921	0.1516	0.0853	0.0492	0.0290
15	0.4929	0.3749	0.3276	0.2866	0.2511	0.2202	0.1933	0.1700	0.1318	0.0711	0.0393	0.0223
16	0.4694	0.3504	0.3033	0.2630	0.2283	0.1984	0.1726	0.1504	0.1146	0.0593	0.0315	0.0171
17	0.4471	0.3275	0.2809	0.2412	0.2075	0.1787	0.1541	0.1331	0.0997	0.0494	0.0252	0.0132
18	0.4258	0.3060	0.2601	0.2213	0.1886	0.1610	0.1376	0.1178	0.0867	0.0411	0.0201	0.0101
19	0.4055	0.2860	0.2408	0.2031	0.1715	0.1451	0.1229	0.1042	0.0754	0.0343	0.0161	0.0078
20	0.3862	0.2673	0.2230	0.1863	0.1559	0.1307	0.1097	0.0923	0.0655	0.0286	0.0129	0.0060
21	0.3678	0.2498	0.2064	0.1709	0.1417	0.1177	0.0980	0.0816	0.0570	0.0238	0.0103	0.0046
22	0.3503	0.2335	0.1912	0.1568	0.1288	0.1061	0.0875	0.0722	0.0495	0.0198	0.0082	0.0035
23	0.3336	0.2182	0.1770	0.1438	0.1171	0.0956	0.0781	0.0639	0.0431	0.0165	0.0066	0.0027
24	0.3177	0.2039	0.1639	0.1320	0.1065	0.0861	0.0697	0.0566	0.0375	0.0138	0.0053	0.0021
25	0.3026	0.1906	0.1517	0.1211	0.0968	0.0776	0.0623	0.0501	0.0326	0.0115	0.0042	0.0016
26	0.2882	0.1781	0.1405	0.1111	0.0880	0.0699	0.0556	0.0443	0.0283	0.0096	0.0034	0.0012
27	0.2745	0.1665	0.1301	0.1019	0.0800	0.0629	0.0496	0.0392	0.0246	0.0080	0.0027	0.0010
28	0.2614	0.1556	0.1205	0.0935	0.0727	0.0567	0.0443	0.0347	0.0214	0.0066	0.0022	0.0007
29	0.2489	0.1454	0.1115	0.0858	0.0661	0.0511	0.0396	0.0307	0.0186	0.0055	0.0017	0.0006
30	0.2371	0.1359	0.1033	0.0787	0.0601	0.0460	0.0353	0.0272	0.0162	0.0046	0.0014	0.0004
31	0.2258	0.1270	0.0956	0.0722	0.0546	0.0415	0.0315	0.0240	0.0141	0.0038	0.0011	0.0003
32	0.2150	0.1187	0.0885	0.0662	0.0497	0.0374	0.0282	0.0213	0.0122	0.0032	0.0009	0.0003
33	0.2048	0.1109	0.0820	0.0608	0.0452	0.0337	0.0251	0.0188	0.0106	0.0027	0.0007	0.0002
34	0.1951	0.1037	0.0759	0.0557	0.0411	0.0303	0.0224	0.0167	0.0093	0.0022	0.0006	0.0002
35	0.1858	0.0969	0.0703	0.0511	0.0373	0.0273	0.0200	0.0148	0.0081	0.0019	0.0005	0.0001
36	0.1769	0.0905	0.0651	0.0469	0.0339	0.0246	0.0179	0.0131	0.0070	0.0015	0.0004	0.0001
37	0.1685	0.0846	0.0603	0.0430	0.0308	0.0222	0.0160	0.0116	0.0061	0.0013	0.0003	0.0001
38	0.1605	0.0791	0.0558	0.0395	0.0280	0.0200	0.0143	0.0102	0.0053	0.0011	0.0002	0.0001
39	0.1528	0.0739	0.0517	0.0362	0.0255	0.0180	0.0127	0.0090	0.0046	0.0009	0.0002	0.0000
40	0.1456	0.0691	0.0478	0.0332	0.0232	0.0162	0.0114	0.0080	0.0040	0.0007	0.0001	0.0000

Mid-Year Cash Flow, Continuous Interest from Equation 7.9

$$DF = e^{-i*(t-0.5)}$$

Year	Discount Rate											
	5%	7%	8%	9%	10%	11%	12%	13%	15%	20%	25%	30%
1	0.9753	0.9656	0.9608	0.9560	0.9512	0.9465	0.9418	0.9371	0.9277	0.9048	0.8825	0.7408
2	0.9277	0.9003	0.8869	0.8737	0.8607	0.8479	0.8353	0.8228	0.7985	0.7408	0.6873	0.5488
3	0.8825	0.8395	0.8187	0.7985	0.7788	0.7596	0.7408	0.7225	0.6873	0.6065	0.5353	0.4066
4	0.8395	0.7827	0.7558	0.7298	0.7047	0.6805	0.6570	0.6344	0.5916	0.4966	0.4169	0.3012
5	0.7985	0.7298	0.6977	0.6670	0.6376	0.6096	0.5827	0.5571	0.5092	0.4066	0.3247	0.2231
6	0.7596	0.6805	0.6440	0.6096	0.5769	0.5461	0.5169	0.4892	0.4382	0.3329	0.2528	0.1653
7	0.7225	0.6344	0.5945	0.5571	0.5220	0.4892	0.4584	0.4296	0.3772	0.2725	0.1969	0.1225
8	0.6873	0.5916	0.5488	0.5092	0.4724	0.4382	0.4066	0.3772	0.3247	0.2231	0.1534	0.0907
9	0.6538	0.5516	0.5066	0.4653	0.4274	0.3926	0.3606	0.3312	0.2794	0.1827	0.1194	0.0672
10	0.6219	0.5143	0.4677	0.4253	0.3867	0.3517	0.3198	0.2908	0.2405	0.1496	0.0930	0.0498
11	0.5916	0.4795	0.4317	0.3887	0.3499	0.3151	0.2837	0.2554	0.2070	0.1225	0.0724	0.0369
12	0.5627	0.4471	0.3985	0.3552	0.3166	0.2822	0.2516	0.2242	0.1782	0.1003	0.0564	0.0273
13	0.5353	0.4169	0.3679	0.3247	0.2865	0.2528	0.2231	0.1969	0.1534	0.0821	0.0439	0.0202
14	0.5092	0.3887	0.3396	0.2967	0.2592	0.2265	0.1979	0.1729	0.1320	0.0672	0.0342	0.0150
15	0.4843	0.3624	0.3135	0.2712	0.2346	0.2029	0.1755	0.1518	0.1136	0.0550	0.0266	0.0111
16	0.4607	0.3379	0.2894	0.2478	0.2122	0.1818	0.1557	0.1333	0.0978	0.0450	0.0208	0.0082
17	0.4382	0.3151	0.2671	0.2265	0.1920	0.1628	0.1381	0.1171	0.0842	0.0369	0.0162	0.0061
18	0.4169	0.2938	0.2466	0.2070	0.1738	0.1459	0.1225	0.1028	0.0724	0.0302	0.0126	0.0045
19	0.3965	0.2739	0.2276	0.1892	0.1572	0.1307	0.1086	0.0903	0.0623	0.0247	0.0098	0.0033
20	0.3772	0.2554	0.2101	0.1729	0.1423	0.1171	0.0963	0.0793	0.0537	0.0202	0.0076	0.0025
21	0.3588	0.2381	0.1940	0.1580	0.1287	0.1049	0.0854	0.0696	0.0462	0.0166	0.0059	0.0018
22	0.3413	0.2220	0.1791	0.1444	0.1165	0.0939	0.0758	0.0611	0.0398	0.0136	0.0046	0.0014
23	0.3247	0.2070	0.1653	0.1320	0.1054	0.0842	0.0672	0.0537	0.0342	0.0111	0.0036	0.0010
24	0.3088	0.1930	0.1526	0.1206	0.0954	0.0754	0.0596	0.0471	0.0295	0.0091	0.0028	0.0007
25	0.2938	0.1800	0.1409	0.1103	0.0863	0.0675	0.0529	0.0414	0.0253	0.0074	0.0022	0.0006
26	0.2794	0.1678	0.1300	0.1008	0.0781	0.0605	0.0469	0.0363	0.0218	0.0061	0.0017	0.0004
27	0.2658	0.1565	0.1200	0.0921	0.0707	0.0542	0.0416	0.0319	0.0188	0.0050	0.0013	0.0003
28	0.2528	0.1459	0.1108	0.0842	0.0639	0.0486	0.0369	0.0280	0.0162	0.0041	0.0010	0.0002
29	0.2405	0.1360	0.1023	0.0769	0.0578	0.0435	0.0327	0.0246	0.0139	0.0033	0.0008	0.0002
30	0.2288	0.1268	0.0944	0.0703	0.0523	0.0390	0.0290	0.0216	0.0120	0.0027	0.0006	0.0001
31	0.2176	0.1182	0.0872	0.0642	0.0474	0.0349	0.0257	0.0190	0.0103	0.0022	0.0005	0.0001
32	0.2070	0.1103	0.0805	0.0587	0.0429	0.0313	0.0228	0.0167	0.0089	0.0018	0.0004	0.0001
33	0.1969	0.1028	0.0743	0.0537	0.0388	0.0280	0.0202	0.0146	0.0076	0.0015	0.0003	0.0001
34	0.1873	0.0958	0.0686	0.0490	0.0351	0.0251	0.0180	0.0128	0.0066	0.0012	0.0002	0.0000
35	0.1782	0.0894	0.0633	0.0448	0.0317	0.0225	0.0159	0.0113	0.0057	0.0010	0.0002	0.0000
36	0.1695	0.0833	0.0584	0.0410	0.0287	0.0201	0.0141	0.0099	0.0049	0.0008	0.0001	0.0000
37	0.1612	0.0777	0.0539	0.0374	0.0260	0.0180	0.0125	0.0087	0.0042	0.0007	0.0001	0.0000
38	0.1534	0.0724	0.0498	0.0342	0.0235	0.0162	0.0111	0.0076	0.0036	0.0006	0.0001	0.0000
39	0.1459	0.0675	0.0460	0.0313	0.0213	0.0145	0.0099	0.0067	0.0031	0.0005	0.0001	0.0000
40	0.1388	0.0630	0.0424	0.0286	0.0193	0.0130	0.0087	0.0059	0.0027	0.0004	0.0001	0.0000

Individual Binomial Tables											
= BINOMDIST (Success = x, Trials = n, probability, true for cumulative and false for individual values)											
Trials	**Success**	**Probability**									
n	**x**	**0.05**	**0.01**	**0.15**	**0.2**	**0.25**	**0.3**	**0.35**	**0.4**	**0.45**	**0.5**
1	0	0.950	0.900	0.850	0.800	0.750	0.700	0.650	0.600	0.550	0.500
	1	0.050	0.100	0.150	0.200	0.250	0.300	0.350	0.400	0.450	0.500
2	0	0.903	0.810	0.723	0.640	0.563	0.490	0.423	0.360	0.303	0.250
	1	0.095	0.180	0.255	0.320	0.375	0.420	0.455	0.480	0.495	0.500
	2	0.003	0.010	0.023	0.040	0.063	0.090	0.123	0.160	0.203	0.250
3	0	0.857	0.729	0.614	0.512	0.422	0.343	0.275	0.216	0.166	0.125
	1	0.135	0.243	0.325	0.384	0.422	0.441	0.444	0.432	0.408	0.375
	2	0.007	0.027	0.057	0.096	0.141	0.189	0.239	0.288	0.334	0.375
	3	0.000	0.001	0.003	0.008	0.016	0.027	0.043	0.064	0.091	0.125
4	0	0.815	0.656	0.522	0.410	0.316	0.240	0.179	0.130	0.092	0.063
	1	0.171	0.292	0.368	0.410	0.422	0.412	0.384	0.346	0.299	0.250
	2	0.014	0.049	0.098	0.154	0.211	0.265	0.311	0.346	0.368	0.375
	3	0.000	0.004	0.011	0.026	0.047	0.076	0.111	0.154	0.200	0.250
	4	0.000	0.000	0.001	0.002	0.004	0.008	0.015	0.026	0.041	0.063
5	0	0.774	0.590	0.444	0.328	0.237	0.168	0.116	0.078	0.050	0.031
	1	0.204	0.328	0.392	0.410	0.396	0.360	0.312	0.259	0.206	0.156
	2	0.021	0.073	0.138	0.205	0.264	0.309	0.336	0.346	0.337	0.313
	3	0.001	0.008	0.024	0.051	0.088	0.132	0.181	0.230	0.276	0.313
	4	0.000	0.000	0.002	0.006	0.015	0.028	0.049	0.077	0.113	0.156
	5	0.000	0.000	0.000	0.000	0.001	0.002	0.005	0.010	0.018	0.031
6	0	0.735	0.531	0.377	0.262	0.178	0.118	0.075	0.047	0.028	0.016
	1	0.232	0.354	0.399	0.393	0.356	0.303	0.244	0.187	0.136	0.094
	2	0.031	0.098	0.176	0.246	0.297	0.324	0.328	0.311	0.278	0.234
	3	0.002	0.015	0.041	0.082	0.132	0.185	0.235	0.276	0.303	0.313
	4	0.000	0.001	0.005	0.015	0.033	0.060	0.095	0.138	0.186	0.234
	5	0.000	0.000	0.000	0.002	0.004	0.010	0.020	0.037	0.061	0.094
	6	0.000	0.000	0.000	0.000	0.000	0.001	0.002	0.004	0.008	0.016
7	0	0.698	0.478	0.321	0.210	0.133	0.082	0.049	0.028	0.015	0.008
	1	0.257	0.372	0.396	0.367	0.311	0.247	0.185	0.131	0.087	0.055
	2	0.041	0.124	0.210	0.275	0.311	0.318	0.298	0.261	0.214	0.164
	3	0.004	0.023	0.062	0.115	0.173	0.227	0.268	0.290	0.292	0.273
	4	0.000	0.003	0.011	0.029	0.058	0.097	0.144	0.194	0.239	0.273
	5	0.000	0.000	0.001	0.004	0.012	0.025	0.047	0.077	0.117	0.164
	6	0.000	0.000	0.000	0.000	0.001	0.004	0.008	0.017	0.032	0.055
	7	0.000	0.000	0.000	0.000	0.000	0.000	0.001	0.002	0.004	0.008

Area Under Normal Curve, (Probability <)

Z	0.00	0.01	0.02	0.03	0.04	0.05	0.06	0.07	0.08	0.09		0.00	0.01	0.02	0.03	0.04	0.05	0.06	0.07	0.08	0.09
-3.5	0.000	0.000	0.000	0.000	0.000	0.000	0.000	0.000	0.000	0.000	0.0	0.500	0.504	0.508	0.512	0.516	0.520	0.524	0.528	0.532	0.536
-3.4	0.000	0.000	0.000	0.000	0.000	0.000	0.000	0.000	0.000	0.000	0.1	0.540	0.544	0.548	0.552	0.556	0.560	0.564	0.567	0.571	0.575
-3.3	0.000	0.000	0.000	0.000	0.000	0.000	0.000	0.000	0.000	0.000	0.2	0.579	0.583	0.587	0.591	0.595	0.599	0.603	0.606	0.610	0.614
-3.2	0.001	0.001	0.001	0.001	0.001	0.001	0.001	0.001	0.001	0.001	0.3	0.618	0.622	0.626	0.629	0.633	0.637	0.641	0.644	0.648	0.652
-3.1	0.001	0.001	0.001	0.001	0.001	0.001	0.001	0.001	0.001	0.001	0.4	0.655	0.659	0.663	0.666	0.670	0.674	0.677	0.681	0.684	0.688
-3.0	0.001	0.001	0.001	0.001	0.001	0.001	0.001	0.001	0.001	0.001	0.5	0.691	0.695	0.698	0.702	0.705	0.709	0.712	0.716	0.719	0.722
-2.9	0.002	0.002	0.002	0.002	0.002	0.002	0.002	0.001	0.001	0.001	0.6	0.726	0.729	0.732	0.736	0.739	0.742	0.745	0.749	0.752	0.755
-2.8	0.003	0.002	0.002	0.002	0.002	0.002	0.002	0.002	0.002	0.002	0.7	0.758	0.761	0.764	0.767	0.770	0.773	0.776	0.779	0.782	0.785
-2.7	0.003	0.003	0.003	0.003	0.003	0.003	0.003	0.003	0.003	0.003	0.8	0.788	0.791	0.794	0.797	0.800	0.802	0.805	0.808	0.811	0.813
-2.6	0.005	0.005	0.004	0.004	0.004	0.004	0.004	0.004	0.004	0.004	0.9	0.816	0.819	0.821	0.824	0.826	0.829	0.831	0.834	0.836	0.839
-2.5	0.006	0.006	0.006	0.006	0.006	0.005	0.005	0.005	0.005	0.005	1.0	0.841	0.844	0.846	0.848	0.851	0.853	0.855	0.858	0.860	0.862
-2.4	0.008	0.008	0.008	0.008	0.007	0.007	0.007	0.007	0.007	0.006	1.1	0.864	0.867	0.869	0.871	0.873	0.875	0.877	0.879	0.881	0.883
-2.3	0.011	0.010	0.010	0.010	0.010	0.009	0.009	0.009	0.009	0.008	1.2	0.885	0.887	0.889	0.891	0.893	0.894	0.896	0.898	0.900	0.901
-2.2	0.014	0.014	0.013	0.013	0.013	0.012	0.012	0.012	0.011	0.011	1.3	0.903	0.905	0.907	0.908	0.910	0.911	0.913	0.915	0.916	0.918
-2.1	0.018	0.017	0.017	0.017	0.016	0.016	0.015	0.015	0.015	0.014	1.4	0.919	0.921	0.922	0.924	0.925	0.926	0.928	0.929	0.931	0.932
-2.0	0.023	0.022	0.022	0.021	0.021	0.020	0.020	0.019	0.019	0.018	1.5	0.933	0.934	0.936	0.937	0.938	0.939	0.941	0.942	0.943	0.944
-1.9	0.029	0.028	0.027	0.027	0.026	0.026	0.025	0.024	0.024	0.023	1.6	0.945	0.946	0.947	0.948	0.949	0.951	0.952	0.953	0.954	0.954
-1.8	0.036	0.035	0.034	0.034	0.033	0.032	0.031	0.031	0.030	0.029	1.7	0.955	0.956	0.957	0.958	0.959	0.960	0.961	0.962	0.962	0.963
-1.7	0.045	0.044	0.043	0.042	0.041	0.040	0.039	0.038	0.038	0.037	1.8	0.964	0.965	0.966	0.966	0.967	0.968	0.969	0.969	0.970	0.971
-1.6	0.055	0.054	0.053	0.052	0.051	0.049	0.048	0.047	0.046	0.046	1.9	0.971	0.972	0.973	0.973	0.974	0.974	0.975	0.976	0.976	0.977
-1.5	0.067	0.066	0.064	0.063	0.062	0.061	0.059	0.058	0.057	0.056	2.0	0.977	0.978	0.978	0.979	0.979	0.980	0.980	0.981	0.981	0.982
-1.4	0.081	0.079	0.078	0.076	0.075	0.074	0.072	0.071	0.069	0.068	2.1	0.982	0.983	0.983	0.983	0.984	0.984	0.985	0.985	0.985	0.986
-1.3	0.097	0.095	0.093	0.092	0.090	0.089	0.087	0.085	0.084	0.082	2.2	0.986	0.986	0.987	0.987	0.987	0.988	0.988	0.988	0.989	0.989
-1.2	0.115	0.113	0.111	0.109	0.107	0.106	0.104	0.102	0.100	0.099	2.3	0.989	0.990	0.990	0.990	0.990	0.991	0.991	0.991	0.991	0.992
-1.1	0.136	0.133	0.131	0.129	0.127	0.125	0.123	0.121	0.119	0.117	2.4	0.992	0.992	0.992	0.992	0.993	0.993	0.993	0.993	0.993	0.994
-1.0	0.159	0.156	0.154	0.152	0.149	0.147	0.145	0.142	0.140	0.138	2.5	0.994	0.994	0.994	0.994	0.994	0.995	0.995	0.995	0.995	0.995
-0.9	0.184	0.181	0.179	0.176	0.174	0.171	0.169	0.166	0.164	0.161	2.6	0.995	0.995	0.996	0.996	0.996	0.996	0.996	0.996	0.996	0.996
-0.8	0.212	0.209	0.206	0.203	0.200	0.198	0.195	0.192	0.189	0.187	2.7	0.997	0.997	0.997	0.997	0.997	0.997	0.997	0.997	0.997	0.997
-0.7	0.242	0.239	0.236	0.233	0.230	0.227	0.224	0.221	0.218	0.215	2.8	0.997	0.998	0.998	0.998	0.998	0.998	0.998	0.998	0.998	0.998
-0.6	0.274	0.271	0.268	0.264	0.261	0.258	0.255	0.251	0.248	0.245	2.9	0.998	0.998	0.998	0.998	0.998	0.998	0.998	0.999	0.999	0.999
-0.5	0.309	0.305	0.302	0.298	0.295	0.291	0.288	0.284	0.281	0.278	3.0	0.999	0.999	0.999	0.999	0.999	0.999	0.999	0.999	0.999	0.999
-0.4	0.345	0.341	0.337	0.334	0.330	0.326	0.323	0.319	0.316	0.312	3.1	0.999	0.999	0.999	0.999	0.999	0.999	0.999	0.999	0.999	0.999
-0.3	0.382	0.378	0.374	0.371	0.367	0.363	0.359	0.356	0.352	0.348	3.2	0.999	0.999	0.999	0.999	0.999	0.999	0.999	0.999	0.999	0.999
-0.2	0.421	0.417	0.413	0.409	0.405	0.401	0.397	0.394	0.390	0.386	3.3	1.000	1.000	1.000	1.000	1.000	1.000	1.000	1.000	1.000	1.000
-0.1	0.460	0.456	0.452	0.448	0.444	0.440	0.436	0.433	0.429	0.425	3.4	1.000	1.000	1.000	1.000	1.000	1.000	1.000	1.000	1.000	1.000
0.0	0.500	0.496	0.492	0.488	0.484	0.480	0.476	0.472	0.468	0.464	3.5	1.000	1.000	1.000	1.000	1.000	1.000	1.000	1.000	1.000	1.000

INDEX

In searching for a given item in this book, please also refer to the Table of Contents, List of Figures, and List of Tables in the front of this book. The latter two are particularly useful since they show the content of the accompanying material.

A

B

C

D

E

F

G

H

I

J

O

P

INDEX

NOTES:

NOTES:

NOTES: